Introduction to Counseling

An Art and Science Perspective

Michael S. Nystul

New Mexico State University

Allyn and Bacon

Boston ■ London ■ Toronto ■ Sydney ■ Tokyo ■ Singapore

Vice President and Publisher, Education: Sean Wakely
Editorial Assistant: Karen Huang
Marketing Managers: Brad Parkins and Ellen Mann Dolberg
Composition Buyer: Linda Cox
Manufacturing Buyer: Megan Cochran
Production Administrator: Deborah Brown
Editorial-Production Service: Marret Kauffner
Cover Administrator: Jenny Hart
Electronic Composition: Omegatype Typography, Inc.

Copyright © 1999 by Allyn and Bacon
A Pearson Education Company
160 Gould Street
Needham Heights, MA 02494–2310

Internet: www.abacon.com

Library of Congress Cataloging-in-Publication Data
Nystul, Michael S.
    Introduction to counseling : an art and science perspective /
Michael S. Nystul.
        p.   cm.
    Includes bibliographical references and index.
    ISBN 0-205-26827-7
    1. Counseling.   2. Psychotherapy.   I. Nystul, Michael S. Art and science of counseling and psychotherapy.   II. Title.
BF637.C6N97   1999
158'.3—dc21   98–45118
                                                 CIP

Printed in the United States of America

10 9 8 7 6 5 4 3 2   03 02 01 00 99

This book is dedicated to my wife, Laura.
Her love and compassion for others have helped me understand the true
meaning of counseling and the value of the helping profession.

CONTENTS

12   Group Counseling   305

PREFACE

This book provides an overview of the counseling profession. It is written from the perspective of counseling and psychotherapy as an art and a science. This theme is extended throughout the book in an effort to create a balance in terms of the subjective and objective dimensions of counseling. The art and science are reflected in the book in a number of ways. For example, I provide an objective overview of the major topics emerging in the field of counseling. I also attempt to balance this science perspective with the art of counseling as reflected in a number of *Personal Notes,* which are based on over 30 years of clinical experience.

The first part of the book presents an overview of counseling and the counseling process. It attempts to provide a conceptual framework for understanding what counseling is and the counseling process. Chapter 1 presents several models that can be used to conceptualize counseling. These models include the art and science of counseling and psychotherapy, formal versus informal helping, counseling from a historical perspective, and future trends in counseling. Chapter 2 provides information about professional preparation and legal-ethical issues. Chapter 3 presents an overview of the counseling process and a description of the art of listening skills. Chapters 4 and 5 cover the art and science of assessment, diagnosis, research, and evaluation.

Chapters 6 through 9 are directed at providing a frame of reference for developing a personal approach to counseling from a multicultural perspective. A model for formulating a personal approach to counseling is presented, along with an overview of the major counseling theories. Special attention is directed at the need to create a multicultural perspective in conceptualizing and implementing counseling theories and procedures. The importance of considering emerging trends such as spirituality, diversity and multiculturalism, postmodernism, and brief counseling are also addressed.

After counselors have gained fundamental knowledge and skills in counseling, it is common to begin to develop expertise in working with special populations and settings such as counseling children and adolescents in a school setting or working with mental health issues in clinics, hospitals, and private practice. Special approaches to counseling, such as marriage and family, child and adolescent, group, and career counseling can be useful modalities for counselors working with clients to promote optimal development across the life span. Numerous challenges and rewards are associated with developing these special skills and practices associated with the counseling profession. Chapters 10 through 15 provide an overview of counseling specialties of marriage and family, child and adolescent counseling, group, and career counseling. School and mental health counseling are also covered to provide illustrations of two important professional settings for counselors.

The full text of the ACA ethical code and standards of practice is available for reference in Appendix A.

I have attempted to incorporate emerging trends such as postmodernism (which focuses on relational-contextual issues), evolving perspectives on multiculturalism (including spirituality and religion), and brief-solution-focused counseling. Together these emerging perspectives offer opportunities for major paradigm shifts that can redefine important elements of the theory, research, and practice of counseling. The ultimate goal of these changes appears to be developing models of helping that are more inclusive and adaptive as opposed to culturally encapsulated and can be translated into effective, efficient methods of helping in an environment of decreasing resources. It is indeed an exciting and rewarding time to be exploring the field of counseling.

Acknowledgments

I would like to extend my deep appreciation to several individuals who provided feedback regarding chapters in this book: Gerald Corey (group counseling), Martin Greer (assessment and diagnosis), Peggy Kaczmarek (child and adolescent counseling), Bob Myrick (school counseling), Michael Waldo (mental health counseling), and Richard Watts (professional preparation and ethical-legal issues, counseling theories, and marriage and family counseling). Special big thanks are due Richard Watts, who provided detailed suggestions on numerous chapters in this book. His in-depth knowledge of counseling theories and approaches were invaluable.

I would also like to recognize the reviewers of this text who provided valuable feedback and suggestions: Mark J. Miller, Louisiana Tech University; Paul D. Schwartz, Mt. St. Mary College; Edna Mauriello, Salem State College; and Daya Singh Sandhu, University of Louisville. Their efforts and encouragement were very much appreciated. Collectively, these reviewers played an invaluable role in the evolution of this book.

In addition, I would like to acknowledge two mentors from Oregon State University who played instrumental roles in my counselor education: Jerry Becker for helping me appreciate the value and importance of a psychological frame of reference and Frank Zeran for believing in me and providing hope for my future in the field of counseling. I would also like to acknowledge the two individuals who created the opportunity to work on this project—Jon Carlson (thanks for the support and encouragement) and Ray Short, editor for Allyn & Bacon (thanks, Ray, for being flexible and understanding, and for your expertise in developing and publishing quality counseling texts).

Last, but certainly not least, I would like to thank the most important person in my life, my wonderful wife Laura, who has always been there with love, support, ideas, and encouragement. Her positive approach to life has been a sustaining source of energy for this project and an inspiration.

M.S.N.

ABOUT THE AUTHOR

Michael S. Nystul received his Ph.D. in counseling from Oregon State University in 1974. He holds the position of Professor in the department of counseling and educational psychology at New Mexico State University. Professor Nystul is a licensed psychologist, clinical mental health counselor, and school psychologist. He has worked in a variety of clinical settings such as schools, hospitals, community mental health centers, university counseling centers, and private practice. His first position was an elementary school counselor with the Bureau of Indian Affairs in 1970 and he has continued to be very interested in working with children in counseling. Professor Nystul has published over 80 articles in journals and several chapters in books. In addition, he wrote *Art and Science of Counseling and Psychotherapy.* He has three daughters and three grandchildren and relies on his wife, Laura, for his major support system.

1 An Overview of Counseling

CHAPTER OVERVIEW

This chapter provides several models that can be used to conceptualize counseling. Highlights of the chapter include

- The art and science of counseling and psychotherapy
- Counseling as storytelling
- Counseling versus psychotherapy
- Formal versus informal helping
- Personal qualities of effective helpers
- The helping profession
- Counseling from a historical perspective
- Future trends in counseling

Welcome to the Field of Counseling

The field of counseling can be of interest to you even if you do not want to become a professional counselor. It offers tools for understanding, connecting, and helping that can be used to promote self-awareness and self-improvement and to enhance all aspects of life, including interpersonal relations, coping with stress, and problem solving.

Counseling as a career can be exciting and rewarding, and there are many reasons for becoming a counselor. You may think that helping a client work through a crisis or develop a more effective and meaningful lifestyle will be personally gratifying. Perhaps you find people interesting, or you are curious about how the mind functions, or even fascinated by abnormal conditions such as schizophrenia. You may view the challenge of working in a relatively new profession as appealing. Counseling offers numerous opportunities for its practitioners to make a significant contribution to the profession. You can develop new approaches to counseling or become involved in professional issues such as licensure. There are many ways to involve yourself in the counseling profession, and this book tries to help you identify some facet of counseling you would like to explore.

What Is Counseling?

No simple answer addresses the question, What is counseling? Counseling can more appropriately be understood as a dynamic process associated with an emerging profession. It involves a professionally trained counselor assisting a client with particular concerns. In this process, the counselor can use a variety of counseling strategies such as individual, group, or family counseling to assist the client to bring about beneficial changes. These strategies can generate a variety of outcomes. Some of these are facilitating behavior change, enhancing coping skills, promoting decision making, and improving relationships.

This chapter provides several conceptual models through which the different facets of counseling can be understood. Counseling is described first as an art and a science, then from the perspective of narrative psychology or storytelling. The chapter also differentiates counseling from psychotherapy and formal from informal helping, describes the personal qualities of effective helpers, identifies members of the helping profession, and provides information on past and future trends in counseling.

The Art and Science of Counseling and Psychotherapy

Counseling is essentially both an art and a science. The art and science model promoted throughout the book suggests that counseling is an attempt to balance the subjective and objective dimensions of the counseling process. From this perspective, the counselor, like an artist, can sensitively reach into the world of the client, yet on some level maintain a sense of professional and scientific objectivity.

The theoretical origins of the art and science of counseling and psychotherapy can be traced to the scientist-practitioner model set forth in Boulder, Colorado, in 1949. The scientist-practitioner, or Boulder, model (Raimy, 1950) suggests that science should provide a foundation for clinical practice. The Boulder model continues to have a major influence over the structure of university programs in the helping professions (Bernstein & Kerr, 1993; Peterson, 1995). Beutler, Williams, Wakefield, and Entwistle (1995) noted that there is increasing discontent among practitioners with traditional research methodologies and a movement toward alternative research approaches that are more directly linked with everyday clinical practice.

The art and science of counseling and psychotherapy represents an extension of the scientist-practitioner model. From this perspective, the science of counseling generates a knowledge base that has been shown to promote competency and efficacy in counseling. The art of counseling involves using this knowledge base to develop skills that can be applied sensitively to clients in a multicultural society. In addition, the art of counseling relates to the subjective dimension and the science of counseling reflects the objective dimension. The focus of counseling can shift back and forth between these two dimensions as one proceeds through the counseling process. For example, during the initial sessions, the counselor may function more like an artist, using listening skills to understand the client. Later the focus might shift to the science dimension as the counselor uses psychological tests to obtain an objective understanding of the client. Together, the art and science can create a balanced approach to counseling. A more detailed description of these two dimensions to counseling follows.

The Art of Counseling. To a large degree counseling is an art. To call counseling an art suggests it is a *flexible, creative process* whereby the counselor adjusts the approach to the unique and emerging needs of the client. The following *Personal Note* provides an illustration of how a counselor can be flexible and creative in working with a client.

A Personal Note

As a psychologist working for the Public Health Service on a Navajo Indian Reservation, I was asked to work with an autistic child as part of my consultation with the public schools. School personnel had placed the young girl in a classroom for the mentally retarded, not knowing she was autistic. The child was referred to me for counseling and self-concept development. When she came into my office, I had some puppets ready to use with her. These puppets were part of a self-concept program called Developing an Understanding of Self and Others (DUSO) (Dinkmeyer & Dinkmeyer, 1982). I soon realized that she seemed oblivious to me and the puppets. My counseling plans appeared to be useless.

I wanted to make contact with the child and find a way to reach into her world and develop a special relationship with her. I decided to let her be the guide, and I would follow. She walked over and threw the puppets into a neat pile. If she missed the pile, she threw it until it landed right on top of the others. She was very good at throwing puppets into a pile, and she seemed to enjoy doing it. I had identified one of her assets—something she felt good about, something she felt secure with. It was an extension of her world, her way of doing things. It made sense to her.

I wanted to become part of her world by reaching into it. I walked over and put my arms around her pile of puppets, becoming a puppet-basketball net. She continued to throw her puppets on the pile and through my net. For the next 20 minutes, the child threw the puppets into a pile. When she ran out of puppets, she would gather them up and start over, throwing them into a new pile. I would move the "net" as necessary. During this time, she never made eye contact with me or said a word. I became discouraged and walked back to my seat. As I did, I noticed that her eyes followed my movement. At that instant, I knew I had made contact. I had found a way into her world.

Over the next year, she let me further into her world. For the most part, she was the guide and I the follower—a guest in her home. As the relationship grew stronger, she became willing to explore my world. Through our relationship, I helped her reach out into the world of others. For example, I helped her with language development and encouraged her to move away from her ritualistic behavioral patterns. (A more detailed description of this case can be found by referring to Nystul, 1986.)

Another aspect of the art of counseling is the concept of giving of oneself in counseling. This concept is derived from humanistic psychology and emphasizes the importance of counselors being authentic and human in the counseling approach.

Counselors can give of themselves on many levels. They can give concern and support as they empathize with their client. A more intense form of giving is an existential encounter, which involves the process of self-transcendence. In this experience, the counselor moves beyond the self and feels at one with the client (Nystul, 1987). The experience can help a client overcome feelings of aloneness and alienation.

Giving of oneself in counseling may be especially appropriate in situations that involve working with neglected and abused children. These children may be wards of a court, without parents or "significant others." They may feel unloved and lost, lacking a reason to live. In these cases, the counselor may attempt to communicate compassion, kindness, tenderness, and perhaps even love. The following *Personal Note* illustrates the concept of giving of oneself in counseling.

A Personal Note

A five-year-old child was abandoned by her parents and placed in a residential facility for neglected and abused children. On one occasion, the caretakers of the institution became concerned when the child stayed up all night crying and vomiting. They brought her to a hospital the next morning. A pediatrician found nothing physically wrong with the child and referred her to me for mental health services.

After introducing myself to the child, I asked her how she was feeling. She sat down, put her face between her legs, and began to cry. It was the most deep-sorrowful sobbing I had ever heard. I leaned forward and gently touched her head, trying to comfort her. I could feel her pain. She looked up at me and appeared frightened and alone. I reached over and held her hand and told her I wanted to help her feel better. My heart reached out to her. I looked at her and said I thought she was a beautiful person, and I wanted to work with her every day. She nodded in agreement. I worked with her in play therapy for several weeks. During that time, her depression gradually lifted.

Counselors must use safeguards when expressing intense feelings to a client. They must clearly establish their role as a counselor and not a parent. They must avoid becoming overly involved to the point where they lose professional objectivity. Counselors must also be aware that excessive concern or worry about a child could lead to burnout. Giving of oneself in counseling is a very delicate process. It can be enriching and rewarding for the counselor and the child, but it can also be exhausting. Communicating intense emotion may not be practical for some counselors. For others, it is an art that must be developed over time.

The Science of Counseling.   The science of counseling provides a balance to the art of counseling by creating an objective dimension to the counseling process. Claiborn (1987) noted that science provides an important aspect to the identity of counselors in that it can differentiate professional counselors from nonprofessional helpers. He suggested that counselors should strive to be counselors-as-scientists (that is, someone who functions as a counselor and thinks as a scientist). Thinking as a scientist requires the counselor to have the skills to formulate objective observations and inferences, test hypotheses, and build theories (Claiborn, 1987).

Claiborn (1987) also suggested that the scientist-practitioner model, set forth by Pepinsky and Pepinsky (1954), could provide useful guidelines for contemporary counselors. Pepinsky and Pepinsky's model conceptualizes science and practice as integrated, mutually dependent, and overlapping activities. The interrelationship between theory, research, and practice provides an illustration of the complementary nature of science and practice. For example, practice can test a counseling theory that can, in turn, be evaluated by research.

The science of counseling also proposes that counselors develop skills that can promote professional objectivity in the counseling process. These include the observation, inference, hypothesis-testing, and theory-building skills that Claiborn (1987) suggested are necessary for counselors to think as scientists. Other strategies include the use of psychological tests, a systematic approach to diagnosis, and research methods to establish counseling accountability and efficacy. We should not view these as separate entities of counseling. Instead, counselors should integrate these skills and strategies into their overall role and function.

Counseling as Storytelling

Counseling as storytelling is an emerging conceptual model. Howard (1991) and Sexton and Whitson (1994) note that narrative (or storytelling) methods for understanding human behavior have become increasingly popular in psychology. For example, identity development can represent life-story construction and psychopathology can be related to dysfunctional life stories and can involve story repair (Howard, 1991).

Narrative psychology and its application to counseling as a form of storytelling are related to two emerging and complementary trends in counseling. These trends are the theories associated with postmodernism and brief-solution-focused counseling approaches (additional information regarding these trends are provided throughout the text). Narrative approaches to counseling attempt to simplify and demystify counseling by focusing on the client's own language as opposed to psychological jargon (Eron & Lund, 1993). The role of the counselor is to engage in a collaborative, nonimpositional relationship with the client (Eron & Lund, 1993). In this process, the counselor and client work together to create new narratives (or alternative stories) as a means of enhancing the client's well-being.

Howard (1991) goes on to provide a more detailed description of the role of storytelling in counseling.

> In the course of telling the story of his or her problem, the client provides the therapist with a rough idea of his or her orientation toward life, his or her plans, goals, ambitions, and some idea of the events and pressures surrounding the particular presenting problem. Over time, the therapist must decide whether this problem represents a minor deviation from an otherwise healthy life story. Is this a normal, developmentally appropriate adjustment issue? Or does the therapist detect signs of more thoroughgoing problems in the client's life story? Will therapy play a minor, supportive role to an individual experiencing a low point in his or her life course? If so, the orientation and major themes of the life will be largely unchanged in the therapy experience. But if the trajectory of the life story is problematic in some fundamental way, then more serious, long-term story repair (or rebiographing) might be indicated. So, from this perspective, part of the work between client and therapist can be seen as life-story elaboration, adjustments, or repair. (p. 194)

Meichenbaum and Fitzpatrick (1992) provide additional information on storytelling in terms of how people cope with stress. According to Meichenbaum and Fitzpatrick,

- People organize information in terms of stories about themselves.
- Negative, stressful life events affect people's belief systems, thereby altering the nature of their stories.

- How people rescript their stories (that is, engage in narrative repair) will influence how well they cope with stress.
- The literature is beginning to identify what are adaptive and maladaptive narratives and how stress-inoculation training can be used to help clients construct adaptive narratives to stressful life events.

Counseling as storytelling is an intriguing concept that appears to offer much promise to understanding counseling. Russell and Lucariello (1992) note that there is a great need for empirical research to investigate the impact of storytelling on the counseling process.

The following *Personal Note* provides an illustration of the role of storytelling in counseling.

A Personal Note

It seems as if everyone has a story to tell if one is willing to listen. I remember a mailman (whom I did not even know) who stopped me when I was walking around in my backyard. He was visibly angry and preceded to tell me how a policeman had blocked his way on the road while he was giving a ticket. The mailman said, "I asked him to let me by, so I could do my job. But he wouldn't, so I went by anyway driving onto the shoulder. Good grief, some people only think of themselves."

As he talked on, I thought this is a story that this man must tell someone, anyone, to ventilate and to feel understood. I can think of many other examples (such as some planes and bus trips I've had) where people have expressed their desire to tell their stories. I have also been in need of telling my own stories from time to time.

Lately I have become more aware of the role of storytelling in counseling. It has been my experience that most clients have stories to tell. Many of these clients have told their stories to others (such as friends or family members) with disappointing results. In counseling, the clients stories will hopefully be shown the respect and care they deserve.

One example of a client's story that stands out for me is one of pain, struggle, and courage. Pat was a forty-year-old Anglo single parent of four children. She had been in a serious car accident a year before I had my first counseling session with her. Much of our first sessions involved Pat sharing her story of the accident and her anger at the drunk driver who hit her and the lack of support she was feeling from her insurance company.

Pat's story was also one of struggling for her physical and emotional survival. She had to endure numerous operations for her physical injuries, was unable to go back to work due to physical limitations, and had multiple psychological problems that included insomnia, depression, and anxiety. It was therefore necessary to work closely with a psychiatrist to include medication in conjunction with counseling in her treatment program.

Fortunately Pat had a very strong support system, including friends and family members who helped her feel safe and encouraged, which helped her overcome some of her feelings of anxiety and depression. Gradually, Pat was able to work her way out of her sadness and depression and see some hope and possibilities for a better tomorrow. As she struggled to gain control of her life, she appeared to be engaging in a process of narrative repair, replacing words of gloom with feelings of hope.

Counseling and Psychotherapy

In order to understand what counseling is, it is important to understand key terms and concepts such as *counseling* and *psychotherapy*. The counseling literature has not made a clear distinction between counseling and psychotherapy (Corsini & Wedding, 1995), perhaps because the two processes are more similar than different. We can probably best understand their relationship within a continuum, with counseling at one end and psychotherapy at the other. A counselor may actually do both counseling and psychotherapy in one session. The two processes can therefore blend.

We can identify some subtle differences between these two processes. The main difference is that counseling addresses the conscious mental state, whereas psychotherapy also ventures into the client's unconscious processes. An example of relating to unconscious processes is providing insight to a client. Several other differences exist between counseling and psychotherapy in terms of focus, clients' problems, goals, treatment, and setting. These differences are shown in Table 1.1.

As depicted in Table 1.1, the focus of counseling tends to be developmental in nature, whereas psychotherapy has a remediative emphasis. Counseling attempts to empower clients with tools they can use to meet the normal developmental challenges of progressing through the life span. Counseling is therefore preventative in nature and growth facilitating. Psychotherapy, on the other hand, is directed at helping clients overcome the pain and suffering associated with existing problems such as anxiety and depression. Counseling is used with clients whose problems do not stem from a serious mental disorder such as a major depression. Instead, it is more appropriate for clients who have "problems of living," for example, parent-child conflicts or marital difficulties. Goals of counseling tend to focus on resolving immediate concerns such as helping clients work through a relationship difficulty or make a career decision.

TABLE 1.1 Comparison of Counseling and Psychotherapy

	Counseling	Psychotherapy
Focus	Developmental—fosters coping skills to facilitate development and prevent problems.	Remediative—aimed at helping clients overcome existing problems such as anxiety and depression.
Clients' Problems	Clients tend to have "problems of living" such as relationship difficulties, or need assistance with specific problems such as career choice.	Client's problems are more complex and may involve using formal diagnostic procedures to determine if there is a mental disorder.
Goals	The focus is more on short-term goals (resolution of immediate concerns).	The focus is on short- and long-term goals. Long-term goals can involve processes such as helping the client overcome a particular mental disorder.
Treatment Approaches	The treatment program can include preventative approaches and various counseling strategies to assist with the client's concerns.	Psychotherapeutic approaches are complex. They utilize strategies that relate to conscious and unconscious processes.
Setting	Counseling services can be provided in a variety of settings such as schools, churches, and mental health clinics.	Psychotherapy is typically offered in settings such as private practice, mental health centers, and hospitals.

Treatment programs in counseling vary according to the client's concern. For example, counseling might involve a parent education program to help parents learn how to establish a positive relationship with their child. Other counseling strategies might help a client work through marital difficulties. Counseling approaches are usually short-term, involving one session each week for three to twelve weeks. Counseling services may take place in a variety of settings such as schools, churches, and mental health clinics.

Psychotherapy is a process that can be used to assist a client who is experiencing more complex problems such as a mental disorder. Psychotherapy can involve both short- and long-term goals. The focus of short-term goals may be similar to problems addressed in counseling, for example, dealing with marital problems. Long-term goals relate to more deep-seated or involved problems such as depression or schizophrenia.

Psychotherapy is complex and relates to both conscious and unconscious processes. Hypnosis, projective tests, and dream analysis are all examples of techniques that relate to unconscious processes. Psychotherapy requires expertise in several areas such as personality theory and abnormal psychology. Psychotherapeutic approaches are usually long-term, occurring once each week for three to six months, and sometimes even longer. Typical settings for psychotherapy are private practice, mental health centers, and hospitals.

Differentiating Formal from Informal Helping

Another way to answer the question, What is counseling? is to differentiate counseling from the informal helping that can take place between friends. Some individuals who have had no formal training in counseling can provide valuable assistance. These informal helpers usually have some of the personal qualities associated with effective counselors, such as being caring, nonjudgmental, and able to utilize listening skills. Professional counselors may differ from informal helpers in a number of ways.

First, counselors can maintain a degree of objectivity because they are not directly involved in the client's life. Though there are exceptions, informal helpers usually have a personal relationship with the individual, so the assistance they provide is likely to reflect a personal bias. A related fact is that counselors usually do not have a preconceived idea of how a client should behave. Having no previous experience with the counselor, the client is free to try new modes of behaving and relating. This often does not occur with informal helpers, who may expect the person they are trying to help to act in a certain way. The person being helped might easily fall into the habits established in the relationship. This can create a restrictive environment.

Second, counselors are guided by a code of ethics, which is designed to protect the rights of clients (see American Counseling Association [ACA] code of ethics in Appendix A). For example, the information that a client presents to a counselor must be held in confidence, except in extreme circumstances such as when the client plans to do serious harm to self or others. Knowing this, a client might feel more free to share thoughts and feelings with a professional counselor than an informal helper.

Third, formal counseling can be an intense and emotionally exhausting experience. After establishing a rapport, the counselor may find it necessary to confront the client with painful issues. Informal helpers may avoid confrontation to avoid jeopardizing the friendship. They often play a more supportive and reassuring role, at times even attempting to rescue the person they are helping. In doing so, the helper, despite good intentions, does not communicate the all-important belief that the client is a capable person. The helper may also rob the individual of an opportunity to get in touch with feelings.

A final difference lies in the repertoire of counseling strategies and techniques available to professional counselors and their ability to systematically utilize these strategies and techniques to promote client growth. For example, a client may have a phobia such as a fear of heights. The counselor may use a behavioral technique called systematic desensitization, which helps the client replace an anxiety response to heights with a relaxation response. Some clients may not be able to stand up for their rights or state their opinions and could therefore benefit from assertiveness training. Other clients may have marriage or family problems, and the professional counselor may utilize the various schools of marriage and family therapy. Lacking formal counselor training, informal helpers are unfamiliar with and thereby unable to utilize these strategies. Instead, they typically rely on advice giving as their main method of helping.

Personal Qualities of Effective Helpers

The following *helping formula* developed by Brammer (1996) provides yet another conceptual model for answering the question, "What is counseling?"

$$\begin{matrix} \text{Personality} \\ \text{of the Helper} \end{matrix} + \begin{matrix} \text{Helping} \\ \text{Skills} \end{matrix} = \begin{matrix} \text{Growth-Facilitating} \\ \text{Conditions} \end{matrix} \rightarrow \begin{matrix} \text{Specific} \\ \text{Outcomes} \end{matrix}$$

This formula suggests that taking the personality of the helper and adding some helping skills like counseling techniques can generate growth-facilitating conditions. A feeling of mutual trust, respect, and freedom between the counselor and client characterize these growth-facilitating conditions (Brammer, 1996). When such conditions exist, desirable outcomes tend to emerge from the counseling process.

The helping formula emphasizes the importance of the personality of the helper (Brammer, 1996). There is emerging evidence to suggest that the personal characteristics of the counselor play a critical role in the efficacy of counseling (Corey, Corey, & Callanan, 1993; Herman, 1993). As early as 1969, Combs et al. (1969) suggested that the central technique of counseling is to use the "self as an instrument" of change. In other words, counselors use their personality to create a presence that conveys encouragement for, belief in, and support of the client. Rogers (1981) also comments on the importance of the counselor's personal qualities. He notes that the client's perception of the counselor's attitude is more important than the counselor's theories and methods. Rogers' point underscores the fact that clients are interested in and influenced by the personal style of the counselor.

A number of attempts have been made to identify the personal characteristics that promote positive outcomes in counseling. Strong (1968) suggests that clients be perceived as expert, attractive, and trustworthy. Corey, Corey, and Callanan (1993) contend that effective counselors present a positive model for their clients by being actively involved in their own self-development, expanding their self-awareness as they look honestly at their lives and the choices associated with personal growth and development. Beutler, Machado, &

Neufeldt (1994) found some empirical support for other counselor characteristics such as emotional well-being, self-disclosure, and optimism.

It would not be realistic to imply that an effective counselor must be a certain type of person. At the same time, the literature does suggest certain basic qualities tend to be important to the counseling process. I have incorporated these basic qualities into what I believe are the 14 personal characteristics of an effective counselor.

1. *Encouraging.* Being encouraging may be the most important quality of an effective counselor. Encouragement helps clients learn to believe in their potential for growth and development. A number of Adlerian counselors have written about the power of encouragement (for example, Dinkmeyer & Losoney, 1980).

2. *Artistic.* As mentioned, effective counselors tend to be sensitive and responsive to their clients. Being artistic implies being creative and flexible and adjusting counseling techniques to the unique needs of the client. Just as true artists give something of themselves to each thing they create, counselors must give of themselves to the counseling process. Effective counselors cannot insist on maintaining an emotional distance from the client if such a distance inhibits client growth. If necessary, counselors must allow themselves to experience the client's world directly and be personally affected by the counseling process, as they bring their humanness and vulnerability to the moment. Counselors who allow themselves to be human may also promote authenticity and genuineness in the counseling process.

3. *Emotionally Stable.* An emotionally unbalanced counselor will probably do more harm than good for the client. Unfortunately, some counselors enter the counseling profession in an attempt to work through serious mental problems. These counselors may attempt to meet their own needs at the expense of their clients. Langs (1985) goes so far as to suggest that a substantial number of clients spend much of their energy adjusting to the mood swings of their counselor. In some instances, clients might even believe they have to provide temporary counseling for the counselor (Langs, 1985). Role reversals of this type are obviously not in the best interest of the client. An inconsistent counselor will not only waste valuable time but create confusion and insecurity within the client.

4. *Empathic and Caring.* Effective counselors care about people and have the desire to help those in need. They are sensitive to the emotional states of others and can communicate an understanding of their struggles with life. Clients experience a sense of support and kindness from these counselors. This can help the client have the courage to face life realistically and explore new directions and possibilities.

5. *Self-Aware.* Being self-aware enables counselors to become aware of their limitations. Self-awareness can also help counselors monitor their needs, so they can gratify those needs in a manner that does not interfere with the counseling process. Self-awareness requires an ongoing effort by the counselor. The various ways counselors can promote their self-awareness include using meditation techniques and taking time for personal reflection.

Self-awareness appears to be related to a number of other concepts related to the "self" such as self-acceptance, self-esteem, and self-realization. In this regard, as people become more aware of themselves, they are in a better position to accept themselves. Self-acceptance can then lead to enhancement of one's self-image or self-esteem, which in turn can free a person to move toward self-realization.

6. *Self-Acceptance.* Self-acceptance suggests that counselors are comfortable with themselves. Although hopefully they will be working on improvement in their personal growth and development, the discrepancy between the real self and the ideal self is not so great to cause undue anxiety.

7. *Positive Self-Esteem.* A positive self-esteem can help counselors cope with their personal and professional lives and maintain the emotional stability that is central to their job. Also, counselors who do not feel positive about themselves may look for the negative in their clients. Even worse, such counselors may attempt to degrade the client to enhance their own self-image.

8. *Self-Realization.* Bob Dylan (1971) captured the spirit of this personal characteristic when he said, "Those that aren't busy being born are busy dying." Effective counselors are busy being born. They reach out in new directions and explore new horizons. As they do, they realize that growth requires commitment, risk, and suffering. They discover they have to stretch to grow. Counselors can welcome life experiences and learn from them. They develop a broad outlook on life that can help their clients put their problems in perspective. Being alive also means counselors have an enthusiasm for life. This enthusiasm can create energy and optimism that can energize and create hope for a client.

9. *Self-Disclosure.* Effective counselors are constructively open with their thoughts and feelings. When counselors model openness, they encourage their clients to be open. The resulting candidness can be critical to the counseling process.

10. *Courageous.* Although it is important for clients to perceive their counselors as competent, counselors are not perfect, and they should not be viewed as perfect. Instead, they should try to model the courage to be imperfect (Dreikurs & Soltz, 1964). Counselors with the courage to communicate their weaknesses as well as their strengths are disclosing an authentic picture of themselves. They are also presenting a realistic view of the human condition and can help clients avoid self-defeating, perfectionist tendencies. Another facet of the courage to be imperfect is the willingness of counselors to seek out counseling services for themselves if the need arises. Counselors should not feel that they are too good for counseling or they may develop a condescending attitude about counseling that could result in looking down on their clients. Obtaining counseling can also help counselors understand what it feels like to be in the role of client, contributing to a better understanding of the counseling process.

11. *Patient.* Being patient can be valuable in the counseling process. Helping someone change is a complex process and requires significant effort. Clients may make some progress and then regress to old habits. Counselors must be patient with the goal of achieving overall positive therapeutic movement.

12. *Nonjudgmental.* Counselors must be careful not to impose their values or beliefs on the client, even though they may wish to expose clients to new ideas at times. Being nonjudgmental communicates a respect for clients and allows them to actualize their unique potential.

13. *Tolerance for Ambiguity.* This can be an important characteristic of effective counselors. Ambiguity is often associated with the art of counseling. For example, the counselor never knows for sure what the best technique for a client is or exactly what was accomplished during a session. Although the science of counseling can contribute to the objective understanding of the counseling process, counselors must be able to tolerate some ambiguity.

14. *Spirituality.* Spirituality is an emerging trend in counseling. In this sense, the value of addressing and utilizing spiritual-religious processes in the helping process is being recognized. Characteristics of spirituality include capacities such as being sensitive to religious-spiritual issues in oneself and others (such as morality and the soul) and being able to function from and relate to the spiritual world as distinct from the material world.

The Helping Profession

Counseling can also be understood within the context of the helping profession. The term *helping profession* encompasses several professional disciplines, including psychology, counseling, and psychiatry. Each discipline can be distinguished by its unique training programs and resulting specialties. Many individuals from these various groups provide similar services, such as counseling and psychotherapy.

Members of the helping profession often work together on multidisciplinary teams. For example, school counselors and school psychologists join forces to provide counseling services in school settings. Psychiatrists, psychiatric nurses, psychiatric social workers, psychologists, and mental health counselors blend their specialized skills to provide a comprehensive treatment plan in mental health settings. An overview of the degree requirements, specialized skills, and work settings for the members of the helping profession is provided in Table 1.2.

Counseling: Past, Present, and Future

The counseling profession has been characterized by a dynamic evolution. This section describes some of these key events as well as attempting to predict some future trends in counseling.

Counseling from a Historical Perspective

A number of prominent individuals have made unique and lasting contributions to the counseling profession. The pioneering work of Freud, Adler, and Jung (see Chapter 7) can be credited with establishing the foundation for modern clinical practice. These three men were colleagues in Vienna in the early 1900s, and each went on to develop a unique school of counseling and psychotherapy.

Freud developed psychoanalysis, which emphasizes the role of sexuality in personality development. Adler developed his own school of psychology called individual psychology, which emphasizes the importance of social interest in mental health. Jung is credited with originating the school of psychology called analytic psychology. Jung's work was influenced by various disciplines, including theology, philosophy, and anthropology. His

TABLE 1.2   Types of Professional Helpers

Type of Helper	Licensure and Degree Requirements	Skills and Responsibilities	Work Setting
Mental health counselor	Master's degree in counseling or related field. Most states require licensure.	Use of counseling and psychotherapeutic strategies.	Community mental health centers, hospitals, and private practice.
Marriage, child, and family counselors	Usually a master's degree in marriage, child, and family counseling or related field. An increasing number of states require licensure.	Marriage, child, and family counseling.	Private practice.
Psychiatric social worker	Usually a master's degree in social work. Most states require licensure.	Counseling and psychotherapy usually from a family perspective; knowledge about psychiatric service, and ability to assist with social services (food, shelter, child abuse and neglect, foster and nursing care).	Most work in hospitals and social service agencies. Some have their own private practice.
Pastoral counselor	Master's degree in counseling or related field. Some states require certification or licensure.	Counseling and psychotherapy from a religious perspective. Some focus their practice on issues pertaining to marriage and the family (for example, marital enrichment).	Churches or agencies with church affiliation.
Clinical and counseling psychologist	Psy.D., Ph.D., or Ed.D. (Doctor of Psychology, Philosophy, or Education). All states require licensure or certification.	Counseling and psychotherapy, psychological testing, and mental health specialist.	University counseling centers, community mental health centers, hospitals, and private practice.
Psychiatrist	M.D. (Medical Degree) and 3–4 years specialized training in psychiatry in a full residency program. All states require licensure.	Treatment of serious mental disorders usually involving the use of medications, some counseling and psychotherapy, and consultation. Supervision of other mental health workers is usually involved.	Hospitals, community mental health centers, and private practice.
Psychiatric nurse	R.N. (Registered Nurse) degree. All states require licensure.	Assist in the psychiatric treatment of mental disorders by monitoring medication and providing counseling and psychotherapy.	Hospitals, community mental health centers.
School counselor	Many states require a master's degree in counseling. All states require certification or licensure in school counseling.	Personal and career counseling and consultation with school staff and parents.	Elementary, middle, and senior high schools.
School psychologist	Many states require a master's degree in school psychology or related field. All states require certification or licensure as a school psychologist.	Psychological testing, counseling, consulting.	Elementary, middle, and high schools.

theory, is probably, best known for its recognition of a collective unconscious, which suggests that all people share some common memories.

Numerous other schools of counseling have emerged since the pioneering work of Freud, Adler, and Jung. Perhaps more than any other theorist, Rogers has influenced the development of contemporary counseling approaches. His person-centered approach was a testament to the belief in the dignity and worth of the individual (Rogers, 1981). Rogers' approach has held wide appeal among individuals in the helping professions. He was particularly influential in the development of the third force, or humanistic school of counseling and psychotherapy. Cognitive behavioral approaches such as those developed by Albert Ellis (1994) and Aaron Beck (1993) are becoming increasingly popular theories of counseling. These approaches are welcomed by managed care because they tend to focus on symptom relief (such as anxiety or depression) and can be accomplished in a time-limited format.

Recent trends in counseling are reflected in the postmodern theories of constructivism (Mahoney, 1995) and social constructionism (Gergen, 1994) and the brief-solution-focused approaches to counseling (de Shazer, 1994). Postmodern theories create an opportunity for a paradigm shift that recognizes the roles cognition, language, and narratives play in defining truth, knowledge, and reality. Brief-solution-focused approaches create another potential paradigm shift toward a focus on strengths and solutions as opposed to problems, weakness, and pathology,

Many other individuals have played significant roles in the evolution of the counseling profession. Table 1.3 identifies these individuals and their unique contributions to counseling as well as important events affecting the profession.

Key Historic Events.   Several historic events have played important roles in the evolution of counseling. Among these are the vocational guidance movement, the standardized testing movement, the mental health movement, and key legislative acts.

The vocational guidance movement had its inception in the efforts of Frank Parson, a Boston educator who started the Vocational Bureau in 1908. Parson contended that an individual who took the time to choose a vocation, as opposed to a job, would be more likely to experience success and work satisfaction (Brown & Brooks, 1990). Career counseling, which focuses on helping clients explore their unique potential in relation to the world of work, evolved from the vocational movement.

The standardized testing movement can be traced to Sir Frances Golton, an English biologist, and his study of heredity. Golton developed simple tests to differentiate characteristics of genetically related and unrelated people (Anastasi, 1996). Many others have made significant contributions to the testing movement. Cattel set forth the concept of mental testing in 1890 (Anastasi, 1996), and Binet developed the first intelligence scale in 1905.

World Wars I and II played important roles in the testing movement. The army's need to classify new recruits for training programs resulted in the development of mass intelligence and ability testing. Examples are the Army Alpha and Army Beta tests during World War I and the Army General Classification test in World War II. After World War II, the use of tests proliferated throughout American society. Testing soon became an integral part of the public school system. Tests were also used in a variety of other settings, including

TABLE 1.3   Individuals and Events Central to the Evolution of Counseling

Individual	Contribution
Hippocrates (400 B.C.)	Classified types of mental illnesses and personality disorders
Socrates (400 B.C.)	Encouraged self-awareness as the purest form of knowledge
Plato (350 B.C.)	Postulated human behavior in terms of internal states
Aristotle (350 B.C.)	Designed first rational psychology to manage emotions
St. Augustine (400 A.D.)	Prescribed introspection to master emotions
Leonardo da Vinci (1500)	Combined science with art to recreate human reality
Shakespeare (1600)	Created a literature of psychologically complex characters
Philippe Pinel (1800)	Described various forms of neurosis and psychosis
Anton Mesmer (1800)	Used hypnotic suggestion to cure psychological symptoms
Fyodor Dostoyevsky (1850)	Wrote novels with complex character studies of anxiety and dread
Charles Darwin (1850)	Set forth an evolutionary theory of individual differences
Jean Charcot (1850)	Scientifically studied hypnosis to give it respectability
Søren Kierkegaard (1850)	Developed an existential concept of giving meaning to being
G. Stanley Hall (1880)	Began first child guidance clinic
James Cattell (1890)	Coined the term *mental tests;* in 1903 became known for research on mental tests and individual differences
Jesse Davis (1890)	Became the first school counselor
Emil Kraepelin (1900)	Systematized the classification of mental disorders
William James (1900)	Postulated comprehensive theory of emotions
Ivan Pavlov (1900)	Described behavioral theory of conditioned reflexes
Sigmund Freud (1900)	Developed the first systematic form of therapeutic counseling
Alfred Binet (1908)	Developed first intelligence test
Clifford Beers (1905)	Published *A Mind that Found Itself;* became acknowledged leader of mental hygiene movement
Eugen Bleuler (1908)	Proposed the name *schizophrenia* and related the prognosis to the extent of the symptoms
Frank Parsons (1908)	Established field of vocational guidance
Carl Jung (1920)	Developed the school of analytic psychology, which included the concept of the collective unconscious
Alfred Adler (1920)	Developed a school of psychology that emphasized the importance of social interest
J. L. Moreno (1920)	Proposed an approach to therapy that he called *psychodrama*
John Watson (1920)	Proposed a behavioristic theory to predict and control behavior
Hermann Rorschach (1921)	Published *Psychodiagnostics,* initiating usage of ink blots to assess mental disorders
Karen Horney (1924)	Challenged Freud's theory of penis envy with the concept of womb envy

continued

TABLE 1.3 **Continued**

Individual	Contribution
Robert Hoppock (1930)	Studied levels of job satisfaction
Gordon Allport (1937)	Introduced a personality theory that positioned personality traits as the basic components
B. F. Skinner (1940)	Formulated theory of operant conditioning
E. G. Williamson (1940)	Published standard text on school counseling
Stark R. Hathaway and J. C. McKinley (1942)	Published the Minnesota multiphasic personality inventory
Clark Hall (1943)	Introduced the theory of learning
Helene Deutsch (1944)	Extended Freud's analysis of female development to later stages of development
Gregory Batson (1945)	Emphasized family influence on psychological disturbances
Kurt Lewin (1945)	Used training group format for personal development
Wolfgang Kohler (1947)	Founded the Gestalt psychology movement along with Kurt Kollka and Max Werhheimer
Rollo May (1948)	Expanded work on existential therapy
David Wechsler (1949)	Developed the Wechsler intelligence tests
Margaret Mead (1949)	Examined the cultural determinants of sex and sexual behavior
Erick Erikson (1950)	Proposed theory of personality development
Jean Piaget (1950)	Proposed theory of cognitive development
Victor Frankl (1950)	Introduced system of existential therapy
Milton Erickson (1950)	Focused on linguistic aspects of therapeutic encounter
Carl Rogers (1950)	Proposed theory of client-centered counseling
Donald Super (1950)	Proposed career development theory
Anna Freud (1950)	Applied psychoanalytic theory to counseling children
Anne Roe (1951)	Developed a personality theory of career development
Abraham Maslow (1955)	Studied self-actualized individuals
Arnold Lazarus (1958)	First used terms *behavior therapy* and *behavior therapist*
Anne Anastasi (1958)	Measured gender differences and wrote the most widely used textbook on assessment
Passage of National Defense and Education Act (NDEA) (1958)	Provided financial assistance for training counselors
J. P. Guilford (1959)	Proposed a three-dimensional "structure of intellect"
Joseph Wolpe (1960)	Devised systematic theory of behavior therapy
Jay Haley (1960)	Started family counseling movement
Eric Berne (1960)	Introduced Transactional Analysis
Albert Ellis (1960)	Introduced rational-emotive therapy
Albert Bandura (1960)	Emphasized the importance of social modeling in learning

continued

TABLE 1.3 Continued

Individual	Contribution
Betty Freidan (1963)	Wrote *The Feminine Mystique,* which sparked a national examination of the psyche of American women
Rudolf Dreikurs (1964)	Related Alfred Adler's theory to parent education and child counseling
Virginia Satir (1964)	Wrote *Conjoint Family Therapy*
Fritz Perls (1965)	Popularized Gestalt therapy
George Gazda (1965)	Described methods of group counseling
Robert Carkhuff (1965)	Identified specific skills of helping
John Krumboltz (1965)	Published theory of behavioral counseling
William Glasser (1965)	Founded reality therapy
American Psychological Association (1966)	Published *Standards for Educational and Psychological Tests and Manuals*
Donald Blocher (1966)	Presented a model for developmental counseling
Allen Ivey (1971)	Introduced microcounseling as a method of learning counseling skills
Phyllis Chesler (1972)	Wrote *Women and Madness,* which critiqued the male-as-the-normative model of mental health
Jo Ida Hansen (1972)	Applied Holland's theory to the Strong Vocational Interest Blank
Sandra Bem (1972)	Popularized and assessed the concept of androgyny
Aaron Beck (1976)	Developed a cognitive model for treating depression
Jean Baker Miller (1976)	Wrote *Toward a New Psychology of Women* and created the Stone Center, a research center that examines her "relational" theory of women's development
Edna Rawlings (1977)	Wrote extensively on feminist and nonsexist therapy
Hilde Bruche (1979)	Published work on eating disorders
Harriet Lerner (1980)	Brought a feminist perspective to family systems counseling
Derald Sue (1981)	Published work in cross-cultural counseling
Nancy Betz (1981)	Self-efficacy theory applied to women's career development
Counselor Certification (1982)	American Association for Counseling and Development (APGA) establishes the National Board for Certified Counselors to certify counselors
Carol Gilligan (1982)	Challenged the male model of moral development
APGA name change to AACD (1983)	APGA changed name to American Association for Counseling and Development (AACD)
Janet Helms (1984)	Examined the impact of racial identity on the counseling process
Lenore Walker (1985)	Brought attention to the psychology of domestic violence
Kenneth Gergen (1985)	Set the foundations for social constructionism, a postmodern theory of particular interest to family therapists
Steve de Shazer (1985)	Set the stage for new directions in brief-solutions-focused approaches to counseling and psychotherapy

continued

TABLE 1.3   Continued

Individual	Contribution
Laura Brown (1986)	Addressed lesbian and feminist issues in psychotherapy
Louise Fitzgerald and Roberta Nutt (1986)	Wrote *Principles for Counseling Women*
Lucia Gilbert (1987)	Examined dual career issues in counseling
AACD ethical standards (1988)	AACD revised its ethical standards
Christine Courtois (1988)	Addressed counseling issues with incest survivors
AACD name change to ACA (1992)	AACD changed name to American Counseling Association (ACA)
Michael J. Mahoney (1997)	Wrote the *Cognitive and Constructive Psychotherapies,* which infused postmodern thought into psychotherapy
Licensure-Certification for counselors (1997)	Forty-two states instituted licensure or certification laws in professional counseling

Source: From *Introduction to Therapeutic Counseling* (pp. 15–16) by J. A. Kottler and R. W. Brown, 1985, Monterey, CA: Brooks/Cole. Copyright 1985 by Brooks/Cole. Reprinted by permission.

mental health services and employment agencies. The testing movement slowed to some extent during the 1960s, when it became apparent that many standardized tests reflected a cultural bias (Minton & Schneider, 1981). Since that time, there appears to be an increased sensitivity to multicultural issues pertaining to the use of tests.

The mental health movement resulted from the contributions of several forces. In 1908, Clifford Beers wrote *A Mind that Found Itself,* describing the horrors of his three years as a patient in a mental hospital. Beers' efforts resulted in an increase in public awareness of the issues relating to mental disorders. Beers later formed the Society for Mental Hygiene, which promoted comprehensive treatment programs for the mentally ill (Baruth & Robinson, 1987).

Another major factor in the mental health movement was the development in 1952 of medications that could treat serious disorders such as schizophrenia (Rosenhan & Seligman, 1995). Today, it is uncommon for psychiatric patients to remain in a hospital for more than one or two months. Although these medications do not cure mental disorders, they often can control symptoms to the degree that a person can function in society.

Unfortunately, it has been difficult to develop effective follow-up programs for psychiatric patients after their discharge from a hospital. The result has been an alarming number of mentally disturbed people wandering the streets as homeless "street people." Several studies have estimated that 25–50 percent of homeless people are mentally ill (Frazier, 1985; Ball & Harassy, 1984). Many mental health professionals are attempting to develop more effective follow-up and outreach services for the chronically mentally ill.

Key legislative acts have also contributed to the evolution of the counseling profession, in particular, the National Defense Education Act (NDEA) of 1958. This act was designed to improve the teaching of science in public schools, motivated by a popular belief that the United States was lagging behind Russia's achievements in science. This belief developed after Americans learned of the Soviet Union's success in launching the first space satellite, *Sputnik*. The NDEA had a major impact on the counseling profession by providing funds to train school counselors, resulting in a marked increase in the number of counselors employed in U.S. schools.

Future Trends

This section goes beyond describing what counseling is and attempts to predict some trends as we enter the twenty-first century. Although it is difficult to speculate what the future will entail, several researchers have identified possible trends in research, ethics, multicultural counseling, managed mental health services, brief-solution-focused counseling, mental disorders, postmodernism, spiritualism, and cybercounseling.

Research.   Gelso and Fassinger (1990) provided a comprehensive review of the counseling research conducted during the 1980s. They noted that the decade was characterized by increased interest in alternative research methodologies which incorporate more field-based and fewer laboratory-based designs. These authors suggested that the interest in alternative research designs would continue into the 1990s, along with "a trend toward the use of more refined methodological strategies and, in particular, advanced statistical procedures" (p. 374).

There appears to be increasing discontent with the scientist-practitioner model of counseling, which emphasizes the importance of clinicians integrating research into their clinical practice (Stricker & Trierweiler, 1995). The split between science and practice does not appear to be owing to a lack of interest by practitioners but rather that current research tends to offer little use or relevance to the day-to-day practice of counselors (Edelson, 1994; Havens, 1994).

Maling and Howard (1994) suggest that the statistical abstractions associated with quantitative research are of little use for counselors who are struggling with the individualized issues of clients. Alternative (qualitative) research methodologies are gaining increasing interest. They tend to focus on the use of interviews to discover with the subject (client) clinically relevant information (a process that parallels counseling). Qualitative methods appear to represent a blend of the art and science of counseling by providing information on the subjective and objective dimensions of the counseling process.

Ethical and Legal Issues.   Ethical and legal issues are playing an increasing role in the overall role and function of counselors. Counselors are required to apply ethical and legal principles on a daily basis (Davis & Mickelson, 1994). Applying them can be challenging in that they involve values, knowledge, and clinical judgment (Davis & Mickelson, 1994).

Confidentiality and dual (or conflictual) relationships are rated as the two most common type of ethical dilemmas encountered by professional helpers (Pope & Vetter, 1992). Also, in an age of increasing violence, the duty to warn and protect associated with the Tarasoff litigation is becoming a special concern among practitioners (Monahan, 1993).

Multicultural Counseling.   Multicultural counseling is becoming the fourth force in psychology, following psychodynamic, existential-humanistic, and cognitive-behavioral forces (Pedersen, 1991; Sue, Ivey, & Pedersen, 1996). The multicultural counseling movement is directed at reconceptualizing traditional counseling theory and practice. In this regard, Sue, Ivey, and Pedersen (1996) argue that "current theories of counseling and psychotherapy inadequately describe, explain, and predict, and deal with current cultural diversity . . . culture should be defined inclusively and broadly rather than narrowly . . . understanding the cultural and sociopolitical context of a client's behavior is essential to accurate assessment, interpretation, and treatment . . . and a culture-centered metatheory is viable" (p. 2).

Current trends in multicultural counseling do not suggest that traditional theories of counseling have been abandoned (McFadden, 1996; Patterson, 1996). The spirit of this movement appears to be directed at a more comprehensive integration of multiculturalism into all phases of the counseling process from establishing the relationship, to termination, and research and evaluation.

Multicultural counseling and therapy (MCT) (Sue, Ivey, & Pedersen, 1996) provides an example of this emerging trend in counseling. It can be used as a "lens" to conceptualize multicultural issues throughout the counseling process. As multicultural issues are identified, counseling theories, strategies, and other facets of the counseling process can be adjusted as necessary to meet the unique and emerging needs of clients (see Chapter 6 for a description of MCT and other multicultural perspectives).

Managed Mental Health Services.   Managed care for mental health services began in the late 1980s (Freeman, 1995), and continues as a major thrust in contemporary health care. Managed care focuses on managing care rather than managing benefits (Freeman, 1995). It typically involves Health Maintenance Organizations (HMOs), Managed Mental Health Care Organizations (MMHCOs), Independent Provider Organizations (IPOs), and Employer Assistance Programs (EAPs). It is becoming increasingly important for mental health practitioners to affiliate themselves with these organizations in order to be part of the health care system and be able to provide services.

A number of major concerns have been raised about the managed care movement, such as reduced number of visits (usually three to seven sessions), problems with confidentiality, depersonalization, questionable training for those screening mental health problems, and restricted choice of mental health providers (Solomon, 1996).

The Brief-Solution-Focused Counseling Movement.   The brief-solution-focused counseling movement appears to be gaining significant momentum. The pressures of budgetary and time constraints and the shift toward managed care have contributed to the increased interest in brief-counseling approaches. Many of the major counseling theories are being reinterpreted from a brief-counseling perspective (Friedman, 1997). In addition, some brief-counseling models have focused on problem solving (Nystul, 1995) while others are solution-focused (Furman & Ahola, 1992). Brief-counseling models provide opportunities to reconceptualize counseling theories and practice from a strengths perspective. There is little doubt that the trends toward brief-solution-focused counseling models will play a major role in the future evolution of counseling.

Mental Disorders.   Yager (1989) and Pincus et al. (1989) made projections about the impact of advances in science on the diagnosis and treatment of mental disorders. A summary of their predictions follows.

- Genetics will play an increasingly important role in the diagnosis and treatment of mental disorders. For example, scientists could use genetic engineering to alter the gene structure to prevent or treat mental disorders, and clinicians will be able to identify children who are at risk to develop mental disorders.
- Neurobiologists will gain a more complete understanding of the role of neurotransmitters, or agents that facilitate communication between neurons, in the development and treatment of mental disorders.
- Psychopharmacology researchers will develop more effective medications with fewer unwanted side effects to treat mental disorders. Scientists will also develop new medications that will successfully treat mental disorders previously unresponsive to medication. Examples are substance abuse disorders, including alcoholism, personality disorders, and sexual disorders.
- Sociobiologists will identify factors that trigger the onset of mental disorders.
- Advances in computer technology and software development will enable clinicians to make better use of computers in the diagnosis and treatment of mental disorders.

Postmodern Trends.   Postmodern trends are emerging that could have major implications for theory development and paradigm shifts in counseling. Postmodernism recognizes that truth, knowledge, and reality are reflected contextually in terms of social, political, cultural, and other forces that can impact on personal experience. Postmodernism therefore appears to offer opportunities for integrating diversity issues such as the role of culture and economic forces in mental health and counseling. Postmodernism is also associated with an evolving view of the self (Gergen, 1994; Smith, 1994). Postmodernism suggests there is a movement away from the autonomous integral self to a social-community self that extends beyond the individual to all aspects of society.

Postmodern trends are associated with the emergence of two psychological theories (constructivism and social constructionism) that could have major implications for reconceptualizing the counseling process. Constructivism (Mahoney, 1988) emphasizes the role of cognition in interpreting external events, whereas social constructionism (Gergen, 1994) stresses the impact of social forces in constructing reality. Both theories recognize the role that narratives play in creating stories that individuals utilize in defining personal meaning in life. Postmodern trends appear to offer multiple opportunities for theory building, especially in terms of infusing diversity issues in counseling. The implications of these new trends must be carefully investigated through research to determine their usefulness in counseling.

Spirituality.   Spirituality is an emerging trend in counseling that represents an important dimension to diversity, multiculturalism, and the counseling process (Richards & Bergin, 1997). Spirituality can be broadly conceptualized as the "invisible phenomena associated with thoughts and feelings of enlightenment, vision, harmony with truth, transcendence, peak experiences, and oneness with God, nature, or the universe" (Richards & Bergin, 1997, p. 77). From this perspective, all people are believed to recognize the spiritual (but not necessarily religious) realm of existence (Ingersoll, 1995). A number of factors are contributing to the increased interest in the spiritual domain of counseling. Spirituality can be conceptualized as a universal quality of humans as reflected in their search for meaning in their existence (Haase et al., 1992; Ingersoll, 1995). In this regard, one does not have to be religious to be spiritual. Religion can play an important role in spirituality, with 90 percent of the residents of the United States believing in God (Kroll & Sheehan, 1989). Spirituality and religion are interrelated terms, with the religion realm providing a framework in which spirituality can be expressed. This conceptualization suggests that "spirituality becomes an organismic, developmental dimension and religion, a 'culturally flavored' framework that helps develop the organismic spiritual potential" (Ingersoll, 1995, p. 12). From this perspective, spirituality and religion also represent a multicultural-diversity consideration (Pate & Miller-Bondi, 1995).

Aside from the widespread appeal of spirituality, it is recognized as a neglected yet valued dimension to the counseling process (Miranti & Burke, 1995). It is conceptualized as an important force in all phases of the counseling process from establishing a relationship through assessment, goals setting, and treatment (Richards & Bergin, 1997). The spiritual perspective in counseling is also consistent with the movement toward brief-solution-focused counseling in terms of utilizing a strengths perspective. For example, it is common for people to turn to prayer and other forms of spirituality during times of great need to gain strength and support to promote recovery and healing (Miranti & Burke, 1995).

The counseling literature is beginning to provide more empirical support for considering the spiritual domain in counseling. Many clients are indicating that they cannot be effectively helped in counseling unless their spiritual issues are addressed sensitively and capably (Richards & Bergin, 1997; Shafranske, 1996). In addition, there is increasing evidence to suggest that spiritual health plays an important role in physical and psychological health and well-being (Bergin, 1991; Richards & Bergin, 1997). Studies such as these appear to be giving spirituality the scientific credibility that will help propel it into the mainstream of counseling in the twenty-first century and beyond.

Cybercounseling.   Cybercounseling (counseling on the Internet) is becoming an increasingly popular means of providing counseling services (Wiggins-Frame, 1998). Cybercounseling involves counselors creating Web sites such as Shrink Link and Psych Central on the World Wide Web (Hannon, 1996). Counseling on these sites is done with e-mail and typically involves clients submitting questions of up to 200 words to the counselor and the counselor responding to the client in one to three days (Wiggins-Frame, 1998).

Wiggins-Frame identified potential benefits and hazards of cybercounseling. Benefits include providing counseling services to individuals who otherwise might not be able to receive services (such as those who live in rural areas). Cybercounseling may also be more attractive to individuals with disabilities such as the hearing impaired. Hazards include a number of potential ethical problems such as difficulty ensuring confidentiality and client welfare and providing adequate informed consent.

Counselors appear to have some ambivalence regarding participating in cybercounseling. Kirk (1997) conducted a survey that showed that 30 percent would never engage in cybercounseling; 25 percent would consider using it; and 45 percent would use it as an adjunct to face-to-face counseling.

Summary

Counseling is a complex process that does not afford a simple definition. For example, counseling is both an art and science, emphasizing the importance of the subjective and objective dimensions. Counseling also has its basis in narrative psychology, or counseling as a form of storytelling.

Counseling is differentiated from psychotherapy in terms of clients, goals treatment, and settings. It is also part of the helping profession, which includes psychiatrists, psychologists, mental health counselors, and school counselors.

Future trends in counseling include such emerging issues as managed mental health services, brief-solution-focused counseling, postmodernism, spirituality, and cybercounseling.

2 Professional Preparation and Ethical and Legal Issues

CHAPTER OVERVIEW

This chapter provides an overview of professional issues in counseling. It covers important aspects of becoming a professional counselor and major ethical and legal issues. Highlights of this chapter include

- Becoming a professional counselor, including formal study and professional affiliation, certification, and licensure; continuing education; and professional involvement
- Ethical issues, including client welfare, informed consent, confidentiality, and dual relationships
- Legal issues, including privileged communication and malpractice
- Special ethical and legal issues relating to marriage and family counseling, child counseling, group counseling, and AIDS
- Ethical-legal decision making, including clinical examples
- Diversity issues

Some of the major issues associated with becoming a professional counselor include certification and licensure, professional organizations, and ethical and legal issues. Guidelines for ethical decision making and clinical examples can illustrate some applications of ethical and legal principles.

Becoming a Professional Counselor

Deciding to undertake formal study in counseling constitutes the first step toward becoming a professional counselor. Being a professional counselor is an ongoing process that involves work, study, and commitment. This section describes four building blocks that characterize this process, as shown in Figure 2.1.

Formal Study and Professional Affiliation

Formal study in counseling usually involves working toward a master's or doctoral degree in the counseling field. There has been increasing pressure for graduate programs offering these degrees to obtain accreditation from one or more organizations: the American Counseling

FIGURE 2.1   The Building Blocks of Professional Counseling

Association's (ACA) Council for the Accreditation of Counseling and Related Problems (CACREP); the American Psychological Association (APA); and, in some instances, the American Association of Marriage and Family Therapy (AAMFT). Accreditation helps ensure that the programs will maintain an acceptable level of standards. In addition, some certification processes in counseling or psychology require a degree from an accredited program. A current list of graduate programs approved by the ACA, APA, and AAMFT can be obtained by writing directly to each organization at the following addresses.

> The ACA: 5999 Stevenson Ave., Alexandria, VA 22304
> The APA: 1200 17th St., N.W., Washington, DC 20036
> The AAMFT: 1717 K Street, N.W., #407, Washington, DC 20006

Master's degree programs provide the necessary foundations for a career as a professional counselor. Students can also benefit from joining a professional organization such as the ACA or APA, as a student member. Student members can attend conventions and involve themselves in professional issues facing counselors and psychologists. They also receive journals and newsletters that address important counseling issues and receive a copy of the code of ethics that guides clinical practice.

The ACA and APA each have numerous divisions that may be of interest to counselors and psychologists. Selected divisions are listed in Table 2.1.

Certification and Licensure

Certification and licensure are important to all professions, including counseling. They provide professional recognition as well as enabling members of the helping profession to utilize third-party insurance to help clients pay for counseling services. Certified or licensed psychologists can utilize third-party insurance in all 50 states. Counselors, on the other hand, are just beginning to be able to use third-party insurance programs. As of 1993, certified or licensed counselors can utilize third-party insurance in only 10 states. This number is increasing as insurance companies are becoming more aware of the special skills and training of licensed Professional Counselors.

TABLE 2.1 Selected Divisions and Affiliates of the ACA and APA

ACA	APA	
Association for Assessment in Counseling (AAC)	General Psychology	Psychopharmacology and Substance Abuse
Association for Adult Development and Aging (AADA)	Society for the Teaching of Psychology	Psychotherapy
American College Counseling Association (ACCA)	Experimental Psychology	Psychological Hypnosis
Association for Counselors and Educators in Government (ACEG)[1]	The Psychometric Society	State Psychological Association Affairs
Association for Counselor Education and Supervision (ACES)	Evaluation, Measurement, and Statistics	Humanistic Psychology
Association for Gay, Lesbian, and Bisexual Issues in Counseling (AGLBIC)	Behavioral Neuroscience and Comparative Psychology	Mental Retardation and Developmental Disabilities
Association for Humanistic Education and Development (AHEAD)	Developmental Psychology	Population and Environmental Psychology
Association for Multicultural Counseling and Development (AMCD)	Society of Personality and Social Psychology	Psychology of Women
American Mental Health Counselors Association (AMHCA)	Society for the Psychological Study of Social Issues	Psychology of Religion
American Rehabilitation Counseling Association (ARCA)	Psychology and the Arts	Child, Youth and Family Services
American School Counselor Association (ASCA)	Division of Clinical and Abnormal Psychology	Health Psychology
Association for Spiritual, Ethical, and Religious Values in Counseling (ASERVIC)	Clinical Psychology	Psychoanalysis
Association for Specialists in Group Work (ASGW)	Consulting Psychology	Clinical Neuropsychology
International Association of Addictions and Offender Counselors (IAAOC)	Society for Industrial and Organizational Psychology	American Psychology-Law Society
International Association of Marriage and Family Counselors (IAMFC)	Educational Psychology	Psychologists in Independent Practice
National Career Development Association (NCDA)	School Psychology	Family Psychology
National Employment Counseling Association (NECA)	Counseling Psychology	Society for the Psychological Study of Lesbian, Gay and Bisexual Issues
	Psychologists in Public Service	Society for the Psychological Study of Ethnic Minority Issues
	Military Psychology	Media Psychology
	Adult Development and Aging	Exercise and Sport Psychology
	Applied Experimental and Engineering Psychology	Peace Psychology
	Rehabilitation Psychology	Group Psychology and Group Psychotherapy
	Society for Consumer Psychology	Division of Addictions
	Theoretical and Philosophical Psychology	Society for the Psychological Study of Men and Masculinity
	Experimental Analysis of Behavior	International Psychology
	History of Psychology	
	Society for Community Research and Action	

[1]Denotes Organizational Affiliate status

Certification and licensure are similar processes in which the applicant must meet certain requirements in education, training, experience, and clinical competence. Forester (1977) identified several differences between certification and licensure. Certification recognizes the competence of practitioners by authorizing them to use the title adopted by the profession. Unlike certification, licensure is authorized by state legislation and regulates the practice and title of the profession. Since licensure is a legal process, legal sanctions can be imposed on an individual who is licensed. Licensure also has more specific and comprehensive regulations, necessitating greater training and preparation than in the certification process (George & Cristiani, 1990).

Historically, most states have offered school counselors opportunities to be certified or licensed. Along with other school personnel, school counselors are traditionally certified by a state board of education. Most states also require counselors to be certified as teachers. Since 1977, all states have required that psychologists be either certified or licensed by a state board of psychologist examiners (Cummings, 1990).

More recently, there has been a trend to provide certification or licensure for counselors who wish to practice outside the school setting, for example, in mental health clinics, hospitals, or private practice. The counseling profession has made progress in passing legislation at the state level requiring certification or licensure. As of 1998, 44 states and the District of Columbia have passed certification or licensure laws for counselors, as listed in Table 2.2. Certification or licensure in counseling requires 30 to 60 graduate hours, depending on the state; a master's degree in counseling or a closely related field; 2 to 4 hours per week of supervised counseling experience, depending on the state; and passing an examination. There is some concern that current examination processes do not assess an applicant's clinical skills and are therefore in need of modification (Brooks & Gerstein, 1990).

The ACA has taken an active role in certification and licensure for counselors at the state and national levels (Brooks & Gerstein, 1990). For example, the ACA helped create the National Board for Certified Counselors (NBCC) in an attempt to identify national standards for professional counselors. Individuals wishing to obtain recognition as an NBCC counselor must have a master's or doctoral degree in counseling or a closely related field, have at least two years of supervised professional counseling experience, and successfully complete a certification exam.

Counselors may also pursue certification in a specialty field. Some examples are National Certified Career Counselors, Certified Clinical Mental Health Counselors, and Certified Rehabilitation Counselors (Brooks & Gerstein, 1990).

Some animosity has developed among the members of various helping professions over the proper qualifications. In this debate, members of specialties such as psychiatry, psychology, and counseling emphasize the merits of their respective fields. For example, psychiatrists promote the need for medical training. Unfortunately, the real issue appears to be gaining dominance and control. Some examples of this lack of cooperation are psychiatry's failure to support psychology, psychology's contempt for mental health counselors, and the counseling profession's (represented by the ACA) refusing to recognize the standards of the AAMFT as necessary to practice as marriage and family counselors (Cummings, 1990; Everett, 1990). Clearly, there is a need for more cooperation among the helping professions and less concern with special interests (Brooks & Gerstein, 1990; Cummings, 1990).

TABLE 2.2   States That Have Passed Certification or Licensure Laws for Counselors (District of Columbia Is Also Included)

State	Law Passed (Year)	State	Law Passed (Year)
Alabama	1979	Montana	1985
Arizona	1988	Nebraska	1988
Arkansas	1979	New Jersey	1993
California	1989	New Hampshire	1992
Colorado	1988	New Mexico	1993
Connecticut	1997	North Carolina	1983
Delaware	1987	North Dakota	1989
District of Columbia	1994	Ohio	1989
Florida	1981	Oklahoma	1985
Georgia	1987	Oregon	1989
Idaho	1982	Rhode Island	1987
Illinois	1993	South Carolina	1985
Indiana	1997	South Dakota	1990
Iowa	1991	Tennessee	1987
Kansas	1987	Texas	1981
Kentucky	1996	Utah	1994
Louisiana	1987	Vermont	1988
Maine	1989	Virginia	1976
Maryland	1985	Washington	1987
Massachusetts	1987	West Virginia	1986
Michigan	1988	Wisconsin	1992
Mississippi	1985	Wyoming	1987
Missouri	1985		

Continuing Education

Some form of continuing education is essential for the ongoing development of professional counselors. Most certification and licensure regulations also require counselors to take continuing education courses to maintain their professional credentials. This usually involves attending workshops or presentations at conferences or taking courses that have been approved for continuing education credits.

Other professional development activities can help counselors remain current and refine their clinical skills. Some of these are reading professional journals and books, attending in-service training programs, cocounseling with an experienced clinician, seeking ongoing supervision, and attending institutes for advanced training in a counseling specialty.

Professional Involvement

As mentioned, being a professional counselor requires ongoing work and effort. As individuals embark on a career in counseling, they initially draw help and guidance from the profession. As they advance in the profession, they find themselves in a position to make a contribution. Some ways that counselors can contribute are taking an active role in professional organizations, supporting efforts for certification and licensure, and writing in professional journals.

Professional involvement helps support and maintain the profession, but it also enriches the counselor. As counselors become professionally involved, they develop a network of friends who can often become an important support system. The experience can also diversify their interests and professional activities, which can be stimulating and professionally rewarding.

The following *Personal Note* speaks to the importance of professional involvement in counseling.

A Personal Note

I've noticed that colleagues of mine who are active in professional organizations tend to be happier, more productive, and less prone to burnout than those that don't take an active role in professional organizations. It seems as if those who aren't as active tend to get frustrated more easily, have a more negative view about their jobs, and get tired and give up more easily than those who are professionally active. Perhaps one reason for these differences between the professionally active and inactive counselor is that professional organizations provide counselors with a broader sense of the counseling community and help keep things in perspective.

I've made a lot of friends through my involvement in professional organizations and activities. These friends have created an important network and have been helpful in many ways. I've felt a sense of support and encouragement from these people. I've also experienced a number of career opportunities, such as reviewing one of my colleague's books for a book company, which resulted in my obtaining my own book contract. Professional involvement has also been a way for me to contribute to the profession. It has been personally rewarding to give of my time and energy, to participate on committees, editorial boards, and other aspects of the various professional organizations with which I've been affiliated.

Ethical-Legal Issues

The Art and Science of Ethical-Legal Issues

Ethical-legal issues reflect on both the art and science of counseling. To a large degree ethical codes and legal statutes are not written in black-and-white terms but serve as principles to guide one's clinical practice. The art of counseling suggests that practitioners engage in creative approaches to ethical-legal decision making that are sensitive to multicultural issues. The science of counseling also recognizes that ethical codes and legal statutes also have some clear statements as to what is ethical-legal behavior for a practitioner. For example, there are legal reporting duties when child abuse or neglect is suspected.

Meara, Schmidt, and Day (1996) conceptualize ethics in a manner that complements the art and science of counseling. They suggest that there are two dimensions to ethical decision making—principle ethics and virtue ethics. Principle ethics (like the science of counseling) are the overt ethical obligations that must be addressed in clinical situations such as the duty to warn and protect when a client becomes homicidal. Virtue ethics (like the art of counseling) suggest that practitioners go beyond the *obligatory* and strive toward the *ideals* to which professionals aspire. Central to this task is the development of virtuous character traits such as sensitivity to the cultural milieu, which can impact on ethical decision making. These authors go on to suggest that principle and virtue ethics be integrated to create a balance in ethical decision making that is not only ethically and legally correct but also in the best interest of society as a whole.

Ethical-legal issues are becoming increasingly prevalent in the day-to-day practice of the professional counselor. This is as true for school counselors as it is for mental health counselors and other practitioners in the helping profession. The emergence of these issues represents a response to the increased risk of malpractice suits against counselors (Corey, 1996), and to the ACA's 1997 statement that counselors should "respect the integrity and promote the welfare of clients" (Section B.1). It is therefore imperative that counselors have the necessary knowledge and skills to integrate legal and ethical issues into every aspect of the counseling profession. The following *Personal Note* illustrates the importance of considering ethical-legal issues in one's practice.

A Personal Note

For the past six years, I've been working one day a week as a school psychologist for a local school district. In this job I've provided psychological services (which include assessment, consultation, and counseling) to six different elementary schools. It seems like each new year brings more and more legal and ethical issues that affect how I must do my job.

An error in the ethical or legal domain can have disastrous effects for the students, staff, and parents that I serve, as well as the school district and myself. For example, if I tell a parent that his or her child needs to be hospitalized for treatment of a mental disorder, the school district may have to pay for it. Since the bill for a mental health hospitalization can be $20,000 or more per month, such a decision on my part will not win any friends in the superintendent's office or school board. To avoid this dilemma, I work closely with the community mental health center, and when necessary arrange for them to refer students for necessary hospitalization.

Ethical Issues

Ethical codes and standards of practice have been formulated by the ACA (see Appendix A) and the APA. The ACA (1997) code of ethics relates to issues such as general topics of concern, the counseling relationship, measurement and evaluation, research and publication, consulting, private practice, personnel administration, and preparation standards.

The various ethical standards are guidelines for what a counselor can or cannot do. Each clinical situation is unique and may require an interpretation of the particular code of ethics. In this regard, the standards can be viewed as guiding principles that counselors can use to formulate their clinical judgment. In addition, Mabe and Rollin (1986) note that the codes of ethics provide a framework for professional behavior and responsibility and serve as a means for establishing professional identity.

Baruth and Huber (1985) identify three major ethical issues that influence clinical practice: client welfare, informed consent, and confidentiality. An additional major ethical issue relates to dual relationships. An overview of these four ethical issues follows.

Client Welfare. The counselor's primary responsibility is the welfare of the client. In this regard, the ACA and APA codes of ethics suggest that the client's needs come before the counselor's needs, counselors should practice within their area of competence, and counselors should terminate or refer a client who is no longer benefitting from the service. Table 2.3 provides excerpts from the ACA and the APA regarding client welfare and conditions relating to client referral.

Informed Consent. The ethical guidelines relating to informed consent require counselors to provide each client with an overview of what counseling will entail so the client can decide whether to participate. Table 2.4 lists excerpts on this topic from the ACA and the APA. Mardirosian, McGuire, Abbott, and Blau (1990) note that counselors can assist a

TABLE 2.3   Ethical Considerations Relating to Client Welfare and Referral

Client Welfare	Client Referral
ACA (1997) *Primary Responsibility* The primary responsibility of counselors is to respect the dignity and to promote the welfare of clients.	**ACA (1997)** If counselors determine an inability to be of professional assistance to clients, they avoid entering or immediately terminate a counseling relationship. Counselors are knowledgeable about referral resources and suggest appropriate alternatives. If clients decline the suggested referral, counselors should discontinue the relationship.
APA (1992) Psychologists strive to maintain high standards of competence in their work. They recognize the boundaries of their particular competencies and the limitations of their expertise. They provide only those services and use only those techniques for which they are qualified by education, training, or experience. Psychologists are cognizant of the fact that the competencies required in serving, teaching, and/or studying groups of people vary with the distinctive characteristics of those groups. In those areas in which recognized professional standards do not yet exist, psychologists exercise careful judgment and take appropriate precautions to protect the welfare of those with whom they work.	**APA (1992)** Psychologists arrange for appropriate consultations and referrals based principally on the best interests of their patients or clients, with appropriate consent, and subject to other relevant considerations, including applicable law and contractual obligations.

TABLE 2.4   **Ethical Considerations Relating to Informed Consent**

Informed Consent

ACA (1997)

When counseling is initiated, and throughout the counseling process as necessary, counselors inform clients of the purposes, goals, techniques, procedures, limitations, potential risks and benefits of services to be performed, and other pertinent information.

APA (1992)

Psychologists obtain appropriate informed consent to therapy or related procedures, using language that is reasonably understandable to participants. The content of informed consent will vary depending on many circumstances; however, informed consent generally implies that the person (1) has the capacity to consent, (2) has been informed of significant information concerning the procedure, (3) has freely and without undue influence expressed consent, and (4) consent has been appropriately documented.

Source: ACA excerpts reprinted from *Code of Ethics and Standards of Practice* (1997). © ACA. Reprinted by permission. No further reproduction authorized without written permission of the American Counseling Association. APA excerpts from *Ethical Principles of Psychologists and Code of Conduct.* Copyright © 1992 by the American Psychological Association. Reprinted by permission.

client in making an informed consent by providing information on policies, goals, and procedures. In controversial issues such as pregnancy counseling, the authors suggest that counselors should inform the client of their moral-value position.

One way to give a client information to assist with informed consent is by providing a professional disclosure statement. McFadden and Brooks (1983) have provided an example of such a statement, which has been incorporated into the professional disclosure statement shown in Table 2.5. The professional disclosure statement in Table 2.5 can be adjusted to reflect the counselor's professional identity and special theoretical orientation. For example, school counselors might mention that their approach includes consultation with parents and teachers and counseling with students individually and in small and large groups. In terms of theoretical orientation, school counselors might explain the importance of a developmental perspective in addressing the developmental tasks of children at different grade levels.

Confidentiality.   Confidentiality is a critical condition in counseling and psychotherapy (Paradise & Kirby, 1990). The client must feel safe in disclosing information to the counselor for the counseling process to be effective (Reynolds, 1976). Denkowski and Denkowski (1982) identify two purposes of confidentiality in counseling: (a) protecting the client from the social stigma often associated with being in therapy, and (b) promoting the client's vital rights that are integral to the client's welfare. The ACA and the APA provide guidelines relating to confidentiality, as shown in Table 2.6. The major exception to the principle of confidentiality is when clients pose a clear and imminent danger to themselves

TABLE 2.5   Professional Disclosure Statement

Professional Disclosure Statement

(LETTERHEAD)

Milton H. Counselor, Ph.D.
333 Maple Street
Littletown, Alabama 36501
(205) 555-5347
Hours by Appointment

STATEMENT OF PROFESSIONAL DISCLOSURE

Ph.D., Counseling—Bigname State University, 1981
B.A., Group Communication/Psychology—Bigname State University, 1973
B.S., Psychology—Bigname State University, 1972

Certified Clinical Mental Health Counselor, 1980.
Certificate #609
Licensed Professional Counselor, 1980, License #576

Philosophical Base

I utilize a cognitive approach that emphasizes cognitive restructuring to alter affective states. This means that the way we feel and the way we behave are directly related to how and what we are thinking. The past and the future are not as important as living one's life to the fullest in the present. I view counseling as a process by which I facilitate my clients in exploration, clarification, and identification of their needs and help them make changes in their behavior that will result in the attainment of life satisfaction and self-acceptance.

Therapeutic Approach

I use an integrative approach. My core theory is Adlerian. I also utilize techniques and counseling procedures from other schools of counseling to meet the needs of my clients. In addition, I try to be especially sensitive to multicultural issues that may arise in counseling.

In individual counseling, I attempt to help clients focus their awareness on strengths rather than liabilities. Clients are encouraged to accept responsibility for initiating and maintaining change in their lives as those changes are identified through the counseling process. In marriage counseling, I focus on developing a healthy independence and interdependence.

This is accomplished by using the techniques that help to develop self-awareness as well as improving the communication skills of both partners. I view group counseling as an adjunct to individual counseling rather than as a substitute for it. In my work in family counseling and the management of behavioral problems of children, I use an approach that involves encouragement, rational thinking, logical consequences, understanding misdirected goals, and improved parent-child communication. In all cases, I stress the effect of cognition on behavior and emotions and the need to develop control over this function.

continued

TABLE 2.5 Continued

Areas of Competency

Individual counseling

Marriage counseling

Family counseling

Child counseling

Group counseling

Drug abuse counseling

Career counseling

Values clarification and life planning

Organization development

Biofeedback and relaxation training

Ethical Standards

I subscribe to the codes of ethics of the following organizations. Copies are available and will be discussed with the client upon request.

American Counseling Association

American Mental Health Counselors Association

National Academy of Certified Clinical Mental Health Counselors

Alabama Board of Examiners in Counseling

Limits to Confidentiality

All information discussed in counseling will be treated as confidential except in instances when the client becomes a serious threat to self (for example, suicidal) or others (for example, homicidal) or when mandated by law (for example, reporting of child abuse and neglect).

Professional Memberships

American Counseling Association

American Mental Health Counselors Association

Association for Specialists in Group Work

Alabama Association for Counseling and Development

Alabama Mental Health Counselors Association

Fees

Individual, marriage, or family counseling

Group counseling

Career counseling

$75 per session

$40 per session

Fees vary according to tests and services required.

(Ordinarily the above fee schedule will apply. Please feel free to discuss fees and special circumstances regarding fee payments at our first session.)

Please discuss any concerns about the counseling services you receive with me. If these concerns cannot be resolved between us, contact the Alabama Board of Examiners in Counseling, c/o Donald Schmitz, Chairman, Jacksonville State University, Jacksonville, AL 36265, or National Academy of Certified Clinical Mental Health Counselors, Two Skyline Place, Suite 400, 5203 Leesburg Pike, Falls Church, VA 22041.

TABLE 2.6   Ethical Considerations Relating to Confidentiality

Confidentiality

ACA (1997)
Counselors respect their clients' right to privacy and avoid illegal and unwarranted disclosures of confidential information.

APA (1992)
(a) Psychologists discuss with persons and organizations with whom they establish a scientific or professional relationship (including, to the extent feasible, minors and their legal representatives) (1) the relevant limitations on confidentiality, including limitations where applicable in group, marital, and family therapy or in organizational consulting, and (2) the foreseeable uses of the information generated through their services.

(b) Unless it is not feasible or is contraindicated, the discussion of confidentiality occurs at the outset of the relationship and thereafter as new circumstances may warrant.

(c) Permission for electronic recording of interviews is secured from clients and patients.

Psychologists have a primary obligation and take reasonable precautions to respect the confidentiality rights of those with whom they work or consult, recognizing that confidentiality may be established by law, institutional rules, or professional or scientific relationships.

Source: ACA excerpts reprinted from *Code of Ethics and Standards of Practice* (1997). © ACA. Reprinted by permission. No further reproduction authorized without written permission of the American Counseling Association. APA excerpts from *Ethical Principles of Psychologists and Code of Conduct.* Copyright © 1992 by the American Psychological Association. Reprinted by permission.

or others, such as a client who threatens to commit suicide or kill someone (Gross & Robinson, 1987). It is important to ensure that clients are aware of the limits regarding confidentiality before they begin counseling. This can be accomplished in several ways, including the use of a professional disclosure statement.

Dual Relationships.   Dual relationships involve counselors engaging in more than one relationship with a client (Corey, Corey, & Callanan, 1998), for example, a professor also being a student's counselor. Dual relationships can be problematic and violate ethical and legal standards when professional roles conflict (for example, a counselor dating a client) (Corey, Corey, & Callanan, 1998). Table 2.7 provides excerpts from the ACA and APA regarding dual relationships.

Legal Issues

Several legal issues that impact the practice of counseling relate to confidentiality. As mentioned, counselors are ethically obligated to maintain confidentiality unless clients pose a clear and imminent danger to themselves or others. A legal precedent for counselors to take

TABLE 2.7   **Ethical Considerations Relating to Dual Relationships**

ACA (1997)

Counselors are aware of their influential positions with respect to clients, and they avoid exploiting the trust and dependency of clients. Counselors make every effort to avoid dual relationships with clients that could impair professional judgment or increase the risk of harm to clients. (Examples of such relationships include, but are not limited to, familial, social, financial, business, or close personal relationships with clients.) When a dual relationship cannot be avoided, counselors take appropriate professional precautions such as informed consent, consultation, supervision, and documentation to ensure that judgment is not impaired and no exploitation occurs.

APA (1992)

(a)   In many communities and situations, it may not be feasible or reasonable for psychologists to avoid social or other nonprofessional contacts with persons such as patients, clients, students, supervisees, or research participants. Psychologists must always be sensitive to the potential harmful effects of other contacts on their work and on those persons with whom they deal. A psychologist refrains from entering into or promising another personal, scientific, professional, financial, or other relationship with such persons if it appears likely that such a relationship reasonably might impair the psychologist's objectivity or otherwise interfere with the psychologist's effectively performing his or her functions as a psychologist, or might harm or exploit the other party.

(b)   Likewise, whenever feasible, a psychologist refrains from taking on professional or scientific obligations when preexisting relationships would create a risk of such harm.

Source: ACA excerpts reprinted from *Code of Ethics and Standards of Practice* (1997). © ACA. Reprinted by permission. No further reproduction authorized without written permission of the American Counseling Association. APA excerpts from *Ethical Principles of Psychologists and Code of Conduct*. Copyright © 1992 by the American Psychological Association. Reprinted by permission.

decisive action to protect human life was set in the landmark case of Tarasoff versus the Board of Regents of the University of California (1974, 1976). The case involved a psychologist at the University of California at Berkeley who provided counseling services to a student. After the student threatened to kill his girlfriend, Tatiana Tarasoff, the psychologist failed to warn her of the threat. Two months later, the client killed the girl. Her parents filed suit against the university and won on the basis that the psychologist had been irresponsible.

The California Supreme Court went on to determine that there was also a duty to protect in Tarasoff cases. This will typically involve arranging for clients to be hospitalized when they become homicidal. The following *Personal Note* describes some of the difficulties associated with the duty to warn and duty to protect.

Monahan (1993) provides additional guidelines regarding the duty to warn and duty to protect. Monahan emphasizes that the single best predictor of violence is a past history of violence. It is therefore imperative that an in-depth history be taken, including reviewing past hospitalizations and other forms of treatment as well as gathering information from significant others if necessary. Follow-up is also important to ensure that a homicidal client received the necessary treatment to prevent harm to self or others. In addition, Monahan stresses the importance of documentation and consultation.

Corey (1996) identified three other situations in which counselors are legally required to report information: (a) when the counselor believes that a client under the age of 16 is the victim of child abuse, sexual abuse, or some other crime; (b) if the counselor determines that a client is in need of hospitalization; and (c) if information is made an issue in a court action.

The following *Personal Note* provides information on some of the stressors associated with legal issues in counseling.

A Personal Note

As society becomes increasingly violent, it is not surprising that counselors such as myself are dealing with a heightened number of potentially violent situations. I therefore find myself in numerous clinical situations that require instituting the Tarasoff ruling by warning and protecting my client's intended victim. One method that I've used to help determine whether a client presents a serious threat to others is the MMPI (not the test but an acronym for means, motive, plan, and intent). Other factors to consider are past histories of violence, abuse of alcohol and drugs, mental stability, and overall mental status. Consultation with a supervisor or colleague such as a psychologist or psychiatrist can also be helpful determining whether someone represents a homicidal threat.

I have found the actual process of instituting the Tarasoff litigation in a clinical situation to be a very stressful experience for all involved. These situations typically have one or more lives at risk and also involve my client's welfare (including the client's mental health, career, family, and legal status). I find it very stressful to contact the intended victims and inform them that my client appears to be planning to kill them. It is also stressful to attempt to protect the victim by taking the necessary steps, which often involve arranging for hospitalization. Having a client admitted voluntarily or involuntarily to a hospital is often a very difficult and time-consuming process. I'm also amazed at how quickly some of these hospitals discharge these patients back into the community, often creating additional legal-ethical dilemmas and stress for all involved.

Privileged Communication.   Another legal issue that pertains to confidentiality is the notion of *privileged communication.* This term refers to a legal protection for clients, preventing a counselor from disclosing confidential communication in court without their permission (Herlihy & Sheeley, 1987). The privilege exists to protect the rights of the client and not the counselor. The client owns and controls the privilege (Herlihy & Sheeley, 1987) and can therefore determine whether or not a counselor may disclose confidential information in a court of law.

Corey, Corey, and Callanan (1998) have identified the following exceptions in which a client does not own and control the privilege and the counselor must provide information to the court. These instances are when

- A counselor is acting in a court-appointed capacity, such as conducting a psychological examination (Remley, 1991)
- A counselor determines that a client has a high risk of suicide (Bedner et al., 1991)
- A client initiates a lawsuit against a counselor (Denkowski & Denkowski, 1982)
- A client uses a mental condition as a claim or defense in a civil action (Leslie, 1991)
- A counselor suspects that a client under the age of 16 is the victim of a crime such as child abuse or neglect (Everstine et al., 1980)
- A counselor determines that a client requires hospitalization for a mental or psychological disorder (Bedner et al., 1991)
- A client reveals an intent to commit a crime or is assessed to be dangerous to the self or others (Bedner et al., 1991)

Laws relating to privileged communication between a client and a member of the helping profession vary considerably from state to state (Herlihy & Sheeley, 1987). Some states recognize privileged communication between psychologists and their clients but not between licensed counselors and their clients. Practitioners must therefore be aware of their state's laws regarding privileged communication.

Legal Issues in Managed Care.   Some form of managed care is currently present in all forms of health care (Appelbaum, 1993). A number of legal issues have emerged in conjunction with this movement toward managed care. Appelbaum (1993) identified legal issues associated with managed care that affect practitioners and providers. Practitioners have several legal responsibilities associated with managed care. Some of these are the duty to appeal adverse decisions, the duty to disclose, and the duty to continue treatment. The duty to appeal adverse decisions relates to the necessity to write to the managed care provider and appeal a decision to limit or decline services if the counselor believes that it is not in the best interest of the client (for example, the client is suicidal or homicidal). The duty to disclose involves informing clients about the financial limitations of managed care (in terms of payment for therapy being stopped before the counselor or client believes that the goals of therapy have been reached) and the problems associated with confidentiality regarding the provider having access to personal information that the client has disclosed during counseling. There are legal and ethical issues relating to the duty to continue treatment. It is not considered ethical or legal to "abandon" clients who no longer have the financial means for counseling (for example, managed care refuses to pay). Counselors should attempt to refer the client to free or affordable services, see the client for free, or move toward an appropriate termination (Appelbaum, 1993).

Providers also have legal responsibilities regarding managed care. These include the duty to review appeals and other pertinent information regarding the care of clients, the duty to disclose to clients the limits of coverage, and the duty to select qualified providers (Appelbaum, 1993). Together practitioners and providers must work closely together to ensure that clients receive appropriate care and services.

Malpractice. Counselors have an increased risk of being sued for malpractice (Corey, 1996). It is therefore important for counselors to understand what malpractice is and what they can do to prevent legal difficulties.

Knapp (1980) defines malpractice as an act or omission by a counselor that is inconsistent with reasonable care and skill used by other reputable counselors and that results in injury to the client. Knapp (1980) notes that courts do not assume that malpractice exists if a counselor has made a mistake in judgment, since it is possible to make such a mistake and still exercise reasonable care. Keeton (1984) identifies four conditions that must exist for malpractice to have occurred. Applied to a counseling situation, these are (a) the counselor had a duty to a client, (b) the duty of care was not met, (c) the client sustained an injury, and (d) there was a close causal relationship between the counselor's failure to provide reasonable care and the resulting injury.

DePauw (1986) provides guidelines for avoiding ethical violations relating at each phase of the counseling process. These guidelines can minimize the risk of harm to clients and the incidence of malpractice suits for counselors.

Precounseling. Issues during this phase include accurately advertising services, making advance financial arrangements that are clearly understood and serve the best interest of the client, providing services within the counselor's parameters of competency, facilitating the client's informed choice of services, avoiding dual relationships, clearly indicating experimental treatment approaches and taking appropriate safety precautions, and identifying the limits to confidentiality.

Ongoing Counseling. Issues include maintaining confidentiality, seeking consultation as necessary, maintaining adequate client records, taking necessary action regarding clients who pose a clear and imminent danger to themselves or others, and complying with laws that relate to reporting child abuse and neglect.

Termination Phase. Issues at this point include being sensitive to the client's termination and post-termination concerns, initiating termination or referral if the client is no longer benefitting from services, and evaluating the efficacy of counseling services.

Special Ethical and Legal Issues

This section addresses some of the special ethical and legal issues associated with marriage and family therapy, child counseling, and group counseling. Information is also provided on ethical and legal issues relating to Acquired Immunodeficiency Syndrome (AIDS).

Issues Relating to Marriage and Family Therapy. Huber (1994) has identified ethical and legal issues in marriage and family therapy in terms of client welfare, confidentiality, informed consent, and dual relations.

Client Welfare. The AAMFT's (1991) ethical position relating to client welfare is

> Marriage and family therapists advance the welfare of families and individuals. They respect the rights of those persons seeking their assistance, and make reasonable efforts to ensure that their services are used appropriately.

The issue of client welfare can become complex in marriage and family therapy because the counselor is working with more than one client. Margolin (1982) notes that there can be a conflict in the goals of individuals seeking marriage and family therapy. This can occur in marriage therapy, for example, when one person wants a divorce and the other does not. Huber (1994) suggests that a counselor can avoid these problems by utilizing a systems perspective rather than focusing on the problems of individual clients.

Confidentiality. The AAMFT's (1991) ethical position on confidentiality is

> Marriage and family therapists have unique confidentiality concerns because the client in a therapeutic relationship may be more than one person. Therapists respect and guard confidences of each individual client.

Respecting the confidence of clients in marriage and family therapy can often create an ethical dilemma, for example, being asked to keep information about a client's affair from the client's spouse.

Margolin (1982) notes that counselors tend to take one of two positions regarding confidentiality when working with couples and families. One position involves the counselor viewing each marital partner or family member as an individual client. In this approach, the counselor may routinely see the clients individually before seeing them together in couples or family therapy. A counselor who utilizes this approach needs to develop a clear position on confidentiality and to communicate it to the clients. Typically, the counselor will either reserve the right to use professional judgment to maintain individual confidence or avoid disclosing sensitive information unless the client gives permission.

A second approach to confidentiality that Margolin (1982) describes is based on nonsecrecy. From this perspective, the counselor does not feel any obligation to withhold information from the other marital partner or family member. A counselor who utilizes this position usually avoids seeing the clients individually. In addition, the counselor should inform the clients of the policy on confidentiality before they commence counseling.

Confidentiality can also vary in marriage and family therapy in terms of privileged communication. Huber (1994) notes that the concept of privileged communication was originally developed within a context of one-to-one relationships, for example, doctor-patient and attorney-client. It is therefore not surprising that there have been conflicting legal precedents when this concept has been applied to situations involving more than one client.

Several legal cases have tested the validity of privileged communication for clients involved in marriage counseling. Herrington (1979) notes that a Virginia judge ruled that there was no confidentiality because statements were not made in private to a doctor, but were made in the presence of a spouse. Another case reported by Margolin (1982) provides support for privileged communication in marriage counseling. This case involved a man who decided to divorce his wife. He had his counselor subpoenaed to testify in court about statements his wife had made during their conjoint sessions. In this case, the husband was waiving his right of privileged communication, but the wife was not waiving hers. The judge ruled in favor of protecting the wife's right to confidentiality. In view of the varying litigation on this subject, it is important for counselors to determine the laws in their state regarding privileged communication in multiperson therapies (Gumper & Sprenkle, 1981).

Informed Consent.   The AAMFT (1991) provides the following ethical position relating to informed consent:

> Marriage and family therapists respect the right of clients to make decisions and help them to understand the consequences of these decisions. Therapists clearly advise a client that a decision on marital status is the responsibility of the client.

Applying the concept of informed consent can be more difficult in marriage and family therapy than in individual counseling. Margolin (1982) notes that the individuals who undergo marriage and family therapy together do not always begin therapy at the same time. It may therefore be necessary to repeat the procedures associated with informed consent as new clients begin the counseling process.

Dual Relationships.   The AAMFT (1991) provides the following ethical position on dual relationships:

> Marriage and family therapists are aware of their influential position with respect to clients, and they avoid exploiting the trust and dependency of such persons. Therapists, therefore, make every effort to avoid dual relationships with clients that could impair professional judgment or increase the risk of exploitation. Examples of such dual relationships include, but are not limited to, business or close personal relationships with clients. Sexual intimacy with clients is prohibited. Sexual intimacy with former clients for two years following the termination of therapy is prohibited.

Dual relationships can pose problems in all types of counseling, including marriage and family counseling. One potential problem in marriage and family counseling is providing individual counseling and marriage counseling to the same individual and attempting to ensure that confidentiality is maintained.

Issues Relating to Child and Adolescent Counseling.   Child and adolescent counseling can involve special ethical and legal issues in terms of informed consent, confidentiality, and reporting laws that relate to child abuse.

Informed Consent.   Corey, Corey, and Callanan (1998) note that most states require parental consent for minors to receive counseling services. Some states permit minors to enter into a counseling relationship without parental permission in crisis situations, such as those involving substance abuse (Corey, Corey, & Callanan, 1998). Counselors should therefore be aware of the laws relating to informed consent in their state.

Confidentiality.   Ansell (1987) describes confidentiality with minors as a gray area that requires the counselor to proceed with caution. Conflicts can result from the counselor's legal responsibility to respect a parent's right to be informed of counseling services and the ethical responsibility to maintain the confidentiality of the minor (Huey, 1986).

Ansell (1987) suggests that counselors establish guidelines with the parents and the minor regarding the nature of information that can be released to parents. The ACA's (1997) ethical code can be used to structure these guidelines: "When counseling minors or persons unable to give voluntary informed consent, counselors act in these clients' best interest" (Section A:3). The counselor can therefore suggest that confidentiality information will be released to parents when the counselor believes it is in the child's best interest.

Parents are also legally entitled to have access to their child's or adolescent's confidential records (Thompson & Rudolph, 1997). Personal notes are exempt from this requirement when they are kept separate from institutional files; they are not seen by anyone, including clerical staff; and they were not discussed with anyone in the process of decision making (Thompson & Rudolph, 1997).

Child Abuse.   All states have laws relating to child abuse (Thompson & Rudolph, 1997), and most require counselors to report suspected abuse (Congdon, 1987). These laws usually "include penalties for failure to report and provide immunity for the reporter from criminal and civil liability" (Congdon, 1987). Counselors should limit their reporting of information to that which is required by law. Reporting additional information can make the counselor guilty of releasing privileged information (Congdon, 1987).

Issues Relating to Group Counseling.   The Association for Specialists in Group Work (ASGW) revised its ethical standards in 1989 (ASGW, 1990). The highlights of the ASGW's ethical code and legal issues are as follows.

Orientation.   Information is provided to prospective or new members on a variety of issues such as the length of group, role expectations for group members, goal of the group, potential risks, and fees.

Screening of Members.   The counselor "selects group members whose needs and goals are compatible with the goals of the group; who will not impede the group process; and whose well-being will not be jeopardized by the group experience" (ASGW, 1990, p. 121).

Confidentiality.   Group counselors alert members of the limits to confidentiality before counseling begins. These limits relate to when a client poses a serious threat to self or others and when group members are minors. The counselors should also discuss potential problems of group members violating confidentiality.

Voluntary or Involuntary Participation.   "Group counselors inform members whether participation is voluntary or involuntary" (ASGW, 1990, p. 121). Informed consent should be obtained for both voluntary and involuntary groups. In addition, group counselors do not certify successful completion unless a member meets the defined group expectations.

Leaving a Group.   "Provisions are made to assist a group member to terminate in an effective way" (ASGW, 1990, p. 122). Group members have the right to exit a group whenever they choose but should inform the counselor and group members prior to termination. The counselor should also discuss possible risks associated with premature termination.

Imposing Counselor Values.   Group counselors strive to become aware of their needs and values and the impact they may have on clients.

Equitable Treatment.   "Group counselors make every reasonable effort to treat each member individually and equally" (ASGW, 1990, p. 123). Counselors also attempt to ensure that each group member has equitable use of group time.

Dual Relationship.   "Group counselors avoid dual relationships with group members that might impair their objectivity and professional judgment, as well as those which are likely to compromise a group member's ability to participate fully in a group" (ASGW, 1990, p. 123).

Goal Development.   Every effort is made to help each group member develop personal goals.

Consultation.   Policies regarding between-session consultation with group members are specified.

Termination from the Group.   Group members are encouraged to terminate from the group in the most efficient period of time.

Evaluation and Follow-up.   "Group counselors make every attempt to engage in ongoing assessment and to design follow-up procedures for their groups" (ASGW, 1990, p. 125).
    Paradise and Kirby (1990) identify several legal issues relating to group counseling. They suggest that group counselors should take extra precautions regarding confidentiality. It is especially important to clarify the limits to confidentiality and privileged communication for members during pregroup orientation or the first session. Counselors can be sued for negligence if they have given the impression that confidentiality was guaranteed. In addition, group counselors should have all members sign a contract requiring confidentiality and stating that breach of confidentiality will result in the member being dropped from the group (Paradise & Kirby, 1990).
    Legal problems in group counseling can also arise from issues relating to a counselor's duty to protect. As noted earlier in this chapter, the Tarasoff litigation (Tarasoff v. Board of Regents of the University of California, 1974, 1976) mandated that counselors have a legal responsibility to warn anyone who is the subject of a serious threat.
    Corey, Corey, Callanan, and Russell (1982) note that the incidence of verbal abuse and subsequent casualties is higher in group counseling than individual counseling because of the intensity of group work and interaction between members. Paradise and Kirby (1990) therefore suggest that group counselors screen out potentially dangerous clients and continuously monitor clients to ensure their physical and psychological safety.

Multicultural Issues.   Corey, Williams, and Moline (1995) emphasize the importance of recognizing multicultural issues in group counseling. They provide several guidelines for addressing diversity issues in group counseling. These are summarized as follows: group leaders must be respectful and sensitive to multicultural issues in groups, including differences in religious and spiritual issues of group members. Leaders need to be aware of social cultural forces such as racism and help group members recognize when their problems stem from external forces. In addition, leaders must be aware of their own biases and prejudices and work them through so they do not have an adverse effect on group process.

Legal Issues in Group Counseling.   Corey, Williams, and Moline (1995) provide an overview of legal issues in group counseling. They note that the best way to avoid malpractice suits is to practice within the boundaries of one's competency and to practice in a *reasonable, ordinary, and prudent* manner. In addition, they suggest that group counselors understand state laws and how they impact on confidentiality and privileged communication, use written contracts with members to ensure informed consent, secure permission from legal guardians when working with minors, and ensure the rights and safety of group members.

Issues Relating to AIDS.   Many authors have addressed ethical issues that relate to providing counseling services to clients infected by the AIDS virus (Cohen, 1990; Gray & Harding, 1988; Melton, 1988). The main ethical question that emerges from the literature is, What should a counselor do when a sexually active client has AIDS and has not informed any partners of the illness? In these instances, the counselor's ethical dilemma would be whether to maintain confidentiality or inform the client's sexual partners that they are being exposed to the AIDS virus.

Gray and Harding (1988) believe that there are both ethical and legal precedents for breaking confidentiality in these cases. In terms of ethics, the authors cite the 1997 ACA ethical standards, which state that confidentiality can be breached when there is a "clear and imminent danger" to self or others (Section B.1). In addition, the Tarasoff case set forth a legal precedent regarding "duty to warn" (Tarasoff v. Board of Regents of the University of California, 1974, 1976). As a result of the Tarasoff case, professional counselors have a legal duty to warn a person if their client poses a serious threat.

Naturally, counselors should not arbitrarily break confidentiality in cases involving AIDS clients. Instead, they should only do this as a last resort. Gray and Harding (1988) and Cohen (1990) provide several guidelines that can assist counselors in dealing with these sensitive ethical dilemmas. Their recommendations are summarized as follows.

- Clients should be made aware of the limits to confidentiality before they begin counseling.
- Clients who have contracted the AIDS virus should be informed how the virus is spread and what precautions they can take to prevent its spreading.
- Clients should be encouraged to inform any sexual partner that they may have been exposed to the virus.
- If a client is unwilling to inform any partner who may be at risk, the counselor should first alert the client of the need to break confidentiality and then inform the sexual partner in a timely fashion.
- Counselors should limit disclosure of information to general medical information regarding the client's disease.
- Disclosures should only be made to the party at risk or to a guardian in the case of a minor.
- Disclosures should communicate willingness to provide counseling services to the client.
- Medical consultation and referral should be arranged as necessary.

Stanard and Hazler (1995) provide additional information regarding the implications of Tarasoff in HIV cases. They suggest that each case needs to be carefully evaluated for its own unique circumstances. When the case does present medical evidence of the AIDS virus, there is a high-risk relationship, and little likelihood of the client's self-disclosure, "counselors are directed to seek consultation, to make sure no reasonable alternative can be utilized, and even then to release only information that is necessary, relevant, and verifiable" (Stanard & Hazler, 1995, p. 97). In addition, they stress the importance of working with clients to prevent the infection of present and future individuals.

Ethical-Legal Decision Making

Huber (1994) describes a method for ethical decision making that has been incorporated into the following model for ethical-legal decision making. Ethical-legal decision making provides a structure for addressing ethical-legal issues that impact on counseling. It must be emphasized that throughout the decision-making process, it is critical to consult when necessary and to document all significant activities and events such as consultation and treatment efforts (for example, phone calls to a suicidal client).

Step 1: Determine Whether the Situation Requires an Ethical-Legal Decision. Counselors must first determine if an ethical-legal decision needs to be made. This requires an awareness of ethical codes and legal issues and how they may affect clinical practice, for example, the importance of confidentiality in counseling.

Step 2: Considering Diversity Issues. As society becomes increasingly diversified, it is essential to incorporate a multicultural perspective in all phases of clinical practice. As noted earlier, Meara et al. (1996) note that virtue ethics attempts to broaden ethical decision making beyond the self to reflect the interest of community and culture. These authors go on to suggest that "virtue ethics, rooted in the narratives and aspirations of specific communities, can be particularly helpful to professionals in discerning appropriate ethical conduct in multicultural settings and interactions" (p. 4). From this perspective, virtue ethics appears to parallel social constructionism's in terms of broadening the self to include sensitivity to the cultures reflected in the stories that clients tell.

Meara et al. (1996) also note that ethical-legal decision making evolved from a European-American perspective. A number of biases associated with ethnocentrism must therefore be addressed. These authors cite Carol Gillian's (1982) seminal work on the role of gender in moral development as an example of the importance of considering diversity issues in ethical-legal decision making.

Step 3: Formulating an Ethical-Legal Course of Action. Once counselors establish that an ethical-legal dilemma exists, they must determine what form of action to take. Consultation with a legal advisor and/or one's supervisor can be an important first step in formulating a course of action. Legal consultation can be useful to identify potential legal issues and the appropriate action associated with a case. Supervisors can also play a vital role in formulating a course of action. Kitchener (1984, 1985) has identified two levels of ethics that can be used to formulate a course of action: intuitive and critical-evaluative. The intuitive level addresses immediate feelings in response to the situation. An intuitive reaction can be useful in situations that require immediate action, such as crisis intervention.

The critical-evaluative level of ethical reasoning can be used in situations that do not require immediate action. Most situations requiring an ethical decision are complex, with no clear right or wrong way of proceeding. Kitchener (1984, 1985) suggests a three-tiered approach to critically evaluate a particular situation. The first tier involves referring to the code of ethics for guidelines pertaining to the ethical situation. If these guidelines are insufficient, counselors can move to the second tier and determine the philosophical foundations on which the ethical guidelines were based, such as the right to privacy or the right to make free choices. When counselors are still uncertain, they can proceed to the third tier and apply the principles of ethical theory. There are several noted ethical theorists who can help provide a rationale for ethical action (Ableson & Nielson, 1967; Baier, 1958). Huber (1994) surveyed these theorists and identified suggestions that could be of help in ethical decision making. For example, counselors should do what they would want for themselves or significant others in a similar situation, or they should do what would result in the least amount of harm.

Step 4: Overcoming Personal-Professional Conflicts.   This process recognizes that a counselor's personal and professional values may be in conflict, thereby inhibiting appropriate action. For example, a counselor may have a colleague who is also a close friend. The counselor may become aware of unethical behavior on the part of the colleague but may not want to take action because of their friendship. One way for counselors to overcome such an impasse is to remember that they will be acting unethically if they do not take constructive action.

Step 5: Implementing an Action Plan.   Once counselors have determined a course of action and overcome possible personal-professional conflicts, they are in a position to implement an action plan. This will require courage and the willingness to accept personal responsibility for their actions. After implementing a plan of action, counselors may wish to evaluate their professional functioning. Van Hoose (1980) has provided the following guidelines that counselors can use to determine whether their actions are ethically responsible. Counselors have probably acted ethically if they have maintained personal and professional honesty; had the client's best interest in mind; acted without malice or personal gain; and can justify their action as the best judgment according to the current state of the profession.

Clinical Examples

The following clinical examples provide an opportunity to practice ethical decision making. Four ethical dilemmas are presented that relate to a variety of clinical situations. There is no right or wrong way of responding to these examples, but counselors should simply attempt to develop a response that reflects sound clinical judgment. Each example is followed by a description of the way I would respond.

Clinical Example #1.   You are a counselor at a community mental health center. A young woman was convicted of drunk driving and told by the judge that she must attend your alcohol treatment program to keep her driver's license. You are concerned about the issue of informed consent. What would you do in this situation if you were the counselor?

My Response.   Any situation that involves a client who has been court-ordered to undergo counseling creates an ethical dilemma. The ethical code regarding informed consent requires that this client must not be forced to attend counseling. In addition, the client should feel free to terminate counseling whenever she chooses. At the same time, the counselor must inform the judge if the client does not complete the alcohol program. Technically, the client is free to choose counseling and keep her driver's license or choose no counseling and lose her license. At the very least, if the client chooses counseling, she may be doing so under duress.

As the counselor, I would first discuss with the client what the alcohol treatment program entailed and give her a professional disclosure statement. The statement would provide information such as my background, my definition of counseling, and the limits to confidentiality. I would then explore with her the available options, that she may either lose her license or attend the alcohol program. If she did decide to participate in the alcohol program, I would recognize the duress she must be feeling and suggest that we both try to make the best of a difficult situation. I would tell her that she is free to terminate her participation in the program at any time. I would also emphasize that if she decided to do so, I would unfortunately be obligated to inform the judge that she did not complete the program successfully.

Clinical Example #2.   You are an elementary school counselor. After working at the school for a month, you identify several policies that conflict with your ethical code. Two examples of these policies are (1) You are told you must provide counseling services for certain students even if they don't want them; and (2) you are not allowed to maintain confidentiality because you must inform the principal about what certain students tell you during their sessions.

My Response.   The ACA (1997) code of ethics suggests that when an institution functions in a manner that conflicts with the counselor's code of ethics, the counselor should attempt to resolve the differences with the institution. If the institution in this example is not willing to make the necessary changes, you must resign. It would be important for you to remember that even when an institution asks you to act unethically, you cannot defend your action later by saying, "My supervisor told me to do it."

Clinical Example #3.   You are a mental health counselor in a community mental health center. After the second session with a male client, you decide he may be suffering from a serious mental disorder. You don't feel comfortable providing counseling services because you think the client requires help beyond your area of competence. You decide to refer the client to a psychiatrist or other mental health professional. The client refuses to accept your suggestion and insists instead that you continue seeing him. What would you do if you were the counselor?

My Response.   The ACA (1997) and APA (1992) codes of ethics regarding client welfare suggest that a counselor has an ethical responsibility to refer a client who requires help beyond the counselor's level of competency. If the client is reluctant or resistant to pursue a referral, the counselor can help the client overcome these impasses. The counselor may also wish to consult with a supervisor to gain ideas to facilitate the referral process. In addition, the counselor should document all attempts to assist with the referral to provide a "paper trail." This could be useful to be able to document that the counselor did not commit an ethical violation in terms of abandoning the client.

Clinical Example #4.   You have a private practice specializing in marriage, family, and child counseling. You are seeing a married couple, Dan and Mary, in marriage counseling. Your approach to marriage counseling is to see the marital partners individually for 15 minutes each and then together for 30 minutes.

During the initial session, you first talk with Dan. He informs you that he and Mary have been married for two years. Before the marriage, he was an intravenous drug user, "shooting up" heroin at least twice a day for several years. Dan explains that he had been off drugs for two years, but two weeks ago he ran into some of his old buddies and started "using the needle again." He says that he will not tell Mary about his drug habit because he wants the marriage to work out. He fears that if she found out, she would leave him. What would you do in this situation if you were the counselor?

My Response.   As a counselor, I would want to help Dan with his drug problem and help Dan and Mary with their marital difficulties. In addition. I would be concerned about the potential ethical and legal issues, since current research suggests that intravenous drug users are a high-risk group for contracting the AIDS virus.

This case has several ethical issues (client welfare and confidentiality) and one legal issue (relating to the Tarasoff ruling). In terms of client welfare, I would be concerned for Dan regarding his drug problem, for Mary regarding the potential of her contracting the AIDS virus, and for the two of them regarding their marriage. I would also have some ethical and legal concerns regarding confidentiality. Ethically, I need to do whatever I can to ensure my clients' safety when they are in imminent danger (including breaking confidentiality). The Tarasoff ruling of duty to warn and protect also may require me to break confidentiality and take the necessary steps to ensure Mary's safety regarding contracting the AIDS virus from Dan.

In weighing the various legal and ethical issues, I would first explain to Dan how the AIDS virus can be spread by sharing a needle among people who have AIDS or are HIV positive. I would then make sure he understood that he could transmit the AIDS virus to Mary if they had unprotected intercourse. In addition, I would request that Dan get an AIDS test; insist that Dan tell Mary about his drug habit before the end of our first session so that she could decide if she wanted to take the risk of having sex with him; warn him that if he did not tell her, I would, because I view his drug habit as posing a clear and imminent danger to Mary; recommend that Dan enter into a drug rehabilitation program as soon as possible; and continue marital therapy as necessary.

Diversity Issues.   Diversity issues such as culture and spirituality impact on all phases of the counseling process, including ethical-legal decision making. Pedersen (1997) provides a scholarly review of the ACA code of ethics in terms of culture. He concludes that the ACA code of ethics contains cultural bias, favors the dominant culture, and fosters cultural encapsulation. These problems are reflected in the ethical codes' failure to consider the world views of clients and the utilization of a unidimensional (instead of multidimensional) cultural perspective.

Spirituality is an emerging diversity issue that is being incorporated into a multicultural perspective (Bishop, 1995). Spiritual issues in counseling are recognizing the role that values and morality play in ethical-legal decision making and the necessity of addressing these issues from a multicultural perspective (Grant, 1992; Schulte, 1992). This literature suggests that counseling, by its very nature, is a value-laden process (Grant, 1992), whereby clients are aware of their counselors' value systems and counselors help clients explore value-laden issues (Patterson, 1992). Ethical-legal decision making must therefore take into consideration the multiple voices that define what is moral-ethical behavior. In this process counselors can attempt to understand clients' values (including morality) from their world view and guard against imposing universal-unidimensional definitions of morality (Pedersen, 1997).

Summary

Counselors face many professional issues. Exploring the four building blocks of professional counseling: formal study of counseling and professional affiliation, certification or licensure, continuing education, and professional involvement encourages students to become involved in professional issues as soon as possible.

Counselors and psychologists have codes of ethics such as the ACA, APA, and AAMFT to help guide their clinical practice. These ethical codes are not written in black-and-white terms but must be interpreted and applied to each particular clinical situation. Major ethical issues for counselors include client welfare, informed consent, confidentiality, and dual relationships. Special ethical issues relate to marriage and family therapy, child counseling, group counseling, and AIDS.

Several legal issues concern members of the counseling profession. For example, a counselor must break confidentiality when a client poses a clear and imminent danger to self or others. Privileged communication exists to protect the rights of clients in terms of confidentiality in a legal proceeding. This privilege belongs to the client and not the counselor.

Clinical examples provide opportunities to apply various ethical and legal principles. Counselors must also be aware of the diversity issues in ethical-legal decision making.

CHAPTER

3

The Counseling Process

CHAPTER OVERVIEW

This chapter provides an overview of the counseling process as well as a description of some of the common problems that beginning counselors experience. It explores what can occur in a counseling session and some of the special skills utilized in counseling.

Highlights of the chapter include

- The art and science of the counseling process
- The six stages of the counseling process
- Listening skills
- Recent trends in counseling
- Brief-counseling approaches
- Common problems for beginning counselors
- Diversity issues

The Art and Science of the Counseling Process

The counseling process is both an art and a science. For example, it is an art to really listen to a client and to communicate caring and compassion. Through the art of listening, a counselor attempts to enter into the client's world and see things from the client's perspective. The art of counseling requires the counselor to reach sensitively into the world of clients and help them become aware of their strengths and hidden beauty. The art of counseling also recognizes the importance of tuning into and reacting appropriately to diversity issues such as culture, gender, and spirituality. All these issues play important roles in addressing the theory, research, and practice of counseling.

The science of counseling creates an important balance, providing an objective dimension to the subjective art of counseling. Counselors must be able to utilize scientific tools to gain an objective understanding of what is occurring during the various stages of the counseling process, from formulating a counseling relationship to termination and follow-up and research and evaluation. For example, the counseling literature has identified a number of factors associated with establishing a positive counseling relationship, such as core conditions (for example, empathy, respect, genuineness, and immediacy). There are numerous other examples of the role of science in counseling from the use of standardized tests in assessment to research methodology for evaluating efficacy in counseling.

Counseling is not a fixed entity but a fluid process in which the counselor continually tries to adjust course to accommodate the unique and emerging needs of clients. The art and science of counseling should provide a point of reference to chart an effective course through the counseling process.

The Six Stages of the Counseling Process

Most counseling sessions last approximately 50 minutes (Linder, 1954). A counseling session is therefore sometimes referred to as the 50-minute hour. What actually takes place in a session depends on the client's needs and the counselor's personal approach to counseling. Although there is some variation during a session, there is a basic structure that most counseling approaches have in common. This structure is described by Cormier and Hackney (1993) as a five-stage process: relationship building, assessment, goal setting, interventions, and termination and follow-up. These stages have been expanded into the following six-stage model of the counseling process.

Stage one: Relationship building
Stage two: Assessment and diagnosis
Stage three: Formulation of counseling goals
Stage four: Intervention and problem solving
Stage five: Termination and follow-up
Stage six: Research and evaluation

A typical counseling session can involve all six stages except termination, The focus of counseling may shift as the counseling process progresses over time. For example, during

Counseling can be conceptualized as a series of stages or steps that lead one through the counseling process.

the first few sessions with a client, a counselor may place the primary emphasis on building a positive counseling relationship, assessment and diagnosis, and formulating counseling goals. During the later phase of the counseling process, the counselor may shift the emphasis to intervention and problem solving, termination and follow-up, and research and evaluation. A more complete description of these six stages follows.

Stage One: Relationship Building

The counseling relationship is the heart of the counseling process. It supplies the vitality and the support necessary for counseling to work. It is the critical factor associated with successful outcomes in counseling (Kokotovic & Tracey, 1990). Sexton & Whiston (1994, p. 6) commented on the importance of the counseling relationship when they noted that "the quality of the counseling relationship has consistently been found to have the most significant impact on successful client outcome."

Although there appears to be a general consensus that the counseling relationship is important, it is less clear how important it is and in what way (Gelso & Carter, 1985). Research efforts that have attempted to address these issues can be grouped into two general categories, counselor-offered conditions and counselor- and client-offered conditions.

Counselor-Offered Conditions.   Counselor-offered conditions relate to how the counselor influences the counseling process. The majority of the literature on the counseling relationship has focused on counselor-offered conditions relating to core conditions for effective counseling and the social influence model. An overview of the issues associated with these two important topics follows.

Core Conditions.   Rogers (1957) identified what he believed were core conditions for successful counseling: empathic understanding, unconditional positive regard, and congruence. Rogers (1957) suggested that these core conditions were necessary and sufficient for constructive personality change to occur. No other conditions were necessary. Later, Carkhuff (1969, 1971) expanded the core conditions to include respect, immediacy, confrontation, concreteness, and self-disclosure. Carkhuff (1969, 1971) also pioneered the development of listening skills that could be used to promote these core conditions. An overview of the eight conditions is provided in Table 3.1. This table is followed by a description of each of these core conditions.

Empathy.   Empathy is considered the most important core condition in terms of promoting positive outcomes (Orlando & Howard, 1986). Gelso and Fretz (1992) observe that virtually all major schools of counseling note the importance of empathy in the counseling process.

Egan (1994) describes empathic understanding as a process that involves listening, understanding, *and* communicating that understanding to the client. Carl Rogers emphasizes the experiential nature of empathy. He vigorously rejects mechanistic explanations of empathy that focus on techniques such as reflection of feeling (Raskin & Rogers, 1995). According to Rogers, empathy involves entering into and experiencing the client's phe-

TABLE 3.1   Core Conditions

Core Conditions	Description	Purpose
Empathy	Communicating a sense of caring and understanding	To establish rapport, gain an understanding of the client, and encourage self-exploration in the client
Unconditional positive regard	Communicating to clients that they have value and worth as individuals	To promote acceptance of the client as a person of worth as distinct from accepting the client's behavior
Congruence	Behaving in a manner consistent with how one thinks and feels	To be genuine (not phony) in interactions with the client
Respect	Focusing on the positive attributes of the client	To focus on the client's strengths (not weaknesses)
Immediacy	Communicating in the here-and-now about what is occurring in the counseling session	To promote direct mutual communication between the counselor and client
Confrontation	Pointing out discrepancies in what the client is saying and doing (between statements and nonverbal behavior), and how the client is viewed by the counselor and client	To help clients clearly and accurately understand themselves and the world around them
Concreteness	Helping clients discuss themselves in specific terms	To help clients focus on pertinent issues
Self-disclosure	Making the self known to others	To promote increasing counseling-relevant communication from the client, enhancing the client's evaluation of the counselor, and increasing the client's willingness to seek counseling

nomenological world. It is an active, immediate, and ongoing process in which the counselor becomes aware of the client's feelings, experiences those feelings, and creates a mirror through which clients can explore and discover deeper meanings associated with their feelings (Raskin & Rogers, 1995).

Empathic understanding can be understood as a multistage process (Barrett-Lennard, 1981; Gladstein, 1983) consisting of different types of empathy. Gladstein (1983) identifies the following stages of empathy: the counselor has an emotional reaction to the client's situation, the counselor attempts to understand the client's situation from the client's perspective, the counselor communicates empathy to the client, and the client feels a sense of caring and understanding from the counselor.

Several kinds of empathy have also been identified, for example, primary and advanced empathy (Egan, 1994). Egan describes primary empathy as a process that involves the counselor attending, listening, and communicating accurate perceptions of the client's messages. Advanced empathy involves the characteristics associated with primary empathy as well as utilizing the skills of self-disclosure, directives, or interpretations.

Unconditional Positive Regard. Unconditional positive regard involves the counselor communicating to clients that they are of value and worth as individuals. This concept has been referred to by several other names, including nonpossessive warmth, acceptance, prizing, respect, and regard. There has been some controversy regarding the core condition of unconditional positive regard. Gelso and Fretz (1992) contend that this concept is neither desirable nor obtainable. Martin (1989) counters the critics by suggesting that the concept has been misunderstood. According to Martin, unconditional positive regard does not imply that the counselor reacts permissively, accepting all the client's behavior. Instead, it means that the counselor's unconditional positive regard involves acceptance of the client while setting limits on certain behaviors (see Rogers et al., 1967 for additional information on unconditional positive regard).

Congruence. Congruence involves counselors behaving in a manner consistent with how they think and feel. This condition has also been referred to as genuineness. An example of not functioning congruently is a counselor who says, "I'm glad to see you," when a client arrives for an appointment, even though the counselor does not like the client.

Respect. Respect is similar to unconditional positive regard in that it focuses on the positive attributes of the client. Counselors can communicate respect by making positive statements about the client and openly and honestly acknowledging, appreciating, and tolerating individual differences (Okun, 1997)

Immediacy. Carkhuff (1969, 1971) developed the concept of immediacy, which is similar to Ivey's (1971) notion of direct, mutual communication. Immediacy involves communication between the counselor and client that focuses on the here and now. It allows the counselor to directly address issues of importance to the counseling relationship. Immediacy can involve counselors describing how they feel in relation to the client in the moment. For example, if a client does not appear interested in counseling, the counselor might say, "I'm getting concerned that you're not finding our sessions meaningful. How are you feeling about what is going on in counseling now?"

Confrontation. The core condition of confrontation involves the counselor pointing out discrepancies in what a client is saying. There can be discrepancies between what the client is saying and doing (Gazda et al., 1979), between statements and nonverbal behavior (Ivey, 1994), and between how clients see themselves versus how the counselor sees them (Egan, 1994).

Confrontation is a difficult and risky counseling technique that is used most effectively by high-functioning counselors (Berenson & Mitchell, 1968). Confrontation can have a negative effect on the counseling process, for example, when a client misreads the confrontation and feels attacked or rejected by the counselor (Egan, 1994).

Concreteness.   Concreteness refers to the counselor helping clients discuss their concerns in specific terms. Clients can feel overwhelmed with their problems and have difficulty putting things into perspective. When this occurs, concreteness can help the counselor create a focus for the client in the counseling process.

Self-Disclosure.   Jourard (1958) developed the concept of self-disclosure, which involves making the self known to another. Danish, D'Augelli, and Brock (1976) differentiate two types of self-disclosure statements: self-disclosing and self-involving. In self-disclosing statements, counselors disclose factual information about themselves. In self-involving statements, counselors describe what they are experiencing in relation to the client in the counseling process.

A review of the literature suggests support for both types of self-disclosure, with some studies favoring the merits of self-disclosing statements and other studies recognizing the value of self-involving statements in the counseling process (Sexton & Whiston, 1994). In addition, Collins and Miller (1994) conducted a meta-analytic review of the literature on self-disclosure and liking. These researchers found that people are liked more when they engage in intimate self-disclosure (as compared to people who self-disclose at less intimate levels of self-disclosure), self-disclosure increases when people like each other, and people like each other more when they engage in self-disclosure. Current research trends on the various facets of self-disclosure show it to be a complex process subject to influence from mediating variables such as gender, race, and disability (Collins & Miller, 1994; Sexton & Whiston, 1994). For example, Mallinckrodt & Helms (1986) found that counselors are perceived as being more attractive when they disclosed having a disability that is not apparent to the client.

Research on Core Conditions.   As mentioned, Rogers (1957) contends that the core conditions are all that is necessary or sufficient for constructive personality change. Many researchers have conducted studies to evaluate this premise. The early research of Truax and Carkhuff (1967) and Truax and Mitchell (1971) provided support for Rogers' theory. During the 1970s, researchers began to report negative results with criticism of earlier studies for methodological flaws or failure to test the efficacy of core conditions in non-Rogerian approaches (Garfield & Bergin, 1971; Mintz, Luborsky, & Auerbach, 1971; Sloane et al., 1975).

More recent research has overcome many of the methodological flaws and is showing overall support for the importance of the core conditions for enhancing the counseling relationship and fostering positive outcomes in counseling (Beutler, Machado, & Neufeldt, 1994; Sexton & Whiston, 1994). Gelso and Fretz's (1992) review of the literature on core conditions concludes that core conditions are not necessary and sufficient as Rogers suggests but do facilitate positive outcomes in counseling. The recent research trend also suggests that the relationship between the core conditions and the counseling process is more complex than previously believed. It appears to be not so much a counselor-offered condition but a set of variables (such as empathy and respect) that are dependent on both the counselor and client (Beutler, Machado, & Neufeldt, 1994).

Social Influence Model. Strong's (1968) social influence model is another theory that emphasizes the importance of counselor-offered conditions in the counseling process. Strong's model has two stages, representing an integration of social psychology into counseling theory. During the first stage, the counselor attempts to be perceived by the client as expert, attractive, and trustworthy. When this occurs, the counselor establishes a power base. In the second stage of Strong's model, the counselor uses the power base to exert positive influence on the client within the counseling process. Extensive research efforts have been conducted to test both stages of Strong's model (see Corrigan et al., 1980; Heppner & Dixon, 1981; and Heppner & Claiborn, 1989 for literature reviews). For example, Heppner and Claiborn provided an overview of studies that have evaluated each stage of Strong's model.

Studies evaluating the first stage of Strong's model attempt to identify what factors promote the client's perception of the counselor as expert, attractive, and trustworthy. Counselors tend to be perceived as *expert* when they have objective evidence of training and utilize prestigious cues (Angle & Goodyear, 1984; Littrell, Caffrey, & Hopper, 1987); use frequent, consistent, and responsive nonverbal behavior such as touch, smiling, and body leans (Roll, Crowley, & Rappl, 1985; Strohmer & Biggs, 1983; Tyson & Wall, 1983); and use narrative analogies and empathic responses (Suit & Paradise, 1985). Counselors are perceived as *attractive* when they have objective evidence of training (Angle & Goodyear, 1984; Paradise, Conway, & Zweig, 1986), have status (McCarthy, 1982), and are self-disclosing (Andersen & Andersen, 1985; Curran & Loganbell, 1985). Counselors appear more *trustworthy* when they use credible introductions and reputational cues (Bernstein & Figioli, 1983; Littrell, Caffrey, & Hopper, 1987), responsive nonverbal behavior (Hackman & Claiborn, 1982); and verbal and nonverbal cues associated with confidentiality (La Fromboise & Dixon, 1981; Merluzzi & Brischetto, 1983).

As noted, the second stage of Strong's model suggests that once counselors establish a power base by appearing expert, attractive, and trustworthy, they can exert a positive influence on the client. The majority of the studies reviewed by Heppner and Claiborn (1989) provide support for the second stage of Strong's model. For example, expertness, attractiveness, and trustworthiness are related to client satisfaction (Heppner & Heesacker, 1983; McNeill, May, & Lee, 1987), changes in the client's self-concept (Dorn & Day, 1985), favorable counseling outcomes (La Crosse, 1980), and less-premature terminators (McNeill, May, & Lee, 1987).

Counselor- and Client-Offered Conditions. The working alliance is another concept that can be used to describe the counseling relationship. It goes beyond focusing on counselor-offered conditions and includes counselor- and client-offered conditions. Several models of the working alliance have emerged from the literature (Greenson, 1967; Bordin, 1979; Gelso & Carter, 1985). Bordin's model has received considerable attention (Kokotovic & Tracey, 1990). Bordin (1979) suggests that the working alliance is composed of three parts: agreement between the counselor and client in terms of the goals of counseling, agreement between the counselor and client in terms of the tasks of counseling, and the emotional bond between the counselor and client.

Research has suggested that positive outcomes in counseling are enhanced if the working alliance is established early in counseling (Kivlighan, 1990). Al-Darmaki and Kivlighan (1993) also note that the literature suggests that the working alliance is dependent on four factors: client precounseling characteristics such as motivation and interpersonal skills, counselor's personal characteristics, counselor's skills, and the match between the client's needs and the counselor's skills and resources. Gelso and Fretz (1992) and Lazarus (1993) have commented on the fourth factor (the importance of the counselor-client fit). Gelso and Fretz suggest that the strength of the working alliance depends on the degree of agreement relating to goals and tasks of counseling and the level of emotional attachment between the counselor and client. Lazarus (1993) goes on to note that the counseling relationship should be characterized by counselors functioning like "authentic chameleons," adjusting their therapeutic style to the unique and emerging needs of clients.

Stage Two: Assessment and Diagnosis

Assessment and diagnosis contribute to several important aspects of the counseling process. They can help a counselor develop an in-depth understanding of a client and identify mental disorders that require attention. This understanding can facilitate goal setting and also suggest types of intervention strategies.

Assessment procedures can be divided into two categories: standardized and nonstandardized measures (Kottler & Brown, 1996). Standardized measures include psychological tests that have a standardized norm group. Nonstandardized measures do not have a standardized norm group and include strategies such as the clinical interview and assessment of life history.

Diagnosis is a medical term that means "identification of the disease-causing pathogens responsible for a physical illness" (Nathan & Harris, 1980, p. 110). Rosenhan and Seligman (1995) identify four reasons for making a diagnosis: facilitating communication shorthand, indicating possible treatment strategies, communicating etiology, and aiding in scientific investigation. Additional information regarding assessment and diagnosis can be found in Chapter 4.

Stage Three: Formulation of Counseling Goals

Cormier and Hackney (1993) described three functions that goals serve in the counseling process: motivational, educational, and evaluative.

First, goals can have a motivational function, especially when clients are involved in establishing the counseling goals. Clients appear to work harder on goals they help create (Cormier & Hackney, 1993). They may also be more motivated when they have specific, concrete goals to work toward. Concrete goals can help clients focus their energy on specific issues. It is also important for counselors to encourage clients to make a verbal commitment to work on a specific counseling goal. Clients tend to be more motivated to work when they have made a commitment to do so (Strong & Claiborn, 1982).

The second function of a counseling goal is educational. From this perspective, clients can learn new skills and behaviors that they can use to enhance their functioning. For example, a counseling goal might be to become more assertive. During assertiveness training, clients can learn skills to enhance their functioning in interpersonal situations.

The third function of a counseling goal is evaluative. Clear goals allow the counselor and client an opportunity to evaluate progress. Goals can also be useful in implementing research strategies, and they provide a means for counselor accountability.

We can also conceptualize counseling goals as either process or outcome goals (Cormier & Hackney, 1993). *Process goals* establish the conditions necessary to make the counseling process work. These goals relate to the issues of formulating a positive relationship by promoting the core conditions, as described earlier in this chapter. Process goals are primarily the counselor's responsibility. *Outcome goals* specify what the client hopes to accomplish in counseling. The counselor and client should agree on these goals and modify them as necessary. George and Cristiani (1995) identify five types of outcome goals: facilitating behavior change, enhancing coping skills, promoting decision-making, improving relationships, and facilitating the client's potential. The following overview expands on these five outcome goals.

1. *Facilitating behavior change.* Some form of behavior change is usually necessary for clients to resolve their concerns. The amount of change necessary varies from client to client. For example, one client might need counseling to learn how to deal effectively with a child, while another might require psychotherapy to change an unhealthy, stressful lifestyle.

2. *Enhancing coping skills.* Erikson (1968) identified several developmental tasks and associated coping mechanisms unique to the various stages of development. Blocher (1974) later created a developmental counseling approach that identified coping skills necessary to proceed through the life span. For example, intimacy and commitment are developmental tasks of young adulthood. Coping behaviors necessary to meet these developmental tasks include appropriate sexual behavior, risk-taking behavior, and value-consistent behavior such as giving and helping. In more general terms, many clients may require help coping with life. They may have problems dealing with stress, anxiety, or a dysfunctional lifestyle. In these situations, clients may benefit from a stress management program that includes relaxation, meditation, and exercise.

3. *Promoting decision making.* Some clients have difficulty making decisions. They may feel that no matter what they decide, it will be wrong. They may even think they are "going crazy." Difficulty making decisions is often a normal reaction to a stressful life situation, for example, a recent divorce. In these situations, the counselor may want to reassure clients that they are not going crazy. Helping clients feel normal can encourage them and alleviate unnecessary worry. For clients who need help developing decision-making skills, the counselor may wish to take a more active role. It may be appropriate to involve family members if the client is suffering from a serious mental disorder such as an organic brain syndrome.

4. *Improving relationships.* Adler (1964) once suggested that the barometer of mental health is social interest. He believed that a person who did not have a close relationship with anyone was at risk for mental problems. Glasser (1965) supported this notion when he noted that all people need one or more reciprocal relationships in which they feel loved and understood and experience a sense of caring. Counselors can use a variety of counseling strategies to help clients improve their interpersonal relations. These strategies include social-skill training programs (Argyle, 1981), group counseling that focuses on interpersonal relations (Rogers, 1970), couple therapy (Sager, 1976), and marital therapy (Humphrey, 1983).

5. *Facilitating the client's potential.* Goals in this category are more abstract and relate to the concepts of self-realization and self-actualization. Self-realization implies helping clients become all they can be as they maximize their creative potential. There can be roadblocks to self-realization that require the counselor's attention. For example, clients may become discouraged and want to quit at the first sign of failure. In these instances, the counselor can help clients gain a more realistic understanding of what is required to be successful. Maslow (1968) developed the concept of self-actualization, which relates to the need to fulfill one's potential. He believes that as people's basic needs are met, they will move toward self-actualization. Rogers (1980) incorporated the concept of self-actualization into his person-centered counseling approach. He believes that if the counselor establishes certain conditions, such as communicating nonpossessive warmth, unconditional positive regard, and empathy, then the client can move toward self-actualization and become a healthy, integrated person.

Stage Four: Intervention and Problem Solving

Once the counselor and client have formulated a counseling goal, they can determine what intervention strategy to implement. They may choose from a variety of interventions, including individual, group, couples, and family counseling. It may be best to begin with individual counseling for clients with problems of an intrapersonal nature. As clients become more secure, they may be able to benefit from the open dialogue that often characterizes group counseling. Couples or family counseling may be more appropriate for clients with difficulties of an interpersonal nature, as in a marital or parent-child conflict.

Involving clients in the process of selecting intervention strategies has some advantages. For example, Devine and Fernald (1973) note that this approach can help counselors avoid using strategies that a client has already tried without apparent success. Instead, the counselor and client together can select a strategy that seems realistic in terms of its strengths and weaknesses.

Cormier and Cormier (1993) provide the following guidelines, which encourage client involvement in selecting the appropriate intervention strategy. The counselor should provide an overview of the different treatment approaches available, describe the role of the counselor and client for each procedure, identify possible risks and benefits that may result, and estimate the time and cost of each procedure. In addition, it is important for the counselor to be sensitive to client characteristics such as values and beliefs when selecting an intervention strategy (Cormier & Hackney, 1993). This sensitivity should extend to multicultural issues. Counselors should also be aware of a client's personal strengths and weaknesses in selecting a counseling approach. For example, counselors should determine whether a client has the necessary self-control or ego strength to utilize a counseling strategy (Cormier & Hackney, 1993).

Problem-Solving Strategies. One way to conceptualize intervention is within the framework of problem solving. Dixon and Glover (1984) suggest that all counseling or psychotherapy is a problem-solving process, whether it involves individual, group, marriage, or family counseling. They note that since the counseling process is focused on helping a client resolve problems, counselors should develop a systematic approach to problem solving. Dixon and Glover also believe that counselors should attempt to teach clients how to use problem-solving skills in their daily lives. This approach would enable clients to learn skills that could contribute to their personal autonomy.

Several problem-solving approaches can be used in the counseling process (for example, Heppner & Krauskopf, 1987; Kanfer & Busemeyer, 1982). Kanfer and Busemeyer identified a six-stage model for problem solving: problem detection, problem definition, identification of alternative solutions, decision-making, execution, and verification. This model is a behaviorally oriented approach that involves describing a particular problem in behavioral terms, identifying possible solutions associated with the problem, deciding on a course of action relative to the various alternative solutions, implementing the decision, and verifying whether the outcome is consistent with the expected outcome.

Nystul (1995) developed a four-step problem-solving model based on Adler's and Glasser's theories. It can be used with children, adolescents, or adults. It has a built in mechanism to enhance clients' motivation for involvement in counseling and minimize client resistance, and it can be especially useful in brief-counseling approaches. An overview of the Nystul problem-solving method is as follows.

1. Step 1 is based on Glasser's theory (Glasser, 1989). It explores what the client is doing that is problematic and adding an "ing" to it to help the client realize the control he or she has over what he or she is doing (for example, angering).

2. Step 2 is based on Adlerian psychology (Adler, 1969) and involves exploring the purpose or psychology of use of the client's behavior. This process involves asking the client, "I'm sure your angering [or whatever it is that is problematic] has served some purpose and been useful to you or you would not be doing it. I wonder when it all began, . . . when you first remember using angering." Together the counselor and client can then explore some early memories in terms of what needs the client may have met while engaging in the problematic behavior. Maslow's hierarchy of needs can be used to help identify possible needs that were met.

Step 2 is the most important phase of the problem-solving approach. It is respectful in that it recognizes that problematic behavior must be useful or the client would not be doing the angering or whatever. This is in contrast to many approaches that simply say things such as "I hear a lot of shoulds and musts in your statements. These sound irrational and can be the cause of your problems." By showing respect to the psychology of use of the client's inefficient approach, the counselor can minimize resistance to the change process and maximize motivation for change.

3. Step 3 involves helping the client realize the cost of not changing. It is based on Homans' (1962) social exchange theory (from social psychology), which suggests that people will change when they realize that the behavior they are engaged in is costing more than it is getting them. During this step, the counselor can help clients realize that what they did to meet their needs as children does not work to meet their needs as adults. This realization can be a paradoxical point in therapy, shifting the client's motivation toward increased involvement in the change process.

4. Step 4 involves helping the client develop a new approach that meets the needs identified in step 2 without the cost associated with step 3. This may involve helping the client learn new coping skills and other strategies necessary to be successful in his or her new approach.

A Case Example. A brief case example can be used to illustrate the four steps of the Nystul problem-solving method. Tom is a 45-year-old physician who had lost two jobs because of angry outbursts in front of his supervisors and had recently been given an ultimatum from his fiancée that he either get his anger under control or she "will be history." During step 1 of the problem-solving approach, the counselor and client identified angering as the problem that the client needs help with. Tom liked the idea of adding the "ing" to anger, because it gave him a feeling of control over the problematic behavior.

Step 2 involved exploring the psychology of use of his angering. Several early memories were obtained that related to when Tom first remembered engaging in angering. For example, his first early memory was of when he had just moved to a new city and had no friends. On the first day of school he got into a fight and broke another boy's nose. Blood was everywhere, and people gathered around and said he was "one tough guy." After the fight, several other boys wanted to be his friend. Tom's initial experience with angering resulted in enhancing his self-esteem and belonging needs.

Step 3 involved helping Tom become aware of the cost of angering. In this process, the counselor and client did a cost-benefit analysis (what he gets from it versus what it is costing him). Quickly it became clear that his angering worked for him when he was a child to meet his basic needs of self-esteem and belonging, but it did not work for him as an adult. In fact angering was having an opposite effect in that his angering was driving people away and making them think he was immature and "infantile" in his behavior. Recognition of the paradoxical effect of angering helped Tom increase his motivation for letting go of his angering and developing more efficient means of meeting his needs.

The counselor then provided Tom insight into his problematic behavior by noting that what works for people as children often does not work for adults (that is, the primitive tools children use such as angering are not acceptable in adult relationships). But people continue to use these primitive tools because their private logic (which is primarily unconscious) tricks them into thinking that they must use these tools to meet their needs. Providing Tom with this insight seemed to help normalize his angering and minimize his resistance to working through his problem.

Step 4 involved helping Tom learn a new approach to use to meet his needs without the cost associated with angering. Tom saw angering as reactive to conflict situations, and he wanted to be more proactive. Together the counselor and client decided that encouragement could be an approach to avoid conflict and work through conflict from a more positive perspective. Encouragement was also seen as an excellent tool to meet needs such as self-esteem and belonging. The counselor and client then spent two sessions helping Tom develop and implement his new approach, which they called encourag*ing,* to help him realize the control he had with his approach.

Stage Five: Termination and Follow-Up

Perhaps the ultimate goal in counseling is for counselors to become obsolete or unnecessary to their clients. This result can occur when clients have worked through their concerns and are able to proceed forward in their lives without the counselor's assistance. At this point, counseling can be terminated. It is usually best for the counselor and client to agree on a termination date, reducing the chance of premature termination or feelings of ambivalence.

Quintana and Holahan (1992, p. 299) note that research has identified four components of termination that are associated with positive outcomes in the counseling process. These components are discussion of the end of counseling, review of the course of counseling, closure of the counselor-client relationship, and discussion of the client's future, post-counseling plans. Based on the literature, it is clear that counselors should attempt to address these four components to prepare clients appropriately for termination (Lamb, 1985). In this process clients can explore what they have learned in counseling and identify how they will apply that knowledge to enhance their psychological functioning. In addition, clients and counselors can process their feelings regarding the counseling relationship and work toward closure regarding potential affective issues. Counselors can also arrange with clients to have a brief follow-up counseling session (for example, several weeks after the last formal session) to see how they are doing and provide additional counseling services as necessary.

Stage Six: Research and Evaluation

Research and evaluation can occur at any time during the counseling process or after termination. Some behavioral approaches utilize single-case or small-group research designs that require counselors to evaluate counseling whenever they implement an intervention strategy. These research procedures involve face-to-face interaction between the counselor and client. Other research procedures that may or may not involve direct interaction between counselor and client are empirical research involving hypothesis testing and alternative methodology such as the discovery approach. These procedures may be used before or after a client has terminated (see Chapter 5 for a description of research methods).

Research and evaluation are an integral part of the counseling process. They contribute to the science dimension of counseling by promoting an objective understanding of what is occurring in counseling. Counselors can also use research and evaluation to communicate accountability.

Listening Skills

Listening skills play a vital role in virtually all aspects of counseling. Listening is a procedure that helps clients tell *their* story and feel connected and understood by a caring and interested person. It is a complex process that involves a number of strategies. Some of these strategies include attending (or tuning into) the verbal and nonverbal messages of clients, encouraging clients to freely express themselves, developing a phenomenological understanding of clients, and responding in an appropriate manner.

Listening skills can play an important role in all stages of the counseling process. Listening is especially important in terms of establishing a positive counseling relationship because the counselors can communicate care and understanding through listening-skill responses. Listening skills can be used in assessment, diagnosis, and goal setting as the counselor attempts to gain a phenomenological understanding of the client (seeing the client's concern from the client's perspective). Listening skills are useful interventions in the sense that talking in and of itself can have a healing power. This can occur when clients have their thoughts and feelings validated or normalized or can simply result from the letting go of feelings in the process of catharsis. Listening can also be an important tool for counselors during termination and follow-up and research and evaluation to determine how clients conceptualize their progress and the efficacy of counseling.

Listening skills can be conceptualized in terms of primary and secondary skills. Primary listening skills focus on generating the phenomenological understanding of the client and include open-ended questions, paraphrasing, reflection of feeling, minimal encouragers, clarifying remarks, summarizing, and perception check. Secondary listening skills do not promote a phenomenological perspective but can be facilitative (in terms of the counseling process) while the counselor is utilizing listening skills. Secondary skills include normalizing, structuring, and probing. An overview of listening skills follows along with a brief counseling vignette to illustrate these skills.

Primary Listening Skills

Open-Ended Questions.   These are questions such as, "What would you like to talk about?" or "How does this affect you?" These questions cannot be answered with a simple yes or no, but encourage the client to elaborate on responses.

Paraphrasing.   This can be useful after a client has talked at some length about a particular situation or problem. Paraphrasing allows the counselor to communicate that he or she has not only heard the client but understands what has been said. A paraphrase should be "tentatively" worded so the client can correct the counselor if necessary. Paraphrasing, like so many things, takes practice. A key to good paraphrasing is to keep it simple.

Paraphrasing often involves taking one or two key words that the client has said and finding analogous words. For example, if the client says, "I enjoy taking a run with my dog after work," a possible paraphrase is, "You like to jog with your dog." In this example, the counselor has found analogous words for enjoy (like) and run (jog). Another way to paraphrase is to repeat the client's overall message using slightly different words. For example, the client may say, "I like to take a jog after a stressful day, because it helps me unwind." A possible paraphrase would be, "Jogging is a good stress release for you."

Reflection of Feeling.   This involves the counselor reflecting what he or she senses the client is feeling. It communicates that the counselor not only understands how the client is feeling, but also empathizes with the client. For example, if a client tells the counselor how her husband insults her in public, the counselor could respond by saying, "This really makes you mad." Again, as in paraphrasing, it is important to phrase the reflection of feeling statement tentatively so the client can correct the counselor if necessary.

It is also important to be specific in attempting to reflect the client's feelings. For example, the word "upset" is usually too general and may not communicate a clear understanding of the client's feelings. It is therefore useful for counselors to develop a broad repertoire of words associated with various emotional states. Cormier and Cormier (1991) have provided a comprehensive list of words depicting various emotions (see Table 3.2).

TABLE 3.2 Words Depicting Feelings

Level of Intensity	Happiness	Sadness	Fear	Uncertainty	Anger	Strength, Potency	Weakness, Inadequacy
Strong	Excited	Despairing	Panicked	Bewildered	Outraged	Powerful	Ashamed
	Thrilled	Hopeless	Terrified	Disoriented	Hostile	Authoritative	Powerless
	Delighted	Depressed	Afraid	Mistrustful	Furious	Forceful	Vulnerable
	Overjoyed	Crushed	Frightened	Confused	Angry	Potent	Cowardly
	Ecstatic	Miserable	Scared		Harsh		Exhausted
	Elated	Abandoned	Overwhelmed		Hateful		Impotent
	Jubilant	Defeated			Mean		
		Desolate			Vindictive		
Moderate	"Up"	Dejected	Worried	Doubtful	Aggravated	Tough	Embarrassed
	Good	Dismayed	Shaky	Mixed up	Irritated	Important	Useless
	Happy	Disillusioned	Tense	Insecure	Offended	Confident	Demoralized
	Optimistic	Lonely	Anxious	Skeptical	Mad	Fearless	Helpless
	Cheerful	Bad	Threatened	Puzzled	Frustrated	Energetic	Worn out
	Enthusiastic	Unhappy	Agitated		Resentful	Brave	Inept
	Joyful	Pessimistic			"Sore"	Courageous	Incapable
	"Turned on"	Sad			Upset	Daring	Incompetent
		Hurt			Impatient	Assured	Inadequate
		Lost			Obstinate	Adequate	Shaken
						Self-confident	
						Skillful	
Weak	Pleased	"Down"	Jittery	Unsure	Perturbed	Determined	Frail
	Glad	Discouraged	Jumpy	Surprised	Annoyed	Firm	Meek
	Content	Disappointed	Nervous	Uncertain	Grouchy	Able	Unable
	Relaxed	"Blue"	Uncomfortable	Undecided	Hassled	Strong	Weak
	Satisfied	Alone	Uptight	Bothered	Bothered		
	Calm	Left out	Uneasy		Disagreeable		
			Defensive				
			Apprehensive				
			Hesitant				

Source: From *Interviewing strategies for helpers: Fundamental skills and cognitive behavior interventions,* by W. H. Cormier and L. S. Cormier. © 1991, 1985, and 1975, Brooks/Cole Publishing Company, Pacific Grove, CA 93950, a division of International/Thomson Publishing, Inc. By permission of the publisher.

Minimal Encouragers.   This technique allows the counselor to facilitate what the client is saying without changing the client's line of thought. Minimal encouragers include such words of acknowledgement as, "yes," "yeah," "oh," "ah-ha," and so forth.

Clarifying Remarks.   This technique can be used when the counselor either did not hear or does not understand what the client has said. For example, the counselor could say "I didn't understand that," or "Could you go through that again?" Through the use of clarifying statements, the counselor communicates that he or she genuinely wants to understand what the client is saying.

Summarizing.   This involves restating some of the major concerns the client has mentioned during a particular session. Obviously this helps identify the client's areas of concern. Summarizing can also lead to a "perception check" and to the development of problem-solving strategies.

Perception Check.   This technique helps the counselor determine what the client wants to work on. It follows the summary statement as illustrated in the following example: "You seem to be worried about your performance at school, your relationship with your wife, and your lack of money (the summary statement). I know all these problems concern you. I was wondering if you would like to focus on one of these areas, or is there something else that you haven't mentioned that you would like to talk about?"

Secondary Listening Skills

Normalizing.   Normalizing involves helping clients understand that what they are going through is a normal reaction to life (Nystul, 1994). Normalizing can alleviate unnecessary stress and anxiety so that clients can focus their energy on recovery. The opposite of normalizing could be called *pathologicalizing,* which involves overdiagnosing or engaging in other activities with clients that make them feel sicker or discouraged. An example of normalizing is to tell someone whose husband just died and is very sad and indecisive that it is normal to have intense feelings of depression and to have difficulty making decisions after a loved one has died.

Structuring.   Structuring involves describing the role and function of the counselor and client and provides a rationale for what the counselor is doing in counseling (Nystul, 1994). It helps clients understand what is going on in counseling, increasing their motivation and enabling them to take an active role in the counseling process. Structuring can also help them learn how to be their own self-therapist since they are assisted in understanding some of the dynamics of the counseling process.

Probing.   Probing involves asking for specific information such as questions relating to a suicidal assessment. Probing may be necessary during the use of listening skills to obtain specific information that is critical to understanding the client. It is important to minimize the use of probing while using listening skills, because it takes the perspective away from the client's phenomenological field and forces the client to respond to the counselor's frame of reference.

Counseling Vignette

The following brief counseling vignette provides an illustration of how the primary and secondary listening skills can be used.

COUNSELOR: What would you like to talk about today? (open-ended)

CLIENT: My daughter has me really worried.

COUNSELOR: About what? (open-ended)

CLIENT: She's dating someone who is 15 years older than her.

COUNSELOR: That could worry anybody. (normalizing)

CLIENT: I just feel that in some ways he seems old enough to be her father.

COUNSELOR: This really does bother you. (reflection of feeling)

CLIENT: Yes, it does.

COUNSELOR: Could you tell me more how you feel about this? (open-ended)

CLIENT: I really don't know where to begin.

COUNSELOR: Perhaps you could start by telling me the age of your daughter. (probing)

CLIENT: Sure, she's 17 years old.

COUNSELOR: How does it make you feel for your 17-year-old daughter to be dating this 32-year-old man? (open-ended)

CLIENT: I feel like he's taking advantage of her and there is something immoral about it.

COUNSELOR: You are really worried about her. (reflection of feeling)

CLIENT: The whole thing just doesn't make sense to me. . . .

COUNSELOR: Things don't add up. (paraphrase)

CLIENT: It's a crazy world.

COUNSELOR: I don't quite understand what you mean. Could you run that one by me again? (clarifying)

CLIENT: Sometimes I think she's just looking for a father figure.

COUNSELOR: Searching for something she is missing? (paraphrase)

CLIENT: I guess I just feel inadequate.

COUNSELOR: Ah-ha. (minimal encourager)

CLIENT: Yeah, like I'm one big zero.

COUNSELOR: You really do have some strong negative feeling about yourself. (reflection of feeling)

CLIENT: Yes, I could write a book on that one. My ex-wife said I had a BIG inferiority complex.

COUNSELOR: There really is a lot going on there. (paraphrase)

CLIENT: I guess my life is one big mess. I'm probably only supposed to talk about one problem at a time.

COUNSELOR: No, in counseling we want to get an overview of your concerns—especially during the initial stages of counseling. (structuring)

CLIENT: So what do we do now?

COUNSELOR: Well, so far we have identified some concerns about your daughter and her older boyfriend and your feeling about yourself. (summary)

CLIENT: Right.

COUNSELOR: Is there anything else you would like to tell me that you think I should know, or would you like to focus in on one of these concerns? (perception check)

Effective Listening "Don'ts"

This section provides some helpful guidelines for effective listening. Dinkmeyer and McKay's (1989) "roadblocks to effective listening" have been incorporated into the following list of things to avoid.

Avoid Moralizing or Being Judgmental. Imposing one's belief system onto the client can cause defensive reactions and be a demoralizing, dehumanizing experience.

Avoid Premature Analysis. Premature analysis involves identifying meaning behind the message, such as motivational forces associated with a particular action. It can occur when the counselor uses the word "because" in his or her paraphrase. For example, if the client says, "No matter what I do, nothing seems to go right," a counselor engaging in premature analysis might respond with, "Nothing is going right because you lack confidence in yourself."

When a counselor responds in this manner, the client may respond to the counselor's hunches (for example, "Is nothing going right because I lack confidence?"). This may result in redirecting the line of thought from client to the counselor. Once a counselor has gained a phenomenological understanding of the client, he may find it appropriate to analyze the content of the client's message and provide insights to the client (for example, suggest that a lack of self-confidence may be a problem for the client).

Avoid "Parroting." Parroting means repeating exactly what the client has said, just changing the order of the words. This communicates what the counselor has *heard* but may not understand (like a parrot). For example, if the client says, "I really like to jog after work," the counselor responding like a parrot might say, "After work, you really like to jog."

Avoid "Gimmicky" Phrases. Some counselors get into the habit of using a "lead in" phrase such as "Did I hear you say . . ." each time they paraphrase. This often sounds "gimmicky" to a client.

Effective Listening "Dos"

Decide to Be in the Role of the Listener. Effective listening is a skill the counselor must *decide* to take on. It involves utilizing a series of skills: attending and focusing on the client, encouraging the client to freely express him- or herself, attempting to develop a phenome-nological understanding of the client, and implementing an appropriate response.

Try to Sense the Client's Inner Message.   Communication is a complex process. It is important to learn to listen with a "third ear." The counselor needs to learn to go beyond the spoken word and try to listen to what is really being communicated.

Be Aware of Nonverbal Communication.   A large percentage of communication is non-verbal. It often provides the most authentic indicator of the client's emotional state.

Allow Yourself to Correct Impressions.   Being in the role of listener is a tentative process. It is a joint effort in which the counselor works with the client until he or she gains a clear understanding of the client's situation.

A Final Thought Regarding Listening Skills

Becoming an effective listener is an art that takes time to develop. One of the best ways to learn listening skills is to obtain a videotape critique of one's work from an experienced counselor. It can also be helpful to do cocounseling with an experienced counselor and obtain feedback from the counselor regarding one's counseling approach.

Developing listening skills can be discouraging. At times a counselor may even feel he or she is becoming a less effective communicator. During these times, the counselor could consider that he or she is in the process of becoming a more effective communicator. With practice, these new skills will become integrated into the counselor's natural mode of responding.

Recent Trends in the Counseling Process

Two emerging and complementary trends in counseling are postmodernism (and its associ-ated theories) and brief-counseling approaches. Both trends appear to take a strengths per-spective and are solution-focused. In addition, they appear to recognize the role that narratives and storytelling can play in the counseling process. These trends represent important paradigm shifts in the manner in which counseling can be conceptualized and practiced. An overview of postmodernism and brief counseling is provided next.

Postmodern Trends

As noted in Chapter 1, postmodernism represents an emerging trend in counseling. It is contributing to a potential paradigm shift that is creating new opportunities for conceptual-izing the counseling process. Bitter and Corey (1996) differentiate modern from postmod-ern in terms of different ways of viewing reality. Modernists believe in an objective reality that is independent from the observer, whereas postmodernists contend there is a subjective reality that varies contextually in relation to the observer. The modernist position is similar to the behaviorist theory, which focuses on overt measurable behavior such as recognizing the state of depression when a person has problems with sleep and appetite, has a loss of interest doing things that used to be fun, and so forth. The postmodernism position parallels experiential theories and contends that people are depressed when they experience depression as defined within the context of social-cultural forces such as language and narratives internalized by the individual.

Constructivism and social constructionism are two psychological perspectives that have evolved from postmodernism. Constructivism is primarily associated with cognitive behavioral approaches (see Neimeyer & Mahoney, 1995), and social constructionism has become an important dimension of marriage and family counseling (see Anderson & Goolishian, 1992). Gutterman (1996) contrasts constructivism and social constructionism by noting that constructivists contend that knowledge is based on the subjective cognitions of the individual, whereas social constructionists hold that reality is constructed from the conversations of people (see list of Suggested Readings on pages 420–422).

The postmodern theoretical perspectives of constructivism and social constructionism appear to have more in common than they have differences. Both are concerned with issues relating to epistemology—the theory of knowledge, or how we know what we think and what we think we think" (Durrant, 1995, p. 3). These theories appear to suggest that human experience is a highly individualized process based contextually on the interactions of cognition, social-cultural forces, language, and narratives. Knowledge and the concept of "truth" are therefore subjective and generate the possibility of multiple realities best understood from a phenomenological perspective. The postmodernists also emphasize the role that narratives and storytelling play in psychological functioning. According to this theory, people are constantly constructing stories about their lives, creating "storied lives" (Bitter & Corey, 1996).

The process of counseling and psychotherapy is therefore one of exploring life stories to gain insight into how clients generate personal meaning. When necessary, counselors can help clients engage in narrative repair, reauthoring life stories to help clients create opportunities to cope effectively and generate new meaning to life. Other goals of counseling include helping clients generate solution-focused approaches to problem solving and enhancing awareness of the effects of the dominant culture on human life (Bitter & Corey, 1996).

Bitter and Corey (1996) and Carlsen (1995) have identified techniques associated with postmodern counseling theories. These are summarized as follows.

Listening with an Open Mind. The counseling relationship is characterized as one of equality. Counselors avoid preconceived ideas or taking a judgmental position. The counselor attempts to empower clients by conveying optimism and encouragement and respecting and giving voice to the client's stories. The process is similar to qualitative research, where the counselor and client are coinvestigators attempting to discover meanings reflected in their stories and narratives.

An example of listening with an open mind is using listening skills to obtain a phenomenological understanding of the client. In this process, the counselor can convey a nonjudgmental position, encouraging clients to tell their story from their perspective.

Questions That Make a Difference. The counselor engages the client in dialogues or conversations that help clients address questions that can make a difference in terms of positive change. Questions tend to be circular or relational as reflected in the systemic concept of circular causality (for example, exploring the interrelationship between current and past problems).

An example of a question that could make a difference is a counselor asking the client, "Describe what it's like when you don't have this problem?" This type of question can make a difference by getting the client to focus on what works as opposed to what does not work, thus replacing a cycle of defeatism with one of hope.

Deconstruction and Externalization.   Externalization can be used to help clients deconstruct problems associated with their storied lives in two ways. Counselors can help clients gain valuable insights and minimize resistance by having them remove themselves from the problems associated with their storied lives. In the role of external observer, clients may be more open to engage in an adversarial relationship with their problems (deconstruction) and develop new methods for problem resolution (reconstruction). Another technique for deconstruction is similar to that used by feminists. It involves scientifically examining problematic narratives from the dominant culture (such as patriarchy) to provide evidence that refutes (deconstructs) the dominant culture's position.

An example of externalizing could be to ask a client named Sam, "How does this affect Sam?" This process can minimize resistance by providing an indirect voice for Sam to express his concerns. Externalizing techniques such as this also facilitate story deconstruction, since Sam may feel more free to be critical of his story with "Sam" being referred to in the third person.

Alternative Stories, Reauthoring, and Narrative Repair.   Clients are encouraged to rewrite their storied lives, creating alternative stories that are more consistent with their goals and aspirations. Reauthoring and narrative repair can be reflected in numerous ways, such as clients who begin to focus on solutions rather than problems.

Alternative stories, reauthoring, and narrative repair are terms that mean essentially the same thing (they help clients develop more functional or meaningful life stories). For example, a client's story may be one of sorrow, loss, and despair owing to the death of a family member. In time, the client can learn to engage in narrative repair and reauthor an alternative story that reflects purpose and hope in life. The upcoming *Personal Note* describes the "Colombo" technique as a method of helping clients with the process of narrative repair and reauthoring.

Use of Metaphors.   A metaphor is a figure of speech that suggests that one idea is similar or analogous to another idea or concept. Metaphors provide a powerful technique that can be used in counseling processes such as cognitive restructuring and helping clients create alternative stories through narrative repair and reauthoring. Metaphors are especially useful to overcome resistance by providing an indirect means of exploring painful issues and identifying alternative means of overcoming problems. In this regard, clients may not even be aware of the salient messages conveyed by metaphors as they "have a way of dropping below the surface of awareness to influence us in ways that we may not fully acknowledge or understand" (Carlsen, 1995, p. 131). An example of a metaphor can be found in the *Personal Note* in terms of the concept of "going with the flow."

Evaluation of Postmodern Trends. Postmodern trends and theories such as constructivism and social constructionism offer much promise in terms of conceptualizing the counseling process. They create opportunities to recognize the role that narrative psychology and diversity issues such as language and culture play in counseling. The postmodern perspective could provide another dimension to the multicultural counseling evolution.

Sexton and Whiston (1994) identify some concerns about postmodern trends such as social constructivism. For example, they note that social constructivism appears to be a theory that does not connect to any specific research methodology. Sexton and Whiston (1994) also suggest that social constructivism may be nothing more than "a call for relativism in which anything goes" (p. 69). Additional research is necessary to evaluate the postmodern theories and determine how they can be successfully integrated into counseling theory, research, and practice.

A Personal Note

I find the postmodern theories of constructivism and social constructionism to be very interesting. They offer exciting opportunities for developing creative counseling techniques. The "Colombo" technique and the use of metaphors in counseling are two examples of techniques that I have found useful in counseling. I developed the "Colombo" technique as a means of helping clients engage in narrative repair, or coauthoring more meaningful stories. The "Colombo" technique involves having the counselor act like the TV detective Colombo, who appears to lose track of a thought or need help from the suspect to clarify a point that he was confused about. In this process, the counselor can do such things as stop in mid-sentence and let the client finish the sentence, such as "You are really trying to . . . ." The client may respond by saying, "get my act together" and in doing so take responsibility for reauthoring his or her story in a more positive manner. Another "Colombo" technique is when the counselor says to the client, "I got the part about how you are convinced you are such a terrible parent. I'm just a bit confused about how a terrible parent is someone who has always been there for his children financially and emotionally and seems to care so much for his children's welfare. Perhaps you can help me understand that a bit better." As the parent offers his or her explanation, it will help him or her construct cognitions that foster more realistic, healthy narratives.

Metaphors are another counseling technique that are generating increased interest in counseling. I find the use of metaphors to be especially useful in working with children and adolescents. Metaphors involve the use of similes, or implied comparison, to symbolically represent an idea or concept. An example of a metaphor that I am currently using with some of my students in Special Education is "going with the flow." In this metaphor, I suggest that life is like a river. I have the student visualize a river that he or she has seen, such as when going fishing. I have the student try to remember what the river was like and what the student saw floating down the river (such as leaves and so forth). I ask the student if the leaf had a motor to move it down the river, and the student says "no." I say, "You're right, leaves don't need motors to go down the river, they use the current of the river and 'go with the flow.' " I tell my students that they also can go with the flow when they listen to their teacher, follow instructions, get their work done, and try to get along with others in a polite and caring manner. Students that do not follow the rules will have their problems mounting up on them, and life for them will be like swimming against a current. I then have them imagine how it would feel to swim upriver against a current . . . against the flow of life.

Brief-Counseling Approaches

Brief-counseling approaches are becoming increasingly popular and appear to characterize the counseling wave of the future. Koss and Shiang (1994) identify some of the factors that have contributed to the popularity of brief-counseling approaches. These are summarized as follows.

1. People seek counseling for help with specific problems and are only willing to commit to a few counseling sessions to resolve their problems. The mean number of sessions (regardless of theoretical orientation or if counseling is considered brief or nonbrief) is six to eight sessions, and 75 percent of those who are helped by counseling do so during the first six months they are in counseling.
2. Research has shown that brief counseling has efficacy rates similar to traditional approaches to counseling, especially when treating certain types of clients with certain types of disorders. Brief counseling is particularly effective for clients who relate well, are motivated, desire symptom relief, and suffer from a minor problem such as a mild depression or a severe stress reaction such as experiencing a natural disaster.
3. The popularity of brief counseling has to some degree evolved in response to managed care and its emphasis on time-limited, solution-focused counseling. Brief counseling is perceived to be a cost effective alternative to traditional methods of counseling.

The origins of brief-counseling models can be traced to Milton Erickson (1954), who was one of the most influential pioneers of brief counseling. Erickson was a genius for using paradoxical techniques and hypnosis (in as few as one session) to generate solutions to clients' problems. A number of other individuals have contributed to the movement toward brief approaches to counseling. Some of these are Haley (1984), de Shazer's solution-focused brief therapy (1985, 1991), O'Hanlon and Weiner-Davis (1989), and the Brief Therapy Project at the Mental Research Institute (Fisch, Weakland, & Segal, 1982). Forms of brief counseling have also been adapted to most of the major traditional schools of counseling (see Koss & Shiang, 1994; Steenbarger, 1992).

Littrell, Malia, and Vanderwood (1995) identify three main assumptions associated with brief approaches to counseling. The first assumption is that the problem clients present in counseling is the real problem. Although the problem can be related to some unknown deep-seated issues, simple straightforward methods are used whenever possible. The second assumption is that clients are capable of solving their own problems. Counselors need to help clients become aware of their strengths and how they can use them effectively. The third assumption is that change does not need to be large to make a significant difference. Small steps toward change may be all that is necessary to break self-defeating cycles and contribute to problem resolution. Durrant (1995) has identified a number of other assumptions associated with brief-counseling models, which are summarized as follows.

1. All problems have examples of exceptions, such as a person who has a problem with heights but on one occasion was able to go climb an historic landmark with friends.
2. Problems can be reframed in solution-focused terms.

3. If it's not broken don't fix it. Do what is working more and stop doing what is not working.
4. It's not important to know what the problem is, but what things will be like when the problem is solved.

These assumptions taken collectively suggest that brief counseling utilizes a strengths perspective that helps clients solve their problems as quickly and directly as possible.

Brief-Solution-Focused Counseling

The brief-solution-focused counseling model proposed in this text has four stages and is based primarily on brief-counseling models described by Durrant (1995), Koss and Shiang (1994), and Thompson (1996), as well as some of the techniques and procedures associated with postmodern theories of counseling.

Stage One: Establishing the Relationship and Defining the Problem. The counselor and client enter into a collaborative relationship. The counselor offers encouragement and hope and attempts to gain a phenomenological understanding of the client's life. Clients are encouraged to function as cocounselors and are empowered to take an active role in the counseling process from assessment through intervention and follow-up.

Problems are defined in simple direct terms void of complicated psychological jargon. When possible, counselors normalize the client's problems and experience and communicate "wellness" as opposed to using psychological labels that communicate "sickness." Expectations for change and positive action are communicated to foster a positive self-fulfilling prophecy. In addition, most brief counseling is practiced within a time-limited framework. This usually requires that the counselor and client determine as quickly as possible how many sessions will be required (or authorized by managed care) to resolve the problems.

Stage Two: Assessment and Establishing Treatment Goals. Rapid and early assessment is crucial in brief counseling. Assessment procedures serve a number of purposes such as determining whether a client is appropriate for brief counseling (for example, it is contraindicated for people with severe problems such as personality disorders, substance abuse, and psychosis), and it can also be used to obtain an overall understanding of clients and the nature of their problems. Assessment procedures can be directed at intrapsychic (within the person) as well as ecological perspectives (outside of the person). Assessment tends to focus on the here and now and avoid exploration of early life events. Another key aspect of assessment in brief-solution-focused counseling is assessing for strengths and resources and how clients can use these assets to resolve problems.

Standard traditional assessment procedures can be used in conjunction with assessment procedures unique to brief-solution-focused counseling. One commonly used assessment method in brief-counseling approaches is the scaling technique. This procedure involves having a client rate his or her problems on a 1 to 10 scale, with 10 representing resolution of the problem. Scaling questions are used that emphasize change, exceptions to the problem, and future aspirations. For example, a counselor could ask, "So you're a 3 now in terms of your anger management. When were you more than a 3, what was that like, what were you doing then, and how were things different?"

Counseling goals are established that are concrete, observable, and measurable. They allow for ongoing evaluation of the counseling process and establish a point of termination. Goals must be flexible and interface effectively with intervention strategies. Thompson (1996, p. 19) identifies the following key questions associated with counseling goals:

> What will be the very first sign that things are moving in the right direction?
>
> Who will be the first to notice?
>
> Are there small pieces of this that are already happening?
>
> What do you need to do to make it happen more?
>
> What else will you be doing differently when you no longer have this particular problem?

De Shazer's (1991) miracle question can be useful in generating counseling goals. The miracle question involves asking the client to imagine that a miracle occurred while he or she was asleep that solved the client's problem. What would be different in the client's life and how would he or she know that the miracle happened?

Stage Three: Designing and Implementing Interventions.   Interventions are designed to disrupt patterns of problematic behavior by introducing alternative ways of reacting to the problem. Some form of change (no matter how small) is a central component of intervention strategies. Four intervention strategies are commonly used during the intervention stage: reframing, utilization, strategic tasks, and narrative repair and reauthoring stories. Reframing is a cognitive process that involves helping clients "frame" their problems in terms of what is right with their situation as opposed to what is wrong. Utilization involves helping clients find solutions within their problems. Solutions can be developed from the exceptions to the problem (for example, times that the client did not get anxious with heights) or from developing alternative methods of problem solving. Narrative repair involves helping clients reauthor their stories to reflect a positive-strength perspective as opposed to a pathological-defeatist perspective.

Brief-solution-focused counseling is a task-action-results–oriented process whereby counselors and clients perceive their role as "doers" and not just "talkers." Clients are provided opportunities to learn solution-focused strategies and are encouraged to apply these strategies to their problems between sessions. Adjustments are made as necessary at the start of each session to ensure that clients can effectively make progress toward positive change.

Stage Four: Termination, Follow-Up, and Evaluation.   Once clients' problems have been resolved satisfactorily, they can terminate formal counseling. Brief-solution-focused counseling also encourages clients to become their own self-counselor and apply their problem-solving skills to new and emerging problems. In addition, the science of counseling suggests that research procedures can be used to evaluate the efficacy of the counseling experience. During the counseling process, clients can be provided opportunities to take an active role in the research process. In this regard, they can function as coinvestigators with counselors in an ongoing journey of discovery. Clients should be encouraged to continue to take an active role in self-evaluation after termination through processes such as self-monitoring and self-reflection.

Research on Brief Counseling.   Koss and Shiang (1994) provide a comprehensive overview on the research that has been conducted on brief counseling. Results of their findings are summarized as follows. Brief counseling approaches are being successfully applied to individual, group, and marriage and family counseling. Initial research efforts suggested that brief counseling was only suited for less severe problems such as adjustment reactions. More recent research indicates that brief counseling can be used successfully with a wide range of problems, including severe and chronic problems if the treatment goals are reasonable. Some of the problems that brief counseling has been able to successfully treat are depression (Dobson, 1989), panic disorders (Beck et al., 1992), and posttraumatic stress disorder (Foa et al., 1991).

Research efforts have also been directed at determining the client characteristics that are best suited for brief counseling. Koss and Shiang (1994) review this literature and indicate that individuals who appear to benefit most from brief counseling are those whose problem had a sudden or acute onset, were previously reasonably well adjusted, could relate well with others, and had high initial motivation when entering counseling.

Research suggests that brief counseling may be counterindicated for individuals whose personal characteristics are in contrast to those noted above and for some types of psychological disturbances such as substance abuse, psychosis, and personality disorders (Koss & Shiang, 1994). Additional research is necessary to gain a clearer understanding of how brief counseling can be effectively integrated into the counseling process with various traditional and nontraditional counseling theories and techniques.

Common Problems for Beginning Counselors

Beginning counselors tend to experience similar problems in counseling. These problems can manifest themselves as roadblocks to the counseling process. In this section, 15 typical roadblocks that can impede counseling effectiveness are discussed, with suggestions for overcoming each problem.

Focusing on the First Issue in a Session

Some beginning counselors tend to focus on the first problem the client presents in a session, even though a client may not want to work or be capable of working on this problem. The counselor may then spend the rest of the session trying to help the client resolve this particular problem. Counselors can overcome this roadblock by first obtaining an overview of the client's concerns and then selecting a counseling goal with the client.

Overlooking Physical or Medical Issues

Beginning counselors may assume that when a client seeks their services for counseling, counseling is all the client needs (Nystul, 1981). For example, a client may seek counseling to obtain stress management to help alleviate migraine headaches. In this instance, it would be important for the counselor to ensure the client has had a recent physical examination. This will enable the counselor to rule out possible organic causes of the headache such as a brain tumor. A substance abuse problem may be another medical issue that counselors may overlook. A counselor may assume that clients do not have substance abuse problems if they do not raise the issue. Counselors can avoid this problem by obtaining a history of alcohol and drug use when they gather other important background information.

Wanting to Rescue Clients from Their Unhappiness

Some beginning counselors have a naive notion that counseling is a process that makes clients feel happier. It is true that a major goal of counseling can be self-realization and inner peace. The road to that goal, however, will undoubtedly have ups and downs and emotional highs and lows.

Counseling is a process that requires the client to take risks and have the courage to face difficult issues. For example, a client may need to become aware of personal inadequacies or self-defeating patterns of behavior. This can make a client feel uncomfortable or sad and may even result in the client crying. Counselors may falsely conclude that since their client cried, they must have done something wrong. When this occurs, the counselor should consider that helping a client get in touch with inner feelings is an important part of the counseling process.

There are several ways that a counselor may rescue a client. Three common examples follow.

■ *Reassuring clients.* When clients feel bad about their situation, the counselor may be tempted to say, "Don't worry, things will get better." It is important, however, for the counselor and client to have a realistic view of the counseling process. If the client does not make necessary changes, things probably will not get better. In fact, the client's situation may worsen.

■ *Offering instant advice.* When clients are uncomfortable with their situation, the counselor may attempt to rescue the client by offering advice. In counseling, giving advice is usually unproductive, can foster dependency and can be a superficial solution to a complex problem.

■ *Rescuing clients from intense emotions.* Some beginning counselors tend not to allow clients to experience any intense emotions. When clients express intense emotions such as anger or grief, the counselor may want to calm them or get them to think about something else. This type of rescuing prevents clients from getting in touch with and working through their feelings.

Having Perfectionist Tendencies

Some beginning counselors may have perfectionist tendencies. They may fear making mistakes or looking bad. These tendencies may cause several problems, including counselors being reluctant to explore a new idea or technique because they fear not learning or using it correctly, avoiding supervision because they believe seeking assistance might reflect their inadequacy, and being hesitant to refer a client because they think a referral might imply they could not handle the situation.

The following *Personal Note* provides some suggestions for helping beginning counselors overcome perfectionist tendencies.

A Personal Note

I have found several ways to help counselors overcome perfectionist tendencies. First, counselors should avoid absolutistic, or right-versus-wrong, views of the counseling process. Once counselors realize there is no right or wrong way of doing counseling, then they can stop worrying about making mistakes. The model of counseling as an art maintains a realistic, pragmatic view of counseling. This model suggests that when the client seems to be making progress, the counselor and client should continue using that counseling approach. When the client does not appear to be making gains in counseling, the counselor and client should make the necessary adjustments to the counseling process.

I identified the "monkey on the back" phenomenon as another way to help student counselors overcome perfectionist tendencies. The "monkey on the back" symbolizes why it is not productive to try to look perfect while learning new counseling skills. I begin by explaining to students that a counselor training program is in some ways like having a "monkey" put on their back. The "monkey"—instructions from the professor—may tell students to do some things differently from what they would ordinarily do. For example, the instructions might be to use open rather than closed questions during active listening.

When the "monkey" suggests that students stop to consider different ways of responding, they may feel the "monkey" is interfering with their spontaneity. If they focus on their professor perceiving them as spontaneous, they may avoid trying new behaviors. Unfortunately, these students will also not learn much from their counseling program.

I tell students that the feeling of the "monkey" interfering with their spontaneity is a good sign. It indicates that they are trying some new skills and are in the process of becoming a more effective counselor. In time, the new skills will become integrated into their natural way of working with clients and their spontaneity will be restored.

Having Unrealistic Expectations

Some beginning counselors have unrealistic expectations for their clients. They may therefore become frustrated when their client does not make steady progress. When a client has a setback and regresses to old negative patterns of behavior, counselors may feel they have failed the client. In time, the counselor may project these negative feelings onto the client (Nystul, 1979). The art-of-counseling model suggests that counselors develop a balanced set of expectations blending optimism with realism. These expectations involve believing that clients can improve and realizing that change can take time.

Getting Carried Away with the Latest Technique

Some beginning counselors tend to get carried away after learning a new technique, wanting to use this technique with all clients (Nystul, 1981). For example, after attending an extensive training program in hypnosis, a counselor may believe that every client could benefit from hypnosis. This enthusiasm may continue for a period of time until the counselor gets excited about another new technique.

It is important for counselors to get excited and be enthusiastic about their education. At the same time, they must learn to channel these energies into a positive direction rather than imposing their current interest on the client.

Getting Lost in the Counseling Process

Clients often feel overwhelmed with issues when they begin counseling. Each time they come to a counseling session, they may talk about many different concerns. They may describe these concerns in a very interesting manner, and the concerns may begin to seem like an ongoing soap opera from television.

As counselors hear these stories, they may find themselves taking a passive role in counseling. I call this the *popcorn syndrome* (Nystul, 1981). It is as if counselors are eating popcorn at the movies, listening to their client's latest struggle with life. Counselors who find themselves in the popcorn syndrome usually enjoy the counseling sessions, but they often have the feeling they are not accomplishing much. When this occurs, counselors can feel lost in the ongoing storytelling. To overcome this problem, the counselor can create a focus in the counseling process by exploring with the client what has happened in counseling —where they have been, what they are currently working on, and where they seem to be headed. Together they can make the necessary adjustments for future sessions. If the popcorn syndrome is occurring, the counselor may also want to create more of a shared responsibility in the counseling process and work toward clearer counseling goals.

Using Inappropriate Phrases

Although I contend there are no right or wrong ways to approach counseling, I believe that certain phrases are usually inappropriate and unproductive in counseling. Three examples follow.

■ *"Why" questions.* "Why" questions usually provoke a defensive response, causing people to believe they need to justify their behavior. Instead of asking, "Why did you and Tim break up?" the counselor might ask, "Could you tell me what happened regarding your breakup with Tim?"

■ *I know how you feel.* Counselors may use this phrase to show that they have been through a similar situation and can therefore understand the client. Actually, no two people have exactly the same reaction to a situation. For example, take the varied reactions to a house burning down. One person might feel relief at the prospect of insurance money, while another might be heartbroken because of losing priceless family mementos. A client may have negative reactions to a counselor saying, "I know how you feel." The client may think, "No, she does not. She is not me. Who does she think she is?" Another client might react by thinking, "If this counselor knows how I feel, why bother exploring my feelings with him?"

■ *Let me tell you what I would do.* This phrase can lead to instant advice. As mentioned earlier, advice giving usually does not promote positive outcomes in counseling.

Having an Excessive Desire to Help

Many students are drawn to counseling because they truly want to help others. Wanting to help can be beneficial to the counseling process because it communicates enthusiasm, desire, and caring. Some counselors can be excessive in their need to help, however, to the point of being overly invested in the counseling process. A useful indicator that counselors may have gone too far in wanting to help is when they feel they are working harder than the client. Students should also explore their motives for wanting to become counselors. A positive motive would be to enjoy helping a client overcome self-defeating forces to move toward self-realization. A negative motive would be an excessive desire to feel needed by someone. This desire could foster unnecessary dependency in the counseling relationship. Another negative motive would be a need to feel power or control over others. This need could lead to a counselor intimidating clients, undermining their self-esteem, and fostering dependency. When counselors discover they have inappropriate motives for providing counseling services, they should refer the client and seek out counseling for themselves.

Having an Excessive Need to Be Liked

Most people, including counselors, enjoy being liked. At times, however, the counselor may need to do things that could make the client angry or unhappy, such as during a confrontation. It is therefore not necessary for the client always to like the counselor. Instead, it is essential to establish mutual respect to maintain a rapport throughout the counseling process.

Getting Too Emotionally Involved

Some beginning counselors tend to get too emotionally involved with the counseling process. There can be many reasons for developing this tendency. One is what I call the *stray cat syndrome,* which involves counselors wanting to take responsibility for the client's welfare. These counselors may have tendencies to want to go out of their way to help all living creatures—including stray cats—that appear to need assistance. As a result, whenever they see a client suffering, they may want to find a way to take away the pain and fix things, leading to the rescuing process described earlier.

Counselors can become so emotionally invested in their clients that they lose professional objectivity. They can also become emotionally exhausted and burned out. The art-of-counseling model suggests that for counseling to be effective, the counselor must be affected. At the same time, counselors should not assume ownership of the client's problems. They should instead help clients become capable of resolving their own problems.

Taking Things Too Personally

Beginning counselors may take things too personally when a client expresses intense emotions. For example, a client may react as if the counselor were another person with whom the client has had a close relationship, for example, a father or mother figure. During this process of transference, the client may become angry with the counselor. It would be inappropriate for the counselor to take this personally and retaliate against the client. Instead, the counselor should view the transference as an important part of therapy. For example,

Freudian psychoanalysis contends that transference is therapeutic in that it allows the client to work through unresolved emotional trauma (Freud, 1969).

Having Difficulty Differentiating Between Normal and Abnormal

Beginning counselors often have a difficult time deciding whether clients suffer from some form of psychopathology. For example, a counselor may wonder if a client is acutely suicidal and needs hospitalization or mildly suicidal and only requires monitoring. Another dilemma may be differentiating a clinical depression, such as a major depression, from a normal depressive reaction to a life event relating to the death of a loved one.

The reason some beginning counselors have trouble differentiating between normal and abnormal may be their lack of exposure to psychopathology. Student counselors may overcome this obstacle by taking advantage of internships and other clinical placements during their educational placement to obtain experience working with clients who suffer from mental disorders.

Being Uncertain About Self-Disclosure

Another problem that beginning counselors commonly experience is determining how much they should self-disclose. Although there are no hard-and-fast rules on this issue, the following suggestions may be useful.

■ Answer questions about yourself that you feel comfortable with—just answer the questions without elaborating. Feel free to offer information about your professional qualifications. Be willing to share immediate reactions to what is taking place in the session.

■ Don't tell your life story to your clients—they are there to tell you their story, not listen to yours. Don't say, "This is how I handled it." It could lead to ineffective advice giving.

Being Uncertain About Confidentiality

Many beginning counselors are unclear about the limits of confidentiality. One of the most common sources of confusion relates to the question, "With whom can I discuss a client, and what information can I disclose?" Following are some suggestions regarding this issue. A counselor may discuss a case with a supervisor or when required by law, such as reporting child abuse or neglect. It is also permissible to break confidentiality when clients pose a serious threat in terms of harming themselves or others. It is not appropriate to discuss a case with a secretary, friends, or family members even if you change the name of the client.

Diversity Issues

Atkinson and Thompson (1992), Gilbert (1992), and Sue, Zane, and Young (1994) provide an extensive overview of the literature on diversity and the counseling process. These reviews provide specific information on diversity issues such as culture and gender as well as a description of how multicultural issues impact on the counseling process. Research topics that are attracting much interest include the impact of similarity and difference between the counselor and client on the therapeutic alliance, how tests and diagnostic processes can be culturally biased, and how diversity serves as a mediating variable in assessing counseling interventions and outcomes.

Spirituality (including religion) is an emerging area of diversity in the literature that has vast potential for integration into counseling (Bishop, 1995). Spirituality can be broadly defined as "attunement with God, the Spirit of Truth, or the divine intelligence that governs or harmonizes the universe" (Richards & Bergin, 1997, p. 77). From this perspective, all people are believed to recognize the spiritual (but not necessarily religious) realm of existence (Ingersoll, 1995). Richards and Bergin (1997) refer to spiritual trends in counseling as the New Zeitgeist (spirit of our times). This recognition of the role of spirituality in counseling is reflected in the increased interests in the healing power associated with holistic health (Witmer & Sweeny, 1995). Empirical research is also creating a foundation for the acceptance of spirituality in counseling by recognizing the relationship between spiritual wellness and physical and mental health (Chandler, Holden, & Kolander, 1995).

Historically, counseling and spirituality have to a large degree been kept separate. More recently, the counseling literature is suggesting that spirituality is another form of diversity that should be carefully and sensitively addressed to obtain an accurate understanding of a client's world view (Bishop, 1995). Miranti and Burke (1995) suggest that recognition of the spiritual domain in counseling enables counselors to relate to the core essence of a client's being. Spirituality and religion provide strength and support that many people turn to during times of crisis to derive meaning from life. This is especially true for people as they get older (Smith, 1993).

A number of individuals are beginning to provide a structure for how spirituality and religion can be integrated into the counseling process (Ingersoll, 1995; Richards & Bergin, 1997). Ingersoll suggests that counselors should attempt to recognize and affirm clients' concepts of spirituality, enter the clients' spiritual world views to gain a phenomenological perspective, and consult with other "healers" in clients' lives as necessary. Richards and Bergins (1997) provide extensive guidelines such as assessment and intervention for addressing spiritual issues throughout the various phases of the counseling process. For example, spiritual forms of intervention can require special training and may include such strategies as cognitive restructuring of irrational religious beliefs, methods to foster forgiveness, and meditation and prayer.

The spiritual domain of counseling appears to represent a vast, largely untapped reservoir of potential. Additional theory, research, and practice will be necessary to facilitate a meaningful evolution of this important dimension into the counseling process.

Summary

A six-stage approach to counseling involves relationship building, assessment and diagnosis, goal setting, intervention and problem solving, termination and follow-up, and research and evaluation.

Current trends in the counseling process such as postmodernism and brief counseling offer new ways of conceptualizing the counseling process in terms of narrative psychology and counseling as storytelling and brief-solution-focused approaches to counseling. These counseling trends appear to offer special promise for addressing issues in multicultural counseling and managed care. Diversity issues, and the emerging trends in the counseling literature, such as spirituality and religion, offer much hope and promise in terms of enriching the counseling process.

Problems that beginning counselors experience include focusing only on the first issue in a session, overlooking medical issues, wanting to rescue clients, having perfectionist tendencies or unrealistic expectations, getting carried away with the latest technique learned, getting lost in the counseling process, using inappropriate phrases, having an excessive desire to help or to be liked, getting too emotionally involved or taking things too personally, and being uncertain about psychopathology issues, self-disclosure, or confidentiality.

In the final analysis, counseling is a process that varies in length and content according to the concerns of the client. In this process, the client may appear to make some progress and then regress to self-defeating habits. When things appear to be going wrong, the counselor, like a navigator on a ship, can adjust course. Counseling may be considered successful when the overall direction of therapy is positive.

4 Assessment and Diagnosis

CHAPTER OVERVIEW

This chapter provides an overview of assessment and diagnosis. Highlights of the chapter include

- The art and science of assessment and diagnosis
- Evaluation of tests
- Administration and interpretation of tests
- Test bias
- Types of tests
- Historical perspective of diagnosis
- Uses of diagnosis
- The DSM-IV
- Treatment planning
- Diversity and postmodern issues in assessment and diagnosis

The Art and Science of Assessment and Diagnosis

The art of assessment and diagnosis is an emerging dimension of the counseling process. The counselor-as-artist recognizes there are infinite methods and procedures to discover overt and salient aspects of clients. From this perspective, counselors adjust assessment and diagnostic procedures to accommodate the unique and emerging needs of the client. Examples of these procedures include the use of projective techniques to help a resistant client have a less-threatening means of self-disclosure and adjusting test procedures to accommodate issues of diversity.

Assessment and diagnosis represent an important dimension of the science of counseling and psychotherapy. They provide standardized methods such as intelligence and personality tests to obtain an objective understanding of the client's overall psychological functioning. The counselor-as-scientist emphasizes the necessity of comprehensive ongoing education in psychological testing. This training is a prerequisite for accurately administering, scoring, and interpreting tests. In addition, continuing education is necessary to keep up with the revision of tests and the complete revamping of the procedures used in tests (for example, the Exner system for the Rorschach inkblot test).

Virtually all aspects of assessment and diagnosis relate to the art and science of counseling. For example, treatment planning is an art that requires the counselor to creatively integrate vast amounts of information from different sources into a meaningful composite of the client. Treatment planning is also a science that involves organizing this information into a cohesive, effective program that provides structure and direction to the counseling process. Together the art and science of assessment and diagnosis create a balance, bridging the subjective and objective underpinnings on this important aspect of the counseling process.

Assessment and Diagnosis

Hohenshil (1996) notes that assessment and diagnosis tend to be interrelated processes, with assessment providing the necessary information to make a diagnosis. All counselors use some form of assessment to obtain an overall understanding of clients. Most counselors also incorporate diagnosis in their counseling process. Some theoretical perspectives such as reality therapy and person-centered counseling tend to abstain from the diagnostic process because they promote inaccurate and harmful labels. Most counselors find diagnosis essential to formulating treatment strategies and as a means of communication shorthand (Hohenshil, 1996). Key publications associated with diagnosis are also attempting to be more sensitive about the labeling process by referring to someone as a person with mental retardation or schizophrenia, and so on instead of saying that someone is mentally retarded or schizophrenic (Hohenshil, 1996). This certainly makes sense, because no one would be referred to as "a cancer" or "a broken bone." They would be referred to as someone with cancer or with a broken bone.

Hohenshil (1996) suggests that in reality all counselors (regardless of their theoretical orientation) engage in some form of diagnosis. For example, when a person-centered counselor decides that a client has psychopathology that requires the attention of a psychologist or psychiatrist, the counselor is making a diagnosis (Hohenshil, 1996). Hamann (1994) goes on to note that most counselors are actively involved in making diagnoses so that they can communicate effectively with other professional helpers and provide the necessary information to insurance companies, and so forth. Although counselors utilize diagnostic procedures on a regular basis, they often have not had the appropriate training to do so, resulting in serious potential ethical problems (Hamann, 1994).

Assessment

Sundberg (1977) notes that *assessment* first appeared as a psychological term in *Assessment of Men* (Office of Strategic Services, 1948). The term was used to describe the process of selecting men to serve on special missions in World War II. Since that time its meaning has broadened to include a wide range of techniques and processes. These include standardized psychological tests, interviewing and observation strategies, sociocultural assessment, behavioral assessment, and environmental assessment. This section provides a description of these assessment procedures as well as information on evaluating tests and the administration and interpretation of test results.

Evaluation of Tests

Anastasi and Urbina (1997) describe several sources of information that provide valuable means of evaluating tests:

- *Mental Measurement Yearbook,* edited by Burros, which provides information on most tests as well as a critique of each test.
- *Test Collection Bibliographies,* produced by the Educational Testing Service, which provides information on tests pertaining to a particular content such as physical disabilities.
- *Test and Microfiche,* distributed by Test Collection, Educational Testing Service, which provides important information about tests, such as reliability and validity.
- *The APA's Standards for Educational and Psychological Testing,* which provides guidelines for proper test use and interpretation of test results.

Three concepts are especially important in evaluating tests: validity, reliability, and norms.

Validity.   Validity is the degree to which a test measures what it is intended to measure (Anastasi & Urbina, 1997). According to Anastasi and Urbina (1997), validity is the most important characteristic of a test and provides a check on how well the test fulfills its intended function. For example, the Graduate Record Examination could be used to help select students for Ph.D. programs in counseling psychology. The test would have a high validity if the students who scored high were successful in their graduate programs.

The three major types of validity are content, construct, and criterion-related. Anastasi and Urbina (1997) provide a description of these types of validity:

1. *Content validity* involves the examination of a test's content to determine whether it covers a representative sample of the behavior to be measured. Content validity is often used in achievement tests to determine whether the test content is representative of the information that an individual was exposed to (for example, biology concepts in a biology course).
2. *Construct validity* refers to the degree to which a test measures a theoretical construct or trait such as neuroticism or anxiety.
3. *Criterion-related validity* provides an indication of how well a test predicts an individual's performance on a particular criterion. For example, a mechanical aptitude test might be used to predict how well a person will perform as a machinist. There are two types of criterion-related validity. *Concurrent validity* is determined when the criterion is available at the time of testing. *Predictive validity* can be assessed when the criterion is available only after the testing has occurred.

Reliability.   Reliability is another important factor that should be considered in test evaluation. It "refers to the consistency of scores obtained by the same persons when they are reexamined with the same test on different occasions, or with different sets of equivalent items, or under variable examining conditions" (Anastasi & Urbina, 1997, p. 84). Reliability can be determined by the following three methods.

1. *Test-retest reliability* involves administering the same test again to an individual.
2. *Alternate-forms reliability* refers to administering equivalent forms to the individual on separate occasions.
3. *Split-half reliability* involves dividing a test into two equivalent halves and administering each half to the individual. It provides a measure of the test's internal consistency.

Norms. Sundberg (1977) notes that to understand an individual's score, it is necessary to have information on scores made by other people (that is, the norm group). In evaluating the norms used in a test, it is important to determine whether the norm group is representative of the population for whom the test was designed (Sundberg, 1977). For example, a test with norms derived from an upper-class white group may be inappropriate to use with a minority client.

Administration and Interpretation of Tests

Only qualified individuals should administer and interpret tests. Many tests such as the Wechsler intelligence test require specialized training in test administration and interpretation. In addition, the counselor should carefully review the test manual to determine procedures to use in test interpretation. For example, it is important to determine the strengths and limitations of the test and whether the norm group is representative of the individual being tested.

Miller (1982) provides the following guidelines for interpreting test results to clients.

- The counselor should explore how the client felt about taking the test.
- The counselor should review the purpose of taking the test and provide information necessary for test interpretation (for example, norms and percentiles).
- The counselor and client should examine the test results and discuss what the results mean to the client.
- The counselor should help the client integrate the test scores into other aspects of the client's self-knowledge.
- The counselor should encourage the client to develop a plan to utilize the test results.

Goodyear (1990) suggests that counselors should introduce test materials and interpretations in response to specific concerns raised by the client throughout the counseling process rather than at one particular point in counseling. Goodyear contends that a client will achieve better assimilation of information from an approach to interpretation that occurs at various phases of the counseling process.

Several research studies provide useful information regarding interpretation. Jones and Gelso (1988) have found that clients perceive tentative interpretations as more helpful than absolute interpretations. Clients are also more willing to see counselors who use tentative interpretations. Goodyear (1990) cites a study by Taylor and Brown (1988) that found that mentally healthy individuals were more likely to harbor unrealistic positive self-perceptions. Based on these findings, Goodyear warns that clients may be prone to distort test interpretations in an unrealistically positive manner. Other studies have shown that clients prefer individual test interpretations over group interpretations in terms of clarity (Miller & Cochran, 1979), favorability (Oliver, 1977), and helpfulness (Wilkerson, 1967).

Rawlins, Eberly, and Rawlings (1991) note that counselors are ill-prepared to deal with the wide array of potential problems in testing and are in need of better training in measurement. These authors suggest that counselors could overcome some of their problems with testing by infusing counseling skills in test interpretation. Rawlins, Eberly, and Rawlings (1991) suggest that neuro-linguistic programming (NLP) can be integrated with counseling technique and theory to facilitate test interpretation. For example, counselors can use the NLP technique (such as pacing) to gain insight into what the client is experiencing regarding the test interpretation. Pacing involves staying with the client's experience by using counseling techniques (such as listening skills) to determine what sensory modality the client is functioning from (for example, visual, auditory, or tactile), and then matching predicates (such as "I see your point" with a visual learner) and mirroring bodily states (such as breathing rates) to facilitate rapport and understanding in the test interpretation process. In this regard, the use of NLP and other counseling strategies facilitates the art of counseling and test interpretation by helping counselors adjust to the unique and emerging needs of clients.

Computer-based test interpretation (CBTI) is an increasingly popular resource for testing and assessment (Sampson, 1990). A variety of computer software programs have been designed to assist counselors in interpreting the most commonly used tests, such as the Minnesota multiphasic personality inventory (MMPI-II) and the Wechsler intelligence scales. CBTI systems are not intended to replace the counselor's role in the assessment process. Instead, counselors should view CBTI as a basic framework to aid in assessment, diagnosis, and treatment planning (Sampson, 1990).

Test Bias

Watkins and Campbell (1990) note increasing concern in the literature regarding the fairness of tests and assessment methods for clients of culturally diverse backgrounds. Evidence of cultural bias has been found in numerous assessment procedures such as projective techniques, intelligence tests, and self-report measures (Jewell, 1989). Reynolds (1982) identifies the following factors often associated with test bias.

- *Inappropriate content.* Test content is biased toward values and experiences of white, middle-class individuals.
- *Inappropriate standardization samples.* Most norm groups, which tend to be underrepresented by ethnic minorities, are not realistic reference groups for minorities.
- *Examiner and language bias.* Psychologists tend to be white and speak only standard English. As test examiners, they can therefore intimidate ethnic minorities and create communication barriers, which can account for lower performance on tests.
- *Inequitable social consequences.* Ethnic minorities receive unfair labels from tests (for example, low intelligence), which can relegate them to dead-end educational tracks.

- *Measurement of different constructs.* Tests measure significantly different attributes when used with ethnic minorities, for example, the degree of their adherence to the value system of the dominant culture.
- *Differential predictive validity.* Although tests can accurately predict outcomes such as academic attainment for whites, they are much less effective in terms of predicting outcomes for ethnic minorities.

In response to the potential problems in multicultural assessment, Anastasi and Urbina (1997) suggest that testing should be conceptualized within a multicultural perspective. Culture-fair tests have been developed in an attempt to overcome the problems associated with test bias. Penrose and Raven (1936) developed one of the first culture-fair intelligence tests, called the Raven Matrices Test. This test has three versions, allowing for the evaluation of mentally retarded individuals up to normal adults. Each version consists of a non-verbal test in which the examinee must choose which matrix completes a particular pattern. Cattell (1949) developed another culture-fair intelligence test called the Cattell Culture-Fair Intelligence Test. The test is primarily nonpictorial and nonverbal and can be used with individuals from age 4 through adult.

A more current approach to culture-fair testing is the System of Multicultural Pluralistic Assessment (SOMPA), developed by Mercer (1977). This system can be used with children from 5 to 11 years of age. The SOMPA approach has several unique qualities. First, the child is administered several tests, including the Wechsler Intelligence Test for Children—Third Edition (WISC-III). Second, an interview is conducted with the child's primary caregiver to obtain information on how the child functions in various activities and settings (McMillan, 1984). The WISC-III score is then "corrected" after consideration of other test scores and the interview. Mercer contends that the "uncorrected" test scores can be useful in making educational and instructional decisions, but the "corrected" score more accurately reflects the child's intellectual aptitude (McMillan, 1984).

Types of Tests

Assessment procedures can be divided into two major categories: standardized and non-standardized measures (Kottler & Brown, 1996). *Standardized measures* are tests that have a standardized norm group. This category includes a wide variety of psychological tests such as intelligence tests, personality tests, interest tests, aptitude tests, achievement tests, and neuropsychological tests. Nonstandardized measures do not have a standardized norm group and include procedures such as observations, behavioral assessment, and environmental assessment.

Each form has advantages and disadvantages. Standardized assessment procedures provide the counselor with objective information regarding the client. In addition, these tests contain information on validity and reliability, which can be used to evaluate the results. The disadvantages include potential cultural bias, promoting harmful labels, and producing scores that may be oversimplified or misleading.

Nonstandardized assessment procedures also have inherent strengths and weaknesses. One strength of these measures is providing a flexible and individualized approach, which yields information unique to the individual. They can also be easily modified to

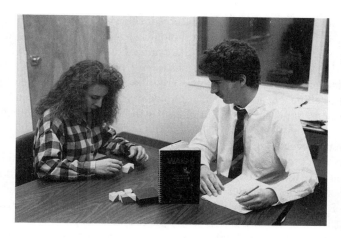

Testing can provide counselors with objective information regarding the client's psychological functioning.

accommodate individual differences, thereby minimizing cultural bias. Weaknesses include a lack of information on reliability and validity to evaluate the assessment procedures and a lack of objectivity in terms of test results. The advantages and disadvantages of standardized and nonstandardized assessment procedures are summarized in Table 4.1.

TABLE 4.1   Comparison of Standardized and Nonstandardized Measures

Type of Test	Advantages	Disadvantages
Standardized	1. Provides objective information regarding the client	1. Is prone to cultural bias
	2. Provides specific information about a client relative to a norm group	2. Often results in "labels"
	3. Contains information on validity and reliability that can be used to evaluate the test	3. Can lead to oversimplified and misleading test results (for example, IQ scores)
Nonstandardized	1. Provides a flexible, individualized approach that yields information unique to the individual client	1. Lacks information on validity and reliability
	2. Fosters an active role for the client in the assessment process	2. Lacks objectivity and ability to generalize to a reference group
	3. Can be easily modified to accommodate individual differences	3. Lacks specific scores and reference groups, which may make assessment results appear confusing to clients

Standardized Measures. Standardized measures include a wide range of psychological tests. Anastasi and Urbina (1997) define a psychological test as "an objective and standardized measure of a sample behavior" (p. 4). "Standardization implies *uniformity of procedure* in administering and scoring the test" (Anastasi & Urbina, 1997, p. 6). Psychological tests can be administered to an individual or a group to assess a wide range of traits and attributes such as intelligence, achievement, aptitude, interest, personality, and neuropsychological impairment. Some commonly used tests in these domains are intelligence tests, achievement tests, aptitude tests, interest inventories, personality inventories, projective techniques, and neuropsychological tests.

Intelligence tests provide information regarding the client's intellectual functioning. The most common individually administered intelligence tests are the Stanford Binet and three Wechsler scales: the Wechsler Pre-School and Primary Scale of Intelligence—Revised (WPPSI-R), the Wechsler Intelligence Scale for Children—Third Edition (WISC-III), and the Wechsler Adult Intelligence Scale—Third Edition (WAIS-III). Two of the more commonly used group-administered intelligence tests are the Otis-Lennon Mental Ability Test and the California Tests of Mental Maturity. Nonverbal intelligence tests are also available, such as the Raven Progressive Matrixes and the Test of Nonverbal Intelligence (TONI). These are especially useful in multicultural testing to overcome language barriers. They can also be used if the counselor has limited time available and only needs to have a rough estimate of the client's intellectual level (Anastasi & Urbina, 1997).

Achievement tests are used primarily in school settings. They provide information on what a person has learned. Three of the more popular achievement tests are the Iowa Test of Basic Skills, the Wide Range Achievement Test, and Woodcock Johnson Psycho-Educational Battery (Anastasi & Urbina, 1997).

Aptitude tests focus on the client's potential in an attempt to predict success. As mentioned, the Graduate Record Examination is an example of an aptitude test, and it is designed to predict whether a person will be able to successfully complete graduate study. Another example is the Differential Aptitude Test, which counselors use frequently in educational and vocational counseling of students in grades 8 through 12 (Anastasi & Urbina, 1997).

Interest inventories help the counselor determine where the client's interests lie. This information can be especially useful to career counselors. Three of the most commonly used interest inventories are the Kuder Preference Record, the Career Assessment Inventory, and the Strong Campbell Interest Inventory.

Personality inventories provide information about personality dynamics and can also be part of the diagnostic process to determine whether there is a mental disorder. The two types of personality tests are objective and subjective. Objective tests require more rigid responses, such as true-false or multiple-choice responses. The most widely used objective personality test is the MMPI-II. It is especially useful in identifying certain mental disorders, for example, depression or schizophrenia. Two popular objective personality tests that provide an overview of the personality are the California Psychological Inventory (CPI) and the 16 Personality Factors Questionnaire (16 PF).

Projective techniques are subjective tests that require clients to project their thoughts and feelings into a variety of ambiguous stimuli, such as the inkblots of the Rorschach test or pictures in the thematic apperception test. Projective tests are sometimes more appropriate in multicultural settings since they minimize the use of words, thereby decreasing tendencies toward cultural bias. Two other commonly used examples are the Draw-a-Person and House-Tree-Person tests. Clark (1995) suggests that projective tests are underutilized by counselors and can provide a valuable means of enhancing the counseling process. Clark notes that projective tests have a variety of uses in counseling, such as overcoming resistance, obtaining a phenomenological understanding of the client, identifying goals, and establishing a treatment plan.

Neuropsychological tests "are used to evaluate the neurologically impaired patients' cognitive, behavioral, and psychological strengths and weaknesses and to determine their relationship to cerebral functioning" (Newmark, 1985, p. 383). Several popular neuropsychological tests and test batteries are in use. One example is the Bender-Gestalt Test, which involves having the client copy nine separate designs. This test can be scored by subjective intuitive means or by utilizing an objective scoring procedure (Anastasi & Urbina, 1997). Another neuropsychological test that clinicians use is the Benton Visual Retention Test, which requires the client to reproduce 10 different geometric figures. Although these two tests can provide an indication of brain damage, they should not be used as a sole means of making a diagnosis. Bigler and Ehrfurth (1981) even suggest that the Bender should be banned as a single neuropsychological technique.

Several neuropsychological test batteries have been developed in an attempt to create a more comprehensive approach to assessment and diagnosis. The two most popular test batteries are the Halstead-Reitan Neuropsychological Test Battery and the Luria Nebraska Neuropsychological Battery. The Halstead-Reitan Neuropsychological Test can be used with individuals ages 15 and older. It is technically comprised of 10 tests, two of which are considered allied procedures (Newmark, 1985). The main battery is comprised of the Category Test, Speech-Sounds Perception, Seashore Rhythm, Tactual Performance Test (TPT), Finger Oscillation, Trail Making A and B, Aphasia Screening, and Sensory Perceptual Examination. The allied procedures are the WAIS-III and the MMPI-II. Compared with the Halstead-Reitan, the Luria Nebraska Battery requires less time to administer (2½ hours as opposed to 6 or more hours), is more highly standardized, and provides a fuller coverage of neurological deficits (Anastasi & Urbina, 1997).

Nonstandardized Measures.   Goldman (1990) refers to nonstandardized measures as qualitative assessment, noting that for the most part these forms of assessment do not yield quantitative raw scores as are found in standardized measures. Goldman suggests that qualitative assessment has a number of advantages over standardized approaches. Some advantages of qualitative assessment procedures are as follows.

- They foster an "active role for the client in the process of collecting and teasing meaning out of data, rather than the role of a passive responder who is being measured, predicted, placed, or diagnosed" (Goldman, 1990, p. 205).
- They emphasize "the *holistic study* of the individual rather than the isolation and precise measurement of narrowly defined discrete elements of ability, interest, or personality" (Goldman, 1990, p. 205).
- They encourage clients to learn about themselves within a developmental framework.

- They are especially effective in group work, in which clients can learn about individual differences as well as gain an understanding about themselves in relation to others in the group.
- They reduce the distinction between assessment and counseling by stimulating rather than hampering counseling methods, as can be the case with standardized assessment.
- They can be easily modified to accommodate individual differences such as cultural diversity and gender since they do not attempt precise measurements from normative samples.

A variety of nonstandardized measures can be used in the counseling process. These include observation skills, behavioral assessment, and environmental assessment. A description of each of these procedures follows.

Observation Skills.   The power of observation can be a very revealing aspect of clinical assessment. Freud attested to the power of observation when he said, "He that has eyes to see and ears to hear may convince himself that no mortal can keep a secret. If his lips are silent, he chatters with his fingertips; betrayal oozes out of him at every pore" (Freud, 1953, pp. 77–78). As Freud noted, the skilled clinician can learn much from observing what occurs during the counseling session.

Ivey (1994) and Baruth and Huber (1985) provide a description of how nonverbal behavior can provide valuable information regarding clients. These observations have been incorporated into the following overview. In reviewing these facets of nonverbal behavior, it is important to consider how diversity issues such as culture and gender can contribute to variation in communication.

- *Touch.* The amount and nature of the physical contact (in terms of touch) can provide information on such things as interpersonal comfort and closeness, capacity for empathic responding, and so forth.
- *Proxemics.* Proxemics is the study of physical space or distance between people. For example, people who seek close physical distance between each other could suggest intimacy, and those that desire more space could be seeking to meet needs such as solace or safety.
- *Kinesics.* Kinesics relates to how body movements contribute to communication. Much can be learned from a client's body language. For example, crossing the arms can suggest reluctance or resistance; leaning forward can imply interest; and leaning away can imply fear or boredom.
- *Autonomic physiological behavior.* Autonomic responses are very expressive and provide uncensored information about the client. For example, rapid breathing can suggest anxiety or nervousness, and blushing can indicate embarrassment.
- *Vocal qualities.* A client's voice quality can provide important information to the counselor. Changes in rate, volume, or pitch can communicate different messages. For example, hesitations and breaks can suggest confusion or stress.
- *Facial expressions.* Grimaces, frowns, smiles, and raised eyebrows all communicate something important about the client's emotional state.

■ *Eye contact.* Pupils tend to dilate when clients are discussing an interesting topic and contract when they are bored or uncomfortable. In addition, clients tend to look away when discussing something that is depressing or disturbing.

Counselors can also learn from observing clients in their natural habitat. Goldman (1990) refers to this process as *shadowing,* which he defines as "following someone through a day or part of a day to observe how the person acts and reacts in various places and in various interactions" (p. 210). Shadowing can provide information on how the client functions in a real-life situation. Numerous possibilities exist for making observations in the field. Some examples include observing a student in a classroom, on a school bus, or on a playground to assess the child's interpersonal skills; observing a mother or father with a newborn to determine the degree of bonding; conducting a marriage or family session in a client's home to observe the family in their natural habitat; and observing a manager role-play administrative functions in an organizational setting.

Sundberg (1977) identifies systematic methods for observing and recording behavior in organizational settings. These methods include the situational test, in-basket test, and critical incidence technique. The situational test involves a contrived situation in which the subject is given a task to accomplish, for example, as a perspective policeman attempting to find a person who has mysteriously vanished. Specific measures of observation are identified to facilitate accurate recording of information.

The in-basket test is a method used to select and train managers and executives (Vernon & Parry, 1949; Lopez, 1966; Bray, Campbell, & Grant, 1974). This test entails observing an individual role-play various administrative tasks. Systematic procedures are then identified for observing and recording behavior.

The critical incidence technique involves an observer recording instances of behavior that indicate good or poor performance. From this information procedures are identified to chart performance or plan training.

Behavioral Assessment.   Behavioral assessment, which evolved from behavioral psychology, involves the systematic measurement of behaviors broadly defined to include attitudes, feelings, and cognitions (Sundberg, 1977). In behavioral assessment, counselors may use a wide variety of procedures, including direct observation in the natural environment, problem checklists, self-reports, and record-keeping (Sundberg, 1977; Anastasi & Urbina, 1997).

Behavioral assessment can be tied directly into treatment by using single-subject designs, such as A-B and A-B-A designs. The A phase involves obtaining a baseline of a problem behavior before treatment. The B phase assesses behavior after treatment. The behaviors recorded during the A and B phases are usually graphed to provide a measure of behavior change before and after treatment. Additional information on single-subject designs such as A-B and A-B-A can be found in Chapter 5.

Environmental/Ecological Assessment

Environmental assessment (also referred to as ecological assessment) involves consideration of environmental factors such as sociocultural forces in the assessment of psychological functioning. It shares common characteristics with other theories such as family therapy, interpersonal psychotherapy, and postmodern theories. Family therapy recognizes the need to assess people from a systemic or systems perspective. Interpersonal psychotherapy is similar to family therapy, emphasizing the role of interpersonal relationships in mental health. Postmodern theories such as social constructionism also emphasize the role of social cultural forces in assessment. Central to this position is a redefining of the self from being an autonomous self to a social self that extends beyond the individual to all aspects of society (Gergen, 1994). Alfred Adler's concept of social interest as the barometer of mental health is an excellent example of the relationship between social embeddedness and psychological functioning (Jones, 1995).

Walsh (1990) observes that any assessment is incomplete without some assessment of the environment. Walsh suggested that counselors include an environmental assessment to determine how clients perceive their environment and how these perceptions influence their behavior. Environmental assessment can be particularly important when determining the etiology, or cause, of psychopathology. A counselor who does not consider environmental factors may attribute a mental disorder to intrapsychic forces, that is, forces within the person, instead of considering environmental factors such as living in poverty.

As counseling becomes increasingly multicultural, it is particularly important to include an assessment of sociocultural factors when conducting an environmental assessment. Social forces that may warrant attention include how clients feel about where they live and with whom they live and their attitudes toward their job, family, and friends. Topper (1985) identifies cultural factors that counselors should address during the assessment process. He notes that it is particularly important to evaluate the client's level of acculturation to determine whether traditional Western counseling approaches will be appropriate. In addition, he suggests that it would be advantageous to determine how the client's condition will be viewed by members of the client's culture and then evaluate the client in terms of patterns of psychological development that are normative to that culture.

Hershenson, Power, and Waldo (1996) provide additional information regarding environmental assessment. These authors note that there has been an increased interest in the role of the environment in psychological functioning. They contend that in many instances, the environment is both the primary source of a client's problem and the potential target for an intervention in counseling. They go on to describe theories and strategies for environmental assessment. Theories include the behavior-setting approach (the environment shapes behavior), need-press theory (the relationship between needs and environmental presses), human aggregate model (the match between the individual and the environment), and social climate models (a systems perspective that also considers the person's perception of environmental events). These theories describe a complex interaction between each individual and the environment. Environments represent numerous tasks of life such as work, marriage and family, social environment, and spiritual environment and are influenced by various forces such as war and peace, poverty and affluence, and oppression and mutual respect. These environmental forces can be reinforcing to an individual and contribute to need fulfillment or be a source of stress and discontent. Individual perceptions of the environment play a key role in what is actually experienced. For some a disorganized work setting is perceived as a challenge and for others a major source of stress.

Strategies for environmental assessment are directed at identifying the ultimate client-environmental fit. In this process it is important to assess how the various environmental forces impact each other, such as stresses at work and functioning at home, and to obtain an accurate reading of individual perceptions of these forces. Hershenson, Power, and Waldo (1996) adapted information from Huebner (1980) in making the following guidelines for environmental assessment.

1. All aspects of the environment must be assessed independently and in relation to each other.
2. Instruments used in assessment should provide information on the sources of pressure within the environment.
3. Locally developed instruments should be considered in intervention planning.
4. Multiple strategies and procedures should be utilized when assessing complex person-environment relationships.
5. The relationship between the objective and perceived environment should be differentiated.
6. Assessment instruments should be reliable and valid for the purpose they are to be used.

Environmental assessment appears to offer another important dimension of the assessment process. It expands the horizons of assessment beyond the individual to include the assessment of people within the context of their social milieu. Environmental assessment appears to offer much promise in terms of generating information on the role of social cultural forces in psychological functioning.

Diagnosis

Historical Perspective

Nathan and Harris (1980) provide information that shows that the process of diagnosis can be traced to the preclassical period in Greece. The Greeks were able to identify the behavioral consequences associated with the aging process and the mental health consequences of alcoholism. Somewhat later during classical times, the Greeks went on to identify and describe psychological disorders that are still recognized today, for example, mania, melancholia, and paranoia.

It was not until much later that a formal classification of psychological disorders was developed. Rosenhan and Seligman (1995) identify several key individuals who contributed to this process. Philippe Pinel (1745–1856), the psychiatric reformer, divided psychological disorders into melancholia, mania (with and without delirium), dementia, and idiotism. In 1896, Emil Kraepelin (1855–1926) developed the first comprehensive system of classifying psychological disorders. He based this system of diagnosis on a medical model. In this regard, Kraepelin believed all medical disorders had a physical origin and diagnosis required a careful assessment of symptoms. Rosenhan and Seligman identify several other individuals, such as Eugene Blueler and Adolf Meyer, who proposed their own systems of diagnosis.

Although there are merits in the various diagnostic systems, the need for one coherent system of diagnosis became apparent. This led to the development of the *Diagnostic*

Statistical Manual of Mental Disorders (DSM) in 1952. The DSM has undergone several revisions since that time, with the DSM-IV being published in 1994.

Uses of Diagnosis.   Diagnosis is an important aspect of the counseling process. Rosenhan and Seligman (1995) describe four reasons for making a diagnosis.

1. *It provides communication shorthand among clinicians.* Diagnosis enables the clinician to incorporate the various symptoms of a client into a single diagnosis that other clinicians can easily understand.
2. *It suggests treatment possibilities.* Diagnosis can help clinicians narrow down the treatment possibilities. For example, a paranoid schizophrenic will usually not respond well to verbal therapies.
3. *It can communicate information about etiology.* Mental disorders are associated with different types of etiology. For example, one of the major causative factors associated with schizophrenia is an excess of the neurotransmitter dopamine in the brain.
4. *It aids scientific investigation.* Diagnosis helps group symptoms together so they can be systematically studied to determine etiology and treatment strategies.

Woody, Hansen, and Rossberg (1989) note that some counselors shy away from diagnosis, because they believe it is a judgmental process that labels clients. These authors counter that diagnosis is more than a process of labeling. It also provides an analysis of the client's functioning to determine the most appropriate treatment.

The DSM-IV

The DSM-IV is a classification system of all recognized mental disorders. It is a multiaxial evaluation system that provides information on five separate axes.

Axes I and II.   These two axes comprise the entire system of mental disorders. All recognized mental disorders will be on either Axis I or Axis II. The DSM-IV provides decision trees that describe the symptoms associated with various mental disorders. Clinicians can use decision trees to rule out certain disorders when conducting a differential diagnosis to determine whether a patient has a particular mental disorder.

Axis I is used for all mental disorders except for personality disorders and mental retardation, which are placed on Axis II. Axis I can also be used to record counseling problems that are not mental disorders but require professional attention or treatment. These are called V-codes and include many so-called problems of living, such as marital difficulty or parent-child problems. It is also important to note that multiple diagnoses can be recorded on both Axis I and Axis II. For example, a 54-year-old male with a history of alcohol abuse is currently experiencing a major depression. In addition, the patient has an antisocial personality disorder. These disorders can be recorded on each axis as follows.

Axis I	296.22	Major depression, single episode, moderate
	305.00	Alcohol abuse
Axis II	301.70	Antisocial personality disorder

Clinicians record the presence or absence of a diagnosis on Axis I and Axis II, as illustrated in the following examples.

A 12-year-old client who is mentally retarded can be recorded as follows:

Axis I   V71.09   No diagnosis or condition an Axis I

Axis II   317   Mild mental retardation

A client who does not have a mental disorder but is receiving help for a marital problem can be recorded as

Axis I   V61.10   Partner Relational Problem

Axis II   V71.09   No diagnosis on Axis II

Another factor for clinicians to consider when making an Axis I or Axis II diagnosis is to determine the principal diagnosis or condition. The principal diagnosis is the condition that is primarily responsible for the evaluation and will be the main focus of attention. When making two or more diagnoses on the same axis, the clinician should list the primary diagnosis first on that axis. When making diagnoses on both axes, the clinician should indicate which is the primary diagnosis, as illustrated in the following example.

Axis I   309.24   Adjustment disorder with anxiety

Axis II   301.20   Schizoid personality disorder (principal diagnosis)

The DSM-IV also provides a mechanism for the clinician to indicate the degree of diagnostic certainty. There may be inadequate information to make a diagnosis on either Axis I or Axis II. When this occurs, the clinician can use the notation, "799.90 Diagnosis or condition deferred," on the appropriate axis, as illustrated in the following example.

Axis I   799.90   Diagnosis or condition deferred on Axis I

Axis II   799.90   Diagnosis or condition deferred on Axis II

The clinician can also make a provisional diagnosis on either axis. This enables the clinician to formulate a tentative diagnosis, which requires additional assessment before a final diagnosis can be made. The following example shows how the clinician indicates a provisional diagnosis.

Axis I   296.22   Major depression, single episode, moderate (provisional)

Axis III.   Axis III allows the clinician to indicate whether there is a current physical disorder or condition that may be relevant to the particular case. For example, a person may be suffering from syphilis, which could be responsible for producing hallucinations. If this is the case, the clinician would record a diagnosis of untreated syphilis on Axis III.

Axis IV.   Axis IV provides information relating to pertinent psychosocial and environmental problems, which can impact the diagnosis or treatment of a mental disorder. Generally these are problems that have occurred during the past year but can extend beyond that time frame if the events appear to have a bearing on the current mental status of the client, such as being a Vietnam veteran. The DSM provides specific categories for reporting psychosocial and environmental problems such as educational problems or occupational problems. The clinician should use these categories to help describe the particular circumstances of the client. The clinician can list more than one problem area. For example, a client who is about to fail out of school and loose his part-time job can be recorded as follows:

Axis IV   Academic difficulties
           Threat of job loss

Some psychosocial and environmental problems can become so significant in the client's treatment they may become the focus of the clinician's attention. When this occurs, they should also be recorded on Axis I as a V code (as noted earlier in the description of Axis I).

Axis I   V62.3   Academic problem
          V62.2   Occupational problem

Axis V.   Axis V allows the clinician to indicate the client's overall level of functioning (in terms of psychological, social, and occupational functioning). A Global Assessment of Functioning (GAF) Scale is provided to rate the client. The scale is rated from 0 to 100, with 100 indicating superior functioning and 1 indicating seriously impaired functioning. The clinician should record the GAF number and what time period it reflects (for example, current, highest level past year, on admission, at discharge). A person with serious suicidal thoughts upon admission to a hospital could be recorded as

Axis V   GAF = 50 (on admission)

A Case Study.   Spitzer et al. (1994) provide an excellent learning tool for counselors to gain expertise in using the DSM. For numerous case studies involving children, adolescents, and adults, the authors follow a format of describing each case study, giving a DSM-III-R diagnosis and explaining the rationale for the diagnosis. The following excerpt from *The DSM-IV Casebook* (Spitzer et al., 1994, pp. 323–325) provides an example of how to apply the DSM diagnostic process to a case (reprinted by permission).

"Sniper"
Leah, age 7, was referred by her teacher for evaluation because of her tearfulness, irritability, and difficulty concentrating in class. Three months earlier Leah had been among the children pinned down by sniper fire on her school playground. Over a period of 15 minutes, the sniper killed one child and injured several others. After the gunfire ceased, no one moved until the police stormed the sniper's apartment and found that he had killed himself. Leah did not personally know the child who was killed, or the sniper.

According to her teacher, before the shooting, Leah was shy but vivacious, well-behaved, and a good student. Within a few days after the incident, there was a noticeable change in her behavior. She withdrew from her friends. She began to bicker with other children when they spoke to her. She seemed uninterested in her schoolwork and had to be prodded to persist in required tasks. The teacher noticed that Leah jumped whenever there was static noise in the public address system and when the class shouted answers to flashcards.

Leah's parents were relieved when the school made the referral, because they were uncertain about how to help her. Leah was uncharacteristically quiet when her parents asked her about the sniping incident. At home she had become moody, irritable, argumentative, fearful, and clinging. She was apprehensive about new situations and fearful of being alone and insisted that someone accompany her to the bathroom. Leah regularly asked to sleep with her parents. She slept restlessly and occasionally cried out in her sleep. She appeared always to be tired, complained of minor physical problems, and seemed more susceptible to minor infections. Her parents were especially worried after Leah nearly walked in front of a moving car without being aware of it. Although she seemed less interested in any of her usual games, her parents noticed that she kept engaging her siblings in nurse games, in which she was often bandaged.

When asked about the incident in the interview, Leah said that she had tried desperately to hide behind a trash can when she heard the repeated gunfire. She had been terrified of being killed, and was "shaking all over," her heart pounding and her head hurting. She vividly told of watching an older child fall to the ground, bleeding and motionless. She ran to safety when there was a pause in the shooting. Leah described a recurring image of the injured girl lying bleeding on the ground. She said that thoughts of the incident sometimes disrupted her attention, though she would try to think about something else. Lately, she could not always remember what was being said in class. She no longer played in the area where the shooting had occurred during recess or after school. She avoided crossing over the playground on her way home from school each day and avoided the sniper's house and street. She was particularly afraid at school on Fridays, the day the shooting had occurred. Although her mother and father had comforted her, she did not know who to tell what it was she was feeling.

Leah continued to be afraid that someone would shoot at her again. She had nightmares about the shooting and dreams in which she or a family member was being shot at or pursued. She ran away from any "popping noises" at home or in the neighborhood. Although she said that she had less desire to play, when asked about new games, she reported frequently playing a game in which a nurse helped an injured person. She began to watch television news about violence, and recounted news stories that demonstrated that the world was full of danger.

Discussion of "Sniper"

Leah experienced a traumatic event that involved actual or threatened death or serious injury to herself and to her classmates and evoked intense fear, helplessness, and horror. Within a few days of the trauma, she began to exhibit the characteristic symptoms of severe Posttraumatic Stress Disorder (DSM-IV, p. 427). Because the duration of symptoms is less than 3 months, we further specify Acute.

Although adults sometimes have "flashbacks" in which they actually experience the situation as if it were currently happening, children rarely reexperience trauma in this way. As is typical for her age, Leah reexperienced the trauma in the form of recurrent, intrusive images and recollections of the event and recurrent, distressing dreams about it. She also incorporated themes from the event into repetitive themes in play.

Leah attempted to avoid thoughts and feelings associated with the trauma and places that reminded her of the event. This formerly vivacious little girl now exhibited numbing of general responsiveness. She became apathetic and uninterested in her schoolwork and detached from her former friends. She displayed persistent symptoms of increased arousal, including exaggerated startle reaction (to loud noises), irritability, difficulty concentrating, and sleep disturbance.

In making a multiaxial assessment, we check on Axis IV Problems Related to Interaction With Legal System/Crime and specify Victim of sniper attack. Because of the serious symptoms and impairment in her social relationships and schoolwork, we assign a current global assessment of functioning score of 45.

A DSM IV diagnosis for Leah is:

Axis I	309.81	Post-traumatic stress disorder
Axis II	V71.09	No diagnosis on Axis II
Axis III		None
Axis IV		Problem related to interaction with the legal system/crime (victim of sniper attack)
Axis V		GAF: 45 (current)

The Clinical Interview

The clinical interview provides a structure for assimilating information pertaining to assessment and diagnosis. May (1990) notes that the clinical interview is one of the most widely used assessment procedures. It serves a variety of purposes such as providing information on the client's presenting problem and concerns; enabling the counselor to gain necessary historical information, including organic factors that could contribute to the client's condition; and aiding in the process of making a differential diagnosis to determine whether a client suffers from a particular mental disorder.

The clinical interview normally takes place early in the counseling process, usually during the first or second session. It allows the counselor to gain important background information and determine whether the client suffers from a mental disorder or is in a state of crisis that requires immediate attention. The clinical interview can be structured according to the counselor's theoretical orientation and the client's unique issues and concerns.

I have developed a four-stage model for the clinical interview: using listening skills, taking the client's history, conducting a mental status exam, and using standardized and nonstandardized measures. These four stages serve overlapping functions and should not be perceived as discrete entities. For example, a counselor may gain useful information about the client's history and mental status while using listening skills. An overview of these four stages follows.

Stage One: Using Listening Skills. Counselors can begin the clinical interview by using listening skills to obtain a phenomenological understanding of the client. Counselors can also use listening skills to determine whether a client is self-referred, what prompted the appointment, and a description of the presenting problem and underlying concerns.

Stage Two: Taking the Client's History. The counselor may take an in-depth history after clients have had a chance to discuss their situation with the counselor. The history can be divided into two parts. The first part involves the client providing background information regarding work, family, social relationships, health, and other areas of interest such as important turning points in the client's life. Counselors may develop or use forms to solicit information on these topics as an efficient method of gathering this part of the history. The second part of the history involves exploring the client's symptoms and concerns, such as difficulty sleeping, loss of appetite, or marital problems, in terms of onset, duration, and severity. This information can help the counselor gain a better overall understanding of the client's condition. It can also be particularly useful in diagnosis, since major systems of diagnosis such as the DSM-IV require this information to make a differential diagnosis.

It is particularly important when conducting a history to explore possible organic factors that could contribute to mental disorders. These factors include the use of alcohol or drugs, prescription medications, and existing or past medical conditions. For example, excessive use of alcohol can create hallucinations, resulting in a mental disorder called alcohol hallucinosis. Many prescription drugs have been known to contribute to the symptoms associated with mental disorders (Othmer & Othmer, 1989). For example, estrogen can cause anxiety and depression; diuretics can produce irritability, restlessness, insomnia, and delirium; and insulin can induce psychosis and confusion. Medical conditions may also be accompanied by symptoms of psychological distress. For example, gout or brain tumors can produce depression; head injury can cause anxiety; and multiple sclerosis can foster anxiety, depression, and episodic psychiatric symptoms. Othmer and Othmer (1989) provide a more complete list of prescription drugs and medical conditions and their associated psychiatric symptoms.

Stage Three: Conducting a Mental Status Exam.   Counselors can conduct a mental status exam to help make a differential diagnosis. For a client who reports hearing voices, a counselor may consider schizophrenia as a possible diagnosis. The counselor could then use the mental status exam to explore whether the client has other symptoms associated with schizophrenia, such as delusions, flat or inappropriate affect, and evidence of a thought disorder.

Trzepacz and Baker (1993) describe six components that should be addressed in a mental status exam. These are summarized as follows.

1. *Appearance, Attitude, and Activity.* Much can be learned from *appearance.* Bizarre dress and overall appearance can suggest disorientation and a mental disorder. Physical appearance can also provide some information regarding the person's physical health (for example, running nose and so forth can suggest a cold or illness). *Attitude* relates to the individual's demeanor during the interview. This can range from cooperative to hostile and can provide indications of the person's interpersonal style and reaction to the counselor. *Activity level* relates to the quality and degree of physical and motor movement. Some clients are constantly pacing, suggesting possible explosive tendencies, whereas others are listless with little movement, which may suggest depression.

2. *Mood and Affect. Mood* is the person's *internal* emotional state such as happy, sad, or anxious. *Affect* is the *external* manifestation of how emotions are expressed. Affect is communicated verbally and nonverbally in numerous ways such as facial expressions, tone of voice, laughter, and crying. Mood and affect can be congruent and appropriate (indicating mental health), such as laughing when one feels happy, or incongruent, such as laughing when one is sad (indicating a possible mental disorder).

3. *Speech and Language. Speech and language* relate to verbal and written communication involving words, concepts, and ideas. Assessment of speech and language can help identify problems with fluency (such as stuttering), communication disorders (relating to information processing), and learning disabilities.

4. *Thought Process, Thought Content, and Perception. Thought processes* relate to how we are thinking and *thought content* is directed at what we are thinking. Normal thought processes tend to be connected (or linear), with one idea contributing to the next idea. Problems with thought processes can occur in schizophrenia when the individual has difficulty staying with one line of thought and instead jumps from one topic to another, unrelated topic. The *content of thought and perceptions* can also suggest mental health or illness. For example, it is common in psychosis to have problems in thought content such as being delusional and problems with perceptions such as hallucinations.

5. *Cognition. Cognition* relates to a wide array of intellectual functions, including memory, ability to think and reason, problem solving, and creativity. Assessment of cognition involves a variety of skills and abilities such as determining a person's degree of orientation (for example, who they are and where they are), and the ability to attend, concentrate and remember, use abstract thinking to solve complex problems, and so forth. Failure to use basic mental facilities can suggest brain damage such as that found in Alzheimer's dementia.

6. *Insight and Judgment. Insight and judgment* involve the use of a variety of higher order functions that can be referred to as emotional intelligence or "EQ." EQ can include such things as having self-awareness, being able to "read social situations" to determine appropriate interpersonal behavior, and utilizing decision-making skills necessary for sound judgment.

Stage Four: Using Standardized and Nonstandardized Measures.   Counselors can use standardized and nonstandardized measures to refine diagnostic considerations and plan treatment. For example, a client's MMPI-II profile might include elevated scales on 2 (depression) and 9 (mania), which could contribute to a diagnosis of manic-depression. In terms of nonstandardized measures, environmental assessment might show that the client feels depressed about living on the East coast, hates working in a retail job, and wants to go back to school. Information from the environmental assessment can be useful in terms of understanding the etiology or cause of the mental disorder as well as in planning treatment. In this example, the client could consider moving and going to school.

Treatment Planning

Treatment planning can be defined as "an organized conceptual effort to design a program *outlining in advance* the specific steps by which the therapist will help the patient recover from his or her presenting dysfunctional state" (Makover, 1992, p. 338). Linda Seligman (1990) conceptualizes treatment planning in terms of an hourglass. Initially, the counselor generates a large amount of information during the assessment phases (such as psychosocial and medical history). This information gets narrowed down, generating one or more diagnoses. The diagnosis then broadens into consideration of treatment goals and associated counseling techniques and strategies.

Seligman (1990) notes that it is important to consider counselor and client variables when formulating a treatment plan. Consideration of counselor and client characteristics can be useful in selecting treatment modalities for client problems and disorders. For example, there is some evidence to suggest that depressed individuals with low social dysfunction respond well to interpersonal therapy and those with low cognitive dysfunction respond well to cognitive-behavioral therapy (Shea et al., 1990). The literature provides a rich description of the client variables (Garfield, 1994) and the counselor variables (Beutler, Machado, & Neufeldt, 1994) on counseling outcomes that can provide additional information for treatment planning.

Treatment planning can be conceptualized from several perspectives. For brief-solution-focused counseling, treatment planning tends to be narrow in nature, focusing on symptom relief and returning the individual to a functional state as quickly as possible. Traditional treatment planning is more comprehensive, with the goal of addressing as many clinical issues and client modalities as necessary to move the client toward optimal development. All perspectives on treatment planning share some common elements. Young (1992) identified two aspects of treatment planning that would seem to be useful for most theoretical perspectives. First, the counselor and client formulate mutually agreed on treatment goals, which are prioritized and associated with counseling strategies. A number of useful treatment planners are available that can be used to identify treatment goals and the associated counseling strategies for common counseling problems (such as anger management) and mental disorders (see Jongsma & Peterson, 1995, *The Complete Psychotherapy Treatment Planner*). Second, the counselor utilizes curative factors to promote success in the treatment planning process. These curative factors are maintaining a positive counseling relationship, enhancing the client's self-efficacy and self-esteem, lowering and raising emotional arousal, increasing hope and expectations, and practicing behaviors and providing new learning experiences. Curative factors such as these appear to offer much promise for promoting efficacy in all phases of the counseling process and warrant in-depth research evaluation to determine the actual effect they have on different phases of the counseling process.

Several comprehensive treatment planning models have emerged from the literature. Seligman's (1990) model is based on the acronym DO A CLIENT MAP. A description of each of the elements of her approach is provided in Table 4.2.

Arnold Lazarus's (1995, 1997) multimodal therapy (MMT) is both a separate school of counseling and a method that can be used in treatment planning. As a school of counseling, Lazarus's (1995) approach is based on social learning theory, general systems theory, and group and communication theory. Lazarus (1997) notes that MMT has always been a brief form of therapy embracing the major trends in brief counseling such as problem-centered, solution-focused, and active-directive. Lazarus (1997) recognizes the pressures from managed health care and strengthens his brief therapy perspective as follows. Brief-MMT is characterized by

- Active-directive strategies that include advice giving and homework assignment
- Didactic-educational focus (such as direct teaching and bibliotherapy) to help clients learn effective coping responses
- Use of the BASIC I.D. modalities in assessment, diagnosis, treatment planning, and to quickly identify key problems and counseling goals
- Using "elegant solutions" (from sources such as Ellis's 1996 brief rational emotive behavior therapy) to provide brief yet comprehensive approaches to problem resolution.

TABLE 4.2   **Overview of Seligman's DO A CLIENT MAP**

Elements of the Model		Description
D	Diagnosis	The overall diagnosis
O	Objective	Treatment goals
A	Assessments	Nature of assessment procedures required
C	Clinician	Counselor characteristics that would be facilitative
L	Location of treatment	Setting of treatment (for example, school or hospital)
I	Interventions	Types of counseling strategies utilized
E	Emphasis of treatment	Behavioral, cognitive, affective, supportive, directive, and so forth
N	Nature of treatment	Individual, group, marriage and family, and so forth
T	Timing	Frequency, duration, and number of counseling sessions
M	Medications	Nature of medication needs
A	Adjunct services	Types of additional services needed such as human services
P	Prognosis	Amount of improvement that is expected

According to Lazarus (1993), MMT is a form of technical eclecticism that is the utilization of a recognized theory along with counseling strategies from other theories. Lazarus (1993) contends that technical eclectic theories such as MMT have an advantage over other approaches in that they provide specific decision-making criteria for treatment planning.

The core of MMT is conceptualized in terms of the acronym BASIC I.D., which addresses seven modalities that provide a basis for treatment planning. Table 4.3 provides an overview of Lazarus's BASIC I.D.

Lazarus (1997) suggests that an assessment of all seven modalities provides an overview of the client's physical and psychological functioning. Additional assessment can be conducted in each modality as necessary to obtain a more in-depth understanding of the client. For example, an exploration of the nature and content of a client's cognition could suggest a pattern of self-destructive behavior (such as statements like "I'm no good. My wife would be better off without me"). Once the modalities have been evaluated, the counselor is in a position to formulate treatment goals with the client.

Makover (1992) provides another model of treatment planning called hierarchical treatment planning. It is a very practical, easy-to-understand approach. Makover suggests that counselors and clients should work together on formulating a treatment plan. Makover goes on to note that agreement on a treatment plan can be facilitated if clinicians generate answers to three questions by the end of the first session. The three questions are: Why did the client come here? Why did the client come now? and What does the client want? These questions can help identify what precipitated the request for counseling, current stressors, and the overall aim of receiving counseling.

Hierarchical treatment planning is composed of a four-tier hierarchy that provides a mechanism for understanding the interrelationship between the counseling process and treatment planning. The hierarchical approach begins with an identification of the final out-

TABLE 4.3   Larazus's BASIC I.D.

Elements of Model		Description
B	Behavior	Actions that people do (such as withdraw or avoid)
A	Affect	Emotional states (such as depression and anxiety)
S	Sensation	Feelings derived from the bodily senses (such as emptiness)
I	Imagery	Visualizations (such as daydreaming and fantasizing)
C	Cognition	Thoughts and ideas (such as I wish I were dead)
I	Interpersonal relations	How people relate to each other (such as encouraging)
D	Drugs	Biophysiological states (such as use of medication)

come or overall aim of counseling (such as enhanced marital relationship). The second tier of the hierarchy is the counseling goals (such as improved communication skills) associated with the overall aim. The third tier is the strategies (such as listening skills) that can be used to meet the goals. The fourth tier is the techniques (such as use of paraphrasing) that are associated with the counseling strategies. It must be emphasized that hierarchical treatment planning begins by identifying the overall aim of counseling and works downward to goals, strategies, and techniques. Counselors who emphasize techniques in counseling can essentially get treatment planning "backward," using a technique-oriented approach to generate what the final outcomes will become.

In the final analysis all three models of treatment planning can be used collectively to provide a comprehensive approach to treatment planning. Together they provide useful information on the counseling process in terms of assessment, diagnosis, and treatment and the interrelationship between aims, goals, strategies, and techniques; they also provide information on client modalities such as affect, cognitions, and interpersonal relations. In this regard, treatment planning provides an organizational structure to promote a sense of direction for the counseling process.

Diversity and Postmodern Issues in Assessment and Diagnosis

It is important to use a multicultural perspective in all phases of counseling, including assessment and diagnosis. A muticultural assessment helps counselors gain an accurate understanding of clients in terms of cultural, gender, spirituality, and other issues of diversity *before* they develop and implement a treatment program. For example, it is necessary to take into consideration cultural issues such as race and degree of acculturation in psychological assessment to avoid inaccurate test results associated with cultural bias.

Fortunately, criteria for recognizing and describing mental disorders such as the Diagnostic Statistic Manual (DSM) are beginning to address issues of diversity such as culture and spirituality. The trend toward cultural sensitivity began with the DSM-IV (Smart & Smart, 1997). The DSM-IV (as compared to the DSM-III-R) demonstrates significant improvement in incorporating cultural considerations in the diagnostic process. According to Smart and Smart (1997), the DSM-IV achieves its enhanced cultural perspective by including "(a) descriptions of specific cultural features that may be present in various disorders, (b) a glossary of 25 culture-bound syndromes, (c) an Outline of Cultural Formulation intended to help counselors in evaluating the impact of the client's cultural background, (d) a broader definition of Axis IV, and (e) the inclusion of new culturally sensitive 'V codes' " (p. 393). For example, the Outline for Cultural Formulation provides culturally relevant information that can be considered in formulating a multiaxial diagnosis, and examples of new "V codes" are V62.4, Acculturation Problem and V62.89, Religious or Spiritual Problems.

Although the DSM is beginning to make advances in terms of addressing diversity issues, additional work is required to establish a realistic understanding of the diagnosis and description of mental disorders within a multicultural perspective (Smart & Smart, 1997).

Postmodern theories such as social constructionism emphasize the role of diversity in assessment and diagnosis. From this perspective, it is important to take into consideration the effects of culture, gender, age, environment, language, and the multiple realities that can be generated from each individual's unique world view. Assessment and diagnosis must therefore involve processes that move beyond the intrapsychic or self-analysis to include a consideration of diversity issues.

Numerous diversity issues are associated with assessment. For example, the importance of being aware of possible cultural bias is described earlier in this chapter. Environmental assessment and assessment of world view provide good examples of how a counselor can look beyond intrapsychic forces to gain a broader picture of the client's world.

Spirituality is an emerging dimension of multiculturalism, which should be considered during the assessment process (Richards & Bergin, 1997). Spiritual assessment is in its infancy stage of development with few formal spiritual assessment instruments available. Richards and Bergin therefore recommend that spiritual assessment be done primarily during the initial history-taking and the clinical interview. Spiritual assessment can be used with all clients to obtain an understanding of their world view regarding spiritual issues (which may or may not include religious beliefs). It may be particularly useful to determine whether clients perceive spirituality as a source of strength and guidance and whether they turn to spiritual processes during times of personal difficulties. In these instances, spirituality can be used to foster a strengths perspective in counseling.

In some instances, counselors may also wish to determine if clients' spiritual beliefs and values are healthy or unhealthy in terms of promoting mental health (Richards & Bergin, 1997). For example, Allport and Ross (1967) differentiate unhealthy and healthy religious practice in terms of extrinsic versus intrinsic motivation. Unhealthy religious practice is characterized by an extrinsic religious orientation and includes people who use religion as a way of impressing others with status and self-righteousness. Healthy religious orientation tends to be intrinsically motivated and is characterized by personal spiritual journeys with individualized goals and aspirations. Clients who have potentially unhealthy spiritual beliefs and values can address these issues in counseling or be referred to specialists for assistance.

Accurate diagnosis also requires sensitivity to issues in diversity. It is especially important for counselors to be aware of the cultural context of language when differentiating mental health from mental illness. What might be considered normal can vary dramatically from one culture to the next. Gergen (1994) points out the role of language and culture in the etiology of mental disorders. He notes that some cultures have survived for centuries without any word or concept for depression, yet cultures that have a term for depression seem to find depression virtually everywhere.

Other important factors to consider in diagnosis include age and gender. Developmental psychopathology has identified how problems such as anxiety and depression manifest themselves differently according to age. For example, it is not uncommon for a child's or adolescent's depression to be "masked" by anger. Gender is also important to consider. For example, a woman who has just had a baby and becomes depressed could be experiencing a postpartum depression.

Summary

Assessment and diagnosis are important parts of the counseling process. They provide critical background information that is necessary before the counselor and client can establish counseling goals. Assessment and diagnosis also contribute to the science dimension of counseling by providing objective information regarding the counseling process.

Standardized assessment procedures include psychological tests that have a standardized norm group, such as the MMPI-II. Nonstandardized tests do not have standardized norm groups, are more subjective in nature, and include a variety of procedures such as observation and environmental assessment. Standardized and nonstandardized assessment procedures have their inherent strengths and weaknesses. For example, the major strength of nonstandardized measures lies in the ease of adjusting these procedures to the unique characteristics of the individual, thereby avoiding tendencies to induce test bias.

The DSM-IV can be used to formulate a multiaxial diagnosis. The clinical interview is a valuable tool for counselors to use in assessment and diagnosis. Counselors can use the interview to establish positive relationships and provide a structure for assessment and diagnosis. The clinical interview can also help the counselor avoid overlooking important issues such as a medical condition, past history of alcohol or drug abuse, and symptoms associated with a mental disorder. Diversity issues such as culture, gender, age, and spirituality should also be considered in assessment and diagnosis.

5 Counseling Research and Evaluation

CHAPTER OVERVIEW

This chapter provides an overview of the issues relating to counseling research and evaluation. In addition to discussing traditional research methodologies, particular attention is focused on field-based methodologies such as alternative and single-subject research designs. These newer methodologies are attracting considerable attention in the literature as being particularly relevant to the practitioner. Highlights of the chapter include

- The art and science of research and evaluation
- The purpose of research and evaluation relative to theory and practice, counselor accountability, and the body of knowledge in the counseling field
- An overview of types of research such as qualitative research methodologies and single-subject designs
- Diversity and postmodern issues in research and evaluation

The Art and Science of Research and Evaluation

Counseling research is both an art and a science, providing subjective and objective means for understanding and evaluating counseling. Traditionally, counseling research has emphasized the science dimension by utilizing experimental/quantitative research methodology involving hypothesis testing and statistical analysis. Experimental/quantitative research continues to hold an important position in the science of counseling, providing counselors with an objective tool for understanding and evaluating techniques and procedures in counseling.

Unfortunately, few practitioners use experimental/quantitative research methods, creating an ever widening gap between practice and research (Peterson, 1995). Goldfried and Wolfe (1996) note that with the changes in health care delivery resulting from managed care, it is becoming increasingly important for clinicians to utilize some form of research to demonstrate accountability.

Recent trends in research have explored how the art of counseling research can be developed as a means of bridging the gap between practice and research. In this regard,

The section on single-subject design was written by Dr. Steven Stile.

qualitative approaches have emerged that provide practitioners with alternative methodologies that are less rigid and involve more clinical skills than are used in traditional research methodologies. For example, qualitative approaches have emerged that focus on the researcher/evaluator and participant functioning as coinvestigators attempting to discover important information relating to a particular subject. In this process, more emphasis is given to awareness and sensitivity to diversity and other social forces and less emphasis is directed at data gathering and statistical analysis.

Both quantitative and qualitative approaches to research and evaluation have their place in counseling. In time there may be an integration of these positions, creating a balance between the art and science of research and evaluation in counseling.

The Purpose of Research and Evaluation

Counseling research serves many functions in the counseling process. This section reviews several of these uses, such as evaluating the efficacy of a counseling approach through the interaction of theory, practice, and research; providing a means for communicating counselor accountability; and contributing to the body of knowledge in the counseling field.

Theory, Research, and Practice

The art and science of counseling and psychotherapy are similar to the scientist-practitioner model, which emphasizes the role that science plays in shaping clinical practice. Unfortunately, the science of counseling has not kept up with the art of counseling. Hill and Corbett (1993) note that practitioners tend to rely on clinical judgment rather than research to formulate which theories and techniques to use.

The art and science of counseling emphasize the interrelationship between theory, research, and practice. Postmodern theories such as social constructionism stress the role of theory in scientific investigation. In this regard, Gergen (1994) suggests that theories are representations of language and culture and provide a paradigm to understand reality.

Figure 5.1 provides an illustration of the relationship between theory, research, and practice. It shows theory to be at the apex of a triangle, thus placing it in the uppermost

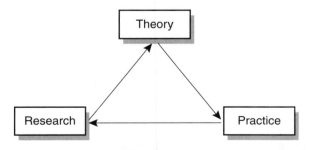

FIGURE 5.1   The Relationship Between Theory, Practice, and Research

position. The interrelationship between theory, practice, and research can be illustrated in the following example. The counseling theory of behavior therapy develops techniques such as assertion training. A counselor may use this technique in clinical practice and later implement research strategies to evaluate its effectiveness. The results of this research can provide useful information to refine the theoretical origins of assertion training.

Research, Evaluation, and Counselor Accountability

Research and evaluation can also be used to communicate counselor accountability. One way to conceptualize how this occurs is through the interaction of research, evaluation, and accountability, as shown in Figure 5.2. This model suggests that counselors can use research strategies to evaluate their individual clinical skills or an entire counseling program. The information obtained from the evaluation process can then provide professional accountability. Even though accountability has been established, however, the process is still incomplete. The counselor should then set up an ongoing accountability program. This may require additional research strategies to evaluate the various facets of one's professional activities.

Gibson (1977) and Hershenson, Power, and Waldo (1996) have provided guidelines regarding evaluation research. These are summarized as follows.

- *Determine the purpose of the evaluation.* It is necessary to identify what type of information needs to be generated from the evaluation. Should the evaluation focus on cost effectiveness or other issues such as quality control?
- *Effective evaluation uses valid measuring criteria.* Once goals have been identified, criteria for measuring these goals must be established. For example, a goal in a mental health center might be to have all counselors initiate a follow-up contact with each client within one to two months after termination of counseling services. The measuring criterion might be the percentage of clients whose follow-up activities were initiated.
- *Effective program evaluation depends on accurate application of the measuring criteria.* Appropriate research strategies should be used to collect and analyze the data.

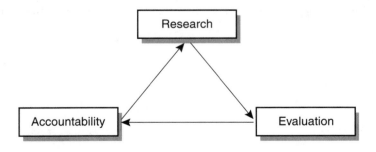

FIGURE 5.2   The Relationship Between Research, Evaluation, and Accountability

- *Program evaluation should obtain input from all people involved in the program.* Opportunities for input from all levels of the organization should be provided. In a mental health center, for example, the evaluation might include information from administrators, clerical staff, counselors, and clients.
- *The evaluation should include feedback and follow-through.* Once the evaluation is complete, the results may be communicated to the staff in a clear and concise fashion. Recommendations should be included to facilitate future program planning and development.
- *Evaluation should be a planned and continuous process.* A program should have an ongoing evaluation process. This enables the staff to monitor strengths and weaknesses. Accountability does not imply that a program has only strengths. Rather, it implies also becoming aware of weaknesses and attempting to rectify them.
- *Program evaluations should be sensitive to the politics of the organization.* All organizational systems have unique political structures that impact the functioning of the organization. It is therefore important to take these political forces into consideration throughout the evaluation process.

Hershenson, Power, and Waldo (1996) go on to identify knowledge and skills necessary for effective evaluation. Effective evaluation requires knowledge of the particular program—its needs, resources, the population it serves, and how the evaluation process can be of use or benefit. Knowledge is also required about creating the best fit regarding program needs and evaluation procedures. Numerous skills are also facilitative, such as communication, interpersonal, organizational, and advocacy skills.

The Contribution of Research to the Counseling Field

Another purpose of conducting research is to contribute to the body of knowledge in the counseling field so that theories can be tested and practices refined.

Hill and Corbett (1993) identify future trends in research relating to process and outcome issues in counseling. These are summarized as follows.

- "The overall goals of process and outcome research should be to develop new theories of therapy, to provide information for practitioners about how to intervene with clients at different points in therapy, and to develop training programs based on the empirical results of what works in therapy" (p. 16).
- Research should be directed at analyzing an entire model of the counseling process such as the one proposed by Hill (1992), which includes the therapist intentions, therapist response modes, client reactions, and client behaviors.
- Research should explore issues relating to competence in counseling (that is, what it means to be a good counselor).
- Research priorities should focus on first determining what the effective process components of counseling are, then developing and evaluating treatment models that emerge from this basic research.
- Additional research is necessary to determine similarities and differences between career and personal counseling.

- Measures need to be developed that can be used to evaluate the content of counseling (for example, interpersonal relations and cultural conflicts) and to measure the strength and healthy functioning of clients as opposed to their psychopathology.
- And finally, researchers across disciplines need to make more effort to work together to communicate methods and results.

Additional research will need to be conducted on these topics as well as others if counseling is to continue to evolve in a meaningful fashion. Counselors can play a vital role in contributing to their profession by engaging in an ongoing research program. The following guidelines can be used to formulate a research program.

1. Do research on topics that interest you rather than selecting a topic to impress someone else.
2. Develop some tenacity when doing research. Once you believe in a project, stick with it and follow it through. There will always be someone to tell you what you can't do. Your job is to tell yourself what you can do and will do.
3. Make a detailed outline before starting to write the research report. This will help you organize your ideas and make your paper easier to read and understand.
4. Don't get discouraged with the publishing process. Once you submit a paper to a journal, it may be accepted, accepted provisionally, rejected with suggestions for resubmission, or rejected. Don't give up if you are requested to revise and resubmit your paper. Only 4 percent of the articles submitted to American Counseling Association journals are accepted without necessary revisions (Seligman, 1986).
5. Finally, never assume your idea is so simple that someone must have published it already. There is a good chance that your idea has not been published, and your contribution might be valuable to the counseling profession.

In the following *Personal Note,* I share some of my personal rewards and struggles with the publishing process.

A Personal Note

I've had my share of ups and downs in conducting research. Some highs include having my first paper accepted for publication and feeling excited about contributing to an area of investigation. I was particularly pleased that this was a theoretical paper about a new dimension of social interest. I remember thinking, "Wow, now I'm part of the evolution of Adlerian theory development." I've also had my share of lows in conducting research. The letters of rejection and critical reviews of articles are still painful to receive today.

To survive the research and publication process, I've had to develop a lot of tolerance, patience, perseverance, and self-discipline. But it's been worth it. I've been able to gain a better understanding of a wide range of topics from stuttering to why children soil their pants. Research has also helped me continually develop my personal approach to counseling, as I carefully examine what occurred in a case study. In addition, research has been a helpful tool to communicate accountability. For example, I have used a single-subject design, a topic discussed later in this chapter, to assess what is occurring with a program I'm using to treat encopresis (soiling the pants).

Overview of the Types of Research

Research can be classified in several ways. One classification system differentiates basic research from applied research. *Basic research* is usually conducted under controlled conditions in a laboratory setting, often in a university. Basic research usually involves university students acting as subjects. Although basic research studies tend to use rigorous research designs, it may be risky to generalize the results of this type of research to the real world. *Applied research* typically tests theories in a field setting. Applied research is therefore reflective of people in their natural habitat. Unfortunately, field studies are not always easy to control and may provide misleading results. Regardless of these limitations, applied research may provide a more realistic alternative for clinicians.

Types of Research Methodologies

Research can also be classified in terms of design. Some of the more common types of research designs are as follows.

Survey Studies.   Survey research typically describes a variable in terms of its frequency in a population (Wilkinson & McNeil, 1996). For example, an investigator might survey a representative sample of professional counselors to determine what counseling approaches are used most often. A potentially influential survey was recently published by Consumer Reports (1995, November). The Consumer Reports survey was reviewed by Seligman (1995). He concludes that the study showed that long-term therapy was superior to short-term therapy; therapy was as effective as medication and therapy; and psychologists, psychiatrists, and social workers were equally as effective as therapists and were more effective than marriage counselors and long-term family doctoring. In addition, Seligman notes that clients whose length or choice of therapy were determined by managed care insurance did worse than those who were not so restricted. Seligman concludes that although the Consumer Reports study has several methodological shortcomings, it should be taken seriously since it provides valuable information regarding counseling efficacy.

VandenBos (1996) goes on to note that the Consumer Reports survey provides encouraging information on the public's perception of psychotherapy in terms of need and efficacy. The survey provides evidence that the public clearly values the use of psychotherapy as a form of mental health treatment. In addition, the survey is to a large degree supportive of previous empirical research.

Correlational Studies.   Correlational studies are used to determine whether two factors are related. A counselor may wish to determine whether there is a relationship between gender and age of clients. A review of the counselor's clients over a two-year period may show that clients over 40 years of age tend to be female and those under 15 tend to be male.

Experimental Methods.   This methodology is also referred to as *quantitative research;* it involves evaluating a particular treatment under controlled conditions to determine whether a cause-and-effect relationship exists. For example, an investigator may wish to evaluate the effects of a parent education program on parental attitudes and parent-child behavioral interactions. Traditional experimental designs involve randomly assigning a group of subjects to a treatment group (subjects receiving parent education) and a control group (subjects who do not receive parent education). The two groups can then be compared before and after the program on attitudes, behaviors, or other measures. Statistical analysis is used to evaluate the degree of change in the particular measures to determine the effects of the parent education program.

Longitudinal Studies.   Longitudinal studies are designed to evaluate a particular group of subjects over an extended period of time. For example, a counselor may wish to analyze how well a group of immigrants adjusts to American society. Using this research design, the counselor might periodically check on variables such as the percent who graduate from high school and college or tendencies toward physical or mental health problems.

Large-Scale Reviews.   This methodology involves reviewing many published research studies. It has usually been conducted in an attempt to assess the efficacy of counseling. Some of the early work of this type did much to challenge the efficacy of counseling. This was especially true for Eysenck (1965), who claimed that counseling was not effective and that people tended to get better regardless of whether they received counseling. Levitt (1957) also challenged the efficacy of counseling in a large-scale review of studies that evaluated the effectiveness of child counseling and concluded that Eysenck's findings were essentially correct.

Several large-scale reviews of outcome research provide support for the effectiveness of counseling and psychotherapy (Elkin et al., 1989; Garfield, 1983; Lambert, 1991; McNeilly & Howard, 1991; Smith & Glass, 1977; Smith, Glass, & Miller, 1980). These large-scale reviews often use a sophisticated form of statistical analysis called *meta-analysis* in an attempt to reduce some of the methodological problems that can result from grouping together numerous studies for analysis. Smith and Glass conducted the first large-scale review that demonstrated strong empirical support for the effectiveness of counseling. Their investigation of 400 studies shows that treated individuals were better off than 75 percent of those who did not receive counseling. Smith, Glass, and Miller reviewed 475 studies and found that treated individuals were better off than 80 percent of those who did not receive counseling. (See Lambert & Bergin, 1994, for additional information regarding the efficacy of counseling.)

Qualitative Methods (Alternative Methods).   This design attempts to understand people and events in their natural setting. It has therefore been referred to as a naturalistic approach. Qualitative methods typically employ nonstandardized measures such as interviews and observations as a means of collecting data. Qualitative methods are oriented to the discovery of insights rather than confirmation of hypotheses. Qualitative methods have been called *alternative methods* because they provide an alternative to more traditional experimental designs. A more in-depth description of alternative methods appears later in this chapter.

Case Studies and Single-Subject Designs.   This method involves an intensive study of one individual or a group of individuals. Information is obtained from interviews, observations, and client self-reports (Wilkinson & McNeil, 1996).

Case studies can be expanded to incorporate some of the principles of experimental design. These designs are sometimes referred to as *single-subject designs* and are presented later in this chapter. They can increase the counselor's ability to evaluate counseling outcomes objectively. Case studies are also a popular means for counselors to illustrate new concepts in counseling theory and practice.

Shortcomings of Traditional Counseling Research

Although the scientist-practitioner model appears to be a goal in the counseling profession, it is not yet a reality. University programs have historically advocated the merits of the scientist-practitioner model, yet clinicians failed to integrate these positions (Peterson, 1995). Clinicians have essentially taken the position that research relates to statistical abstractions and not the average person and therefore has little relevance to the challenges of clinical practice (Beutler et al., 1995).

Beutler and his associates make several recommendations that could help overcome the split between science and practice. These are summarized as follows. Scientists need to become more knowledgeable about the issues of clinicians by maintaining ongoing relationships with clinicians, the role of science in practice needs to be reevaluated, new research methods must be developed to make research more relevant to clinicians, and new vehicles are needed to communicate research findings to practitioners.

It is obvious that changes are required to make research more relevant to the needs of practitioners. Qualitative research methodologies represent an emerging trend in the field of social sciences that offers much promise to practitioners (Garfield & Bergin, 1994).

Qualitative Research Methodologies. As mentioned, qualitative (alternative) research methods have evolved in response to disillusionment with traditional basic research methodologies, which typically utilize experimental designs, for example, subjects and control groups. In addition, advocates of alternative research methodologies suggest that basic research designs are unnecessarily restrictive and yield results that have little relevance to practitioners (Mahrer, 1988).

Hoshmand (1989) and Hill, Thompson, and Willams (1997) provide an extensive overview of qualitative methodologies. They present information relating to the purpose of alternative methods, the roles of the researcher and participants, the process of inquiry, the types of inquiry, and data analysis. This information has been summarized as follows.

- *Purpose.* Qualitative research designs are characterized by the purpose of developing an understanding of the essence of human experience. They emphasize description and discovery rather than theory testing. In this regard, Goldman (1989) points out that researchers using alternative methods are more concerned with what topics they want to learn about and explore than with what instruments to use or how to obtain participants.
- *Role of the researcher and participants.* The researcher takes a more active role in the research process than simply observing and recording data. This role may involve engaging in dialogue and interacting with the participants as a means of exploring and discovering significant events that the client has experienced. Participants also

take a more active role, becoming coinvestigators in a collaborative and reciprocal relationship with the researcher. From this perspective, research activity is not controlled by the researcher. In addition, participants are consulted as to what they consider meaningful and relevant research questions and whether the interpretations and conclusions are valid for the participants. In this context, reality can be defined from the perspective of the participants.

■ *The process of inquiry.* Inquiry is characterized as an emergent, ongoing process that includes responsiveness to feedback from the participants. The course of inquiry is therefore determined by collaboration between the researcher and participant. The emphasis is also on process and outcome rather than outcome alone.

■ *Data gathering.* Data-gathering procedures vary according to the methodology employed. Typical methods include observation in the client's natural setting for extended periods of time, in-depth interviews from a phenomenological perspective, and oral histories such as recording myths and legends.

■ *Data analysis.* The methods of data analysis can be described as interpretive, with the goal of recognizing meaningful patterns. A number of comparisons can be made between qualitative and quantitative data analysis. Phenomena are described rather than manipulated; emphasis is on descriptions rather than explanations; focus is on emergence of concepts as opposed to relating findings to existing theories; results are expressed linguistically rather than numerically; scientific knowledge is viewed as tentative, not fixed; and data is conceptualized contextually, not as isolated-controlled entities.

Types of Qualitative Research Methodologies.   This section presents four types of qualitative methodologies: naturalistic-ethnographic, discovery-oriented, representative-case methods, and consensual qualitative research.

Hoshmand (1989) describes *naturalistic-ethnographic* methodologies as involving the observation of participants in their natural context to obtain an understanding of the factors that influence human behavior. This approach requires prolonged contact and immersion in a particular setting to enable the researcher to obtain an understanding of the members in that setting. Data gathering may incorporate activities such as observation, interviews, oral histories, reviews of existing research documents and literature, and the use of critical incidence. Kidder, Judd, and Smith (1986) and Lincoln and Guba (1985) provide detailed descriptions of these procedures. The selection of a particular data-gathering procedure involves a consideration of how to relate effectively to the population under study. For example, one investigation used "rap" groups in a data-gathering method with mentally retarded adults (Hoshmand, 1985). Data analysis entails constant recording, categorizing, sorting, and re-sorting in an attempt to create emergent core categories of meaning. Field notes are transcribed verbatim and analyzed during repeated readings of the data to identify key phrases and concepts. Independent judges identify categories of meaning and sort them into themes to check for reliability. The researcher then collaborates with the participants for their opinion on the data that were generated.

McKenzie (1986) provides an example of a naturalistic-ethnographic study, which investigated the attitudes of West Indian American youths toward counseling. In the first phase of the study, a counselor spent six months immersing himself in the schools, homes, peer groups, and other activities of students under study. The researcher spent an average of forty hours with each student. During the second phase, the researcher conducted in-depth interviews with the students and counseling staff, exploring issues such as development and attitudes toward counseling and toward seeking help. The data were then analyzed to identify meaningful patterns. Results of the study showed that West Indian Americans had strong taboos against seeking counseling, their cultural background affected their career choices, and biculturalism induced conflict within their families.

Mahrer (1988) has developed another type of qualitative methodology, which he calls *discovery-oriented psychotherapy research.* The purpose of the discovery-oriented approach is to take an in-depth look at psychotherapy and attempt to discover important aspects of what is occurring in counseling, for example, what prompted a personality change in a client. Mahrer described the following method for using the discovery-oriented approach.

1. Select the target of investigation. Start off by identifying some aspect of counseling of interest, no matter how large or insignificant it may seem. Avoid getting sidetracked by technical jargon such as "transference" or "locus of control."
2. Obtain instances of the target being investigated. Obtain as many instances as possible of the target under investigation. For example, a researcher may be interested in what can be discovered about early childhood memories. The researcher can attempt to obtain examples of these memories in a variety of ways, such as video recordings of sessions and narratives provided by clients.
3. Obtain an instrument to take a closer look. Once incidences of target behavior are obtained, the researcher can develop an instrument to take a closer look at the target being investigated (for example, early memories). A category system can be used for this purpose. This can begin with a search of the literature. Next, a group of judges can review the sample incidences of the target under investigation (for example, videotapes) and continuously review this material until meaningful themes or categories of data emerge. The themes and categories obtained can provide the researcher with an instrument to systematically evaluate the target of investigation.
4. Gather data. This step involves obtaining the necessary data for the study and applying the instrument to the data. This may involve analyzing the original data obtained during step 2 or obtaining new examples of the target of investigation (for example, additional early memories).
5. Make discovery-oriented sense of the data. This step involves interpreting the data to determine what can be learned from the study. This process requires the characteristics associated with the art of counseling. The investigator must be sensitive to the discoverable by being open to what appears new, unexpected, challenging, or disconcerting in the data.

Gordon and Shontz (1990) have developed a case-study type of qualitative methodology called *representative-case research.* This method can be used to gain an in-depth understanding of people with various problems, such as children who are terminally ill, school dropouts, and single parents. Gordon and Shontz described representative-case research as a process that involves carefully examining "chosen persons one at a time, in depth, to learn how each experiences and manages an event, situation, or set of circumstances or conditions that is important in human life" (p. 62).

Representative-case research is considered a qualitative methodology because it requires the active involvement of the client, who is considered to be an expert on the problem under study and a coinvestigator. It is a process that attempts to discover what a client has learned about a particular experience or set of circumstances. The assistance of supervisors or advisors can also promote objectivity and monitor different aspects of the research process. These individuals can help with various activities such as data analysis and interpretation. They can also assist with the relationship between the counselor and client—the investigator and coinvestigator.

Hill, Thompson, and Williams (1997) developed consensual qualitative research as a method that can provide structure and a degree of objectivity to qualitative research. This model attempts to maintain the central qualities associated with qualitative research. At the same time it offers systematic procedures that can add in teaching qualitative procedures and enable qualitative researchers to replicate studies. In addition, this model advocates the use of three to five investigators to engage in consensual decision making during data analysis to encourage diversification of opinions. One or two auditors are also employed to ensure that the investigators did not overlook important data.

Three general steps are utilized in consensual qualitative research. These are

1. Responses to open-ended questions from questionnaires or interviews for each individual case are divided into domains (that is, topic areas).
2. Core ideas (that is, abstracts or brief summaries) are constructed for all the material within each domain for each individual case.
3. A cross analysis, which involves developing categories to describe consistencies in the core ideas within domains across cases, is conducted (Hill, Thompson, & Williams, 1997, p. 523).

Consensual qualitative research appears to be a step toward the integration of qualitative and quantitative research in terms of attempting to standardize some of the highly subjective procedures associated with qualitative research. An integrative, "middle ground" form of research methodology provides another valuable research alternative for the art and science of counseling.

Evaluation of Qualitative Methodologies.   Qualitative methods appear to offer much promise for practitioners as a viable research method, but they also seem to pose some potential problems. One way to assess this new form of research is to relate it to nonstandardized measures, as described in Chapter 4. The same strengths and weaknesses apply to both, since alternative research methods typically utilize nonstandardized measures, such as observation and environmental assessment.

In terms of weaknesses, both nonstandardized assessment and qualitative research methods lack objectivity, the ability to generalize to a reference group, can create confusing results, and often lack acceptable levels of validity and reliability. The advantages common to both nonstandardized measures and qualitative research methods are that they provide a flexible, individualized approach, which generates information unique to the individual, can be easily modified to accommodate individual differences, and fosters an active role between the counselor (researcher) and the client (participant).

These advantages make qualitative research methods particularly attractive to multicultural counseling research (Helms, 1989). Another advantage of alternative methods is that they require some of the same skills associated with effective counseling, as Goldman (1989) wrote.

> . . . these new methods are not for the faint of heart. They demand imagination, courage to face the unknown, flexibility, some creativeness, and a good deal of personal skill in observation, interviewing, and self-examination—some of the same skills, in fact, required for effective counseling, but now systematically directed toward the education of principles and generalizations, rather than effective change in individuals. (pp. 83–84)

Qualitative research methodologies can be viewed as an emerging form of counseling research. These methods should be viewed as alternatives, not as replacements for other forms of research. Additional research and development are necessary to refine these methodologies. In particular, investigators need guidelines for data gathering and analysis. At present, many of these procedures appear vague, lacking in structure, and confusing. In addition, clinicians may get the impression that these alternative research methods must involve a lengthy investigative process that includes living in the particular setting under study. These impressions could discourage active clinicians from considering this form of research. It is hoped that the problems associated with qualitative methodologies can be overcome because many benefits could evolve from this intriguing new approach. Emerging models such as consensual qualitative research may play an important role in the evolution of alternative methodologies in terms of integrating the best aspects of qualitative and quantitative research.

Single-Subject Designs. Single-subject designs constitute another emerging form of research that offers much promise to the practitioner. According to Charles (1995), such research is often seen in studies of students with exceptionalities where it would be inappropriate to use an experimental treatment with subjects who do not have special needs. Single-subject designs may be used to investigate the effectiveness of counseling with one client or a small group of clients. These designs may be classified into three distinct families or groups: ABA or "withdrawal" designs, multiple baseline designs, and comparative treatment designs (Stile, 1993). Table 5.1 describes eight major steps involved in applying single-subject design strategies to counseling research or evaluation. These steps are the same regardless of the design used.

ABA Designs. This family of designs gets its name from the simplest single-subject experimental design, which requires *withdrawal* of a treatment in order to measure its effects when it is introduced and again when it is removed.

The five most common ABA designs are the A, the B, the A-B, the A-B-A, and the A-B-A-B. The first three designs have been termed *preexperimental* (the A and B designs) and *quasi-experimental* (the A-B design) in relation to their abilities to establish cause-and-effect relationships. The A-B-A and A-B-A-B designs are classified as *experimental* designs, since they can be used to establish cause and effect with single subjects or small groups.

TABLE 5.1   **Steps in Applying Single-Subject Strategies**

Step	Procedure
1. Identification	Identify which skills or behaviors will be targeted for change (for example, "irresponsibility").
2. Definition	Define the targeted skill or behavior in such a way that it can be observed and measured (for example, "staying out late" provides a more adequate unit of measurement than "irresponsibility").
3. Selection of dependent variable or measure	Select the characteristic of the behavior to be measured and the counseling objective. For example, the *number* of occurrences of staying out late can be measured in relation to a particular treatment. Zero occurrences may be established as the outcome.
4. Identification of independent variable or treatment	Identify the treatment (for example, counseling technique) to be applied to the dependent variable. For example, logical consequences may be applied to occurrences of staying out late.
5. Completion of planning	Complete all related planning. Decisions made at this step should include who will record the occurrence of the behavior (for example, staying out late) and how the occurrence of the behavior will be recorded (for example, tally marks on a simple recording instrument).
6. Training	Train (if appropriate) all other participants to consistently carry out data collection/treatment procedures. For example, all observers should practice collecting data until they reach close agreement on recording of the dependent variable.
7. Intervention and data collection	Intervene by withholding, applying, or withdrawing the treatment while continuously collecting data on the dependent variable (for example, number of occurrences).
8. Graphing	Graph the results of the treatment by plotting data points on graph paper and connecting the points to represent trends.

The A Design.   This design has also been referred to as the *case study method.* According to Borg and Gall (1989), "the case study . . . involves an investigator who makes a detailed examination of a single subject or group or phenomenon" (p. 402). Although case studies have long been considered unscientific because of a lack of control and subjectivity, Borg and Gall have recently noted an increased acceptance of qualitative methods such as "ethnography and participant observation." The A design can be thought of as an extended period during which data are collected on the dependent variable—the behavior you hope to change—but treatment is withheld.

The B Design.   The B design is closely related to the A design. In this design, no baseline observations are made, but dependent variables are monitored throughout the course of a treatment. The B design is generally considered to be an improvement over the uncontrolled case study method.

The A-B Design.   The A-B design corrects for some of the weaknesses of the A and B designs. The inquirer begins by selecting a subject or subjects, pinpointing a problem, selecting a dependent variable, and choosing a treatment. Next, the dependent variable is measured during a minimum of three baseline (A) observations. In the second and final phase of this design, the investigator applies the treatment (B) and measures its effect on the dependent variable. In this design the baseline can be thought of as a control since it predicts future behavior without intervention. The major objection to this design is the possibility that some other variable may be operating simultaneously with the treatment to bring about change in skills or behavior.

The A-B-A Design.   The A-B-A design addresses objections to the A-B design by employing a second baseline (A2) as a control. If withdrawal of treatment results in trends in A2 that approximate A1, arguments for a cause-and-effect relationship between the independent and dependent variables gain considerable support.

The A-B-A-B Design.   The A-B-A-B design addresses the major shortcoming of the A-B-A design because it ends in a second treatment condition, or B2. The A-B-A design is rarely the original design of choice anymore. In fact, it is usually used only when attrition prevents the final phase of the A-B-A-B design. Since no limitation exists regarding the length of B2, a successful treatment may be left in place for a lengthy period to help ensure maintenance of change. The major shortcoming of the A-B-A design is that it often ends on a "negative note" (Borg and Gall, 1989), since a presumably effective treatment is withdrawn.

The following case illustrates the steps in the application of a member of the ABA family of single-subject designs (the A-B) to evaluate the efficiency of a counseling program. The steps refer to those listed in Table 5.1. The A-B design was chosen because it is easy to apply. Beginning counselors may wish to use this design in a pilot study of a new counseling technique.

The Case of Ann.   Ann was a 17-year-old girl enrolled in a large urban high school. The target behavior identified (step 1 in Table 5.1) in this case was "school phobia." The school principal defined Ann's behavior (step 2) as often refusing to go to school or failing to remain there once she arrived. Ann was referred to the school counselor for assistance with this problem. Before seeing Ann, the school counselor examined her attendance records. These records showed that she had attended school for the entire day only 40 percent, 60 percent, and 20 percent during the first, second, and third weeks of school, respectively. At this point, the counselor identified percent of attendance as the dependent variable and established the therapeutic objective (step 3) that Ann would attend school 95 percent of the time every week unless she had a legitimate excuse such as a family emergency. Next, the counselor identified a treatment package consisting of individual and group counseling sessions as the independent variable and completed all prior planning (steps 4 and 5). Since training (step 6) was not necessary in this case, the next step was to begin the intervention and data collection (step 7).

A behaviorally oriented approach was used in individual sessions. In these sessions, Ann was helped to understand how school had become threatening to her and how certain physical symptoms including nausea, diarrhea, and dizziness were related to her anxiety. After four sessions, Ann was able to enter the counselor's office and attend one class independently. She was then invited to attend weekly group sessions with the school's five other school-phobic students to discuss feelings toward school and related issues.

Over a four-month period, the counselor observed that Ann developed a caring attitude toward other group members. She met with them before school, and they often walked home together. Beginning with the first group session, Ann was asked to monitor her own school attendance. By the beginning of Christmas vacation (week 15), she reported to the group that her attendance (that is, the dependent variable) had increased to 100 percent. Periodic checks at monthly intervals revealed that her attendance remained at this level. The graph developed by Ann and her counselor (step 8) is shown as Figure 5.3.

Multiple-Baseline Designs.   A variation of the A-B design is the multiple-baseline design. Frequently, withdrawal designs such as A-B-A or A-B-A-B are inappropriate for a given behavior. For example, a counselor might be viewed as unethical for beginning a second baseline phase when it appears that treatment (for example, self-monitoring) is associated with a significant reduction of aggressive behavior in the client. In such cases, multiple-baseline designs should be considered.

The three major multiple-baseline designs are multiple baseline across behaviors, multiple baseline across settings, and multiple baseline across subjects. All three may be thought of as extensions of the A-B design illustrated by the case of Ann.

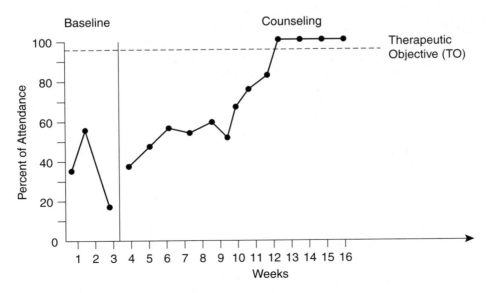

FIGURE 5.3   A-B Design for the Case of Ann

Multiple Baseline Across Behaviors.   This design is intended for use with single subjects or groups. When used with groups, arithmetic means are calculated, and the group is treated as a single subject. When using the across-behaviors design, the inquirer is cautioned to select behaviors that are independent of one another. Borg and Gall (1989) explain as follows.

> Independence is demonstrated by a change in the target behavior to which the treatment is being applied while other target behaviors (or controls) maintain a stable baseline rate. If other behaviors change reliably from baseline, the multiple-baseline design is invalid. (p. 585)

Multiple Baseline Across Settings.   The across-settings design is also intended for use with single groups or subjects. In this design, the effect of a treatment on a dependent variable is studied in independent temporal and/or physical settings.

Multiple Baseline Across Subjects.   The across-subjects design is used for inquiry with matched groups. For example, Gardill and Browder (1995) use this methodology to examine the effectiveness of training students with severe behavior disorders and developmental disabilities to use money independently.

The following case illustrates the steps in implementing the design of multiple baseline across behaviors in a counseling situation. As shown in Figure 5.4, this design requires that the counselor apply a treatment (B) to a *succession* of behaviors that are being baselined (A). The steps refer to those shown in Table 5.1.

The Case of Drew.   Drew was an 18-year-old college freshman living at home with his mother and father. The target behavior identified (step 1) by counselor and parents was "irresponsibility." Irresponsible behavior was defined as (a) staying out too late on school nights, (b) not parking the car in the garage, and (c) not putting his father's tools away after use (step 2). After closely observing these behaviors for five days, Drew's father established the number of occurrences of irresponsible behavior as the dependent variable and set zero occurrences of the behavior as the therapeutic objective (step 3). After a lengthy discussion, the counselor and family decided that logical consequences (Dreikurs & Soltz, 1964) would be the treatment approach used in response to Drew's irresponsible behaviors (step 4). Logical consequences involve experiencing the consequences of one's behavior, as in losing the use of a car if one gets a citation for driving while intoxicated. Planning was completed (step 5) when it was decided that Drew would experience a logical consequence immediately upon occurrence of an irresponsible behavior. In addition, application of the logical consequences would be applied sequentially as follows: (a) first only with staying out late; (b) second, it would be applied to inappropriate car parking; and (c) finally it would be applied to all three behaviors (staying out late, parking the car, and not putting away the tools). Drew's father and mother were then trained by the counselor to tally occurrences of the three behaviors on a simple record-keeping instrument (step 6).

The treatment began (step 7) with Drew being told that he would lose the privilege of going out on school nights (Sunday through Thursday) if he came home after 11:00 P.M. After five more days, the logical consequence treatment was also applied to his parking the car. That is, if he did not park the car in the garage, he would be unable to use it. Finally, after an additional five days (day 16), the logical consequence strategy was applied to putting his father's tools away. If Drew failed to put his father's tools away after using them, he would be unable to borrow them. Thus beginning on day 16, the treatment was applied to all three behaviors with Drew's mother and father continuing observations and data collection. His father charted Drew's progress on a graph (step 8), as shown in Figure 5.4. The use of logical consequences appears to have resulted in the elimination of each of the problem behaviors targeted for change. In addition, the zero rate of occurrence was maintained until the treatment and monitoring were withdrawn after 40 days.

Evaluation of Single-Subject Designs.   Single-case designs offer much value to the active clinician. They provide an objective means to evaluate what is occurring in the counseling process with one client at a time. A counselor can use this information to adjust the treatment program throughout the counseling process. It also can provide a useful tool to keep the client informed as to what is occurring in counseling. These designs have been used primarily in conjunction with behavioral approaches. Additional research and development is necessary to expand their use to accommodate other schools of counseling.

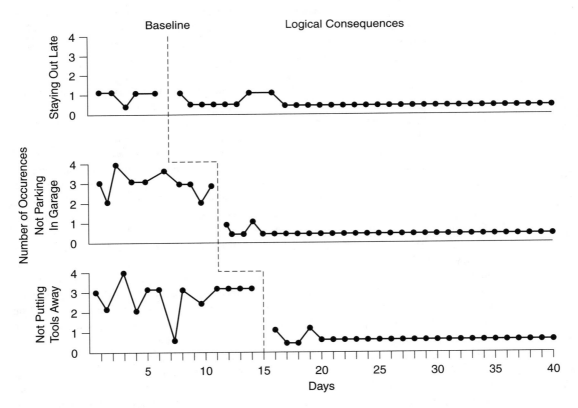

FIGURE 5.4   Multiple Baseline Across Behavior Design for the Case of Drew

Diversity and Postmodern Issues
in Research and Evaluation

All aspects of the counseling process (including research and evaluation) must be conceptualized from a multicultural counseling perspective. The multicultural perspective enables counselors, like artists, to sensitively navigate diversity issues that may impact on scientific investigations. For example, it is common to consider issues of gender, culture, and socioeconomic level when designing a research study.

Another issue relating to diversity and research is the role of white researchers in multicultural counseling. There appears to be some concern that the field of multicultural counseling has been dominated by white researchers at the expense of minority individuals (Mio & Iwamasa, 1993). Atkinson (1993) contends that the major issues in this debate relate to ethics and turf. The ethical issues are directed at determining who is in the best position to realistically evaluate multicultural counseling. The answer to this question will no doubt impact issues of turf. Pedersen (1993) contends that a central problem in the debate relates to an oversimplification and polarization of categories such as majority-minority and the need for all researchers to work toward a common ground characterized by shared interests.

Postmodern trends are based on a subjective view of reality and appear to parallel characteristics of qualitative research and the art of counseling. Case studies and in-depth interviews are examples of postmodern research, since they provide opportunities to discover meanings from a participant's stories. Modernism adheres to an objective view of reality and therefore has more in common with quantitative research and the science of counseling. The modernism's fixed view of reality characterizes quantitative research. Quantitative research is characterized by statistically focused hypothesis testing, which attempts to seek out the "truth" in definitive black-and-white terms.

Gergen (1994) posits a case for postmodern research and its subjective view of truth. Gergen contends that research that adheres to universal assumptions regarding reality and knowledge may convey inaccurate, misleading, and potentially harmful information about what is to be regarded as the truth. Gergen suggests that researchers should be aware of how sociocultural forces and language create multiple realities. For example, many Western cultures recognize depression, with millions being treated with antidepressant medications, whereas individuals from other cultures have survived for centuries without the concept of depression reflected in their language.

Summary

Research and evaluation are an ongoing facet of the counseling process. Research strategies serve several functions, such as offering a means to evaluate the efficacy of a counseling approach, communicate accountability, and contribute to the body of knowledge relating to the counseling profession. Research and evaluation can also be conceptualized as contributing to the science-of-counseling model by providing objective information regarding the counseling process. The practice of research and evaluation is both an art and a science, with approaches such as qualitative methodologies and single-subject designs encouraging clinicians to develop flexible, creative strategies of evaluation.

6 Developing a Personal Approach to Counseling with a Multicultural Perspective

CHAPTER OVERVIEW

This chapter provides guidelines for formulating a personal approach to counseling and addresses issues relating to multicultural counseling. Highlights of the chapter include

- The art and science of developing a personal approach to counseling with a multicultural perspective
- Developing a personal approach to counseling
- An eight-stage model for developing a personal approach
- Multicultural counseling
- Potential challenges in multicultural counseling
- Suggestions for incorporating a multicultural perspective

The Art and Science of Developing a Personal Approach to Counseling with a Multicultural Perspective

Developing a personal approach to counseling with a multicultural perspective is both an art and a science. It is an art to draw together multiple factors such as personal preference, diversity issues, and client characteristics in developing and implementing a counseling approach. The art of counseling suggests that the process of developing a personal approach to counseling begins with self-assessment to identify strengths, weaknesses, attitudes, and beliefs that can promote or inhibit the counseling process. Counselors are then encouraged to work toward developing personal characteristics that promote optimal development in the client. The science of developing a personal approach relates to the importance of using research to determine the efficacy of theories and procedures to maximize the use of proven approaches throughout the counseling process.

The multicultural perspective contributes a critical dimension to a personal approach to counseling. It can be conceptualized as a lens that can bring multicultural issues into focus throughout the counseling process. The art of multicultural counseling is related to the counselor's skill in adjusting the multicultural lens to accurately assess and respond to diversity issues such as socioeconomic status, culture, gender, and sexual orientation. A related challenge in the art of counseling is learning how to adjust traditional counseling theories and procedures to meet the unique and emerging needs of clients from a multicultural perspective. This can involve recognizing the value of alternative methods to helping, including the use of traditional healers such as medicine men with American Indians. In addition, the art of counseling suggests that counselors create opportunities to experience and be enriched by multiculturalism. This can involve a wide variety of activities from taking an interest in the traditional art of a culture (such as Navajo rugs) to exploring issues such as acculturation, world view, and identity development to gain an awareness of individual differences and relational-contextual issues that can affect clients.

The science of multicultural counseling is entering into an exciting phase in the evolution of counseling. Traditional schools of counseling and research methodology are being reassessed from a multicultural perspective in an attempt to overcome problems such as bias toward the white middle class male model of counseling. Theories basic to counseling (such as developmental theories) are being modified to accommodate diversity issues such as gender and culture. Carol Gilligan's (1982) seminal work on female moral development is an excellent example of these exciting new trends.

Multicultural counseling and therapy (MCT) (Sue, Ivey, & Pedersen, 1996) provides another example of the evolution of theory development within counseling. MCT is perhaps the first comprehensive theory of multicultural counseling. It can be used in the science of counseling to provide an objective framework to explore multicultural issues in terms of theory, research, and practice. For example, diversity issues such as consideration of contextual-relational issues in hypothesis development are being incorporated into a number of emerging trends in research.

Developing a Personal Approach to Counseling

All counselors and counselors in training have a personal approach to counseling. Some put a considerable amount of time and effort into the process while others simply "do counseling." Using a personal approach that results from careful planning enhances the complex process of counseling.

Over the years, there has been a proliferation of counseling approaches. Lynn and Garske (1985) observed more than 130 different approaches, many of which they say were far from the mainstream and of questionable value. The authors believe there appears to be a shift in emphasis from more to fewer theories, creating an optimal climate for integrating theories.

Patterson (1989) and Lazarus and Beutler (1993) support this view, suggesting there is a trend toward integration and eclecticism. Norcross and Newman (1992) go on to identify several other factors that appear to be contributing to this trend. These factors are summarized as follows. No one theory can possibly address the diversified needs of clients, research has shown similar efficacy rates for counseling theories, and trends for short-term counseling have required modification in how theories are implemented. With so many forces at work, it is not surprising that 30 to 50 percent of the surveys of clinical and counseling psychologists consider themselves eclectic or integrative (Norcross & Newman, 1992) and 64 percent of counselors claim to be eclectic (Norcross, Prochaska, & Gallagher, 1989).

Numerous models of eclecticism and integration have emerged. Historically, eclecticism has been considered by some to be a disjointed approach, whereby a counselor utilizes various theories and techniques without the benefit of an internally consistent psychological frame of reference (Wachtel, 1991). Students of the eclectic approach often lack a clear sense of structure or direction in the counseling process, struggling with problems such as how to shift from one therapeutic modality to another (Wachtel, 1991). Lazarus and Beutler (1993) refer to this type of eclecticism as *unsystematic eclecticism,* and contend that this smorgasbord approach to counseling lacks clinical precision and contributes to confusion in counseling.

Lazarus and Beutler (1993) go on to describe technical eclecticism as a practical and effective method of conceptualizing a personal approach to counseling. They summarize the basic tenets of technical eclecticism as follows: "technical eclectics select procedures from different sources without necessarily subscribing to the theories that spawned them; they work within a preferred theory (Dryden, 1987) but recognize that few techniques are inevitably wedded to any theory. Hence, they borrow techniques from other orientations, based on the proven worth of these procedures" (p. 384). In addition, technical eclecticism favors the restriction of use of theories and techniques to those that have proven efficacy in research and those that contribute to systematic decision making in treatment planning. In this regard, Lazarus (1995) has developed a school of counseling called multimodal therapy. It is based on social learning theory, general systems theory, and group and communication theory. Central to his approach is his concept of the BASIC I.D., which provides a conceptual model for treatment planning (see Chapter 4).

Theoretical integration represents another recognized model for formulating a personal approach to counseling. Norcross and Newman (1992) describe theoretical integration as an approach that involves the synthesis of two or more counseling theories. The recent trend toward integrating cognitive and behavioral counseling would be an example of theoretical integration. Several other individuals have suggested that theoretical integration should be based on a core counseling theory such as Adlerian or existential to promote internal consistency and a sense of structure and direction for counseling (Ginter, 1988; McBride & Martin, 1991; Wachtel, 1991; Watts, 1993).

Utilizing the "core approach to theory integration" when developing a personal approach to counseling represents an integration of technical eclecticism and theoretical integration. The major feature of this approach is to first obtain an in-depth understanding of one counseling theory to establish a core theory. The classic theories of Freud, Adler, and Jung described in Chapter 7 are ideal for this purpose, since they also have a comprehensive theory of personality to complement their theory of counseling. The core theory will help establish a degree of internal consistency in the personal approach. The counselor can then select components from other counseling theories to meet the unique and emerging needs of clients from a multicultural perspective. Techniques and procedures utilized should have support from research and lead to appropriate treatment planning.

An Eight-Stage Model for Developing a Personal Approach

The following eight-stage model can be used to develop a personal approach to counseling. The eight stages of this model are self-assessment, survey of supportive disciplines, overview of major counseling theories, intensive study of one (core) counseling theory, sensitivity to individual differences, integration of techniques from counseling theories, implementation, and research and evaluation.

Stage One: Self-Assessment

Self-assessment helps counselors understand their values, beliefs, strengths, and weaknesses. With self-awareness, counselors can avoid overreacting in counseling and use their strengths to maximize their effectiveness. Vontress (1988) notes that self-knowledge may be the best predictor of effective living because it provides a clear direction in life and is necessary to make meaningful decisions. Richardson and Molinaro (1996) go on to note that multicultural sensitivity can be enhanced by counselors engaging in self-awareness exercises that explore their values, cultural identity, and world view. McWhirter (1994) expands on the need for multicultural self-awareness. McWhirter notes that counselors should pay more attention to the *person of the counselor* in terms of how counselors can be vehicles of cultural oppression.

Counselors can undertake a self-assessment in numerous ways. Perhaps the most comprehensive approach is to obtain formal counseling. Through the use of tests and other counseling strategies, counselors can gain information about their self-concept, personality, interests, values, aptitude, and other important aspects of the self. Many training programs, for example, in psychiatry require students to undertake analysis by a psychotherapist for one year or longer. The underlying belief in this requirement is that the experience can help provide students with personal insights necessary to become effective helpers.

Self-assessment through personal counseling or other procedures can generate an understanding of personal characteristics that may or may not be helpful in counseling. Chapter 1 provides an overview of the personal characteristics of effective counselors. These include qualities such as being encouraging, empathic and caring, patient, nonjudgmental, and flexible. These characteristics can enable counselors to use the "self as an instrument of change." In this regard, counselors can facilitate the counseling process by fostering core conditions such as unconditional positive regard, self-disclosure, empathy, and respect.

Stage Two: Survey of Supportive Disciplines

A variety of disciplines can contribute to the development of a personal approach to counseling, but psychology and medicine are perhaps the most relevant. Other disciplines that may be useful are philosophy, theology, anthropology, sociology, and literature. A brief description of each of these disciplines follows.

Psychology. Psychology is vital as a discipline for counselors to draw from since it encompasses the major schools of counseling and psychotherapy, which are the topics of

Chapters 7, 8, and 9. Psychology also has a number of specialties that can contribute to a counselor's personal theory. The following list summarizes the relevant aspects of some of these specialties.

- *Clinical and counseling psychology* investigates how psychological tests and other helping skills can be used in the counseling process.
- *Developmental psychology* helps counselors gain an understanding of how human growth and development take place over the life span. The counseling profession emphasizes the importance of utilizing a developmental perspective. This perspective enables counselors to adapt their approaches to the unique needs of clients progressing through the life span.
- *Experimental psychology* provides an important link to the science-of-counseling model by identifying research strategies to evaluate counseling approaches and processes.
- *Abnormal psychology* provides an overview of mental disorders and helps counselors learn how to use that information in the process of assessment and diagnosis.
- *Multicultural psychology* explores how psychology varies across cultures. This knowledge can be particularly important in developing a counseling perspective.
- *School psychology* focuses on the use of psychological tests in the school setting to assess personality, intelligence, aptitude, and achievement.
- *Physiological psychology* explores the physiological foundations of psychology. It can contribute a frame of reference for understanding physiological factors associated with behavior, cognition, and emotions.
- *Social psychology* explores psychology from a social perspective. It provides much promise to counseling research in terms of identifying paradigms relating to the social forces that influence the counseling process.

Medicine.   Medicine is another important discipline for counselors to study to develop some theoretical grounding. The mind and body are not separate entities but an interrelated whole. To understand one, it is essential to have some knowledge of the other. The following *Personal Note* illustrates how some physical illnesses can cause psychiatric symptoms such as hallucinations.

A Personal Note

A doctor suspected that a female patient had a schizophrenic disorder, since she was having auditory hallucinations (was hearing voices), and referred the woman to me. My psychological evaluation of the patient did not suggest that she was suffering from schizophrenia. In reviewing her hospital chart, however, I noticed that she had been diagnosed as having syphilis more than 10 years earlier and that there was no record of her successfully completing treatment for the condition. I knew that syphilis can cause hallucinations, so I referred the patient back to the physician to begin medical treatment for syphilis. I also arranged for the patient to see a consulting psychiatrist, who gave her medication for the auditory hallucinations.

Psychiatry is a medical specialty that has direct relevance to counseling. The three "classic" theorists who will be discussed in Chapter 7 were all psychiatrists. Psychiatry is the study of human behavior from a medical perspective. Psychiatrists have a special interest in how pathology, or abnormality, in the brain and nervous system can cause mental disorders such as schizophrenia and major depression. They also have special training in the use of medications to treat these mental disorders. A basic background in psychiatry can help counselors differentiate a medical problem from a psychological problem so the client can receive the appropriate treatment. It can also assist counselors in understanding physiological factors associated with mental disorders.

Philosophy.   Philosophy can provide a valuable foundation for counselors in developing a personal approach. It can help them broaden and enrich how they see life and clarify beliefs, attitudes, and values. The following issues may be useful to explore in undertaking a study of philosophy.

1. Do people have free will?
2. What is the purpose of anxiety in life? Is it something to be avoided at all cost?
3. In order to experience love and joy, must one also be able to bear pain and sorrow?
4. Are people inherently good or bad, or is their nature primarily determined by environmental forces?

The study of philosophy can help counselors explore these and other relevant issues. It can also help counselors become aware of personal biases to avoid imposing them on clients.

Existentialism is a major school of philosophy that may be particularly interesting to counselors. Existentialism contends that people are self-determined and have free will, which they can use to make choices in life. Shakespeare (1938) summed up the spirit of existentialism when he wrote, "To be or not to be—that is the question."

The writings of several noted philosophers can be used to develop a philosophical perspective. A list of recommended reading is provided at the end of this chapter. One example is Gibran's (1965) popular book *The Prophet,* which expresses philosophical views that are easy to understand. It covers a wide variety of topics from children to love. The following is an excerpt from the section on children.

On Children
And a woman who held a babe against her bosom said, Speak to us of Children. And he said: Your children are not your children. They are the sons and daughters of life's longing for itself. They come through you but not from you. You may give them your love but not your thoughts, for they have their own thoughts. You may house their bodies but not their souls, for their souls dwell in the house of tomorrow, which you cannot visit, not even in your dreams. You may strive to be like them, but seek not to make them like you. For life goes not backward nor tarries with yesterday. You are the bows from which your children as living arrows are sent forth. The archer sees the mark upon the path of the infinite, and he bends you with his might that his arrows may go swift and far. Let your bending in the archer's hand be for gladness; for even as he loves the arrow that flies, so he loves also the bow that is stable. (pp. 17–18)

Theology.   Theology is the study of spirituality and religion, and various schools of theology incorporate theories of philosophy. Theological concepts have traditionally not played a significant role in counseling. Most counselors have viewed the client's religion as a personal, private matter that is not necessary or appropriate to explore with a client. An exception to this view is pastoral counseling, in which counselors practice from a particular religious perspective. In those situations, the client often seeks counseling from a religious orientation. Many churches employ counselors for this purpose.

Spirituality is an emerging trend in counseling that can be used to provide a theological foundation for a personal approach to counseling and also represent an important diversity consideration in multicultural counseling (Bishop, 1995; Richards & Bergin, 1997). Spirituality is considered to be endemic to all people, whereas religion can be used to create a structure and focus for the spiritual realm (Ingersoll, 1995). Recognition of the strength and support people draw from spirituality is contributing to its acceptance as an important dimension of the counseling process (Miranti & Burke, 1995). When religious issues do come up in counseling, clients tend to expect counselors to be supportive of the client's religion or attend to psychological issues and not challenge the client's religious beliefs (Morrow, Worthington, & McCullough, 1993).

Worthington (1989) identifies five reasons why counselors should make more of an effort to include spiritual and religious considerations in formulating a counseling approach.

1. A high percentage of people in the United States are religious.
2. People often turn to religion during an emotional crisis.
3. Clients (especially religious clients) are reluctant to mention religious issues during secular therapy.
4. Counselors do not tend to be as religiously oriented as their clients.
5. Since many counselors are not as religiously oriented as their clients, they tend to be less informed about religion and are therefore less helpful to these clients.

Worthington (1989) provides guidelines for incorporating spiritual and religious issues into the counseling process. In these guidelines, he provides information on spiritual and religious faith across the life span in terms of implications for counseling and research.

Theological issues can impact on virtually all aspects of the counseling process. Smith (1993) suggests that it is especially important to explore the religious-spiritual needs of the dying. Smith notes that 79 percent of people surveyed believed that spiritual issues would play an important role in attaining a "healthy" death. In addition, 50 percent of people who were dying reported that they did not have an affiliation with an organized religion but felt the need to discuss religious-spiritual issues. Smith goes on to provide a description of theological counseling tools that can be used with dying clients. For example, the client can be asked to write a "healthy death story" in which the individual describes the ideal death. Smith recommends that counselors use these tools to explore clients' theological concerns, struggles, and resources.

Multicultural counseling provides another impetus for incorporating a theological perspective in counseling (Pate & Bondi, 1992). According to Pate and Bondi, spiritual and religious beliefs are related to clients' cultural background and should therefore be incorporated into a multicultural perspective. MCT (Sue, Ivey, & Pedersen, 1996) provides additional evidence of the need to address religious and spiritual issues in multicultural counseling. According to MCT, counselors need to modify conventional helping roles to accommodate various cultural groups. The need for alternative styles of helping that focus on spiritual issues appears especially important for non-Western cultures. In this regard, Lee, Oh, and Mountcastle (1992) surveyed 16 counties and found that the three main sources of healing were the use of communal groups and family, spiritualism and religion, and traditional healers (such as the medicine man with Native Americans). Counselors can effectively broaden their helping role by addressing these important sources of healing by providing interventions (such as family counseling and support groups), addressing theological issues, and recognizing the value of culturally relevant healers.

The holistic health movement also recognizes the value of addressing all aspects of the mind and body (including spiritual issues) in fostering health and wellness. In this regard, Westgate (1996) suggests that spiritual issues can contribute to a holistic approach to prevention and treatment of depression. According to Westgate, spiritual void is associated with depressive symptomology such as meaninglessness, emptiness, alienation, and hopelessness. The spiritually well person is able to draw strength from religion to gain meaning and a sense of direction in life. Westgate (1996) goes on to identify four spiritual dimensions that counselors can use to overcome problems with depression: "a sense of meaning in life, a transcendent perspective, an intrinsic value system, and a sense of belonging to a spiritual community of shared values and support" (p. 26).

Spirituality is a dimension of counseling that appears to offer many opportunities and challenges. It appears to fit well emerging trends in counseling that use a strengths perspective, such as brief-solution-focused counseling. In this regard, counselors can encourage clients to use their faith (including, if appropriate, prayer) as a strength to help deal with challenges they face. Unfortunately, many counselors appear to be unprepared to relate effectively to spiritual issues in counseling (Genia, 1994). According to Genia (1994), counselor educators can play an important role in enhancing the spiritual dimension to counseling by providing training on spirituality in counseling. This can include activities such as course work on religion (for example, the psychology of religion) and supervised experience in counseling religious clients (Genia, 1994). Additional research on counseling and spirituality seems warranted.

Anthropology. Cultural anthropology is the study of cultures. Mental health cultural anthropology is a specialty that investigates mental health issues unique to a particular culture. For example, Topper (1985) has explored Navajo alcoholism in terms of drinking, alcohol abuse, and treatment in a changing cultural environment. The mental health–cultural anthropology perspective can be particularly useful in addressing cross-cultural issues in counseling.

Sociology. Sociology is the study of social group behavior. A basic premise is that behavior is primarily determined by a person's social interaction. For example, during the socialization process, a person is encouraged to conform to the norms and laws of society. Many different groups and institutions can exert a significant influence on personality development. Some of these are family, friends, church, the work place, and school. A counselor may be interested in how these forces affect the client.

Literature.   The roads of literature and psychology have often crossed, creating new perspectives for understanding the psychology of people and exploring the counseling process. Adler emphasized the importance of literature in the development of individual psychology, as illustrated in the following excerpt.

> Some day soon it will be realized that the artist is the leader of mankind on the path to the absolute truth. Among poetic works of art which have led me to the insights of Individual Psychology, the following stand out as pinnacles: fairy tales, the Bible, Shakespeare, and Goethe. (Ansbacher & Ansbacher, 1956, p. 291)

Numerous possibilities exist for exploring the implications for counseling to be found in literature. For example, Adlerian psychotherapy and the life-style analysis have been related to the investigative strategies employed by Sherlock Holmes (Nystul, 1978). Kopp (1971) provides another example of understanding literature from a counseling perspective in his analysis of *The Wizard of Oz*. He notes that Dorothy is similar to a client in search of herself, and the Wizard can be perceived as her counselor. As Dorothy journeys through the Land of Oz, she encounters the Scarecrow, the Tin Woodsman, and the Cowardly Lion, who become her support system.

Kopp (1971) identifies several insights into life that Dorothy and her friends may have realized, as the following excerpt shows.

> Acquiring wisdom involves risking being wrong or foolish; being loving and tender requires a willingness to bear unhappiness; courage is the confidence to face danger, though afraid; gaining freedom and power requires only a willingness to recognize their existence and to face their consequences. We can find ourselves only when we are willing to risk losing ourselves to another, to the moment, to a quest, and love is the bridge. (p. 98)

Bibliotherapy provides another example of how the roads of literature and counseling cross (see Chapter 8). Bibliotherapy involves having clients read books or other literary works to promote different outcomes associated with counseling, for example, anxiety reduction and stress management. Gelso and Fassinger (1990) suggest that counselors should consider client characteristics to determine the appropriateness of self-help literature.

Stage Three: Overview of Major Counseling Theories

It is necessary to study the major schools of counseling to obtain an overview of the various counseling theories (see Chapters 7, 8, and 9). This understanding alerts counselors to the various theoretical perspectives that are available to use with different clients. One central or core theory can then be selected as the foundation of an integrative approach.

Stage Four: Intensive Study of One Counseling Theory

A solid foundation in theory is necessary for developing a personal approach. The importance of a theoretical foundation is evident in all disciplines. For example, music students usually benefit from studying music theory and learning to read music before creating their own musical composition. The same is true in counseling. After students have established an in-depth theoretical foundation, they are ready to develop their own personal style and approach.

Stage 4 suggests that counselors undertake an in-depth study of the particular school they have selected. The core theory should include a comprehensive theory of personality to provide an understanding of the dynamics of behavior. The theory should be a well-thought-out approach to counseling that includes an understanding of the counseling process. The core theory can provide internal consistency in terms of how counselors understand and work with a client.

Counselors who do not have a well-thought-out core theory are prone to superficial and fragmented personality assessment. They are likely to have a technique-oriented approach to counseling, thinking, for example, "With this client, I'll use this theory's suggested technique." It is important for counselors to read books and articles written by the founder of the school they have selected. Reading about an approach in a textbook will not provide an in-depth understanding. Training in an institute associated with the theory, such as the Gestalt Institute in Arizona, can also help counselors develop expertise in a particular school of counseling. It may be useful to join a professional organization associated with the chosen theory. An example is the North American Society of Individual Psychology for counselors interested in Adlerian psychology.

Stage Five: Sensitivity to Individual Differences

Counselors should not force a client to fit into their personal approach. I refer to this as "forcing square pegs into round holes" (Nystul, 1981). On the contrary, a counselor's approach should be adjusted to the unique and emerging needs of the client. In this regard, the counselor should be sensitive to the individual differences of clients. It is particularly important to address multicultural issues to make the counseling process relevant to the needs of the client. The next section of this chapter describes multicultural issues that can be used to formulate one's personal approach to counseling.

It is also important to assess the client's personal characteristics to help determine what type of counseling approaches may be appropriate. One way of doing this is by trying to identify how the client tends to engage in problem solving in terms of "spaces of perception." This theory suggests there are three spaces of perception: near-, mid-, and far-spaced (Nystul, 1981). *Near-spaced* clients tend to want a lot of detail in problem solving. For example, they want to know exactly what and how they are supposed to do something. These clients may be better able to utilize behavioral approaches that incorporate the monitoring of behavior with graphs and other objective procedures.

At the other extreme are *far-spaced* clients. These are people who hate to be pinned down with a lot of details. They do not want to be locked into a preconceived method of problem solving. An existential or humanistically oriented approach may be more in keeping with their mode of problem solving.

Mid-spaced clients are characterized by having difficulty making decisions. They tend to want others to make decisions and resolve problems for them. Reality therapy or

Gestalt therapy may help these clients become aware of choices and accept responsibility for their behavior.

Garfield (1994) provides an extensive review of the literature on client variables in counseling and psychotherapy in terms of continuation in counseling and outcome. For example, clients from upper socioeconomic status tend to stay longer in counseling and have less of a tendency to engage in premature termination. A number of variables have also been investigated in terms of outcome. There is some evidence to suggest that degree of disturbance is related to outcome, with extreme disturbance being negatively correlated with positive outcomes in counseling.

Stage Six: Integration of Techniques from Counseling Theories

To develop an integrative counseling approach, counselors may draw from different counseling theories to add to their repertoire of counseling techniques. In reviewing the various schools of counseling, students may find that these theories have more in common than they have differences. Subtle differences do exist, however, enabling counselors to adjust their approach to the particular problems that present themselves in the counseling session.

Stage Seven: Implementation

As counselors make the transition from theory to practice, they will begin to implement their approach. The application of one's approach is an art. It is a creative process that varies according to the particular clinical situation.

Stage Eight: Research and Evaluation

Research and evaluation enable counselors and counselors in training to determine the efficacy of their approach, use the literature to refine their approach, and contribute to the literature on a topic of interest. Chapter 5 provides information pertaining to this important topic.

Multicultural Counseling

The preceding discussion suggests that a personal approach to counseling should incorporate a multicultural perspective sensitive to the individual differences that reflect contemporary society. In this regard, Pedersen (1991) contends that multicultural counseling has become a fourth force, which follows psychodynamic, behavioral, and humanistic counseling. It is relevant to all aspects of counseling as a generic rather than exotic perspective (Pedersen, 1991).

This section describes key terms and concepts of some of the major issues in multicultural counseling. The next two sections provide an overview of MCT theory, identify potential problems associated with multicultural counseling, and provide guidelines for developing a multicultural perspective.

Terms and Concepts

Many terms relating to multicultural counseling can be difficult to differentiate and can therefore obscure its meaning. The following explanations help clarify some common terms and concepts.

- *Culture* is an ambiguous concept that defies definition. In a broad sense, it can be thought of as "things a stranger needs to know to behave appropriately in a particular setting" (Pedersen, 1988, p. viii).
- *Race* "refers to a pseudobiological system of classifying persons by a shared genetic history or physical characteristics such as skin color (Pedersen, 1988, p. viii).
- *Minority* "generally refers to a group receiving differential and unequal treatment because of collective discrimination" (Pedersen, 1988, p. viii).
- *Ethnicity* "includes a shared sociocultural heritage that includes similarities of religion, history, and common ancestry" (Pedersen, 1988, p. viii).
- *Cross-cultural counseling* is "any counseling relationship in which two or more of the participants differ with respect to cultural background, values, and life style" (Sue et al., 1982, p. 47).
- *Multicultural counseling* has a broader definition of culture than implied in cross-cultural counseling. Pedersen (1988) defined multicultural counseling as a situation in which two or more persons with different ways of perceiving their social environment are brought together in a helping relationship" (p. viii). Pedersen (1991) prefers the broader definition of culture associated with multicultural counseling, because it "helps counselors become more aware of the complexity in cultural identity patterns, which may or may not include the obvious indicators of ethnicity and nationality" (p. 11).
- *Diversity* refers to the variables such a age, gender, culture, spirituality, and sexual orientation, which are addressed within the context of multicultural counseling.

Theoretical Perspectives for Multicultural Counseling

MCT represents the first comprehensive theory of multicultural counseling (Sue, Ivey, & Pedersen, 1996). MCT was developed in an attempt to overcome multicultural limitations associated with contemporary counseling theory, research, and practice. According to Sue, Ivy, and Pedersen (1996), the major problem with existing schools of counseling is that they are culture bound and do not adequately provide conceptual tools to incorporate a multicultural perspective. Sue, Ivy, and Pedersen (1996) go on to suggest that a *culture-centered theory* is necessary to broaden the theoretical foundations of counseling to make it relevant to the needs of a multicultural society.

MCT can be used to provide a perspective or lens to conceptualize diversity issues such as gender, culture, age, and sexual orientation in all phases of counseling. Throughout the counseling process, the MCT lens must be continuously adjusted to promote a clear understanding of emerging multicultural issues. Once diversity issues are identified, then counseling theories and procedures can be modified to reflect an MCT perspective.

Sue, Ivy, and Pedersen (1996) identify six propositions for MCT that provide an overview of the basic assumptions from which this theory is based.

Proposition 1.   MCT can be used to provide an organizational framework for understanding Western and non-Western theories and methods of helping.

Proposition 2.   Counselors' and clients' identities are reflected in various levels of human experience (individual, group, system, and universal). Contextual issues in treatment must therefore be addressed as necessary.

Proposition 3.   Cultural identity development affects how the counselor and client view the self and others and how they formulate counseling goals and interventions. It is therefore important to be cognizant of how cultural identity development is impacting the counseling process, including an awareness of the different sociocultural forces that influence its development.

Proposition 4.   The efficacy of MCT is enhanced when counselors use procedures congruent with the values and experiences of the client. Counselors are encouraged to broaden their helping responses so that they demonstrate multicultural sensitivity throughout the counseling process.

Proposition 5.   MCT encourages counselors to expand their helping roles to include conventional and alternative methods of helping as necessary to meet the cultural needs of clients.

Proposition 6.   A fundamental goal of MCT theory is the liberation of consciousness from a relational-contextual perspective. In this regard, MCT attempts to provide opportunities to promote an awareness of how cultural and relational issues (such as self in relation to family) impact present concerns.

Potential Challenges in Multicultural Counseling

Many studies have identified potential challenges in multicultural counseling. This research addresses a wide range of topics, including counseling as a white middle-class activity, social class, gender, the intrapsychic perspective, sexual orientation, prejudice, stereotyping, communication problems, faulty assumptions, test bias, and the efficacy of multicultural counseling.

Counseling as a White Middle-Class Activity

A major criticism of contemporary counseling is that its theories and techniques have been developed primarily by people from a white middle-class culture. As a result, contemporary counseling is not directly applicable to ethnic minorities because its theories and techniques do not address their specific issues and concerns (Sue, Ivey, & Pedersen, 1996). In addition,

Ponterotto and Casas (1991) note that traditionally trained counselors are encapsulated in a culturally biased framework and consequently tend to engage in culturally conflicting and oppressive counseling approaches. It is therefore not surprising that counseling services are not utilized as much by minorities as by whites (Sue & Sue, 1990). In addition, the rate of dropping out of counseling after attending one session is 50 percent for ethnic minorities versus 30 percent for whites (Sue & Sue, 1990).

Social Class

Social-class differences may be more profound than cultural differences (Baruth & Manning, 1991). For example, whites in the lower socioeconomic class may have more in common with Hispanics in the same class than with whites in the middle or upper class.

Diagnostic and treatment bias is one concern that has been associated with social class. In one of the earliest studies on this subject, Lee (1968) found that clients from the lower socioeconomic class received a diagnosis of mental illness at a higher rate than clients from the upper socioeconomic class. Some evidence also suggests that counselors become more involved with clients from the upper class than with clients from the lower class (Garfield, Weiss, & Pollack, 1973). Considering these findings, it is not surprising that clients with a lower socioeconomic status tend to drop out of counseling after one or two sessions (Berrigan & Garfield, 1981; Weighill, Hodge, & Peck, 1983). With these concerns in mind, Atkinson, Morten, and Sue (1998) note that social class is an important variable to consider when formulating a treatment approach.

Gender

A proliferation of research has emerged suggesting that women's issues have not been adequately addressed in terms of the theory, practice, and research of counseling. Gender bias in theory begins with developmental theories (a theoretical foundation for counseling). In this regard, Carol Gilligan's (1982, 1991) seminal work on female moral development and identity development provides evidence of the need to create developmental theories that address men's *and* women's issues.

Feminists have also identified systematic bias in traditional counseling theories and theories of psychopathology (Enns, 1993). From a feminist's counseling perspective, counseling theories have been written from a white-male perspective, acknowledging values of autonomy and independence over relational considerations. In addition, assessment of psychopathology tends to ascribe causality to a lack of internal conditions (such as autonomy and independence) as opposed to a recognition of external forces (such as sociopolitical oppression from a male-dominated society). The practice of counseling can therefore be a process of cultural-encapsulation, whereby women are controlled and manipulated to conform to expectations of a white-male counseling perspective. It is therefore not surprising that research evidence suggests that women tend to prefer women counselors to discuss relationship issues such as love, closeness, and sexual behavior (Snell, Hampton, & McManus, 1992).

Lucia Gilbert (1992, p. 387) also notes that "sexism and gender bias characterize psychological research and theory to the extent that unexamined assumptions about the sexes or untested distinctions based on gender enter into the hypotheses, rationale, norms of adjustment, or coverage of the field." Gilbert goes on to suggest that in order to overcome gender bias in research, it is essential to begin by accurately describing the experiences of men *and* women. In addition, Ballou (1996) posits that women's experiences deserve to be valued and recognized as offering alternative views of knowledge and reality. This postmodern perspective would include an understanding of relational-contextual issues that define women's existence and concept of "self" as important considerations for counseling research.

The Intrapsychic Perspective

The intrapsychic perspective focuses on internal forces such as the unconscious processes and endopsychic conflicts described by Freud (see Chapter 7). The multicultural counseling perspective suggests that traditional schools of counseling rely on an overemphasis of intrapsychic forces in conceptualizing the dynamics of behavior. The multicultural perspective suggests that external forces such as oppression, racism, and discrimination can also have a direct bearing on psychological functioning (Sue & Sue, 1990).

Postmodernism offers an alternative perspective for understanding the human condition. From a postmodern perspective, issues such as language and narratives provide a relational-contextual perspective for defining what truth, knowledge, and reality are. This can be particularly true in terms of gender and culture, since women tend to emphasize relational issues and minorities are directly impacted by sociopolitical forces. A relational-contextual perspective can therefore provide an important frame of reference in counseling women and minorities.

Sexual Orientation

Sexual orientation is an important diversity issue in counseling. Fassinger (1991) defines several key terms associated with sexual orientation. Sexual orientation (or preference) refers to the complex set of behaviors, attitudes, and lifestyle factors associated with choosing a sexual partner. Homosexuality refers to sex with a same-sex partner, and the etiology of homosexuality is to a large degree considered to be genetic or biologically based. Gays (males and females) and lesbians (females) tend to be preferred terms (rather than homosexuality), because they promote a more positive image that extends beyond sexual activity and includes the cultural considerations associated with gay/lesbian lifestyles. Homophobia is another common term associated with sexual orientation. It can be defined as the negative attitudes of fear and hatred that people may direct at gay people.

The counseling literature has to some degree been negligent in addressing issues associated with gays and lesbians, even though these individuals represent 10–15 percent of the general population (Fassinger, 1991). Literature is beginning to emerge that provides models for conceptualizing developmental, treatment, and spiritual issues of gay and lesbian clients. Several gay-identity development models have been developed (for example, Cass, 1979; Minton & McDonald, 1984). According to Fassinger (1991), these models tend to have three central stages—recognition, acceptance, and affirmation. The process of "coming out" (sharing one's sexual orientation with friends and family) is perceived to be an important step in promoting a positive gay identity and fostering optimal development (Fassinger, 1991). The process of coming out varies according to a number of factors such as age, gender, and culture. For example, in terms of age, younger individuals may have to be especially cautious in coming out, because they are still financially dependent on their parents. Black and Underwood (1998) comment on additional issues associated with adolescents coming out. They note when the circumstances are right, coming out can be a very positive experience, promoting self-acceptance and psychological well-being. Premature coming out can be associated with numerous problems such as rejection by friends and family. Adolescents should wait to come out until they have worked through self-doubt and have a clear sense of identity, feel self-worth, and have an established support system. It may be difficult to achieve some of these foundations for coming out since they are also associated as a consequence of coming out.

Browning, Reynolds, and Dworkin (1991) address treatment issues pertaining to lesbian women and Shannon and Woods (1991) provide information on counseling gay men. These scholars emphasize that it is important to look beyond sexuality when thinking about gays and consider the special diversity and lifestyle issues that contribute to the unique features of this cultural group. For example, lifestyle considerations include career considerations, such as considering selecting careers where coming out could jeopardize job security and or advancement (for example, the military). It is also important to help gays adjust to same-sex relationships in a heterosexual-homophobic world. This can involve helping gay clients work through feelings of isolation, oppression, abandonment, and anger. In addition counselors should strive to develop an understanding of the unique relationship issues associated with gays (for example, sexuality, communication, and parenting).

Ritter and O'Neill (1995) provide an overview of spiritual issues in counseling gays. They note that traditional organized religion has offered little positive and much negative in terms of the psychological functioning and development of gays. Essentially, most of the organized religions (for example, Judeo-Christian) have promoted the message that homosexuality is wrong, a sin, and a form of perversion. Obviously, the evidence that homosexuality is primarily determined by biological forces does not tend to be recognized by these religious groups (Ritter & O'Neill, 1995). Gays' only acceptable response to church doctrine tends to be conversion, repentance, celibacy, or attempting to function in spurious heterosexual relationships (Ritter & O'Neill, 1995). Gays who fail to measure up to church policy tend to receive little support or empowerment in terms of involvement in church functioning (for example, not being married as gays in the church). Without access to church functions, it is also difficult to use the church as a source of strength and support during difficult times, such as working through loss due to death, divorce, and other adverse life events.

Ritter and O'Neill (1995) suggest that gays experience numerous psychological and developmental problems resulting from exclusionary church doctrine and policy. On a psychological level, gay people can struggle with negative feelings such as guilt, shame, and isolation, which in turn can interfere with self-acceptance and identity development. Feelings of isolation are endemic to gays. It is therefore not surprising that gays often feel like invisible people, living in an existential void beyond the recognized fringes of society. Counselors must take care to consider the vast array of special needs of gays, so they can be afforded opportunities for spiritual development and enhancement.

Stereotyping

Stereotyping can be defined as "rigid preconceptions we hold about *all* people who are members of a particular group, whether it be defined along racial, religious, sexual, or other lines" (Sue & Sue, 1990, pp. 47–48). Examples of stereotyping are "Native Americans live on reservations and get drunk," "African Americans are musical," and "Asians are good with numbers." Stereotyping has negative effects on the counseling process (Sue, 1988). Some potential concerns are that stereotyping causes counselors to apply a perceived characteristic of a group to all members of that group without regard for individual differences, fail to take logic or experience into consideration, and distort all new information to fit preconceived ideas (Sue & Sue, 1990).

Communication Problems

Pedersen (1988) notes that much of the criticism directed at multicultural counseling relates to communication problems that interfere with the counseling process. Language differences can result in a variety of challenges in counseling (Sue, 1988). For example, Vontress (1973) has found that counselors who experience language difficulties with a client have trouble establishing a positive counseling relationship with the client. Sue and Sue (1977) also warn that counselors who use only standard English with a bilingual client may make an inaccurate assessment of the client's strengths and weaknesses.

The style of nonverbal communication may also vary across cultures, creating communication problems. For example, African Americans tend to utilize more direct eye contact when speaking than whites and as a result have been labeled as more angry (Sue & Sue, 1990). Native Americans tend to avoid direct eye contact when listening, causing them to be incorrectly perceived as inattentive (Sue & Sue, 1990). Herring (1990) notes the particular importance of counselors being able to assess nonverbal communication accurately, because this type of communication is more ambiguous and culturally bound than verbal communication.

Westwood and Ishiyama (1990) provide the following guidelines regarding the communication process in multicultural counseling.

1. Counselors should check with the client on the accuracy of their interpretation of nonverbal communication.
2. Counselors can promote catharsis by encouraging clients to use their own language to express a particular feeling when another language cannot accurately describe it.
3. Counselors should try to learn culturally meaningful expressions of the client to accurately describe the client's inner process.
4. Counselors should use alternative modes of communicating, such as art, music, and photography.

Faulty Assumptions

Pedersen (1987) identifies 10 faulty assumptions that can impede progress in counseling. Later in this chapter these assumptions are used to evaluate the appropriateness of counseling theory in multicultural counseling. These 10 faulty assumptions are summarized as follows (repeated by permission).

Misconceptions of Normal Behavior.   A tendency exists for people to assume that the definition of *normal* is universal across social, cultural, economic, and political backgrounds. Pedersen (1987) suggests that "what is considered normal will vary according to the situation, the cultural background of a person or persons being judged, and the time during which a behavior is being displayed or observed" (p. 17). Counselors can make an error of diagnosis if they fail to consider how the definition of normalcy can vary.

Emphasis on Individualism.   Counselors with a traditional Western approach tend to emphasize the importance of the welfare of the individual. Self-awareness, self-fulfillment, and self-discovery are often used as indices of success in counseling. In addition, the task of the counselor is often perceived as "changing the individual in a positive direction even at the expense of the group in which that individual is a member" (Pedersen, 1987, p. 18).

This emphasis on the interests of the individual over the group may not be consistent with the value system of some cultures. In the Chinese culture, it would be inappropriate to put the welfare of an individual before the welfare of that individual's family (Pedersen, 1987). Counselors should therefore take cultural issues into consideration before promoting the virtues of individualism in counseling.

Fragmentation by Academic Disciplines.   Some tendency exists for counselors to isolate themselves from related disciplines such as sociology, anthropology, theology, and medicine. This can result in a narrow view of people and an inability to understand individual differences. Cultural anthropology can be a particularly useful area for a counselor to study in terms of addressing multicultural issues.

Use of Abstract or Out-Of-Context Concepts.   Many counseling principles contain abstract concepts, which can be easily misunderstood across cultures. In addition, the meaning of a concept will vary from one context or situation to another. It is therefore important to determine what a concept means as it relates to a particular client.

Overemphasis on Independence.   A common goal in counseling is to help the client become autonomous and independent. Pedersen (1987) warns that some cultures, such as the Japanese, believe that dependency is not only healthy but necessary. Some examples of relationships in which the Japanese culture views dependency as appropriate are those between employer and employees, mother and son, and teacher and student. Counselors should therefore be sensitive to cultural issues in determining whether a client's dependence is excessive.

Neglect of Client's Support System.   A client who enters counseling may want the counseling relationship to become a substitute for existing support systems. To ensure that this does not occur, counselors should include the client's support system in treatment planning. This can be especially important for a minority client who may already feel a high degree of isolation because of cultural differences.

Dependence on Linear Thinking.   Traditional Western counseling approaches tend to be characterized by linear thinking whereby each cause has an effect and each effect has a particular cause. Some cultures are not tied to the linear model of analysis. The concept of Yin and Yang from Eastern culture does not differentiate between cause and effect but sees them as interrelated. In counseling it is therefore important to attempt to communicate in a manner that is consistent with the client's way of viewing the world.

Focus on Changing the Individual, Not the System.   "In many minority groups counseling has a bad reputation for taking the side of the status quo in forcing individuals to adjust or adapt to the institutions of society" (Pedersen, 1987, p. 22). To overcome this obstacle, counselors should broaden their intervention strategies to include a community psychology perspective. This can include trying to change the system if it appears the system is having a detrimental effect on the client. If a client's depression appears to be related to high unemployment in the community, the counselor may become active in efforts to create employment opportunities.

Neglect of History.   Counselors may focus only on the most recent precipitating events that lead up to a crisis or mental disorder and fail to consider the client's problems from a historical perspective. For some minority clients, a historical perspective may be more appropriate because it can help the counselor understand sociocultural forces that have contributed to shaping a client's approach to problem solving and outlook on life. Many African Americans, for instance, have experienced years of poverty, oppression, prejudice, racism, and exploitation. This can cause some to develop limited horizons and affect the way they view themselves and others, for example, with a sense of despair, helplessness toward self, or hostility or suspicion toward others.

Dangers of Cultural Encapsulation.   *Cultural encapsulation* is a process in which counselors cannot see beyond their belief system and fail to address cultural issues with the client. Multicultural counselors must move beyond "parochial concerns and perspectives" and develop a comprehensive perspective that integrates contrasting assumptions from other cultures (Pedersen, 1987, p. 23).

Test Bias

Lonner (1985) provides a comprehensive overview of testing and assessment in multicultural counseling. The author identifies a variety of potential problems in multicultural testing that could contribute to test bias. These include difficulties in reactions to test-taking situations and problems that relate to validity, reliability, and norms.

Regarding test-taking situations, Lonner (1985) notes there could be cultural differences in terms of use of time, language difficulties, and the manner of response to test questions. As an example of the effect of culture on an individual's manner of response, it may be culturally appropriate for some to agree with nearly every statement out of politeness. For others, it may be appropriate to give only socially desirable answers. Some individuals may view tests as unimportant and respond carelessly (Lonner, 1985).

Validity, reliability, and norms are critical in determining the use and effectiveness of tests, as discussed in Chapter 4. Validity may be the most important factor in evaluating a test. Construct validity is one type of validity that may vary across cultures (Lonner, 1985). Construct validity is the extent to which a test measures a theoretical construct or trait such as intelligence and verbal fluency (Anastasi & Urbina, 1997). The meaning and importance of these constructs may vary from one culture to another. Tests that utilize the same constructs across cultures may therefore have invalid construct validities.

Sociocultural factors may influence a test's reliability. Different opportunities in learning may vary across cultures, affecting a test's reliability. One culture may require formal education, for instance, and another may not (Lonner, 1985). It is therefore best to develop separate indices of reliability for each culture (Lonner, 1985).

Another potential problem in using psychological tests multiculturally relates to norms. Most standardized tests utilize a white, middle-class norm group in determining standards or points of comparison. These standards often vary considerably across cultures. The norms are therefore only relevant for the particular reference group or culture in which they were developed. If the test is to be used multiculturally, new norms should be established based on the population (Lonner, 1985).

It is also important to ensure that the test results are used in an appropriate fashion. Cronbach (1984) warns that the central issue in the test-bias controversy relates to decision making and how the inappropriate use of a test can create an unfair advantage for one culture over another. For example, using a culturally biased test in job selection could create an unfair advantage for some prospective employees. Culture-fair tests have been developed in an attempt to overcome some of the problems associated with test bias. Several of these tests are described in Chapter 4.

Prejudice

Sandhu and Aspy (1997) suggest that prejudice and prejudice reduction and prevention are important considerations in multicultural counseling. These scholars adapt Gordon Allport's (1954) definition of prejudice: "thinking ill of others without sufficient warrant" (p. 7). Prejudice is believed to emanate from a variety of individual, social, and political forces such as oppressive attitudes (for example, stereotyping and racism), life-societal events (for example, loss of job due to foreign competition), and fear (Sandhu & Aspy, 1997). Geoseffi (1993) provides an alternative explanation for the etiology of prejudice, suggesting it can be traced to self-hatred. From this perspective, prejudice results from feelings of inadequacy that are projected onto others. Maslow's (1968) hierarchy of needs can also be used to understand prejudice. In this context, prejudice can be seen as a reflection of unmet needs (Sandhu & Aspy, 1997).

Prejudice can have adverse effects on the overall functioning of society and the peoples of the world, playing a major role in discrimination, oppression, violence, and even war. Sandhu and Aspy (1997) suggest that prejudice in the form of discrimination, cultural alienation, and restricted access to opportunities can also have detrimental effects on individuals' optimal development and self-actualization. In the final analysis, prejudice is a form of negativity that imparts a destructive force on anything in its path.

Sandhu and Aspy (1997) provide a comprehensive model for conceptualizing and addressing issues of prejudice in counseling (the multidimensional model of prejudice prevention and reduction [MMPPR]). From an MMPPR perspective, prejudice is the result of individual, social, and political factors. Although eclectic in nature, the model draws heavily from Maslow's (1968) need hierarchy theory (people tend to meet their needs in a hierarchical manner—that is, needs of physiological, safety, love and belonging, and self-actualization). According to this theory, when people believe their need gratification is being interfered with, they attribute blame (in the form of prejudice) to the perceived source of the need inhibition. Conversely, people who have healthy need systems and can satisfy their needs tend to have self-actualizing tendencies such as harmony with self and others. The process of prejudice prevention and reduction, reduced to its most basic elements, is directed at helping clients meet their needs in a responsible manner. Sandhu and Aspy (1997) provide numerous assessment and intervention methods that can be used by counselors to address the complex individual, social, and political issues to overcome prejudice.

Prejudice prevention and reduction appears to offer much promise as an emerging dimension to the multicultural literature. It suggests that counselors become proactive and promote multidimensional roles and interventions in fighting the tide of prejudice. This can involve activities and initiatives such as addressing prejudice in all phases of the counseling process and becoming advocates for social reform regarding prejudice. Additional research and investigation are needed to determine how models for addressing prejudice can be effectively incorporated into multicultural counseling.

The Efficacy of Multicultural Counseling

After reviewing the potential challenges in multicultural counseling, one may wonder whether any counselor could overcome these barriers. Research in this area has tended to focus on the role of similarity between the counselor and client on the counseling process and counseling outcome. Atkinson and Thompson (1992) provide an overview of the literature on racial/ethnic similarity, attitude similarity, and educational dissimilarity. They note that clients tend to rate counselors as more attractive when they are similar to them, except when dissimilarity is valued (such as the counselor having more education than the client). Attitudinal similarity is found to be more important to perceived counselor attractiveness than ethnic/cultural similarity. The literature on ethnic/cultural similarity is conflicting, with some studies favoring similarity and others suggesting clients would prefer dissimilar counselors in terms of the ethnic/cultural status. There is some evidence that similar attitudes and counselor credibility are rated as higher priorities for clients than is ethnic/cultural similarity.

Cultural mistrust, level of acculturation, and stages of identity development may be variables that should be considered in determining preference for ethnic/cultural similarity. In terms of cultural mistrust, Atkinson and Thompson (1992) describe several studies that indicate that African American clients who rated high on cultural mistrust engaged in premature termination when paired with white counselors and rated white counselors as less credible, accepting, expert, and trustworthy. Level of acculturation also appears to play a role in preference for similar ethnic/cultural counselors. A review of these studies shows clients rated low in acculturation preferring counselors who have similar ethnic/cultural status (Atkinson & Thompson, 1992). Stages of identity development provide another example of a variable that can influence clients' preference for counselors with similar ethnic/cultural status (Atkinson, Morten, & Sue, 1998). This line of research is beginning to determine how clients' preference for counselors with similar ethnic/cultural status depends to some degree on their current stage of identity development.

Several other studies have investigated the relationship between personality similarity between counselor and client and the counseling process. Berry and Sipps (1991) researched the relationship between personality similarity, client's level of self-esteem, and premature termination. They found that clients who had low self-esteem tended to engage in premature termination when they also rated high on similarity with their counselor in terms of the Myers-Briggs Type Indicator. These researchers suggest that clients with low self-esteem may have a tendency to project their feelings of inadequacy onto their similar counselors, reducing these counselors' credibility and increasing tendencies toward premature termination. Towberman (1992) provides additional information on the relationship between personality similarity on the counseling process. She finds that similarity between the counselor and client (as measured by the California Psychological Inventory) is related to clients' positive perception of the counseling relationship in terms of degree of involvement, support, and expressiveness.

Beutler, Machado, and Neufeldt (1994) provide a review of the literature regarding gender similarity and counseling outcome. They note that the literature does not present a clear statement regarding the efficacy of male versus female counselors or whether gender similarity between the counselor and client promotes superior efficacy over diverse gender pairings in counseling. Research is beginning to differentiate styles of counseling between males and females, with males using counseling approaches that tend to be more directive and controlling than females (Nelson & Holloway, 1990; Wogan & Norcross, 1985). Feminist counselors are investigating issues such as male dominance and control and women's oppression in the counseling process (Enns, 1993). From a feminist perspective, it is not surprising that there is preliminary evidence to suggest that women prefer women counselors for assistance with relationship issues (Snell, Hampton, & McManus, 1992). Additional research seems required to gain a clearer understanding of the role of gender in the counseling process.

This literature, taken collectively, appears to suggest that clients first and foremost want a counselor that is credible (someone they believe can help them with their problems). Clients also place a high value on having a counselor that has a similar personality and attitudes (someone who they can relate to and feel comfortable with). Ethnic/racial similarity becomes important for clients who are experiencing high levels of cultural mistrust and low levels of acculturation and are processing issues of identity development. Gender also is an important variable, with women showing some tendency to prefer same-sex counselors to explore relationship issues. In addition, there appear to be some salient variables (such as self-esteem) that should be considered to gain a more in-depth understanding of the role of similarity in the counseling process.

The following *Personal Note* illustrates how a counselor can turn potential challenges in multicultural counseling into an advantage.

A Personal Note

I was surprised to discover that some of the barriers I envisioned in multicultural counseling turned out to be benefits. When I was a psychologist at a public health hospital on the Navajo Indian reservation, I was especially concerned about language barriers. I was told that I would need an interpreter since some Navajos could not speak English. This proved to be true in individual counseling with clients who did not speak English. In family therapy, however, I often found that some family members could not speak English but others were bilingual. In these situations, I would have the bilingual family members act as interpreters, so an "outside" interpreter was not necessary.

Several positive outcomes resulted from having clients act as interpreters. First, they seemed to listen very carefully since they did not know when I would ask them to interpret. These clients seemed to take their responsibility as interpreter very seriously. Perhaps it allowed them to show respect for what other family members said. Second, clients were taking an active role in the counseling process, since interpreting is basically paraphrasing.

I believe that many of the potential challenges in multicultural counseling can be overcome if the counselor develops a positive attitude and is sensitive in adjusting the approach to the unique needs of the client.

Suggestions for Incorporating a Multicultural Perspective

This section identifies suggestions for counselors to incorporate a multicultural perspective into their personal approach to counseling. It presents information on beliefs, knowledge, and skills necessary for multicultural counseling; describes the concept of *world view* as a construct that can be used to individualize multicultural counseling; provides an overview of identity development; presents methods for determining the appropriateness of traditional counseling theory; and provides general guidelines for implementing a multicultural approach.

Gaining knowledge about a culture can be important to multicultural counseling.

Beliefs, Knowledge, and Skills

The Division of Counseling Psychology of the American Psychological Association has established a task force that identified beliefs and attitudes, knowledge, and skills of the culturally skilled counselor (Sue et al., 1982). The following overview provides a summary of the task force's findings.

Beliefs and Attitudes.   To be effective in a multicultural setting, counselors should be aware of how their beliefs and attitudes may impact the counseling process. Sue (1981) notes that counselors who are not aware of their beliefs and attitudes may unknowingly impose their values and standards on others and engage in cultural oppression. It is therefore important to develop appropriate attitudes and beliefs. Sue et al. (1982) suggest that culturally skilled counselors

- Are aware of and sensitive to their cultural heritage and have learned to value and respect differences
- Are aware of their own values and biases and how those attitudes may affect minority clients
- Are comfortable with differences that exist between themselves and their client in terms of race and beliefs
- Are sensitive to circumstances such as personal biases, stages of ethnic identity, and sociopolitical influences that may dictate a referral of a minority client to a counselor of the client's culture (Sue et al., 1982)

Knowledge.   An effective multicultural approach to counseling requires some knowledge about the client's culture. In addition, Sue et al. (1982) note that culturally skilled counselors

- Have a good understanding of the sociopolitical system's operation in the United States with respect to its treatment of minorities
- Possess specific knowledge and information about a particular group they are working with
- Have clear, explicit knowledge and understanding of the generic characteristics of counseling and therapy
- Are aware of institutional barriers that prevent minorities from using mental health services

Skills.   Some counseling strategies, such as being a good listener, are usually effective regardless of the culture. At the same time, as Sue (1981) warned, different cultural groups usually have different counseling goals and therefore require different counseling strategies to be effective. In addition, Sue et al. (1982) suggest that culturally skilled counselors

- Are able to generate a wide variety of verbal and nonverbal responses
- Are able to send and receive both verbal and nonverbal messages accurately
- Are able to exercise institutional intervention skills on behalf of their clients when appropriate (Sue et al., 1982)

World View

Although it is important to have a knowledge of the client's culture, it is also essential to be able to understand the client as a unique individual. World view, a concept with increasing recognition in the multicultural literature, is a construct that can be used to individualize the counseling process (Ibrahim, 1991; Sue, 1978, 1981).

World view, which extends beyond culture or ethnic group, can be defined as assumptions and perceptions regarding the world (Sire, 1976; Sue, 1978). World view is directly related to thoughts, feelings, and perceptions of social relations and the world (Ibrahim, 1991). It also has a direct effect on ability to solve problems, make decisions, and resolve conflicts (Ibrahim, 1993). Knowledge of a client's world view can promote a better understanding of the client and can lead to more sensitive and effective counseling strategies (Ibrahim, 1991).

Ibrahim (1991) suggests that a client's world view should be determined during the initial client assessment. One effective tool for determining a client's world view is the Scale to Assess World Views (SAWV) (Ibrahim & Kahn, 1984, 1987). The SAWV assesses information regarding the client's view of human nature, social relations, relations with nature, time orientation, and activity orientation. The SAWV can help the counselor explore the client's values, beliefs, and assumptions; gain an understanding of the client's concerns; and differentiate between the client's world view and cultural views (Ibrahim, 1991).

More recently, Trevino (1996) proposed a model for conceptualizing the change process that has a multicultural perspective. It is based primarily on the concept of world view and also incorporates concepts from anthropology and research on the counseling process. Trevino's model of change recognizes both a general and specific world view for both the counselor and client. According to this theory, it is advantageous for the counselor and client to have congruent general world views (one's basic understanding of the world in a broad abstract sense) and discrepant specific world views (more definite thoughts and opinions based on life experiences). Throughout the change process in counseling, similarity about general outlook on life is believed to promote empathy and foster a positive counseling relationship; discrepant specific world views promote alternative perspectives for problem solving.

Identity Development

Identity development is "a process of integrating and expanding one's sense of self" (Myers et al., 1991, p. 54). Establishing a positive self-identity can be difficult to attain (Myers et al., 1991). Helping clients clarify or enhance their self-identity can be a central task in counseling.

Identity development models have emerged as a means of understanding the process of identity formation and determining where clients are functioning in that process. Several models have emerged to describe the stages of identity development for racial-ethnic groups, for example, those for African Americans (Cross, 1995), Hispanic Americans (Casas & Pytlulk, 1995), Asian Americans (Sadowsky, Kwan, & Pannu, 1995), white Americans (Helms, 1995; Rowe, Behrens, & Leach, 1995), and biracial Americans (Kerwin & Ponterotto, 1995).

Myers et al. (1991) note that racial-ethnic identity development models may have several limitations. For example, they may not take into account multiple oppressive factors such as socioeconomic status and minority status (for example, lowerclass Mexican Americans) or multiracial backgrounds (for example, Amerasians). In an attempt to overcome some of these limitations, these authors developed the Optimal Theory Applied to Identity Development model (OTAID). The OTAID model does allow for consideration of multiple oppressive factors that can influence identity development. In addition, it is based on a world view rather than being restricted to racial-ethnic considerations.

Myers et al. (1991) describe the OTAID model as a six-phase process:

- *Phase 0: Absence of Conscious Awareness.* In this phase, individuals lack a sense of the self as a separate individual. Individuals do not develop self-awareness until one or two years of age (Dworetzky, 1996).
- *Phase 1: Individuation.* During this phase, individuals adhere to a personal identity that was generated by early familial and societal experiences. They utilize an egocentric view of themselves, which does not take into account the negative views of others.
- *Phase 2: Dissonance.* In phase 2, individuals begin to consider the opinions of others regarding who they are, even if these opinions are negative. Their perceptions of negative views from others create dissonance, and they begin to wonder who they really are.
- *Phase 3: Immersion.* Individuals who feel devalued by others may immerse themselves in the customs and way of life of the devalued group and react angrily toward the dominant group. For example, a 20-year-old Asian-American woman who had identified with anglo customs now rejects those customs and immerses herself in Asian customs if she hears whites talking about her in derogatory ways (for example, "silly chink").
- *Phase 4: Internalization:* During this phase, individuals incorporate a number of salient aspects of the self in formulating their personal identity. This broadened self-image enables them to be more tolerant and accepting of the criticisms of others.
- *Phase 5: Integration.* As individuals gain deeper self-understanding, they begin to change their assumptions regarding the world. Their world view is broad and accepting of individual differences. At this point, they choose friends on the basis of shared values and interest instead of ethnic-racial criteria.
- *Phase 6: Transformation.* In the transformation phase, the self is redefined according to a world view that appreciates the interrelatedness of all aspects of life. This emerging personal identity incorporates a spiritual awareness regarding the order of life and the universe and fosters a sense of wholeness or completeness in the individual.

Methods to Evaluate Counseling Theories

To formulate a personal approach to counseling, it is necessary to determine the appropriateness of traditional counseling theory in multicultural counseling. Several methods can be used to assist with this process.

Acculturation Theory.   Acculturation theory can be used to determine the appropriateness of traditional counseling approaches (Atkinson & Thompson, 1992). According to this model of evaluation, it is important for counselors to assess the client's level of acculturation early in the counseling process. This method contends that the more acculturated a client is, the more appropriate it is to use traditional approaches (Topper, 1985). Counselors can estimate a client's level of acculturation by examining how much the client has assimilated into the mainstream society. Lee (1991) has noted the factors that influence acculturation include educational level, socioeconomic status, length of time lived in the United States, and extent of exposure to racism.

Acculturation theories are being developed for different ethnic/cultural groups to obtain an understanding of the process of acculturation (for example, for American Indians, Choney, Berryhill-Paapke, & Robbins, 1995). In addition, acculturation scales are available for African Americans (Helms, 1986), American Indians (Hoffman, Dana, & Bolton, 1985), Asians (Suinn et al., 1987), and Hispanics (Mendoza, 1989).

Acculturation theory appears to offer much promise to the counseling literature. Researchers are beginning to use this theory to explore issues that extend beyond evaluating the appropriateness of traditional counseling procedures with minority clients. For example, "acculturative stress" is being investigated by a number of researchers. Smart and Smart (1995) define acculturative stress as the "psychological impact of adjusting to a new culture" (p. 25). Moyerman and Forman (1992) provide a meta-analytic analysis of 49 studies of acculturation and adjustment and conclude that stress is more intense at the beginning of the acculturation process. Smart and Smart (1995) go on to identify health factors and counseling implications associated with acculturative stress of Hispanic immigrants. They find acculturative stress to be related to such phenomena as impaired physical health, decision making, occupational functioning, and utility of the counseling relationship. Acculturation theory will undoubtedly stimulate additional research activity on a wide range of issues relevant to counseling within a multicultural perspective.

Usher's Model.   Usher (1989) presents another method to evaluate the appropriateness of a theory. She suggests that the 10 faulty assumptions identified by Pedersen (1987) can be used to determine whether a traditional counseling theory can be used in multicultural counseling. A counseling theory that appears to foster one or more of these faulty assumptions could either be modified or avoided in a multicultural context. Usher (1989) illustrates this method by using the 10 faulty assumptions to evaluate Rogers' (1951) person-centered therapy. Her analysis shows Rogers' theory to have some strengths and weaknesses in terms of its use in multicultural counseling.

Usher (1989) identifies two facets of Rogers' theory that appear to promote multicultural counseling. First, since clients define the goals and determine the evaluation process, there is less chance of their being judged in terms of the dominant culture's view of normality. Second, Rogers' approach contains elements of circularity, allowing clients to express themselves within a framework that is nondirective and nonjudgmental.

Usher (1989) also identifies some potential problems with person-centered counseling in multicultural settings. One problem relates to Rogers' emphasis on individualism and independence from others. Rogers does not recognize the view of healthy dependencies that some cultures hold for authorities and family members. A second problem could arise from Rogers' belief that the locus of control and responsibility resides within the client. This position does not take into account environmental factors such as poverty, which can contribute to the client's growth process. Another potential problem relates to Rogers' emphasis on the here and now. Such a frame of reference may not be adequate to understand problems such as oppression that may impact on culturally different clients.

Etic-Emic Model.   A third method that can be used to evaluate the efficacy of counseling theory in multicultural counseling involves the concepts of *etic* and *emic*, terms linked to linguistics (Lee, 1984; Ridley, Mendoza, & Kanitz, 1994). Etic relates to phonetics, which is something common to all languages. Etic is associated with concepts in counseling theory that are universal to all cultures. An example of an etic concept is the contention in rational emotive behavioral therapy (REBT) that irrational beliefs contribute to negative emotional consequences. Emic relates to phonemics, which is something unique to that particular language. Emic is associated with concepts that emphasize individuality. An example of an emic concept is neuro-linguistic programming, since it is an approach that varies with each individual (Bandler & Grinder, 1975).

There may be some advantages in using emic concepts as opposed to etic concepts in multicultural counseling. Emic concepts encourage the counselor to treat each client as an individual, thereby avoiding tendencies to engage in prejudice or stereotyping. Etic concepts, on the other hand, must be truly universal to be applied to different cultures without bias. Problems can surface with etic concepts when the theory assumes the concept is universal when in fact it is not. This could occur in REBT, since it suggests that irrational thinking will generate emotional difficulties regardless of the culture (Bandler & Grinder, 1975). REBT does not appear to take into consideration the possibility that the definition of irrational ideas may vary from one culture to another. The efficacy of REBT would therefore be significantly reduced in situations in which a counselor was imposing inappropriate standards regarding what is rational, irrational, and self-defeating.

Guidelines for Multicultural Counseling

This section provides 10 guidelines for incorporating multicultural counseling strategies into a personal approach to counseling.

Establish Mutual Respect.   Mutual respect forms the foundation for all relationships (Dinkmeyer & McKay, 1989). This may be especially important in multicultural counseling when a counselor from the majority culture counsels a minority client. In these situations, clients may feel they are being looked down upon and consequently resist participating in counseling.

Counselors can create opportunities to communicate respect to the client by honoring the client's unique way of perceiving and interacting with the world. Counselors can also communicate an acceptance of their client whenever possible. For example, some clients may become embarrassed because they have difficulty speaking English. When this occurs, a counselor can tell these clients that it is impressive that they are becoming bilingual when most people can speak only one language.

As clients experience acceptance and respect, they may become more relaxed with and accepting of their counselor. The resulting mutual respect can contribute to a relationship of equality in the counseling process.

Don't Impose Your Belief System.   When working in multicultural counseling, it is important for the counselor to be nonjudgmental. Each culture has its own norms and value system. This may influence how clients see important issues pertaining to counseling, such as their understanding of mental health. For example, the Navajos do not differentiate between physical and mental health (Harrar, 1984). They see mental problems resulting when a person is "out of harmony" with the traditional Navajo culture (Harrar, 1984).

Treat Clients as Unique Individuals First and as People from a Particular Culture Second.   It is important to consider that all people are unique, even in terms of what it means to be part of a particular culture. Focusing on the unique characteristics of a particular client will help counselors overcome stereotyping and other self-defeating processes.

Determine Whether Traditional Counseling Approaches Would Be Appropriate for a Particular Client.   The counselor can use the three methods described in this chapter to determine the appropriateness of traditional counseling theory in multicultural settings.

Provide Accessible, Dependable Services.   It is important for counseling services to be adequately staffed so clients will know someone will be there if they come for help. This is especially important in rural areas, where a client may have traveled a long distance to come for counseling services. On the Navajo reservation, it was not uncommon that clients may have journeyed 100 miles and may have had to get a ride from a friend or hitchhike. It would not be very welcoming for these clients to be told that they would have to come back the next day or wait a long time to receive help. It is essential for the counseling center to develop a reputation for being reliable and responsive, or clients will stop coming.

Some clients may feel that their problems are not "big enough" to warrant counseling services. These are often the clients who need help the most. They need to be reassured that the counseling service is there for them to use and that they are not "in the way," as they might feel, but are welcome.

Use a Flexible Approach.   Counselors should adjust their approach to the client's unique needs in all cases, but flexibility is especially important in multicultural counseling. In many minority cultures, such as Mexican Americans, African Americans, and Native Americans, a high percentage of people are struggling against the elements of poverty. These individuals may therefore need assistance with basic needs such as food, shelter, and safety. When this occurs, counselors should adjust their approach to meet these needs, becoming more action-oriented and focused in the present (Sue, 1981). Counselors may even function to some degree as advocates for the client's basic rights. This may involve helping clients obtain benefits from social services or other agencies.

Be Perceived as a Doer, Not Just a Talker.   Counselors should show they are capable of accomplishing something concrete with the client as early as possible in the counseling relationship. A counselor who is perceived as a doer and not just a talker will be valued and sought after by clients, especially those struggling to fulfill basic needs.

Conduct an Environmental Assessment.   It is important to avoid an overemphasis on intrapsychic forces in assessment and diagnosis. An environmental assessment will enable the counselor to explore sociocultural factors that could also be contributing to the client's problems. This will not only contribute to more accurate assessment and diagnosis but also help the counselor and client identify realistic treatment goals.

Allow Yourself to Be Enriched by the Client's Culture.   Multicultural counseling can be rewarding and exciting. It can involve living and working in a different culture or simply providing a multicultural counseling service. Regardless of the degree of a counselor's multicultural experience, many opportunities exist for cultural enrichment. A counselor may soon discover some of the special facets of a culture such as types of food, styles of dress, differences in family life, and approaches to physical and mental health.

Each culture also has its special customs, beliefs, heritages, and creative arts. It may be helpful to study a culture to appreciate its special beauty. This can involve reading, going to art exhibits and other cultural events, and, of course, learning from clients.

You Don't Have to Be a Minority to Counsel a Minority.   There can be potential problems in multicultural counseling such as language barriers, stereotyping, and a lack of awareness of the value systems of a cultural group. At the same time, counselors can overcome these problems by being sensitive to the unique needs of the client and attempting to gain the beliefs, knowledge, and skills necessary to counsel in multicultural settings.

Summary

Developing a well-thought-out personal approach to counseling creates the necessary structure to work within the counseling process. An eight-stage model, including the merits of using an integrative approach, provides guidelines for formulating a personal approach responsive to a multicultural society. This model suggests that counselors who utilize a central or core theory will have a solid foundation to approach the counseling process. This foundation will provide internal consistency for the counselor's approach.

Some of the potential challenges associated with multicultural counseling include a tendency for diagnostic and treatment bias. These concerns can be overcome when the counselor treats the client as a person first and a member of a particular culture second; sensitively relates to the special needs and circumstances of the client; and gains the necessary beliefs, knowledge, and skills associated with the populations the counselor intends to serve.

7 The Classic Theories of Freud, Adler, and Jung

CHAPTER OVERVIEW

This chapter provides a description of the three classic theories of Freud, Adler, and Jung. Highlights of the chapter include

- The art and science of the classic theories
- Background information regarding the three classic theories
- The theory of personality regarding the three classic theories
- The theory of counseling and psychotherapy regarding the three classic theories
- Contemporary issues for the classic theories
- Brief-counseling approaches for the classic theories
- Diversity issues for the classic theories

The Art and Science of the Classic Theories

The art of counseling owes much to the classic theories. Freud was one of the first clinicians to really listen to clients' stories through processes such as free association and dream analysis. It was a creative process that involved reaching into the clients' world and attempting to discover hidden or symbolic content that could be interpreted to the client. Adlerian psychology provides another dimension to the art of counseling. Adler referred to the center or nucleus of the person as the creative self, emphasizing the creative capacity to interact with the world in a manner that reflects each person's uniqueness. Jung's theory more than any other counseling theory may capture the spirit of the art of counseling. He was a very sensitive individual who would adapt his approach to meet the needs of his client. For example, Jung found that by mirroring the gestures of his psychotic clients he could attempt to understand what they were trying to communicate (Douglas, 1995). In addition, Jung frequently used different modalities within the creative arts, such as having a client draw an image from a dream to provide additional means for analysis (Douglas, 1995).

The classic theories also provide a strong foundation for the science of counseling. From a science perspective, these theories have played an integral role in the evolution of current psychotherapies. Some of the concepts generated by the classic theorists that are commonly used by clinicians include the conscious-unconscious continuum, defense mechanisms, the importance of early life experiences on personality development, the therapeutic alliance, lifestyle, and the relationship between wholeness and psychological balance to psychological growth and self-healing.

There has been a wide array of research endeavors directed at the classic theories. Henry, Strupp, Schacht, & Gaston (1994) have reviewed research on Freud's theory and found that current trends in research are directed at gaining a better understanding of transference relationships, interpretation, and the therapeutic alliance. Adlerian theoretical constructs continue to receive interest in the literature (for example, birth order, Sullivan & Schwebel, 1996; and lifestyle, Kern, Gfroerer et al., 1996). Current research trends in Jungian psychology include recognition of the importance of affect, feelings, and body awareness in the analytic process (Douglas, 1995).

As noted in Chapter 6, the art and science of counseling recommend using a multicultural perspective to conceptualize diversity issues throughout the counseling process. It is especially important to utilize a multicultural perspective with the classic theories, because some concepts may appear dated and out of step with contemporary values and beliefs. The art and science of the classic theories involve making the necessary modification to these theories by utilizing multicultural research findings and maintaining a sensitivity to the evolving needs of clients.

An Overview of Freud, Adler, and Jung

The classic psychological theories of Sigmund Freud, Alfred Adler, and Carl Jung laid the foundation for modern clinical practice. Their influence transcended psychology, making a significant impact on the arts, education, child-rearing practices, and numerous other aspects of daily living.

Freud's masterpiece *The Interpretation of Dreams,* which was published in 1900, caught the interest of Adler and Jung. Adler and Jung were colleagues of Freud who became central figures in the psychoanalytic organization. They eventually broke ranks with Freud when they believed he overemphasized the role of sexuality in personality development. Adler and Jung proceeded to develop their own psychological theories. The three distinct schools of psychology that evolved have a number of commonalities. Each emphasizes the importance of early life experiences on personality development and also views insight as an important prerequisite to change.

The Freudian, Adlerian, and Jungian schools of psychology can be considered the "classic schools," because each developed its own comprehensive theory of personality and approach to psychotherapy. They can be used as the central or core theory from which to develop an integrative counseling approach. Table 7.1 presents an overview of these three theories. This is followed by an overview of the three classic theories, each with background information on the theorist and information on his theory of personality and theory of counseling and psychotherapy. The chapter concludes by addressing diversity issues and brief-counseling perspectives of the classic theories.

TABLE 7.1   Freud, Adler, and Jung

Theory	Key Concepts	The Counseling Process	Techniques
Freud's psychoanalytic theory	Endopsychic conflicts resulting from the id, ego, and superego; defense mechanisms; the conscious–unconscious continuum; and the effects of traumatic experiences in childhood on personality development	Has the major aim of resolving intrapsychic conflicts to restructure the personality as necessary	Dream analysis and free association can be used to explore unconscious processes; confronting, clarification, and interpretation provide necessary insight
Adler's individual psychology	The creative self; behavior as goal directed and purposeful; social interest; striving for significance as a motivational force; and the family constellation	Is educationally oriented, provides information, guides and attempts to encourage discouraged clients	The lifestyle analysis as an assessment technique, motivation modification to modify underlying motivational forces, and techniques to reorient clients from basic mistakes
Jung's analytic psychology	The collective unconscious, archetypes, and personality types	Explores unconscious processes to help the self emerge so clients can be free to move toward self-realization	Analysis of the interrelationship of several dreams for their symbolic content and cues to the various systems of the personality

Freud's Psychoanalytic Theory

Background Information

Patterson (1986) describes some of the significant events of Freud's life. These observations have been incorporated into the following overview.

Sigmund Freud (1856–1939) was born in Freiberg, Moravia, a town in what is now Czechoslovakia. He was the oldest of eight children and moved with his family to Vienna when he was four.

Freud obtained a medical degree in 1881 from the University of Vienna. After graduation, he went to Paris to study with Charcot, who was known for his work with hypnosis in the treatment of hysteria. Freud then returned to Vienna and married Martha Bernays. They had six children; the youngest was Anna, who later became a distinguished child analyst.

In 1882, Freud began a private practice in medicine, initially specializing in nervous diseases. He later broadened his practice into what is known today as psychiatry. At this

Sigmund Freud

point in his career, Freud became interested in the "talking cure," which was being developed by the prominent Viennese physician, Joseph Breuer. Breuer believed that a client could be helped by simply talking about his problem. This concept contributed to Freud's free association technique and is an important part of the evolution of the counseling profession.

The most creative period in Freud's life was also a period during which he experienced serious emotional problems. He was tormented by psychosomatic disorders and phobias such as an exaggerated fear of dying. At one point he was even afraid to cross the street. During this time Freud engaged in extensive self-analysis by studying his dreams. The insights Freud gained from his self-analysis became very influential in the development of his own theories such as the Oedipus complex. He remembered that as a child he felt hostility toward his father, whom he perceived as an overbearing authority figure. On the other hand, Freud had sexual feelings for his mother, whom he remembered to be loving, attractive, and protective.

Freud's rise to prominence required perseverance and an ability to withstand severe criticism. As he developed his revolutionary theory, he was initially met with scorn and ridicule from all corners of the academic and scientific community. Alone, he forged on, typically working for 18 hours a day. Finally, with his publication of *The Interpretation of Dreams* in 1900, he became "respectable" again. Shortly thereafter, Freud was welcomed back to the intellectual community and regarded with great esteem.

In his later years, Freud's struggles turned to his personal health. His fondness for cigars apparently contributed to the development of jaw cancer. During the last 20 years of his life, he was in almost constant pain and underwent 33 operations. Somehow, he still managed to maintain an active professional life. Hall and Lindzey (1978) note that Freud was a prolific writer, with his collective works filling 24 volumes. His work also stands out from a literary point of view. Freud's eloquent writing style did much to popularize his ideas.

Theory of Personality

Freud's theory of personality was well developed, providing information on how behavior manifests itself in terms of the id, ego, and superego; the unconscious-conscious continuum; defense mechanisms; and other useful psychological constructs.

View of Human Nature.   Freud had a deterministic view of human nature. He was convinced that behavior was determined by unconscious biological urges of sex and aggression and psychosexual experiences during the first six years of life.

Key Concepts.   Freud's theory of personality is characterized by several key concepts (Strachey, 1953–1974). Some of these are the structure of the personality, endopsychic conflicts, defense mechanisms, the conscious-unconscious continuum, and psychosexual stages of development. These concepts, as described by Freud (Strachey, 1953–1974), are incorporated into the following overview.

The Structure of the Personality.   In Freud's view, the personality is made up of three autonomous yet interdependent systems: the id, ego, and superego.

The *id* is the original system of the personality from which the ego and superego emerge (Hall & Lindzey, 1978). It is the reservoir of psychic energy, supplying energy to the other two systems. The id can be considered the "hedonistic branch" of the personality (Hall, 1954). It is driven by the pleasure principle, which attempts to reduce tension by gratification of sexual and aggressive impulses.

The *superego* is the other extreme of the personality. It can be considered the "judicial branch" and is concerned with moralistic issues determining what is right or wrong (Hall, 1954). It represents the values and ideals of society as handed down from parent to child. The superego has three purposes: to inhibit the impulses from the id, to alter the ego's orientation from realistic to moralistic, and to encourage the personality to strive for perfection.

The *ego* can be considered the "executive branch" of the personality (Hall, 1954). It is ruled by the reality principle, which attempts to exert a realistic, reality-based influence over the id and superego.

Endopsychic Conflicts.   An *endopsychic* conflict is a conflict within (from *endo*) the psyche. Endopsychic conflicts result from the interaction of the three parts of the personality: the id, ego, and superego. According to Freud, there is only so much "psychic energy" for the three parts of the personality to function. All three systems are therefore in constant competition for this energy to take control and dominate the personality. As the three parts of the personality compete for psychic energy, they create conflicts within the psyche, called *endopsychic conflicts*. These conflicts create anxiety, which the organism can attempt to alleviate by creating defense mechanisms.

Endopsychic conflicts always involve the ego and the id or superego (or both the id and superego). Several possible examples of endopsychic conflicts are

- *Id versus ego:* (Id:) "I want to rape or murder." (Ego:) "If you do, you will go to jail."
- *Id versus superego and ego:* (Id:) "I want to rape or murder." (Superego:) "You shouldn't because it is wrong" and (Ego:) "You will go to jail."
- *Ego versus superego:* (Ego:) "I would like to go to bed with my lover." (Superego:) "Don't do it, because it is a sin to have sex unless you are married."

Defense Mechanisms.   Freud's concept of defense mechanisms was one of his most important theoretical achievements. Defense mechanisms develop unconsciously when the ego feels threatened by an endopsychic conflict. When this occurs, defense mechanisms can be utilized to deny, falsify, or distort reality so the ego can cope. The role of the counselor can therefore be to help strengthen the client's ego to minimize stress from endopsychic conflicts and the resulting defense mechanisms. This process of strengthening can involve psychoeducational interventions that provide clients with information they can use to take a more realistic position regarding stresses in their environment.

Some of the more common defense mechanisms are projection, reaction formation, fixation, regression, and repression.

Projection is an attempt to attribute to another person one's own thoughts or feelings. For example, instead of saying you hate someone, you say, "That person hates me." In this example, projection occurs because the ego is threatened by aggressive id impulses. Projection can therefore be seen as an attempt to "externalize the danger."

Reaction formation is a way of coping by creating an extreme emotional response that is the opposite of how one actually feels. This results in a "falsification of reality." For example, a man may hate his wife and want a divorce. At the same time, he may have intense feelings of guilt, since he believes divorce is morally wrong. If the man tells others how wonderful his wife is and how much he loves her, a reaction formation may be operating.

Fixation can occur if the demands of life become too threatening. In an attempt to avoid new responsibilities, a person can avoid growing up and fixate, or stand still, in terms of development. When this occurs during adolescence, the individual's personality would remain like an adolescent for the remainder of life.

Regression is an attempt to cope by moving back to a point in one's development that was less threatening. For example, a person who has a major business failure may feel life is falling apart. In an attempt to cope, the person may try to escape these feelings of failure by moving back to a point in time that was not so threatening. When this occurs, the person may assume the role of a child to avoid adult responsibilities.

Repression is an attempt to cope by creating an avoidance response. In repression, the stressful situation is pushed from the conscious to the unconscious dimension of the mind.

The Conscious-Unconscious Continuum.   Freud was one of the first to explore the unconscious dimension of the human psyche. He believed it held the key to understanding behavior and problems within the personality. It is therefore not surprising that the majority of the techniques associated with psychoanalysis are used to explore unconscious processes (for example, free association and dream analysis).

Freud conceptualized conscious and unconscious processes in terms of a continuum. The analogy of the iceberg can be used to understand this continuum, as illustrated in Figure 7.1.

As shown in Figure 7.1, most of the psyche involves unconscious processes. The *conscious* dimension contains material that the person is aware of and can readily retrieve. The *preconscious* relates to material that the person is almost consciously aware of but that is just out of mental awareness (for example, almost being able to remember a person's name). The *unconscious proper* includes all memory traces that the person is not consciously aware of (for example, a repressed traumatic experience such as childhood incest).

Psychosexual States of Development.   Freud contended that personality development was determined to a large degree by early life experiences. His theory suggests that problems in the personality can result if the child has a traumatic experience or the child's basic needs

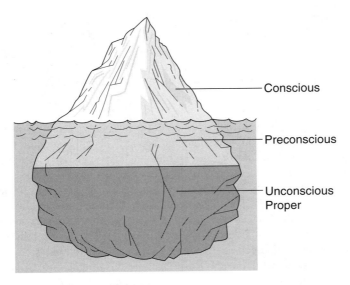

FIGURE 7.1   Iceberg Analogy

are not met. When this occurs, the person could attempt to achieve indirect gratification by displacement or sublimation to restore equilibrium to the organism. Displacement is indirect gratification, such as a baby sucking a thumb when not allowed to eat. Sublimation is also indirect gratification, but it results in some form of social recognition. An example of sublimation is a sexually frustrated person creating a beautiful, sensuous painting.

Freud was one of the first theorists to identify stages of development that a person progresses through. He called them psychosexual stages, emphasizing the role of sexuality in the developmental process. Freud divided these stages into three periods: the pregenital period, which lasts until age six; the latency period, which spans from age six to adolescence; and the genital period, which continues for the rest of a person's life.

The pregenital period is composed of the oral, anal, and phallic stages and the latency period. Freud believed that the *oral stage* occurs during the first 18 months of life. It is called the oral stage because the child appears preoccupied with oral functions (for example, sucking the mother's breast and exploring objects by putting them into the mouth). Problems that occur during the oral stage (such as extreme frustration of oral gratification) could result in the individual developing an oral personality as an adult. Adult nail-biting could be an example of displacement of latent oral needs. Becoming a teacher or orator could result from sublimation of oral needs.

The *anal stage* occurs from eighteen months to three years of age. This stage emphasizes the impact of toilet training on personality development. Problems that can occur during the anal stage may result in an anal-explosive or anal-retentive personality. The anal-explosive personality is an aggressive type of person. This style of personality could result when a child went to the toilet all the time as a means of keeping a parent's attention. The anal-explosive personality could develop skills in football or boxing as a form of sublimation. An anal-retentive personality could occur if a parent used severe punishment when the child had an "accident." Out of fear, the child could develop a pattern of not going to the toilet. An example of sublimation for the anal-retentive personality could be a person who is good at saving money.

The *phallic stage* occurs between the ages of three and six. According to Freud, it is a time when male children become sexually interested in their mothers (the Oedipus complex), and female children become attracted to their fathers (the Electra complex). The boy eventually resolves his Oedipus complex out of fear of castration from his father. Problems could occur if a father had jealous tendencies and threatened to hurt his son if the boy did not stop "pestering mother." This threat could intensify the boy's fear of castration. According to Freud, this fear could then inhibit any future thoughts of the opposite sex, promoting homosexual tendencies.

Unlike the male child, the female does not have a dramatic means of resolving her Electra complex, such as fear of castration. Instead, she may resolve her sexual feelings by reacting to the realistic barriers that are established to prohibit incestuous relationships. A problem could result during this stage if a child felt emotionally rejected by her father, possibly causing her to avoid relationships with males in the future. On the other hand, if an incestuous relationship were allowed to occur, the child could experience even more profound difficulties in her personality, such as low self-image and perhaps promiscuity.

The *latency period,* which occurs between the ages of six and twelve, is a period of relative calm. The child has emerged from the turbulence of the pregenital period with the basic structure of the personality largely formed. During this period, the child develops new interests to replace infantile sexual impulses. Socialization takes place as the child moves from a narcissistic preoccupation to a more altruistic orientation. Problems could occur during this period if the parents did not encourage the child's interest in establishing positive social relationships. As a result, the child might not be able to develop the social skills necessary for successful interpersonal relationships.

The *genital period* begins at puberty and continues for the rest of life. The focus of this period is an opposite-sex relationship leading to the experience of intimacy. Problems during this period could occur for an individual who was discouraged from socializing or began sexual relationships before being emotionally ready to handle them.

Theory of Counseling and Psychotherapy

Freud's approach to counseling and psychotherapy is called *psychoanalysis,* emphasizing the analysis of the mind. It is a time-consuming approach that can typically involve 4 one-hour sessions each week over a period of several years (Arlow, 1995).

The major aim of psychoanalysis is to restructure the personality by resolution of intrapsychic conflicts. The actual process of traditional psychoanalysis involves the patient lying on a couch and engaging in free association, saying whatever comes to mind. In this process, the analyst is seated out of the patient's view behind the couch and listens and reacts in a noncritical manner. Arlow (1995) describes four phases of psychoanalysis: the opening phase, the development of transference, working through, and the resolution of transference.

The Opening Phase.   The analyst obtains important history from the patient. Gradually, over a period of three to six months, the analyst obtains a broad understanding of the patient's unconscious conflicts.

The Development of Transference.   During this phase, the patient begins to experience a transference relationship with the analyst. This involves projecting thoughts and feelings onto the analyst that are associated with significant others such as a father or mother. Transference is encouraged during psychoanalysis. It plays a key role in bringing unresolved conflicts (which typically originated in childhood) to the surface, so they can be worked through and resolved within the safety and support of the therapeutic relationship.

Analysis of the transference is a cornerstone of the psychoanalytic process. It provides the patient with insight into how past relationships and experiences are creating problems in present relationships. Analysis of transference also helps the patient learn how to use insight to have appropriate, mature decisions regarding current relationships.

Countertransference may also occur in therapy and results when analysts unconsciously begin to see qualities in the client that remind them of someone from their past. Countertransference can interfere with the analyst's objectivity and destroy the therapeutic process. When this occurs, the analyst may need psychoanalysis to work through these tendencies.

Working Through.   This phase is essentially a continuation of the previous phase. It involves additional analysis of transference aimed at generating more profound insights and consolidating what can be learned from them.

Resolution of Transference.   During the final phase of therapy, the analyst and patient work toward termination. This can involve working through resistance from the patient regarding termination or preparing the patient to function independently once termination is complete.

Techniques

Freud developed many techniques that could be used in psychoanalysis (Strachey, 1953–1974). Their primary purpose is to make the unconscious conscious. Some of the more commonly used techniques are as follows.

- *Free association* is the primary technique used in psychoanalysis. As discussed earlier, it is used throughout the counseling process. Free association encourages the patient to discuss whatever comes to mind, thereby overcoming the patient's tendencies to suppress or censor information.
- *Dream analysis* is a technique Freud developed as a means to explore unconscious processes. He suggested that elements of dreams contained symbolic meaning, such as a screwdriver being a phallic symbol, representing a penis.
- *Confrontation and clarification* are feedback procedures to help the patient become aware of what is occurring and in need of further analysis (Prochaska, 1984).
- *Interpretation* involves providing insight to the patient regarding inner conflicts reflected in resistance, transference, and other processes.

Contemporary Issues

Contemporary Freudian psychology reflects several changes and modifications from Freud's original theory. These changes evolved primarily in response to what was considered to be his overemphasis on the role of sexuality in personality development and the excessive time required to complete psychoanalysis.

Strupp (1992) describes several recent trends in psychoanalysis. These are summarized as follows.

1. The role of the therapist will shift from the detached-impersonal classical Freudian position to the more humanistic interactive model associated with the therapeutic alliance.
2. The role of the Oedipus complex in psychopathology will be deemphasized, with earlier developmental periods playing a more central role in psychological dysfunction.
3. Treatment considerations will shift from neurotic conditions such as obsessive compulsive disorders and phobias to the treatment of personality disorders.
4. Transference and countertransference are being reconceptualized in terms of interpersonal theory, which emphasizes the dyadic quality of the counseling relationship. Within this context, the therapist and client will continually contribute to transference and countertransference processes as a natural outcome of their ongoing relationship. Thus negative connotations of transference and countertransference are being replaced by a more robust and positive view of how the counseling relationship can provide opportunities for insights and analysis.

Strupp (1992) identifies several additional trends in psychoanalysis. They include a recognition of the importance of interpersonal relations in psychological health, a reassessment of the role of the ego in psychological functioning, and the movement toward time-limited psychoanalysis.

The Interpersonal Perspective. The interpersonal perspective contends that psychoanalytic theory overemphasizes intrapsychic forces (such as inner conflicts over sexuality) and does not recognize the importance of environmental forces (such as the quality of interpersonal relationships). Interpersonal psychotherapy is an emerging form of psychotherapy based on the work of Harry Stack Sullivan (1953) and his collaborators (for example, Adolph Meyer, 1957, and John Bolby, 1973). This approach recognizes the effect of early life experiences (such as the degree of parent-child attachment) on the quality of interpersonal relationships later in life and the role that interpersonal functioning plays in depression (Prochaska & Norcross, 1994). Interpersonal psychotherapy is a time-limited approach that focuses on enhancing social skills and improving interpersonal relationships (Prochaska & Norcross, 1994).

Chapter 9 provides additional information on interpersonal psychotherapy, with transactional analysis featured as an example of this school of counseling and psychotherapy.

Ego-Analytic Theory. The ego-analytic position incorporates theories associated with ego psychology and object-relations theory. Ego psychology is associated with the work of

Erikson (1950) and Rapaport (1958) and represents a shift in focus from the id to the ego as the primary driving force of personality (Prochaska & Norcross, 1994). In this new role, the ego is viewed as capable of functioning independently from the id in its attempt to adapt to reality and master the environment (Prochaska & Norcross, 1994).

Object-relations theory, as proposed by Kernberg (1976) and Kohut (1971), emphasizes the self and objects (people) as the primary organizing force in personality functioning (Prochaska & Norcross, 1994). Object relations are intrapsychic structures based on the mental representations of the self and others (Prochaska & Norcross, 1994).

Baker (1985) identifies the following six characteristics of the ego-analytic position.

1. Noninstinctual factors are emphasized.
2. The ego is conceptualized as a separate autonomous structure that operates independently of the id.
3. The function of the ego has been expanded to include the role of adaptation to the environment by developing coping and mastery skills.
4. Psychosocial and interpersonal variables are emphasized over biological-instinctual variables.
5. Developmental stages that occur after puberty are considered as important as those occurring before puberty.
6. Psychopathology occurs as a result of not meeting the needs associated with developmental tasks and other forces that could cause defects in the personality structure of the individual.

Freudian Brief Approaches to Counseling

With the emergence of managed care, long-term open-ended psychoanalysis is a luxury that few individuals and insurance companies can afford (Strupp, 1992). There will therefore be increasing pressure for all forms of psychotherapy (including psychoanalysis) to be directed toward the treatment of specific mental disorders within the context of a limited number of sessions (Strupp, 1992). Brief psychodynamic psychotherapy evolved as an alternative to classic psychoanalysis. Among the brief psychodynamic approaches are Malan's (1976, 1980) focal therapy, Mann's (1973, 1981) time-limited psychotherapy, Sifneos's (1979, 1984) short-term dynamic psychotherapy, and Davanloo's (1978, 1984) short-term dynamic psychotherapy. Garske and Molteni (1985) note that all brief psychodynamic approaches share several characteristics. The approaches are all based on psychoanalytic theory, suggest similar efficacy, and modify psychoanalytic procedures for use in a briefer format.

The aim of brief psychodynamic psychotherapy is to go beyond symptom relief and bring out necessary changes in the client's personality (Garske & Molteni, 1985). The number of sessions required in brief psychodynamic psychotherapy tends to be limited to 12 and depends on the nature of the client's problem and the type of therapy utilized (Garske & Molteni, 1985). Mann's (1973) time-limited model has a duration of between 1 and 12 sessions. Davanloo's (1978, 1984) short-term dynamic approach varies the number of recommended sessions from 2 to 5 sessions, 6 to 15 sessions, 16 to 25 sessions, or 26 to 40 sessions depending on the nature of the client's problem.

Garske and Molteni (1985) identify the following six factors seen to promote change in brief psychodynamic psychotherapy.

1. A contract is established with the client, which includes a description of the client's problems in psychoanalytic terms.
2. A statement of goals and objectives is established, along with a time limit on the number of sessions.
3. The therapist takes an active, probing approach, clarifying and confronting the client's resistance.
4. The therapist interprets the links between the client's current problems, relationship with the therapists and significant others, and past conflicts.
5. The time-limited aspect of therapy arouses issues relating to separation and individualization within the client.
6. The termination phase of therapy is characterized by working through problems associated with separation and individualization.

Research efforts have attempted to determine what factors contribute to efficacy of brief psychodynamic psychotherapy. Nergaard and Silberschatz (1989) found that high measures of shame and guilt (especially guilt), as measured by the Therapy Shame and Guilt Scale, correlated with positive therapy outcomes. Mills, Bauer, and Miars (1989) note that transference reactions should be addressed quickly and energetically by the therapist to maximize their impact.

Goldfried, Greenberg, and Mormar (1990) review the literature on brief psychodynamic psychotherapy. They note the approach has been effective for treating stress and bereavement disorders (Mormar & Horowitz, 1988); late-life depression (Thompson, Gallagher, & Breckenridge, 1987); and adjustment, affective, and personality disorders (Marziali, 1984). In addition, Barth et al. (1988) evaluated 34 short-term dynamic psychotherapy cases. They found significant gains in symptom relief, adaptive functioning, and personality change at termination and over a 2-year follow-up period.

Summary and Evaluation

Sigmund Freud's place in history is secure. He is widely regarded as one of the most prominent intellectual figures of all time. His contributions to psychology and other fields are phenomenal. His most remarkable achievements include the concept of defense mechanisms as a means for coping with anxiety, the mapping of the conscious-unconscious continuum, and his methods for exploring unconscious processes in psychoanalysis. Weaknesses of Freud's theory are what has been considered his overemphasis of the role of sexuality in personality development and the excessive length of time required to achieve the aims of psychoanalysis. New advances in Freudian theory as reflected in the ego-analytic position and in brief psychodynamic psychotherapy are attempts to overcome these problems.

Adler's Individual Psychology

Background information

Alfred Adler (1870–1937) received a medical degree from the University of Vienna in 1895. In 1902, he began what was to develop into a rather stormy relationship with Sigmund Freud. Adler quickly took an active role in Freud's psychoanalytic society and was elected as its president in 1910. He and Freud cofounded and became coeditors of the *Journal of Psychoanalysis*. Shortly thereafter, Adler broke ranks with Freud over several important theoretical issues. These differences culminated in Adler's resigning from his positions as president of the society and coeditor of the journal. At this point, Adler disassociated himself from the Freudian circle and founded his own school, which he called *individual psychology.*

After serving as a medical officer during World War I, Adler returned to practice medicine in Vienna. In 1922, he turned his attention to the problems of children and established a child guidance clinic in the Vienna public schools (Dinkmeyer & Dinkmeyer, 1985). Eventually more than 50 similar guidance clinics were opened before political turmoil restricted the growth of Adlerian psychology in Europe (Dinkmeyer & Dinkmeyer, 1985). By 1935, political unrest forced Adler to flee Europe, and he settled in the United States. Adler died two years later while on a lecture tour in Aberdeen, Scotland.

Adler maintained a busy schedule throughout his career. He was particularly known for his extensive lecture tours, during which he would often work with a client in front of an audience. This was revolutionary at the time, because therapy was not practiced with such openness (Dinkmeyer & Dinkmeyer, 1985). Today, Adlerians continue the tradition of demonstrating counseling strategies in front of live audiences.

Adler was a prolific writer, publishing more than 100 books and articles during his lifetime. *The Practice and Theory of Individual Psychology* (Adler, 1969) is an excellent introduction to Adlerian psychology.

Alfred Adler

Theory of Personality

Adler's theory of personality is a comprehensive in-depth analysis of how people function. It emphasizes the importance of early life experiences within the family of origin, or as Adler referred to it, the family constellation. From this perspective, factors such as birth order, sibling rivalry, and social interest played important roles in the formulation and functioning of the personality.

View of Human Nature.   Adler held an optimistic view of people. He believed people were basically positive, with the capability of self-determination. This view of human nature stimulated the development of the humanistic movement in psychology, which focuses on the dignity and worth of the individual. Adler also emphasized that behavior is holistic, or interrelated; teleological, in that it has a purpose and is directed toward a goal; and phenomenological, because it can best be understood from the client's frame of reference.

Key Concepts.   Adler (1969) and Ansbacher and Ansbacher (1956, 1964) have described a number of key concepts that make up the structure of Adler's theory of personality. The following 10 principles are central to this theory.

The Creative Self.   This concept was Adler's "crowning achievement as a personality theorist" (Hall & Lindzey, 1978. p. 165). It lies at the heart of Adlerian theory of personality. The creative self is the center or nucleus from which all life movement generates (Ansbacher & Ansbacher, 1956). Freud called this center the ego. For Adler, the creative self emphasized that each person has the potential to creatively interact with the world. Adler expressed the potential for self-determined behavior when he said:

> . . . the important thing is not what one is born with, but what use one makes of that equipment . . . To understand this we find it is necessary to assume the existence of still another force, the creative power of the individual. (Ansbacher & Ansbacher, 1964, pp. 86–87)

The Concept of Teleological Movement.   Adler saw all behavior in terms of movement: nothing was static. This movement is teleological in nature since it has a purpose and is directed toward a goal. According to Adler, a person can move on the useful or useless side of life. Movement on the useful side is characterized by cooperative efforts, whereas movement on the useless side is narcissistic in nature (Ansbacher & Ansbacher, 1956).

Adler also believed that life movement was from a sensed minus to a sensed plus. According to their private logic, individuals will behave in a manner that appears to improve their position (Ansbacher & Ansbacher, 1956). This concept can be useful to understand the motivation behind misbehavior. For example, a child may move toward a goal of power to gain recognition. In this instance, the private logic may be, "I can be somebody if I fight with others."

Behavior Can Be Understood from an Interpersonal Perspective.   Adler emphasized that behavior can best be understood from an interpersonal perspective (Ansbacher & Ansbacher, 1956). This spirit was captured by the poet John Donne (1952) when he said, "No man is an island" (p. 441). Adler believed that people do not behave in isolation from others but in relation to others. This reasoning can be used to identify goals of misbehavior. For example, parents can develop a tentative hypothesis by asking themselves how they feel when their child misbehaves. Feeling annoyed could indicate their child has a goal of attention; feeling angry or threatened could suggest a goal of power; feeling hurt could indicate a goal of revenge; and feeling desperate or hopeless could suggest a goal of a display of inadequacy (Dinkmeyer & McKay, 1989; Dreikurs & Soltz, 1964).

The Psychology of Use.   Adler stressed that all behavior has a use or payoff that is usually unconscious in nature (Ansbacher & Ansbacher, 1956). Emotions serve a use in helping propel a person toward a goal. This concept can also be used to understand the symptoms associated with psychopathology, as the following *Personal Note* illustrates.

A Personal Note

Don was a 22-year-old assistant accountant. One day while he was working, his hand became numb and he was unable to move it. Don was taken to a hospital where I was the staff psychologist. The patient received a complete medical evaluation, including numerous neurological tests. After the doctors decided there was nothing physically wrong with the patient's hand, they referred him to me. When I asked Don how he liked his work, he said he hated it, largely because he wanted to go to medical school. After some additional assessment, I decided to hypnotize him. I told him he was a doctor and asked him to take my blood pressure. At this point, he was able to move his hand.

The psychology of use was quite apparent in this case, since the patient's inability to move his hand could help him avoid a job he hated. It is important to point out that Don wasn't consciously aware of trying to avoid his job. He was actually relieved to discover there was nothing physically wrong with his hand.

Together, we decided that Don would try to go back to college, so he could be doing something he wanted to do. With this in mind, I spent the next few sessions helping him apply for admission into college. It is interesting to note that Don could not voluntarily move his hand until he received a letter of acceptance from the college.

Don's disorder is known in the literature as a *conversion disorder.* It involves losing a bodily function such as the use of a hand or sight due to psychological, not physical, reasons. As illustrated in this case, the disorder can also be understood in terms of the psychology of use.

A Phenomenological Psychology.   The phenomenological perspective provides an understanding of clients from their internal frame of reference. Adler suggested that what individuals perceive is biased according to past experiences (Ansbacher & Ansbacher, 1964). He referred to this phenomenon as an *apperception.* A phenomenological perspective is therefore necessary to understand clients' interpretations of their experiences.

Emphasis on Social Interest.   Adler's term *Gemeinschaftsgefühl* has been translated into English as social interest (Ansbacher & Ansbacher, 1964). It refers to an inborn tendency to cooperate and work with others for the common good (Ansbacher & Ansbacher, 1964). Adler related this concept to mental health when he observed that social interest is the barometer of mental health (Ansbacher & Ansbacher, 1964). Glasser (1965) supports this position when he suggests that all people need love and affection to be fulfilled. Social interest is considered a major motivational force in Adlerian psychology.

The Life Style. Hall and Lindzey (1978) suggest that lifestyle became the recurrent theme in Adler's later writings and the most distinctive feature of his psychology. "The term *life style* refers to the person's basic orientation to life—the set of patterns of recurrent themes that run through his or her existence" (Dinkmeyer & Dinkmeyer, 1985, p. 123). According to Adler, the lifestyle is relatively fixed by age four or five. Once established, the individual's lifestyle guides the assimilation and utilization of future experiences (Hall and Lindzey, 1978).

A Holistic Psychology. Adler's individual psychology means the individual is indivisible and undivided. It is therefore a holistic psychology, which attempts to understand the overall lifestyle as a unified whole. Adlerians are interested in assessing how the person organizes the self as a whole person with interrelated and coherent beliefs, perceptions, and goals (Dinkmeyer & Dinkmeyer, 1985). This position is similar to the holistic health concept, which views the mind and body as an interacting system, not as separate entities.

Striving for Significance. Adler believed that people have a basic tendency to avoid feelings of inferiority by striving for superiority (Ansbacher & Ansbacher, 1956). A person could therefore compensate for feelings of inadequacy in one area by excelling in another aspect of life. In this example, striving for superiority should not be viewed as an attempt to feel superior over others. Instead, it amounts to a striving for significance and worth as an individual and is a major motivational force (Dinkmeyer & Dinkmeyer, 1985).

The Family Constellation. The family constellation encompasses many factors associated with a person's family of origin, such as birth order, family size, and the relationship between family members. Adler believed that each person's family constellation was unique and could therefore make a significant impact on the development of the lifestyle. Adler was particularly interested in birth order and how it would affect a person's development (Ansbacher & Ansbacher, 1956). For example, first-born children tend to be bossy and talkative, since they are used to telling their brothers and sisters what to do. They also tend to be conservative, since they are born into a world of adults and therefore tend to affiliate with adults and adult values.

With the arrival of a second child, first-born children can feel temporarily dethroned, since they have to share their parent's attention. This can cause them to be suspicious and tend to protect themselves from sudden reversals of fortune. Middle-born children tend to be very ambitious as they attempt to compete with the oldest. This can result in the "race-course syndrome," which can foster an achievement orientation in middle-born children. It can also promote sibling rivalry or competition between siblings, which is another Adlerian principle. In addition, middle-born children can grow up having difficulty feeling a sense of belonging, since they don't have the special place of being the oldest or youngest. They also tend to be observers and mediators interested in what is going on between the siblings and willing to mediate when a conflict occurs.

The youngest child of the family is the "baby." Parents tend to be more lenient and give special favors to the baby. Youngest children usually appreciate these special considerations and learn early in life that other people will take care of them and protect them from life's difficulties.

Dinkmeyer and Dinkmeyer (1985) note that birth-order characteristics are only tendencies, which may or may not occur. Whether they manifest themselves depends on how parents relate to a child and how children interpret their ordinal position. When a person does not have the typical characteristics of a particular birth order, it can be interesting to determine what familial factors could account for the differences. For example, a middle-born female with three brothers and no sisters will usually not lack a sense of belonging, because she feels special as the only girl. A middle-born male may act like a first-born child as a result of the first-born being disowned from the family because of doing something extreme, such as committing murder.

Theory of Counseling and Psychotherapy

Adlerian counseling and psychotherapy stresses the role of cognition in psychological functioning. It begins by using the lifestyle analysis to gain an understanding of the client. Through various techniques and procedures such as encouragement and acting as-if, clients are helped to reorient themselves toward more positive ways of functioning.

Adlerians attempt to go beyond overt behavior and understand the motivation behind the behavior (Nystul, 1985). This approach is therefore more concerned with modifying motivation than with modifying behavior. Sonstegard, Hagerman, and Bitter (1975) elaborated on this position when they said:

> The Adlerian counselor is not preoccupied with changing behavior, rather he is concerned with understanding the individual's subjective frame of reference and the identification of the individual's mistaken notion or goal within that framework. Indeed, the behavior of an individual is only understood when the goals are identified . . . (p. 17)

Mosak (1995) summarizes the major goals of Adlerian psychotherapy as

- Increasing clients' social interest
- Helping clients overcome feelings of discouragement and reducing inferiority feelings
- Modifying clients' views and goals and changing their life scripts
- Changing faulty motivation
- Helping clients feel a sense of equality with others
- Assisting clients to become contributing members of society

The counseling process is educationally oriented, providing information, guiding, and attempting to encourage discouraged clients. The approach attempts to reeducate clients, so they can live in society as equals, both giving and receiving from others (Mosak, 1995).

The counseling relationship is based on equality. Adlerians avoid placing the client in a subservient position as in a doctor-patient relationship. They consider a sense of mutual respect to be vital to all relationships, including the counseling relationship.

Dinkmeyer and Dinkmeyer (1985) identify four phases of Adlerian psychotherapy: establishing the relationship, performing analysis and assessment, promoting insight, and reorientation. The authors observe that these phases are not intended to be separate or distinct processes but instead tend to overlap and blend in clinical practice. This can be especially true in the process of establishing a positive relationship. Adlerians believe it is important to maintain a positive relationship throughout the counseling process.

Techniques

Adlerian techniques can be described in terms of the four phases of Adlerian psychotherapy.

Phase One: Establishing the Relationship. Adlerians utilize many techniques to establish a positive relationship. Three of these techniques are

1. *Use of listening skills.* Dinkmeyer, Dinkmeyer, and Sperry (1987) note that effective listening skills are necessary to promote mutual trust and mutual respect—two essential elements of the Adlerian counseling relationship.
2. *Winning respect and offering hope.* Nystul (1985) suggests that a counselor can increase the client's motivation for becoming involved in counseling by winning the client's respect and offering hope.
3. *Encouragement.* Encouragement communicates a sense of support and can also help clients learn to believe in themselves. Dinkmeyer and Losoncy (1980) identify important skills that are involved in the encouragement process. Some of these skills are focusing on the client's assets; communicating respect and confidence; being enthusiastic; helping the client become aware of choices; combating self-defeating, discouraging processes; and promoting self-encouragement.

Phase Two: Performing Analysis and Assessment. Adlerians typically do an in-depth analysis and assessment as early as the first session. This usually involves conducting a lifestyle analysis to explore how early life experiences can contribute to the adult personality.

Dream analysis can be a part of the lifestyle analysis (Mosak, 1995). Adlerians do not attempt to analyze dreams in terms of their symbolic content, as do Freudians. Instead, they see dreams as an attempt to deal with the difficulties and challenges of life. In this sense, dreams become a problem-solving activity, allowing the person a chance to rehearse for some future action (Mosak, 1995).

The lifestyle analysis can also be used to identify the client's strengths or assets that can be used to overcome the client's problems. It can also be used to identify faulty or irrational views that may interfere with the client's growth. These are referred to as *basic mistakes,* and the following descriptions of these statements by Mosak (1995) are listed with examples.

- *Overgeneralizations:* "People can't be trusted."
- *False or impossible goals of security:* "I must please everybody."
- *Misrepresentations of life and life's demands:* "I never get any breaks."
- *Minimization or denial of one's worth:* "I'm dumb."
- *Faulty values:* "It doesn't matter how you play the game as long as you win."

Phase Three: Promoting Insight.   Adlerians believe that insight is an important prerequisite to long-term change. Insight allows clients to understand the dynamics of self-defeating patterns so they can be corrected during the reorientation process. The main tool for providing insight is interpretation, which focuses on creating awareness of basic mistakes that are impeding the client's growth.

Counselors can use confrontation techniques during the insight process if they encounter resistance from clients. Shulman (1973) notes that confrontation can challenge a client to make an immediate response or change or examine some issue. It can also foster immediacy in the relationship by enabling a client to know how the therapist is experiencing the client at the moment (Dinkmeyer & Dinkmeyer, 1985).

Phase Four: Reorientation.   The final phase of Adlerian psychotherapy involves putting insight into action. Clients are encouraged to make the necessary changes in their life as they develop more functional beliefs and behaviors. Counselors can use the following techniques during the reorientation phase.

1. *Spitting in the client's soup.* This technique can be used when clients engage in manipulative games such as acting like a martyr. Spitting in their soup involves determining the payoff of the game and interpreting it to the client. For instance, a client may say, "My husband is such a drunk. I don't know why I put up with him." The counselor could respond by saying, "You must get a lot of sympathy from others, because you have to put up with so much." As this client realizes that someone is aware of the payoffs she is receiving from her martyr syndrome, the game may seem less enjoyable.

2. *The push-button technique.* This technique is based on Ellis's (1962) rational emotive therapy. It involves having clients concentrate on pleasant and unpleasant experiences and the feelings they generate (Dinkmeyer & Dinkmeyer, 1985). When clients discover that their thoughts influence their emotions, they recognize that they can take control of their emotional responses. The push-button concept symbolizes the amount of control clients can exert when they "push the button" and put a stop to self-defeating processes. They can then create a constructive way of reacting to their situation, producing a more positive emotional response.

3. *Catching oneself.* Clients can use this technique to avoid old self-defeating patterns. Initially, clients may catch themselves in the process of self-defeating behavior, such as playing a manipulative game. Eventually, they can catch themselves just before they start playing the game. Clients can be encouraged to use humor when they catch themselves, learning to laugh at how ridiculous their self-defeating tendencies are.

4. *Acting as-if.* This technique involves clients acting as if they could do whatever they would like to do, such as being more confident or being a better listener. The technique promotes a positive "can-do" spirit and a self-fulfilling prophecy, which can help clients experience success.

5. *Task setting and commitment.* Adlerians do not believe that change occurs by osmosis. They believe instead that it takes work and effort to change. Task setting and commitment are therefore essential aspects of Adlerian psychotherapy. Homework assignments can be useful in this regard by providing a structure through which clients can try out new modes of behaving.

Contemporary Issues

Many contemporary Adlerian concepts derive from the work of Rudolph Dreikurs (1897–1972). Dreikurs was a student of Adler's. In 1939, just two years after Adler's death, Dreikurs moved to Chicago and established the Alfred Adler Institute of Chicago (Dinkmeyer & Dinkmeyer, 1985). In many ways, he picked up where Adler left off (Dinkmeyer & Dinkmeyer, 1985). He continued the development of Adlerian theory, especially in terms of parent education and child guidance. Dreikurs had a gift for taking Adler's writings and reworking them into concepts that are easy to understand and apply. In addition, he developed his own concepts based on Adlerian principles, such as the four goals of misbehavior (Dreikurs, 1949; Dreikurs & Soltz, 1964), encouragement (Dinkmeyer & Dreikurs, 1963), logical and natural consequences (Dreikurs & Soltz, 1964), and social equality (Dreikurs, 1971). Dreikurs maintained an active lecture tour during which he would demonstrate his approach. He is credited with having a great deal to do with the popularization and acceptance of Adlerian psychology as a major school of counseling and psychotherapy (Dinkmeyer & Dinkmeyer, 1985).

Don Dinkmeyer is another key individual in the evolution of Adlerian psychology. Dinkmeyer and his associates have incorporated a number of Adlerian and Dreikurserian concepts into programs relating to children, adolescents, parents, and teachers. These programs have gained popularity and wide usage among counselors and other members of the helping professions. Some of these programs are systematic training for effective parenting (STEP) (Dinkmeyer & McKay, 1989), systematic training for effective teaching (Dinkmeyer, McKay, & Dinkmeyer, 1980), training in marital enrichment (TIME) (Dinkmeyer & Carlson, 1984), and developing understanding of self and others (DUSO-R) (Dinkmeyer & Dinkmeyer, 1982).

Several other individuals have made significant contributions to contemporary Adlerian psychology. Ray Corsini (1977, 1979) developed an educational system based on Adlerian principles, which he called individual education. Dreikurs et al. (1959), Sherman and Dinkmeyer (1987), and Oscar Christenson have done much to promote the popularity of Adlerian family counseling.

A recent trend is a movement toward integrating Adlerian psychology with other schools of thought. In this regard, Shulman suggests that Adlerian psychology needs to develop further to incorporate new advances in the field of child development, neurochemical processes in the brain, and cognitive psychology (Nystul, 1988). Watkins (1984) provides another example of integration in terms of similarities between Adler's theory and vocational counseling. For example, Watkins notes that Adler's construct of lifestyle and Holland's personality types (such as realistic and investigative) both acknowledge the role that individual difference plays in psychological functioning.

The movement toward integration appears to be gaining momentum among the Adlerian ranks. A special issue of *Individual Psychology: The Journal of Adlerian Theory, Research, and Practice* focused on exploring the issues relating to "beyond Adler." In this special issue, Carlson (Nystul, 1991) suggests that the Adlerian movement has become isolated, focusing too much on well-developed concepts such as the four goals of misbehavior and logical consequences. Carlson contends that broader, more permeable boundaries are needed for Adlerian psychology to become part of the mainstream of contemporary psychology (Nystul, 1991). Carlson also suggests that Adlerian approaches could be developed to reach nontraditional, non-YAVIS (young, attractive, verbal, intelligent, and sensitive) clients; clients who are victims of family violence; clients infected with the AIDS virus; and clients who require sex therapy. Mosak (1991) echoes the call for change by noting that Adlerian theory focuses too much on the psychology of abnormalcy and not enough on the psychology of normalcy.

Adlerian Brief Approaches to Counseling

According to the Adlerian scholar Ansbacher (1989), Adlerian counseling and psychotherapy was the first form of brief counseling. Adler believed that time limits in counseling could be beneficial and typically restricted his sessions over a 10-week period with two sessions per week (Ansbacher, 1989). A number of Adlerian constructs are particularly relevant to brief-counseling theory and practice. For example, the use of encouragement and focusing on clients' assets is consistent with the strengths perspective advocated in contemporary brief-counseling models. Kurt Adler (Adler's son) suggested that although Adlerian counseling is a forerunner in brief-counseling methods, it is neither a short- or long-term form of counseling, but a flexible approach that can be adjusted to the unique and emerging needs of clients (Adler, 1972).

Contemporary Adlerians are making innovative advances in terms of developing brief-counseling approaches. Sperry (1987) was one of the first Adlerians to set forth specific procedures for conducting brief counseling. He developed a simple cognitive map that clinicians can use to organize all forms of brief consultations, including "sidewalk consults" and emergency phone calls. More recently, Maniacci (1996) developed a brief-counseling model for treating personality disorders. He notes that Adlerian procedures such as the lifestyle assessment are particularly useful to understanding core personality issues. Sperry (1989) edited a special issue on brief counseling in *Individual Psychology: The Journal of Adlerian Theory, Research, and Practice* that provides numerous other examples of brief counseling in Adlerian psychology.

Postmodern Trends and Adlerian Psychology

The postmodern trends of constructivism and social constructionism appear to have much in common with Adlerian psychology. Adlerian psychology has been recognized as laying the theoretical foundations for constructivism (Mahoney, 1991; Mahoney & Lyddon, 1988; Shulman, 1985). Jones (1995) and Scott, Kelly, & Tolbert (1995) identify several psychological constructs that constructivism and Adler's theory have in common. For example, both theories emphasize the role of cognition in psychological functioning, noting the active role people play in creating their own reality. In this regard, Adler contends that the creative self allows each person an opportunity to make a unique response based on one's past experiences and the capacity for self-determination.

Adlerian psychology also appears to share commonalties with social constructionism. Social constructionism stresses the role of social forces such as the narratives reflected in cultures in creating personal meanings or "storied lives." Adler's construct of social interests also reflects an ecological perspective. In this regard, Adler contends that mental health and meaning to life is to a large degree achieved through interest, concern, and involvement with others.

Summary and Evaluation

Adler was a man ahead of his time. His psychological insights stressed the importance of phenomenology, holism, and social interest. These concepts are incorporated into most contemporary counseling theories. Adlerian psychology is perhaps best known for concepts that can be used to understand individual differences such as lifestyle, family dynamics, birth order, and sibling rivalry. Another strength of Adlerian psychology is its influence on programs such as STEP, TIME, and other guidance programs.

A criticism is that Adlerian counselors may be trying too hard to adhere to Adler's original concepts in terms of theory, research, and practice. As Shulman recommends, Adlerian psychology must be responsive to ongoing advances in counseling and psychology if it is to remain a viable theory for contemporary practitioners (Nystul, 1988).

Another criticism can be directed at Adlerian psychotherapy in terms of its narrow focus and use of the concept of basic mistakes (Nystul, 1994). Jones (1995) notes that Adlerian psychology focuses on cognitions rather than behaviors, emotions, and cognitions. It would seem that a more comprehensive treatment program would focus on all three of these domains of psychological functioning.

There also appear to be problems in the manner in which cognitions are conceptualized in Adlerian psychotherapy. From an Adlerian perspective, cognitions are primarily conceptualized in terms of the concept of basic mistakes (Jones, 1995; Nystul, 1994). Jones notes that basic mistakes are key to understanding lifestyle and emotional disorders. Nystul (1994) goes on to suggest that to a large degree Adlerian psychotherapy involves reorienting clients from their basic mistakes. It is unfortunate that so much emphasis has been placed on the concept of basic mistakes, because the concept may be inconsistent with Adlerian theory of personality and discouraging to clients (Nystul, 1994).

Jung's Analytic Psychology

Background Information

Carl Gustav Jung (1875–1961) was born in Kesswil, Switzerland. His father was a pastor, which may have contributed to his fondness for religion. Jung's intellectual interests were by far the most varied of the three classic theorists. As a young man, he became intrigued by mythology, philosophy, religion, history, literature, and archeology. While Jung was struggling to decide what to study at the university, he had an unusual dream that somehow compelled him to pursue medicine (Hall & Lindzey, 1978). Jung went on to obtain a medical degree from the University of Basel in 1900, the same year Freud published *The Interpretation of Dreams*. Freud's work may have influenced his decision to specialize in psychiatry. Shortly thereafter, Jung obtained a position at the University of Zurich and worked under Eugene Bleuler, who was well known for his theories on schizophrenia. During this time, Jung was also fortunate to study with Pierre Janet, who was conducting research on hysteria and multiple personality disorders.

By 1907, Jung had his first meeting with Freud. They found many areas of common interest as they talked continuously for 13 hours. Freud believed that Jung was his crown prince and successor (Hall & Lindzey, 1978). It was therefore not surprising that in 1910 Jung became the first president of the International Psychoanalytic Association. Their initial

Carl Jung

compatibility was short-lived, as Jung began to differ with Freud on important theoretical issues. Like Adler, Jung became particularly disenchanted with Freud's emphasis on the role of sexuality in personality development. By 1914, Jung felt he could no longer participate in the Freudian movement and resigned from the presidency of the Psychoanalytic Association.

At this point, Jung decided to develop his own school of psychology, which he called analytic psychology. It is interesting to note that some of Jung's most creative years occurred during a time of personal distress between 1913 and 1916, as with Freud. Jung was able to make the most of difficult times. During this period, Jung did extensive self-analysis through the interpretation of his dreams. He obtained a number of insights that had a profound effect on the development of his theory. An example is the importance of gaining an understanding of unconscious processes during psychotherapy.

Jung's analytic theory was unique in its varied theoretical foundation. Jung was able to integrate his early interests in religion, mythology, archeology, literature, history, and philosophy into the study of psychology. This work resulted in what may be the most comprehensive understanding of the human condition (Hall & Lindzey, 1978). His collective works are extensive, filling 20 volumes (Read, Fordham, & Adler, 1953–1978). Jung's work holds particular interest for those who wish to integrate mystical ideas from the Far East with analytical concepts from the Western European and American traditions.

Jung's Theory of Personality

Jung's theory of personality is very robust, incorporating elements from various disciplines such as eastern philosophy, theology and religion, medicine, and psychology. Harris (1996) contends that Jung's ideas are becoming increasingly popular and can even be found in such best-selling books as Estes' (1992) *Women Who Run with the Wolves*. An overview of Jung's theory of personality follows.

View of Human Nature.   Jung (1928) had a positive view of the human condition, believing that people had inherent tendencies toward individualization—becoming unique individuals capable of wholeness and self-realization. This process of individualization is characterized by a union or integration of conscious and unconscious processes (Jung, 1928).

Key Concepts.   Jung identified the following concepts, which were associated with his theory of personality (Read, Fordham, & Adler, 1953–1978).

The Ego, the Personal Unconscious, and the Collective Unconscious.   According to Kaufmann (1989), Jung believed that the psyche is made up of autonomous yet interdependent subsystems of the ego, the personal unconscious, and the collective unconscious. The ego represents the conscious mind and the personal unconscious and collective unconscious make up the unconscious domain of the psyche.

The *ego* is the center of consciousness and is made up of conscious perceptions, memories, thoughts, and feelings (Kaufmann, 1989). It provides consistency and direction in people's lives (Fadiman & Frager, 1976).

The *personal unconscious* is similar to Freud's preconscious, containing thoughts based on personal experience just beyond the reach of conscious recall (Feist, 1985). It contains forgotten or repressed material that had once been conscious and could become conscious in the future (Hall & Lindzey, 1978). The information in the personal unconscious clusters around several complexes (Kaufmann, 1989). Complexes revolve around themes such as prestige or control, which can interfere with effective living (Corey, 1982). For example, a client could have a "mother complex," whereby he behaves as if he were under his mother's domination or control.

The *collective unconscious* is sometimes referred to as the transpersonal or nonpersonal unconscious, since it is not associated with personal experiences. It is considered the most provocative yet controversial aspect of Jung's theory (Hall & Lindzey, 1978). The collective unconscious is made up of memory traces inherited from one's ancestral past. Jung called it *collective* because he believed that all people shared common images and thoughts regarding such things as mother, earth, birth, and death.

Jung referred to these universal thoughts as archetypes. He believed that the collective unconscious creates the foundation for the personality. Starting from birth, the collective unconscious guides an individual's life experiences, thereby influencing perceptions, emotions, and behavior. It is therefore the most powerful and influential aspect of the personality (Hall & Lindzey, 1978).

Jung suggested that the collective unconscious was not directly amenable to the conscious but could be observed indirectly through its manifestations in eternal themes in mythology, folklore, and art (Kaufmann, 1989). Jung visited numerous "primitive" cultures to test his theory in Africa and the American Southwest. He found that even though these cultures evolved independently, they shared intricate memories that could have been transmitted only by a collective unconscious.

Archetypes.   Jung discovered that several archetypes evolved so completely that they could be considered separate systems within the personality (Hall & Lindzey, 1978). These are the persona, the anima and animus, the shadow, and the self.

The *persona* is the public self one projects as opposed to the private, personal view of oneself. The persona is reflected in various roles such as work, marriage and family, and social situations. According to Jung, awareness of the persona has an inverse relation to awareness of one's personal self or individuality. For example, the more aware one is of the persona, the less aware that person will be of individuality and the private, personal self.

The *anima* and *animus* refer to the suggestion that people have both masculine and feminine dimensions to their personality. The *anima* is the feminine archetype in men, and the *animus* is the masculine archetype in women. Jung believed these archetypes resulted from years of men and women living together (Hall & Lindzey, 1978). Fadiman and Frager (1976) note that this archetype appears in dreams and fantasies as figures of the opposite sex and functions as the primary mediator between unconscious and conscious processes.

The *shadow* represents the negative or evil side of the personality that people do not want to recognize. The shadow is associated with thoughts that originate from animal instincts inherited through the evolutionary process.

The *self* is the center of the personality, including the conscious and unconscious parts of the mind (Feist, 1985). The self provides the personality with a sense of unity, equilibrium, and stability (Hall & Lindzey, 1978). The self cannot emerge until the other systems of the personality have fully developed, which is usually not until middle age (Corey, 1982). The emergence of the self occurs when the center of the individual shifts from the conscious ego to the midpoint between conscious and unconscious (Hall & Lindzey, 1978). This midpoint region becomes the domain of the self. It is not surprising that Jung discovered the existence of the self when he was studying Eastern meditation practices, which emphasize the interaction between conscious and unconscious processes.

Personality Types.   Jung noted that personality types could be differentiated in terms of attitudes and functions. He identified two types of attitudes: extroverted, or outgoing; and introverted, or introspective. According to Jung, people have both attitudes in their personality makeup. The dominant attitude is represented in the conscious mind and the subordinate attitude exists in the unconscious psyche (Hall & Lindzey, 1978).

Jung also described four functions that provide additional means to differentiate personality types. These functions include thinking, feeling, sensation, and intuition. Jung contended that although people rely on all these functions to react to events, the function that is the best developed will be relied on most and becomes the superior function.

Theory of Counseling and Psychotherapy

Jung's approach to counseling and psychotherapy is called analytic psychotherapy. It emphasizes the role of unconscious processes in psychological functioning. Through dream analysis and other procedures, the client becomes aware of unconscious processes and learns to use that understanding to maximize mental health and wellness.

The overall aim of analytic psychotherapy is to help the self emerge so the client can be free to move toward self-realization. For this to occur, the analyst must help the client develop the other major systems of the personality. Much of psychotherapy therefore involves exploring unconscious processes in order for clients to gain insight into the structure of their personality (Kaufmann, 1989). In time, clients can learn how to make the various systems develop to their fullest and function in a complementary fashion. For example, a client who describes himself as a real "macho-type" person seeks help for marital problems. The analytic psychotherapist may encourage the client to recognize the feminine (anima) dimension to his personality. According to analytic theory, this will help the client become a more fully functioning person and develop a better understanding of life.

Jung had a unique conception of psychopathology. He did not view it as a disease or abnormal state (Kaufmann, 1989). Instead, he believed the symptoms associated with psychopathology could be instructive for both the client and analyst (Kaufmann, 1989). They could serve as warning signals that something was wrong and could also provide clues into the functioning of the personality (Kaufmann, 1989). Jung was therefore reluctant to use medication to treat mental disorders, because he was afraid it might mask important messages that symptoms could communicate.

The nature of the therapeutic relationship is also unique in analytic psychotherapy. Analysts are required to undertake their own analysis, which helps them gain a respect for what is involved in being a client. They do not see the counseling relationship as a healthy therapist treating a sick patient. Instead, Jungian analysts view therapy as one person who has journeyed into the unconscious helping another person develop a meaningful dialogue with unconscious processes (Kaufmann, 1989). The Jungian analyst also believes it is critical for the client to feel a sense of acceptance during therapy (Kaufmann, 1989).

Fadiman and Frager (1976) describe two major stages utilized in Jungian psychotherapy. In the *analytic stage,* clients attempt to identify unconscious material. This is followed by the *synthetic stage,* which initially involves helping clients use insight to formulate new experiences. The final phase of the synthetic stage is called *transformation,* in which clients engage in self-education and thus become more autonomous and responsible for their own development.

Techniques

Jung advocated a flexible approach to psychotherapy, believing that the method of treatment should be determined by the unique features of each client (Harris, 1996). His approach shares the characteristics associated with the art-of-counseling model described in Chapter 1, in that he recommended the analyst be creative and flexible in working with the client.

Jungian psychotherapy is a practical approach based on the guiding principle that anything goes, as long as it seems to work (Kaufmann, 1989). When one patient complained of difficulty falling asleep, for example, Jung simply sang the client a lullaby (Kaufmann, 1989).

Jung, was skeptical of using techniques in therapy, because he thought they could be unnecessarily restrictive. At the same time, he believed dream analysis could be a useful vehicle for helping clients explore unconscious processes. Unlike Freud, Jung found little value in analyzing a single dream. He believed it was essential to investigate the interrelationship of several dreams recorded over a period of time. In this process, Jung would help the client understand the symbolic meaning of dreams, and how they provide clues to the various systems of the personality.

Contemporary Issues

Harris (1996) suggests that an emerging trend is the conceptualization of Jungian psychology from a paradoxical perspective. According to Harris (1996), Jung's theory is founded on the concept of paradox and paradox implies "ambiguity, a puzzle or dilemma, a tension between opposite poles of an issue, even incongruity between elements of a larger whole"

(p. 4). She suggests that there are no simple answers in Jungian psychology. Instead balance and wholeness can evolve from working with opposing-paradoxical forces. In this regard, analytic psychotherapy involves helping clients seek out painful opposing forces in their lives to generate creative new solutions to old problems (Harris, 1996).

Additional trends in Jungian psychology are directed at diversification and integration. Samuels (1985) notes that there are three schools of Jungian psychology: classical, developmental, and archetypal. The classical school emphasizes the role of the self as the major personality construct, the developmental school focuses on the use of transference and interpretation to work through problems associated with childhood experiences, and the archetypal school relates primarily to issues pertaining to archetypes (Spiegelman, 1989). Samuels (1989) suggests that the emerging schools of Jungian psychology need not be viewed as a form of conflict. He believes differences should be encouraged to foster creative developments in Jungian psychology. Jungian psychology is also expanding its horizons in an attempt to incorporate other theories and approaches. Saayman, Faber, and Saayman (1988) provide an example of this by exploring how family systems theory could be integrated into Jungian marital therapy.

Jungian concepts have also been incorporated into other psychological theories and systems. Myers and McCaulley (1985) incorporate Jung's concept of attitudes and functions (for example, introvert, extrovert, thinking, feeling) into the development of the Myers-Briggs Type Indicator (MBTI). The MBTI has become a popular personality instrument for individuals who want to gain self-understanding and for use in organizational and industrial psychology (McCrae & Costa, 1989). Unfortunately, research evidence has emerged suggesting that Jung's theory was inaccurately incorporated into the MBTI and therefore should not be used to interpret test results (McCrae & Costa, 1989).

Jungian Brief-Counseling Approaches

Harris (1996) notes that analytic psychotherapy has traditionally been a long term form of treatment directed at maximizing the functioning of the personality. Harris suggests that owing to the restrictions on length and nature of counseling imposed by managed care, Jungian clinicians must develop flexible practices and approaches. She contends that Jungian principles and strategies have been successfully adapted for use in time-limited counseling, focused on resolving specific problems with clients of various ages and socioeconomic status. Harris also notes that Jungian counselors use strategies such as sandplay, art therapy, and dance therapy, which can be valuable adjuncts to brief-counseling approaches. Harris also believes that Jungian long-term counseling and psychotherapy can also be valuable, especially in cases requiring personality restructuring. In these instances, the counselor may work with a client to provide the necessary services outside of the restrictions imposed by managed care.

Summary and Evaluation

The fundamental strength of Jung's approach lies in his comprehensive view of the human condition. In this regard, Hall and Lindzey (1978) observed

> The originality and audacity of Jung's thinking have few parallels in recent scientific history, and no other person aside from Freud has opened more conceptual windows into what Jung would choose to call the "soul of man." (p. 149)

Jung has had a major influence on "contemporary religious, cultural, and sociological thought, as well as art, literature, and drama" (Douglas, 1995, p. 97). For example, Jung's theories and interest in Eastern philosophy and spirituality such as yoga and mediation appear to be playing a key role in the emerging interest in holistic health. In this regard, Jung believed that wholeness and psychological balance will occur when the conscious and unconscious mind learn to work in harmony, and people have the inherent capacity for psychological growth and self-healing (Douglas, 1995).

Jung's theories have also played a role in the evolution of psychological theories. For example, Jung's notion of individualization over the life span have been incorporated into life-span theories such as those of Gilligan, Erikson, and Kohlberg (Douglas, 1995). Jung's deep caring for his patients and sense of hope and optimism have also laid the foundation for the humanistic theories of Maslow, Rogers, and others (Douglas, 1995).

Jungian concepts have also played a role in counseling procedures, especially the creative arts such as art therapy, dance therapy, and sand-tray therapy (Douglas, 1995). Jung utilized these creative arts modalities in his own therapeutic procedures. For example, he would encourage patients to express themselves through art or expressive movement and would also engage in these processes to better understand the patient (Douglas, 1995). In his own self-analysis, Jung constructed a stone village as a means of working through some of his own issues (Douglas, 1995). This concept was later modified into what is currently known as sand-tray therapy (see Allan & Brown, 1993, and Carmichael, 1994, for more information on sand-tray therapy).

Several criticisms have been directed at Jungian psychology. The existence of a collective unconscious has been challenged more than any other. Glover (1950) insists that the concept is metaphysical and incapable of proof. Glover (1950) further suggests that Jung's theory lacks development concepts necessary to explain the growth of the mind. Hall and Lindzey (1978) observe that many psychologists have found Jung's writing to be "baffling, obscure, confusing, and disorganized" (p. 148).

The Classic Theories and Their Use in Contemporary Practice

The classic theories of Freud, Adler, and Jung may be criticized as outdated and of little use to clinicians. Concerns can be directed at the degree these theories have effectively kept up with recent trends such as brief counseling and diversity issues. Although these concerns have some validity (which needs to be taken into consideration in clinical practice), the classic theories also have some strengths that can be of use to practitioners. The following section provides a brief overview of the classic theories in terms of diversity issues and brief-counseling approaches.

Diversity Issues in the Classic Theories

The classic theories of Freud, Adler, and Jung pose special considerations in cross-cultural counseling. Freudian theory may have the most limitations from a cross-cultural perspective. Freud tended to overemphasize intrapsychic forces such as the endopsychic forces resulting from competition between the id, ego, and superego at the expense of understanding sociocultural forces that can play a role in human functioning. On the positive side, Freud was a genius for describing intrapsychic forces, and a recognition of these forces is essential to the understanding of people regardless of culture.

Adler and Jung appear to have achieved more of a balance between the intrapsychic and sociocultural perspective. This may be especially true for Adler, who emphasized cognitive processes (intrapsychic forces) and social interest (social embeddedness), both playing key roles in psychological functioning. Jung also sought out balance in his theory as he attempted to integrate the intrapsychic working of the conscious and unconscious mind with ontological issues of spirituality, transcendence, wholeness, and healing.

Gender issues should also be considered when addressing the classic theories. Freudian psychology has come under fire by feminists and others for a number of reasons. From a feminist perspective, Freudian psychology is one of the best examples of how male dominance is overtly displayed in the psychological literature. This anti-female spirit is perhaps captured best in his concept of penis envy, which women are supposed to have as they progress through the psychosexual stages of development. Adler (and his colleague Dreikurs) and Jung would appear to fare much better than Freud in terms of gender considerations. Adler and Dreikurs have played an important role in promoting social equality between the sexes (Dreikurs, 1971). Jung's work also appears to have utility across the sexes in terms of his Eastern concepts, which have been integrated into the holistic health-and-wellness movement.

Brief Counseling and the Classic Theories

Although the classic theories (perhaps with the exception of Adlerian) were originally developed as a form of long-term therapy, they hold much promise for clinicians interested in brief counseling. First and foremost, the classic theories offer counselors a comprehensive means to understand the personality dynamics of the client before they develop their treatment plan and implement their interventions. Although brief-counseling approaches are not designed for personality restructuring, some comprehensive means of understanding the dynamics of behavior would seem essential in any approach to counseling.

The classic theories offer other useful concepts and procedures that could be used in brief counseling. For example, the Adlerian/Dreikurserian concept of encouragement stands out as a critical counseling concept for clinicians. It can foster a positive counseling relationship and help clients begin to believe in their own inherent strengths and abilities. This strengths perspective is a focal point for brief counseling. Jung's focus on psychological health and wellness is also consistent with the brief counseling in terms of taking a positive approach with clients. Freudian psychoanalysis has also made great gains in terms of its appropriateness in brief counseling by revising its approach to fit within a time-limited format.

Summary

The theories of Freud, Adler, and Jung are considered classic theories because of their historical significance and comprehensiveness. These theories share some elements. Freud and Adler both noted the importance of early life experiences on adult personality formation. Freud and Jung both emphasized the role of unconscious forces in personality functioning.

Each theory also has its unique psychological constructs and orientation. Freud stressed the role of sexuality and developed a psychosexual model for personality development. Adler favored the importance of social interest as a major motivating force for understanding the dynamics of personality. Jung was known for his formulation of the collective unconscious, proposing that all people inherit a common set of memories from birth that are passed on from generation to generation.

The three classic schools of psychology continue to evolve in terms of theory, research, and practice. In addition, each has had a major impact on the evolution of current psychotherapies. Most contemporary counseling theories have incorporated psychological constructs from Freud, Adler, and Jung. Most noticeable is the wide recognition of the importance of early life experiences and the existence of unconscious processes. Some of the principles of Adlerian psychology have been particularly influential in the evolution of modern clinical practice (Corey, 1996). Adlerian concepts of holism and phenomenology are reflected in experiential theories. Adler's emphasis on cognition (for example, basic mistakes) has also contributed to the current cognitive behavioral approaches.

The strength of the classic schools is their foundation in personality theory. They tend to be more limited in terms of their approaches to counseling and psychotherapy. In this regard, the classic schools of psychotherapy need further development and integration with modern counseling practice to enable practitioners to develop comprehensive treatment programs. The Suggested Readings on pages 420–422 contain additional information regarding the classic theories of Freud, Adler, and Jung.

CHAPTER

8 Experiential Theories and Approaches

CHAPTER OVERVIEW

This chapter provides an overview of experiential theories and approaches to counseling. Highlights of the chapter include

- The art and science of experiential counseling
- Person-centered theory of personality and theory of counseling
- Gestalt theory of personality and theory of counseling
- Existential theory of personality and theory of counseling
- Overview of the creative arts therapies of music, art, dance, drama, bibliotherapy and multimodality CAT
- Research trends
- Brief experiential approaches
- Diversity issues

The Art and Science of Experiential Counseling

The art and science of counseling and psychotherapy are reflected in experiential theories and approaches. The art of counseling plays a key role in experiential counseling. Experiential counselors, like artists, attempt to bring out the hidden beauty in their clients. In this regard, experiential counselors often use creative arts modalities (such as music, art, dance, drama, and bibliotherapy) to help clients discover strengths they can use to enhance their psychological functioning.

The counseling relationship is based on humanistic psychology, which recognizes the benefits of allowing one's humanness to stimulate and enhance interpersonal relationships. Open, candid interactions are common and encourage immediacy and authenticity in the counseling process. The art of experiential counseling also allows for intense therapeutic encounters. In these instances, the counselor may utilize the process of self-transcendence to move beyond empathy and understanding to enable the counselor to directly *experience* the client's joy or suffering.

The science of experiential counseling provides objectivity as a necessary balance to the art of counseling. Experiential counseling can be emotionally exhausting and taxing for both counselors and clients. The science of experiential counseling monitors the degree of psychological intensity and like a navigator on a ship, enables the counselor and client to chart a realistic and productive course for therapy.

The science of experiential counseling also has direct ties to research methodology. Experiential theorists such as Carl Rogers (and his person-centered approach) have played a key role in counseling research. Rogers was keenly aware of the interrelationship between theory, research, and practice (Heppner, Rogers, and Lee, 1984). Rogers developed his person-centered theory based on empirical research and extensive clinical practice. Rogers pioneered the research procedure of listening to counseling tapes to gain an understanding of the change process in counseling (Greenberg, Elliott, & Lietaer, 1994). Much of the recent interest in the change process can be traced to Rogers' early work (Greenberg, Elliott, & Lietaer, 1994).

Other recent research trends in experiential counseling are focused on analyzing the impact of specific experiential counseling strategies (such as the Gestalt empty-chair technique) on the change process. This line of research is qualitative in nature, whereby the counselor and client attempt to discover (as coinvestigators) the subtle nuances associated with the change process. Much of the current research in experiential counseling is directed at this type of methodology (Greenberg, Elliott & Lietaer, 1994).

As noted in Chapter 6, the art and science of counseling recommend using a multicultural perspective to conceptualize diversity issues throughout the counseling process. Experiential theories such as existentialism appear to be compatible with multicultural issues since they encourage an exploration of philosophical concepts such as the meaning of life. The art and science of the experiential theories involve making the necessary modifications to these theories by utilizing multicultural research findings and maintaining a sensitivity to the evolving needs of clients.

Experiential Counseling

This chapter presents theories and approaches to counseling that emphasize experiential processes. It begins by providing an overview of three major schools of counseling: person-centered, Gestalt, and existential. The last part of the chapter describes the major creative arts therapy (CAT) modalities of music, art, drama, and dance therapy, bibliotherapy, and multimodality CAT. The common thread among these theories is their emphasis on the importance of the *experiential* aspect of counseling.

Experiential Theories

The experiential theories focus on what the client is experiencing during the counseling process. In person-centered counseling, the client is encouraged to experience the self in an open and flexible manner (Raskin & Rogers, 1995). The focus of Gestalt counseling is to help clients become aware of what they are thinking and feeling in the here and now. Existential therapy suggests that a client can obtain personal meaning by experiencing both the joys and sorrows of life. From an existential point of view, even anxiety can be instructive.

The experiential theories maintain a humanistic orientation regarding the nature of people. These theories tend to view people as inherently positive with self-actualizing tendencies. The experiential theories can therefore be particularly attractive to counselors who share this optimistic point of view. An overview of these three theories is provided in Table 8.1.

TABLE 8.1   Overview of Experiential Approaches

Theory	Founder(s)	Key Concepts	The Counseling Process	Techniques
Person-Centered	Carl Rogers	Trust in the inherent self-actualizing tendencies of people; the role of the self and the client's internal frame of reference in personality dynamics.	Involves an if-then process: if certain conditions are established (such as communicating empathic understanding), then the client will move toward self-actualization.	Although no techniques are identified, the approach requires the use of listening skills to communicate empathic understanding and establish other core conditions.
Gestalt	Fritz Perls	An existential–phenomenological perspective; moving from dependence to independence; and being integrated and centered in the present.	Involves a dialogue between the therapist and client whereby the client becomes aware of what is occurring in the here and now.	The therapist models authenticity and uses techniques to help the client become aware and centered in the present. Some of the techniques include the empty-chair technique and the use of personal pronouns.
Existential Therapy	Victor Frankl, Rollo May, and James Bugental	Uniqueness of the individual, search for meaning, role of anxiety; freedom of responsibility; and being and nonbeing.	Emphasizes the role of the counseling relationship over techniques. Counseling goals can include searching for personal meaning and becoming aware of choices.	Paradoxical reflection, dereflection, and existential encounter.

Carl Rogers

Person-Centered Therapy

Background Information

Carl Rogers (1902–1987) was the fourth of six children. He was raised in a closely knit family with strict religious standards (Rogers, 1961). In 1931 Rogers obtained a Ph.D. degree in clinical psychology from the Teachers College of Columbia University.

Rogers then embarked on his professional career, taking a position as a psychologist with the Child Guidance Clinic of Rochester, New York. Shortly thereafter, in 1939, he wrote his first book, *The Clinical Treatment of the Problem Child,* which was based on his experience at the guidance center. This led to his appointment as a full professor in psychology at The Ohio State University. It was there during the 1940s that Rogers began to formulate his own approach to counseling and psychotherapy, culminating in the publication of *Counseling and Psychotherapy* in 1942.

From 1945 to 1964 Rogers held academic positions at the University of Chicago and the University of Wisconsin. During this time, he was able to continue developing his personal approach and explore its implementation in education, group process, and counseling and psychotherapy. Rogers noted that he had a somewhat negative experience with his academic peers at the Ohio State University and the University of Wisconsin (Heppner, Rogers, & Lee, 1984). He felt he was not liked by his colleagues, although he did not have a particularly high regard for them either. Not surprisingly, he preferred graduate students or people outside the department as friends (Heppner, Rogers, & Lee, 1984). In 1964 Rogers left academia permanently. During the last years of his career, he worked at the Institute for the Study of the Person in La Jolla, California. Today, the institute continues to provide training opportunities in person-centered counseling.

Theory of Personality

The theory of personality in person-centered counseling is humanistically oriented, focusing on phenomenology and the role of the self in psychological functioning. An overview of Rogers' theory of personality follows.

View of Human Nature

Rogers (1951) held a positive view of human nature, noting the inherent self-actualizing tendencies of people. He believed that if the right conditions existed, people would naturally proceed toward self-actualization. In addition, Rogers' theory emphasizes the phenomenological perspective by suggesting that an individual's internal frame of reference is the best vantage point to understand the person.

Key Concepts

Raskin and Rogers (1995) note that trust is the most fundamental concept in person-centered therapy. This theory contends that clients can be trusted to establish their own goals and monitor their progress toward these goals. In addition, counselors trust that all individuals have inherent self-actualizing tendencies.

Many other key concepts can be derived from Rogers' (1951) theory of personality, which is described in 19 propositions. The key concepts emphasize the role of a person's internal frame of reference and the self in understanding the dynamics of behavior. Four propositions that characterize Rogers' personality theory are

1. *People react to the phenomenal field as they experience and perceive it.* A person's phenomenal field is the internal frame of reference for perceiving the world. This proposition suggests that what a person perceives will be influenced according to past experiences.
2. *The best point to understanding behavior is the internal frame of reference of the person.* This proposition is logically related to the first proposition. Since each person's perception is unique, it can only be understood from the person's internal frame of reference. Rogers therefore advocated developing a phenomenological perspective when working with clients, which involves understanding things from the client's perspective.
3. *People tend to behave in a manner consistent with their concept of self.* The self is the center of the organism and consists of how a person sees the self in relation to others. The self attempts to foster consistency within the organism by promoting behavior that is compatible to one's view of the self.
4. *The more people perceive and accept experiences, the more they will tend to be accepting and understanding of others.* Self-acceptance and understanding are viewed as contributing factors in understanding and accepting others as unique individuals.

Theory of Counseling and Psychotherapy

Rogers' person-centered theory can be described as an "if-then" approach. If certain conditions exist in the counseling relationship, then the client will move toward self-actualization

(Rogers, 1961). Rogers (1957) identified the following three core conditions as necessary and sufficient for personal growth to occur:

1. *Counselor congruence.* Counselor congruence means counselors are congruent in terms of what they are experiencing and what they communicate. For example, when counselors feel threatened by a client, it would be inappropriate for them to say they enjoy being with the client. This would communicate a confusing double message and the counselor would not be genuine or authentic.
2. *Empathic understanding.* The counselor attempts to understand the client from the client's internal frame of reference. This phenomenological perspective involves understanding what the client is thinking, feeling, and experiencing and communicating this understanding to the client.
3. *Unconditional positive regard.* Rogers believed that it is essential for the counselor to communicate a sense of acceptance and respect to the client. There has been some misunderstanding of what Rogers meant by unconditional positive regard. He did not mean the counselor should tolerate and accept anything the client did (Martin, 1989). He instead believed the counselor should try to "separate the deed from the doer" (Martin, 1989). The counselor should accept the client as a person worthy of respect even though the client's behavior may be inappropriate (Rogers et al., 1967).

In addition to these therapist-offered core conditions, Rogers (1957) identified three other conditions that must occur for successful counseling to occur. The first two are considered preconditions for therapy: the therapist and client are in psychological contact, or aware of each other's presence, and the client is experiencing some discomfort in life to be motivated for therapy. The third condition is that the client must be able to accurately perceive and experience the core conditions set forth by the therapist.

A number of goals and therapeutic outcomes emerge from the person-centered therapy. This style of counseling is unique in that it does not attempt to resolve the client's presenting problem (Rogers, 1977). It instead assists the client in the growth process to become a fully functioning individual. Rogers (1961) identified the following changes that tend to occur as the client moves toward self-actualization.

- *Open to experience.* Clients are capable of seeing reality without distorting it to fit a preconceived self-structure. Instead of operating from a rigid belief system, clients are interested in exploring new horizons.
- *Self-trust.* Initially clients tend to have self-doubts. Clients may believe that no matter what they decide, it will be wrong. As therapy progresses, clients can learn to trust their own judgment and become more self-confident.
- *Internal source of evaluation.* Person-centered therapy fosters the development of an internal locus of control. This occurs as clients are encouraged to explore their inner choices and discouraged from looking to others for a sense of direction or locus of evaluation.
- *Willingness to continue growing.* As a result of person-centered therapy, clients will realize that self-actualization is a process and not an end goal. In this sense, no one ever becomes self-actualized. Instead, a fully functioning person is always in the state of becoming.

Techniques

Rogers (1951, 1961) minimizes the importance or use of techniques. Instead of relying on techniques, he emphasized the importance of the counseling relationship. He believed that the counseling relationship can create core conditions that are the necessary and sufficient conditions for the client's self-actualization. In addition, the person-centered therapist uses listening skills to communicate empathic understanding and help the client explore inner choices. Chapter 3 contains a vignette that provides a Rogerian-oriented example of listening skills and additional information regarding Rogers' concept of core conditions in counseling.

Summary and Evaluation

Carl Rogers made a phenomenal contribution to counseling. He was the major figure behind the humanistic movement in counseling. In addition, many principles of his person-centered therapy have been incorporated into other current psychotherapies. For example, listening skills are frequently used to help establish a positive relationship, obtain a phenomenological understanding of the client, and promote the core conditions identified by Rogers.

Several studies have provided support for Rogers' theory and its application to a wide range of counseling procedures. Watkins (1993) notes that person-centered theory can be used in the contemporary practice of psychological testing. He notes that Rogers' theory could have numerous applications in testing procedures, such as maintaining a client-centered focus to ensure that the client understands and can use test results and using facilitating conditions (such as listening skills and core conditions) to maximize the client's readiness for positive involvement throughout the assessment process. A study by Cramer (1994) examines the relationship between self-esteem and having a friend who communicates the core conditions of empathy, unconditional acceptance, and congruence. The study shows a positive relationship between self-esteem and having a friend who communicates all of these core conditions. Merrill & Andersen (1993) provide a qualitative study on Rogers' theory. They find that when Rogers' core conditions are applied to CAT, the clients have gains in self-awareness, self-confidence, risk taking, and self-exploration.

One limitation associated with the person-centered approach is that counseling goals are unclear, creating ambiguity in the counseling process. Usher (1989) also notes the person-centered approach could be prone to cross-cultural bias in terms of its emphasis on independence and individualism. In addition, research suggests that Rogers' core conditions are not necessary and sufficient but can more accurately be viewed as facilitative for personality change (Gelso & Carter, 1985; Gelso & Fritz, 1992).

Gestalt Therapy

Background Information

Frederick "Fritz" S. Perls (1883–1970) was the founder of Gestalt therapy. Born in Berlin, Perls was initially a student of psychoanalytic theory. In 1946, he moved to the United

States and began to develop Gestalt therapy. Perls went on to help establish a Gestalt Institute in New York in 1952 and another one in Cleveland in 1954.

Perls is best known for the work he did at the Esalen Institute of Big Sur, California. He was a resident associate psychiatrist at Esalen from 1964 to 1969. This was Perls' most productive and creative period. In 1969, he published two of his most popular books, *Gestalt Therapy Verbatim* and *In and Out of the Garbage Pail*. Perls died a year later, after leaving the Esalen Institute to establish a Gestalt community on Vancouver Island in British Columbia.

Theory of Personality

The theory of personality in Gestalt therapy emphasizes the concepts of phenomenology, independence, and being integrated and centered in the now. An overview of Perls' theory of personality follows.

View of Human Nature

The Gestalt view of human nature is similar to the person-centered position. According to Perls, people are self-determined, striving for self-actualization, and best understood from a phenomenological perspective. The term Gestalt also relates to a particular view of human nature. It draws from the principles of Gestalt psychology, which suggests that people are a whole compiled of interrelated parts of body, emotions, thoughts, sensations, and perceptions. Each of these aspects of a person can be understood only within the context of the whole person.

Key Concepts

Perls (1969a, 1969b) described the following three key concepts associated with Gestalt therapy.

1. *An existential-phenomenological perspective.* The Gestalt therapist functions from an existential-phenomenological perspective. From this perspective, the therapist attempts to understand clients from the clients' perspective and helps clients gain personal meaning to their existence.
2. *Helping a client move from dependence to independence.* Perls (1969a) referred to this concept when he said Gestalt therapy helps clients make the transcendence from environmental support to self-support. When clients seek counseling, they tend to expect environmental support such as reassurance from the counselor. The Gestalt therapist avoids reinforcing clients' dependency needs and helps the client become an independent person. Clients will often resist moving toward self-support because change is threatening. When this occurs, the Gestalt therapist will usually frustrate and confront clients to help them work through the impasse.
3. *Being integrated and centered in the now.* Perls (1969a) believed that nothing exists except the now, since the past is gone and the future is yet to come. From this perspective, self-actualization is centered in the present rather than oriented to the future. It requires that clients become centered in the now and aware of what they are

experiencing. Anxiety can result when clients are not centered in the now but are preoccupied with the future (Perls, 1969a). When this occurs, clients may develop excessive worry about what might happen and lose touch with what is happening. Unresolved difficulties from the past can also cause problems, resulting in emotional reactions such as anger, guilt, or resentment. Being unaware of this "unfinished business" can interfere with one's functioning in the now. Resentment is seen as the most frequent and worst kind of unfinished business. Perls (1969a) believed that unexpressed resentment often converts to guilt. For example, a man finds out his wife has had an affair and becomes angry and resentful. Unfortunately, he doesn't express his resentment. Instead, he wonders what he could have done to prevent the affair, resulting in feelings of guilt.

Theory of Counseling and Psychotherapy

The counseling process in Gestalt therapy is experiential. It focuses on what is occurring in the here and now of the moment (Yontey & Simkin, 1989). "Explanations and interpretations are considered less reliable than what is directly perceived and felt" (Yontey & Simkin, 1989, p. 323). Gestalt therapy involves a dialogue between the therapist and client in which the client experiences from the inside what the therapist observes from the outside (Yontey & Simkin, 1989).

The goals that emerge from Gestalt therapy are not specific to a client's concerns. The only goal is awareness, which includes knowledge of the environment, taking responsibility for choices, self-knowledge, and self-acceptance (Yontey & Simkin, 1989).

Passons (1975) identifies common problems that can impede a client's progress in Gestalt therapy. Problems can occur with clients who are overly dependent on others and lack self-responsibility, become out of touch with the world around them, allow unresolved experiences from the past to interfere with being aware of what is occurring in the now, disown their own needs, or define themselves in absolutistic, *either-or* terms.

Techniques

Levitsky and Simkin (1972) note that authenticity symbolizes the Gestalt approach. These authors suggest that it is essential for therapists to be authentic since they cannot teach what they do not know. Gestalt institutes focus their training efforts on trainees playing the role of client. Aside from being authentic, the Gestalt therapist also utilizes several techniques: assuming responsibility, using personal pronouns, and using the *now I'm aware* and empty-chair techniques.

Assuming responsibility is a technique that requires the client to rephrase a statement to assume responsibility. For example, a client can be asked to end all statements with: ". . . and I take responsibility for it." The client may also be requested to change "can't" to "won't" or "but" to "and." For example, instead of saying, "I want to get in shape *but* I don't exercise," the client says, "I want to get in shape *and* I don't exercise."

Using personal pronouns encourages clients to take responsibility by saying *I* or *me* instead of making generalizations using *we* or *us,* or *people,* for example. Clients will tend to feel they own their thoughts and feelings more by saying, "It scares *me* to think of going to college" than by saying, "It scares *people* to go to college."

Now I'm aware is a technique that can help clients get in touch with the self. One way to use this technique is to have clients close their eyes to encourage them to get in touch with their inner world and say, "Now I'm aware" before each statement. For example, "Now I'm aware of my breathing"; "Now I'm aware of some tension in my stomach"; "Now I'm aware of feeling embarrassed and self-conscious of having my eyes closed"; "Now I'm aware of feeling afraid of something, but I don't know what." The exercise can continue after clients open their eyes to help them become aware of themselves in relation to their environment.

The *empty-chair* technique can be used to help clients work through conflicting parts of the personality, such as in an approach avoidance conflict. For example, a client wants to ask a girl out but is afraid of rejection. The empty-chair technique involves placing an empty chair in front of the client. The client is then told that sitting in the empty chair is the part of his personality that does not want to ask the girl out. The client is then encouraged to start a conversation with the empty chair by stating the reasons why he wants to ask the girl out. After the client expresses the positive side of the argument, he is asked to sit in the empty chair and respond with the reasons why he does not want to ask her out. The client continues to move back and forth until he has resolved the issue. The empty-chair technique can be useful in helping clients work through unfinished business so they can be centered in the now.

Summary and Evaluation

Gestalt therapy can be particularly appropriate for clients who lack self-awareness and feel "out of touch" with themselves. Several research studies provide some support for the efficacy of Gestalt therapy. Guinan and Foulds (1970) found clients to have increased self-actualization and self-concepts after Gestalt therapy. Clarke and Breeberg (1986) found the empty-chair technique to be more effective than problem-solving techniques in resolving decisional conflict.

The main weakness of the Gestalt approach is that it lacks a strong theoretical base. It appears to emphasize techniques of therapy, rather than providing an in-depth theoretical foundation for understanding human behavior or providing a comprehensive approach to psychotherapy. Additional research on Gestalt techniques and principles appears warranted.

Existential Therapy

Background Information

No single individual is responsible for the development of existential therapy. The theoretical origins of existential therapy can be traced to existentially oriented philosophy. In this regard, Nietzsche, Heidegger, Sartre, and Buber have played influential roles. For example, Buber (1970) proposes an interesting view of existence. He contends that people do not exist as isolated individuals but instead function in a state of existence that is between the I or oneself and others. In addition, several individuals have written books on existential therapy: Victor Frankl (1963, 1967, 1971, & 1978); Rollo May (1953, 1961, & 1977); and James Bugental (1976). To a large degree, the basic concepts and other tenets of existential therapy identified in this section represent an integration of these major existential theorists.

Theory of Personality

The theory of personality in existential therapy sees each person as a unique individual who is struggling to derive meaning in life. An overview of existential therapy follows. Existential therapy focuses on attempting to understand the human condition. It rejects a fixed view of human nature but instead contends that each person must ultimately define his or her own personal existence.

Key Concepts

The following five key concepts form the basis for existential therapy.

1. *Uniqueness of the individual.* The existential position suggests that no two people are alike—each one is unique. To become aware of one's uniqueness, it is necessary to encounter oneself as a separate and distinct individual. An important part of this process is to have the experience of existential aloneness. This can be a painful experience as a person attempts to encounter the meaning of one's existence. It can also help a person discover the capability of becoming autonomous.

2. *The search for meaning.* Victor Frankl's (1963, 1967, 1971, 1978) logotherapeutic approach evolved out of his experience as a prisoner of war in a Jewish concentration camp during World War II. He described these experiences as well as the basic principles of logotherapy in his book *Man's Search for Meaning* (Frankl, 1963). Logotherapy suggests that the most prominent psychological problem facing people is a lack of meaning in life, which he called the *existential vacuum.* Frankl (1978) believed that a person can experience meaning by feeling valued or needed, which in turn can create a purposeful existence. In this regard, Frankl (1963) cited the words of Nietzsche, who said, "He who has a *why* to live can bear almost any *how*" (p. 121).

3. *The role of anxiety.* Existential therapy differentiates between two types of anxiety. One is normal or healthy anxiety called *existential anxiety,* and the other is unhealthy anxiety referred to as *neurotic anxiety.* Neurotic anxiety is not healthy because it is an anxiety reaction that is not in proportion to the situation and can overwhelm the person. Existential anxiety suggests that some degree of anxiety can be positive, since it can motivate a person to make the necessary changes in life. Another positive aspect of anxiety is that it often occurs when a person faces a difficult situation. A person that flees from this anxiety will not be able to learn from the challenges of life. From this perspective, existentialists believe one can draw meaning from pain and suffering. Nietzsche also related to this point when he said, "That which does not kill me, makes me stronger" (Hollingdale, 1978, p. 23).

4. *Freedom and responsibility.* Existential therapy contends that freedom and responsibility are interrelated. Although people are free to choose their own destiny, they must take responsibility for their actions. Existentialists help clients become aware of their choices and the control they can exert over their own destiny.

5. *Being and nonbeing.* Being and nonbeing are also interrelated. The reality of death brings meaning to life. Being and nonbeing are also related to freedom and responsibility. People are free to be or not to be. If individuals choose to be, they must assume responsibility for their existence.

Theory of Counseling and Psychotherapy

The goals of existential therapy relate directly to the key concepts. They can be directed at helping clients (a) discover their own uniqueness, (b) find personal meaning in life, (c) use anxiety in a positive sense, (d) become aware of their choices and the need to take responsibility for choices, and (e) not see death as a nemesis but as an eventual reality that gives meaning and significance to life.

The actual process of existential therapy emphasizes the role of the counseling relationship over the use of specific techniques. This approach is similar to the person-centered position in that both attempt to obtain a phenomenological understanding of the client and encourage the client to become aware of inner choices. The two approaches differ on the nature of the counseling relationship. Whereas Rogers focuses on the client, the existentialists focus on the therapist and the client. Counseling from an existential point of view is therefore a shared responsibility, with the counselor and client taking an active role in the counseling process.

Buber's "I-thou" concept can be used to provide insight into the nature of the counseling relationship in existential therapy. Buber suggests that counseling relationships can be experienced at different levels that reflect different degrees of humanness and authenticity. For example, the "I to it" is a depersonalized relationship in which the counselor relates to the client as an object. Buber contends that the "I-thou" relationship (which is characterized by authenticity and humanness) is necessary for a genuine encounter to occur between the counselor and client. Brace (1992) goes on to note that Buber's "I-thou" concept can be used to enhance counseling relationships from various theoretical perspectives such as interpersonal psychotherapy.

Techniques

Some existential theories such as Frankl's (1963, 1967, 1971, 1978) logotherapy utilize specific techniques. Frankl (1963, 1978) described two techniques that are central to his approach. The first technique Frankl described is *dereflection,* which is a procedure that involves helping clients focus on strengths rather than weaknesses. This technique seems more closely aligned to the cognitive school of counseling than to existential theory. The second technique associated with logotherapy is *paradoxical intention,* which involves asking clients to do what they fear doing, such as asking them to stutter if they fear stuttering. It is not entirely clear what makes this technique existential. Paradoxical intention is simply a technique that helps a client overcome anticipatory anxiety by redefining success and failure.

Several research studies provide support for the efficacy of paradoxical intention. It appears to be particularly effective for cases that do not respond to behavior therapy (Ascher, 1979; Ascher & Efran, 1978). One particularly well-controlled study by Turner and Ascher (1979) also shows paradoxical intention to effectively treat insomnia.

More recently, Dowd and Sanders (1994) have suggested that paradoxical techniques can be useful with resistant clients who are highly reactant (have high control tendencies). Two types of paradoxical techniques can be used with these individuals (symptom prescription and restraining). *Symptom prescription* involves requiring the client to experience the symptom they are trying to overcome. This technique creates a no-lose situation for control-seeking clients. Either they experience the symptom as prescribed (and feel that they now have control over their symptom), or choose to foster resistance toward the suggestion (and do not experience their problem). *Restraining* involves asking clients to change slowly or not to change at all. In this case, clients' need for control can manifest itself in a form of resistance that results in the client changing very quickly and overcoming his or her problem.

Frankl (1963) also referred to the process of self-transcendence, which means moving beyond the self. This is a uniquely existential concept, which can allow the therapist to transcend the limit of the self and directly experience the client's inner world of pain or joy. When this occurs, it can be referred to as an *existential encounter.* Unfortunately, Frankl (1963) did not describe a technique that could facilitate the existential encounter.

Summary and Evaluation

Existential therapy focuses on issues such as individuality and searching for meaning in life. These issues become increasingly important especially in light of advances in cloning. Existential theory will play a key role in helping people define themselves as unique individuals in an ever-changing world.

The major weakness of this approach lies in its lack of a well-formulated theoretical foundation. Another weakness is that there are few, if any, unique existential techniques that can be utilized in the counseling process. In addition, Goldfried, Greenberg, and Mormar (1990) note a significant decline in research on experiential therapies and thus a danger of their becoming extinct or being integrated into other schools of counseling.

Creative Arts Therapy

Creative arts therapy can be defined as promoting psychological and physiological well-being through the use of creative modalities such as art, music, dance, or drama. Two groups of individuals use CAT: members of the helping professions who use it as an adjunct to counseling and psychotherapy, such as counselors and psychologists; and CAT professionals who are certified or registered in a particular CAT modality, such as music and art therapists. CAT can be used with clients of all ages across a wide array of therapeutic modalities such as individual, group, and marriage and family counseling (Sherwood-Hawes, 1995).

According to Fleshman and Fryrear (1981), CAT has been referred to by many names over the years. These include expressive therapy, expression therapy, and creative therapy. CAT has been shown to (a) facilitate communication of cognitively impaired and nonverbal patients with their therapists, (b) enable therapists to readily explore patients' affect, and (c) foster therapeutic bonding (Johnson, 1984a; Robbins, 1985).

CAT is not a recognized school of counseling because it lacks a clear theoretical foundation of its own. Creative arts therapists do utilize the major psychological theories and procedures to facilitate therapeutic outcomes. Freudian, Jungian, and existential theories are three theories with special appeal and utility in CAT. For example, art therapists often utilize Freudian concepts to interpret drawings and other artwork. Jungian psychology (especially Jung's concept of the collective unconsciousness) can be useful to help clients explore the symbolic nature of unconscious processes that emerge from creative expression (Sherwood-Hawes, 1995). Existential concepts of self-transcendence and the existential encounter can also provide opportunity for creative arts practitioners. In this regard, CAT can foster self-transcendence, enabling the counselor to feel at one with the client (Nystul, 1987). When this occurs, the counselor directly experiences the client's inner emotional state, resulting in an existential encounter. The case of Ron, described in a *Personal Note* later in this chapter, provides an illustration of the use of CAT and the existential encounter.

Professional Issues

The profession of CAT is made up of individuals who have undertaken formal study in the therapeutic use of a particular creative arts modality such as music or drama. Professional recognition is achieved by obtaining certification or registration in a particular CAT modality. Requirements for registration or certification vary according to the CAT specialty from a bachelor's to a master's degree and from six months to two years of supervised clinical training. Current requirements for certification or registration can be obtained by writing to the CAT professional organizations listed in Table 8.2.

Certified and registered CAT professionals work in a variety of settings that include hospitals, nursing homes, and private practice. Their role in mental health services has been primarily as "an adjunctive, secondary form of psychotherapeutic treatment" (Johnson, 1984a, p. 212). Johnson (1984a) identifies several changes that need to be made for CAT to emerge as an independent profession. These include (a) using CAT to advance the knowledge of psychology, (b) identifying the unique contribution CAT can make in the helping process, (c) overcoming CAT's dependency on other disciplines such as psychology and psychiatry by broadening the role and function of professional creative art therapists, and (d) taking a more assertive position with other professional groups and legislative agencies.

The remaining sections of this chapter present an overview of the prominent modalities associated with CAT. Information is provided in terms of key concepts, procedures and outcomes, and special populations. These are summarized in Table 8.3.

Music Therapy

Music is the oldest form of art associated with curing the ill, according to Fleshman and Fryrear (1981), who cite instances of primitive tribes and other people using songs and chants to obtain divine assistance.

Key Concepts.   Fleshman and Fryrear (1981) identify the following three key concepts associated with music therapy.

1. Music is intrinsically part of a culture.
2. Music can help clients get in touch with thoughts and feelings and communicating emotions that cannot be described by words.
3. Music has a basic structure characterized by rhythm, melody, pitch, and tempo that can be used to promote structure in clients whose thoughts are disorganized and chaotic (for example, schizophrenics).

TABLE 8.2   **Addresses for CAT Professional Organizations**

Music Therapy
>   Music Educators National Conference
>   1902 Association Drive
>   Reston, VA 22091
>
>   National Association for Music Therapy and Company
>   P.O. Box 610
>   Florence, KS 66044

Art Therapy
>   American Art Therapy Association and Company
>   428 East Preston Street
>   Baltimore, MD 21202
>
>   National Art Education Association
>   1916 Association Drive
>   Reston, VA 22091

Dance Therapy
>   American Dance Therapy Association
>   2000 Century Place
>   Columbia, MD 21044

Drama Therapy
>   National Association for Drama Therapy
>   c/o Barbara Sandberg, Recording Secretary
>   Theatre Department
>   William Paterson College
>   Wayne, NJ 07470
>
>   American Theatre Association
>   1000 Vermont Avenue NW
>   Washington, DC 20005

Bibliotherapy
>   Association of Hospital and Institution Libraries
>   Committee on Bibliotherapy
>   American Library Association
>   50 East Huron Street
>   Chicago, IL 60611
>   (Division of Health and Rehabilitative Library Services)

Miscellaneous CAT Addresses
>   American Association for Psychotherapy and the Arts
>   175 Fifth Avenue
>   New York, NY 10010
>
>   Institute for Psychotherapy and the Arts
>   175 Fifth Avenue
>   New York, NY 10010

TABLE 8.3 CAT Modalities

CAT Modality	Key Concepts	Procedures and Outcomes	Special Populations
Music Therapy	1. Music is intrinsically part of a culture. 2. Music can help clients get in touch with their thoughts and feelings. 3. Music has a basic structure in terms of rhythm, melody, and so forth, which helps clients overcome problems with thought disorders.	Use of a musical experience to enhance and facilitate counseling goals.	Can be used with all types of clients of all ages but can be particularly effective with young children and the elderly.
Art Therapy	1. Art offers a form of sublimation whereby clients can achieve indirect gratification of unconscious needs. 2. Visual symbols in art can be useful diagnostic tools. 3. Art allows for the expression of unconscious thoughts and feelings. 4. Art promotes a sense of internal equilibrium.	The process of art therapy varies according to theoretical orientation but typically includes color analysis and spontaneous drawings.	Can be used with clients of all ages but can be particularly useful with children and adolescents.
Drama Therapy	1. Offers an opportunity to externalize and learn from experiences. 2. Allows for the expression of strong feelings. 3. Deals directly and openly with functions of the personality. 4. Emotional conflicts can be better understood by expressing them in action through drama.	Spontaneous role-play is the heart of drama therapy. A variety of procedures are used in drama therapy such as movement, mime, and puppet plays.	Drama therapy can be used with clients of all ages. Its main use is with children who are physically, emotionally, or mentally handicapped.

continued

TABLE 8.3 Continued

CAT Modality	Key Concepts	Procedures and Outcomes	Special Populations
Dance Therapy	1. Dance therapy involves the integration of mind and body. 2. Can reflect a client's mood and indicate flexibility or rigidity. 3. Clients can channel self-expression into dance.	Dance procedures vary according to the outcomes desired. It can involve spontaneous or structured dance experiences. It can be used to improve motor skills and interpersonal relationships; facilitate expression of moods, attitudes, and ideas; and stimulate, energize, and relax the body.	Dance therapy can be used with clients of all ages.
Bibliotherapy	Bibliotherapy can be used to foster universalizing, identification, catharsis, and insight.	Books or some form of literature are read to promote particular counseling outcomes.	Any client who can read can benefit from bibliotherapy.
Multimodality CAT	Multimodality CAT involves using the full range of CAT modalities. It can broaden the client's ability to respond to creativity.	Procedures vary according to the theoretical orientation and can include: counselors setting the stage for creativity, setting an example, setting themselves at ease, and developing insights from creativity after a client has finished a creative expression.	All clients can benefit from multimodality CAT.

Procedures and Outcomes. Bruscia (1987) notes that music therapy involves using musical experiences and the therapeutic relationship to enhance the client's state of well-being. According to Bruscia (1987), musical experiences can include a wide range of activities that include improvising, performing, composing, and listening to music. Bruscia (1987) contends that improvising is the fundamental approach to music therapy and involves creating and playing simultaneously.

Fleshman and Fryrear (1981) suggest that music therapy involves four basic activities: (a) recreational and entertainment-oriented experiences to foster socialization; (b) therapeutic listening groups to promote group cohesion; (c) an adjunct activity to psychotherapy to stimulate emotions, encourage discussions, promote self-understanding, and facilitate socialization; and (d) individual and group music therapy to address a client's particular problem, for example, asking clients to play a duet to foster cooperation.

Several studies have been conducted on music therapy and its implication for the counseling process. Some of this research shows that music therapy facilitates the counseling process in terms of assessment and diagnosis (Isenberg-Grzeda, 1988; Wells & Stevens, 1984). Other studies have found music therapy exerts positive influence on perceived locus of control (James, 1988) and as a stimulus to promote group cohesion (Wells & Stevens, 1984). Moreno (1988) suggests that all procedures used in music therapy should reflect a multicultural sensitivity since musical traditions vary from culture to culture.

Special Populations. Music therapy can be used with people of all ages. Gibbons (1988) suggests that music therapy can be particularly effective when working with the elderly. Gibbons (1984) notes that elderly people prefer active involvement in music and can learn new musical skills such as the guitar or piano at a level comparable to much younger people.

Music therapy has also been used successfully with children and adolescents. Eidson (1989) has utilized a behaviorally oriented music therapy program to help emotionally disturbed middle school students improve their classroom behavior. Cripe (1986) provides guidelines for how to use music therapy with children with attention deficit disorder. Wells and Stevens (1984) find that music stimulates creative fantasy in young adolescents during group psychotherapy.

Fleshman and Fryrear (1981) identify other special populations, such as the mentally retarded and physically disabled, who can be served by music therapy. According to Fleshman and Fryrear (1981), music therapy can be useful with mentally retarded individuals to provide stimulation and teach social skills. In addition, regimental music, such as a march, can be used to help mentally retarded individuals obtain control over their impulses. Physically disabled clients can also benefit from music therapy. Fleshman and Fryrear (1981) cite examples such as using wind instruments to help clients with lung disorders and using certain instruments that require finger dexterity to help clients overcome motor control dysfunctions.

Melodic intonation therapy represents an emerging use of music therapy. According to Sparks and Deck (1994), it can be especially useful to treat aphasia (weakening or loss of language ability, which can include speech problems). Melodic intonation therapy utilizes music to stimulate portions of the brain that are associated with language functioning. The actual process of melodic intonation therapy involves teaching the person with aphasia to sing in a unique manner based on music from the Judeo-Christian period. Family members are encouraged to participate in this process (Sparks & Deck, 1994).

Art Therapy

Art therapy is one of the oldest and most established forms of CAT. Some of the earliest examples of art therapy can be traced to the prehistoric era, when people painted pictures on the walls of their caves to express their relationship with the world (Wadeson, 1980). Art therapy encompasses many of the visual art forms, including painting, sculpture, crafts, and photography (Kenny, 1987).

Key Concepts.   The key concepts associated with art therapy are that art

1. Offers a form of sublimation whereby clients can achieve indirect gratification of unconscious needs (Kramer, 1987)
2. Has visual symbols that can be useful diagnostic tools (Wilson, 1987)
3. Allows for the expression of unconscious thoughts and feelings (Rubin, 1987)
4. Promotes a sense of internal equilibrium (Fleshman & Fryrear, 1981)

Procedures and Outcomes.   The origins of art therapy can be traced to psychoanalytic theory (Rubin, 1987). More recently, however, it has been applied to most other major schools of psychology and counseling. Some examples are Gestalt (Rhyne, 1987); behavioral (Roth, 1987); and cognitive (Silver, 1987). A brief review of these applications follows.

Psychoanalytic.   Art can be analyzed for its symbolic content (Fleshman & Fryrear, 1981; Rubin, 1987).

Gestalt.   Art allows the client "to experience and express immediate perceptions and awareness" (Rhyne, 1987, p. 173).

Behavioral.   The behavioral approach to art therapy involves applying the principles of behavior modification to traditional art therapy techniques (Roth, 1987). In this process, principles of reinforcement are used to involve the client in art therapy and other desirable behaviors (Roth, 1987).

Cognitive.   Cognitive art therapy involves both the assessment and development of cognitive processes (Silver, 1987). Based primarily on Piaget and other cognitive psychologists, Silver (1987) identifies different ways art can be used to foster cognitive and creative skills. For example, Silver (1987) describes how the concept of sequential order can be developed through painting. Several other individuals have described procedures that are common to all approaches to art therapy. For example, color analysis can be traced to the work of Jung (1959), who noted that the use of color is related to perceptions and judgment. According to Jung (1959), yellow is associated with intuition; red is related to feeling; green suggests sensation; and blue represents thinking. In addition, Kenny (1987) suggests that color selection is also associated with emotional states, with blacks and grays indicating depression and white suggesting emotional rigidity.

Stabler (1984) provides additional guidelines for analyzing art. He notes that proportion, form, detail, movement, and theme could be used to obtain an estimate of a client's psychosocial and cognitive development and level of maturity (see Chapter 11).

Stabler (1984) also identifies three types of drawings that can be useful in art therapy: self-portraits, free drawings, and family drawings. Bertoia and Allan (1988) emphasize the role that *spontaneous drawings,* which are essentially free drawings, can play in art therapy by providing a direct link to unconscious processes.

Special Populations. Art therapy can be used with clients of all ages. Fleshman and Fryrear (1981) note it can be particularly useful with disadvantaged ghetto youth, children with sexual identity problems, mentally retarded children, schizophrenics, and suicidal patients. For example, the "suicide slash," which is a slip of the pen or an inappropriate line in a picture, and powerful repetitious images can indicate suicide ideations (Fleshman & Fryrear, 1981).

The following *Personal Note* provides an example of how I used art therapy as an adjunct to my counseling approach.

A Personal Note

"Sam" was a 21-year-old self-referred client I saw at a university counseling center in Australia. He had a severe stuttering problem and also complained of loneliness and boredom. During our second session, I asked Sam to draw whatever came to his mind. Sam drew the picture shown in Figure 8.1.

After Sam finished drawing, I asked him to describe himself in terms of his picture. Soon we began to acquire information regarding Sam's motivation for therapy, possible counseling goals, and barriers to the goals. The picture seemed to provide an overview of what Sam wanted from counseling. He mentioned that he had never had a girlfriend and hadn't even kissed a girl. The catapult suggested he was very motivated to have a girlfriend. Unfortunately, he didn't believe this was possible since there were several barriers standing in his way, as illustrated by the sharks swimming between him and the girl.

We went on to identify what these barriers were in terms of *basic mistakes,* as discussed in Chapter 7. For example, he thought he could not get

FIGURE 8.1   Sam's Picture

continued

a girlfriend if he was a stutterer. I then helped Sam overcome the basic mistakes as well as other self-defeating processes during the reorientation phase of counseling. (See Nystul and Musynska, 1976, for a more detailed description of this case.)

Source: Nystul, M., and Musynska, E. (November 1976). Adlerian treatment of a classical case of stuttering, *Journal of Individual Psychology, 32*(2), 194–202; by permission of the University of Texas Press.

Drama Therapy

Moreno (1946) was the founder of psychodrama, which was one of the first systematic uses of drama as a form of therapy. Later, drama therapy emerged as a more flexible alternative to psychodrama. Irwin (1987, p. 277) notes that drama therapy is less verbal, less structured, and less oriented toward the theater than psychodrama. Johnson (1984b, p. 105) defines drama therapy "as the intentional use of creative drama toward the psychotherapeutic goals of symptom relief, emotional and physical integration, and personal growth." Drama therapy includes any use of role-playing, but it is especially associated with the use of creative theater as a medium for self-expression (Johnson, 1984b).

Key Concepts.   Although drama therapy is in its formative stage of development, the following four key concepts characterize its current status.

1. Drama offers an opportunity to externalize and learn from experiences, both real and imagined (Irwin, 1987).
2. Drama allows for the expression of strong feelings, thinking, impulses, and action (Irwin, 1987).
3. Drama deals directly and openly with different functions of the personality (Fleshman & Fryrear, 1981).
4. Emotional conflicts can be better understood by expressing them in action through drama (Irwin, 1987).

Procedures and Outcomes.   As in all CAT modalities, the procedures of drama therapy will vary according to the theoretical orientation of the practitioner. Irwin (1987) notes that drama therapists draw from a variety of theoretical orientations such as psychoanalytic, behavioral, Gestalt, Jungian, and Rogerian.

Several authors have identified what can be considered common procedures associated with drama therapy. First, spontaneous role-playing is the heart of drama therapy and can be found in all its forms (Fleshman & Fryrear, 1981). Second, the therapist uses a variety of procedures such as movement, mime, and puppet plays to involve the client in action so inner conflicts can be expressed and better understood (Irwin, 1987). Third, drama therapy contributes to assessment and diagnosis by analyzing roles that are enacted or rejected, themes and conflicts that emerge in fantasies and stories, and the process of the session in terms of emotional release (Irwin, 1987).

Special Populations.   Drama therapy can be used with people of all ages. Its main use appears to be with children, and numerous programs have been developed for children who

Various moods can be expressed in drama therapy.

are physically, emotionally, or mentally disabled (Fleshman & Fryrear, 1981). Drama therapy can be particularly useful in school settings to teach students how to deal with pressures relating to dating or drug and alcohol use.

Dance Therapy

The origins of dance therapy can be traced to modern dance, which began early in the twentieth century (Fleshman & Fryrear, 1981).

Key Concepts.   Fleshman and Fryrear (1981) identify these three key concepts associated with dance therapy.

1. The fundamental concept in dance therapy is the integration, or more specifically the reintegration, of mind and body.
2. Movement can reflect a client's mood and indicate either flexibility or rigidity.
3. Dance therapy provides an opportunity for clients to express themselves in movement, channeling self-expression into dance form.

Procedures and Outcomes.   Dance therapy may involve clients dancing by themselves or with other clients. The dance method can be spontaneous or more structured in nature. Particular attention is paid to what the client communicates or discovers from the dance. Other factors worth noting are how the client interacts with others, the client's awareness of space, and how the dance may relate to a particular problem that the client is experiencing.

Fleshman and Fryrear (1981) and Lasseter et al. (1989) identify goals associated with dance therapy, which include

- Improving motor skills
- Enhancing the relationship between the client and therapist

- Increasing the client's movement repertoire to facilitate expression of moods, attitudes, and ideas
- Allowing for the sublimation of erotic and aggressive impulses
- Encouraging interpersonal relationships
- Stimulating, energizing, and relaxing the client's body

Special Populations.   Dance therapy can be used with people of all ages. Lasseter et al. (1989) note that dance therapy has been a primary treatment strategy for children with mental, physical, and emotional problems. In this regard, dance therapy has been used successfully with autistic children (Cole, 1982), psychotic children (Gunning & Holmes, 1973), children with cerebral palsy (Clark & Evans, 1973), mentally retarded children (Boswell, 1983), and emotionally disturbed and learning-disabled children (Polk, 1977; Wislocki, 1981).

Bibliotherapy

The earliest uses of bibliotherapy can be traced to the Grecian times where a sign was hung over the entrance of a library proclaiming "the healing place of the soul" (Zaccaria & Moses, 1968). Riordan and Wilson (1989, p. 506) define bibliotherapy as "the guided reading of written materials in gaining understanding or resolving problems relevant to a person's therapeutic needs." There appears to be an increase in use of bibliotherapy as an adjunct to counseling (Riordan & Wilson, 1989), with 60 percent of psychologists prescribing self-help books occasionally; 24 percent often, and 12 percent regularly (Starker, 1988).

Key Concepts.   According to Fleshman and Fryrear (1981), the key concepts of bibliotherapy are derived from psychoanalytic theory and include

1. *Universalizing.* Clients minimize feelings of guilt, shame, and isolation when they discover others share similar problems in life.
2. *Identification.* Clients can identify with characters in books, which provide a positive role model regarding attitudes and values.
3. *Catharsis.* Bibliotherapy group discussions provide clients with opportunities for self-disclosure and catharsis.
4. *Insight.* Clients can obtain insight by having an external frame of reference for comparison.

Procedures and Outcomes.   Bibliotherapy involves asking clients to read a book or some form of literature to promote certain outcomes associated with the counseling process (for example, career awareness and exploration). The nature of the reading assignment will depend on the desired outcomes. For example, *What Color Is Your Parachute?* could be used to assist a client with career choice. Four of the most commonly prescribed books by psychologists are *What Color Is Your Parachute?, The Relaxation Response, Your Perfect Right,* and *Feeling Good* (Starker, 1988). Once clients have read a book or other literature, they can discuss what they learned with the counselor.

Counselors can share their creative outlets in multimodality creative arts therapy (CAT).

Special Populations.   Bibliotherapy can be used with any client who knows how to read. Research on the efficacy of bibliotherapy has provided mixed results. The most recent studies showed support for bibliotherapy in effecting behavioral change (Riordan & Wilson, 1989).

Multimodality CAT

A relatively recent addition to the CAT approaches involves the use of multiple CAT modalities instead of relying on a single modality such as dance or music. This broad-based approach to CAT has been called various names, including creative-expressive arts, mixed-media arts, and multimedia approach to the expressive arts (Fleshman & Fryrear, 1981; Talerico, 1986). The term *multimodality CAT* indicates using whatever CAT modality the therapist and client want to use.

Key Concepts.   The major premise behind multimodality CAT is that it creates limitless possibilities for creative expression, whereas using one modality can be unnecessarily restrictive, discouraging creative responses from the client (Talerico, 1986).

Procedures and Outcomes.   A four-phase model of CAT can be used with all types of creative media, for example, art, music, or dance, with clients of all ages (Nystul, 1980, 1985, 1987). The four phases of this model are

1. *Set the stage.* The counselor sets the stage for creative process by either having creative arts material available to use or encouraging the client to bring a creative outlet (for example, a guitar) to the next counseling session.
2. *Set an example.* The counselor may wish to share a creative outlet with the client to set an example of risk taking and self-disclosure.

3. *Set yourself at ease.* The counselor should initially avoid analyzing a client's creative expression for psychological insights before the client is finished. This can cause a client to become self-conscious and interfere with the counselor directly experiencing the client's creative expression.

4. *Obtain a phenomenological understanding of the client.* Once the client has completed the creative expression, for example, a song or drawing, the counselor can attempt to gain a phenomenological understanding of the client. This can be accomplished by asking clients to describe what the creative expression said about them or describe themselves in terms of the creative expression.

The use of multiple CAT modalities in counseling and psychotherapy can promote the following outcomes (Nystul, 1980, 1985, 1987). Multimodality CAT can provide assessment and diagnostic information by having clients project their thoughts and feelings into a creative expression, promote self-disclosure in counselors and clients as they share their creative outlets. It can also increase clients' social interest as they discover the support that can result from sharing a creative expression, develop a phenomenological understanding of clients as they describe themselves in terms of their creative expression, and promote an existential encounter as counselors directly experience their clients' emotions through the release of their creative expressions.

Special Populations.   Multimodality CAT can be used with clients of all ages. Some examples are autistic children (Nystul, 1985), emotionally disturbed children (Nystul, 1978, 1980), a young adult stutterer who felt socially isolated (Nystul & Musynska, 1976), and a student in a university counseling center who had a sexual identity problem (Nystul, 1979). In addition, the counselor is not restricted to one modality such as art therapy, so clients have more opportunities to explore and discover creative outlets.

The following *Personal Note* provides an example of how I used multimodality CAT.

A Personal Note

One case that was very special to me involved a first-grader named Ron. I was an elementary school counselor and Ron was referred to me for counseling services. The reason for the referral was that he spent most of his time daydreaming in class and appeared to have no friends at school.

Ron was unresponsive to my questions during our first counseling session, so I decided to see him in a play therapy setting. As described in Chapter 11, my approach to play therapy involves two parts: a self-concept program and the four-stage model associated with multimodality CAT (Nystul, 1980).

After we finished our self-concept program, Ron was humming a song. I asked him to make up a song about how he was feeling. I attempted to accompany him on the guitar, and he responded by singing a deep, sorrowful song. These were the words to Ron's song

My mom comes home and daddy stays home
Momma goes home, daddy stays
Momma stays in the city when she wants to
Momma stays in the city when she wants to

Momma daddy, Momma daddy
I just can't seem to go.

Daddy keep care of the baby
Daddy keep care of the baby
Daddy keep care of the baby

Please help me
I want no!
I need help!

I can't seem to stop
Daddy keep care of the baby
Good-bye, good-bye.

As Ron sang, I did not try to identify any psychological insights from the words of the song. Instead, I went with the music and allowed myself to get caught up with his creative energy. When Ron finished singing, I felt I had gone beyond attempting to understand or empathize with Ron's pain or sorrow. Instead, I had to some degree experienced these feelings as he sang.

As a result of our existential encounter, Ron and I had established a special counseling relationship. He therefore felt free to discuss his thoughts and feelings with me. Later that day, we listened to his song again, which I had tape-recorded. This time, I was interested in exploring the song for possible psychological significance. I asked Ron what the song might say about him. He responded by telling me different facets of his past.

As I listened, I began to identify basic mistakes, which are described in Chapter 7—faulty views that may interfere with what a person wants out of life. For example, he said his father was black, and his mother said black men are all no good. This was a basic mistake, since his view of being black would have a detrimental effect on feeling good about himself and others (something he wanted out of life).

To help reorient Ron from this basic mistake, I enlisted the help of Bill, a black counselor from another school, who agreed to co-lead some of my play therapy groups. The students loved Bill. Soon Ron began to believe that being even part black could be beautiful. (See Nystul, 1980, for a more complete description of this case.)

Summary and Evaluation of CAT

Creative arts therapy is a dynamic and powerful tool. CAT can be viewed as an emerging profession or adjunctive strategy associated with counseling and psychotherapy. It can have many uses such as promoting socialization, communicating thoughts and emotions, enhancing the counseling relationship, and as a projective device in assessment and diagnosis. A weakness is the lack of empirical research to determine its precise effect on psychological functioning and the counseling process.

Research Trends in Experiential Counseling

Greenberg, Elliott, and Lietaer (1994) provide an overview of research trends in experiential counseling approaches. Their review includes summaries of studies directed at determining who benefits most from experiential therapies and treatment trends in experiential therapy. Studies examining the effects of client characteristics on success with experiential therapy show that

- Clients who rate high in social skills, affiliation, and assertiveness tend to respond well in person-centered therapy.
- Clients with high reactance (including high dominance) or resistance to influence appear to do better in person-centered therapy, whereas those low in reactance do better in Gestalt therapy.
- Internally oriented clients (open clients who are interested in inner experience) appear to do well in person-centered therapy.

Treatment trends in experiential therapies are summarized by Greenberg, Elliott, and Lietaer (1994) as follows.

- Experiential therapies appear to be useful across a broad range of treatment considerations from the "worried well" to the treatment of disorders such as anxiety and depression.
- Therapists should be aware of factors in experiential therapy (such as lack of direction and intrusiveness) that can hinder therapeutic progress.
- Therapists need to move away from uniform use of an experiential theory and adapt the theory to treat specific disorders such as depression or panic attacks.
- Task interventions for therapists and clients can be developed, implemented, and processed to provide a focused means of treating specific problems and then analyzing their efficacy.

Research trends are also generating support for CAT. Sherwood-Hawes (1995) notes that the various CATs are currently being used to successfully treat a wide array of clinical problems. For example, art therapy is being successfully used to treat sexual abuse. Dance therapy has been proved useful in treating eating disorders. Music therapy is used in a wide array of treatments from dementia and Alzheimer's disease to treating chronic pain and immune system disorders. And drama and poetry therapy have been found to be effective in treating post-traumatic stress disorders and substance abuse.

Brief Approaches to Experiential Counseling

Although experiential theories were not originally developed for brief counseling, they appear to offer much promise in terms of providing a useful adjunct to a time-limited format. Person-centered therapy can be of use in establishing the counseling relationship through the use of listening skills and facilitating the core conditions. Gestalt therapy has several useful concepts and techniques that could be of use in brief counseling. The key concept of awareness would seem to be a useful goal in brief counseling to maximize a client's readiness for counseling. Gestalt offers numerous useful techniques that can be used in brief counseling, such as the use of personal pronouns to help clients take responsibility for their behavior. The existential concepts of freedom, choice, and responsibility empower clients and enhance their motivation for involvement in the change process.

CAT is ideally suited for brief counseling. Any of the creative arts modalities can be used successfully in as little as one session (such as patients in a hospital listening to music) or can be used as an adjunct to brief-counseling models designed to treat specific disorders. CAT can make an instant impact because of the healing power of the CAT experience. In this regard, Hale (1990) notes that CAT often provides a superior method of healing over more traditional methods.

Diversity Issues in Experiential Counseling

Experiential theories hold both promise and concern in terms of diversity issues such as culture and gender. In terms of culture, Carl Rogers (in his later years) provided training throughout the world in how his counseling theory could be used to foster positive interpersonal relations and overcome conflict. Rogers hoped that his theory could provide a means to alleviate interracial tension and foster world peace (Corey, 1996). Rogers was recognized for this effort by being nominated for a Nobel Peace Prize just before he died.

Corey (1996) notes that Gestalt therapy can make positive contributions in terms of cultural issues. Gestalt therapy can be useful in cross-cultural counseling by helping clients integrate the opposing forces (or polarities) that they can face such as working through the conflicts between their culture and the dominant culture. In addition, Gestalt therapy emphasizes the importance of nonverbal communication as an authentic means of communication. Nonverbal communication can help overcome confusing misunderstandings that result from language differences in cross-cultural counseling. The various creative arts modalities (such as art, music, and dance) also rely on nonverbal communication, which enhances their cross-cultural utility.

Corey (1996) also describes how existential therapy can play an important role in cross-cultural counseling in terms of bringing personal meaning to life and feeling a sense of control over one's destiny. For example, experiential counseling can help clients who feel oppressed and victimized by forces such as racism or sexism realize that on some level there are choices and decisions that they are making that are influencing the direction of their lives. Awareness of choices can foster a sense of control and responsibility, which in turn can contribute to meaning in life.

Ingersoll (1995) posits that diversity issues associated with spirituality are associated with Frankl's (1963) existential theory of logotherapy. In this theory, Frankl stresses the relationship between the mind, body, and spirit with the spirit playing the key role in one's search for meaning. Processes such as self-transcendence and ontological at-oneness with others would appear to be an example of the role of spiritual issues in logotherapy.

Experiential counseling has also been criticized in terms of diversity issues such as culture and gender (Corey, 1996; Prochaska & Norcross, 1994). These authors note that experiential theories overemphasize the intrapsychic forces as being responsible for psychological health and wellness and underestimate environmental forces. Experiential counseling techniques and procedures are reflected in this narrow intrapsychic focus, failing to incorporate current "ecological" trends such as social constructionism, systemic theory from marriage and family counseling, and environmental assessment. For example, social constructionism emphasizes the role that social forces (such as language, narratives, and culture) play in influencing how people construct reality (Gergen, 1994).

Experiential counseling appears to be somewhat naive, with a very narrow and unrealistic focus. It fails to recognize the significant role that environmental factors such as unemployment, poverty, overcrowding, sexism, racism, and other oppressive forces can play in psychological functioning. For example, from a feminist perspective, experiential theories can be seen as the male's way of controlling and blaming women for the women's problems such as depression (that is, depression is due to an "intrapsychic defect" and not forces such as political and gender oppression arising from a male-dominated and -controlled society and culture).

In the final analysis there is promise, yet work still to be done, regarding the utility of experiential counseling with issues of diversity. It is hoped that future research will focus on how experiential theories can be broadened to create a more comprehensive, inclusive explanation for human growth and development, including psychological health and wellness.

Summary

Some theories and approaches are called *experiential* because of their common view that therapeutic gains result from what the client experiences during the counseling session. The three major experiential theories, person-centered, Gestalt, and existential, reflect the spirit of humanistic psychology in conceptualizing human nature as inherently positive, self-determined, and having self-actualizing tendencies.

The strength of experiential therapies lies in their ability to help clients become aware of their thoughts and feelings, discover their inner choices, and promote personal responsibility. The weakness of experiential therapies can be their overemphasis on feelings and underemphasis on cognition and behavior. Experiential therapies may therefore lack some of the counseling strategies necessary to promote a comprehensive treatment program.

Creative arts therapy is an emerging profession with opportunities for professional certification and registration in various CAT modalities such as music, art, and drama. CAT is also an adjunctive counseling strategy, which can be used to facilitate the counseling process. Multimodality CAT is a relatively new addition to the CAT field. It has the advantage of utilizing whatever CAT modality the counselor or client prefers to use.

Information on research trends, brief approaches, and diversity issues in experiential counseling shows that experiential theories and approaches can be flexible and useful in various counseling formats from long term to brief. Research trends and issues of diversity help identify some of the strengths and weaknesses of this school of counseling.

The Suggested Readings on pages 420–422 contain additional information regarding the experiential theories and approaches.

CHAPTER

9 Cognitive-Behavioral Theories

CHAPTER OVERVIEW

This chapter provides an overview of cognitive-behavioral theories and approaches to counseling. Highlights of the chapter include

- The art and science of cognitive-behavioral counseling
- An overview of each cognitive-behavioral theory in terms of a theory of personality and a theory of counseling and psychotherapy (that is, of behavior therapy, rational-emotive behavioral therapy, cognitive therapy, transactional analysis, and reality therapy)
- Trends in brief counseling
- Diversity issues
- Postmodern trends

The Art and Science of Cognitive-Behavioral Counseling

The goal of cognitive-behavioral counseling is to help clients identify how their thoughts and behaviors generate negative emotional consequences and to assist them with the necessary interventions to foster positive growth and development. The art of this theoretical approach is twofold. First, counselors can work *with* clients to help them discover dysfunctional thoughts from the perspective of the *client's* worldview and not from the *counselor's* view of what is rational or functional. Second, counselors can attempt to create a balance in terms of exploring the etiology of dysfunctional thoughts, addressing both intrapsychic forces and postmodern considerations that are reflected contextually between clients and sociocultural and political forces in their environments.

Behavioral counseling (which focuses on overt, observable, and measurable behavior) is founded on principles associated with the science of counseling. This position was articulated by B. F. Skinner (1990) in his ongoing goal of promoting the science of behavioral psychology. Cognitive-behavioral counseling continues the strong tradition in science.

In this regard, the cognitive-behavioral school of counseling has the strongest research base of any school of counseling.

New trends in the science of counseling are reflected in postmodern theories such as constructivism and social constructionism. These trends are creating new perspectives for understanding concepts that are fundamental to science (for example, knowledge and reality). From a postmodern perspective, knowledge and reality are relative terms that must be understood contextually. For example, the definition of reality can vary according to culture as reflected in the culture's language and narratives. The science of cognitive-behavioral counseling can draw on qualitative research's discovery method, in which the counselor and client attempt to discover the personal meaning generated from the client's stories.

As noted in Chapter 6, the art and science of counseling recommend using a multicultural perspective to conceptualize diversity issues throughout the counseling process. Cognitive-behavior theories can create special concerns regarding diversity. For example, from a postmodern perspective the nature and content of cognitive and behavioral processes vary contextually according to variables such as gender. In this regard, developmental researchers such as Carol Gilligan (1982, 1990) have clearly shown that women think and behave differently with regard to processes such as moral decision making and identity development. The art and science of the cognitive-behavioral theories involve making the necessary modifications to these theories by incorporating multicultural research findings and maintaining a sensitivity to the evolving needs of clients.

Cognitive-Behavioral Theories

Cognitive-behavioral theories emphasize the role of cognition and/or behavior in psychological functioning and well-being. The recent trend toward diversifying and integrating counseling theories has altered the focus of some cognitive-behavioral theories. Theories that originally had a cognitive focus have incorporated behavioral techniques (for example, cognitive therapy and rational-emotive behavior therapy) and behaviorally oriented theories have incorporated cognitive techniques and concepts (for example, behavior therapy and reality therapy).

The integration of theories represents an attempt to develop a more comprehensive approach as opposed to highlighting what is unique about a particular school of counseling. It is hoped that this trend will continue, replacing unnecessary barriers between theories with compatible concepts and procedures.

This chapter provides a description of the following theories: behavior therapy, rational-emotive behavior therapy, cognitive therapy, transactional analysis, and reality therapy. Table 9.1 provides an overview of these theories in terms of key concepts, the counseling process, and techniques.

Behavior Therapy

Background Information

The historical roots of behavior therapy can be traced to three learning theories: classical conditioning, operant conditioning, and social learning theory. Classical conditioning evolved

TABLE 9.1 The Cognitive-Behavioral Theories

Theory	Founder(s)	Key Concepts	The Counseling Process	Techniques
Behavior Therapy	Pavlov, Skinner, Bandura, Wolpe, and Meichenbaum	Incorporation of principles from learning theories; grounding in the scientific method; focus on overt, observable behavior; view of psychopathology primarily in behavioral terms.	Attempts to establish clear and precise counseling goals such as modifying maladaptive behavior, strengthening desired behavior, and helping clients learn effective decision making.	Assertive training, systematic desensitization, token economy, cognitive behavior modification, and self-control.
Rational-Emotive Behavior Therapy	Ellis	Basic premise that emotional disturbance results from illogical or irrational thought processes.	Helps the client learn how to dispute irrational or illogical thoughts.	Cognitive restructuring emotive techniques, shame attacking exercises, bibliotherapy, and behavioral techniques.
Cognitive Therapy	Beck	The role of cognition in mental health, cognitive vulnerability, cognitive distortions, systematic bias in information processing, cognitive triad of depression, and the cognitive model of anxiety.	Offers a short-term treatment program for depression, anxiety, and other mental disorders. Its ultimate goal is elimination of systematic bias in thinking.	Cognitive techniques such as decatastrophizing, reattribution, redefining, decentering; and behavioral techniques such as skill training, progressive relaxation, behavioral rehearsal, and exposure therapy.
Transactional Analysis (TA)	Berne	The three ego states (parent, adult, child), transactional analysis, games people play, life scripts, the four life positions, and strokes.	Educative method to teach the client how to use TA concepts to make positive decisions regarding their lives.	Structural analysis, transactional analysis, script analysis, and analysis of games.
Reality Therapy	Glasser	Success and failure identity, emphasis on responsibility, avoidance of labels associated with mental disorders, positive addiction, and control theory.	Has primary aim to help client develop a success identity through responsible action; teaches clients how to use control theory to fulfill basic needs and not interfere with the rights of others.	Incorporates an eight-step approach that includes creating a relationship, focusing on current behavior, having client evaluate behavior, making an action plan, obtaining a commitment, not accepting excuses, not using punishment, and refusing to give up.

from Ivan Pavlov's experiments with dogs. In these experiments, Pavlov (1906) demonstrated that he could condition a dog to salivate to the sound of a bell. This was the first demonstration of what Pavlov called *classical conditioning,* the principle of conditioning people to respond to a stimulus. Pavlov's principles of classical conditioning were later applied to counseling. Joseph Wolpe (1958, 1973) played a key role in this process, integrating the principles of classical conditioning into a systematic desensitization process to treat phobias. This technique continues to be one of the most popular approaches for the treatment of phobias.

B. F. Skinner developed the second major field of learning theory, operant conditioning. Skinner (1938, 1953, 1961) proposed that learning cannot occur without some form of reinforcement. He contended that behaviors that are reinforced will tend to be repeated, and those that are not tend to be extinguished. Compared to classical conditioning, operant conditioning is a more active process of learning in that the person must do something to be reinforced.

Skinner developed the principles of operant conditioning in his now-famous Skinner Box experiments, which involved training a rat to press a bar for food. More recently, the principles of operant conditioning have been utilized in programmed learning, self-control, behaviorally oriented discipline procedures, and management of clients in institutions by use of token economies.

The third major learning theory that helped formulate behavior therapy is social learning theory. Along with the various cognitive theories, social learning theory represents a more recent dimension to the behavioral school. Among the individuals associated with these new trends are Beck (1991), Meichenbaum (1986), Mahoney (1991), and Bandura (1986). In particular, Bandura was instrumental in the integration of cognition into behavior therapy.

Bandura's (1977) early work on social learning theory focused on how learning occurs from observation, modeling, and imitation. The idea that learning could occur entirely as a function of cognitive control was a direct challenge to the traditional behavioral stimulus-response model (Mahoney & Lyddon, 1988). In addition, Bandura's (1974) "endorsement of an interactional reciprocity between person and environment marked a pivotal shift from exclusive environmental determinism" (Mahoney & Lyddon, 1988, p. 196).

More recently Bandura (1982, 1986, 1989) developed a theory of self-efficacy, which related to a person's belief in the ability to successfully accomplish a particular task. Perceived self-efficacy plays a central role in mediating constructive behavior change (Bandura, 1986). Bandura's theory contends that self-efficacy can directly influence what activities people will choose to engage in, how much effort they will exert, and how long they will continue when faced with adversity (Johnson et al., 1989).

Theory of Personality

The theory of personality of behavior therapy is integrated into its theory of counseling and psychotherapy. In this sense assessment and intervention are interrelated. For example, counselors and clients chart changes in behaviors to assess the relative impact of various intervention procedures.

View of Human Nature.   Historically, behaviorists viewed human nature as neutral. A person was not inherently good or bad but would become what the environment dictated. This position was in direct contrast to the humanistic stance, which suggested people were capable of self-determination. The more recent behavioral point of view recognizes the possibility of self-determined behavior (Bandura, 1986; Meichenbaum, 1986). In this regard, individuals can take an active role in their destiny.

Key Concepts.   Behavior therapy is currently in a state of rapid change and evolution (Wilson, 1995). Rimm and Cunningham (1985) identify common elements that characterize behavior therapy. Five of their observations are incorporated into the following overview.

1. *Behavior therapy concentrates on overt, observable behavioral processes and cognitions.* The early behaviorists focused on overt behavior. More recently, the cognitive realm is also viewed as an important mediating factor in relation to behavior.
2. *Behavior therapy focuses on the here and now.* Information about past experience is considered important only as it relates to current treatment issues. The focus is on understanding and treating current problems relating to behavior and cognitions.
3. *Maladaptive behaviors are primarily the result of learning.* Models of learning (operant, classical, and social learning theories) can be used to understand the etiology of maladaptive behavior. Learning principles can therefore be used to change maladaptive behavior.
4. *Well-defined, concrete goals are used.* Goals are stated in observable, measurable terms whenever possible.
5. *Behavior therapy is committed to the scientific method.* Behavior therapy utilizes the principles of scientific method to evaluate techniques and procedures. Assessment and treatment are viewed as part of the same process, creating a built-in mechanism for research and accountability.

Theory of Counseling and Psychotherapy

The Counseling Process.   The counselor utilizes an active and directive approach, which often incorporates problem-solving strategies (Wilson, 1995). The client is also expected to take an active role in the counseling process in terms of assessment by engaging in processes such as self-monitoring and treatment by acquiring new skills and behaviors through work and practice.

A misconception regarding behavior therapists is that they view a positive counseling relationship as unimportant to the counseling process (Wilson, 1995). Brady (1980) notes, however, that the nature of the counseling relationship can have a direct bearing on the outcome of behavior therapy. In addition, Swan and MacDonald (1978) have found that behavior therapists reported that relationship-building procedures are among the most frequently used.

Behavior therapy has concrete, specific goals that include acquiring necessary behaviors and coping skills and overcoming self-defeating cognitive processes. When possible, clients assume primary responsibility for determining treatment goals. The therapist's role and function are therefore directed at how to accomplish goals in therapy rather than focusing on which goals to work on (Wilson, 1995).

Techniques.   Most behavior therapy procedures are short-term in duration, although some may extend as long as 25 to 50 sessions (Wilson, 1995). Behavior therapists use a wide variety of techniques and procedures: cognitive behavior modification, self-management and self-control, self-efficacy, participant modeling, assertiveness training, systematic desensitization, and token economy.

Cognitive Behavior Modification.   Donald Meichenbaum's (1986) cognitive behavior modification has several useful strategies such as self-instructional therapy and stress-inoculation training. Self-instructional therapy is a form of self-control therapy in which clients learn to use tools to take control of their lives. Behavior change occurs "through a sequence of mediating processes involving the interaction of inner speech, cognitive structures, and behaviors, and their resultant outcomes" (Meichenbaum, 1977, p. 218).

This theory suggests that people have a set of beliefs or cognitive structures that influence how they react to events in terms of an inner speech or self-talk. To a large degree, cognitive structures and inner speech determine how people behave. The focus of therapy is on restructuring faulty cognitive structures, altering inner speech so that it triggers coping behaviors, and if necessary using behavior therapy to teach coping responses.

Stress-inoculation training is another useful approach that utilizes a number of cognitive-behavioral techniques such as "cognitive restructuring, problem-solving, relaxation training, behavioral and imaginal rehearsal, self-monitoring, self-reinforcement, and efforts at environmental change" (Meichenbaum, 1985, p. 21). It can be used to treat different disorders, but is especially useful to treat anxiety. The procedure focuses on helping clients learn coping mechanisms that they can use to "inoculate" or protect themselves from stress-related reactions. A major premise of this approach is that clients can be taught to cope with stressful situations and enhance their performance by modifying their self-statements. Stress-inoculation training is comprehensive, attempting to go beyond symptom relief and teach skills that can be useful to prevent problems in the future, including relapse. The actual process of implementing stress inoculation typically involves three stages: conceptualization, skill acquisition and rehearsal, and application and follow-through.

Self-Management and Self-Control.   Kanfer and associates (Kanfer & Goldstein, 1986), Bandura (1986), and Meichenbaum (1986) are associated with self-management and self-control procedures which are directed at helping clients become their own agents for behavior change (Gintner & Poret, 1987). In this process, the therapist provides support and expertise in terms of behavioral management. The client assumes responsibility for implementing and carrying out the program (Kanfer & Goldstein, 1986).

A wide range of skills can be used to promote self-management and self-control. For example, Kanfer and Goldstein (1986) identify skills in (a) self-monitoring, (b) establishing rules of conduct by contracting, (c) obtaining environmental support, (d) self-evaluating, and (e) generating reinforcing consequences for behaviors that promote the goals of self-control. Wilson (1995) describes other self-control skills such as progressive relaxation to reduce stress; biofeedback to treat psychophysiological disorders; and self-instructional training for control of anger, impulsivity, and other coping problems.

Self-Efficacy.   As noted earlier, self-efficacy is a theory developed primarily by Bandura (1982, 1986, 1989) that relates to a person's belief in the ability to accomplish a particular task. Self-efficacy is not a behavioral technique. It can be better viewed as a concept that should be considered when implementing a technique. Rimm and Cunningham (1985) note that treatments that foster the greatest change in self-efficacy should be the most effective.

Albert Bandura

They suggest that treatment efficacy can be increased by promoting methods that foster efficacy information to clients. In this regard, Bandura, Reese, and Adams (1982) note that efficacy information can be transferred to clients by (a) actual performance, which is the most powerful information source; (b) vicarious learning or modeling; (c) verbal persuasion; and (d) psychological arousal.

Self-efficacy theory has stimulated a proliferation of research activity. It has been shown to predict many behaviors such as depression (Davis-Berman, 1988); cessation after treatment (Gooding & Glasgow, 1985; Nicki, Remington, & MacDonald, 1984); recovery from heart attacks (Bandura, 1982); sports performance (Lee, 1982; McAuley, 1985); and success in weight-reduction programs (Weinburg et al., 1984). Based on a review of the literature on self-efficacy, Johnson et al. (1989) conclude that "across varied behavioral domains, self-efficacy has predicted differences in the degree to which people choose, present, and succeed in performing targeted behaviors" (p. 206).

Participant Modeling.   Participant modeling is based on Bandura's (1977, 1986, 1989) social learning theory, which emphasizes the role of observation and imitation in learning. It is used primarily to treat phobias and fears (Rimm & Cunningham, 1985). Participant modeling involves two stages, observation and participation. During the observation stage, the client observes a model engaged in the feared behavior, for example, petting a dog. Research suggests that efficacy increases when the model is similar to the client in terms of age and gender (Raskin & Israel, 1981) and the manner in which the model approaches the feared task (Meichenbaum, 1972). The second stage involves the client participating or engaging in the feared behavior. During this process, the counselor guides the client through a series of exercises relating to the feared task (Rimm & Cunningham, 1985).

Assertiveness Training.   Assertiveness training can be used for clients who find it difficult to stand up for their rights or who are unable to express their feelings in a constructive manner (Wilson, 1995). Rimm and Cunningham (1985) describe the following steps involved in assertiveness training. First, the therapist and client determine whether there is a need for assertiveness training. Second, the therapist describes how increased assertiveness can be beneficial. The third step is the most important and involves a process of behavioral rehearsal. During behavioral rehearsal, the therapist models an assertive behavior, then asks the client to "rehearse" the assertive behavior, and finally provides feedback and appropriate reinforcement.

Systematic Desensitization. Systematic desensitization is a technique developed by Wolpe (1958, 1973) to treat problems resulting from classical conditioning such as phobias. It has also been used to treat a variety of other maladaptive behaviors including excessive fears about issues such as death, injury, and sex (Kazdin, 1978).

The following steps can be used to implement this technique.

1. *Teach deep relaxation.* Systematic desensitization utilizes the principle of counterconditioning by introducing a relaxation response to replace the previously conditioned adversive response. It is based on the assumption that a person cannot be anxious and relaxed at the same time. The client is therefore taught to experience a state of deep relaxation when the therapist describes a relaxing scene.
2. *Develop a hierarchy.* The therapist and client develop a hierarchy of situations that elicit a fear response. The situation that elicits the lowest level of anxiety is the first item in the hierarchy, and the one that elicits the highest level of anxiety is last. It is important that the statements are specific enough that the client will be able to visualize the situation. An example is, "I walked up a flight of stairs to the fourth floor and looked out the window."
3. *Proceed through the hierarchy.* The therapist helps the client enter into a state of deep relaxation. The therapist then asks the client to imagine the first item in the hierarchy. By introducing a relaxation response to a situation that previously elicited a fear response, the therapist helps the client become desensitized by the counterconditioning process.
4. *Address the fear in vivo.* This step involves desensitizing the client to *in-vivo* or real-life situations associated with the fears. For example, if the client has a snake phobia, an item on the hierarchy may be to imagine looking at a snake. During the *in-vivo* experience, the client will be asked to look at a real snake.
5. *Follow up and evaluate.* The final step is to evaluate the client's success in dealing with the fear response in a variety of situations over an extended period of time.

Token Economy. Ayllon and Azrin (1968) developed the technique of *token economy* to teach psychiatric patients to become more responsible. It has been used primarily in hospitals, residential settings, and schools. The technique is based on the principles of operant conditioning and involves giving tokens to reinforce a desired behavior such as cleaning one's room. After collecting enough tokens, clients can exchange them for goods or privileges such as being able to watch TV. To increase intrinsic motivation, the tokens must be gradually eliminated and replaced by social reinforcers such as encouragement. This will enable clients to maintain newly acquired behaviors after they leave the treatment setting.

Summary and Evaluation

Behavior therapy focuses on overt behavior. The counseling process emphasizes the importance of establishing clear goals stated in behavioral terms. Progress in therapy is indicated when there is a change or modification in behavior. Treatment and assessment are seen as part of the same process, creating a built-in mechanism for research and accountability.

Emmelkamp (1994) summarizes the research on behavior therapy and concludes that it has been shown to be effective to treat a number of mental disorders and client concerns such as

- Anxiety disorders such as phobias, post-traumatic stress disorder, generalized anxiety, aggressive-compulsive disorder
- Depression (behavioral counseling is especially effective when used in conjunction with cognitive approaches such as cognitive therapy)
- Alcoholism (including treatment of controlled drinking)
- Sexual disorders (behavioral counseling is quite useful to treat sexual dysfunctions such as premature ejaculation and missed orgasm but not so effective in treating paraphilias such as exhibitionism and pedophilia)

Some weaknesses are associated with the behavioral approach. Behavior therapy tends to disregard the importance of feelings and emotions in the counseling process, ignore historical factors that can contribute to a client's problem, and minimize the use of insight in the counseling process.

Rational Emotive Behavior Therapy (REBT)

Background Information

Albert Ellis (b. 1913) received M.A. and Ph.D. degrees in clinical psychology from Columbia University and went on to practice in the areas of marriage, family, and sex therapy. Ellis initially developed his theory of counseling in the 1950s which he called rational therapy.

In 1962, Ellis published *Reason and Emotion in Psychotherapy,* which laid the foundation for his revised theory which he called rational emotive therapy (RET). Ellis changed the name of his theory in 1993 to rational emotive behavior therapy (REBT) to acknowledge the interrelationship between thoughts, feelings, and behaviors in human functioning (Ellis, 1993, 1995).

Ellis is a very prolific writer, active clinician, and the Executive Director of his institute for REBT since 1960. The following *Personal Note* provides additional information about his interests and professional activities.

A Personal Note

I had the privilege of interviewing Albert Ellis when he was 71 years old, and I found him to be very energetic (Nystul, 1985). He noted that his typical daily schedule involves providing individual and group counseling and psychotherapy from 9:30 A.M. until 11:30 P.M. Ellis' other activities include directing his institute, supervising numerous therapists, making many presentations, conducting workshops, and writing approximately 20 articles and 1 or 2 books each year.

continued

Although Ellis had already written more than 45 books and 500 articles, he had no intention of retiring. At the end of our interview, he said:

All this activity is infinitely more enjoyable to me than would be lying on a beach, sightseeing, or reading romantic novels. I hope that my good health continues, in spite of the diabetes that I have had for the last 30 years, and that I shall die in the saddle a few decades from now.

Many years ago, I reluctantly came to the conclusion that when I die I shall still have at least 100 books unwritten and that is a frustration I had better realistically accept. I would prefer to live forever and to keep exploring the realm of human disturbance and potential realms to happiness and self-fulfillment for eons to come, but no such luck! One of these days in the not-too-distant future, I shall run down. Too damned bad! But hardly awful and terrible. (Nystul, 1985, p. 254)

Theory of Personality

The theory of personality for REBT emphasizes the role of cognitions (and to some degree behaviors) on emotions. REBT contends that people can be best understood in terms of the nature of their self-talk (internal cognitive dialogue).

View of Human Nature.   Ellis (1995, 1996) believes that humans have a potential to be rational or irrational—to be self-preserving or self-destructive. He contends that people perceive, think, emote, and behave simultaneously. Thus, to understand self-defeating conduct, it is necessary to understand the interrelationship between thinking, feeling, and behavior (Ellis, 1995, 1996).

Key Concepts.   The major concepts in REBT (Ellis, 1962, 1995, 1996) relate to the role of cognition and how irrational thoughts can create self-defeating, emotionally disturbing outcomes.

The Role of Cognition.   The basic premise of REBT is that emotional disturbance results primarily from cognitive processes that are fundamentally irrational or illogical in nature

Albert Ellis

(Ellis, 1995). Ellis and Harper (1975) defined *rational* as anything that promotes happiness and survival for the individual and *irrational* as anything that inhibits personal happiness and survival.

One way to identify illogical or irrational thought processes is to look for statements that contain the unconditional *should* or the absolutistic *must* or *ought* (Ellis, 1995; Ellis & Harper, 1975). Examples of these self-defeating statements are

- "I should get all A's, and if I don't, I'm stupid."
- "I ought to know better when it comes to choosing a boyfriend. The ones I pick are all duds."
- "I must do well at my job, and if I don't, I'm no good."

Ellis (1977, 1995) notes that not all statements of irrational beliefs contain shoulds, oughts, and musts. According to Ellis (1984), irrational thoughts can also be in the form of other self-defeating self-statements such as

- *Self-damnation:* "I am a worthless good for nothing."
- *I-can't-stand-it-itis:* "I can't stand the thought of loosing my girlfriend."
- *Awfulizing:* "I would never want to bring a child into this insane and awful world."

The A-B-C-D-E Acronym.   In part, REBT's popularity is due to its simplicity. The basic procedures associated with REBT can be taught to the client by using the A-B-C-D-E acronym. The letter "A" in the acronym stands for the activating event. This can be whatever the client may be reacting to, such as a recent phone conversation or a report that was received by a supervisor. "B" represents the client's belief system or cognitive reaction to the activating event. "C" is the emotional consequence that the client is experiencing, such as feeling anxious or depressed. "D" suggests that the client learn to dispute self-defeating thought processes, and "E" is the effect of the disputing process.

Ellis (1962, 1995) contends that it is not "A" that causes a serious emotional reaction ("C"). For "C" to occur, a self-defeating thought process must occur at "B." The client is therefore taught how to dispute self-defeating processes ("D") to generate a positive effect ("E").

Ellis (1962, 1995, 1996) also suggests that self-defeating cognitive reactions follow a predictable pattern. People usually start with a sane or rational reaction to the activating event. Next, they tend to engage in self-talk that is illogical or irrational. Finally, they grossly overreact to the situation, making it seem like a catastrophe.

It is important to note that for REBT to be effective, counselors must be careful to not just focus on the client's sentences and self-statements. They should also help clients explore and dispute self-defeating "meanings, evaluations, images, and other forms of cognitions" (Ellis, 1986, p. 648). From this perspective, Ellis contends that REBT has always been consistent with postmodern trends, which recognize the multiple voices reflected in social forces such as culture, language, and narratives (Ivey, 1996). The following *Personal Note* provides an illustration of REBT.

A Personal Note

Tim was a 30-year-old, self-referred male who came to a mental health clinic complaining of anxiety and depression and threatening suicide. Tim told me he had recently started a new job as an accountant for a firm. Two days earlier, his boss had returned a report he had written with several suggestions and one or two indications of possible errors in his statistics. His boss had asked him to look over the suggestions and revise the report accordingly. Tim told me all he could think about since then was the report and how his boss "*must* be out to get me."

I decided to use REBT, so I provided Tim with an overview of the A-B-C-D-E acronym. Together, we decided that the activating event "A" was the boss returning the report; "B" was his cognitive reaction to "A" (that is, My boss must be out to get me); and "C" represented his feelings of being anxious, depressed, and suicidal. Since REBT focuses on cognition, we then explored his cognitive reactions to "A." Tim's thought process followed the predictable pattern described earlier. He started with a sane reaction, "It looks like there are some mistakes here." He then began to think irrationally and said things like, "He *must* be out to get me. I know he has decided he made a mistake in hiring me and is looking for a way to let me go." Finally, his thoughts became catastrophic as he concluded, "It's just a matter of time until he fires me, and I'll never get another job. I guess there is just no hope for me."

We also explored how social cultural forces could influence the personal meanings, evaluation, and images associated with his story. In this regard, he mentioned that he could be overreacting to this situation, owing to repeated parental messages of "no matter what, you have to do well at work."

When I asked Tim how he felt when he said these things to himself, he replied, "Terrible." He began to realize that his thoughts could cause an intense emotional reaction at "C." Tim and I then attempted to restructure his cognitive reactions. We disrupted "D," his irrational reactions with rational reactions. For example, he changed "My boss *must* be out to get me" to "My boss seems to have some concerns about my report." We also co-constructed new narratives that were more realistic in terms of how to conceptualize work in terms of success and failure.

By the end of our first counseling session, Tim no longer had intense feelings of being anxious, depressed, or suicidal. He said he had no idea how much power thoughts could have on emotions, and he was glad he had a tool he could use to help control his emotional reactions. Tim also commented that he still felt somewhat uncomfortable about his relationship with his boss. He wanted to know how his boss thought he was doing in his job. Tim agreed to ask his boss this question as a homework assignment. At the start of our next session, Tim smiled and said, "I guess I caused myself a lot of needless worry. My boss said he thought I was doing just fine, and he really appreciated me revising my report." Counseling was terminated shortly thereafter.

Theory of Counseling and Psychotherapy

The Counseling Process.   The primary goal of REBT is "minimizing the client's central self-defeating cognitions" and helping the client acquire "a more realistic, tolerant philosophy of life" (Ellis, 1995, p. 177). The actual process of therapy is educational and confrontational in nature. The therapist teaches the client how to dispute irrational thoughts and also confronts and even attacks, if necessary, the client's self-defeating belief system. Once clients become aware of negative self-talk, they can create a cognitive reaction that generates a more positive emotional consequence.

In terms of the counseling relationship, Ellis (1995) does not believe that a warm relationship is a necessary or sufficient condition for personality change. He believes the therapist must fully accept clients but must also point out discrepancies in their behavior when necessary (Ellis, 1995, 1996).

Techniques.   The techniques that Ellis (1962, 1995, 1996) identified for therapists to utilize in REBT include the following cognitive, emotive, and behavioral techniques.

Cognitive Techniques.   To a large degree, REBT focuses on helping clients overcome self-defeating cognitions. Cognitive restructuring is the main technique used in REBT. It involves restructuring irrational and illogical cognitions through the A-B-C-D-E acronym. Other cognitive methods utilized in REBT include techniques such as reframing, which involves redefining (or reframing) a negative situation into a more positive perspective, and referenting, which involves helping clients conceptualize problems in a holistic rather than fragmented perspective (Livneh & Wright, 1995). Bibliotherapy is also used in REBT to help clients learn how to apply REBT in everyday life.

Emotive Techniques.   Emotive (or emotive-evocative) techniques focus on the client's affect or emotional domain. These techniques can play a major role in helping clients learn how to accept themselves (Corey, 1996). For example, humor can be used to help clients put their situation in perspective and stop putting themselves down. Other emotive techniques include the use of imagery to create more positive emotional patterns (for example, imagining what it would feel like to overcome fear) and shame-attacking exercises, in which clients learn to overcome shame by becoming less concerned about how they are perceived by others.

Behavioral Techniques.   REBT utilizes the full range of behavioral techniques to help clients achieve their goals. Examples of behavioral techniques include the use of operant conditioning (for example, behavior modification), assertiveness training, systematic desensitization, relaxation therapy, and self-management (including self-monitoring). Homework assignments play an integral role in the application of behavioral techniques, whereby clients try out and practice what they learn in counseling in their day-to-day life activities.

Summary and Evaluation

Weinrach (1995) provides a literature review on REBT and concludes that there is some encouraging support for the efficacy of REBT. For example, Lyons and Woods (1991) conducted a meta-analysis of 70 REBT studies that showed REBT to be significantly superior to no treatment and having similar efficacy to other approaches such as cognitive behavior modification and cognitive therapy.

REBT is an educationally oriented approach that attempts to teach a client how to overcome self-defeating cognitive reactions. One of the strengths of REBT is its simplicity. It can be taught to the client in terms as simple as the A-B-C-D-E acronym. In time, clients can learn to use the tools necessary to become their own self-therapists and gain control over their mental health.

The major weakness of REBT may be to overemphasize the role of cognition in the etiology of mental disorders and emotional disturbances. In addition, it may be an oversimplified approach in terms of what is required to effectively restructure cognition. For many clients, much more may be required than simply changing irrational statements to rational statements. REBT also avoids exploring other factors such as traumatic early-life experiences, which could represent important treatment considerations. Ellis (1995) identifies limitations of REBT in that it is not appropriate for clients who are not capable of engaging in a cognitively oriented process, for example, people who have mental retardation, brain injuries, psychosis, or mania.

Cognitive Therapy

Background Information

During the mid-1950s Aaron Beck developed a cognitive-oriented approach to treat mental disorders, rejecting his early training in psychoanalysis. Beck is best known for his work on depression (Beck, 1987, 1991; Beck et al., 1979) and anxiety (Beck & Emery, 1985). Beck's early work on depression resulted in the development of the Beck Depression Inventory, which is widely used as a clinical and research instrument.

Theory of Personality

The theory of personality for cognitive therapy emphasizes the role of cognitive processes on the development of mental disorders such as depression and anxiety. Cognitive therapy contends that the etiology of many mental disorders can be directly traced to cognitive dysfunctions such as misinterpreting environmental cues (for example, "My friend did not show up, so he must not like me").

View of Human Nature.   Beck contends that people are a product of the interaction of innate, biological, developmental, and environmental factors (Beck & Weishaar, 1995). He also suggests that people have the capacity for self-determination by emphasizing the role of cognition in mental health.

Aaron Beck

Key Concepts.   Beck and Weishaar (1995) describe the following key concepts associated with cognitive therapy.

The Role of Cognition in Mental Health.   Emotions and behaviors are determined primarily by how a person perceives, interprets, and assigns meanings to events.

Cognitive Vulnerability.   Personality structures have vulnerabilities that predispose them to psychological distress. These vulnerabilities are characterized by schemata, which are fundamental beliefs and assumptions that develop early in life and are reinforced by learning situations throughout life. They create beliefs, values, and attitudes about oneself, others, and the world. A schema can be functional or dysfunctional. Examples of statements indicating dysfunctional schemes of a borderline personality are: "There is something fundamentally wrong with me," "People should support me and should not criticize, abandon, disagree with, or misunderstand me and my feelings" (Beck & Weishaar, 1989, p. 294), "I am powerless and vulnerable," and "I am inherently unacceptable" (Beck & Weishaar, 1995, p. 237). A dysfunctional schema can contribute to cognitive distortions, systematic bias in information processing, and other problems associated with emotional distress.

Cognitive Distortions.   A cognitive distortion is a systematic distortion in reasoning that results in psychological distress. Cognitive distortions identified by Beck and Weishaar (1995) include

- *Arbitrary inference,* which involves making a conclusion that has no supportive evidence or contradicts existing evidence.
- *Selective abstraction,* which occurs when taking information out of context or ignoring other information.
- *Overgeneralization,* which results when making a general rule on the basis of one or more isolated incidents and then applying it to unrelated situations.
- *Magnification and minimization,* which involves viewing something out of proportion, as either less or more significant than it actually is.
- *Personalization,* which occurs when attributing external events to oneself without evidence of a causal connection.
- *Dichotomous thinking,* which involves conceptualizing an experience in either-or terms, such as seeing it as good or bad.

Systematic Bias in Information Processing.   Mental disorders are characterized by a bias in information processing. Typically, the bias begins when a person "misreads" external events, thereby creating dysfunctional responses. For instance, someone who suffers from claustrophobia may "misread" taking an elevator as a very dangerous situation. The systematic bias then tends to shift to internal messages such as physiological responses. In this example, the person may "misread" feelings of tension and apprehension as an impending anxiety attack.

Cognitive Triad of Depression.   The cognitive triad is characterized by a negative view of the self, the world, and the future. Psychological and physical symptoms of depression can evolve from the cognitive triad. Beck and Weishaar (1995) cite several examples of this phenomenon. A feeling of being unable to cope or control events can lead to a paralysis of will. Negative expectations about life can contribute to physical symptoms of depression such as low energy, fatigue, and inertia.

Cognitive Model of Anxiety.   Anxiety results when a person's information processing is faulty, resulting in perceptions of danger when no danger exists. People with this anxiety have difficulty correcting their misconception by recognizing safety cues or other evidence. The cognition of anxious individuals is characterized by themes of danger and the likelihood of harm.

Theory of Counseling and Psychotherapy

The Counseling Process.   Beck sums up the major thrust of cognitive therapy in an interview by Weinrach (1998, p. 160).

> Cognitive therapy is a short-term treatment that was developed primarily for the treatment of depression and anxiety. It is now being used for personality disorders, eating disorders, and some of the other types of problems that have been more refractory to psychotherapy in the past. It is based on a view of psychopathology that stipulates that people's excessive affect and dysfunctional behavior is due to excessive or inappropriate ways of interpreting their experiences. It is also based on the notion that people who are depressed or anxious have in some way a distorted image of themselves and their external situation. (p. 160)

Beck and Weishaar (1995) provide information relevant to the counseling process, which is incorporated into the following overview. The counselor initially attempts to promote a positive relationship by establishing the core conditions identified by Rogers: warmth, accurate empathy, and genuineness. The client is then encouraged to take an active role in the counseling process in setting goals, recounting cognitive and behavioral reactions to problem situations, and doing homework assignments.

    The counselor functions as a guide in the counseling process by helping the client understand the role of cognition in emotions and behaviors. The counselor also acts as a catalyst by promoting corrective experiences that result in necessary cognitive restructuring and skill acquisition. In this process, counselors avoid the role of passive expert. They instead engage in a process of collaboration with the client with the ultimate goal of eliminating systematic biases in thinking. In addition, counselors do not tell the client that a particular belief is irrational or wrong. Instead, they explore with the client the meaning, function, usefulness, and consequences associated with the belief. The client then decides whether to retain, modify, or reject a belief.

Techniques.   Beck and Weishaar (1995) describe the following techniques associated with cognitive therapy.

Decatastrophizing.   This process is also known as the *what-if* technique and involves preparing clients for feared consequences by identifying problem-solving strategies.

Reattribution Technique.   This technique encourages challenging thoughts and assumptions by exploring other possible causes of events.

Redefining.   Redefining helps mobilize clients who feel they have no control over a problem by rephrasing the problem in a manner that promotes action. For instance, a student could change "I'm not a good student" to "I'm going to study more."

Decentering.   This technique involves having the client make observations to obtain a more realistic understanding of other people's reactions. It can alleviate anxiety by helping clients realize that they are not the center of attention.

Behavioral Techniques.   Cognitive therapy utilizes a wide range of behavioral techniques to help clients acquire necessary skills (for example, skill training), relax (for example, progressive relaxation), prepare for difficult situations (for example, behavioral rehearsal), and expose themselves to feared situations (for example, exposure therapy).

Summary and Evaluation

Cognitive therapy has become an increasingly popular form of counseling. It has primarily been a short-term treatment for depression. More recently cognitive therapy has been used to effectively treat a variety of disorders such as anxiety (Chambless & Gillis, 1993), eating disorders (Wilson & Fairburn, 1993), and substance abuse (Beck et al., 1993).

Its popularity is due in part to the massive research efforts that have evaluated the efficacy of cognitive therapy in the treatment of depression. Beck and Weishaar (1995) conducted a literature review that showed that cognitive therapy is superior to drug therapy (Blackburn et al., 1981; Maldonado, 1982; Hollon et al., 1992) or equal to drug therapy (Blackburn, Eunson, & Bishop, 1986; Hollon, Evans, & DeRubeis, 1983; Murphy et al., 1983; Simons et al., 1986). Studies indicate that a combination of cognitive therapy and antidepressant medication is the most effective treatment for depression (Blackburn et al., 1981; Blackburn et al., 1986; Maldonado, 1982; Teasdale et al., 1984). Cognitive therapy also appears to have stronger long-term effects than drug therapy (Blackburn et al., 1986; Hollon et al., 1983; Kovacs et al., 1981; Maldonado, 1982).

Dobson (1989) conducted a meta-analysis of the efficacy of cognitive therapy for the treatment of depression. He analyzed 28 studies that used the Beck's Depression Inventory as the outcome measure. Results of Dobson's (1989) study indicate that cognitive therapy clients do better than 98 percent of the control subjects, 70 percent of the drug-therapy clients, and 70 percent of the other psychotherapy clients. These results were consistent with the results of an earlier meta-analysis study by Nietzel et al., (1987).

Hollon and Beck (1994) caution that the literature that suggests that cognitive therapy is superior to drug therapy may be an oversimplification and prone to methodological problems. Their extensive review of the literature cast doubts on the claims that cognitive therapy is superior to drug therapy in the treatment of depression. Methodological problems include a lack of placebo controls to allow for adequate comparisons between treatment groups. In addition, severity of symptomology may play an important role in the efficacy of cognitive therapy as a treatment of depression. In this regard, there is some indication that cognitive therapy may be less effective than drug therapy with individuals who have severe depression and more effective than drug therapy with individuals with mild or moderate depression (see the National Institute of Mental Health's Treatment of Depression Collaborative Research Program, Elkin et al., 1989).

There is some indication in the research that the effectiveness of cognitive therapy depends to some degree on the personal characteristics of the client. Prochaska and Norcross (1994) provide a review of this literature and conclude that clients who were depressed and tended to externalize did better in cognitive therapy and clients who were depressed and internalized tended to do better in supportive/self-directed counseling. In addition, clients who rated low on defensiveness seemed to do better in cognitive therapy than those who were high in defensiveness.

Transactional Analysis (TA)

Background Information

Eric Berne (1910–1970) is the originator of transactional analysis (TA). He received an M.D. degree from McGill University in Montreal in 1935 and then completed psychiatry training at Yale University.

TA is unique in its effort to avoid psychological jargon. Instead, the language of TA is easy to understand, using terms such as parent, adult, child, strokes, games, rackets, decisions, and redecisions. Its use of clear, simple language helped TA become attractive not only as a form of therapy but also as a self-help approach. As evidence of its popularity, two major books on the topic were international best sellers at various times: *Games People Play* (Berne, 1964) and *I'm OK, You're OK* (Harris, 1967).

More recently, TA has been cited as an example of an emerging school of counseling that emphasizes the role of interpersonal relationships in psychological functioning (Prochaska & Norcross, 1994). In this regard, TA can be considered one of the first major theories of counseling that focuses on interpersonal relations (Adlerian psychology also stresses the importance of the interpersonal perspective). The interpersonal orientation is depicted in the name of this theory (that is, transactional analysis, suggesting that people can learn to understand and enhance the transactions and communication patterns between people).

TA's interpersonal focus shares commonalties with another interpersonally oriented theory of counseling, interpersonal psychotherapy, which is gaining recognition as an important new counseling approach (Prochaska & Norcross, 1994). Interpersonal psychotherapy is based primarily on the work of Harry Stack Sullivan (1968) and his interpersonal school of psychoanalysis. Sullivan posited a different version of Freud's theory that emphasizes social relations over drives for sex and aggression as being primarily responsible for mental health and well-being. Adolph Meyer (1957) and individuals associated with the family therapy movement, such as John Bowlby (1973, 1988) and his work on attachment, also contributed to the early development of interpersonal psychotherapy. Together they provide additional information on how environmental factors (such as psychosocial stressors) and family interaction patterns can influence psychological functioning.

Several other individuals have gone on to develop interpersonal psychotherapy as a short-term, present-centered approach to treat depression (for example, Klerman et al.,

1988; and Klerman & Weissman, 1993). Teyber (1997) summarizes the basic premises in interpersonal psychotherapy as follows.

1. Problems are conceptualized from an interpersonal perspective.
2. Familial interaction patterns are the best means of understanding oneself and others.
3. The counselor-client relationship can be used to work through relationship issues.

Interpersonal psychotherapy appears to offer much promise as an emerging theory of counseling. A more detailed description of this approach is beyond the scope of this text. For additional information and an excellent overview of interpersonal psychotherapy, the reader is directed to Teyber's *Interpersonal process in psychotherapy* (1997).

Theory of Personality

TA provides a rich tapestry of concepts that can be used to generate a theory of personality. TA concepts that can be used to provide an in-depth understanding of personality dynamics include stroking, the games people play, and the four life positions.

View of Human Nature.   Berne (1961, 1964) believes that people have the capacity to determine their own destiny. He contends that few people acquire the necessary self-aware-ness to become autonomous. Berne (1961) also stresses the importance of early-life expe-riences in contributing to personality development. His theory suggests that people develop scripts that are played throughout life. These scripts are derived from parental messages and other sources such as fairy tales and literature.

Key Concepts.   Berne (1961, 1964), Dusay and Dusay (1989), and Prochaska and Nor-cross (1994) provide an overview of the key concepts associated with TA.

The Interpersonal Perspective.   As noted earlier, TA is considered one the first major the-ories of counseling that emphasizes the role of interpersonal functioning in mental health. Many of the key concepts in TA (such as transactional analysis and analysis of games) are directed at understanding and enhancing interpersonal relations.

Prochaska and Norcross (1994) note that in TA psychopathology is understood as a manifestation of intrapersonal (within the individual) and interpersonal (between people) forces. Regardless of the origins of psychological disorders, it is always interpersonal in terms of its expression (Prochaska & Norcross, 1994). TA is therefore usually conducted in group counseling to encourage interpersonal expression. In this format, clients can gain valuable insights into their problems and learn how to use TA techniques and other coun-seling strategies to overcome their difficulties (Prochaska & Norcross, 1994).

Transactional Analysis.   The concept of transactional analysis involves analyzing the transactions between people. It entails assessing the three ego states of parent, adult, and child of each person to determine whether the transactions between the people are comple-mentary, crossed, or ulterior.

Complementary transactions occur when each person receives a message from the other person's ego state that seems appropriate and expected. Figure 9.1 provides three examples of complementary transactions. In each example, both people are sending and receiving messages as expected.

Crossed transactions occur when one or more of the individuals receives a message from the other person's ego state that does not seem appropriate or expected. Figure 9.2 illustrates two examples of crossed transactions.

Ulterior transactions occur when a person's communication is complex and confusing. In these transactions, a person sends an overt message from one ego state and a covert ulterior message from another ego state. The ulterior message can be communicated verbally, nonverbally via body language, or by tone of voice. Figure 9.3 gives examples of each possibility.

Games People Play.   Berne (1964) defined *games* as "an ongoing series of complementary ulterior transactions progressing to a well-defined, predictable outcome" (p. 48). These games are usually played at an unconscious level, with the people not aware they are playing a particular game. Some of the different games people can play are "Now I've got you, you SOB" and "Kick me."

Although game playing results in bad feelings for both players, it also offers payoffs for the participants (Dusay & Dusay, 1989). The following example illustrates what might occur during the game of "Kick me."

FIGURE 9.1   Complementary Transactions

FIGURE 9.2   Crossed Transactions

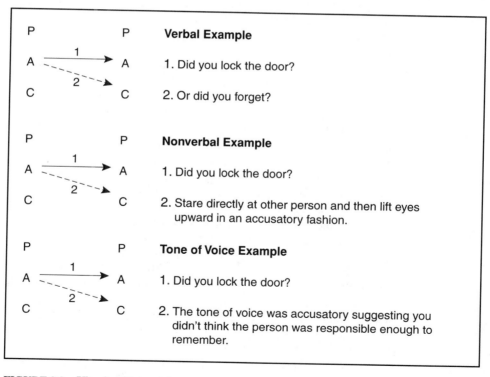

FIGURE 9.3   Ulterior Transactions

Note: Solid lines indicate overt messages; dotted lines indicate covert messages.

Mary fears dating because she believes things will never work out. She reluctantly accepts a date with John, whom she finds attractive. Within the first 10 minutes of the date, she criticizes John's hair style and then complains about the movie they are going to see. After the movie, John gets tired of Mary's insults and takes her home. As he pulls up to her house, he proceeds to tell her off ("kicks her"), saying what an ungrateful person she is.

Although Mary initially feels hurt by John's comments, she will receive a payoff from her game. As she goes into the house, she can ask herself, "Why do I always get rejected? Things never work out. I guess dating isn't for me." The game therefore provides Mary with the payoff of having an excuse to avoid dating in the future. John also receives a payoff in that her rudeness made him feel free to "kick her."

The Four Life Positions.   Berne (1961) says that in developing life scripts, people put themselves in the role of being "OK" or "not OK." They also tend to see others as basically friendly (OK) or hostile (not OK). The following four possible life positions represent combinations of how people define themselves and others.

1. "I'm OK, you're OK" represents people who are happy with themselves and others.
2. "I'm OK, you're not OK" suggests people who are suspicious of others; could have a false sense of superiority; or may be suffering from a mental disorder such as paranoia.
3. "I'm not OK, you're OK" indicates people who have a low self-concept and feel inadequate in relation to others.
4. "I'm not OK, you're not OK" implies people who have given up on themselves and life and may even be suicidal.

Ego States.   Berne identified the three ego states of the parent, adult, and child. The *parent ego state* represents the person's morals and values and can be either critical or nurturing. The critical parent attempts to find fault, whereas the nurturing parent is supportive and promotes growth. The *adult ego state* is the rational-thinking dimension. It is devoid of feelings and acts as a mediator between the child and parent ego states. The *child ego state* is the uninhibited side of the personality, characterized by a variety of emotions such as fear, happiness, and excitement. The child ego state has two dimensions, the free child and the adapted child. The *free child* is uninhibited and playful whereas the *adapted child* is rebellious and conforming.

An egogram can be used to assess the relative strengths and weaknesses of the various ego states. The egogram "reflects the type of person one is, one's probable types of problems, and the strengths and weaknesses of the personality" (Dusay & Dusay, 1989, p. 420). Interpreting an egogram is a complex process that requires specialized training. Clinicians are especially interested in ego states that are particularly high or low relative to the client's other ego states. For example, low critical parent (CP) suggests problems with exploitation; low nurturing parent (NP) implies loneliness; low adult (A) indicates difficulty concentrating; low free child (FC) suggests a lack of zest for life; and low adapted child (AC) indicates a person who is rigid and difficult to get along with (Dusay & Dusay, 1989). A healthy egogram is indicated when there is relative balance between the strength of the ego states as illustrated in Figure 9.4.

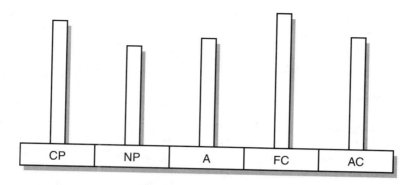

FIGURE 9.4   An Egogram with Relative Balance

Life Scripts.   A major part of personality structure relates to the life scripts that are created beginning in childhood. A life script is composed of parental messages, for example, a parent saying, "You're my darling angel," and complementary messages from other sources that may include fairy tales, movies, and literature. These messages create a role that a person identifies with and acts out throughout life. For instance, a person could identify with the Superman character and play the role of the "good person who comes to the rescue" in interpersonal relations. Another possible life script is identifying with the Cinderella character, which might lead to feelings of self-pity, being taken advantage of, and never having a chance to get out and have fun.

Strokes.   TA suggests that the basic motivation for social interaction is related to the need for human recognition or *strokes* (Dusay & Dusay, 1989). Strokes can be physical, verbal, or psychological and can be positive, negative, conditional, or unconditional. Positive strokes tend to communicate affection and appreciation and are essential to psychological development.

TA attempts to identify what types of strokes are important to clients and encourages them to take an active role in getting these strokes. For instance, after having a rough day, people could tell their partner that they need some extra strokes that evening.

Theory of Counseling and Psychotherapy

The Counseling Process.   Berne (1961) notes that the ultimate goals of TA are to help clients become autonomous, self-aware, and spontaneous, and have the capacity for intimacy. To promote these ultimate goals, some of the short-term goals of TA are that it helps clients

- Make new decisions, called *redecisions,* regarding their behavior and approach to life
- Rewrite their life script so they feel OK about themselves and can relate effectively with others

- Stop playing games that confuse communication and interfere with authentic interpersonal functioning
- Understand their three ego states of parent, adult, and child and how they can function in an effective and complementary fashion
- Avoid communicating in a manner that promotes crossed or ulterior transactions
- Learn how to obtain and give positive strokes

The counseling process in TA is educative in nature. The therapist takes on the role of teacher, providing clients information on how to use the TA concepts. TA emphasizes cognition in its approach by showing clients how they can use their intellect in applying TA principles to overcome mental disorders.

TA utilizes an active counseling process that emphasizes the importance of clients doing something outside of counseling via homework assignments. TA also relies on the use of a counseling contract, which the therapist and the client develop together. The contract is very specific in identifying the counseling goals, treatment plan, and roles and responsibilities for achieving these goals.

Techniques.   The following techniques of TA relate to the key concepts described earlier.

- *Structural analysis* is a technique that helps clients become aware of their three ego states and learn to use them effectively.
- *Transactional analysis* helps clients learn to communicate with complementary transactions (for example, adult to adult).
- *Script analysis* is a process that explores the type of life script the client has developed and how it can be rewritten in a more effective manner.
- *Analysis of games* involves clients identifying what games they play and how the games interfere with interpersonal functioning.

Summary and Evaluation

TA is an educative, cognitively oriented process in which clients learn to apply TA principles so they can become self-therapists and lead autonomous, fully functioning lives. TA was one of the first theories of counseling whose goal was to focus on the role that interpersonal relations play in mental health and well-being. TA provides valuable tools such as analysis of games, which can help clients understand and enhance their interpersonal functioning as an important step in overcoming their psychological problems. The strength of TA is that the concepts are written in easily understandable words, such as parent, adult, child, strokes, and games, instead of psychological jargon. One weakness of TA is the possibility of focusing too much attention on self-analysis and intellectualization. When this occurs, clients may become self-absorbed and calculating in their relationships with others.

There is evidence to suggest that TA is becoming more popular with practitioners as they begin to integrate other schools of counseling such as Gestalt and psychodrama (Poidevant & Lewis, 1995). This wider base of application has enabled TA to be used in corporate settings such as airlines and utility companies (Poidevant & Lewis, 1995).

TA has also been shown to be useful in enhancing wellness, communication skills, family counseling, and school functioning (Poidevant & Lewis, 1995). For example, there appears to be a positive relationship between getting strokes and overall physical and psychological wellness (Allen & Allen, 1989). In addition, TA has been found useful in enhancing communication skills and productivity (Nykodym, Rund, & Liverpool, 1986; Spencer, 1977). In terms of family counseling, TA has been shown to enhance the self-esteem of parents in parent education programs (Bredehoft, 1990) and concepts and procedures such as ego states and transactional analysis were found useful in family counseling (Zerin, 1988). Miller and Capuzzi (1984) provide additional support for TA in terms of school functioning. They find that TA can be used to enhance the self-esteem of elementary school students, increase rates of attendance of high school students, and promote positive academic performance in higher education students. Poidevant and Lewis (1995) also point out that TA does not seem to be appropriate for some populations, such as people who suffer from schizophrenia and severe anxiety disorders such as phobias.

Prochaska and Norcross (1994) provide an extensive review of the TA research literature including the meta-analysis from Smith, Glass, and Miller (1980). Prochaska and Norcross find overall support for TA, suggesting "it was consistently more effective than no treatment and usually more effective than placebo treatments in adult samples" (p. 217). Prochaska and Norcross (1994) also identify limitations with TA. They suggest that a major problem with TA is that many of the concepts (such as parent, adult, and child) are difficult to evaluate empirically. In addition, these concepts (while easy to understand) may be an oversimplification of Freud's theory. This appears to have resulted in leaving major theoretical constructs "lost in the translation" (such as the id as the major driving force in the personality). From a postmodern perspective, TA may also be lacking in terms of not going far enough with its interpersonal perspective. For example, additional emphasis should be made of sociocultural forces that can impact on psychological functioning.

Reality Therapy

Background Information

William Glasser (b. 1925) is the founder of reality therapy. Glasser was a consulting psychiatrist for the Ventura School for Girls in California when he attempted his first large-scale implementation of reality therapy. His program was well received, prompting an interest in the merits of reality therapy. It appeared to be a realistic approach, especially for clients who had a pattern of being irresponsible, for example, delinquent children and substance abusers.

In 1961 Glasser published his first book, *Mental Health or Mental Illness?* He took an antipsychiatry position, exploring how labels such as *mental disorder* and *schizophrenia* can be harmful to a client. Glasser has since persisted with this position by not recognizing the various mental disorders described in the DSM-IV.

Glasser wrote several other books that contributed to the evolution of reality therapy. In 1965, he published *Reality Therapy,* which established his approach as a major force in counseling and psychotherapy. *In Schools Without Failure,* Glasser (1969) attempts to apply the principles of reality therapy to education. His more recent publications have attempted to broaden the theoretical base of his approach. In *Positive Addiction,* he describes how positive addictions can be substituted for negative addictions (Glasser, 1976). In *Stations of the Mind,* he describes the neurological and psychological basis of reality therapy (Glasser, 1981). In the mid-1980s, Glasser's interests began to focus on the role of control in mental health. Reality therapy was therefore expanded to include control theory (Glasser, 1984, 1985). More recently, Glasser (1998) replaced control theory with choice theory. Choice theory recognizes the importance of helping clients learn how to make effective choices to meet their needs in a responsible manner. Glasser has also applied the concepts of control theory to education (1986, 1990).

Wubbolding (1991, 1995) should also be recognized as a key individual in the evolution of reality therapy. He has been influential in expanding on Glasser's theory in terms of counseling procedures. His work on the four stages of reality therapy and the questions associated with these stages (for example, "What are you doing?" and "Is what you doing working for you?") are very useful in terms of providing a structure to the process of reality therapy.

Theory of Personality

Reality therapy emphasizes the role of choice and responsibility in human functioning. Reality therapies' theory of personality proposes that enhanced awareness of choices helps clients assume responsibility for their behavior. As clients learn to make appropriate choices, they can create "quality worlds" characterized by success identities and appropriate need gratification.

View of Human Nature.   Glasser believes that the primary motivational force of people is directed at fulfilling basic physiological and psychological needs of survival, love, belonging, power, freedom, and fun. He emphasizes the choice people have over fulfilling their needs and creating their own destiny.

Key Concepts.   Glasser (1965, 1985, 1998), Glasser and Wubbolding (1995), and Wubbolding (1995) have identified several key concepts that characterize reality therapy.

Success and Failure Identity.   A *success identity* results when a person is able to fulfill the psychological needs of loving and of feeling worthwhile to the self and others in a manner that does not interfere with the rights of others. When a person is unable to meet these basic psychological needs, a *failure identity* results. Failure identities are associated with problematic approaches to life such as delinquency and mental disorders.

Emphasis on Responsibility.   Reality therapy encourages clients to evaluate their behavior in terms of whether it is helping or hurting themselves and others. When people make an honest evaluation of their behavior, they can assume responsibility for it. Glasser believes that responsibility is critical to mental health and therefore a primary goal of reality therapy.

View of Psychopathology.   As mentioned earlier, Glasser (1961) set the stage for his antipsychiatry stance regarding mental disorders with the publication of his first book,

Mental Health or Mental Illness? Since that publication, he has consistently maintained that there are no mental disorders and that the labeling process can do more harm than good.

In addition, Glasser believes that people are in control of their mental health. According to this theory, a person must behave in a manner associated with depression in order to be depressed. When clients say they are depressed, Glasser would suggest that they say instead, "I'm depressing." As a result, clients will realize the control they have over their mental health.

Positive Addiction.   Glasser's (1976) *Positive Addiction* was an innovative attempt to redefine the concept of addiction. Up to that time, the tendency was to understand addiction as something negative and to be avoided. Glasser observed that there were some positive behaviors, for example, jogging and meditation, that appeared addictive, since the person would become uncomfortable if these behaviors were not allowed to occur. Glasser suggested that people with a negative addiction such as alcoholism could try to discover a positive addiction that could become a substitute for it.

Control Theory.   Control theory was a central concept in reality therapy. This theory suggests that each person has a control system that serves to exert control over the environment. It represents a direct challenge to the traditional stimulus—response notion, which suggests that people's responses are conditioned by the environment. Glasser (1986) insisted that "what goes on in the outside would never 'stimulate' us to do anything. All of our behavior, simple to complex, is our best attempt to control ourselves to satisfy our needs" (p. 17). Simply stated, people feel good when they believe they have control of their lives and feel bad when they feel their lives are out of control.

The basic tenet of control theory is that all behavior results from people attempting to satisfy basic needs. These include the psychological needs of belonging, freedom, power, and fun and the physiological need for survival.

Choice Theory.   Glasser (1998) recently made a major revision in reality therapy by replacing the concept of control theory with choice theory. The overall aim of choice theory is to help clients learn to make choices that can help them meet their needs in a responsible manner, and get what they want in terms of creating a "quality world." Glasser emphasizes the role of behavior in learning how to make appropriate choices and contends for the most part behavior is intrinsically motivated.

Glasser (1998) identifies the following 10 axioms of choice theory.

- People can only control *their* own behavior.
- Information is essentially all that people exchange, and people must choose how they deal with the information they get from others.
- Long-lasting problems tend to be relationship problems.
- Problem relationships affect our *present* lives.
- Focusing on the *past* can do little to improve current significant relationships.
- People are motivated to fulfill needs of survival, love and belonging, power, freedom, and fun.
- Need satisfaction is dependent on satisfying pictures in their "quality world."

- People engage in behaviors relating to acting, thinking, feeling, and physiology throughout life.
- Awareness of choice associated with behavior is enhanced by the use of language such as "I am choosing to feel anxiety" or ("I'm anxieting") as opposed to "I am suffering from anxiety."
- People have direct control over their acting and thinking and indirect control over feelings and physiology.

Theory of Counseling and Psychotherapy

The Counseling Process.   The primary goal of reality therapy is to help clients choose to live their lives in a manner that is responsible and does not interfere with the rights of others.

The counseling process is educational in nature, and clients learn how to apply choice theory to effective living. Reality therapy contends that a positive counseling relationship will promote efficacy in the counseling process. In addition, reality therapy focuses on present behavior and makes no attempt to explore past events such as childhood trauma. It also does not recognize mental disorders, because they represent harmful labels.

Techniques.   The main technique in contemporary reality therapy is teaching clients how to use choice theory to meet their basic needs in a responsible manner (Glasser, 1998). Glasser (1980, 1984) set forth an eight-step approach for implementing reality therapy: create a relationship, focus on current behavior, invite clients to evaluate their behavior, make a plan of action, get a commitment, refuse to accept excuses, refuse to use punishment, and refuse to give up. Glasser (1984) suggests using a flexible approach when applying these steps and notes that the steps are interrelated and overlapping processes rather than discrete steps.

A more recent version of reality therapy emphasizes "two major components: a friendly, firm, trusting environment and a series of procedures that leads to change" (Wubbolding, 1995, p. 386). The procedures, to a large degree, involve a four-stage approach that is expressed in the acronym WDEP (Glasser & Wubbolding, 1995; Wubbolding, 1995). A brief overview of these four steps is as follows.

1. "W" stands for the client's wants, needs, and perceptions. In this first stage of counseling, the counselor explores what the client wants out of life by asking questions such as "What do you want" from your job, spouse, and so forth. Various techniques and procedures can be used in this process, such as exploring the client's inner "picture album," which reflects perceptions of his or her wants and needs.
2. "D" stands for what the client is doing and the direction he or she is taking in his or her life. In stage 2, the counselor can ask "What are you doing?" or "Where are you going with your life if you continue doing what you are doing now?" This step focuses on evaluating the client's current behaviors as expressed in the here and now (rather than delving into the past).
3. "E" stands for self-evaluation, which Glasser believes is the central concept in reality therapy. Self-evaluation involves helping the client engage in a process of self-analysis to determine whether "what they are doing is working for them." Self-evaluation is a

critical stage in counseling in terms of helping clients get motivated to engage in the change process.

4. "P" involves helping clients plan to make the necessary changes to meet their needs more effectively. Plans are directed related to the insights gained from the self-evaluation. Wubbolding (1986) identifies characteristics of effective planning, which are simple, attainable, measurable, immediate, involved, controlled by the client, committed to, and consistent.

Summary and Evaluation

Reality therapy is a popular short-term form of intervention that focuses on behavior that is occurring in the present. It is a particularly attractive type of treatment with people who have a pattern of acting irresponsibly, such as delinquent children, students with school-related behavioral problems, and people with substance abuse problems.

There appear to be a limited number of recent studies that have evaluated the efficacy of reality therapy. Most of the studies cited in Glasser and Wubbolding (1995) and Wubbolding (1995) as evidence of the effectiveness of reality therapy were published before 1990. One study by Honeyman (1990) was cited as providing support for reality therapy. It suggested that reality therapy could be used in group counseling with addicts to enhance their self-esteem, help them take more responsibility for their behavior, and improve their relations with others. Additional research efforts seem warranted to provide an evaluation of the key concepts and procedures of reality therapy (for example, choice theory).

Special Issues in Cognitive-Behavioral Counseling

Cognitive-Behavioral Theories from a Brief-Counseling Perspective

Cognitive-behavioral theories have particular utility as a form of brief counseling because their techniques and procedures can easily be integrated into a brief-counseling format (for example, they are solution focused). The following list highlights some of the characteristics cognitive-behavioral theories share with the brief-counseling perspective.

Behavior Therapy. Behavior therapy is well suited for brief counseling. Wilson (1995) notes that behavior therapy tends to be time-limited, with the counselor contracting with the client to resolve the concerns within a 2–3 month period (8–12 sessions). Many of the techniques and procedures used in behavior therapy fit well with the brief-counseling model in that they are solution focused (for example, they use systematic desensitization and stress inoculation to treat anxiety).

Rational Emotive Behavior Therapy. Ellis (1995) notes that REBT is an ideal form of brief counseling. Although REBT can be used as a form of brief therapy for all clients, it is especially productive for clients who have a specific problem such as sexual inadequacy or hostility toward a boss but do not have a serious disturbance (Ellis, 1995). Ellis (1995) contends that REBT can help clients in as few as 1 session but typically between 1 and 10 sessions. Ellis (1995) believes that the efficacy of REBT as a form of brief counseling can be enhanced by having the client listen to tape-recorded sessions to process how they can apply therapy and to use the REBT Self-Help Form to help clients learn how to apply REBT to a variety of problems the client encounters between sessions.

Cognitive Therapy.   Beck and Weishaar (1995) describe cognitive therapy as a highly structured form of short-term counseling that usually lasts from 12 to 16 sessions. It is a solution-focused approach that attempts to address problems with depression and anxiety and to some degree other disorders such as eating disorders and substance abuse. Cognitive therapy has received substantial research support as an effective short-term treatment approach to treating specific disorders. Managed-care organizations have therefore recognized the utility of cognitive therapy (Beck & Weishaar, 1995).

Reality Therapy.   Reality therapy has not traditionally been considered a form of brief counseling. The recent revisions of the theory appear to have made it more attractive as a brief-counseling approach. Some of these revisions have been choice theory and how clients can learn how to meet their needs in a manner that does not interfere with the rights of others; the concepts of success identity and failure identity and positive addictions; and Glasser's new way of conceptualizing the counseling process in terms of "What are you doing?" "Is it working for you?" and so forth. Each of these concepts and processes can be used to create a brief-time limited-solution-focused approach to counseling. In addition, Palmatier (1990) identifies common characteristics that reality therapy shares with the brief-counseling perspective. Some of these characteristics are that current behavior is the focus for change (the past is avoided); psychological jargon is minimized, and the client is encouraged to take an active role in their therapy; and the counseling process is solution focused.

Transactional Analysis.   Although TA was not initially designed as a brief-counseling approach, many of its concepts and procedures could be incorporated into a brief-counseling model. The techniques and concepts in TA can be particularly useful in brief counseling to generate a solution-focused approach to counseling. For example, concepts and strategies such as stroking, game playing, ego states, and transactional analysis (analyzing the transactions between people in terms of parent, adult, and child) can play a useful role in helping clients enhance their interpersonal function and foster mental health and well being.

Diversity Issues

Diversity issues in counseling suggest that it is important to be aware of issues such as the client's degree of acculturation, identity development, cultural background (including values and beliefs), and worldview before implementing counseling theories. For example, degree of acculturation can suggest how appropriate traditional theories may be (the higher the acculturation, the higher the probability of appropriateness).

Behavior Therapy.   Tanaka-Matsumi & Higginbotham (1994) suggest that the essence of behavior therapy is to assess the relationship between the environment and the client's behavior and to adjust counseling to address environmental conditions such as culture as necessary. Prochaska and Norcross (1994) go on to note that although behavior therapy attempts to include environmental assessment, it often falls short of this goal, especially in terms of expressing sensitivity to cultural or family systems perspectives.

Rational Emotive Behavior Therapy and Cognitive Therapy.   REBT and cognitive therapy focus on the role of cognition in mental health and well-being. It is important to consider diversity issues such as gender, culture, and worldview in applying these theories. Prochaska and Norcross (1994) note that cognitive therapies may reflect a male bias valuing "rational thinking" over what could be considered female characteristics, such as intuition and connection, and therefore be inappropriate and offensive to females. Cultural problems could emanate from REBT's notion that absolutistic thinking (characterized by shoulds, oughts, or musts) creates emotional distress. It is critical to ensure that a client's culture does not value absolutistic thinking as a sign of mental health before trying to dispute this type of thinking. In addition, worldview recognizes that each person has a unique way of understanding and viewing the world. It is therefore important to gain a phenomenological perspective when conceptualizing a client's cognitions.

Reality Therapy.   Several concepts in reality therapy may be problematic in terms of cultural issues. Three of these concepts are control, choice, and responsibility. Although these concepts may be valued in Western culture (since they promote individualism), they may not fit well with Eastern cultures (which value the group). In this sense, Eastern cultures are not as concerned with who broke something (identifying who must take responsibility) but how to fix or correct what is wrong.

Wubbolding (1990) recognizes the differences between East and West and recommends that reality therapy be adjusted to fit the needs of the client's milieu. This can include being sensitive to language differences ("I'll try" in Japan may be equivalent to "I'll do it" in the United States). Some of the newer trends in reality therapy may be well suited for cross-cultural counseling. One example is structuring counseling along themes such as "What are you doing?" and "Is it working for you?" enables clients to take an active role in personalizing counseling from the standpoint of their worldview.

Transactional Analysis.   On the positive side, TA has done a good job in moving beyond intrapsychic forces by recognizing the role of relational issues in psychological functioning. Prochaska and Norcross (1994) suggest that TA could go further in this regard by incorporating a systemic perspective and being more sensitive to cultural issues. Although TA has a number of concepts that could have wide appeal cross-culturally (for example, the need for strokes), some of the terminology may be difficult to understand from a cross-cultural perspective.

Postmodern Trends

Postmodern trends such as narrative psychology, constructivism, and social constructionism are beginning to play a key role in the evolution of cognitive-behavioral counseling (Mahoney, 1995). Central to this new perspective is a reevaluation of basic concepts such as knowledge and reality. From a postmodern perspective, knowledge and reality are relative concepts varying according to sociopolitical forces as reflected in the narrative of cultures. Gergen (1982) emphasizes the social dimension to cognition when he says that "knowledge is not something that people possess in their heads, but rather something that people do together" (p. 270).

Postmodern trends are creating a paradigm shift within cognitive-behavioral counseling, changing its focus from intrapsychic causality to a recognition of contextual forces that impact on human functioning. The process of counseling is therefore becoming more of a creative than a corrective endeavor (Lyddon, 1995). It is less concerned with overcoming internal cognitive deficits and more concerned with the counselor and client creating new narratives that no longer are of concern to the client (Lyddon, 1995).

Summary

Several theories emphasize the role of cognition and/or behavior in the counseling process. Cognitive-behavior approaches utilize an integration of concepts and counseling strategies. This is especially true for behavior therapy, rational-emotive behavior therapy, and cognitive therapy. These three theories have a common focus on the integral role that cognition plays in the development of mental disorders. They also incorporate behavioral techniques to teach the skills and behaviors necessary for a comprehensive treatment program. Subtle differences also exist among these three theories. Ellis's REBT focuses on confronting and disputing the client's irrational and illogical thoughts. Beck's cognitive therapy is concerned with whether a client is making a functional or dysfunctional interpretation of an event. For Meichenbaum, the central issue in behavior therapy is the nature of the client's inner speech or self-talk. He contends that a client must learn self-talk that triggers effective coping mechanisms.

Transactional analysis emphasizes the relational aspect of human behavior and how clients can use its concepts to enhance their interpersonal functioning. Reality therapy stresses the role of choice in mental health and how clients can be helped to make appropriate choices to meet their needs in a manner that does not interfere with the rights of others.

Cognitive-behavioral counseling is particularly well suited for use in a brief-counseling format. Cognitive therapy stands out in this regard in terms of providing a time-limited approach to treat specific disorders such as depression and anxiety. Cognitive-behavioral theories have both strengths and weaknesses in terms of effectively addressing diversity issues. Postmodern trends in cognitive-behavioral counseling appear to be providing an important paradigm shift that will accommodate emerging diversity issues such as gender and culture.

The Suggested Readings on pages 420–422 contain additional information regarding the cognitive-behavioral theories.

10 Marriage and Family Counseling

CHAPTER OVERVIEW

This chapter provides an overview of the field of marriage and family counseling. Highlights of the chapter include

- The art and science of marriage and family counseling
- The evolution of marriage and family counseling
- Theoretical foundations, including systems theory and the family life cycle
- Marriage counseling
- Family counseling
- Postmodern trends
- Diversity issues in marriage and family counseling
- Evaluation of marriage and family counseling

The Art and Science of Marriage and Family Counseling

Marriage and family counseling is both an art and a science. It is an art to attempt to formulate and maintain a positive counseling relationship with a couple or family and understand and work with the complex issues that emerge within the family system. This process requires patience, flexibility, creativity, and all the other dimensions associated with the art of counseling.

The spirit of the art of counseling appears to be incorporated into the recent postmodern/social constructionist trends in marriage and family counseling. This approach recommends that marriage and family counselors enter family systems not as experts but as inquisitive learners that want to discover how the family defines their strengths and weaknesses. It is a process similar to the discovery-oriented methods used in qualitative research, whereby the investigator and participant function as coinvestigators. The focus of marriage and family counseling from this perspective is on helping couples and families discover new options and opportunities for effective family living through analysis of family stories and narratives. The postmodern/social constructionist approach to marriage and family counseling may represent a bridge between art and science (that is, between counseling and qualitative research).

The science of marriage and family counseling can be found in processes such as the use of assessment and research procedures. Assessment instruments such as marital satisfaction inventories provide objective information on areas in which the couple is satisfied or dissatisfied. Research strategies such as qualitative and quantitative methodologies help provide information on the effectiveness of marriage and family counseling. Recent advances in quantitative research have done much to overcome methodological weaknesses and clearly demonstrate the efficacy of marriage and family counseling (Shadish, Ragsdale, & Glaser, 1995). Qualitative research also seems to offer promise to marriage and family research in that it is congruent with system theory (Moon, Dillon, & Sprenkle, 1990). In this regard qualitative research and system theory emphasize "social context, multiple perspectives, complexity, individual differences, circular causality, recursion, and holism" (Moon, Dillon, & Sprenkle, 1990, p. 364).

Evolution of Marriage and Family Counseling

The field of marriage and family counseling has evolved over the last 60 years (Everett, 1990). Goldenberg and Goldenberg (1996) identify key events associated with this evolution, which are incorporated into the following overview.

Psychoanalysis.   Nathan Ackerman's (1937) work on the family as an important psychosocial unit set the stage for the adaptation of Freudian concepts to family counseling. Prior to Ackerman's work, psychoanalysis was strictly a process of individual psychotherapy.

General Systems Theory.   Ludwig Von Bertalanffy developed general systems theory in the 1940s. This theory contends that seemingly unrelated phenomena represent interrelated facets of a larger system (Von Bertalanffy, 1968). General systems theory was later applied to marriage and family counseling, providing an important theoretical foundation.

Research on Schizophrenia.   Since the late 1940s numerous studies have been conducted to investigate the relationship between family dynamics and schizophrenia. Although this massive research effort has determined nothing conclusive as yet, it has drawn interest to family therapy as a potentially useful treatment modality.

Marriage Counseling and Child Guidance.   Marriage counseling and child guidance represent the first counseling approaches to recognize that problems relate to both intrapersonal (within the person) and interpersonal (between people) forces. The inclusion of the interpersonal perspective prompted the necessity for counselors to work with the parent and child or husband and wife together in a counseling session.

Group Therapy.   Around 1910, Morino developed what can be considered the earliest uses of group processes in counseling. Since then, many other forms of group counseling have evolved. The evolution of group counseling influenced marriage and family counseling in terms of how marriage and family counselors could use effective group-leadership skills, how the knowledge of group process could contribute to the understanding of interactions between family members, and how the concept of "the group" as a change agent could be applied to "the family" as a change agent.

Changing Family Structure. The traditional intact family characterized by a wage-earning father, a homemaker mother, and biological children is now in the minority. Current family structures in the United States represent a wide range of alternative family systems that include single parents rearing children; blended families, where the husband and wife live with children from a previous marriage; cohabiting couples, or unmarried individuals living together for an extended period of time; and gay couples living together rearing children.

Numerous problems emerge as family members attempt to adjust to changing family structures. For example, a family often experiences financial problems following a divorce (especially women with children). Marriage and family counseling has to some degree evolved as a means of assisting with these common problems of modern family life.

Professional Issues and Organizations

The field of marriage and family counseling is both a professional discipline and a specialized counseling strategy practiced by various members of the helping profession. Smith (1994) recommends that the appropriate sequence for becoming a marriage and family counselor is to first master personal and human relation skills, then to develop general counseling skills and theory, and finally to specialize in marriage and family skills and theory.

The two main professional organizations for marriage and family counselors are the American Association for Marriage and Family Therapy (AAMFT) and the American Counseling Association (ACA)—formerly known as the American Association for Counseling and Development (AACD). The AAMFT has a much longer history; it was originally called the American Association of Marriage Counselors in 1942. As of 1990, there were approximately 15,000 members (Everett, 1990). The current address of AAMFT is

> 1717 K St., N.W.
> Suite 407
> Washington, DC 20006

In 1989, the ACA established division status to the International Association of Marriage and Family Counselors. As of 1995, there are approximately 8,000 members (Smith et al., 1995). The current address of the ACA is

> 5999 Stevenson Ave.
> Alexandria, VA 22304

The AAMFT and ACA have done much to promote the professionalism of marriage and family counseling. Some of these activities have been to establish ethical codes (see Chapter 2) and promote state licensure in marriage and family counseling. By 1996, 35 states had licensure laws regarding marriage and family counseling.

Theoretical Foundations

Several important theoretical foundations have contributed to marriage and family counseling. Theories described in this section include systems theory and the family life cycle.

Systems Theory

Systems theory is the foundation and integrating force in marriage and family counseling (Smith et al., 1995). The systems perspective is based on the principle of circular causality (Everett, 1990). According to this principle, actions caused by one family member influence the actions of all other family members, affecting the functioning of the family system, including the person who was responsible for the initial action (Goldenberg & Goldenberg, 1996). In addition, systems theory focuses on the function of the system rather than the individual. From this perspective, problematic individuals are understood in terms of family interaction patterns and are therefore conceptualized within the social context in which their problems occurred (Hazelrigg, Cooper, & Borduin, 1987).

Key Concepts

Goldenberg and Goldenberg (1996) and Sperry and Carlson (1991) identify key concepts associated with systems theory. The following overview of these concepts incorporates their descriptions.

Organization.   The organizational structure of the family system can be understood in terms of wholeness, hierarchies, and boundaries (Gurman & Kniskern, 1981). *Wholeness* relates to the recurrent patterns reflected in the family system as opposed to individual elements of the family (Sperry & Carlson, 1991). Wholeness suggests that the family is more than the sum of its parts, with the family system having a life of its own (Everett, 1990). *Hierarchies* involve the different levels of subsystems that make up the family system, for example, parents, siblings, and relatives. *Boundaries* are "the invisible lines of demarcation that separate a system, subsystem, or individual from outside surrounding" (Goldenberg & Goldenberg, l996, p. 55). Extreme separateness between family members can occur when boundaries are rigid, and extreme togetherness is associated with diffuse boundaries (Sperry & Carlson, 1991).

Communication.   All behaviors, verbal and nonverbal, are considered important aspects of communication. Systems theory also attempts to identify and assess familial communication patterns.

Family Rules.   Families are governed by rules that influence how family members interact and how well the family functions. For example, an alcoholic family might have an unwritten rule that no one may talk about a family member's drinking problem.

Family Homeostasis.   Family homeostasis is the tendency of family systems to maintain equilibrium or restore balance if the system becomes disrupted. Family systems can resist change in an attempt to maintain homeostasis.

Information Processing.   Information processing involves the exchange of information between the family and the outside world. It provides essential feedback for families to make necessary alterations in functioning. A family system is considered open if there is sufficient opportunity for information processing and closed if there is insufficient opportunity. Healthy family systems are neither too open nor too closed (Sperry and Carlson, 1991).

Change.   Watzlawick, Weakland, and Fisch (1974) note that there can be first-order or second-order change. First-order changes are alterations that leave the organizational structure unchanged, whereas second-order changes result in fundamental change to the system's organization (Sperry & Carlson, 1991).

The Functional Family System.   It would be presumptuous to set forth a definitive description of what constitutes a functional family, since any definition would vary from culture to culture and family to family. Therefore, findings from the following studies on this topic are presented with that caution.

Fisher and Sprinkle (1978) surveyed 310 members of AAMFT in terms of what they believe constitutes a healthy family. The results of the survey suggest that the fully functioning family is one in which the family members feel valued, supported, and safe. In addition the researchers note that "They can express themselves without fear of judgment, knowing that opinions will be attended to carefully and emphatically. Family members are also able to negotiate when necessary" (Fisher & Sprinkle, 1978, p. 9).

Ebert (1978), Stinnet and DeFrain (1985), and Watts, Trusty, & MeGaik (in press) identify many additional characteristics of healthy family functioning. These characteristics are summarized as follows.

- *Sharing of feelings.* Family members feel free to openly share positive and negative feelings with each other.
- *Social interest.* Healthy families tend to have many of the characteristics associated with the Adlerian concept of social interest (for example, social relatedness and sense of connectedness to others, community feeling, and empathy).
- *Adaptability.* These families take a flexible-adaptive approach to problem solving and problem prevention as opposed to a rigid-restrictive approach to the challenges of life.
- *Boundary clarity.* These families allow for a balance between promoting a sense of community, cohesion, and belonging and encouraging family members to grow up as autonomous individuals.
- *Understanding of feelings.* All members of the family sense that they are being understood by the other family members.
- *Acceptance of individual differences.* Individual differences among family members are permitted and even encouraged so all family members can develop their unique potential.
- *Highly developed sense of caring.* Family members communicate a sense of love and caring to each other. This contributes to family members feeling valued and having a sense of belonging within the family.
- *Cooperation.* Each family member is willing to work in a cooperative manner to help the family function effectively

- *Sense of humor.* Family members are capable of laughing at themselves and joking about family events.
- *Provision for survival and safety needs.* The basic needs of food, shelter, and clothing are provided.
- *Nonadversary problem solving.* Problems are usually solved in a democratic fashion.
- *Overall philosophy.* The family has a set of values that provides a structure for family living.
- *Commitment.* Family members are committed to each other's well-being.
- *Expression of appreciation.* Family members regularly express appreciation to each other.
- *Communication.* Good communication patterns are established between family members.
- *Time spent together.* Family members spend time together to foster positive relationships and a sense of family unity.
- *Spirituality.* Family members can draw strength from their spirituality.
- *Coping skills.* The family has the coping skills necessary to meet the challenges of family life.

These characteristics collectively suggest that a functional family system creates a positive environment for individuals to grow and develop. It is characterized by love, caring, and mutual respect. Family members can effectively communicate with each other and be responsive to forces outside the family. The family has the necessary coping mechanisms to be successful in meeting the developmental tasks of family life.

Evaluation of Systems Theory

Systems theory has added an important dimension to the counseling literature. It has contributed to the understanding of how systems work and their influence on psychological functioning. The systems perspective has been particularly useful in describing the structure and process of family life, and how the family system creates an entity which is greater than the sum of its individual parts (Goldenberg & Goldenberg, 1995). According to Goldenberg and Goldenberg (1995, p. 357), "This broad view directs attention to the relationship between interacting parts within a larger context, emphasizing the system's unity and organizational hierarchy." Systems thinking provides a mechanism for seeing wholes: relationships rather than isolated units and patterns of change rather than static snapshots (Senge, 1990).

Enns (1988) and Epstein and Loos (1989) also identify five weaknesses of systems theory. First, systems theory has been accused of overlooking the importance of intrapsychic issues, ignoring clients' emotions and affect, and failing to address issues of responsibility (Golann, 1987; Nichols, 1987a, 1987b). Second, feminists contend that systems theory does not take into account important familial issues such as power, equality, and sex roles function (Enns, 1988; Goldner, 1985). Third, the systems perspective does not adequately consider factors that occur outside the family system, such as at a job or in school (Elkaim, 1982). Fourth, the systems approach is not realistic in that it attempts to "heal the cracked bones of a whole number of people rather than stop the hand of those delivering the blows"

(Elkaim, 1982, p. 345). Finally, systems concepts and practices are in need of empirical validation (Liddle, 1982; Shields, 1986).

Ecosystems theory (Sherrard & Amatea, 1995) and postmodern/social constructionist trends in family counseling (Anderson & Goolishian, 1992; White & Epston, 1990) represent new opportunities to overcome some of the criticisms of systems theory. Ecosystems theory emphasizes holism and is concerned with the relationship between the individual, couples, family, and sociocultural environment (Sherrard & Amatea, 1995). Ecosystem theory appears inclusive, attempting to create a balance between intrapsychic and interpersonal forces. It recognizes the individual and expands systemic horizons beyond the family to include sociocultural forces that represent the individual's social and physical environment. Postmodern/social constructionist trends are consistent with ecosystem theory. From a postmodern/social constructionist perspective, individuals construct their own reality based on the languages and narratives passed on from culture to culture. Ecosystem and postmodern/social constructivist theories represent important trends in counseling, especially in terms of creating a more inclusive, comprehensive model for marriage and family counseling.

The Family Life Cycle

Duvall (1957) has proposed an eight-stage model for understanding family life, which provides another important theoretical foundation for marriage and family counselors. The eight stages begin with marriage and end with the death of both spouses. The model identifies developmental tasks associated with each stage as well as the approximate number of years that each stage will last. Table 10.1 provides an overview of Duvall's family life cycle model.

Duvall's family life cycle model has been integrated into theories of marriage and family counseling (Carter & McGoldrick, 1988; Haley, 1971, 1973; Kovacs, 1988; Solomon, 1973). Carter and McGoldrick (1988) note that Duvall's model could be useful for practitioners to identify past, present, and future developmental tasks associated with family life. Solomon (1973) suggests that failure to master the developmental tasks associated with a particular stage could have adverse effects on family's functioning. Wilcoxon (1985) also notes that marriage and family counselors could play an important role in assisting families to develop the necessary coping skills associated with particular developmental tasks.

Haley (1973) provides additional information on the therapeutic implications of the family life cycle. He notes that the transition points between stages are the most stressful times for the family and that familial problems typically occur during these periods. In addition, Haley (1973) contends that a central therapeutic task is to help families resolve developmental issues so that they can move forward in the family life cycle.

Evaluation of the Family Life Cycle

The family life cycle is a valuable model for understanding how family life proceeds through time. It has also been used extensively in family research, including how it can be integrated with systems concepts (Kovacs, 1988). In addition, the family life cycle provides a focus for counseling by identifying developmental tasks that require assistance from the counselor.

Goldenberg and Goldenberg (1996) also identify weaknesses of the family life cycle model. They point out that it does not take into account the wide array of contemporary

TABLE 10.1   Duvall's Model of the Family Life Cycle

Stage of the Family Life Cycle	Positions in the Family	Stage-Critical Family Developmental Tasks	Approximate Number of Years in Stage
1. Married Couples (without children)	Wife Husband	Establishing a mutually satisfying marriage Adjusting to pregnancy and the promise of parenthood	2 years
2. Childbearing families (oldest child birth–30 months)	Wife-mother Husband-father Infant daughter or son or both	Giving birth to, adjusting to, and encouraging the development of infants	2–5 years
3. Families with preschool children (oldest child 30 months–6 years)	Wife-mother Husband-father Daughter-sister Son-brother	Adapting to the critical needs and interests of preschool children Coping with energy depletion and lack of privacy as parents	3–5 years
4. Families with school children (oldest child 6–13 years)	Wife-mother Husband-father Daughter-sister Son-brother	Fitting into the community of school-age families Encouraging children's educational achievements	7 years
5. Families with teenagers (oldest child 13–20 years)	Wife-mother Husband-father Daughter-sister Son-brother	Balancing freedom with responsibility as teenagers mature Establishing postparental interests and careers as parents of growing children	7 years
6. Families as launching centers (first child gone to last child leaving home)	Wife-mother-grandmother Husband-father-grandfather Daughter-sister-aunt Son-brother-uncle	Releasing young adults into work, military service, college, marriage, with appropriate rituals and assistance Maintaining a supportive home base	8 years
7. Middle-aged parents (empty nest to retirement)	Wife-mother-grandmother Husband-father-grandfather	Rebuilding the marriage relationship Maintaining kin ties with older and younger generations	15± years
8. Aging family members (retirement to death of both spouses)	Widow/widower Wife-mother-grandmother Husband-father-grandfather	Coping with bereavement and living alone Closing the family home or adapting it to aging needs Adjusting to retirement	10–15± years

Source: From *Marriage and Family Development* (5th ed.), by E. Duvall, 1977, Philadelphia, PA: Lippincott. Copyright 1977 by Lippincott. Reprinted by permission of Addison Wesley Educational Publishers Inc.

family structures that result from divorce and remarriage. In addition, Goldenberg and Goldenberg (1996) note that Duvall's model does not provide enough information on the transition points between stages, which can be especially problematic for families.

Marriage Counseling

Marital problems rank highest as the reason for referral to mental health services (Sperry & Carlson, 1991). Sholevar (1985) estimates that 75 percent of all clients entering counseling are seeking assistance with marital difficulties, as well as help with other problems. Goldenberg and Goldenberg (1996) note that people tend to seek marriage counseling when a family system is experiencing a state of disequilibrium owing to problems such as infidelity, sexual incompatibility, disagreements over child-rearing practices, concerns of divorce, ineffective communication, and issues relating to power and control.

The Counseling Process

Marriage counseling tends to be brief, problem-centered, and pragmatic (Goldenberg & Goldenberg, 1996). The most popular form of marriage counseling currently is *conjoint marriage counseling* (Nichols & Everett, 1986), which involves the counselor working with the couple together. Humphrey (1983) describes a slight modification of the conjoint session, suggesting that the counselor see each individual separately before the conjoint session. He contends that when the individuals are seen separately, they will more openly discuss sensitive issues such as an extramarital affair. When this approach is used, the counselor must establish a clear policy regarding confidentiality. The counselor must clarify with the client what information from individual sessions can be introduced during conjoint sessions, and how it will be conveyed.

The actual process of marriage counseling will vary according to the theoretical orientation of the counselor. Marriage counselors utilize a wide variety of counseling theories, such as psychoanalytic, cognitive-behavioral, strategic, and structural (Sperry & Carlson, 1991). To a large degree these theories can be considered adaptations of those utilized in individual counseling, as discussed in Chapters 7, 8, and 9, and those associated with family counseling, as presented later in this chapter.

There also appear to be some commonalities in marriage counseling. Sperry and Carlson (1991) note that all approaches utilize a systems perspective. Goldenberg and Goldenberg (1996) suggest that marriage counselors "address the affective, cognitive, and behavioral aspects of the husband-wife relationship within the context of marital and family systems" (p. 83).

In addition, several integrative models of marriage counseling have been developed that provide a broad, flexible approach. For example, Glick, Clarkin, and Kessler (1987) and Nichols (1988) contend that marriage counseling has three stages: early, middle, and termination. Nichols' (1988) model has three tasks associated with the early stage: establishing a positive relationship, assessment and goal setting, and providing immediate assistance to the couple. The middle stage is primarily concerned with using intervention strategies to resolve counseling goals. The termination stage allows for the transition toward termination once the counseling goals have been achieved.

Marital Assessment

Marital assessment is one aspect of the counseling process that deserves special attention. Comprehensive assessment is essential in marriage and family counseling (Sperry & Carlson, 1991), since 83 percent of treatment failures are associated with inadequate assessment (Coleman, 1985). Sperry (1989) suggests that comprehensive assessment in marriage counseling involves assessing the situation, the system, each spouse, and the suitability of the couple for marriage counseling. A description of these four factors follows.

1. *The situation.* Assessing the situation involves identifying stressors, precipitating factors to marital discord, and other factors that affect the situation.
2. *The system.* Systems theory can be used to assess the marital system to gain an understanding of its functional and dysfunctional characteristics.
3. *Each spouse.* Each spouse is evaluated to determine the level of physical and psychological health and the personality style.
4. *Suitability for treatment.* It is also important to determine if marriage counseling is appropriate for a couple. Beutler (1983) suggests that clients need to be motivated to change and have reasonable expectations regarding outcomes to be suitable for marriage counseling.

Commonly used assessment procedures include the clinical interview in marriage counseling (Framo, 1981); the use of enactment, which involves getting clients to act out conflicts or problems during a counseling session (Nichols, 1988); and the use of standardized tests designed for marriage counseling (Boen, 1988).

Marital assessment instruments have become popular in marriage counseling. These instruments are especially useful during the initial counseling sessions, but they can also be used throughout the counseling process as the need arises (Boen, 1988). Boen (1988) has provided an overview of the most widely used marital assessment instruments.

Stuart's Couples Precounseling Inventory (SCPI).   The SCPI was developed by Stuart (1983). It identifies 15 areas in which the couple is satisfied or dissatisfied, for example, child-rearing practices or sexual practices. The SCPI also identifies the amount of commitment each member has to the relationship, and which individual has more to gain or lose by maintaining the relationship.

Russell and Madsen's Marriage Counseling Report (MCR).   The MCR was developed by Russell and Madsen (1985). It is based on the 16 Personality Factors Questionnaire, which was developed by Raymond Cattell, as discussed in Chapter 4. The MCR provides information on the personality of each spouse, how these personalities may be contributing to marital difficulties, and how the marriage may be exacerbating psychological problems of the spouses.

Taylor-Johnson Temperament Analysis (TJTA).   The TJTA (Taylor & Morrison, 1984) represents a revision of the Johnson Temperament Analysis developed by R. H. Johnson in 1941. It "can be used to show where a couple are similar or different to the normal population as well as where they are similar or different to each other and the degree of understanding they have for each other's personality characteristics" (Boen, 1988, p. 485).

Snyder's Marital Satisfaction Inventory (MSI). The MSI was developed by Snyder (1981). It identifies basic areas in which the couple is satisfied or dissatisfied, for example, communication or problem solving. The MSI is particularly useful for couples who do not know where to begin in terms of dealing with their concerns.

Assessment of Divorce. One intriguing method of assessing marriages is to identify factors that predict divorce. Gottman and associates have conducted a series of studies that have identified the following variables to predict divorce.

- Criticism, contempt, defensiveness, and emotional withdrawal during conflict resolution (Gottman, 1994)
- Lack of positive affect such as humor, interest, and affection (successful marriages have higher rates of positive affect interactions, and their ratios of positive to negative affect during conflict resolution is 5:1 as compared to unstable marriages, which have ratios of 0.8:1) (Gottman, 1994)
- Husband rejects the wife's influence during a conflict (Gottman, Coan, Carrere, & Swanson, 1998)

Gottman et al. (1998) identified the following variables to predict marital satisfaction.

- Wives soften the startup of addressing the potential conflict (for example, they take a more tentative rather than confrontational approach)
- Husbands deescalate low-intensity negative affect of wives (for example, anger, sadness, and tension)
- Wives deescalate high-intensity negative affect of husbands (for example, contempt, defensiveness, or belligerence)
- Physiological soothing for self or partner for stress management (especially important for males, who are considered to have higher levels of autonomic arousal during conflict than women)

In addition, Gottman et al. (1998) found that listening skills may not be very useful during a conflict. They may be too direct and confrontational and require spouses to empathize with a partner when they are emotionally unable to do so (for example, after a spouse has just gotten angry at them). In this regard, listening skills may result in a celebration of the conflict. Gottman and associates went on to note that negative emotions such as anger are not predictors of divorce. In fact successful marriages need to have the expression of positive and negative emotions. What appears to be important is "gentleness, soothing, and deescalation of negativity (negativity of one spouse followed by the partner's neutral affect)" (Gottman et al., 1998, p. 16).

Skills-Based Marriage Counseling

Sperry and Carlson (1991) describe a skill-based approach to marriage counseling adapted from Dinkmeyer and Carlson's (1984) earlier work on marital enrichment. It is a practical approach that could be utilized by practitioners of different theoretical orientations. The skill-based approach to marriage counseling evolved from the following principles:

(a) healthy productive marriages require time and commitment, (b) the skills necessary for a satisfying marriage can be learned, (c) change requires each partner to assume responsibility, (d) positive feelings such as love and caring can return with behavior change, and (e) small changes can help bring about big changes.

According to Sperry and Carlson (1991, p. 45), the 10 skills that are believed to contribute to effective marriages are that both partners

1. Individually accept responsibility for their behavior and self-esteem
2. Identify and align their personal and marital goals
3. Choose to encourage each other
4. Communicate their feelings with honesty and openness
5. Listen emphatically when feelings are expressed
6. Seek to understand the factors that influence their relationship
7. Demonstrate that they accept and value each other
8. Choose thoughts, words, and actions that support the positive goals of their marriage
9. Solve marital conflicts together
10. Commit themselves to the ongoing process of maintaining an equal marriage

The skill-based approach to marriage counseling is educative in that it provides the couple opportunities to learn how to use the 10 skills associated with effective marriages. For example, the couple can learn how to use some of these skills in a four-step approach to conflict resolution. The four steps are show mutual respect, pinpoint the real issue, seek areas of agreement, and mutually participate in decisions. Additional guidelines for conflict resolution include be specific and oriented in the present and future, use good communication skills such as "I" messages and active listening, avoid using absolutes, and avoid attempting to determine who was right or wrong (Sperry & Carlson, 1991).

Family Counseling

No clear definition of family counseling has emerged. Its hallmark, however, is that the process involves problems experienced by an individual that seem to indicate more fundamental problems within the family system (Horne & Ohlsen, 1982). The systems perspective continues to characterize family counseling in that family counselors treat problems within a relationship context rather than working separately with individuals (Goldenberg & Goldenberg, 1996).

This section first provides an overview of six prominent theories used by family counselors, as summarized in Table 10.2. Following this overview is a discussion of the counseling process in family counseling.

Psychodynamic Family Counseling

Ackerman (1937, 1956, 1966, 1970) is credited with integrating Freud's psychoanalytic theory into family counseling. His model emphasizes the importance of both intrapersonal and interpersonal forces. Ackerman (1970) viewed the family as a system of interacting personalities, with each family member representing a subsystem. The primary aim of Ackerman's

TABLE 10.2 Theories of Family Counseling

Theory	Founder(s)	Key Concepts	Process	Goals
Psychodynamic Family Counseling	Ackerman, Framo	Intrapsychic forces are believed to play a key role in family dysfunction; object relations such as meaningful relationships are primary motivational force in life	Focuses on intrapersonal and interpersonal forces (for example, strengthening the ego, clarifying roles, helping clients obtain more satisfying relationships)	Promote change and growth by altering patterns of communication, resolving pathological inner conflicts, and defining roles of family members in complementary fashion
Experiential Family Counseling	Satir, Whitaker, Bumberry	Self-actualization, awareness, choice, and responsibility	Free family members to move toward self-actualization; experiential focus; relates to here and now rather than past issues	Promote clear communication, help family members become authentic–autonomous individuals, promote a positive family climate
Structural Family Counseling	Minuchin	Systemic concepts such as boundaries and reframing	Counselor joins the family to alter structure of the interaction between family members	Clarify boundaries, increase flexibility of family interactions, modify dysfunctional family structure
Strategic Family Counseling	Haley, Madanes	Communication patterns and power struggles determine the nature of the relationships between family members	Attempts to directly resolve presenting problems with little attempt to provide insight from past events	Resolve symptomology of family members by redefining relationship between family members
Adlerian/Dreikursian Family Counseling	Adler, Dreikurs	Family constellation, mutual respect, goals of misbehavior, use of consequences, encouragement, communication	Educational focus to help parents learn skills to foster positive parent–child relationships	Understand the dynamics of problems occurring within the family and promote positive parent–child relationships
Postmodern/Social-constructionism	Andersen, White, and others	Problems are conceptualized in terms of language and narratives	Stories reflecting family life are developed and rewritten, creating new opportunities for more meaningful family life	Help families create new stories, which fosters family functioning

approach is to promote change and growth by altering patterns of communication, resolving pathological inner conflicts, and helping family members define their roles in a complementary manner (Goldenberg & Goldenberg, 1996).

More recently Framo (1992) integrated object relations theory (see Chapter 7) into psychodynamic family counseling. The basic premise of object relations theory is that the fundamental motivation in life is the drive to satisfy object relations, for example, satisfying relationships (Goldenberg & Goldenberg, 1996). In addition, object relations theory contends that intrapsychic conflicts that evolved from the family of origin play a key role in relationship difficulties. As part of the overall treatment program, psychodynamic family counselors may conduct individual counseling, couples counseling, and family counseling that includes members of the client's family of origin (Goldenberg & Goldenberg, 1996).

Experiential Family Counseling

The theoretical origins of experiential family counseling can be traced to the humanistic-existential schools of counseling, as discussed in Chapter 7. Satir (1983, 1988), Whitaker (1976, 1977), and Bumberry (Whitaker & Bumberry, 1988) are credited with incorporating the major concepts of the humanistic-existential schools into family counseling. The basic premise of this approach is that if the individual family member can be freed to move toward self-actualization, then the family will function effectively. The goals of experiential family counseling include promoting clear communication among family members; helping family members become authentic, autonomous individuals; assisting the family in developing a positive family climate characterized by encouragement, caring, and intimacy; and promoting awareness of choice and responsibility in family members.

The counseling process in experiential family counseling focuses on the here and now instead of dealing with problems from the past. The emphasis within counseling is on experiencing rather than intellectualizing. In this regard, the counselor utilizes a variety of techniques such as sculpting, confrontation, communication skill training, and Gestalt exercises to help family members become aware of their feelings. For example, the technique of *sculpting* involves having one person physically arrange the other family members to create a "sculpture." The person creates the sculpture by using space and form to represent perceptions of family relationships, for instance, placing a child between the mother and father to symbolize interference between the marital dyad. All family members are then invited to discuss the creation. Typical themes that result from such discussions are closeness, isolation, alignment, intimacy, and power.

Structural Family Counseling

Salvador Minuchin (1974, 1984) is credited with developing structural family counseling. The role of the counselor in this approach is to join the family in a position of leadership. The goals are to clarify boundaries between family members, increase flexibility of family interactions, and modify dysfunctional family structure (Goldenberg & Goldenberg, 1996).

Minuchin (1974, 1984) has developed several innovative concepts that have played a key role in the evolution of systems theory (Goldenberg & Goldenberg, 1996). One example is the concept of *boundaries,* which are the unwritten rules that help define roles and functions of family members. Boundaries determine what will be allowed to occur between family members, and they can ensure privacy or allow for intimacy. Family dysfunctioning can result when boundaries become rigid, confused, or conflicting.

Another concept that Minuchin (1974, 1984) developed is *reframing,* a family counseling technique to help the family see things from a more positive perspective. For example, an adolescent might complain that his mother spends too much time working. Using the technique of reframing, the counselor might help the adolescent focus on the fact that his mother enjoys her job and that it makes her a pleasant person to be with.

Strategic Family Counseling

Jay Haley (1963, 1971, 1973, 1976, 1980) and individuals such as Madanes (1981, 1984) have played key roles in the development of strategic family counseling. This approach focuses on communication patterns between family members and views intrapsychic forces as unimportant. Haley (1976, 1980) contends that the relationship between family members can be determined by the manner in which they communicate and how they position themselves in terms of power issues.

This approach is considered strategic because it focuses on resolving the presenting problem directly, with little attempt to provide insight from past events. To resolve the presenting problem, counselors use procedures oriented to concrete actions including homework assignments, teaching new skills, and advice giving. They also use paradoxical techniques, which involve prescribing the symptom. For example, if a husband and wife have a habit of yelling at each other, the counselor might ask them to spend 10 minutes yelling at one another every day.

Strategic family counseling can be a powerful and effective form of counseling. Strategies such as advice giving and paradoxical techniques must be used carefully, however, or they may do more harm than good to the family (Nichols, 1984).

Adlerian Family Counseling

Alfred Adler's school of psychology and the later writings of Rudolph Dreikurs (see Chapter 7) have been applied to a variety of helping processes, including family counseling and parent education. Adlerian family counseling focuses on individual family members as well as the overall functioning of the family. The main goal of this approach is to improve parent-child relationships (Lowe, 1982).

The role and function of the counselor is psychoeducational—helping parents learn principles and understand the dynamics of problems occurring within the family (Lowe, 1982). The approach is therefore educative in nature. In this process, the counselor identifies basic mistakes, teaches the parents concepts that will help them understand misbehavior, helps parents deal effectively with discipline problems, and assists in establishing positive parent-child relations.

The key concepts of this approach are family constellation, goals of misbehavior, use of natural and logical consequences, encouragement, and communication. Although these Adlerian concepts are discussed in Chapter 7, they are presented here in light of the family counseling approach.

Family Constellation.   The family constellation relates to the overall structure of the family. Particular attention is paid to how birth-order characteristics can be used to understand the personality of the children (for example, first-born children tend to be bossy).

Goals of Misbehavior.   Children's misbehavior is seen as movement toward one of four goals of misbehavior: attention, power, revenge, and display of inadequacy. Additional goals of misbehavior for teenagers include excitement, peer acceptance, and superiority (Dinkmeyer & McKay, 1990).

Use of Natural and Logical Consequences.   Parents are taught to use natural and logical consequences as opposed to punishment to discipline children. Among the advantages of this approach over punishment are that consequences are more logically tied to misbehavior, promote choice and responsibility in the child, and minimize animosity between the parent and child.

Encouragement.   Parents are taught to use encouragement with their child. Offering encouragement focuses on effort and helps build self-esteem, confidence, and self-efficacy.

Communication Skills.   Parents learn how to use effective communication skills with their child. A philosophy of mutual respect is essential for effective communication. When parents respect the child, they will tend to communicate empathic understanding of the child's point of view. Parents may also be taught listening skills and problem-solving skills, which can be used to help their child deal with personal problems.

The concepts utilized in Adlerian family counseling have also been incorporated into parent education programs such as Dinkmeyer and McKay's (1989, 1990) systematic training for effective parenting (STEP) programs. Parent education programs typically involve small groups of individuals meeting to discuss parenting concepts and concerns, usually for approximately 1½ hours each week over a 10-week period. Research efforts show that the effectiveness of parent educators is not related to whether the educators have been parents themselves (Schultz, Nystul, & Law, 1980). Research also suggests that it is important to include role-play activities to allow for the internalization and transfer from attitudes to behaviors (Schultz & Nystul, 1980).

I developed an approach to family counseling called *marathon family counseling* while working on the Navajo Indian reservation. The approach evolved out of my work with Katherine Hillis, a Navajo mental health counselor. Marathon family counseling shares the following characteristics with Mara Selvini-Palazzoli's (1980) approach. Both utilize extended family sessions lasting up to eight hours approximately once a month, and both serve clients who live in rural areas and have had to travel hundreds of miles for the session.

Marathon family counseling is based on the principles of Adlerian family counseling, including the use of encouragement, establishing mutual respect, identifying basic mistakes, and reorientation from basic mistakes. The following *Personal Note* illustrates this approach.

A Personal Note

A 74-year-old grandmother arrived at the mental health center at the Navajo Indian reservation where I was working. Accompanied by a daughter, the woman appeared depressed and tearful during the initial interview. She lived with her husband 100 miles from the center and had three daughters, two sons, and twelve grandchildren.

The grandmother complained that two of her grandchildren had wrecked four of her automobiles over the years. She thought that the situation was hopeless and it would probably happen again because "kids will be kids . . ." While she talked, my Navajo mental health aide and I identified some basic mistakes. As discussed in Chapter 7, the Adlerian concept of a basic mistake is a self-defeating idea, such as an overgeneralization, false goals of security, misconception of life's demands, or minimization of one's worth.

The client's basic mistakes were as follows.

1. Others can't survive without me.
2. The children of my family aren't responsible, so I'll have to take care of everything.
3. I'm not important. Other people are more important than me.

At this point, my aide and I decided that the client could benefit from marathon family counseling because of the great distance she and her daughter had traveled and the depth of her distress. We then discovered that the grandchild who had most recently wrecked her car was in jail for a D.W.I. citation. Since we wanted to include that family member in the session, we decided that we would have the family counseling session at the local jail. We phoned several other family members, and they agreed to meet us there.

We began the session by asking the grandmother to share how she was feeling. She started to cry and said she was so sad. She didn't feel her grandchildren cared about her but just wanted to use her and her cars. She said she felt they had no respect for her or her feelings. I asked how the family members felt about what grandmother was saying. The two grandchildren that had wrecked her cars seemed uneasy and defensive. After these feelings were explored, they were able to make some statements that seemed to express genuine concern.

I mentioned that all people make mistakes and have room for improvement. The family members agreed. My aide and I then explored ways each

family member had contributed to the current problem and what they could do to help. With much encouragement, each person was able to make a specific plan for improvement.

At the end of the session, I asked the family members to express how the session affected them and what they wanted to do differently to help their family. I arranged to see them all in two weeks at the grandmother's house. We finished the session by thanking the family members and shaking their hands. Several family members also shook hands with one another and gave each other warm embraces.

We then talked with the grandmother privately and explored how she was feeling. She said she was relieved but still felt somehow responsible for her family's behavior. At this point, we discussed the basic mistakes we had identified earlier. We then used a variety of procedures to reorient the grandmother from her basic mistakes. For example, we read the section on children from *The Prophet* (Gibran, 1965). This helped her realize that she was not responsible for her grandchildren. Her job was to provide guidance and love and let them—like arrows—fly freely into the challenges of life. She began to realize that if she didn't let go, they wouldn't have the opportunity to become responsible people. She had a very positive response to the reading from *The Prophet* and wanted a copy of the book. I let her borrow mine until she could get a copy. She then left for home with her daughter.

After the initial marathon counseling session, my mental health aide and I provided counseling services for the family over an 18-month period. The grandmother was eventually able to let go of her tendency to feel responsible for her grandchildren's behavior. Her signs of depression were gone after one month. The two grandchildren who had wrecked her cars both had minor problems with the law (e.g., public intoxication) during the counseling period. On the positive side, however, they didn't wreck any more cars during that time.

Source: From "Marathon Family Counseling" by M. Nystul, 1988, *Individual Psychology: The Journal of Adlerian Theory, Research, & Practice, 44*(2), pp. 210–216, by permission of the University of Texas Press.

Postmodern/Social Constructionist Trends in Family Counseling

Bitter and Corey (1996) note that the postmodern/social constructionist perspective is associated with recent trends in family therapy. As noted earlier, social constructivism represents a paradigm shift that recognizes the multiple realities reflected in the languages of different cultures and the stories internalized by individuals in those cultures. Social constructionism therefore parallels the postmodern position, which recognizes a subjective reality based on the context of the observational process used. The social constructionist perspective is therefore particularly useful in infusing issues of diversity (such as gender, feminism, and culture) into family counseling.

The process of counseling in postmodern/social constructionism is similar to the qualitative research method of discovery. The counselor enters the relationship without preconceived ideas of what should be or should happen in therapy but instead attempts to discover with clients what is important from their phenomenological perspective. In this process, families are encouraged to engage in conversations that explore the meanings family members have given to their problems (Goldenberg & Goldenberg, 1996). In this process, "past experience is viewed as helpful not as a source of objective fact but as a source for determining and understanding the language, assumptions, and views of clients" (Giblin & Chan, 1995, p. 326). The counseling relationship is a collaborative relationship that fosters empowerment in clients. Goals and procedures vary according to the needs of clients and theoretical perspective of counselors but typically focus on helping families create new stories which enlarge perspective and options and can bring new meaning to family life (Bitter & Corey, 1996). "Clients are invited into a reflective process, and the goal is to open up new meanings and possibilities for alternative behaviors" (Giblin & Chan, 1995, p. 326).

Bitter and Corey (1996) identify the following postmodern/social constructionist approaches to family counseling.

The Reflecting Team. Tom Anderson (1991, 1992) proposes that family therapy can be enriched by the dialogues that are generated between families and professionals who are observing and processing the family counseling session. The overall process and goal of the reflecting team approach is to help families create new life stories through dialogue and reflection.

For example, a reflecting team that has observed a family session through a one-way mirror can then join the family and process the central story that characterized the session. The story can be one of concern that family members don't seem to care about each other. Together, counselors and family members can reflect on issues such as when the family does get along. The resulting dialogue can create new stories that promote hope and encouragement for the family.

The Linguistic Approach. Harlene Anderson and Harold Goolishian (1992) are the key individuals associated with the linguistic approach to family counseling. They contend that narratives emerge from social interactions over time, and the nature of the narrative is associated with the meaning experienced in life. In this approach, the counselor enters into the session with compassion and caring and a keen interest in discovering meaning from the families' stories. The goal of counseling is to help the family create alternative stories that can enhance meaning for the family.

The linguistic approach involves helping families explore the evolution of stories that characterize family life. For example, dysfunctional stories can emerge from the narratives shared between family members, which are then passed on from generation to generation (for example, "blacks don't trust whites or vice versa"). Families can use these insights to help overcome dysfunctional elements in their stories (such as stereotyping and prejudice) and then create more meaningful and functional stories.

The Narrative Approach. Michael White and David Epston (1990) and the earlier work of Foucault (1980) are associated with the narrative approach. The narrative approach contends that narratives are a reflection of the dominant culture and therefore must be challenged to ensure they are sensitive to diversity issues such as gender, sexual orientation, and culture. The process and goal of the narrative approach is to help families deconstruct dysfunctional narratives (from the dominant culture) and reauthor new, more functional narratives.

The narrative approach encourages families to question the assumptions on which their stories are based in terms of potential influence from the dominant society. For example, a family member who is "coming out" with his or her family in terms of sexual orientation may encounter excessive resistance from the family. In some instances, this may result in tearing the family apart and psychological abandonment of the homosexual individual. Counselors can help these families separate their value, wants, and needs from external forces that may perceive things in rigid, either-or terms. This process may contribute to more functional family narratives that are based on their cultural identities and worldviews and not the worldviews projected by the dominant society.

Solution-Oriented Therapy. De Shazer (1991) and O'Hanlon and Weiner-Davis (1989) are among some of the individuals who have promoted solution-oriented approaches to counseling. This approach can be used across all domains of counseling from individual to group to marriage and family. The solution-oriented approach suggests that it is more productive to focus on solutions and strengths than on problems and weakness, and families can be assisted in creating narratives that reflect positive change.

The solution-oriented approach focuses on family strengths and problem resolution. An example would be in Adlerian/Dreikurserian family counseling. In this psychoeducational approach, parents are taught to use encouragement to foster children's self-efficacy, and consequences to overcome discipline problems by promoting choice and responsibility.

Feminist Psychotherapy. Enns (1993), Rawlings (1993), Avis (1986), and others have set forth the major issues associated with feminist psychotherapy. Feminist psychotherapy applied to family counseling contends that the family system is a male-dominated, patriarchal system. Male domination exists even when the father is absent from the family. From a feminist perspective, male domination and control are maintained by public patriarchy as represented by government organizations such as welfare and other family assistance programs. Male-dominated narratives are perpetuated in many ways such as the media, research, and even the theories that describe normal family life and human development. Carol Gilligan's (1982) seminal work on moral development of women provides an example of how male-dominated research can ignore gender difference in human growth and development.

The overall aim of feminist family therapy is to help family systems overcome oppressive forces and foster mutual respect, equality, and gender sensitivity between the sexes. Some of the goals of therapy include deconstructing patriarchy narratives and reconstructing narratives that recognize gender differences and the special needs of women in all aspects of living, empowering women within the context of egalitarian families, valuing what is considered feminine or nurturing, and promoting a positive attitude toward women.

The Counseling Process

The counseling process in family counseling will vary according to the theoretical orientation of the practitioner. Many aspects, however, are common to family counseling approaches regardless of the theoretical perspective. Friedlander and Highlen (1984) and Friedlander, Highlen, and Lassiter (1985) identify some commonalities associated with family counseling. Some of these are that family counselors

- View the marital subsystem as the most stressed
- Align themselves with the family's established hierarchy, interacting more with parents than children
- Focus on the nuclear family, especially the parental subsystem
- Avoid direct confrontation with family members, preferring to direct messages to other family members (such as asking the wife why she thinks her husband is afraid of her)
- Actively engage in interpretation and educational processes

In addition, the authors found that family counselors make few references to the future, parents emphasize current issues, and children tend to relate to here and now issues regarding sibling relationships.

Goldenberg and Goldenberg (1996) note there is interest in developing integrative models for family counseling that can be responsive to different populations. L'Abate (1986) set forth the following four-stage integrative model for family counseling.

Stage One: Stress Reduction.   The tasks associated with this stage are establishing a positive relationship, reducing stress and conflict, resolving an existing crisis if necessary, and reducing symptomatic behavior to a tolerable level.

Stage Two: Training and Education.   This stage involves helping the family learn the skills necessary to function effectively. Counselors frequently use homework assignments during this stage for family members to practice the skills they are learning.

Stage Three: Issue of Termination.   During this stage, the family is given an opportunity to deal with issues that have not been resolved, such as dealing effectively with intimacy. When all issues have been resolved, the counselor helps the family move toward termination of the counseling process.

Stage Four: Follow-Up.   Follow-up involves determining the efficacy of counseling and allowing for additional counseling as needed.

Diversity Issues in Marriage and Family Counseling

Diversity issues are becoming increasingly important in all aspects of counseling, including marriage and family counseling (Hayes, 1995; Paniagua, 1996). Marriage and family counselors must be sensitive to a wide array of diversity issues such as gender, culture, age, sexual orientation, and socioeconomic status to be effective in their practice. Hayes (1995) notes that Rothenberg's (1995) book on race, class, and gender may be particularly useful to marriage and family counselors. It has numerous personal narratives that depict the struggles of families with issues such as racism, oppression, and sexism. Hayes (1995) goes on to note that Linda James Myers' (1988) optimal theory offers promise to family therapists to help overcome oppression through self-knowledge and positive identity development.

As noted earlier, feminist therapy has much to offer marriage and family counseling. Giblin and Chan (1995) describe several common themes in the feminist literature that they believe have relevance for marriage and family counselors. Some of these themes are communicating respect; validating feelings; supporting social and political change to overcome oppression; promoting social equality over power, control, and dominance; understanding behavior contextually; awareness of the relational connectedness associated with being human; and promoting mutual empathy, mutual engagement, and mutual empowerment.

Johnson (1995) identifies 10 resiliency mechanisms in culturally diverse families. Johnson defines family resiliency as the manner in which the family renews itself each day and maintains homeostasis and a sense of collective identity as a unique living system. It also relates to the ability for family members to cope with everyday problems without compromising their moral or cultural values. These resiliency mechanisms are summarized as follows. The family serves as a "sacred ark" protecting its members from the storms of adversity and providing safety and refuge for them. These families utilize multiple support systems that include spirituality, the recognition of what the elders of the family or society can offer, and the role of the extended family in daily family life. Other resiliency characteristics include the use of native language, a high value on family socialization and communication, insulation from racism and the adverse effects of migration, and the support of individual resiliency of each family member.

Paniagua (1996) provides suggestions for incorporating a cross-cultural perspective in family counseling. First, the definition of the extended family can vary considerably from culture to culture. For example, in the Hispanic culture the extended family can include the comadre (comother) and the compadre (cofather) and folk healers. Family counselors should therefore have families define what their concept of the extended family is and how their extended family impacts on the overall role and function of the family.

Second, family counselors should assess for levels of acculturation in the family. Significant discrepancies in acculturation between family members (for example, children and parents or husband and wife) can create family dysfunction and should be identified and addressed as necessary. It is also important to recognize that although a family is from a particular ethnic minority, its members may not feel that way (they may be identifying with the majority culture) (Dana, 1993). Acculturation scales have been developed for different cultures (see Chapter 6) that can be used to determine the degree of acculturation for a family member.

Third, Paniagua (1996) notes that it is not critical for a family and a counselor to have the same racial origin. It is more important for the counselor to have some compatibility in terms of lifestyle and values and to be sensitive to cultural variables in the assessment and treatment of family dysfunction. It is also important to have the necessary skills to be successful in cross-cultural counseling. Paniagua (1996) provides some suggestions in terms of what should be communicated cross-culturally during the first and subsequent family sessions. For example, during the first session it is important to demonstrate expertise and authority with Asian families, avoid discussing the behavior of African American parents in the presence of their children, and explore levels of acculturation and provide concrete and tangible advice to all groups. In subsequent sessions, family counselors can focus on other issues associated with a cultural group or all groups such as being sensitive to the family's sense of powerlessness (for all families, especially African Americans) and personalizing the session through the use of first names and handshaking (Hispanic families).

Brown (1997) advocated using a cross-cultural perspective in consulting with parents. Consultation with parents frequently involves the use of parenting programs to help parents improve parent-child relationships and foster optimal development in children. Brown (1997) suggests that cross-cultural parenting consultants "be aware of their personal values and biases, be culturally empathic, be aware of their consulting paradigm, and be able to make culturally sensitive adaptations to their approach to consultation" (p. 29).

Evaluation of Marriage and Family Counseling

At least 20 literature reviews of marriage and family counseling were conducted between 1970 and 1990, involving the analysis of approximately 300 studies (Raffa, Sypek, & Vogel, 1990). Unfortunately, methodological flaws in many of these studies drew questions concerning the efficacy of marriage and family counseling. Some of these methodological problems included a lack of clear description of intervention strategies used in marriage and family counseling studies (Bednar, Burlingame, and Masters, 1988) and a lack of controlled studies, inadequate research design, the use of assessment instruments with questionable reliability and validity, and a lack of replication of results (Raffa, Sypek, and Vogue, 1990).

More recent research and the utilization of meta-analysis to analyze multiple studies at once have been able to adequately address these methodological problems and clearly provide evidence of the efficacy of marriage and family counseling (Dunn & Schwebel, 1995; Lebow & Gurman, 1995; Shadish et al., 1995). Shadish et al. (1995) conducted a meta-analysis of 163 marriage and family counseling studies (62 marital and 101 family). Results of their investigation provide clear support for the efficacy of marriage and family counseling, no evidence of one theoretical approach being superior over others, and no evidence that marriage and family counseling is superior over individual counseling.

Dunn and Schwebel (1995) focused on an evaluation of marriage counseling suggesting that conducting meta-analysis of marriage and family counseling could obscure the results. These researchers evaluated 15 methodologically rigorous marital outcome studies. They found that behavioral marital therapy, cognitive-behavioral marital therapy, and insight-oriented marital therapy are all successful in bringing about positive change in spouses' relationship-related behavior; insight-oriented marital therapy was the most successful in enhancing the spouses' assessment of the quality of their relationship; and cognitive-behavioral marital therapy was the best at contributing to the spouses' posttherapy relationship-related cognitions.

Lebow and Gurman (1995) provide an extensive review of research (including meta-analytic reviews) and conclude that there has been an enormous enhancement of the quality of the research on marriage and family counseling between 1985 and 1995. These individuals note that much of the research has focused on behavioral approaches, but non-behavioral methods are beginning to receive more attention in the literature. In addition, marriage and family counseling is becoming more integrative in terms of theoretical approaches and in its recognition of the merits of designing treatment approaches that are directed at the individual, family, and larger systems such as cultural, societal, and economic (Lebow & Gurman, 1995).

Summary

The field of marriage and family counseling is both an emerging profession and a counseling specialty practiced by various members of the helping profession. Systems theory and the family life cycle model are important theoretical foundations for marriage and family counseling.

Although theories differ with regard to key concepts, goals, and counseling, commonalities in the field exist. In this regard, marriage and family counseling focus on the relationship between family members and the overall family system rather than individual family members. There also appears to be a trend toward integration of theories in an attempt to meet the needs of different populations.

Major reviews of the research that has been conducted on marriage and family counseling note that recent studies provide strong support for the efficacy of marriage and family counseling.

11 Child and Adolescent Counseling

The young . . . are full of passion, which excludes fear; and of hope, which inspires confidence.

—Aristotle, Rhetoric Book II

CHAPTER OVERVIEW

This chapter provides an overview of child and adolescent counseling. Highlights of the chapter include

- The art and science of child and adolescent counseling
- Children and adolescents from a historical perspective
- Developmental theories
- Emerging developmental theories: optimal development, attachment theory, resiliency, and emotional intelligence
- Special approaches to child and adolescent counseling: play therapy and conflict resolution
- Special problems of children and adolescents, including child abuse and neglect, depression, and antisocial behavior
- Diversity and postmodern issues in child and adolescent counseling

Child and adolescent counseling is an emerging specialty within the counseling profession. Some of the most promising advances in counseling and psychology are occurring in this field. These are reflected in our understanding and treatment of common problems that children and adolescents experience, including child abuse and neglect, child/adolescent depression, and antisocial behavior. In this chapter, information is presented on these types of problems as well as other conceptual and treatment issues.

The Art and Science of Child and Adolescent Counseling

Child and adolescent counseling, like all aspects of counseling, is an art and a science. It is an art to discover the private world of children and adolescents. For working with children, the challenge is finding ways to communicate that are not restricted by language and cognitive development. Challenges for working with adolescents are keeping lines of communication open and maintaining trust. Possible venues that can be used to transcend these potential barriers include play therapy, conflict resolution, parent education, family therapy, consultation with teachers and parent, and ecological-environmental approaches directed at enhancing the world of children and adolescents.

One way of conceptualizing the art of child and adolescent counseling is "reaching in–reaching out" (Nystul, 1986a). In this process, the counselor attempts to meet children or adolescents from the perspective of their internal frame of reference—the world that makes sense to them and that they feel safe in. As trust and respect are established, the child or adolescent may then feel encouraged to reach out into the world of others. This may be characterized by a movement toward success-oriented rather than failure-oriented activities in school. Throughout this process, the counselor communicates a wide range of emotions such as caring, compassion, and perhaps even anger to provide the structure and emotional support necessary for the optimal development of children and adolescents.

The science of child and adolescent counseling is grounded in developmental theory, research, and practice. It recognizes that counseling across the life span must be cognizant of the physical, cognitive, and psychosocial aspects of development and their impact on the counseling process. From a developmental perspective, children and adolescents need assistance in acquiring the coping skills necessary to master the various developmental tasks necessary to move forward in their development. Counseling strategies can be directed at helping children and adolescents achieve these coping skills by fostering resiliency, positive attachment relationships, emotional and intellectual intelligence, and other qualities that promote optimal development. Recent research in diversity issues and postmodernism must also be addressed in formulating counseling strategies with children and adolescents.

Children and Adolescents from a Historical Perspective

Children

The concept of childhood as a distinct developmental stage is relatively new (LeVine & Sallee, 1992). Children had been viewed as miniature adults and forced to work alongside adults in the fields and in factories and to fight in wars. Children had no special privileges, lacking the protection of child labor laws or the advantage of formal education. They were to be "seen and not heard" and used in whatever way the parents dictated (LeVine & Sallee, 1992).

Children were often lucky to survive long enough to become adults. Until the nineteenth century, parents had the right to kill a newborn child who was deformed, sickly, retarded, or even the "wrong" sex (Radbill, 1980). If children survived that possibility, there was still a very good chance they would die of illness or accident. In the 1600s, 59 percent of the children in London died before they were five years old, and 64 percent died before they turned 10 (LeVine & Sallee, 1992). Kanner (1962) presents the following story of Emerentia to illustrate how a seven-year-old girl was viewed and treated in 1713.

> This 7-year-old girl, the offspring of an aristocratic family, whose father remarried after an unhappy first matrimony, offended her "noble and god-fearing" stepmother by her peculiar behavior. Worst of all, she would not join in the prayers and was panic-stricken when taken to the black-robed preacher in the dark and gloomy chapel. She avoided contact with people by hiding in closets or running away from home. The local physician had nothing to offer beyond declaring that she might be insane. She was placed in the custody of a minister known for his rigid orthodoxy. The minister, who saw in her ways the machinations of a "baneful and infernal" power, used a number of would-be therapeutic devices. He laid her on a bench and beat her with cat-o'-nine-tails. He locked her in a dark pantry. He subjected her to a period of starvation. He clothed her with a frock of burlap. Under these circumstances, the child did not last long. She died after a few months, and everybody felt relieved. The minister was amply rewarded for his efforts by Emerentia's parents. (p. 97)

LeVine and Sallee (1992) cite the following events as forces that contributed to the recognition of children as a distinct stage of development. In 1744, Pestalozzi published the first scientific record of the development of a young child. In the late nineteenth century, two books served as models for observational and experimental approaches to analyze child development: Charles Darwin's *Biographical Sketch of an Infant* in 1877 and Wilhelm Preyer's *The Mind of a Child* in late 1892. Also during the latter part of the nineteenth century, G. Stanley Hall studied the physical and mental capabilities of children at Clark University. In the early 1900s, child guidance clinics emerged to provide counseling and guidance services to children. In 1910, the Stanford-Binet IQ tests were published. In 1917, John B. Watson conducted his now-famous "Little Albert" experiments, which demonstrated that a child could be conditioned to cry at the sight of a furry object.

Although children have come a long way from the dark ages of the past, there are still signs that being a child is not easy. Wagner (1994) notes that children are faced with a wide array of sociocultural conditions that often have an adverse effect on their development. For example, 25 percent of children under five years of age are living in poverty and the number of children born into a single-parent home has increased from 4 percent to 25 percent from 1950 to 1988 (Wagner, 1994). There has also been an increase in the amount of time parents are spending at work, resulting in a significant reduction in their investment in child rearing (Committee for Economic Development, 1991). Several negative forces appear to be attempting to fill the void left by a lack of parental involvement. Some of these activities include watching television, which is often ladened with sex and violence (three to four year olds watch an average of two or more hours a day [Sroufe & Cooper, 1996]); escaping into substance abuse; and attempting to meet basic needs such as love, becoming, and self-esteem through gang involvement.

Adolescents

Sroufe and Cooper (1996) note that it was not until the twentieth century that adolescence was considered a separate stage of development. Before that time (and in some underdeveloped countries today), puberty marked the transition from childhood to adulthood.

G. Stanley Hall (1904) was one of the first to recognize adolescence as a distinct stage of development. Hall's view of adolescence was characterized as a conflict-ridden period resulting from rapid and profound physical changes set off by the onset of puberty.

Contemporary views of adolescence have modified Hall's position, contending that adolescence is not normally a period of "storm and stress" but a time of relatively healthy development (Sroufe & Cooper, 1996; Wagner, 1996). Current estimates suggest that 80 percent of adolescents manage very well in terms of their overall psychological functioning with the remaining 20 percent having significant behavioral difficulties requiring some form of clinical intervention (Weiner, 1992). More specifically, Weiner notes that 20 percent pass through adolescence with virtually no recognized mental disorders, 20 percent have mental disorders, and the remaining 60 percent have mild psychological problems that do not significantly interfere with daily functioning.

Although adolescence is typically not the stormy period professed by Hall, evidence suggests it is a time of increasingly high risk for problems that adversely affect healthy development, such as substance abuse, teenage pregnancy, depression, and violence (Takanishi, 1993; Wagner, 1996). Takanishi (1993) provides evidence that suggests that approximately 25 percent of U.S. adolescents face serious risk and 25 percent pose a moderate risk for health- and safety-related problems and that these problems appear to be increasing at an alarming rate. For example, more U.S. children and adolescents are experimenting with alcohol and illegal drugs than ever before and at a younger age (15 and younger); depression affects between 7 percent and 33 percent of adolescents; suicide rates tripled between 1968 and 1985 for 10- to 14-year-olds and doubled during that time period for 15- to 19-year-olds; homicide rates have escalated, especially for African American males between 15 and 19 years of age, increasing by 111 percent from 1985 to 1990; and pregnancy rates have also increased 23 percent from 1973 to 1987 for 10- to 14-year-olds (Takanishi, 1993). With all the challenges facing adolescents, it is not surprising that there has been a resurgence of interest in the counseling profession in the field of adolescent counseling [see special issues on adolescence in *The American Psychologist,* 48(2), 1993 and *The Counseling Psychologist,* 24(3), 1996].

Collins and Collins (1994) have noted that approximately 12 percent of individuals under the age of 18 have a serious emotional or behavioral disorder and a minority receive adequate mental health services. These authors suggest that the current mental-health delivery system for children and adolescents is inadequate, and it is necessary to develop a community-based system of care. The community system should be ecological in nature, attempting to unite community organizations and agencies to promote family strength and optimal development.

Developmental Theories

Providing counseling services to children and adolescents differs dramatically from working with adults. Unlike adults, children and adolescents are undergoing constant change in their physical, cognitive, and psychosocial abilities. A child or adolescent may therefore express certain symptoms at one stage of development and entirely different symptoms at another stage (LeVine & Sallee, 1992). For example, a child at age three may resort to temper tantrums when under stress. The same child at age 13 may turn to drugs as a means of dealing with stress (LeVine & Sallee, 1992).

It is therefore important to utilize a developmental perspective when working with children. This section will provide an overview of developmental theories relating to cognitive, moral, and psychosocial development as well as issues that relate to psychopathology and the classic theories of personality (summarized in Table 11.1). A more detailed description of developmental characteristics (physical, cognitive, and social-emotional) and associated counseling and consultation strategies for early childhood through the adolescence stages of development can be found in Stern and Newland (1994) and Vernon (1995).

TABLE 11.1   Developmental Theories

Developmental Theories	Founder	Key Concepts	Implications for Counseling
Cognitive theory	Piaget, Elkind	Divided cognitive development into four distinct stages: sensorimotor (birth to 2), preoperational (2 to 7), concrete operations (7 to 11), and formal operations (begins after 11).	Counselors should adjust the counseling approach to the child or adolescent's level of cognitive functioning.
Theory of moral development	Kohlberg, Gilligan	Identified three levels of moral development beginning with an egocentric view regarding morality (that is, a child controls behavior out of a fear of punishment).	An understanding of moral reasoning can be useful to promote self-control.
Psychosocial development theory	Erikson	Identified seven psychosocial stages and their associated developmental tasks (for example, from birth to 1 year of age the central task is trust).	Counselors can help clients obtain the coping skills necessary to master the developmental tasks so they can move forward in their development.
Developmental psychopathology	Kazden, Kovacs, and others	Study of child and adolescent psychopathology in the context of maturational and developmental processes.	Provides a framework for understanding child and adolescent psychopathology as unique from adult psychopathology and to aid in accurate assessment, diagnosis, and treatment.
The classic theories	Freud, Adler, and Jung	The theories of personality posited by the classic theorists emphasize the role of early life experiences on child and adolescent development.	These theories provide useful information for counselors to understand the dynamics of behavior *before* they begin to use counseling techniques to promote behavior change.

Cognitive Theories

Many theories have attempted to explain how cognitive development occurs throughout the life span (Piaget, 1952; Bruner, 1973). Among these, Piaget's theory has received significant attention in literature. Piaget (1952) divided cognitive development into four distinct stages: sensorimotor (birth to two years of age); preoperational (two to six years of age); concrete operational (ages seven to eleven); and formal operational (age twelve through adulthood).

According to Piaget, the cognitive development of children and adolescents becomes more sophisticated as they progress from one stage to the next. For example, children are usually unable to understand cause and effect during the preoperational stage. Concepts such as divorce or death may therefore be difficult for children to understand during this stage, from two to six years old. When faced with divorce or death during this stage, they may become confused and even blame themselves. It is important for counselors to be aware of a child's and adolescent's level of cognitive development during the counseling process.

Cognitive development can also play an important role in how children respond to questions. The cognitive style of children seven to eleven tends to be concrete in nature (concrete operational stage). The children therefore tend to respond well to questions that ask for specific information (probing questions), such as "Do you like school?" Open-ended statements such as "How are you doing?" can be difficult for children, often resulting in limited responses such as "Fine." Adolescents typically are functioning at the formal operational stage and have the ability to think abstractly. This enables them to be able to generate more robust responses to open-ended questions than children. Most of the other listening skills discussed in Chapter 2 can be used with children and adolescents (for example, reflection of feeling, paraphrasing, clarifying, minimal encouragers, summarizing, and so forth).

Elkind (1984) extended Piaget's theory of cognitive development to include information on adolescent egocentrism. According to Elkind, adolescent thinking tends to be quite self-centered or egocentric in nature. This egocentricism of adolescents is characterized by several tendencies in adolescents that can impede communication processes and psychological functioning. For example, since adolescents tend to see things from their point of view, they tend to argue with opposing positions (especially with adults). Two other characteristics associated with adolescents' egocentricism are the "imaginary audience" and "personal fable." "Imaginary audience" relates to the adolescents' tendency to be self-conscious about what they do. For example, when adolescents are playing tennis, they may think everyone's eyes are on them, leading to frequent bouts of giggles and other forms of embarrassment. "Personal fable" involves adolescents' feeling invulnerable because they believe that what they do is so special no harm will come to them. From this perspective, adolescents may feel that it is impossible to get pregnant, because they are so in love, and their love is so perfect, that nothing bad can happen.

Counseling implications of the egocentricism of adolescents include being aware of this tendency and guarding against it by not overreacting (for example, getting angry at an adolescents' self-centered point of view). Counselors can also try to be patient and help adolescents discover the value of appreciating different points of view as a means of enhancing communication. Group counseling with adolescents may be particularly useful in this process. Counselors may also wish to use reality testing to help adolescents overcome the tendency to be self-conscious and feel invulnerable. This can involve objectively examining various activities (such as playing tennis or engaging in sex) to help them develop a realistic understanding of the consequences of their behavior.

Theories of Moral Development

Counselors are faced with an increasing number of children and adolescents who are out of control and engaging in various acts of misbehavior (McMahon & Forehand, 1988). Theories of moral development can be used to gain a better understanding of children and adolescents who misbehave in terms of their moral reasoning.

Piaget (1965) and later Kohlberg (1963, 1973, 1981) presented theories of moral development. Kohlberg's theory is based on Piaget's work and is widely accepted in the literature. Kohlberg suggests that moral development could be conceptualized in terms of three levels, with each level containing two stages. These levels and stages are hierarchical, requiring a person to move through them one at a time without skipping any of them.

According to Kohlberg, children functioning at Level 1 have an egocentric point of view regarding morality. They control their behavior out of fear of punishment. Individuals who have reached Level 2 of moral development control their behavior and abide by laws out of a concern about how others will view them as a person, and also how they will view themselves. At Level 3, people control their behavior and abide by laws out of a rational decision to contribute to the good of society. Individuals who have reached the age of eleven or twelve are often capable of functioning at Level 3.

Carol Gilligan (1982, 1987, 1990) contends that Kohlberg's theory does not take into account gender issues associated with moral development. According to Gilligan (1982, 1987), Kohlberg's theory is based primarily on the way males perceive morality, as a set of values and moral principles that can be applied to all situations regardless of the social context and that are concerned with what is fair and equitable. Female moral reasoning is more concerned with caring for the needs of others than with equity. It is also directly related to the social context in that an individual's moral reasoning is influenced by how one will be viewed by significant others.

Parr and Ostrovsky (1991) went on to describe how theories of moral development could be used to provide directions for counseling children and adolescents. For example, a behavior modification such as a token economy may be useful with first graders, since their moral decision making is strongly influenced by a fear of being punished and obeying the rules. The same approach may not be as effective with adolescents, since they may be more concerned with social issues such as how their behavior conforms to shared norms, and how their decisions will be perceived by their peer group. Group counseling can provide teens with a social milieu to work through their concerns and facilitate moral decision making.

Psychosocial Theories

Children's and adolescents' psychosocial development is another important issue in counseling. Erikson (1963, 1968) identified seven psychosocial stages from birth to death. In his theory, each stage involves a particular task that must be accomplished before the individual can proceed effectively to the next developmental task. From birth to age 1, for example, the central task is to experience a sense of trust from the environment. Without that experience, an infant will develop a mistrustful attitude toward the environment. To accomplish each task, the individual must master various coping skills associated with that task. Counselors can help children and adolescents develop these coping skills to promote positive psychosocial development (Blocher, 1987; Stern & Newland, 1994). Chapter 14 provides a more detailed description of the role of developmental tasks in the counseling process.

Developmental Psychopathology

A recent trend in counseling is an attempt to view psychopathology from a developmental perspective (Bergman & Magnusson, 1997; Kazdin, 1993; Sroufe, 1997; Wakefield, 1997). Kazdin (1989) defines developmental psychopathology as "the study of clinical dysfunction in the context of maturational and developmental processes" (p. 180). Kovacs (1989) notes that developmental psychopathology attempts to address three issues: (a) how the developing organism mediates the development of mental disorders; (b) the impact of mental disorders on age-appropriate abilities; and (c) whether mental disorders develop continually or in stages.

According to Kazdin (1989), the greatest advance in developmental psychopathology occurred with the publication of the DSM-III and later DSM-III-R (American Psychiatric Association, 1980, 1987). "It represented a quantum leap in the attention accorded disorders of infancy, childhood, and adolescence" (Kazdin, 1989, p. 183). Advances in the DSM include recognizing the variations from childhood to adulthood in the nature and course of psychopathology. For example, the DSM-IV notes that it is common for a depressed child also to experience problems that are usually not found with adult depression. Some of these are somatic, or bodily, complaints; psychomotor agitation; and mood-congruent hallucinations.

Sroufe (1997) goes on to note that it is common for comorbidity (two or more diagnoses) to occur concurrently with children and adolescents. When this occurs, multiple diagnoses can obscure or mask a psychological problem, making it difficult to obtain an accurate assessment. For example, if a child has a substance abuse problem, an opposition defiant disorder, and an anxiety disorder, the focus can be on the drug and oppositional problems, and the clinician could miss the anxiety problem.

Research and theory development in developmental psychopathology appear to be proliferating. Recent research initiatives have explored a wide range of topics such as the role of nature and nurture (Rutter et al., 1997), transition and turning points (Rutter, 1996), and emotions (Cicchetti, Ackerman, & Izard, 1995) in developmental psychopathology. For example, Cicchetti and associates investigate the role of emotional regulation in developmental psychopathology. They contend that the primary function of emotional regulation is to initiate, organize, and motivate adaptive behavior, thereby preventing abnormal conditions and responses.

One area of research that has been lacking appropriate research emphasis has been in developmental psychopathology directed at adolescence. In this regard, Kardin (1993) notes that developmental psychopathology has tended to focus on children and overlook adolescence. Adolescence was viewed as a transitional period between childhood and adulthood that was in constant change due to biological flux, making it difficult to identify clear mental health patterns. This is beginning to change, as the unique developmental characteristics of adolescence are being recognized and accepted as an important domain for scientific investigation (Kazdin, 1993).

Developmental psychopathology holds promise in terms of refining the process of assessment and diagnosis in child and adolescent counseling. Additional research is required to determine how different developmental levels may influence symptom expression and treatment (Kazdin, 1989).

The Classic Theories

The classic theories of personality posited by Freud, Adler, and Jung (see Chapter 7) can also provide useful information on understanding children and adolescents. These theories all emphasized the role of early life experiences in child and adolescent development. Freud was one of the first to look at stages of development in children and adolescents. His psychosexual stages of development consist of the oral, anal, and phallic, latency, and genital. This theory suggests that traumatic experiences during any of these stages can fixate development at that level. Adults can spend the rest of their lives attempting to resolve unmet needs of childhood or adolescence. For example, if children do not have opportunities to meet their oral needs, they can grow up continually attempting to meet those needs. In this process, they can become an orally fixated personality. This could manifest itself in positive tendencies, such as becoming an orator, or negative ones, such as nail biting.

Adler and his colleague Dreikurs and others have also much to offer in terms of child and adolescent development. These individuals have developed numerous psychological constructs that can be used to understand and counsel children and adolescents. Some of these constructs include birth order, the family constellation, lifestyle, goals of misbehavior, encouragement, and the use of consequences as a disciplinary technique.

Jungian psychology can provide another valuable dimension to conceptualizing the development of children and adolescents. For example, Jung's concepts of holism and balance have been integrated in Jungian forms of play therapy, described later in this chapter.

Emerging Developmental Trends

The strengths perspective has become a major paradigm shift in counseling. The shift is characterized by a change in orientation from pathology to wellness. It represents a recognition that strength is required to overcome adversity. The strengths perspective is playing a central role in virtually all aspects of counseling from holistic health (which suggests that clients develop a wellness orientation) to brief-solution-focused counseling, which encourages clients to use what has worked before (exceptions to the problem) to overcome current difficulties. With the ongoing emphasis on strengths, it is not surprising that developmental theories and concepts are beginning to take on a strengths perspective. This section reviews four emerging developmental trends that have a strengths perspective (optimal development, resiliency, attachment theory, and emotional intelligence) (see Table 11.2). These developmental trends appear to be interrelated in that resiliency, secure attachment, and emotional intelligence facilitate optimal development.

Optimal Development. The roots of optimal development can be traced to humanistic psychologists such as Carl Rogers (1951) and Abraham Maslow (1968), who proposed a

TABLE 11.2   Emerging Developmental Trends

Developmental Theories and Concepts	Founder	Key Concepts	Implications for Counselors
Optimal development	No one individual: contributors include Rogers, Maslow, & Wagner	A view of human development that focuses on positive, healthy development as opposed to a pathological view of development	Optimal development can help counselors take a strengths perspective by focusing on what people can do rather than what they cannot do. This perspective will promote a positive, self-fulfilling prophecy.
Resiliency	No one individual: Werner's research stands out	A research trend that is attempting to identify coping mechanisms that provide a buffer to harmful stress and obstacles to development	Resiliency characteristics can provide useful survival responses to stress that can promote optimal development. Counselors can promote resiliency characteristics in their approach with clients.
Attachment theory	Ainsworth, Bowlby, and others	A study of the relationship between the emotional bond between a parent and child and that child's psychosocial development over the life span	An understanding of a client's present and past attachment relationships can provide useful insights into how to move towards optimal psychosocial development.
Emotional intelligence (EQ)	Salovey and Mayer	A study of the role that social emotions play in psychological functioning	Counselors can promote emotional intelligence in clients by helping them gain a better understanding of how emotions foster optimal development. Counselors can also help clients enhance their EQ through such activities as social skills training in groups.

model of human growth and development based on inherent self-actualizing tendencies. In this regard, Rogers contends that a person will move toward self-actualization (optimal development) if the right conditions are established. More recently, Wagner (1996) has presented optimal development as a developmental perspective that emphasizes health and wellness over pathology. Wagner (1996) notes that what constitutes optimal development would to some degree vary contextually in terms of culture and so forth. Wagner goes on to review the literature to identify biophysical, cognitive, and psychosocial competencies that appear to characterize optimal development in adolescence. These research findings are summarized as follows.

- *Biophysical:* "Upon reaching the age of 18, an adolescent will be alive and healthy, physically mature, and engaged in health-enhancing behaviors, including proper diet and regular exercise" (Wagner, 1996, p. 364).
- *Cognitive:* "Upon reaching the age of 18, adolescents will engage in efficient and purposively idiosyncratic thinking of a more hypothetical, multidimensional future-oriented and relative nature that is based on prior life experiences, including the completion or near completion of at least 12 years of formal education" (Wagner, 1996, p. 368).
- *Psychosocial functioning:* "Upon reaching the age of 18, adolescents will be emotionally aware, feel secure and self-confident, be determined and optimistic about the future, and possess the resilience needed to overcome adversity" (Wagner, 1996, p. 371).

Several authors have proposed a person–environmental fit model of development that can be used to understand how optimal development occurs (Chu & Powers, 1995; Eccles et al., 1993). According to this model, a person will move forward toward optimal development when there is a good fit between his or her needs and the social environment. Chu and Powers (1995) go on to note that synchrony occurs when the social environment is responsive to the individual in terms of promoting personal independence, self-determination, and decision making. In addition, synchrony plays a key role in promoting important competencies in children and adolescents, such as attachment, autonomy, and social competency.

When the fit between the social environment and the individual is strained, the person can become discouraged and lack motivation for positive involvement (Eccles et al., 1993). This can lead to disruptions in the developmental process, such as excessive rebelliousness during adolescence, dropping out of school, and drug abuse. The person–environmental fit model can be used to provide a possible explanation for why early and middle adolescence can be particularly problematic for adolescents. According to Chu and Powers (1995), once an adolescent goes to middle school, parents tend to renegotiate rules relating to autonomy and control (for example, how late the teen can stay out). At the same time, it is not uncommon for middle school teachers to also place a high premium on discipline and control. When the adolescent no longer feels a sense of empowerment, he or she can feel discouraged and lack motivation for involvement in family life or school, resulting in a variety of serious problems.

Van Slyck, Stern, and Zak-Place (1996) suggest that optimal development can be facilitated in children and adolescents by building strengths in resiliency, coping, and problem solving. These authors go on to note that preventative programs that focused on conflict resolution are effective interventions for fostering these strengths. This is especially true for adolescents, since they are prone to having problems that stem from interpersonal conflicts.

Chu and Powers (1995) provide guidelines for promoting synchrony in child- or adolescent-adult relationships. For example, adolescent-adult synchrony should be flexible and open to change, sensitive, and active in terms of encouraging problem solving and decision making. These characteristics would also seem to be valuable in promoting strengths associated with optimal development in children.

Resiliency. Resiliency is a term that has been used to describe why some at-risk children and adolescents thrive while others experience disruptions in their development. It can be defined as a tendency to overcome adverse conditions as a result of having growth-facilitating characteristics that promote optimal development. Research investigations have attempted to understand the dynamics of resilience. Perhaps the most significant study on resiliency was one conducted by Werner and her colleagues (Werner, 1992; Werner & Smith, 1982, 1992), which attempted to identify resiliency characteristics for 200 at-risk children in Hawaii over a 32-year period. These children had experienced at least four risk factors such as family dysfunction, parental alcoholism, and poverty. Surprisingly, one out of three of these at-risk children grew into competent, happy, productive young adults.

Rak and Patterson (1996) provide an overview of the literature on resilience in terms of its characteristics and implications for counseling and development. Some of these resiliency characteristics are a positive self-concept, an optimistic outlook, good interpersonal skills resulting in positive social experiences, good problem-solving and decision-making skills, a well-developed sense of personal autonomy, an environmental support system (within or outside of the family), and a significant other who can provide adequate mentoring. Adams (1997) conducted a qualitative study that involved interviews with ten individuals 85 years or older. Results of this study suggested that resiliency was related to a wide array of health factors (for example, emotional, physical, spiritual, social, and internal).

Resiliency research poses a new way of conceptualizing counseling and development. According to Rak and Patterson (1996), resiliency characteristics act as a buffer to help children and adolescents cope with stress so they can move toward optimal development. Counselors can take a strengths perspective by fostering resiliency characteristics in their clients, thereby promoting survival responses and maximizing developmental opportunities. The field of resiliency research appears to offer opportunities for counselors to utilize a strengths perspective in counseling.

Attachment Theory. Attachment theory was originally developed by Mary Ainsworth and associates (Ainsworth et al., 1978), John Bowlby (1969, 1982), and others as an investigation into the emotional bond between the parent and infants and the implications that bond had on psychosocial development. Securely attached infants were believed to have a number of developmental strengths compared to insecurely attached infants. Some of these strengths are being able to from a strong emotional bond with the caregiver and maintain meaningful ongoing relationships, being cooperative and relatively free of anger, and having superior fine and gross motor skills (Papalia & Olds, 1995).

Ainsworth (1989, 1991) and Bowlby (1988a, 1988b) also advocate what is known as a continuity theory regarding attachment. According to this theory, the nature of the attachment in early life influences development throughout the life span. A proliferation of research over the past decade has tested this hypothesis and has also investigated the relationship between attachment styles and affect regulation and social competence in adults (Lopez, 1995). Lopez (1995) notes that there has been some evidence to support the continuity hypothesis. For example, securely attached infants and children tend to become adults who have secure attachment styles (Brennan, Shaver, & Tobey, 1991; Carnelley, Pietromonaco, & Jaffe, 1994), and also become parents who are able to establish secure attachments with their family members (Ricks, 1985). Lopez (1995) posits that the true test of the continuity hypothesis will require longitudinal studies that investigate the relationship between early attachment on development throughout the life span.

Lopez (1995) also presents a compelling body of research that suggests there is a relationship between adult attachment styles and adult affect regulation and social competence. For example, securely attached adults tend to have superior communication and problem-solving skills (Pistole, 1993; Shaver & Brennan, 1992), higher levels of marital adjustment (Kobak & Hazan, 1991), and the ability to provide more emotional support to distressed partners and solicit emotional support when they need it (Simpson, Rholes, & Nelligan, 1992).

One intriguing area of application of attachment theory is in career development. Blustein, Prezioso, and Schultheiss (1995) provide evidence that securely attached individuals tend to have adaptive characteristics that promote success in career exploration and decision making. Some of these characteristics are enhanced ego identity development (Rice, 1990); enhanced adult work behavior (Hazan & Shaver, 1990); and enhanced exploratory behavior (Hazan & Shaver, 1990).

Attachment theory represents a strengths perspective for counseling by providing a view of healthy personality in terms of relational issues in development (Lopez, 1995). Opportunities are beginning to emerge that offer concrete strategies for applying attachment theory in counseling practice. In this regard, several instruments have been developed that can provide an assessment of the nature and scope of a person's attachment style (for adolescent and adult attachment instruments see Lyddon, Bradford, & Nelson, 1993, and Bradford & Lyddon, 1994). Krause and Haverkamp (1996) also advocate that it may be productive to assess adults' current attachment relationships with their parents to gain insights into adult or child–older parent relationships. Clients that appear to have problematic histories or current problems with attachments may wish to address attachment issues in counseling to free the way for optimal development (Blustein et al., 1995).

Emotional Intelligence.   Salovey and Mayer (Salovey & Mayer, 1990; Mayer & Salovey, in press) are credited with coining the concept of emotional intelligence. The term has also been referred to as EQ, although it never was intended to be a measurable quantity similar to intelligence quotient (IQ) (Gibbs, 1995). Salovey and Geher (in press) trace the origins of emotional intelligence to Thorndike's (1920) work on social intelligence. Social intelligence essentially explores how people make judgments regarding others and examines the accuracy of those judgments (Mayer & Geher, in press). Emotional intelligence has evolved into a more complex process that has been defined as "the ability to perceive accurately, appraise and express emotions; the ability to access and/or generate feelings when they facilitate thought; the ability to understand emotions and emotional knowledge; and the ability to regulate emotions to promote emotional and intellectual growth" (Mayer & Salovey, in press).

Goleman (1997) provides information on the practical applications of emotional intelligence to everyday life. He suggests that emotional intelligence may be more important in determining personal success than intellectual intelligence. According to Goleman, IQ may get you hired but it is EQ skills that are primarily responsible for promotions and other job-related successes. Goleman went on to note that self-awareness may be the cornerstone of emotional intelligence, since it is necessary for a wide range of prosocial behaviors such as self-control. Other key characteristics that have been linked to success are empathy and interpersonal skills (Goleman, 1997), optimism (Seligman, 1991), practical intelligence or common sense (Sternberg et al., 1995), and delay of gratification (Mischel, Shoda, & Rodriguez, 1989; Shoda, Mischel, & Peake, 1990). For example, Seligman contends that optimistic responses to setbacks have been associated with job-related success such as increased sales in the life insurance profession. Sternberg and associates provide additional support for the role of EQ in work success by concluding that practical intelligence or common sense is a better predictor of success in employment than intellectual intelligence.

Mischel and associates' (Mischel, Shoda, & Rodriguez, 1989) classic study on delay of gratification provides another example of the effects of emotional intelligence on psychological functioning. In this study, four-year-olds were told they could have one marshmallow now or two when the researcher returned from an errand. Those that waited for two marshmallows utilized a variety of delay-of-gratification coping skills such as singing, playing games, and so forth. The researchers then conducted a longitudinal study that extended from childhood into adolescence (Mischel, Shoda, & Rodriguez, 1989; Shoda, Mischel, & Peake, 1990). They found that the four-year-olds who waited for two marshmallows were rated as more intelligent, better able to concentrate, and more goal oriented than those who preferred instant gratification. In addition, children who could delay gratification went on to become adolescents who tended to have significantly higher SAT scores (Shoda, Mischel, & Peake, 1990).

Gibbs (1995) notes that much of what is being studied in the field of emotional intelligence is also being explored in the emerging field of evolutionary psychology. Evolutionary psychology is based on the work of Charles Darwin and explores all aspects of development in terms of survival of the human species (Daly & Wilson, 1983; Wright, 1994). From an evolutionary perspective, human emotions such as anger may trigger a fight-or-flight response (Goleman, 1997), empathy can act as a buffer to cruelty (Goleman, 1997), and facial beauty and attractiveness can be related to reproductive capacity (Johnston & Oliver-Rodriguez, 1997). The research on evolutionary psychology appears to offer promise in terms of understanding human development, including the realm of emotional intelligence.

Emotional intelligence provides a strengths perspective for counselors by recognizing the vital role that social emotions play in human functioning. For example, counselors can help clients use the power of encouragement to foster self-efficacy in self and others. In addition, Goleman (1997) contends that there is a great need for preventative programs in schools that promote strengths in emotional literacy to overcome negative tendencies such as violence, loneliness, and despair. School counselors appear to be in an ideal setting to promote emotional intelligence through classroom presentations, counseling (especially group), and consultation with parents and teachers.

Treatment Issues

This section addresses treatment issues in child and adolescent counseling. It begins by describing some of the commonly used assessment procedures. The chapter then provides information on treatment in terms of research findings and a description of special counseling approaches with children and adolescents.

Assessment Procedures

Child and adolescent counseling encompasses the full range of standardized and nonstandardized assessment procedures described in Chapter 4. In addition, two child and adolescent assessment procedures warrant additional attention. The first involves the use of drawings as an assessment tool, a procedure clinicians have used for some time. The second is the use of clinical interviews with children, adolescents, and parents. Although clinical interviews have been used with adults for many years, their use with children and adolescents has begun more recently (Edelbrock & Costello, 1988), representing a major advance in the assessment of childhood and adolescent disorders (Kazdin, 1989).

Drawings.   Drawings can be used both in standardized and nonstandardized assessment procedures. One standardized procedure is the Goodenough-Harris Drawing Test (Harris, 1963). This test requires children and adolescents to make a picture of a man or woman (depending on the sex of the child) and a picture of themselves. Another commonly used standardized test is the House-Tree-Person Test (Buck, 1949), in which children and adolescents first draw a house, then a tree, and last a person. More recently, Knoff and Prout (1985) developed the Kinetic Drawing System for Family and School. Children and adolescents draw one picture of their family and another that relates to school. This test assesses important relationships at home and school.

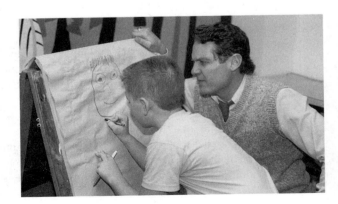

Drawings can provide valuable assessment information.

Stabler (1984) provides information on the nonstandardized use of drawings with children and adolescents. He notes that drawings can be used to obtain an estimate of a child or adolescent's cognitive and psychosocial development and level of maturity. Stabler (1984) identifies the following five factors that are important in assessing drawings.

1. *Proportion or form.* Do figures in the drawings have appropriate proportion or form?
2. *Detail.* What is the degree of detail in the drawing (are there ears, eyes, mouth, and a nose on the face)?
3. *Movement or action.* Is there movement or action depicted in the drawing, such as having the appearance of a three-dimensional person?
4. *Theme.* Is there a theme or story conveyed in the picture, such as two people in love or Superman stopping a villain?
5. *Gender identity.* Is there evidence that the child or adolescent has a clear concept of gender identity?

Stabler (1984) also posits guidelines for assessing drawings in terms of cognitive functioning and overall maturity for children and adolescents in three age groups: five to seven, eight to nine, and ten to twelve. For example, children from age five to seven tend to be able to draw pictures that are more or less proportional; have limited detail; some evidence of gender identity emerging; rather poor movement or action; and typically no theme. Figure 11.1 provides an illustration of a typical drawing by a six-year-old and a twelve-year-old.

Six-Year-Old

Twelve-Year-Old

FIGURE 11.1   Typical Drawing by a Six-Year-Old Child and Twelve-Year-Old Adolescent

Source: From *Children's Drawings* (pp. 5, 8) by B. Stabler, 1984, Chapel Hill, NC: Health Sciences Consortium. Copyright 1984 by Health Sciences Consortium. Reprinted by permission.

Stabler (1984) went on to describe three types of drawings that are particularly useful in the assessment process. These are free drawings, where children are encouraged to draw whatever they like; self-portraits; and family drawings, in which children draw themselves with their family. These drawings enable the counselor to make hypotheses about what to explore with a child. Some possibilities follow. A free drawing may have themes that represent children's concerns. For example, a child who repeatedly draws a house with a child by a mother and father in the home could suggest the child is concerned with issues relating to home and family life. A self-portrait with no arms or legs could indicate a sense of lack of control over the environment. Children who draw a self-portrait without a mouth may think that others do not value their views. A family drawing that has a significant distance between the child and other family members could suggest a feeling of isolation or alienation.

Clinical Interviews.   The clinical interview has become an increasingly popular tool to assist with assessment and diagnosis (see Chapter 4 for a description of the clinical interview). The clinical interview is not designed to replace other forms of assessment but can be best viewed as an adjunct to the process of assessment and diagnosis. In this regard, the clinical interview has been shown to increase diagnostic reliability (Robins et al., 1981).

Although clinical interviews have been used with adults for some time, their development and use with children and adolescents have occurred primarily during the last 10 to 15 years. Interest in the utilization of clinical interviews for children and adolescents corresponds to the increased differentiation of mental disorders for children and adolescents during the past decade.

Edelbrock and Costello (1988) identify several advantages and disadvantages of clinical interviews as compared to other child and adolescent assessment procedures, such as observation and psychological tests. Advantages of clinical interviews include establishing rapport, clarifying misunderstandings, and obtaining self-report data from parents, children, and adolescents. The primary disadvantages relate to questionable levels of validity and reliability owing to the newness of these instruments and the consequent lack of time to empirically evaluate them.

Many clinical interviews for children and adolescents are currently available. Edelbrock and Costello (1988) describe commonly used clinical interviews for children and adolescents. They vary in terms of structure, and the more structured interviews require less training to administer (Edelbrock & Costello, 1988). Three examples are

1. *The Diagnostic Interview for Children and Adolescents* (Herjanic & Reich, 1982). This is a highly structured diagnostic interview that can be used with children six years of age or older. It covers a broad range of childhood symptoms in terms of frequency and duration. There is also a version for parents, which solicits pertinent developmental and family history.
2. *The Interview Schedule for Children* (Kovacs, 1982). This is a semistructured interview for children ages eight to seventeen. It is a symptom-oriented interview that focuses primarily on depression, although it also assesses other diagnostic criteria. A separate interview can be conducted with parents, children, and adolescents.
3. *The Diagnostic Interview Schedule for Children* (Costello et al., 1982). This is a highly structured interview for children and adolescents ages six to eighteen. It provides infor-

mation on a wide range of symptoms and behaviors in terms of onset, duration, and severity. A parallel version can be used with parents and children or adolescents.

Child and Adolescent Counseling Research

Weisz, Weiss, and Donenberg (1992) and Kazdin (1993) provide an overview of a number of meta-analyses on child and adolescent counseling (for example, Hazelrigg, Cooper, & Borduin, 1987; Kazdin et al., 1990). Both research investigations report strong support for the efficacy of child and adolescent counseling. For example, Kazdin finds that the effects of child and adolescent counseling are superior to no treatment, the degree of positive change is comparable to adult counseling, there is little variation in efficacy of treatment modalities such as behavioral versus nonbehavioral, and treatment outcomes are similar for internalized problems such as depression and externalized problems such as aggression.

Research suggests that a developmental perspective is critical in identifying appropriate counseling interventions with children and adolescents. For example, behavioral approaches such as behavior modification have been useful in treating children (Kazdin, 1994), and adolescents (owing to their ability to think abstractly) are able to utilize cognitive-behavioral approaches better than children (Durlak, Fuhrman, & Lampman, 1991).

Kazdin (1993) also notes that there is strong support for preventative programs with children and adolescents (Goldston et al., 1990; Weissberg, Caplan, & Harwood, 1991). For example, programs that provide support to a family during a child's formative years appear to prevent problems such as engaging in antisocial behavior later in childhood and adolescence. Research also suggests that school-based programs appear to be effective in preventing a wide array of problems such as substance use and abuse and school dropout. Kazdin (1993) posits that the success of preventative programs depends to some degree on the ability to not only change attitudes but also to change behavior. Shultz and Nystul (1980) found in an earlier study on parent education that the internalization and transfer from an attitude to a behavior requires some form of action such as role-play.

Special Counseling Approaches for Children and Adolescents

Most counseling approaches used with children and adolescents (such as behavioral and cognitive-behavioral) are adaptations of strategies used with adults (Tuma, 1989). Play therapy and conflict resolution represent two counseling approaches that have been specifically designed for working with children and adolescents. This section will provide an overview of these unique methods of counseling children and adolescents.

Play therapy.   Play represents an important developmental tool for children and adolescents. It provides a natural form of communication (Campbell, 1993) and an expression of creativity linked to learning, coping, and self-realization (Rogers & Sharapan, 1993). It is through play that children and adolescents are able to enhance cognitive, physical, and psychosocial development (Papalia & Olds, 1995). For example, playing hide and seek involves deciding where and how to hide (cognitive); mobility, such as running and squatting (physical); and cooperating with others (psychosocial). For adolescents and adults, sports such as basketball and baseball become favored forms of play and continue to provide opportunities to enhance development.

Play therapy is a counseling strategy that has been confined primarily to children. It has a number of uses such as relationship building, assessment, promoting communication, psychological healing, and fostering growth (Orton, 1997). Play therapy involves the utilization of play media such as sand play, art, and music to learn skills and work through problems so the children move forward in their development. Sand play is an emerging form of play therapy (Carmichael, 1994). It involves the use of two 20-by-30-by-4-inch trays (one with wet sand and one with dry sand). Children are provided numerous objects that represent everyday life (people, fences, animals, and so forth) and are encouraged to use the objects to express themselves in fantasy play. Allan and Brown (1993) describe three stages of play therapy (including what one would expect in sand play): chaos, struggle, and resolution. During the initial stage (chaos), children tend to express negative feelings such as anger and confusion and project those feelings onto their play activities. As play therapy progresses, the therapist encourages children to utilize play as a means of working through their struggles. The last phase of play therapy is characterized by creative expressions that are more positive in nature (such as cooperation), reflecting resolution of conflicts.

The historical roots of play therapy can be traced to two major schools of counseling, Freudian and Rogerian. Anna Freud (1928), the daughter of Sigmund Freud, was perhaps the first to use play therapy with children. Melanie Klein (1960) went on to provide further development of the psychoanalytic school of play therapy. These clinicians incorporated the major principles of psychoanalysis in their approach, for example, strengthening the ego to minimize endopsychic conflicts and utilizing the transference relationship to help children overcome traumatic experiences.

The psychoanalytic counselor conceptualizes play in a manner similar to free association. From this perspective, play allows children to express themselves freely and spontaneously. The counselor's role in this process is passive and interpretive. For example, if a child painted a picture with dark objects, the counselor might ask, "Are you feeling sad or gloomy today?"

The second major school of play therapy was developed by Virginia Axline (1974). Its theoretical foundation can be traced to Carl Rogers' person-centered school of counseling, and it is therefore a humanistic-phenomenological approach. Axline's (1964, 1974) approach suggests that the counselor conveys a warm and accepting attitude toward the child and encourages the child to freely explore the different play materials. The role of the counselor is similar to that in person-centered counseling. As the child plays, counselors attempt to convey empathic understanding by reflecting what they sense the child is experiencing. A more detailed description of Axline's approach can be found in *Dibs: In Search of Self* (Axline, 1964).

Contemporary forms of play therapy are based on a number of theoretical orientations such as Rogerian (Landreth, 1993), Jungian (Allan & Brown, 1993), and Adlerian (Kottman & Johnson, 1993; Nystul, 1980). For example, current trends in Rogerian child-centered play therapy are similar to the earlier model developed by Axline and are being used to treat a wide range of problems such as regressive behavior, depression, abuse, and socially inappropriate behavior (Landreth, 1993).

Jungian play therapy involves an application of the major Jungian principles (see Chapter 7). Allan and Brown (1993) provide an overview of Jungian play therapy. It utilizes the therapeutic alliance to help the child work through unconscious struggles and conflicts reflected in play. One central struggle in Jungian play therapy is to help the child create a balance between the inner world of feelings, drives, and impulses and the demands of the outer world as reflected in school, peers, and family. A major goal in Jungian play therapy is to strengthen the child's ego so it can become an effective mediator between the child's inner and outer world. Jungians have found sand play to be particularly useful as a means of strengthening the child's ego to create a balance between the child's inner and outer world (Carmichael, 1994).

Adlerian play therapy is based on the work of Alfred Adler (1930) and Rudolf Dreikurs and associates (Dreikurs & Soltz, 1964). Adlerian play therapy is used to foster a positive counseling relationship, help parents and teachers gain a better understanding of children, enable children to gain insight and self-awareness, and provide skills and experiences necessary for children to work through conflict and enhance their development (Kottman & Johnson, 1993; Nystul, 1980).

Consultation with parents and teachers can be an important adjunct to Adlerian play therapy (Kottman & Johnson, 1993; Nystul, 1987). In this process, counselors can use Adlerian/Dreikurserian concepts to help parents and teachers develop tools they can use to better understand and work with their children. Some of the more popular concepts are the goals of misbehavior, the birth-order factor in personality development, encouragement versus praise, and consequences versus punishment. Programs such as systematic training for effective parenting (STEP) by Dinkmeyer and McKay (1989) provide an excellent summary of these ideas and structured activities to apply them.

I have developed my own approach to play therapy (Nystul, 1980). It is grounded in Adlerian/Dreikurserian psychology and also integrates the four phases of multimodality creative arts therapy described in Chapter 8: set the stage, set an example, set yourself at ease, and obtain a phenomenological understanding of the child.

My approach to play therapy is based on the following seven assumptions.

1. The counselor attempts to establish a feeling of mutual respect with the child.
2. The counselor uses encouragement whenever possible.
3. The counselor attempts to understand the child by exploring the child's private logic.
4. The counselor tries to redirect the child's teleological movement to increase the child's motivation for change.
5. The session starts with 15–30 minutes of self-concept development and ends with 15–30 minutes of multimodality creative arts therapy.
6. The counselor uses logical and natural consequences to establish realistic limits.
7. The counselor recognizes the importance of parent and teacher involvement as an adjunct to play therapy.

Guidelines for Play Therapy. The following guidelines may be useful when implementing a play-therapy program.

Play therapy can be conducted individually or in small groups of two or three children. The play-therapy room should be approximately 15 by 15 feet. It should be big enough for two adults and four children, but small enough to promote a sense of closeness between the counselor and the child. If the room is too large, for example, the child may wander off. The counselor should ensure privacy. No one should be permitted to come into

Puppets can help children express themselves in play therapy.

the play-therapy room while a session is in progress. Interruptions can be a major distraction from the counseling process.

The counselor should obtain different play materials, for example, play houses, puppets, babies, and other family members. It is also useful to have art supplies such as molding clay and watercolors and musical instruments such as bongo drums and a tambourine.

The counselor should establish limits with the child during the first session regarding time and behavior. In terms of time, the session length can vary according to the time available but should not exceed one hour. The length of time should be determined before the first session and adhered to as much as possible. Regarding behavior, the counselor should restrain a child who acts in an aggressive, hostile manner. It may even be necessary to discontinue the play-therapy session if the child persists in being hostile. When a child abuses a toy, the counselor can use a logical consequence. For example, a counselor might say, "It looks like you're not ready to use the drum today. I'll put it up for now. Some other time, you can try to use it the way it is supposed to be used."

In communicating, counselors should use a friendly, kind voice, especially if they sense a child feels insecure; not talk down to a child in terms of tone of voice; and use an appropriate vocabulary level so that the child will understand the words. While it may be necessary to be firm with a child, it is probably counterproductive to be stern. Counselors should let themselves laugh and have fun with the child, and they should talk from a positive perspective, using encouragement whenever possible.

Play therapy offers a means to reach into the world of the child and help the child reach out to the world of others. It can be used to treat a wide range of problems and concerns. For example, I used play as a means to help an autistic child learn language and other skills necessary to overcome some of her autistic tendencies (Nystul, 1986). Campbell (1993) suggests that play therapy can provide an important dimension to comprehensive developmental counseling programs by helping children overcome tendencies toward reluctance and resistance, fostering problem solving, and so forth. Cochran (1996) goes on to note that play therapy has cross-cultural potential by creating a universal language through play and involvement in the creative arts. Play therapy can help overcome language barriers and other sources of resistance to foster school success in children and adolescents (Cochran, 1996). Reams and Friedrich (1983) conducted a meta-analysis of 15 research reports on play therapy. Results of their investigation show that play therapy is superior to nontreatment and promotes general adaptation and intellectual skills. Additional research seems warranted to provide a clearer understanding of how play therapy can be used with children.

Conflict Resolution.   Youth-oriented conflict resolution procedures can be used with children (Stern & Newland, 1994) and adolescents (Van Slyck, Stern, & Zak-Place, 1996). As noted in Chapter 14 (school counseling), conflict resolution is particularly useful in middle school counseling, where problems tend to be related to interpersonal conflict.

Youth-oriented conflict resolution is an emerging specialty field in school and mental health counseling with its own unique theories, techniques, and training requirements (Van Slyck, Stern, & Zak-Place, 1996). Van Slyck and associates (1996) provide an overview of this field that is summarized as follows. Youth-oriented conflict resolution is considered distinct from adult conflict resolution in that the youth takes an active role in the process by learning how to manage his or her own conflicts, and adults tend to take a more passive role by bringing in a mediator to resolve the conflict (for example, divorce mediation). The overall goal of youth-oriented conflict resolution is to foster problem-solving skills, coping skills, and resiliency characteristics that can be used to overcome conflict and foster optimal development.

Youth-oriented conflict resolution programs can be both preventative and remedial in nature. Preventative programs are directed at helping youth learn how to apply conflict-resolution theory and skills to foster a life with minimal adverse conflicts and stress. Large and small group guidance activities on conflict resolutions as well as adaptations in the school curriculum can play a major role in implementing preventative programs. Remedial conflict resolution relates to overcoming currently existing conflicts. This can involve the use of peer counseling (for example, peer mediation) or direct intervention by teachers, staff, and counselors. Regardless of the level of intervention (prevention or remedial), the focus is on helping youth use problem-solving skills to successfully mediate and negotiate problems of living.

Dysinger (1993) describes a conflict resolution model that can be used with youth. It has several steps that have been incorporated into the following framework for conflict-resolution problem solving. Step 1 is "take a positive approach." It begins by encouraging the youth to approach conflict resolution from a win-win perspective. Ground rules are established that promote a positive, strengths perspective rather than an adversarial approach (for example, no name calling or threatening). Step 2 is "listen and respond appropriately." It involves helping the conflicting parties learn to use listening skills to understand opposing points of view and learn how to respond constructively. Ground rules include no interrupting while the other is talking (so they can be in the role of listener and learner) and respond from a position of caring. Step 3 is "become aware of choices and responsibility." The youth are encouraged to become aware of the choices they have made and responsibility they must assume in relation to the conflict. Ground rules include no blaming or whining. Use of personal pronouns can be encouraged to help youth take responsibility for their behavior.

Step 4 is "create solutions that promote friendship." This step identifies a new approach, which can be used to overcome the conflict. The nature of the new approach will vary with the situation and people involved. For some, assurance that the other person will not engage in a certain behavior will be enough, for others simply understanding the other person's point of view can resolve the conflict. Step 5 is "follow up." Follow-up involves checking to see whether the conflict has been resolved and encouraging the youth to engage in conflict-resolution problem solving if there continues to be a problem. Through cooperation and caring, friendships can be enhanced and conflicts and stress can be minimized.

The following *Personal Note* provides some additional thoughts regarding counseling children and adolescents.

A Personal Note

Working with children and adolescents has been a specialty for me throughout my career. I started off as an elementary and middle school counselor for the Bureau of Indian Affairs between 1970 and 1972. For the past seven years, I have worked one day a week as a school psychologist for a local school district. Sandwiched in between these years were other rewarding experiences such as working as a psychologist for Indian Health Service on the Navajo reservation and promoting parent education in Australia.

As I reflect on what I have learned about counseling children and adolescents, five things seem to stand out.

First, I will always remember what a woman who specialized in working with adolescents told me. She said the most important thing in counseling adolescents is to always maintain a line of communication. It is very easy to lose that connection with adolescents due to their rebelliousness, parental rigidity, and so forth. Without communication, problems cannot be resolved and bad situations only get worse.

Second, I recently went to an Adlerian conference and attended a presentation by Professor James Croake. During the presentation, he said that having a solid grounding in theory could be very beneficial in helping relationships, and it should be emphasized over technique. I could not agree with him more. I have found that theories (such as theories of personality and theories of child development) promote understanding of why the child

is misbehaving or whatever. And understanding tends to promote interest and compassion, which in turn can foster positive outcomes such as problem resolution.

Because I am a school psychologist, teachers often ask me what they should do to deal with a student's misbehavior. My consultation with these teachers usually focuses on helping them understand the dynamics of the child's or adolescent's misbehavior. In this process, we explore the application of simple, practical theories such as Glasser's (1969) concept of success versus failure identity and Dreikurs' concepts of goals of misbehavior and encouragement versus praise (Dreikurs & Soltz, 1964). These theories are great because they have stood the test of time.

I tend to have the most success with theories I have developed myself. One of these is my "hidden reason theory for children's misbehavior" (Nystul, 1986b), which emphasizes the importance of creating positive opportunities for parental involvement with children so they feel like they are "somebody." A more recent theory of mine is "the role of parental emotions in parenting" (Nystul, in press), which describes how parents strive for emotional balance in parenting, thereby avoiding the extremes of emotional enmeshment and emotional abandonment.

Third, I have found that one of the best ways to make a positive impact on children and adolescents is by providing parent education (Nystul, 1980, 1982a, 1984) and a parent-centered approach to counseling children and adolescents (Nystul, 1987). I have been amazed how simple, direct parenting can help overcome parent-child or parent-adolescent conflict and promote optimal development.

Fourth, I believe that choice and responsibility are two of the most important words in promoting optimal development in children and adolescents and minimizing animosity in adult-child and adult-adolescent relationships. Parents, teachers, and others can help children and adolescents become aware of their choices and assume responsibility for those choices. Personal and relational benefits can occur when the choice-responsibility approach is used. Personal growth resulting from choice-responsibility can include self-efficacy, self-control, self-esteem, and internal locus of control. Relational benefits can include minimizing conflict between the adult and child or adolescent (since the parent is focusing on the child or adolescent's choices rather than getting sidetracked into issues such as power and control).

Fifth. One of the best ways I have been able to conceptualize counseling children and adolescents is the "reaching in–reaching out" model I developed when I was working with an autistic child (Nystul, 1986a). I discussed this case briefly in a Personal Note in Chapter 1. It involved trying to find a way to connect with this child to overcome the resistant tendencies associated with her autism.

When I first saw her I was not aware that she was autistic. I had brought puppets that I was going to use to present self-concept material and other activities. Her idea of using the puppets was to throw them all in a pile and redo a throw if it didn't land right on the other puppets (that type of ritualistic behavior is common with autistic children). As I attempted to reach into her world (a world she felt safe with and understood), I became a "puppet basketball net." I circled my arms around her pile of puppets and yelled "two points" when she threw one in my circle. Over time, she felt safe with me and began to welcome my company. I used this interest to encourage her to reach out into the world of others by fostering her language development and eventually finding ways to help her break out of some of the rigidity of her autistic world.

Over the years I have reflected on this case and have come to believe that to some degree all counseling is a reaching in–reaching out process. Initially in counseling, I find ways to reach into my client's world. With children it can be through play therapy, with adults perhaps creative arts therapy or listening skills to discover the personal meaning of my clients' stories. After a while, we establish a positive counseling relationship and that provides the basis for encouraging my clients to reach out in new directions, expand their horizons, and foster their optimal development.

Special Problems of Children and Adolescents

This section provides an overview of some of the special problems experienced by children and adolescents: child abuse and neglect, depression, and antisocial behavior. For each type of problem, information is presented on incidence, assessment, causes, effects, and treatment.

Child Abuse and Neglect

Children have been abused and neglected throughout history, but it was not until the early 1960s that child abuse and neglect became recognized as social problems that require comprehensive treatment (Wolfe, 1988). This section reviews some of the issues associated with child abuse and neglect.

Incidence. The incidence of child abuse and neglect continues to increase at an alarming rate in the United States, with current estimates to be as high as two million children a year (Papalia & Olds, 1995). Many of these abused children have been sexually abused (Papalia

& Olds, 1995). The incidence of sexual abuse in the United States is also staggering. Current estimates suggest that one in every four girls and one in every seven to ten boys will have a sexual experience with an adult before reaching eighteen years of age (England & Thompson, 1988). In addition, psychological abuse may be the most prevalent and destructive form of child abuse (Dworetzky, 1996).

Assessment.   Early identification and treatment of child abuse and neglect is critical to minimize negative effects on the child. Salkind (1994) identified the following warning signs of the various forms of child abuse and neglect.

- *Physical abuse.* Signs of bruises, burns, and broken bones.
- *Child neglect.* Poor health and hygiene and excessive school absenteeism.
- *Sexual abuse.* Use of sexually explicit terminology, nightmares, genital injury, and sexually transmitted disease.
- *Psychological (emotional) abuse.* Depression, self-deprecation, somatic (bodily) complaints such as headaches or stomachaches, and fear of adults.

The assessment of child abuse and neglect is a multistage process (Wolfe, 1988). The process usually begins with impressionistic data from the reporting and referral source. That stage is followed by a refinement of information during interviews with parents and the child (Wolfe, 1988). Much of the initial information regarding the functioning of the parent and child can be obtained in a semistructured interview with the parent (Wolfe, 1988). The Parent Interview and Assessment Guide can be used to structure the interview and provide information on family background, marital relationship, areas of stress and support, and symptomatology (Wolfe, 1988). Several instruments have been developed that can be used to survey the attitudes of parents on topics relating to marriage and the family. The Child Abuse Potential Inventory (Milner, 1986) identifies familial patterns associated with child abuse. The Childhood Level of Living Scale (Polansky et al., 1981) measures the degree of positive and negative influences in the home and is particularly useful for assessing neglect (Wolfe, 1988).

Causes.   Current research shows that child abuse results from a complex interaction of events. Wolfe (1988) summarizes the research by noting that child abuse is a special type of aggression resulting from proximal and distal events.

   Proximal events are those that precipitate abuse. A proximal event can involve a child's behavior or an adult conflict that triggers the abuse. Common child behaviors that can trigger child abuse are aggression, unspecified misbehavior, lying, and stealing (Kadushin & Martin, 1981). Straus, Gelles, and Steinmetz (1980) suggest that marital problems and violence are also associated with child abuse.

   Distal events are those that are indirectly associated with child abuse. Indirect factors that have been shown to contribute to child abuse include low socioeconomic status and poverty, restricted educational and occupational opportunities, unstable family environment, excessive heat, overcrowding, ambient noise level, and unemployment (Wolfe, 1988).

   Other research efforts have attempted to identify characteristics of abusive parents as a means of understanding the causes of child abuse. Talbutt (1986) summarizes this research by noting that abusive parents tend to be abused as children, have difficulty coping with stress, suffer from substance abuse problems, be immature and hold unrealistic expectations of children, and have children with special needs that require extra time and energy.

Sroufe and Cooper (1996) describe a typical profile of parents at high risk for child abuse. They tend to be young, poorly educated, single, living in poverty, and socially isolated, and feel little support from a significant other. The authors also note that abusive mothers tend to have a negative attitude toward their pregnancy. Compared to nonabusive parents, they had less understanding of what was involved in caring for an infant, were less prone to plan for pregnancy; did not attend childbirth classes, did not have special living quarters for the baby to sleep, and had unrealistic expectations about raising an infant.

Effects.   Sroufe and Cooper (1996) describe the effects of child abuse and neglect on the child. Physical neglect that results from not meeting the child's basic needs, such as food and shelter, tends to produce a lack of competency in dealing with the tasks of daily living, such as personal hygiene. Physical abuse and emotional unavailability often result in behavioral and emotional problems, for example, avoidance of intimacy in relationships, aggressiveness with peers, and blunted emotions. Psychologically abused children can develop neurotic traits, conduct disorders, negative self-image, and distorted relations with others (Craig, 1996; Hart & Brassard, 1987).

Sexual abuse can have traumatic and enduring effects. Feinauer (1990) notes that children who have been sexually abused can develop symptoms associated with post-traumatic stress disorder, for instance, flashbacks of the trauma and nightmares. These symptoms also tend to persist into adulthood (Feinauer, 1990). In addition, sexually abused individuals have a high risk of developing psychiatric problems as adults (Herman, 1986).

O'Brien (1983) identifies several ways that sexual abuse can damage a child.

- *Psychological effects.* Sexual experiences can be confusing for children because they are unable to understand the strong emotional feelings associated with sex.
- *Low self-esteem.* Children may blame themselves for permitting the sexual contact or may feel dirty or ashamed as a result of the experience.
- *Exploitation.* Sexually abused children may feel used and develop a hostile, suspicious attitude toward others.
- *Vulnerability.* Because children are dependent on adults, they are vulnerable to and trusting of adults. When that trust is broken, children may develop a negative attitude toward vulnerability, making it difficult to develop trust and intimacy in relationships.
- *Distorted view of sexuality.* It is common for sexually abused children to develop a very negative or perverted attitude toward sex. As they grow up, they may avoid sex or become sexually promiscuous.
- *Violation of the child's privacy.* After an incestuous relationship is discovered, the abused child must cooperate with the authorities. This violation of the child's privacy can be very traumatic and anxiety-provoking.
- *Distorted moral development.* Sexual abuse often occurs between the ages of nine and eleven when a child's moral development is also being formulated. Children can become quite confused about what is right and wrong when an adult is allowed to violate them sexually.

The following *Personal Note* illustrates how difficult it can be for a child to deal consciously with the trauma of sexual abuse.

A Personal Note

When I was a psychologist at a hospital, I worked with several girls who had babies as a result of incestuous relationships with their fathers. These girls tended to use denial as a means of coping with what had happened.

For example, I met a fourteen-year-old girl the day before she had her baby. She insisted that she was not even pregnant. After she had the baby, she said that the baby was not hers. This patient required extensive counseling and psychotherapy to develop a realistic approach to her situation.

Treatment.   Brockman (1987) has suggested that the most hopeful treatment for abusive parents involves "resocialization" tasks, which help parents overcome isolation and foster interpersonal relations and support. These efforts can include encouraging parents to join Parents Anonymous or other self-help groups. Brockman (1987) also identified several preventive programs that could be promoted in schools. These programs include adult education, interpersonal training for students, courses on sexuality and parenting in high school, and guest speakers for students from organizations such as Parents Anonymous.

Thompson and Wilson (1995) go on to note that there is little empirical evidence to support the social isolation theory of child abuses, citing numerous examples of parents that are provided social support that continue to engage in child abuse because of many other stressors such as substance abuse problems. They contend that child abuse and neglect is a cross-disciplinary problem that should be addressed by research and intervention teams composed of disciplines such as psychology, social work, and sociology. Together they can gain a more comprehensive understanding of the causes and treatment strategies associated with child mistreatment.

Treatment efforts can also be directed at the abused child. Group counseling can be especially effective in working with abused and neglected children (Damon & Waterman, 1986) and adolescents (Hazzard, King, & Webb, 1986). Kitchur and Bell (1989) note that group counseling can be useful with this population to foster self-esteem, overcome problems with trust, correct distorted cognitions, and enhance self-control skills.

White and Allers (1994) also note that play therapy has been used extensively with abused children. A review of this literature shows a pattern of unique behaviors that emerged in conducting play therapy with abused children. Some of these behaviors are developmental immaturity; repetitive and compulsive behavior; opposition and aggression; withdrawal and passivity; self-depreciation and self-destructive behavior; hypervigilance; sexual behavior; and dissociation (an unconscious denial of abuse). The nature of play is also unique. Abused children are not very imaginative in their play, and their play does not seem to elevate their anxiety.

Orenchuk-Tomiuk, Matthey, and Christensen (1990) identify special treatment considerations relating to sexual abuse. The authors propose a three-stage model for treating sexual abuse called the resolution model. The three stages are (a) the noncommittal or oppositional stage, (b) the middle stage, and (c) the resolution stage. The model differentiates treatment issues for the child, the nonoffending parent, and the offending parent at each stage, as follows.

The child feels responsible for the abuse during the noncommittal or oppositional stage; feels angry and experiences symptoms associated with post-traumatic stress disorder during the middle stage; and no longer feels responsible for the sexual abuse or experiences problematic symptoms during the resolution stage.

The nonoffending parent denies occurrence of sexual abuse, blames the child for disclosure, and defends the offender during the noncommittal or oppositional stage; believes the abuse has taken place and begins to become an ally for the child during the middle stage; and becomes a positive ally for the child and works through guilt associated with not protecting the child during the resolution stage.

The offender refuses to accept responsibility for abuse and/or denies its occurrence during the noncommittal or oppositional stage, is able to admit to the abuse but may blame the child during the middle stage, and assumes responsibility for the abuse and establishes a more positive parental role during the resolution stage.

The resolution model recommends that individual and group counseling can be useful during the noncommittal or oppositional stage. Couples and family counseling should not be used until the middle or resolution stages and should involve the child only if the child is ready.

England and Thompson (1988) provide additional guidelines that counselors can use with children who have been sexually abused. Counselors should take on the role of advocate for sexually abused children; help them overcome feelings of guilt and shame, emphasizing that the abuse was not their fault and that it will stop; use open-ended questions when assessing for sexual abuse and thus avoid leading questions; and take their accusations seriously, since children tend not to lie about sexual abuse, and psychological harm can occur if they are not taken seriously.

Depression

The recognition of childhood and adolescent depression is a relatively recent occurrence (Petersen et al., 1993; Wagner, 1994, 1996). This section reviews some of the major issues associated with depression in children and adolescents.

Incidence.   Research investigations suggest that children are as capable of experiencing clinical depression as adults (Alper, 1986; Kovacs, 1989). Serious depression has been found in infants (Field et al., 1988; Spitz, 1946), preschool and school-age children (Digdon & Gotlib, 1985; Kazdin, 1988; Kovacs, 1989), and adolescents (Petersen, et al., 1993; Rice & Meyer, 1994; Wagner, 1996). The average duration of a major depression in children and adolescents is seven to nine months, and a dysthymic depression lasts an average of three or more years (Kovacs, 1989). Manic disorders are rare and hard to diagnose accurately for children and adolescents (Strober, Hanna, & McCracken, 1989).

Assessment.   As noted earlier in this chapter, developmental psychopathology provides a framework for understanding how mental disorders such as depression vary over the life span (including childhood and adolescence). Sakolske and Janzen (1987) identify some major symptoms associated with childhood depression. Changes in mood and affect are the most obvious indications. Examples are children who were relatively happy and had positive self-images suddenly saying they are sad, miserable, and no good. Another indication is that depressed children tend to lack interest in activities that were previously enjoyable, such as hobbies and sports. They may also lose interest in friends and family members. Other symptoms include physical complaints such as headaches and abdominal discomfort; sleep disturbances including nightmares; changes in appetite; impaired cognitive processes such as difficulty concentrating; and problems in school, work, and interpersonal relationships.

Petersen et al. (1993) provide a description of adolescent depression. They suggest that depressed adolescents typically show signs of unhappiness and have a number of fears and worries such as a fear of not being loved, not having friends, and worry about their appearance and relationships. In addition, it is estimated that adolescents experience major depression at a much higher rate than children (Petersen et al., 1993).

To obtain a diagnosis for a major depression a person (regardless of age) must meet the established criteria. For example, the DSM-IV (American Psychiatric Association, 1994) includes such things as depressed mood, decreased ability to experience pleasure, weight loss (or failure to thrive in children), loss of energy, thoughts of death, and so forth. The DSM also notes that "certain symptoms such as somatic (bodily) complaints, irritability, and social withdrawal are particularly common in children, whereas psychomotor retardation, hypersomnia are less common in prepuberty than in adolescence and adults" (American Psychiatric Association, 1994, pp. 324–325).

Multiple diagnoses (comorbidity) are common with depressed children and adolescents. When this occurs, it is sometimes referred to by clinicians as a "masked depression," since the symptoms of depression are obscured by the additional diagnosis (Kovacs, 1989). The DSM-IV notes that major depression in children normally does occur with other mental disorders such as anxiety disorders, disruptive behavioral disorders, and attention deficit disorders. Comorbidity in adolescents is often associated with mental disorders such as eating disorders, substance abuse disorders, and disruptive behavioral disorders (American Psychiatric Association, 1994).

Several instruments have been designed specifically to assess childhood and adolescent depression. For example, diagnostic interviews have been developed to assess child and adolescent mental disorders (Edelbrock & Costello, 1988). Most other instruments are directed at children. The most widely used instrument for children is the Children's Depression Inventory (Kovacs, 1981), which was developed from the Beck Depression Inventory. It assesses the cognitive, affective, and behavioral signs of depression. Other instruments include the Short Children's Depression Inventory (Carlson & Cantwell, 1979); the Children's Depression Scale (Lang & Tisher, 1978); and the Schedule for Affective Disorders and Schizophrenia for School-Age Children (Chambers, Puig-Antich, & Tabrizi, 1978). Kazdin (1988) provides a description of each of these instruments.

Causes.   Several factors have been associated with childhood depression. These include parents who have high standards and do not express positive affect to the child (Cole & Rehm, 1986); children who have negative cognitive schemata characterized by self-deprecation, hopelessness, and despair (Hammer & Zupan, 1984); and social-skill and problem-solving deficits (Altmann & Gotlib, 1988).

Wagner (1994) goes on to provide an ecological perspective for conceptualizing mental health problems of children. He describes the "povertization of childhood" by noting that 25 percent of children five or younger are living in poverty and a great number of these children are born to single mothers. This "povertization" has been associated with impeding the development of children and having a devastating effect on their well-being (Wagner, 1994).

Petersen et al. (1993) identify causes associated with adolescent depression (many of which would also seem relevant to childhood depression). Major causes of adolescent depression include pessimistic-negative cognitions; genetic predisposition (a parent has a history of depression); and social-systemic factors such as excessive environmental stress, problems with home (including family and marital discord), school, and peer-group. It is interesting to note that one of the best predictors of adult depression is impaired peer-group relations during adolescence.

Effects.   Depression in childhood and adolescents can have serious consequences. Some problems with childhood and adolescent depression are impaired cognition (Kovacs et al., 1988; Petersen et al., 1993); problems with social and educational progress (Kovacs et al., 1988; Petersen et al., 1993); and suicidal tendencies (Kovacs, 1989; Garland & Zigler, 1993). Even if a person does not become depressed as a child, childhood experiences can make the individual prone to depression as an adult. Brown and Harris (1978) found that children who experience the death of their mother before they are 11 years of age are more prone than other children to develop depression as adults.

Treatment.   Several counseling approaches are available to treat childhood depression. Cognitive approaches have been shown to be particularly effective (Reynolds & Coats, 1986). Another approach is parent education, which can be used to help parents learn skills to promote a positive environment for the family. Play therapy is another option, which enables children to work through traumatic experiences and enhance their social skills and self-image. Antidepressant medication can also be considered in the treatment of depression, although there are mixed reports regarding its efficacy for children (Puig-Antich et al., 1987).

Petersen et al. (1993) provide an overview of the major treatment modalities for adolescent depression. They note that antidepressant medication has not been shown to be effective with adolescents, perhaps due to the dramatic physiological changes associated with adolescents or the comorbid conditions that may complicate treatment responses. A number of counseling and psychotherapeutic approaches have been used to successfully treat adolescent depression. Some of these approaches include cognitive-behavioral, psychodynamic, family therapy, social skill training, and group counseling. In addition, preventative programs show promise as a means of treating adolescent depression (Rice & Meyer, 1994). For example, Rice and Meyer (1994) developed a psychoeducational intervention program that can be used in schools to enhance coping responses to stress.

Antisocial Behavior

Antisocial behavior in children and adolescents includes acts that violate major social rules, including aggression, lying, stealing, and truancy (Kazdin et al., 1989). This section reviews some of the major issues associated with antisocial behavior in children and adolescents.

Incidence. The incidence of children engaging in antisocial behavior is high and involves one-third to one-half of all mental health clinical referrals (Kazdin et al., 1989). Rates of antisocial behavior in the form of delinquency are also staggering, with 6 percent of serious crimes in the United States (such as rape and murder, assault, and robbery) being committed by youth under 15 and 16 percent committed by adolescents 15 to 18 years of age (Berger & Thompson, 1995). In addition, worldwide, a person is more likely to be arrested during adolescence and young adulthood than at any other time.

Assessment. Children or adolescents who engage in a well-established pattern of antisocial behavior for at least six months tend to receive a DSM-IV diagnosis of either conduct disorder or oppositional defiant disorder. Conduct disorder is the more serious mental disorder and requires that the individual has violated the rights of others and age-appropriate norms or rules of society. McMahon and Forehand (1988, p. 107) note that most behaviors associated with conduct disorder involve "direct confrontation or disruption of the environment" and "are basically the same type of behavior that Patterson (1982) and Loeber and Schmaling (1985) have labeled 'overt antisocial behavior.'" The major feature of oppositional defiant disorder "is a recurrent pattern of negativistic, defiant, disobedient, and hostile behavior toward authority figures that persists for at least 6 months . . ." (American Psychiatric Association, 1994, p. 91).

McMahon and Forehand (1988) identify instruments that can be used to assess antisocial behavior. Several structured interviews have been developed for children. For example, the Diagnostic Interview Schedule for Children is a highly structured interview that can be used with children ages six to eighteen and their parents (Costello et al., 1984). It provides scores that correspond to DSM-IV diagnosis of conduct disorder and oppositional defiant disorder.

Several behavioral rating scales are also available for assessing antisocial behavior in children and adolescents. The Child Behavior Checklist (Achenback & Edelbrock, 1983) is one of the most popular rating scales in use. It can be used with children ages two to sixteen and provides a comprehensive assessment of behaviorally disordered children (McMahon & Forehand, 1988). An advantage of this scale is that it has parallel forms for the child, parent, teacher, and observer. The Revised Behavior Problem Checklist (Quay & Petersen, 1983) is a rating scale that can be used to detect tendencies toward conduct problems, personality problems, inadequacy and immaturity, and socialized delinquency. This scale is completed by parents or teachers.

Causes. Patterson, DeBaryshe, and Ramsey (1989) suggest that antisocial behavior is a developmental trait that begins in childhood and often continues into adolescence and adulthood. These authors utilize a social-interactional perspective, which suggests that family members train children to engage in antisocial behaviors (Patterson, 1982; Snyder, 1977; Wahler & Dumas, 1987). According to this theory, parents do not adequately reinforce prosocial behavior or effectively punish deviant behavior. On the contrary, these children learn to use antisocial behaviors to stop aversive intrusions from other family members. From this perspective, antisocial behavior can be viewed as the manifestation of survival skills necessary to cope with a dysfunctional family.

McMahon and Forehand (1988) provide an overview of studies that identify factors associated with conduct disorders and antisocial behaviors. These studies suggest that children with conduct disorders also tend to exhibit impaired peer relationships (Achenback & Edelbrock, 1983), misattribute hostile intentions to others (Milich & Dodge, 1984), have deficits in social problem-solving skills (Asarnow & Calan, 1985), lack empathy (Ellis, 1982), are prone to hyperactivity (Loeber & Schmaling, 1985) and depression (Chiles, Miller, & Cox, 1980), have low levels of academic achievement, and have a genetic predisposition to develop antisocial tendencies (Kazdin, 1985). Kazdin et al. (1989) also note that antisocial children have deficits in interpersonal cognitive problem-solving skills (such as formulating solutions to problems), impaired cognitive development (such as moral reasoning), and maladaptive cognitive strategies (such as impulsiveness). Another series of studies has found a link between the influence of the peer group and acts of delinquency and substance abuse (Elliott, Huizinga, & Ageton, 1985; Huba & Bentler, 1983; Kandel, 1973).

Effects. Kazdin et al. (1989) suggest that the effects of antisocial behavior tend to prevail from childhood to adulthood. In addition, individuals diagnosed with antisocial behavior disorders tend to experience disproportional problems as adults, including criminal behavior, alcoholism, and antisocial personality disorders.

Patterson, DeBaryshe, and Ramsey (1989) note that children who engage in antisocial behavior are also prone to become delinquents. Approximately one-half of antisocial children become delinquent adolescents, and one-half to three-fourths of delinquent adolescents become adult offenders. The cost of delinquency transcends the offender, with $500 million spent annually on school vandalism alone (Feldman, Caplinger, & Wodarski, 1981).

Patterson, DeBaryshe, and Ramsey (1989) also suggest that many factors that are typically seen as causes of antisocial behavior, for example, academic failure and peer rejection, can more accurately be understood as effects. For example, research has shown that childhood aggression leads to rejection by the peer group, not the reverse (Cole & Kupersmidt, 1983; Dodge, 1983).

Treatment. Providing counseling to antisocial individuals can be a very difficult endeavor. It can involve trying to stop a pattern of behavior that has begun during childhood and has evolved into a lifestyle. By the time these individuals are adolescents, many are active in gangs and find the possibility of getting out of a gang either undesirable or not possible. It is therefore not surprising that there has been limited success in attempting to overcome different forms of antisocial behavior (Kazdin, 1987; Wilson & Herrnstein, 1985).

One treatment modality that has been successfully used with antisocial youth is special education programs, which provide services to seriously emotionally disturbed–behaviorally disordered students (Thompson & Rudolph, 1997). In the United States, public schools provide closely supervised educational experiences for students with serious emotional disturbance and behavioral disorders (many have a history of antisocial behavior). These classes utilize a number of procedures such as behavioral contracting, token economy, individual and group counseling, parent consultation, and individualized instruction. Several studies provide evidence that teachers can make a difference in overcoming antisocial tendencies (Kupersmidt & Patterson, 1991; Tremblay, LeBlanc, & Schwartzman, 1988). The following *Personal Note* provides an example of my involvement in these programs.

A Personal Note

Over the past eight years I have been involved in working with special education students in elementary schools who have been placed in a classroom for students with serious emotional disturbance and behavioral disorders. During this time, I have been amazed by the "miracle" that special education programs can achieve with students. The miracle is that the students go from what Glasser (1969) would refer to as a failure identity to a success identity. When they come into the program, they have a failure identity. They hate school because they have never been successful at school. Many are a step away from dropping out. They are some of the best blamers and whiners I have ever encountered. Their problems are always someone else's fault. In addition, they are usually so busy trying to avoid doing school work and having fun that they are constantly running into problems with their teachers and are experiencing adverse consequences, such as not having the privileges that others are getting.

With these programs, in time these students begin to gain a success identity. They learn to follow the rules and get their work done. Gradually, they begin to feel pride in accomplishment, which plants the seed for intrinsic motivation. In addition,

they become aware of choices regarding their behavior and learn to assume responsibility for what they have done. An example of this is when I walked into a class and was talking with a student. I asked him how he was. He told me, "I got caught hitting some guy on the bus and got a level drop." That was it, no whining or blaming. Becoming responsible leads to self-respect, which in turn earns the respect of others.

Perhaps, the best example that illustrates the success of these programs was what I experienced at a Christmas party. I was observing a new boy who had only been in the program for about 10 weeks. When he came into the program he hated everything, and his parents had to "drag him to school." Now he was doing really well in the program and felt pride in his achievements (instead of frowning, he was usually beaming). When the Christmas show finished, it was about 2:00 P.M. and school got out at 3:00 P.M. As his mom was about to leave, the teacher asked the boy if he wanted to go home with his mom. To my surprise, he said "No, I want to stay until school gets out." Now that indeed is a miracle, to see a boy go from hating school and wanting no part of it, to taking pride in school and enjoying it!

Cashwell and Vacc (1996) provide some new directions for preventing and overcoming delinquency problems with adolescents. Their research found that two of the strongest predictors of adolescent delinquency are being involved with delinquent peers and a lack of family cohesion. They suggest that preventative programs should be started during elementary school to promote social skills training and an awareness of the dangers of involvement in antisocial groups such as gangs. In addition, counseling could be directed at enhancing family cohesion through such efforts as parenting training and family counseling.

Additional research and development appears warranted in the area of providing counseling and mental health services for children and adolescents with antisocial behavior problems. The casualties extend beyond the victim, infusing fear and negativity into society itself. Much needs to be done to develop realistic and effective means to defeat needless violence, aggression, and hostility.

Diversity and Postmodern Issues in Child and Adolescent Counseling

Diversity and postmodern issues are playing a major force in the evolution of child and adolescent counseling. Diversity and postmodernism are redefining the foundation and evolution of child and adolescent counseling in terms of theory, research, and practice. From a theoretical perspective, the foundation of child and adolescent counseling is grounded in developmental theory. Carol Gilligan's (1982) seminal work on female moral development is credited with generating an awareness of the male bias in development theory.

Gilligan's (1982, 1991) research has contributed to a wave of interests in reassessing gender issues in developmental theory. Gilligan, Surrey (1985), and more recently Allen and Stoltenberg (1995), Horst (1995), and Wastell (1996) have begun to reassess other developmental theories. For example, they contend that Erickson's (1968) theory of psychosocial development is in need of modification to overcome gender bias favoring males. From a feminist perspective, two of Erickson's stages stand out in need of revision (identity formation during adolescence and intimacy during young adulthood). For example, during identity formation, Erickson appears to recognize male values of autonomy and individualism over relational issues favored by females. A more accurate conceptualization of female identity development would describe the self as being organized around the goal of establishing and maintaining meaningful relationships.

Sexual orientation can be another important diversity issue in counseling across the life span. This is especially true as adolescents and young adults strive for identity formation and intimacy. According to Kottman, Lingg, and Tisdell (1995), gay and lesbian adolescents face a wide array of obstacles to development, such as homophobia, discrimination, negative stereotyping, and even violence. The grip of homophobia often extends into the adolescents' support system, with friends and family often unable to recognize and accept a homosexual orientation. This often leaves the homosexual adolescent feeling alienated and isolated with self-esteem and self-acceptance problems (fundamental building blocks for identity development and intimacy).

Kottman, Lingg, and Tisdell (1995) note that with so much negativity to contend with, it is not surprising that homosexual adolescents are at risk for mental health problems. For example, Remafedi (1987) reported that approximately one-third of gay teens in a study had attempted suicide and/or been hospitalized for mental health problems, 48 percent had run away from home, and 58 percent regularly abused substances. In addition, O'Connor (1992) notes that approximately one-third of all successful adolescent suicides are individuals with homosexual orientations.

Hammon and Yung (1993) address ethnic minority issues that impact on violence and death of adolescent youth. They suggest that African American male adolescents experience a disproportionate risk of death or injury due to violence. Perhaps the most telling statistic regarding this problem is that the number one reason for the death of an African American male adolescent is assaultive gunshot by a friend or acquaintance. These authors go on to provide an overview of causes of violence among African American adolescent males. Some of the contributing forces identified are psychosocial, cognitive-behavioral, and environmental. Environmental-ecological forces appear to play a major role in promoting violence in the lives of these adolescents. For example, many of these individuals live in the inner city, where violence and crime are a part of everyday life. Hammond & Yung (1993) go on to suggest that preventative programs need to be directed at overcoming the legacy of violence that perpetuates this ethnic minority group. They describe a multifaceted program that is directed at challenging beliefs and assumptions regarding violence, overcoming sociopolitical and ecological barriers to optimal development (for example, family and community instability), and fostering cultural awareness and sensitivity.

Gender issues should also be considered when conceptualizing mental health issues such as depression in children and adolescents. For example, Petersen et al. (1993) note that female adolescents are more prone to depression than males. Female adolescents also engage in different responses to depression because they tend to internalize (ruminate) whereas males tend to externalize (distract themselves with activities). Comorbity in depression also tends to vary between male and female adolescents, with female depression often occurring with eating disorders and males having disruptive disorders co-occurring with depression (Petersen et al., 1993).

Postmodern considerations such as culture and environmental-ecological forces also impact the assessment and treatment of mental disorders of children and adolescents. The prevalence of mental disorders varies from culture to culture. Some cultures (such as Native American) have significantly high rates of depression and suicide owing in part to environmental forces such as extreme levels of unemployment (Harrar, 1984). Community psychology that utilizes an ecological perspective can provide a useful dimension to mental health services with Native Americans (Harrar, 1984). In addition, the experience of mental disorders may vary widely from culture to culture in terms of the language and knowledge bases associated with mental health and mental illness. For example, some cultures (such as Latino) experience depression in mainly somatic terms such as complaints of nerves or headaches, whereas other cultures (such as Asian) may relate to feelings of being tired or being off-balance (American Psychiatric Association, 1994). It is therefore important to consider cultural forces reflected in the language and narratives used by children and adolescents as a means of assessing and treating problems such as depression.

Summary

Child and adolescent counseling is an emerging counseling specialty and many new trends and innovations in the assessment and treatment of children and adolescent disorders. The concept of childhood and adolescence as distinct developmental stages is relatively new, and previously the special needs of children and adolescents were generally ignored. More recently, theories of child and adolescent development have been formulated, providing information on the cognitive, moral, psychosocial, and mental health development of children and adolescents. These theories provide an important conceptual framework for understanding and treating children and adolescents.

Assessment procedures unique to this field of counseling include the use of drawings and clinical interviews. Other treatment issues are play therapy, conflict resolution, cognitive-behavioral therapy, and the use of psychotropic medications.

Information on child abuse and neglect, childhood and adolescent depression, and antisocial behavior is provided in terms of incidence, assessment, causes, effects, and treatment to illustrate some of the current trends in child and adolescent counseling.

12 Group Counseling

CHAPTER OVERVIEW

This chapter provides an overview of group counseling. Highlights of the chapter include

- The art and science of group counseling
- Group counseling from a historical perspective
- Comparison to individual and family counseling
- Types of groups and goals
- Problem solving and group process
- Group size, composition, and duration
- Use of coleaders
- Pregroup screening and orientation
- Stages in group counseling
- Brief-solution-oriented group counseling
- Dealing with disruptive group members
- Common mistakes of group leaders
- Qualities of effective group leaders
- Diversity issues

The Art and Science of Group Counseling

Group counseling is both an art and a science. It is an art in the sense that the group facilitator must be flexible and creative in adapting to the ongoing movement within the group process. Groups are dynamic entities and in that regard have a life and purpose of their own. Facilitators need to let go of preconceived ideas of what will occur within a group and allow the group to move toward the realization of its own unique potential. In addition, facilitators must be sensitive to issues of diversity that present themselves in the group. In doing so, facilitators, like artists, can help members create opportunities for sharing and learning.

The science of group counseling is directed at a number of important issues relating to group work. Contemporary group work emphasizes the importance of structure in the group to give individuals and the group a focus to enhance motivation and productivity within the group. Structure can include ensuring that prospective members are appropriate for the group, establishing rules or guidelines for the functioning of the group, encouraging members to formulate personal counseling goals, and using a conceptual frame of reference for facilitating the group (such as a solution-focused brief-counseling perspective). The science of group counseling can also involve research and evaluation to determine the efficacy of group theory and practice. A recent effort was made to create a balance between the art and science of group counseling through a special issue in the *Journal for Specialists in Group Work* (November 1997). It provides numerous articles that encourage collaboration between science and practice in group work.

Group Counseling

Group counseling is an important specialty within the counseling profession. The practice of group counseling is found in most counseling programs and is therefore an integral part of the counselor's identity (Fuhriman & Burlingame, 1990). Several organizations have done much to advance the professionalization of group counseling. The American Counseling Association (ACA) charted a special division for group counseling in 1973 called the Association for Specialists in Group Work (ASGW). Ethical guidelines were established in 1980 and revised in 1989. Several other professional organizations have furthered the cause of group counseling, including the American Group Psychotherapy Association, the International Group Psychotherapy Association, and the American Association of Group Psychotherapy, Psychodrama, and Sociometry.

This chapter provides an overview of group counseling. It begins by describing group counseling from a historical perspective. Group counseling is then differentiated from individual and family counseling. Information on the practice of group counseling and a description of the stages of group counseling are also provided.

Group Counseling from a Historical Perspective

Group counseling has a rich and fascinating history. The group movement can be traced to the pioneering work of J. L. Morreno and Kurt Lewin in the 1920s and 1930s (Bonner, 1959). Lewin's field theory provided an important theoretical foundation for group work, and Morreno developed a unique approach to group counseling called psychodrama.

Initially, group counseling was met with skepticism in the professional community. Some perceived this new technique as a radical, unorthodox procedure that would undermine confidentiality. In addition, it conflicted with the basic definition of counseling, that of counselors working with individual clients. Gradually, however, group counseling gained respectability. In 1946, the National Training Laboratory (NTL) was founded in Bethel, Maine (Baruth & Robinson, 1987) and soon became a major training institute for group work. The institute focused on how to use group dynamics to promote personal growth and interpersonal functioning.

During the 1960s encounter and sensitivity groups became popular in general, and the "in" thing on many college campuses. The spirit of the group movement seemed to blend with the cultural revolution also taking place in the 1960s. Both encouraged self-exploration, mind expansion, spontaneity, openness, honesty, and confrontation when necessary.

Perhaps in part due to its association with the hippies of the 1960s, the group movement came under criticism. Because of a few unusual encounter groups that were conducted in Northern California with nude participants, implications were made that all group counseling evolved into sex orgies. In addition, charges were made that the group movement was a contributing factor to social unrest among youth. As a result, an anti-group movement began in California in the late 1960s.

Some of its leaders even suggested that group counseling was part of a communist conspiracy to undermine the minds of youth. Patterson contended that there were legitimate criticisms of many of the groups run in the 1960s (Vacc, 1989). He believed that problems resulted from inadequate training of group leaders; too much emphasis on uncovering people's problems and doing whatever "feels right" without concern for one's effect on other group members; and the use of gimmicky, manipulative techniques and games.

During the 1970s and 1980s, several factors contributed to group counseling's return to respectability. The major factor was a shift away from the lack of structure associated with sensitivity and encounter groups, which was seen as a contributing factor not only to negative perceptions about the specialty but also to "casualties" in counseling. Professionals believed that groups based on clear goals and objectives could generate more productive outcomes.

Commenting on the future of group counseling in the 1990s, Gazda (Elliot, 1989) said there would be a continuing emphasis on family group work, social-skills training, and life-skills training groups. In addition, he believed that the popularity of self-help groups would grow faster than that of any other type.

Horne (1996) related to current trends in group counseling by noting that group practices are accommodating increasingly diverse populations in various types of settings. In addition, group counseling is incorporating current paradigm shifts such as the solution-focused brief-counseling perspective.

Comparison to Individual and Family Counseling

Group counseling is a specialty that has unique features in terms of theory and practice. At the same time, it has common elements with other forms of counseling such as individual and family counseling. This section describes the similarities and differences between group counseling and individual or family counseling. It also identifies advantages and disadvantages of group counseling.

Group Versus Individual Counseling

Fuhriman and Burlingame (1990) suggest that there are few differences between group and individual counseling. This is not surprising, since theories and techniques tend to be transferred from individual to group counseling.

Although the techniques used in group and individual counseling are similar, the counseling process varies in group counseling to accommodate the increased complexities that result from multiple clients. Drawing primarily from Yalom's (1995) 11 therapeutic factors for group work, Fuhriman and Burlingame (1990) identify the following six factors that differentiate group counseling from individual counseling.

1. *Vicarious learning.* Group counseling offers opportunities for members to learn from observing other group members as they explore their concerns.
2. *Role flexibility.* Clients in group counseling can function both as helpers and helpees. Clients in individual counseling can only maintain the role of helpee.
3. *Universality.* Group counseling creates opportunities for clients to discover that other group members have similar concerns, fears, and problems. This experience of universality can help clients put their problems in perspective and not overreact to them.
4. *Altruism.* During group counseling, members are encouraged to offer help to other group members. Clients who engage in altruistic behavior can provide support for other group members and enhance their self-image.
5. *Interpersonal learning.* Interaction between group members creates opportunities to enhance interpersonal skills.
6. *Family reenactment.* The therapeutic climate created in a group can be similar to what was experienced in a client's family of origin. Group counseling can therefore be particularly useful in working through early familial conflicts.

The following *Personal Note* is an illustration of how I helped a client work through an early familial conflict in group counseling.

A Personal Note

I was a counseling psychologist at a university counseling center, and a client in the group was a young man in his early twenties. "Tom" was having problems, feeling a lack of confidence and courage.

During one session, Tom told the group about an experience he had as a teenager. He said his father was an alcoholic, who verbally and physically abused Tom's mother. Tom described one instance that he often thought about. He and his mother were sitting in the living room when his father started yelling terrible things at his mother, then went over and slapped her on the face. Tom just sat and watched. He felt angry at his father, but also at himself because he couldn't help his mother. As he reflected on the incident, he said he just wished he would have had the courage to "stand up like a man" and come to the aid of his mother.

I suggested that we reenact the situation. I arranged to have a group member play the role of mother; Tom would be himself; I would play the role of father; and the rest of the group members would be the audience and provide feedback.

When we started the scene, Tom initially had a difficult time taking his role seriously. He started to laugh and said, "You don't look like my father." I intensified my yelling and abusive language toward his "mother." I then went over and started to shake her. The next thing I realized was that Tom was standing in front of me. He grabbed my shoulders and told me to leave his mother alone. His face was bright red with anger. He was breathing hard and then started to cry.

At this point, I stopped the reenactment and held the client for a few moments and encouraged him to cry and get his feelings out. We then discussed the experience with the group members. Tom said something seemed to snap in him when I began to yell at his "mother." He really felt he was there with his mother and father. Tom said it made him feel better to be able to tell his father how he felt and stand up for his mother. He went on to say that his tears were tears of relief, that he was finally able to let go of his feelings of helplessness and shame.

This case provides an illustration of the intense emotions that can result from group counseling procedures. The procedures should therefore be used carefully. It is especially important not to push clients to the point where they are forced to deal with emotions that they are not ready to handle.

Group Versus Family Counseling

Group and family counseling also have similarities and differences. In terms of similarities, both "bring people together to resolve problems by emphasizing interpersonal relationships" (Hines, 1988, p. 174). The processes of group and family counseling are also similar. The focus of the initial sessions in both is for the counselor to define the presenting problem from an interpersonal perspective (Hines, 1988; Whitaker & Keith, 1981; Yalom, 1995). In addition, the working stage in both is an interactive process in which the client and counselor are actively engaged (Hines, 1988; Whitaker & Keith, 1981; Yalom, 1995).

Hines (1988) identifies differences between group and family counseling in terms of inclusion, structure, and interrelatedness. According to Hines (1988), inclusion must be gained by participation in a group, whereas it is a biological given in a family. Structurally, group members have equal power, whereas family members have hierarchical power (Couch & Childers, 1989; Hines, 1988). Group members have a lesser degree of interrelatedness than family members, who have spent years living together (Hines, 1988). As a result, family members have well-established interpersonal processes, whereas group members are strangers to one another when they form the group (Couch & Childers, 1989).

Another difference between group and family counseling is the role of the counselor. During the initial stage of group counseling, the leader attempts to assist group members with the process of inclusion (Hines, 1988; Schultz, 1977). The reverse is true in family counseling, since the counselor initially feels like an outsider and attempts to be included in the family (Hines, 1988). The counselor's role also varies between group and family counseling in terms of establishing norms (Couch & Childers, 1989; Hines, 1988). During the initial phase of group counseling, the leader plays an active role establishing group norms (Couch & Childers, 1989; Hines, 1988). This is not the case in family counseling because the family already has a well-established norm system (Couch & Childers, 1989; Hines, 1988).

Perhaps the biggest difference between group and family counseling lies in the goals of each process. Couch and Childers (1989) note that group counseling has goals for the group, such as creating a climate of trust and acceptance, as well as specific goals for each individual member. In contrast, the goal of family counseling is to improve the overall functioning of the family unit.

Although there are differences between group and family counseling, there are also opportunities for integration (Vinson, 1995). A systemic perspective can be used in group and family counseling to enhance awareness of the interactional processes between clients and the system as a whole (Horne, 1993). Vinson (1995) identifies numerous examples of how family therapy can be integrated into group counseling such as psychoeducational-support groups (Gregg, 1994) and separation-divorce adjustment groups (Addington, 1992). Vinson also suggests that there are numerous techniques from family counseling that can be used in group counseling, such as the use of the genogram to explore family-of-origin issues.

Advantages and Disadvantages of Group Counseling

As with any counseling strategy, group counseling has potential advantages and disadvantages. The main advantage of group counseling is that it provides a safe environment for clients to try out and experience new behaviors with other group members. Other advantages are that

- Clients can learn from other group members as they explore their personal concerns.
- The process is more economical in terms of time, since several clients can be seen during a session.
- Clients can have an opportunity to help others during the session, thereby minimizing tendencies to be overly concerned with their own problems.
- Problem solving for a client can be enhanced by the ideas generated by other group members.
- The group can foster energy and enthusiasm, which can help motivate a client to pursue personal goals.

The main disadvantage of group counseling is that it may be inappropriate for some clients. This is especially true for clients with a serious mental disorder or a low self-concept. It may even be dangerous for these clients to participate in a group because they may feel threatened or personally attacked by the feedback they receive from other group members. In these cases, the client may first need to participate in individual counseling to be able to utilize group counseling successfully. Corey and Corey (1997) also identify risks associated with group counseling, including problems with confidentiality that can arise in groups; inappropriate self-disclosing owing to group pressure; feeling attacked as a result of confrontation; and negative emotional consequences that can occur from scapegoating.

Group Goals and Processes

The science of counseling recognizes the structure that goals can bring to the counseling process. Goals create a focus for individuals and the group itself, enhancing motivation and constructive action. There are group goals and individual goals. Group goals vary to a large extent according to the type of group. Some groups will focus on providing guidance information on such topics as parent education and others, such as group counseling and psychotherapy, will have the goal of overcoming mental problems such as depression.

Group goals can also relate to the counseling process and include fostering trust and acceptance, and promoting self-disclosure, feedback, and risk taking (Corey & Corey, 1997). Most approaches to group counseling also encourage group members to formulate individualized goals (Couch & Childers, 1989). Members are then assisted in learning problem-solving strategies they can utilize outside the group setting (Couch & Childers, 1989).

Waldo and Bauman (1998) suggest that it is critical to describe groups in terms of the interrelationship between group goals and processes. These scholars suggest that a new method of categorizing groups, the Goals and Process Matrix (GAP), could be used as a classification system for group work. This model attempts to define (or classify groups) by answering the question, "Which group process is best for pursuing which group goal?" (Waldo & Bauman, 1998).

The GAP appears to promote individualized description of groups, which allows for integration of group formats (for example, task groups and guidance groups) in terms of their goals and processes. At the very least, the GAP model would seem to offer opportunities to enhance existing models for categorizing group counseling by recognizing the overlapping function of groups in terms of their goals and processes. Additional research on the GAP seems warranted to obtain a clearer understanding of how it can be used to describe the types of groups used in group counseling.

Types of Groups

The ASGW revised its *Professional Standards for Training of Group Workers* in 1993. This publication broadly conceptualizes group counseling within the context of group work. Group work is defined as processes that involve giving help and accomplishing tasks in a group setting. The ASGW went on to identify the major types of group work utilized by people in the helping profession. These are summarized as follows.

Task/Work Groups encompass all the different types of groups utilized in contemporary society to accomplish various tasks. Examples of task/work groups include committees, study groups, and discussion groups.

Guidance/Psychoeducation Groups are focused on providing information that can be used to facilitate human growth and development and prevent problems from occurring. These groups are widely used in schools and other settings. They provide an opportunity to explore a variety of topics such as how to avoid involvement in gangs and how to be an effective parent.

Counseling/Interpersonal Problem-Solving groups use interpersonal support and problem-solving methods to help individuals with problems of living. These groups also attempt to help group members learn how to use various counseling strategies so they can work through or prevent future problems.

Psychotherapy/Personality Reconstruction groups are designed to help individuals overcome in-depth personal or mental health problems such as anxiety or depression. These groups attempt to remediate or overcome significant psychological difficulties by a variety of processes, which can include personality restructuring.

Nelson-Jones (1992) and Jacobs, Harvill, and Masson (1997) have identified additional types of groups, which are summarized as follows.

Life-skills training groups, also called education groups, are defined as "time-limited, structured groups in which one or more leaders use a repertoire of didactic and facilitative skills to help participants develop and maintain one or more specific life skills" (Nelson-Jones, 1992, p. 6). These groups are characterized by an emphasis on wellness versus sickness, systematic instruction, an experiential focus, and participant involvement. Life-skills training groups promote skills relating to all aspects of life, for example, parenting, intellectual development, self-management, and physical development.

Mutual-sharing groups, also called support or self-help groups, are composed of people with similar concerns providing support for one another. The fundamental goal of mutual-sharing groups is to provide support to members. Examples of these groups are children of divorced parents, adult children of alcoholics, and adults who are prone to engage in child abuse.

Growth groups are designed to help group members increase self-awareness. Their goal is to assist members in improving their lives by clarifying their values, personal concerns, and interpersonal relationships.

Family groups involve inviting different families to a group setting to discuss issues of concern. The primary goal is to enhance the functioning of the family system. Multiple-family group work can be used when a counselor wants to work with several families at a time. Family network groups can be established with the goal of providing information and support to families.

Discussion groups provide an opportunity to discuss a topic of interest rather than the personal concerns of group members. Examples of discussion group topics are the pros and cons of having children, the effects of drug abuse, and attitudes toward marriage. The goal of discussion groups is to have members share ideas and knowledge regarding a particular topic.

Problem Solving and Group Process

Group counseling is characterized by two dimensions that are critical to the success of the group: problem solving and group process. These dimensions are interrelated, and success in one dimension fosters success in the other.

The problem-solving strategies of individual counseling, as discussed in Chapter 3, can also be used in group counseling. These strategies typically involve the group leader and members first listening to a particular concern of a group member and then helping that member resolve the concern. The member taking action and assuming responsibility is an important part of the problem-solving process (Burlingame & Fuhriman, 1990).

Burlingame and Fuhriman (1990) identify the following four factors associated with group process.

1. *Engagement.* Engagement entails members sharing their feelings with one another. This practice is believed to foster cohesion (Aiello, 1979) and universality (Brabender, 1985).
2. *Group versus individual focus.* Opinions vary as to whether the process in group counseling should focus on the group, the individual, or alternately on the group and the individual (Burlingame & Fuhriman, 1990). A more equitable position might be to focus simultaneously on the individual and the group. Having coleaders is a useful format, with one leader focusing on the concerns of an individual client and the other on issues that relate to the group process.
3. *Here-and-now focus.* Most approaches to group counseling emphasize the importance of maintaining a focus on the here and now in terms of group process (Burlingame & Fuhriman, 1990). Yalom (1995) suggests that a primary task of the group leader is to encourage group members to relate in the here and now, and then to have the group

reflect on the here-and-now behavior that has just transpired. The here-and-now focus is believed to help group members learn about themselves through self-disclosure and feedback as they interact with each other (Sklare, Keener, & Mas, 1990).

4. *Goals of the group.* To some degree, a group's goals will determine the nature of the group. For example, a group designed to discuss parenting may have a didactic emphasis, whereas groups designed to improve interpersonal relationships will tend to be experiential in nature.

Group Size, Composition, and Duration

The appropriate group size varies according to the type of group and the ages of its members. For example, a play-therapy group should not exceed four children for the counselor to be effective. In contrast, an education may have an entire classroom full of people and the counselor can still work effectively with the group. For group counseling and psychotherapy, the average group size ranges from four to ten members (Burlingame & Fuhriman, 1990). This range is large enough to create a diversity of ideas, yet small enough to provide an opportunity for each member to participate.

Group composition is another important issue to consider in formulating a group. Groups can be either heterogeneous or homogeneous. Heterogeneous groups are composed of a diversity of individuals of different ages, gender, cultures, socioeconomic status, and so forth. These groups can help promote a diversity of ideas for group members to consider. Heterogeneous groups are also believed to foster greater individualization because of the wide range of issues they can address (Unger, 1989). Heterogeneous groups are commonly used in schools, where a counselor might conduct a session on alcohol and drug use with an entire classroom, or in community mental health centers, where a counselor might have several clients participate in group counseling to resolve personal problems. Homogeneous groups are composed of individuals who have something in common, for example, parents who want to learn about parenting or clients who suffer from eating disorders. An advantage of homogeneous groups is that they enhance universality by bringing together individuals with similar problems or concerns. Homogeneous groups are also believed to promote more cohesion and identification than heterogeneous groups (Unger, 1989).

Duration relates to three issues: whether the group is open or closed, the length of each session, and the number of sessions. *Open groups* are ongoing with no termination date, and they allow new members to join at any time. Alcoholics Anonymous uses an open-group format, encouraging new members to start attending sessions whenever they can. *Closed groups* have a specific starting date, and they do not allow new members to join after the first session. Closed groups are often utilized when the members want to learn certain principles and do not want to have to keep reviewing what was covered in an earlier session. A parent education group designed to help members learn about parenting might be an example of a closed group. Burlingame and Fuhriman (1990) found that hospital outpatient groups tend to be about half open and half closed, whereas inpatient groups tend to be open to accommodate new patients as they are admitted to the hospital.

For most groups, each session lasts approximately 90 minutes (Burlingame & Fuhriman, 1990). The group leader and members should determine the length of the session in advance and adhere to it as much as possible so group members can plan accordingly.

The number of sessions associated with group work varies according to the type of group, the needs of the group members, and the theoretical orientation of the group leader. Education groups might require from six to ten sessions or extend over an entire school year. For counseling and psychotherapy groups, the number of sessions varies according to the setting. Groups for inpatient psychiatric patients usually meet at least once each day while the patients are in the hospital. Counseling and psychotherapy groups that are conducted in schools, private practice, and counseling centers typically meet once a week over a period of several months, with an average of thirteen sessions (Burlingame & Fuhriman, 1990).

Use of Coleaders

Several advantages are associated with having a leader and coleader in group counseling. First, group members can benefit from the expertise of two counselors. Second, there may be an advantage in having male and female counselors to create a more balanced perspective. Third, at the end of a session, the leader and coleader can spend time debriefing, or sharing ideas about the session. As a result, they can gain a more comprehensive understanding of what occurred. A fourth advantage is that the leader can focus on helping a client work through a personal problem while the coleader focuses on the group process. Facilitating the group process can involve creating a positive, trusting climate; keeping the group on task; helping each member feel valued; assisting reluctant clients in becoming involved in the group; and dealing with difficult members who may want to monopolize or sabotage the group.

Corey and Corey (1997) identify additional advantages of using coleaders in groups. These include avoiding burnout, allowing for coverage if a group leader is ill, processing strong emotional reactions of group leaders, and working through countertransference if it occurs. Corey and Corey also note that there can be potential disadvantages to utilizing coleaders. Many of the problems can deal with a lack of trust and cooperation between the leaders. When this occurs, a leader can compete with the other leader for the support and admiration of the group members. Problems between group leaders can take up group time as the leaders deal with their unresolved issues.

Pregroup Screening and Orientation

There appears to be a positive correlation between the amount of time spent in preparation for a group and positive outcomes occurring from the group (Lynn & Frauman, 1985). A pregroup interview is typically utilized to help screen and orient prospective group members. Couch (1995) identifies four steps in conducting a pregroup screening interview. These steps are identifying needs, expectation, and commitment; challenging myths and misconceptions; conveying information; and screening. The screening process typically excludes individuals who suffer from severe psychopathology such as psychoses, extreme paranoia, or sociopathy (Burlingame & Fuhriman, 1990). The same qualities that are considered desirable for inclusion in individual counseling apply to groups. These include high motivation, adequate ego strength, a satisfactory past relationship with other individuals, the presence of an acute problem, and realistic expectations (Burlingame & Fuhriman, 1990).

Pregroup orientation is designed to help members prepare for entry into the group. Corey and Corey (1997) provide a list of the following issues that should be discussed with prospective group members before they join the group.

- Describe the purpose of the group.
- Provide information on the group format, procedures, and ground rules.
- Determine whether the group is appropriate for the client.
- Explore client concerns.
- Provide information regarding the leader's education, training, and qualifications.
- Discuss possible psychological risks that could result from the group.
- Provide information on fees and expenses.
- Discuss limits of confidentiality.
- Clarify what services can be provided by the group.

Stages in Group Counseling

Several authors have attempted to delineate stages in group counseling (Corey, 1995; Gazda, 1989). These authors contend that a model of the stages in group counseling provides a structure to the process that helps us better understand it.

Corey and Corey (1997) developed the following model, which consists of four stages: the initial transition, working, and final stages.

Stage 1: The Initial Stage.   The initial stage of group counseling involves screening, orientation, and determining the structure of the group. The major functions of the group leader during this stage are establishing ground rules and norms for the group, helping members express their fears and expectations, being open and psychologically present, assisting group members in identifying concrete personal goals, and sharing expectations and hopes for the group. During the initial stage, members attempt to create trust; learn to express their feelings and thoughts, including fears or reservations about the group; become involved in establishing group norms; establish personal goals; and learn about the dynamics of the group process.

Stage 2: The Transition Stage.   The transition stage is characterized as a time when group members experience anxiety and defensiveness as they begin to question the value of the group. The major functions of the leader during this phase are encouraging members to express their anxiety, dealing openly with conflicts that occur in the group, and helping group members become autonomous and independent. During this stage, it is common for group members to become concerned about being accepted by the group. A central task for members is to recognize and express feelings of resistance toward the group process.

Stage 3: The Working Stage.   The working stage occurs when group members feel free to explore their thoughts and feelings and work on their concerns. The major functions of the group leader are encouraging members to translate insight into action and helping them make the necessary changes to achieve their goals. The working stage is characterized by group members introducing personal issues that they are willing to work on, providing and receiving feedback, applying what they learn in the group to their daily lives, and offering support and encouragement to other group members.

Stage 4: The Final Stage.   The final stage is a time that should offer members a smooth transition toward termination of the group. The major functions of the leader during the final stage are to assist clients in working toward termination, provide opportunities for them to receive additional counseling if necessary, and help them gain a useful understanding of what they have learned. This stage is often characterized by sadness and anxiety regarding the termination of the group. Members may begin to decrease their intensity of participation to prepare for termination, and they may also evaluate how they experienced the group.

Some authors have questioned whether group counseling actually has stages. Yalom (Forester-Miller, 1989) claimed that stages are merely a way of imposing a type of structure that does not exist in groups. Patterson (Vacc, 1989) also expressed a negative view of the stage model of group counseling. He contends that group counseling is a continuous process that does not have discrete stages (Vacc, 1989). In addition, Patterson believes that the stage model creates expectations for group members that can interfere with the normal development process of the group (Vacc, 1989). Burlingame and Fuhriman (1990) also note that the various stage models of group counseling have not been supported by research. Additional research on this topic appears warranted.

Brief-Solution-Focused Group Counseling

The trend in counseling is for brief-solution-focused approaches. Group counseling has therefore been conceptualized within this framework. Coe and Zimpfer (1996) apply the basic principles of brief counseling (described by Shazer, 1985, 1988; Walter & Peller, 1992) to group counseling. Coe and Zimpfer contend that group counseling is particularly well suited to incorporate the major tenets of the brief model, which are solution focused and have a strengths perspective. For example, group members can help identify when a person does not have a problem such as controlling anger. These "exceptions" to the problem can then be explored by group members to help the individual learn how to use what works in isolated situations to problem situations.

Solution-focused brief models of group counseling are being applied to specialty groups such as small-group debriefing for victims of violence or disaster (Juhnke & Osborne, 1997; Mitchell & Everly, 1993; Thompson, 1993). Critical incident stress debriefing is an intensive (1–3 hour) session that helps victims of violence and disaster process and debrief issues associated with their traumatic experience (Thompson, 1993). These groups have both experiential and didactic components, enabling participants to work through issues as well as obtain useful information regarding pertinent topics such as post-traumatic stress disorder.

Juhnke and Osborne (1997) integrated critical incident stress debriefing with solution-focused counseling techniques as an alternative method of counseling victims of violence. Their model is a structured program that extends over a three-week period. This approach utilizes solution-focused techniques to promote positive change and recovery as quickly as possible. Some of these strategies are identifying behaviors that promote change and using scaling questions to identify the degree of positive change between sessions.

Brief group counseling may not be appropriate for all clients. Couch (1994) suggests that individuals who need long-term supportive care would not be suited for the brief group counseling model. Certain aspects of the brief model, such as its focus on a strengths perspective, appear to hold promise for all models of group counseling.

Dealing with Disruptive Group Members

Kottler (1994) notes that there is at least one difficult member in every group. He suggests that regardless of the screening procedures, difficult members will end up in groups, creating challenges. The most difficult types of group members that Kottler has encountered are those who feel entitled, are manipulative, or have character disorders. Kottler contends that difficult members can benefit from honest and caring feedback from other group members and compassionate and firm interventions from the group leader. Group leaders also need to be open to possible contributions they are making to the difficulties group members are experiencing.

I have also been challenged by difficult group members. When this occurs, I try and understand each group member as a unique individual. At the same time, I have found there are several typical problematic behaviors that present themselves. Individuals who engage in these behaviors are referred to as aggressors, obstructors, storytellers, and attention seekers.

Aggressors may be overt or covert in their aggressive behavior toward other group members or the leader. When this occurs, the leader should try not to become angry or threatened. The aggressor is often trying to create a conflict, so an angry reaction may only reinforce that behavior. An approach that may be more productive is to inform the aggressor firmly but kindly that group process is based on a philosophy of encouragement and support. It may also be productive to explore and work through the aggressor's feelings.

Obstructors tend to be negative and obstruct the group process. They often find ways to sidetrack the issues being discussed and prevent the group from staying on task. This may involve a variety of disruptive behaviors, for example, constantly trying to change the topic or complaining that nothing seems to be happening in the group. Obstructors often engage in their disruptive behavior as a means of gaining power and control. It is therefore important for the counselor to avoid reacting with anger, since that reaction may only create a power struggle. When the obstructor tries to change the topic, the leader might say, "No,

Group members can obstruct group progress by acting as if they are not interested.

let's not change the focus of our work. We need to spend more time with this so we can reach a meaningful conclusion."

Storytellers often like to monopolize the group by telling drawn-out stories about things that have happened months ago. What they say usually holds little interest for the group, because they typically have already resolved the issue or have no desire to do anything about it. When this occurs, the leader can ask what the storyteller is thinking and feeling at the moment. The leader can emphasize that it is important to try to stay in the here and now so the group can have something concrete to work on.

Attention seekers find different ways to draw attention to themselves. Since their goal is typically gaining attention, the counselor must be careful not to reinforce the behavior. Two strategies can be used in working with attention seekers. The leader should first attempt to channel the attention seeker's need for attention in a positive direction by asking for assistance when possible. When that fails, the leader should ask the attention seeker to refrain from the behaviors that are creating a problem. For example, if the behavior is making frequent, inappropriate jokes, the leader might say, "Turning a serious issue into a joke does not allow the group to work on issues realistically."

Common Mistakes of Group Leaders

Jacobs, Harvill, and Masson (1997) identify the following common mistakes group leaders make in therapy groups.

- *Attempting to conduct therapy without a contract.* It is important to ensure that a member wants help with a particular problem by directly inquiring if the client would like assistance. Assuming a client wants help may waste valuable time with a member who is not ready to make a commitment to work on his problem.
- *Spending too much time on one person.* Group time can be dominated by difficult group members or members who are interesting and attractive and are eager for assistance during *each* session. Group leaders have an ethical responsibility to ensure that all members have an opportunity to participate.
- *Spending too little time with one person.* Group leaders can spend too little time with a member during the problem-solving process in an attempt to give everyone a chance to talk. While it is important to ensure that all members be encouraged to participate, this does not mean they all need to talk. Problem solving requires that one member be the focus of attention for a sufficient period of time.
- *Letting members rescue each other.* There can be a tendency for group members to rescue other members when they sense pain or sorrow. Emotional rescuing is not productive in any form of counseling, because it communicates sympathy. Group counselors should instead encourage members to convey support, concern, and empathy.
- *Letting the session turn into advice-giving.* Premature advice-giving can be particularly prevalent when group members attempt to offer help to other members during problem solving. Premature advice-giving is not productive in any counseling including group counseling. When this occurs, the leader could suggest that members take more time using listening skills to gain a better understanding of the problem before attempting to solve it.

Qualities of Effective Group Leaders

Perhaps the most important factor in effective group counseling is the personal qualities of the group leader. The art of counseling model emphasizes the role of the self as an instrument of change. Several authors have identified leadership qualities that promote positive outcomes in group counseling. Ohlsen (1970) notes that effective group counselors are in tune with the group process. They can then make the necessary changes to ensure positive therapeutic movement. Corey (1995) identifies personal qualities associated with effective group leadership, which include presence, personal power, courage, willingness to confront oneself, self-awareness, sincerity, authenticity, a sense of identity, belief in the group process, enthusiasm, inventiveness, and creativity. Yalom and Lieberman (1971) suggest that the group leader sets the emotional climate for the group. When the leader acts in an autocratic, confrontational, or emotionally distant fashion, the group experience may actually do more harm than good to members. These authors point out that a leader with moderate amounts of executive function and emotional stimulation and high amounts of caring and meaning attribution contributes to improvements in group members. Taken collectively, the literature suggests that the qualities of effective group leaders are having a positive presence, which can instill trust and enthusiasm; being sensitive to the group process and capable of making adjustments as necessary; and setting a positive and encouraging therapeutic climate.

Diversity Issues

Horne (1996) notes that populations being served in group counseling are becoming more diverse. Group-counseling paradigms are expanding to accomodate these diverse populations and settings. McRae (1994) suggest that counselors need to be aware of how cultural diversity can impact group dynamics. For example, individuals with similar worldviews can formulate coalitions or alliances within the group. These alliances can evolve between or within races. McRae recommends that counselors avoid stereotyping group members along racial lines and attempt to understand members as individuals functioning within a group environment.

Johnson et al. (1995) suggest there are both challenges and opportunities in multicultural group counseling. Challenges can evolve from prejudice, difficulty communicating, misunderstandings, and fear between group members. These types of challenges can impede or enhance group growth. The authors suggest that when problems present themselves, they should be directly dealt with in the group. Within this context, the group process can be used to help members develop new levels of communication, understanding, trust, and sensitivity with other cultural groups (Johnson et al., 1995). Opportunities also present themselves in terms of how diverse individuals in groups can broaden the perspective for problem solving and decision making.

Feminist group therapy is one example of infusing diversity issues into group work. Rittenhouse (1997) notes that the feminist perspective could be useful in survivor groups to help women recover from sexual trauma or other adverse life experiences. Rittenhouse describes the following principles of feminist group therapy. The key to achieving success in feminist group counseling is to create an egalitarian relationship between the group members and the members and the counselor. Fostering equality and empowerment can play important roles in encouraging members to take an active role in their recovery and in overcoming oppressive forces that have impeded their development.

A second major principle is to help members look beyond intrapsychic causality and explore problems from an ecological perspective. This process can help members shift from internalizing and self-blaming to exploring sociocultural and political forces such as oppression in family roles and the work place. It does not imply a shift in blame from self to others but an attempt to identify how members can "reinvent their world" in a more gender sensitive and meaningful manner. This process of discovery can involve activities such as understanding the self in more gender-accurate terms such as Carol Gilligan's (1982) seminal work on female moral development. The group format is ideal for the discussion of such material since it allows for experiential processing of ideas and concepts.

Diversity is not restricted to gender or culture but can include other attributes such as individuals with disabilities. There are 43 million disabled Americans, making them the largest minority group in the United States (Patterson, McKenzie, & Jenkins, 1995). Unfortunately, this large group of individuals has historically been systematically excluded from many opportunities, including group counseling because of attitudinal and environmental barriers (Patterson, McKenzie, & Jenkins, 1995). The Americans with Disabilities Act of 1990 provided rights for the disabled in terms of inclusion in the mainstream of society (Brown, 1995).

Specialists in group work are beginning to make strides in breaking down the barriers that the disabled face in participating in group work (Horne, 1995). Patterson, McKenzie, and Jenkins (1995) note that group counselors must sensitize themselves to the needs of the disabled. They must practice disability etiquette by treating all people of diversity as people first and foremost and adjusting the group process, such as ensuring that a person with a hearing impairment can see the speaker's lips. It is also the responsibility of the leader to address attitudinal and environmental barriers that could impede the growth of the disabled member and have an adverse effect on the group process. In the final analysis, diversity in all its forms can create unique opportunities for group counselors and members alike.

Summary

The art and science of group counseling is a dynamic and interesting dimension of the counseling process. As artist, counselors can adjust counseling approaches to the unique and emerging needs of diverse clients in a group milieu. As scientist, counselors can engage in pregroup screening to ensure that prospective group members are appropriate for group work and to incorporate appropriate structuring such as ensuring that group members have personal counseling goals and the group functions from a clear theoretical perspective.

Professional helpers routinely utilize group work in their counseling practice in all types of settings, including schools, hospitals, agencies, and private practice. It can be used as the only form of counseling intervention, such as in parent education or Alcoholics Anonymous. Groups can also provide an important adjunct to other counseling processes, especially individual counseling. In this regard, clients can try out what they have learned in individual counseling within the context of a group milieu.

13 Career Counseling

CHAPTER OVERVIEW

This chapter provides an overview of career counseling, a challenging and evolving specialty that helps individuals with career planning and decision making throughout the life span. This chapter provides information on the following topics

- The art and science of career counseling
- Evolution of career counseling
- Theoretical foundations in terms of career development and decision making
- Treatment issues, including personal versus career counseling, assessment instruments, intervention strategies, and the process of career counseling
- Special issues, including career counseling for women and computer-assisted career counseling
- Diversity issues in career counseling

The Art and Science of Career Counseling

A recent trend in career counseling is to integrate career theory and practice. These two dimensions of career counseling parallel the art and science dimensions of counseling with career theory representing the science and practice reflecting the art. Krumboltz (1996) provides a rationale for the movement toward integration of career theory and practice when he notes that the reason that career theories have been largely ignored by practitioners is that they have focused on career development and not on intervention strategies. They therefore have provided little practical information on what career counselors can *do* during the counseling process.

Herr (1996) points out that theorists such as Holland, Super, and Krumboltz have made progress toward this integration. One obvious example is the assessment instruments developed by Holland (Vocational Preference Inventory), Super (Career Development Inventory), and Krumboltz (Career Beliefs Inventory). Several other individuals have attempted to bridge the gap between career theory and practice (for example, Chartrand, 1996; Harmon, 1996; Holland, 1996; and Savickas, 1996). For example, Savickas (1996) provides a framework that can be used to link career theories to practice. His model is an adaptation of "Wagner's (1971) theory of structural analysis of personality to the domain of vocational psychology" (Savickas, 1996, p. 196). It is a comprehensive model that includes six types of career services: occupational placement, vocational guidance, career counseling, career education, career therapy, and position coaching (Savickas, 1996). Although progress is being made toward integrating, Savickas and Walsh (1996) contend that more work needs to be done to bridge the gap between theory and practice.

Another dimension of the art and science of career counseling is the trend toward integrating traditional career counseling with personal counseling. Traditional career counseling has relied to a large extent on the use of assessment instruments such as interest inventories, which can be used with or without computer assistance. Career assessment instruments represent an important dimension of the science of career counseling, providing objective information that can enhance the counseling process. The art of career counseling is to attempt to interface objective information with the subjective, ever-changing world of the client. Central to this process is the art of addressing personal issues and problems that may arise during the counseling process. From this perspective, career issues are not viewed as separate, isolated entities but interrelated to the person's overall psychosocial functioning.

Evolution of Career Counseling

The world of work has changed dramatically over the centuries along with the evolution of the human species. Our early ancestors had limited opportunities and choices regarding work (Axelson, 1997). What people did was primarily restricted to preserving the survival of the species. Today, people work for many reasons that go beyond obtaining money for food and shelter. Some work to enhance their self-esteem, others have a goal of independence, some want to help people, and others work to experience power and control. As people's needs change over the life span, so too does the type of work they find rewarding. This in turn can account for the career changes that can take place throughout one's life.

Career counseling has evolved as a means of assisting individuals in developing career planning and decision-making skills to facilitate career choice. It has been referred to by several different names over the years, including occupational counseling, vocational guidance, and vocational counseling. These names tended to have a narrower focus than career counseling, since they emphasized the importance of obtaining occupational information in selecting a particular career. Career counseling is a more comprehensive concept, incorporating the various career development theories to formulate a strong theoretical foundation.

Career counseling can be defined as "a series of general and specific interventions throughout the life span, dealing with such concerns as self-understanding; broadening one's horizons; work selection, challenge, satisfaction, and other interpersonal phenomena; and lifestyle issues, such as balancing work, family, and leisure" (Engels et al., 1995, p. 134).

Career counseling, as with all counseling specialties, must begin with general counseling competencies to ensure the necessary foundations for specialization (Engels et al., 1995).

Career counseling is practiced by professional counselors in schools and agencies. Some counselors incorporate career counseling into their repertoire of helping skills to assist clients in exploring career issues and personal problems. Counselors can also specialize in this field and identify themselves as career counselors or career development professionals. In 1952, the American Counseling Association recognized the special skills and professional interests associated with career counseling by creating a special division for career counselors called the National Career Development Association (NCDA).

The NCDA took an active role in establishing credentials for career counseling. These efforts resulted in career counseling becoming the first specialty designation offered by the National Board of Certified Counselors. Requirements for certification include

- Becoming certified by the National Board of Certified Counselors (see requirements in Chapter 2)
- Earning a graduate degree in counseling or a related profession
- Working at least part-time in career counseling for three years following graduate study
- Passing the National Career Counselor Examination

As we approach the twenty-first century, the world of work is evolving into a constant state of flux, creating opportunities and challenges. Stoltz-Loike (1996) identifies some of the defining features of the present work environment as well as some recommendations to be successful in the new millennium. Current work environments are characterized by downsizing and a lack of job security, reduced opportunities for lifetime employment within the same industry, and increased global competition and expanding global marketplaces. According to Feller (1995), the modern workplace is a "joint venture between the employer with problems to be solved and tasks to be done, and the employees who have the skills to sell and needs to be met" (p. 158). Individuals who develop these skills will be successful. Factors critical to this skill development are broad-based flexible skills, educational credentials that promote life-long learning, adaptability, and problem-solving skills (Stoltz-Loike, 1996).

Theoretical Foundations

Several individuals have provided theories of career development and career decision making. These theories provide a description of how career development occurs over the life span and what is entailed in the process of career choice and decision making.

Career Development Theories

Career development theories relate to how career issues develop over the life span. This section provides an overview of three prominent career development theories, those of Super, Holland, and Roe.

Super's Theory.   Super (1990, p. 199) describes his theory as "a loosely unified set of theories dealing with specific aspects of career development, taken from developmental, differential, social, personality, and phenomenological psychology." Super's (1957, 1980,

1990) theory emphasizes the role of self-concept in career development. He contends that how individuals define themselves will have a major effect on their career choices. For example, a person with a self-image of a strong, hard worker but not particularly intellectual may be attracted to a physical job such as an auto mechanic.

Super's (1957) theory can be considered developmental because he suggested that there are five stages of career development, each with corresponding developmental tasks: growth, exploration, establishment, maintenance, and decline. An overview of these stages follows.

The *growth stage* spans from birth to 14 years of age. The self-concept develops as the individual identifies with significant others. Developmental tasks during the growth stage include gaining self-understanding and obtaining an overall understanding of the world of work.

The growth stage has three substages. The *fantasy* substage occurs from age 4 to 10 and involves the child role-playing various fantasies regarding the world of work, for example, playing doctor or nurse. The *interest* substage extends from age 11 to 12. During this period, a child's likes and dislikes have a major impact on career aspirations. The third substage is *capacity,* which takes place from age 13 to 14. The capacity substage is characterized by a more realistic view of the world of work as individuals consider their abilities and job requirements.

Super's second stage is the *exploration stage,* which spans from 14 to 24 years of age. This is a period of self-examination in relation to the world of work. During this time, the individual also begins to directly experience work by involvement in part-time jobs. Developmental tasks associated with the exploration stage include crystallizing, specifying, and implementing a career preference.

The exploration stage has three substages. The *tentative* substage extends from age 15 to 17 and involves identifying appropriate fields of work. The *transition* substage begins at age 18 and continues to age 21. During this substage, the individual may pursue special educational or vocational training related to a field of work or enter directly into the job market. The third substage is referred to as *trial–little commitment* and ranges from age 22 to 24. During this period, the individual usually begins a first job. The commitment is usually tentative as the person decides whether the career choice was appropriate.

The third major stage is the *establishment stage,* spanning from 24 to 44 years of age. During this stage, individuals have identified an appropriate field of work that they want to make a long-term commitment. The key developmental task involves consolidation and advancement.

Two substages are associated with the establishment stage. First is *trial-commitment and stabilization,* which occurs from age 25 to 30. During this substage, the individual either settles down with a particular occupation or becomes dissatisfied and begins to explore other occupational possibilities. *Advancement* is the second substage and extends from age 31 to 44. This is typically a time for stabilization, during which seniority is required. It also tends to be a very creative, productive period.

Super's fourth stage is the *maintenance stage,* which spans from 44 to 64 years of age. This is a time for the individual to enjoy the security of seniority while attempting to maintain status as a current and productive professional. The major developmental task is preservation of achieved status.

The final stage in Super's model is the *decline stage,* which begins at age 64. During this stage, the individual adjusts to retirement as well as declining mental and physical skills and abilities. The key developmental tasks are deceleration, disengagement, and retirement.

The decline stage is composed of two substages. First is *deceleration,* which occurs between 60 and 65 years of age. This is a time when the individual begins to adjust to impending retirement, perhaps pursuing part-time jobs as a transition from full-time work. *Retirement* is the second substage and usually begins at age 61 or later. During this time, the individual may continue some part-time work or discontinue work and devote time to leisure activities.

Super (1980, 1990) refers to his theory as a life-span, life-space approach to career development. Its purpose is to add role theory into the five-stage model to create a model composed of multiple-role careers (Super, 1990). According to this theory, "career is defined as the combination and sequence of roles played by a person during the course of a lifetime" (Super, 1980, p. 282). These roles vary as a person proceeds through the life span and include such possibilities as student, worker, husband, wife, and parent (Super, 1980).

Many research studies have tested various aspects of Super's theory. Osipow (1996) concludes that most of the literature has provided support for Super's model. Savickas (1994) recognizes Super's impact on career counseling in a special issue of *The Career Development Quarterly* that highlighted his contributions to career theory and practice. For example, Savickas (1994) notes that Super helped shift the field from a focus on occupational choice to career development and extended vocational guidance into career counseling. It is therefore not surprising that Super's work has generated a wide range of research activity on topics such as the role of the self-concept in career development (Betz, 1994), work values (Zytowski, 1994), and career adaptability (Goodman, 1994).

Super's theory appears to share some commonalties with current trends such as recognizing the contextual nature of career decision making (Phillips & Blustein, 1994). In this regard, Super notes that career decision making takes place within the context of a broad landscape of issues such as economic, cultural, family, peers, and historic (Phillips & Blustein, 1994). Jepsen (1996) observes that Super's description of the role of the self-concept in decision making provides valuable information on the subjective-phenomenological dimension of career counseling.

Holland's Theory.   Holland's (1973, 1985a, 1992, 1996) theory suggests that career choice results in an attempt to obtain a satisfactory fit of the person with the environment. Job satisfaction results when there is a congruence of personality type and work environment (Holland, 1996). In addition, Weinrach and Srebalus (1990) note several practical applications of Holland's theory in terms of career counseling instruments, for example, Holland's (1985b) Vocational Preference Inventory and Holland's (1994) Self-Directed Search.

Holland's (1973, 1985a, 1992, 1996) theory is based on the following four assumptions.

1. *People tend to be characterized by one of six personality types.* Holland (1973) originally believed that people could be characterized by six personality types. Holland (1985a) expanded this conception of personality types to include the possibility of

subtypes or patterns that would provide further differentiation of a person's personality characteristic. The original six personality types with brief descriptions are as follows.

- *Realistic* individuals take a logical, matter-of-fact approach to life.
- *Investigative* people use an investigative, analytic approach to problem solving.
- *Social* individuals tend to be social, cooperative, and people-oriented.
- *Artistic* people tend to be sensitive, creative, spontaneous, and nonconforming.
- *Conventional* individuals are conforming, inhibited, and have a preference for structured situations.
- *Enterprising* individuals tend to take an extroverted, aggressive approach to problem solving.

2. *There are six kinds of environments that correspond with the six personality types (realistic, investigative, artistic, social, enterprising, and conventional).* Most environments attract workers with corresponding personality types. For example, artistic people work in places such as the theater. A congruent person-environment fit tends to promote job satisfaction.

3. *People seek out work environments that enable them to use their skills, express their values, and enter into agreeable roles.* People are motivated to work in settings that have complementary personality structures.

4. *The interaction of the environment and personality determines behavior.* An individual's behavior, for instance, career choice and achievement, is determined by the nature of the person-environment fit.

Walsh & Srsic (1995) report that Holland's theory continues to generate a substantial amount of research interests investigating constructs such as personality types (Holland, Johnston, & Asama, 1994) and person-environment congruence (Thompson, Flynn, & Griffith, 1994). Holland (1996) notes that studies support the theory that people do well in their careers when there is a good fit between personality types and the environment. In addition, evidence suggests people experience dissatisfaction, poor job performance, and disruption in career path when there is incongruence between personality types and environmental fit (Holland, 1996).

Osipow (1987) posits that Holland's theory has generated more research activity than any other career development theory. Weinrach and Srebalus (1990) emphasize this point by observing that more than 450 studies of Holland's theory were conducted between 1959 and 1988. Fitzgerald and Rounds (1989) provide a literature review of some of these studies and conclude that Holland's congruence hypothesis relating to the person-environment fit has received the most empirical support. In addition, Brown (1987) suggests that Holland's theory is well defined and had substantial research support. Osipow notes that Holland's revision of his theory should generate another extended period of research investigation.

Roe's Theory.   The major principles of Roe's theory evolved from Maslowian and psychoanalytic theory (Roe, 1956; Roe & Lunneborg, 1990). Simply stated, Roe contends that unmet needs in childhood can have a major influence on career choice as an adult. In addition, her theory suggests that people can fulfill all basic and higher-order needs associated with Maslow's hierarchy in their careers. These include needs related to physiology, safety, love and belonging, self-esteem, and self-actualization.

Roe (1956) identifies three types of parent-child relationships that could foster need satisfaction in particular careers. Osipow (1996) provides an overview of these relationships as follows.

1. *Overprotective or excessively demanding parents.* Parents who are overly protective or make excessive demands tend to satisfy physiological needs, but they may be less prone to gratify psychological needs such as love and self-esteem. These parents foster dependency within their children since gratification of psychological needs is contingent on children engaging in socially desirable or high-achieving behaviors. Their children grow into adults with an excessive need for recognition and approval. As a result, they may choose highly visible occupations, for instance, politics or a branch of the performing arts such as acting.
2. *Rejecting parents.* These parents either neglect or reject their children. Their children will tend to have many unfulfilled needs and may become suspicious or untrusting of others. They may therefore select careers where their needs can be met in activities that involve working with things, for example, computers, rather than people.
3. *Accepting parents.* These parents tend to be very accepting and loving toward their children. They engage in unconditional rather than conditional love. Their children's basic and higher-order needs are therefore met, promoting a sense of autonomy and independence in the children as they grow into adulthood. Since these individuals tend to feel secure with themselves, they may choose a profession such as teaching or medicine, in which they can assist others in moving toward their own self-realization.

Osipow (1990) notes that Roe's theory is almost impossible to test empirically because of the subjective nature of the constructs on which the theory is based. Additional refinement of the theory and empirical investigation of its principles appear warranted.

Career Decision-Making Theories

Career decision-making theories provide another theoretical foundation for assisting with career counseling. These theories provide "guidelines for collection, processing, and utilization of information in order to improve decision making" (Gati, 1990a, p. 508). Several theories have been developed on career decision making. This section provides an overview of decision-making theories based on cognitive dissonance theory, social-learning theory, and a multiple-career decision-making theory.

Cognitive Dissonance Theory. Hilton (1962) was one of the first to suggest that career decision making is based on the theory of cognitive dissonance. According to Festinger (1957), cognitive dissonance occurs when an individual has two incompatible cognitions. For example, an individual may contend, "I don't like my job, and it has low pay." The person may then attempt to remove the dissonance by changing one of the cognitions or by aiding dissonance-reducing cognitions, saying, "I like my job even though it does not pay well."

Osipow (1996) identifies the following implications of cognitive dissonance theory on career decision making.

- *It is important for counselors to identify factors that can increase occupational dissonance.* One example is a person with an interest in an occupation that has limited opportunities, for example, wanting to be a professor in a field that has few academic positions available. If the dissonance cannot be resolved, the counselor might advise the client to avoid that occupation.
- *Counselors should develop strategies to deal with dissonance.* This can involve a career counselor introducing "counter-dissonance agents." For example, the counselor might tell a premedical student who lacks the aptitude for medical study that being a physician involves long hours resulting in little time for family life.
- *Counselors can help clients avoid making a premature choice.* One way to accomplish this is by noting that modifying a choice in the future may cause excessive dissonance. This in turn can interfere with making a more appropriate choice in the future. For example, a person with a strong need to be perceived as having clear goals and objectives may decide to pursue a career as a computer analyst. After several courses on the topic, the person might discover an aversion to computers and want to consider other occupations. This would create dissonance with the need to be perceived as "having clear goals and objectives." To avoid such perceptions and reduce dissonance, this individual may then decide to continue working in an undesirable career.

A Personal Note

I entered college as a predental major. I had wanted to be a dentist because my father was a dentist. As part of my predental studies I had to take a lot of chemistry and biology courses, which I hated and in which I had limited ability. This created dissonance, since I thought I wanted to be a dentist but discovered I did not have the aptitude to do so.

I soon found myself changing my attitude toward becoming a dentist. Before I knew it, I began to think, "I don't want to be a dentist." I soon began to think of a lot of good reasons for not wanting to be a dentist, including not wanting to bend over all day and stick my hands in people's mouths. At this point, I had begun to resolve my dissonance by creating a new attitude. I was able to conclude, "I don't want to be a dentist, and I don't have the ability to become one." During my next semester at the university I was attending, I took a psychology course and quickly became interested in the subject. I also discovered that I had the aptitude to become a psychologist.

Social Learning Theory.   Krumboltz (1979) and Mitchell and Krumboltz (1990) have developed a career decision-making model based on social learning theory. The social learning model contends that learning experiences play a key role in occupational selection. Krumboltz (1979) suggests that career choice is influenced by the following factors.

- Genetic endowment creates limits to career choice.
- Environmental factors, such as the economy and educational requirements, will determine occupational choice to some degree.

- Learning experiences, for example, being reinforced for pursuing intellectual endeavors, will influence one's interest and aspirations.
- Task-approach skills, such as work habits and interpersonal skills, will affect one's ability to be successful in a particular occupation.

Mitchell and Krumboltz (1990) have expanded their model to include cognitive behavioral theory. From this perspective, career decision making is also influenced by cognitions and behaviors of clients. Mitchell and Krumboltz (1987) provide empirical support for the importance of cognitive behavioral strategies in career counseling. They have found that cognitive behavioral approaches contributed to appropriate career decisions and also reduced anxiety regarding career decisions.

More recently, Krumboltz (1996) has attempted to integrate his theory of career decision making into a theory of career counseling. The overall goal of his model "is to facilitate the learning of skills, interests, beliefs, values, work habits, and personal qualities that enable each client to create a satisfying life within a constantly changing work environment" (Krumboltz, 1996, p. 61). In this regard, Krumboltz (1994) developed the Career Beliefs Inventory (CBI) as a tool that counselors can use to help clients identify beliefs and assumptions that can impede career decision making. It can be used during the early phases of counseling to help clients develop cognitions and behaviors that enhance career progress (Krumboltz, 1994).

Multiple Career Decision-Making Theory.   Gati (1986) and Gati and Tikotzki (1989) have developed a multiple career decision-making theory. They contend that all career decision-making theories can be described in terms of three major models. These models are prescriptive in nature, using logic and rational approaches to identify the best way to make career decisions (Sharf, 1997). A detailed description and analysis of these models is provided by Gati and Tikotzki (1989), Carson and Mowsesian (1990), Gati (1990a, 1990b), and Gati, Fassa, and Houminer (1995). Reduced to their most basic elements, these three models can be summarized as follows.

- *Expected Utility Model.* This model suggests making separate evaluations of the advantages and disadvantages of various occupations and comparing them to other occupational alternatives. The individual then chooses the occupation with the highest overall value.
- *Sequential Elimination Model.* This model involves identifying attributes of an ideal occupation, for example, working outdoors, and ranking the attributes in terms of importance. Minimal levels of acceptability regarding these criteria are established. Occupations are evaluated on the basis of this criterion and sequentially eliminated if they do not meet the established criterion.
- *Conjunctive Model.* In this model, occupational alternatives are given consideration only when they meet basic occupational requirements, for instance, a minimal salary level.

Gati (1986) suggests that no single model of career development is superior to another. Instead, the models should be empirically investigated to determine the conditions that would be most appropriate for their use.

Treatment Issues

This section provides an overview of several important treatment issues that relate to career counseling. Information is provided on personal versus career counseling, assessment instruments, intervention strategies, and the process of career counseling.

Personal Versus Career Counseling

There appears to be a shift in interest from career counseling to personal counseling (Birk & Brooks, 1986; Spengler, Blustein, & Strohmer, 1990; Watkins et al., 1986; Watkins et al., 1987). For example, Birk and Brooks (1986) surveyed 300 members of the division of Counseling Psychology of the APA on their attitudes toward various counseling activities. Personal counseling was ranked as the most important activity, whereas career counseling was ranked tenth. Watkins et al. (1986) also surveyed members of the division of Counseling Psychology of the APA regarding their attitudes relating to career counseling. Results of this study showed that members in private practice spend 59.2 percent of their time conducting psychotherapy and only 3.5 percent of their time conducting career counseling. The study also suggested that counseling psychologists are minimally engaged in career counseling and view it as an uninteresting and unattractive alternative to personal counseling.

With career counseling receiving less interest than personal counseling, an apparent treatment bias in favor of personal counseling is not surprising. Spengler, Blustein, and Strohmer (1990) find that counselors who prefer personal counseling over career counseling engage in diagnostic and treatment overshadowing. In this process, issues relating to personal counseling overshadow the importance of diagnostic and treatment issues relating to career counseling. Other studies have shown that vocational problems receive poorer prognosis and less counselor empathy than personal problems (Hill, Tanney, & Leonard, 1977) and less of the core conditions and affective and exploratory responses (Melnick, 1975).

A recent trend in the literature suggests it is not necessary to conceptualize career counseling and personal counseling in dichotomous terms. Several authors have contended that career counseling should be integrated into nonvocational treatment approaches (Blustein, 1987; Blustein & Spengler, 1995; and Richardson, 1996). Blustein (1987, p. 794) provides a rationale for integration by noting that "separating work issues from other psychosocial concerns creates an artificial distinction between aspects of life that are clearly interrelated." In addition, the manner in which a person relates to career issues involves coping strategies similar to those utilized in other life concerns (Blustein, 1987).

Blustein and Spengler (1995) describe a comprehensive model that can be used to integrate personal counseling with career counseling. It is a model that incorporates a number of the recent trends in counseling such as social constructivism and problem-oriented brief psychotherapy. Richardson (1996) suggests that an important first step in overcoming the personal counseling–career counseling split is to change the name of career counseling to counseling/psychotherapy and work, jobs, and careers. By placing counseling and psychotherapy first, it acknowledges the role that counseling and psychotherapy theories can play in career development, and it may also encourage more counselors and psychotherapists to address career issues (Richardson, 1996).

Blustein (1987) identifies guidelines for integrating career counseling with psychotherapy. He recommends that counselors take a first step of incorporating a detailed work history during the intake process to obtain important diagnostic considerations. The next step is to gain a comprehensive understanding of career development and career decision-making theories to broaden one's understanding of human behavior. In this process, counselors could select career theories that are compatible with their theories relating to personal counseling. For example, Super's theory of career development with his emphasis on the self could supplement Rogers' person-centered approach. As another example, Krumboltz's social-learning theory might be used in conjunction with the cognitive-behavior school of counseling. Blustein (1987) also notes that it is important to integrate career counseling with personal counseling in cases that involve substance abuse problems, since clients with these problems often have trouble with work and personal issues.

Other individuals have attempted to integrate career counseling with personal counseling. Raskin (1987) integrates career counseling with interpersonally oriented schools of counseling; Yost and Corbishley (1987) conceptualize career counseling from a cognitive-behavior perspective; and Gysbers and Moore (1987) describe career counseling within a broad framework that includes marriage and family counseling and cognitive psychology. It is hoped that this trend toward integration will promote more interest in career counseling so that these vital issues and concerns of clients will receive the attention they deserve.

Some individuals may have difficulty with career decision making even though they have been provided ample opportunity to obtain information regarding their interests, aptitude, the world of work and so forth (Larson et al., 1994). In these instances, Larson et al. (1994) suggest that these individuals may have psychological blocks associated with problematic behaviors, cognitions, or feelings (for example, fear of success or failure and fear of change). These psychological blocks can in turn contribute to problems within the personality structure such as low-esteem, lack of self-awareness, external locus of control, and anxiety, which can undermine the career decision-making process (Larson et al., 1994). Larson et al. (1994) note that the Career Decision Diagnostic Assessment (CDDA) (Bansberg & Sklare, 1986) instrument can identify potential psychological blocks that can interfere with career decision making. The CDDA can be used as a screening device to alert counselors that more intense personal counseling may be required to help these clients overcome impasses to the career counseling process. Kjos (1995) goes on to provide suggestions for career-focused interventions and treatment planning for individuals that are in need of personality restructuring.

Assessment Instruments

Career counseling has historically placed a major emphasis on assessing interests, abilities, and personality traits (Phillips et al., 1988). These assessment procedures play a vital role in career planning and decision making by increasing self-understanding and providing information on careers and educational programs.

Zunker (1997) and Drummond (1992) provide an overview of standardized assessment instruments used in career counseling to assess aptitude, achievement, personality, values, and career maturity. These instruments are summarized as follows.

- *Aptitude.* Aptitude tests provide a measure of a particular skill or the ability to acquire a skill. Aptitude tests can be used by career counselors to predict a person's success in career/education training. Examples of aptitude tests are the General Aptitude Test Battery (GATB), the Differential Aptitude Test (DAT), the Flanagan Aptitude Classification Tests (FACT), and the Armed Services Vocational Aptitude

Battery (ASVAB) (see Zunker, 1994, for information and addresses regarding these instruments).

■ *Achievement.* Achievement tests assess current level of functioning regarding abilities such as reading, arithmetic, and language usage. Career counselors use achievement tests to determine academic areas of strengths and weaknesses to assist with educational and career planning and placement. The three major types of achievement tests are diagnostic, broad survey, and subject area tests. Diagnostic tests can be used to assess strengths and weaknesses to determine whether the individual has the essential skills and competencies to be successful in an educational program. Survey tests can provide a general assessment of fundamental skills and competencies with little information on skills in a particular subject. Subject area tests are designed to assess functioning in specified subject areas such as chemistry and biology. Examples of achievement tests are the Wide Range Achievement Tests (an example of a diagnostic test), the National Assessment of Education Progress (NAEP) (an example of a survey test), and the College Board Achievement Tests (an example of a subject area test).

■ *Interests.* Interest inventories, perhaps more than any other assessment instruments have been associated with career counseling. Interest inventories are used to assess personal and career interests to facilitate education/career planning and placement. Many of these interest inventories can be useful to provide information regarding the person-environmental fit discussed by Holland. Examples of interest inventories are the Self-Directed Search (Holland, 1994), the Strong Interest Inventory (Harmon, et al. 1994), and the series of Kuder interest inventories based on the Kuder General Interest Survey (Kuder, 1964) (for example, the Kuder Occupational Interest Survey (Zytowski, 1985).

■ *Values.* Values inventories have emerged in the past two decades to assess the interface between personal values and the world of work. Mid-life career changes that correspond to radical lifestyle changes are examples of the potent force that values can have on career choice. Congruence between values and career choice is considered an important component in career success and satisfaction. Examples of values inventories are the Work Values Inventory (WVI), (Super, 1970), the Study of Values, the Survey of Interpersonal Values, the Survey of Personal Values, and the Values Scale (see Zunker, 1994, for the address and current information regarding these instruments).

■ *Personality.* Career development theorists such as Roe and Super recognized the importance of considering personality in career counseling. Roe's (1956) theory suggests that early personality development within the context of the family influences career direction. Super (1990) formulated a theory based on the relationship between self-concept and career development. Although the relationship between personality and career choice has been established, there has been limited use of personality inventories in career counseling. The movement toward integrating personal counseling with career counseling could provide a venue for more meaningful use of personality inventories in career counseling. Some of the personality instruments that are used in career counseling are the California Test of Personality, the Edwards Personal Preference Schedule (EPPS), the Guiford-Zimmerman Temperament Survey, the Minnesota Counseling Inventory, the Sixteen Personality Factor (16PF), Temperament and Values Inventory, and the Myers-Briggs Type Indicator.

Diversity issues such as culture and clients with disabilities should be considered in career assessment. In terms of culture, several interest inventories have been evaluated to determine whether they are valid for ethnic minorities. Carter and Swanson (1990) conducted a literature review of studies that investigated the validity of the Strong Interest Inventory (Hanson & Campbell, 1985) for African American clients. This review found little evidence of the validity of the Strong Interest Inventory for blacks. These findings are particularly significant, because this instrument is the most frequently used interest inventory in college counseling centers (Zytowski & Warman, 1982). On a more positive note, Haviland and Hanson (1987) found that the Strong Campbell Interest Inventory (Hanson & Campbell, 1985) has adequate criterion validity for American Indian college students. Additional research on the cross-cultural use of interest inventories appears warranted.

Levinson (1994) addresses career assessment issues for students with disabilities. A number of programs and initiatives have been implemented in an effort to meet the special needs of students with disabilities. Transition planning is one example of the need for career assessment with these individuals. According to the 1990 Public Law 94-142, schools are required to formulate transition plans for students with disabilities by the time the students reach the age of 16. The overall goal of transition planning is to assist students in making a successful adjustment from school to work and facilitate effective community living.

Contemporary career assessment for students with disabilities is typically structured in terms of three levels. Level 1 begins in elementary school and is focused on building self-awareness. During this time, students explore needs, interests, values, and careers, and receive assistance in developing decision-making skills. Level 2 starts in middle or junior high school. Its aim is to assist students in making tentative career choices based on assessment of interests, aptitudes, career maturity, and work habits. Level 3 begins when students reach high school. During this time, assessment can involve a wide range of activities relating to career planning and decision making such as refinement of issues associated with career choice and assistance with post secondary education, training, employment, and community living.

Central to the task of counseling students with disabilities is to first and foremost treat them as people who have more in common with others than they have differences. It is also important to be aware of the special needs and requirements associated with their disabilities to facilitate the self-realization of their full career potential.

Intervention Strategies

A wide range of intervention strategies can be used in career counseling. These include strategies associated with career planning and decision making, assisting with vocational adjustment, and helping clients overcome personal problems. Career counseling can also take place in a variety of formats, including individual, group, self-help, and computer-assisted programs.

A large body of research has evaluated the various forms of career interventions. These studies have been summarized in several annual reviews (Fitzgerald & Rounds, 1989; Morrow, Mullen, & McElvoy, 1990; Osipow, 1987; Phillips et al., 1988; Savickas, 1989; Slaney & Russell, 1987). Oliver and Spokane (1983, 1988) conducted two meta-analyses of career counseling that have received considerable attention in the literature. Both studies provided support for the efficacy of career counseling. Their 1988 review involves an analysis of 58 studies on career counseling published from 1950 to 1982. It attempts to gain a more precise understanding of the variables associated with efficacy in terms of types of intervention, client characteristics, and outcome measures. Results of the study showed differences in type and intensity of intervention. In terms of type of intervention, individual career counseling produced the most gain per hour of any intervention strategy. Group career counseling and workshops were the least effective intervention per hour of treatment. The study also shows intensity of intervention to be important. Efficacy improved with increased length of sessions and number of sessions.

A study by Kivlighan and Shapiro (1987) also shows that it is important to consider client characteristics when formulating treatment strategies in career counseling. This study finds that the clients most likely to benefit from self-help career counseling are rated as realistic, conventional, and investigative on the Vocational Identity Scale of Holland's Vocation Situation (Holland, Daieger, & Power, 1980).

Oliver and Spokane (1988) suggest that future research on career intervention would gain a more realistic understanding of the counseling process by relying more on clients who have sought out career counseling and less on solicited clients who have responded to an ad. These authors also suggest that research efforts should include multiple outcome measures relating to career decision making, effective role functioning, and client satisfaction.

The Process of Career Counseling

Frank Parson was one of the first individuals to identify stages of career counseling. Parson (1909) described his three-stage approach as follows. To make an appropriate career decision, the person needs "(1) a clear understanding of aptitudes, abilities, interests, ambitions, resources, limitations, and their causes; (2) a knowledge of the requirements and conditions of success, advantages and disadvantages, compensations, opportunities, and prospects in different lines of work; and (3) true reasoning on the relations of these two groups of facts" (Parson, 1909, p. 5).

Salomone (1988) has added two stages to Parson's (1909) three-stage model. These additional stages focus on interventions that counselors can use after a client makes a career decision. The first stage involves helping the client implement educational and career decisions. This stage might involve helping the client with job-seeking skills and assisting with job placement. The second stage involves helping the newly employed individual adjust to the new job. This process might involve helping the client deal effectively with job stress, fear of failure, or other barriers to a successful job placement.

Salomone (1988) provides additional information on how to conceptualize these stages. He suggests that counselors do not necessarily have to proceed through these stages sequentially, but can work in several stages simultaneously. Salomone (1988) also notes that many counseling strategies are available for counselors to use in helping clients move through these stages. Some of these strategies are establishing a positive counseling relationship; helping clients assess their abilities and aptitudes regarding work, including promoting self-assessment; providing information about careers and the world of work; and offering assistance with career placement.

Special Issues

This section covers two special issues in career counseling: career counseling for women and computer-assisted career counseling.

Career Counseling for Women

A major criticism of career counseling is that the majority of its theories and approaches have been based on men and are therefore not sensitive to the special issues of women (Brooks, 1990). Several recent theories have attempted to make career counseling more responsive to the special needs of women. This section provides an overview of two theories and identifies their implications for career counseling for women.

Self-Efficacy Theory.   Self-efficacy, as described in Chapter 9, is the belief in one's ability to successfully perform a particular behavior (Bandura, 1986, 1989). Self-efficacy has been related to which behaviors will be initiated, the amount of effort that will be exerted, and how long the behavior will continue in the face of difficult circumstances (Luzzo, 1996). The origins of career self-efficacy can be traced to the work of Hackett and Betz (1981) and Betz and Hackett (1986). It can be broadly defined as the relationship between self-efficacy and various behaviors associated with career choice and adjustment (Lent & Hackett, 1987).

Hackett and Betz (1981) contend that self-efficicy theory has particular relevance to career counseling for women. A central factor to this position is that women and men acquire different efficacy expectations owing to differential gender-role experiences and limited access to efficacy information (Lent & Hackett, 1987). This in turn can contribute to the limited positions women hold in the labor force (Brooks, 1990). In addition, Bonett (1994) notes that the career aspirations of women may be restricted by the perception that they lack the necessary job-related skills associated with male-dominated professions and that pursuing those professions may be in conflict with home and family responsibilities.

Career self-efficacy has stimulated a wide range of research activity. Lent and Hackett (1987) have conducted a literature review of the research on career self-efficacy. The authors conclude that research has provided consistent support for the notion that "self-efficacy beliefs are predictive of important indices of career entry behavior such as college major choices and academic performance in certain fields" (Lent & Hackett, 1987, p. 362).

Morrow, Mullen and McElvoy (1990) describe two studies that identify gender differences in self-efficacy and career behavior. Matsui, Ikeda, and Ohnishi (1989) found that men report equal levels of self-efficacy in male- and female-dominated occupations, whereas women have higher self-efficacy perceptions in female-dominated fields than male-dominated occupations. A second study shows women have lower self-efficacy perceptions than men in mathematical activities although mathematical accomplishments are equivalent for men and women with similar preparatory backgrounds (Lapan, Boggs, & Morrill, 1989).

Watkins and Subich (1995) identify current trends in career self-efficacy research such as integrating career self-efficacy with social cognitive career models (for example, Lent, Brown, & Hackett, 1994, and Hackett & Byars, 1990) and the role of self-efficacy in work and nonwork settings as a coping mechanism (Matsui & Onglatco, 1992). Watkins and Subich (1995) conclude that career self-efficacy is a robust theoretical construct that has only begun to be realized.

Brooks (1990) describes implications of self-efficacy theory for career counseling for women. She suggests that its primary use could be to broaden career options for women and facilitate the pursuit of those options. Brooks (1990) also identifies several counseling strategies that can be used to promote these outcomes. These include cognitive strategies to help clients view their abilities more realistically; reattribution training to enable clients to attribute success to internal rather than external causes (Fosterling, 1980); the use of incremental graded success experiences (Lent & Hackett, 1987); vicarious learning, which can be promoted by arranging experiences for clients to "shadow" successful career women; and desensitization procedures to reduce anxiety that relates to career choice and performance.

Gottfredson's Theory.   Gottfredson's (1981) theory of occupational operations was one of the major vocational theories to emerge in the 1980s (Hesketh, Elmslie, & Kaldor, 1990) and applies to both men and women (Brooks, 1990). Hesketh, Elmslie, and Kaldor (1990) note that this theory is important to career counseling for women because it explains how compromise takes place in vocational decision making, identifies factors associated with social identity, and explores the difficulties that women face entering nontraditional careers.

Brooks (1990) identifies the following major principles associated with Gottfredson's (1981) model.

- People differentiate occupations in terms of sex type (job preferences relating to gender), work level, and field of work.
- People determine the appropriations of an occupation in terms of their self-concept.
- Self-concept factors that have vocational reliance include gender, social class, intelligence, values, interest, and abilities.
- Vocationally relevant self-concept factors emerge in the following developmental sequence. From age 3 to 5, individuals understand the concept of being an adult; from age 6 to 8, they develop the concept of gender; from age 9 to 13, they understand the abstract concepts of social class and intelligence; and beginning at age 14, they refine their attitudes, values, traits, and interests.
- People reject occupations on the basis of self-concept as they proceed through the developmental stages.
- The reasons for rejecting occupations have the following hierarchy. Individuals reject occupations when they are not suitable, first, in terms of gender; second, for social class and ability reasons; and third, on the basis of interests and values.
- Occupational preferences result from compatibility between the job and self-concept and from judgments about job accessibility.
- Compromise in job choice follows a predictable pattern. People will first sacrifice their interests, then prestige, and finally sex type, or job preferences related to gender.

Gottfredson's (1981) theory has stimulated a wide range of research activity. Brooks (1990) has identified several studies that provide general support for Gottfredson's (1981) model (Henderson, Hesketh, & Tuffin, 1988; Holt, 1989; Taylor & Pryor, 1985). Two more recent studies do not support Gottfredson's theory regarding the predictable nature of compromise in job choice. Leung and Plake (1990) found that prestige and not sex type is the most important factor in job choice. Hesketh, Elmslie, and Kaldor (1990) further challenge Gottfredson's (1981) position regarding the process of compromise. Results of their study suggest that interests incorporate attributes of prestige and sex type and are therefore the most important factor in job choice and compromise. Swanson (1992) and Watkins and Subich

(1995) have reviewed the literature on Gottfredson's theory and suggest that it is in need of modification in terms of the role of compromise in career decision making. They conclude that compromise appears to be a complex factor in career decision making, varying according to gender, sex-role attitudes, and interests.

Brooks (1990) identifies several implications of Gottfredson's (1981) theory for career counseling for women. First, Gottfredson's model suggests that clients may experience problems with indecision when they do not have an awareness of the effects of sex type, prestige, and interests on career choice and compromise. Counselors can assist these clients by helping them clarify their vocational priorities regarding these factors. Second, clients may need assistance in identifying occupations that are acceptable in terms of their self-concept. Third, clients may have aspirations that are incongruent with their abilities or interests. In these instances, counselors can evaluate the client's aspirations to determine whether the aspirations are associated with self-defeating processes, such as trying to live up to other people's standards.

Computer-Assisted Career Counseling

Computer-assisted career counseling (CACC) has become an important dimension to the delivery of career counseling in North America (Sampson, 1994). Although most clients can benefit from CACC, Kivlighan et al. (1994) have found that clients with stable goals make the most gain in vocational identity as the result of using CACC. Sampson (1994) identifies several factors that have contributed to the increased use of CACC. Some of these are reduced hardware costs, improved hardware and software capabilities such as color graphics and more comprehensive and diversified programs, and increased expertise by counselors and other professional helpers in using CACC.

Several authors have commented on the importance of including direct counseling services when utilizing computerized career counseling. Sampson, Shahnasarian, and Reardon (1987) identify the following problems that could occur when computerized career counseling is used without direct counselor contact: inappropriate clients can use the system, clients may not understand the purpose or operation of the system, and clients may not be able to integrate their computerized counseling experience into their decision-making process.

In addition, Johnston, Buescher, and Heppner (1988) note that ethical standards require orientation of information prior to and following administration of tests, including those utilized in computer-assisted career counseling programs. Dungy (1984) provides further support for the importance of direct counseling by noting that it enhances the effectiveness of subsequent computer-assisted program use.

CACC can be viewed as an adjunct to direct career counseling. It provides a useful starting point from which clients can gain information to narrow down their career choice (Sampson, 1994). Gati (1994) goes on to note counselors must monitor the client's use of CACC by engaging in an ongoing dialogue with the client and assisting with the integration and interpretation of information to foster appropriate decision making.

Numerous computerized career programs are currently available. Heppner and Johnston (1985), Maze (1984), and Zunker (1997) provide a description and comparative analysis of the major programs. Table 13.1 incorporates computer-assisted career programs described by Zunker (1997) and some of the most current programs available.

TABLE 13.1 Computerized Career Programs

Program Name	Publisher & Year	Program Overview	Special Features	Role of Counselor Client
Elementary Careers Software	Kansas Careers, 1988	Takes students on a tour of Careerville, traveling from building to building to explore different careers.	Suggestions for classroom activities are provided including games, puzzles, and practical problems relating to career issues.	Some aspects require assistance of a counselor or teacher.
Computerized Career Assessment and Planning Program (CCAPP)	Cambridge Career, 1989 (Updated every two years)	Assists with career assessment, selecting alternatives, career planning, and career exploration.	Information on over 1200 occupations; a list of college majors or vocational courses relating to career interest; and an individual career plan and a job-hunting plan.	Some aspects can be used independently by client, but counselors explain how a counselor can use the program to assist the client.
The Perfect Career	James Couyes, Mindscope, 1988	Assists with personal assessment, decision making, occupational exploration, and career planning.	Contains an interest/ability inventory of 144 sample work activities; career analysis; and suggested career goals based on scores in 12 career fields.	Can be used with minimal counselor assistance.
C-LECT	Chronicle Guidance, (Updated annually) 1991	Assists with career awareness, exploration, decision making, and educational planning.	Connects 14 school subjects with over 700 occupations; describes 717 occupations; has 5 self-assessment options; provides information on financial aid; and answers questions on specific colleges and universities.	Can be used with minimal counselor assistance.

Choices	Human Resources Development-Canada 1997	Assists with self-knowledge and assessment; career exploration, planning, and decision making.	Matches interest with careers; identifies schools that have programs and majors associated with career choice; and provides information on schools.	Can be used with minimal counselor assistance.
DISCOVER	The American College Testing Program, Version 4.3, 1990	Assists with career choice and decision-making skills; and enhances the general adjustment of the client.	Opportunities to take interest, ability, and value inventories, producing scores that are used to conduct job search and search for college majors or programs of study; provides information regarding various occupational fields and educational institutions.	Can be used in conjunction with career planning, curriculums, or workshops.
The Guidance and Information System (GIS)	Riverside, Houghton and Mifflin, 1991	Provides information on 1200 primary occupations and 3000 related occupations. Grouped according to the U.S. Office of Educational Occupational Clusters and the Dictionary of Occupational Titles (DOT).	Accessibility through a telephone and teletypewriter or display terminal that receives signals and prints or displays copy, thus does not require an institution to have its own computer.	Not designed to be the sole source of career and educational information but can be a meaningful tool for the career counselor.

The wide variety of computer-assisted career programs can overwhelm counselors, making it difficult to select one for use. Maze (1984) provides the following guidelines for selecting the most appropriate program.

- *Obtain staff input.* Perform a needs assessment with the staff, identifying areas that could be improved by computerized programs.
- *Obtain relevant information about the programs under consideration.* Evaluate each program in terms of cost, software packages, hardware requirements, and user population.
- *Arrange for demonstrations of software programs.* If possible, preview all software before purchasing a program.
- *Evaluate samples of the system's output.* Review sample printouts produced from each module or component of the system before deciding on a program.
- *Determine the total cost of the system.* Calculate the total cost of each software and hardware system under consideration.
- *Determine the cost per user.* Calculate the maximum, minimum, and average estimates for potential users to determine the cost-effectiveness of the system.
- *Determine one-time charges and ongoing charges.* Examples of one-time charges are the cost of a printer and a telephone adapter. Ongoing charges include the costs of renewing software packages and maintaining equipment. There may also be ongoing expenses associated with mainframe or centralized systems that should be determined.

Diversity Issues in Career Counseling

Diversity issues such as culture, socioeconomic status, education, gender, age, and sexual preference are becoming increasingly important in career counseling. Hackett and Byars (1996) note that there are no comprehensive models of career development for ethnic and racial minorities. Practitioners must therefore take care when extrapolating from theory to practice and infuse culturally sensitive issues when appropriate. Arbona (1996) believes that education and socioeconomic status are critical variables in the utility of career-counseling theories with ethnic minorities. Arbona (1996) suggests that career-counseling theories can be useful cross-culturally with individuals who are progressing educationally or those who are middle or upper class. On the other hand, career-counseling theories that emphasize career choice appear to have less utility for individuals who live in poverty and/or are school dropouts. In these instances, a more appropriate approach may be to foster cognitive, academic, and socioemotional development (Arbona, 1996).

Leong and Chou (1994) have identified additional cultural considerations in career counseling that relate to Asian Americans and other ethnic minorities. They contend that identity development, acculturation, and assimilation are key variables in career counseling that can impact prejudice, stress, and educational and career aspirations and expectations. For example, Asian Americans who rate low on acculturation and assimilation tend to score high on perceived prejudice and stress. Issues of prejudice and stress should therefore be monitored and addressed with these individuals as potential barriers to career counseling.

Asian Americans also tend to suffer the highest degree of career stereotyping and segregation of all minorities. Asians tend to be perceived as having skills in the fields of science and mathematics but not in careers that emphasize language and interpersonal relations. It is therefore not surprising that they are underrepresented in careers such as law and overrepresented in science and engineering. Acculturation and assimilation levels may be important intervening variables in this process. Individuals who have low levels of acculturation appear to be more vulnerable to the adverse effects of stereotyping and segregation than people who have assimilated more into mainstream society. In this regard, movement toward assimilation and acculturation may promote a corresponding stage of identity development that rejects stereotypical views of career choice and decision making.

Asian Americans, African Americans, and Hispanics experience a potential career barrier that relates to educational and career aspirations and expectations. These individuals tend to experience a higher discrepancy between their educational and career aspirations (for example, goals) and the degree to which they expect to achieve these goals. This discrepancy is owing in part to perceived education and career barriers associated with discrimination against minorities. Career counselors must therefore be cognizant of these perceptions and associated issues such as problems with motivation and discouragement. In addition, counselors can take a proactive role in helping clients overcome discriminatory practices that are having adverse effects on clients.

Gender issues are perhaps more important in career counseling than in other specialty areas of counseling. This is in part owing to a long history of sexual discrimination in the work force and practices of sex-role stereotyping with its adverse consequences on career choice and decision making. Self-efficacy theory and Gottfredson's theory are described earlier in this chapter as theories that can be useful in addressing career issues in women. For example, Hackett and Byars (1996) have found that one of the most important issues that career counselors should address when working with African American women is how experiences of racism impact on their self-efficacy expectations.

Age is another important consideration in career counseling. Career counseling has historically focused on helping high-school-age students with the process of career choice and decision making. In a rapidly changing technological world and an era where people are living longer, it is becoming increasingly common for individuals to change careers numerous times throughout their life span. Career counseling is therefore broadening its base to include a life-span perspective. Watts (1996) suggests that the concept of career needs to be redefined in order to facilitate the developmental perspective in career counseling.

According to Watts (1996) the old concept of career as a progression up a hierarchical ladder within a profession or organization is obsolete. Watts (1996) suggests that a more realistic concept of career is that it is a subjective experience that is a lifelong progression in learning and work. This definition recognizes that people are ultimately responsible for defining their existence in terms of the world of work, and the focus of their experience is on what they have learned and what they have contributed in their work. Seligman (1994) provides additional information regarding the theory, research, and practice of career counseling across the life span (childhood, adolescence, early adulthood, middle adulthood, and late adulthood). For example, self-esteem enhancement and career education can be important components of career counseling with children and postretirement issues of work and leisure can become a focus in career counseling during late adulthood.

Issues of sexual orientation represent another example of diversity in career counseling. It is especially important for career counselors to be aware of the special career issues that relate to lesbian, gay, and bisexual individuals. Sexual orientation and degree of openness relating to sexuality (for example, being open about one's homosexuality) can influence the type of job and work environment one chooses (Chung, 1995). Unfortunately, there has been a lack of theoretical development regarding the career development of lesbian, gay, and bisexual individuals (Chung, 1995). Several researchers have attempted to fill this void, such as Fassinger's (1995) study on lesbian identity in the workplace and Prince's study of career development of gay men. For example, Fassinger's research describes how lesbian women's identity development and theoretical constructs of vocational psychology of women could be integrated with vocational issues of lesbians. Fassinger goes on to provide useful information regarding career counseling with lesbians that can help sensitize counselors to lesbian issues. For example, lesbians do not tend to rely on men for financial support and therefore tend to seek employment where they can be more financially independent than their heterosexual female counterparts.

Summary

Career counseling is represented by several emerging issues such as the use of computer technology in career counseling. Popular career programs are described along with information that can aid in selection of computer software. Diversity issues such as gender, age, culture, and sexual orientation must also be carefully considered in career counseling. This chapter provides an overview of diversity issues with considerable attention directed at women's issues in career counseling.

CHAPTER

14 School Counseling

CHAPTER OVERVIEW

This chapter provides an overview of the issues relating to school counseling. Highlights of the chapter include

- The art and science of school counseling
- A comprehensive developmental model for guidance and counseling
- The role and function of school counselors
- Special skills and problems, including counseling exceptional students
- Future trends in school counseling

The Art and Science of School Counseling

School counseling is an art and science. It is an art to try to reach a reluctant or resistant student who has problems with drugs, gang involvement, and family. School counselors work closely with community agencies and organizations and consult with parents, teachers, and staff to provide services for these and other problems that students face. The art of counseling suggests that school counselors be sensitive to individual differences and embrace diversity as an opportunity to expand educational horizons. Flexibility and creativity is another dimension of the art of counseling. In this regard, counselors can adjust their counseling approach by using innovative strategies such as play therapy (Campbell, 1993), music therapy (Newcomb, 1994), and sand play (Carmichael, 1994).

The science of school counseling complements the art of counseling by offering the objective-scientific dimension to the counseling process. One research study provides empirical support for the science of school counseling. A meta-analysis of school counseling research suggests that school counseling activities (such as individual and group counseling) play an important role in enhancing students' academic and personal development (Borders & Drury, 1992). Baker (1995) notes that qualitative research such as the use of semistructured interviews is an emerging trend in school counseling research. These more naturalistic forms of research offer a practical alternative to the more traditional statistical hypothesis testing associated with quantitative research. Capuzzi (1988) emphasizes that research has an essential role in the future of school counseling. He identifies nine problem areas that students commonly face: self-esteem, eating disorders, child and adolescent suicide, depression, teenage pregnancy, drug abuse, physical and sexual abuse, stress, and divorced parents. The author notes that a school counselor's expertise on these issues is critical because the problems present roadblocks to children's psychosocial development. He suggests that additional research is required for school counselors to deal effectively with these problems.

A Comprehensive Developmental Model for School Counseling

The recent literature suggests that school counseling should be conceptualized in terms of a comprehensive developmental model (Paisley & Benshoff, 1996; Paisley & Borders, 1995; & Paisley & DeAngelis-Peace, 1995). The term *comprehensive* refers to the notion that school counseling programs should function as an integrated part of a K–12 program, not as separate entities. The *developmental* focus suggests that school counseling programs should be organized from a life-span perspective. Developmental school counseling represents a shift from remediation and crisis intervention to learning and development (Paisley & DeAngelis-Peace, 1995). "The developmental program is proactive and preventive, helping students acquire the knowledge, skills, self-awareness, and attitudes necessary for successful mastery of normal developmental tasks" (Paisley & DeAngelis-Peace, p. 87, 1995).

Robert Myrick and Norman Gysbers are two individuals who have played key roles in formulating comprehensive developmental school counseling. Myrick (1987) has identified a number of goals and objectives of his model that show counselors to be focused on personal and social development, decision making and problem solving, career education, and educational planning. Gysbers (Good et al., 1994) notes that unique features of his model include information on student competencies, organizational framework, resources, time management, developmental linking from K–12 and linking between counseling and administration, and a comprehensive evaluation program. Gysbers spent considerable time developing his program in 75 schools in Missouri between 1984 and 1988, resulting in his model being referred to as the Missouri model (Good et al., 1994). Gysbers estimates that the Missouri model is being used in some form in approximately 30 states in the United States.

Neukrug et al. (1993) set forth a developmental school counseling and guidance model that has been supported by the American School Counseling Association (ASCA). It was designed as a simple yet flexible model that school counselors could use to address the special needs of the students they serve. The model is grounded in developmental theory, encouraging counselors to implement interventions consistent with students' developmental tasks. It is a proactive model "whose primary emphasis is fostering the learning and growth of all students, with a secondary emphasis on assisting individual students with the resolution of special problems and concerns" (Neukrug et al., 1993, p. 358).

Bergin et al. (1990) identified some of the states that have comprehensive K–12 developmental guidance programs: Arkansas, Illinois, Iowa, Missouri, New Hampshire, North Carolina, Ohio, Oklahoma, and Wisconsin. A limited amount of research has been conducted to evaluate these programs. A study by Bergin et al. (1990) evaluated a developmental guidance model called *Building Skills for Tomorrow* (Oklahoma State Department of Education, 1988) that was being implemented in a rural school district. The study found that the program elicited positive responses from parents, teachers, and community leaders.

Hughey, Gysbers, and Starr (1993) provide additional support for the comprehensive developmental model for school counseling. These scholars surveyed the attitudes of students, teachers, and parents regarding the Missouri Comprehensive Guidance Program. Results of the survey indicate that school counselors were perceived as caring individuals that students could freely go to for assistance for career and college planning and individual and group counseling. In addition, students, parents, and teachers believed that schools should hire additional school counselors.

Paisley and Borders (1995) contend that school counselors have had difficulty implementing comprehensive developmental school-counseling programs because they do not clearly understand the concept and have difficulty translating these ideas into practice. Paisley and Benshoff (1996) identify the knowledge and skills necessary to implement a comprehensive developmental school-counseling program. Knowledge necessary for program implementation includes being well grounded in developmental theory (including understanding how change occurs); being familiar with programs such as peer helping programs, which have successfully fostered development; and being aware of emerging strategies such as person-to-environment fit (Paisley & DeAngelis-Peace, 1995). Skills to promote program implementation include using developmental theory in assessment to determine appropriate interventions and skills in consultation with parents and teachers. Other new strategies include dilemma discussions to help students explore difficult situations and the reasoning they use relative to their choices (Paisley & Benshoff, 1996).

Casey (1995) suggests that technology could play a key role in the implementation of developmental school counseling. Casey contends that modern technology must be integrated into all aspects of the school-counseling program (for example, individual counseling, small- and large-group counseling, and consultation). Casey provides examples of how technologies such as interactive CD-ROM and the Internet can be used with students of different ages. For example, a possible technology strategy with 10-year-olds is to develop a technology club, since fostering friendships is an important priority of students at this age.

A Developmental Perspective

The developmental perspective is central to the comprehensive developmental school-counseling model. This perspective represents a shift from an orientation of counselors as clinicians to a role of counselors promoting prevention (Gysbers & Henderson, 1988). In this role, counselors work closely with teachers to promote developmental guidance and counseling as an integral aspect of the overall school program. Myrick (1987) notes that the goals of developmental school counseling can never be fully realized unless teachers take an active role in offering guidance activities in the classroom.

Several individuals have applied the developmental perspective to counseling theories, for example, Blocher's (1974, 1987) developmental counseling and Ivey's (1986) developmental therapy. These theories suggest that counselors should first identify a client's developmental level and then implement an approach that addresses the needs for that level. Developmental counseling approaches incorporate various theories of development. Ivey

(1986) emphasizes Piaget's (1955) theory of cognitive development, whereas Blocher (1974, 1987) focuses on Havighurst's (1972) concept of developmental tasks and Erikson's (1963) psychosocial theory. Developmental theories are becoming increasingly sensitive to diversity issues such as Carol Gilligan's (1982) seminal work on gender issues in moral development.

Blocher's (1974) model suggests that there are certain developmental tasks associated with each stage of development. In addition, clients must master coping skills to meet the challenges of these tasks to successfully move forward to the next developmental task. Blocher (1974) contends that counseling goals and strategies can be developed to help individuals master the necessary coping skills as they proceed through the life span.

According to Blocher (1974, 1987), elementary school students face the developmental tasks of industry and initiative. These tasks can be facilitated by counseling goals that help students implement activities on their own and feel competent when competing with peers. Counselors can promote industry and initiative in students by helping them value themselves and feel a sense of control over their environment. Counseling strategies (such as consultation, and individual and group counseling) that foster self-concept development and encouragement can be used to facilitate these counseling goals.

Blocher's (1974, 1987) theory can also be applied to middle school students. The main developmental task during these years is identity formation. Counseling goals can be developed to assist with this task, such as helping students enhance their self-awareness and clarify their values. Consultation, and individual and group counseling can be used to address these issues as well as other problems that require attention.

The primary developmental task for high school students is intimacy. This task requires developing the skills necessary to establish close, trusting relationships with siblings, peers, parents, and others. The counseling goals associated with this task include promoting students' concern and interest in others and enhancing interpersonal relationship skills. Consultation, individual counseling and group counseling that focuses on social-skills training can be particularly useful as a strategy to promote interpersonal effectiveness.

An overview of these developmental tasks, counseling goals, and associated counseling strategies according to Blocher's model is provided in Table 14.1.

The developmental tasks and their associated counseling goals and strategies shown in Table 14.1 can be useful in providing a focus for counseling services. At the same time, counselors should not limit their programs to these tasks and related counseling strategies. A comprehensive developmental school-counseling program should address the wide array of issues that concern school-age children, for example, divorced parents, drug and alcohol abuse, and teenage pregnancy.

Role and Function of School Counselors

One of the most controversial issues in school counseling has been the role and function of school counselors. The controversy has centered around the difficulties that school counselors have faced in trying to establish a clear professional identity (Paisley & Borders, 1995) and what steps should be taken to overcome these problems. One way to make a clear statement about the role and function of school counselors is to describe the main mission of school

TABLE 14.1   Developmental Tasks, Goals, and Counseling Strategies

Age Level	Developmental Tasks	Counseling Goals	Counseling Strategy
Elementary School	Industry and initiative	Foster independence and self-autonomy	Consultation, and individual and group counseling to promote self-concept development; encouragement strategies to help students believe in their capabilities and implement activities on their own; and self-control interventions for students whose impulse control interferes with their ability to complete tasks
Middle School	Identity formation	Help students gain a clear understanding of who they are as individuals	Consultation, and individual and group counseling to promote self-awareness and value clarification
High School	Intimacy	Promote social interest and interpersonal effectiveness	Consultation and individual, group, and family counseling to promote social interest and compassion for others. Group counseling to foster interpersonal effectiveness. Career counseling to relate to the world of work

counseling in terms of enhancement of learning. Ultimately, all school counseling activities maximize learning potential in students. For example, self-concept and school achievement has been shown to have a positive correlation (Hamachek, 1995). Therefore, a counselor that enhances a student's self-concept will contribute to the student's learning potential.

This section addresses the central issues associated with the school counselor's role and function, such as counseling from a historical perspective, the current ASCA role statement, and the role and function of school counselors working in elementary, middle, and high schools and in rural schools.

A Historical Perspective

A historical perspective can be useful for understanding how the school counselor's role and function have evolved. Gysbers (1988) has provided a description of the history of school counseling, and his observations have been incorporated into the following overview.

The period from 1909 to 1920 represents the beginning of school counseling as a specialty. Its origins can be traced to the pioneering work of Frank Parsons (1909), who provided vocational guidance services in schools.

During the 1920s the emphasis shifted from vocational guidance to assistance with personal adjustment.

The 1930s was an era in which there was an attempt to differentiate guidance from vocational guidance. The term *guidance* was broadly defined as assisting individuals with problems of adjusting to any aspect of life, including health or family and friends as well as work. *Vocational guidance* was more narrowly defined as helping people with choice, preparation, placement, and advancement in a vocation. During this period, school counselors also began to use more formal terms, for example, counseling, assessment, information, placement, and follow-up, to describe what occurred in the helping process.

The counseling profession experienced the initial impact of Carl Rogers' views of counseling in the 1940s. Rogers' (1942) *Counseling and Psychotherapy* had a dramatic effect on the role and function of the school counselor. His person-centered approach provided a theoretical framework for personal counseling and resulted in school counselors utilizing a clinical emphasis in their overall role and function. Rogers' work continues to have a major impact on contemporary school counselors as they attempt to assist students with an ever-increasing array of personal problems.

During the 1950s support for school counselors increased with the passage of Public Law 85–864, the National Defense Education Act. This act allocated funds for colleges and universities to train students to become secondary school counselors.

In the 1960s the focus shifted from guidance as adjustment to developmental guidance. Developmental guidance stresses the importance of understanding and working with students from a developmental perspective. It also places greater emphasis on preventing the occurrence of problems rather than merely helping students adjust to their existing problems. School counselors continue to utilize the developmental perspective.

The 1970s involved an expansion of the developmental perspective to include a K–12 comprehensive developmental guidance model. During this period, there was also a national effort to integrate career education into the overall school program. This effort was met with resistance from some teachers and administrators because they believed it took valuable time away from necessary academic endeavors. Career education therefore had limited success in terms of being integrated into the public schools. The passage of Public Law 94-142, the Education for All Handicapped Children Act, in 1975 (Public Law 94-142, 1975) also affected the role of the school counselor. As a result of this act, school counselors expanded their role to include coordinating the testing and placement of exceptional students and assisting with the development and implementation of individual education programs for each student. Another force that impacted the role and function of the school counselor during this period was the use of personal computers in scoring tests, scheduling, and career counseling. In addition, school counselors began to incorporate group counseling in their guidance and counseling programs in the early 1970s.

During the 1980s career guidance received renewed federal support. The Carl D. Perkins Vocational Education Act was passed in 1984 in response to the belief that public schools were not providing adequate preparation for students to obtain employment or continue post-secondary education. Several states have utilized funds from the Perkins bill to develop K–12 counseling and guidance programs. To qualify for these funds, states must provide opportunities for students to acquire employability skills. Another force that occurred in the 1980s was an awareness of the importance of multicultural issues in counseling. School counselors therefore began to modify their counseling approaches to include a multicultural perspective.

The decade of the 1980s was also a time of changes in the fabric of society that dramatically affected school-age children. During this period, school counselors witnessed substantial increases in divorce, suicides, drug and alcohol abuse, teenage pregnancies, and eating disorders. School counselors invested increasing amounts of energy in implementing prevention and treatment programs addressing these complex issues. Some examples are drug prevention and awareness programs, group counseling for children of alcoholics and children of divorce, parent education, and family counseling. Also during this time, financially conscious educational systems began to scrutinize the effectiveness of school counseling. As a result, schools placed greater emphasis on counselor accountability.

School counseling in the 1990s faced many opportunities and challenges. Counselors continued to deal with an ongoing array of social problems that students faced, such as drug use, violence in the schools, teenage pregnancy, and school dropout. Diversity issues were also emphasized as counselors conceptualized their role and function.

Numerous challenges and opportunities face school counselors in the twenty-first century. One central challenge relates to job security for school counselors. Paisley and Borders (1995) note that one threat to school counselors is the trend toward downsizing and the movement to hire part-time employees to provide school counseling. The school-based mental-health movement is one example of how external funding is being used to bring in people from different disciplines in the helping profession to provide counseling services in schools.

The American School Counselor Association (ASCA) is taking a role in defining the role of a school counselor as a distinct and vital educational professional. The National Standards for School Counseling Programs (Cambell & Dahir, 1997) provides vision and goals for school counseling into the twenty-first century (Dahir, 1997). It will be a useful frame of reference for promoting quality school counseling programs on a national level (Dahir, 1997).

Increased federal legislation (especially regarding students with exceptionalities) and other legal considerations are also having a major impact on education and the role and function of school counselors as we enter the twenty-first century. For example, school counselors must be aware of the impact of legislative acts such as Section 504 of the Rehabilitation Act and the Individuals with Disabilities Education Act (IDEA) to ensure that issues of disability are considered in the educational process, including the manner students are disciplined.

The Current ASCA Role Statement, Definition, and Standards

In 1990 the ASCA revised its role statement of 1981. A significant change in the revised statement was the absence of the earlier differentiation in the role and function of counselors working in elementary, middle, and high schools. Instead, the statement identified five interventions that apply to all school counselors. The motivation for this change was to promote a clearer and more concise understanding of the overall role and function of school counselors.

In the statement, the ASCA recognized and supported the comprehensive developmental guidance and counseling model. In this regard, school counselors should adjust the counseling approach to the developmental levels of students as they progress through the educational system. The aim of school counseling is to promote educational, social, career, and personal development so that students can become responsible, productive citizens.

The statement also identified five basic interventions common to all school counselors. These are individual counseling; small-group counseling, which involves five to eight students; large-group guidance, which includes nine or more students such as in a classroom; consultation; and coordination of the counseling program.

More recently, in 1997 ASCA adopted a new definition of school counseling.

> Counseling is a process of helping people by assisting them in making decisions and changing behavior. School counselors work with all students, school staff, families, and members of the community as an integral part of the education program. School counseling programs promote school success through a focus on academic achievement, prevention and intervention activities, advocacy and social/emotional and career development.

This definition of school counseling is consistent with the comprehensive developmental school-counseling movement, which is focused on prevention and maximizing the learning potential of all students.

As noted earlier, Campell and Dahir (1977) assisted ACA in setting forth National Standards for School Counseling. The national standards conceptualize school counseling in terms of academic, career, and personal/social development. It provides a clear description of the elements and components of a comprehensive K–12 developmental school-counseling program. The standards provide a useful framework for counselor educators and school counselors to develop, organize, implement, and evaluate school counseling services. It is hoped that the National Standards will provide a clear description of concepts and tools necessary for all students to move forward toward their optimal development.

Role and Function by Grade Level and Setting

The literature provides extensive information about the specific goals and strategies for school counselors working with students at various levels and in various settings. For example, Hardesty and Dillard (1994) surveyed 369 school counselors in terms of the activities they perform at elementary, middle, and high school. Results of the survey showed that elementary school counselors focus on consulting with teachers, staff, and parents and engage in small- and large-group guidance programs that have a preventative focus (for example, drug prevention). Middle school counselors direct their efforts primarily on relationships counseling (such on conflict resolution between students). Scheduling and other administrative tasks also rated high on the middle school counselors' activity list. High school counselors' top priorities include assisting with college or trade school admission (including help with scholarships and financial aid), career counseling, and scheduling and other administrative tasks. More specific information regarding the role and function of elementary, middle, and high school counselors follows.

Elementary School Counseling.   Elementary school includes students from kindergarten through the fifth grade. The emphasis of elementary school counseling is on prevention (Muro, 1981). In this regard, counselors spend a large percentage of their time consulting with teachers and parents to promote the child's mental health and in group guidance activities (such as self-concept development).

Several authors have attempted to describe the role and function of elementary school counselors. Morse and Russell (1988) surveyed 130 elementary school counselors in terms of how they perceive their current role and their ideal role. Their findings are summarized in Table 14.2, with actual and ideal roles each shown in rank order of importance to counselors.

Three interesting observations can be made from the survey results shown in Table 14.2. First, three of the top five functions listed as actual roles involve consultation. Second, these counselors ranked the function of helping teachers understand students' needs first as an ideal role, but only fourth as a function they currently perform. Third, four of the top five ideal roles indicate these counselors want to engage in more group counseling involving activities such as social-skills training. Results of this study emphasize the importance of elementary school counselors obtaining skills in consultation and group counseling.

Ginter, Scalise, and Presse (1990) conducted a study that surveyed 313 teachers in terms of their perceptions of elementary school counselors' role and function. Results of this study show that teachers view elementary school counselors as functioning primarily with the dual role of helper and consultant. The helper role entails activities such as individual and group counseling, assessment, interpreting tests, and conducting guidance activities. The consultant role involves providing technical advice and expertise to school staff and parents. The authors conclude that there appears to be congruence between how teachers and elementary school counselors view their role and function.

TABLE 14.2   Actual Versus Ideal Roles of Elementary School Counselors

Rank Order of Actual Role	Rank Order of Ideal Role
Assist students with special needs by making appropriate educational referrals	Assist the teacher to better understand the needs of individual students
Work with school psychologist and educational specialist to meet the special needs of individual students	Provide group counseling to help students learn effective social skills
Provide individual counseling for students to help them understand their feelings	Work with students in groups to promote a positive self-concept
Help teachers better understand the needs of individual students	Counsel students in groups to help them become aware of their feelings
Work with students individually to promote a positive self-concept	Conduct groups to help students learn problem-solving skills

Note. Reprinted from Morse, C. L. and Russell, T., "How Elementary Counselors See Their Role: An Empirical Study," 1988, *Elementary School Guidance & Counseling, 23*(1), pp. 44-62. © ACA. Reprinted with permission. No further reproduction authorized without permission of the American Counseling Association.

In another study, Miller (1989) surveyed teachers, principals, and parents to determine their views regarding the role and function of elementary school counselors. The survey identifies 28 functions that elementary school counselors were believed to fulfill. These functions related to six tasks: developmental or career guidance, consulting, counseling, evaluation and assessment, guidance program development, and coordination and management. Results of the survey show that teachers, principals, and parents strongly endorse these six tasks as being relevant functions for elementary school counselors. Miller (1989) believes the study provided grass-roots support for a developmental model of elementary school guidance and counseling. These studies collectively show recognition of the importance of the developmental model of counseling and the necessity for elementary school counselors to develop skills in direct services such as group counseling.

A Personal Note

I enjoyed working as an elementary school counselor. I liked the diversity of activities, which included play therapy, counseling, consulting, and working with parents. I also found children fun and exciting to work with, because they are so open, spontaneous, and interested in exploring the world around them.

When I work with children, I feel a sense of optimism that real and lasting changes can be made.

Their problems have usually not yet become well-established facets of their personality. I firmly believe that early intervention can prevent children's problems from blossoming into major mental disorders and prevent them from becoming school dropouts. I often think that more of the educational and mental health budget should be invested in elementary school counseling. In the long run, I think it would be the most effective approach.

Middle School Counseling.   The middle school phenomenon is a relatively recent occurrence. This level of schooling provides educational opportunities for students from sixth through eighth grades. This concept evolved from the junior high educational system, which encompassed grades 7 through 9. The middle school concept represents an attempt to group students together as they make their transition from childhood to adolescence.

The literature shows that the role and function of the middle school counselor are just beginning to be formulated. As a result, it is not surprising that less research has been conducted on middle school counseling than on elementary and high school counseling (St. Clair, 1989). Bonebrake and Borgers (1984) conducted a study in which they compared the ideal role of middle school counselors as perceived by counselors and principals. Their results show essential agreement between the perceptions of counselors and principals. Both groups ranked individual counseling first in importance. Other tasks ranked high by both groups include consultation, coordination of student assessment, interpretation of tests, and evaluation of guidance programs. This study suggests that middle school counseling is similar to elementary school counseling in terms of the emphasis on consultation and direct services. One difference is that middle school counseling appears to place emphasis on individual counseling, whereas elementary school counseling stresses the importance of group counseling.

Conflict-resolution skills are important for all students. Middle school students seem to be particularly prone to problems with interpersonal conflict such as jealous reactions within peer groups. Conflict-resolution strategies can be used with couples, small groups, or a classroom. Dysinger (1993) provides some goals and objectives for conflict resolution for middle school students. These are summarized as follows. The overall goal is for the participants to attempt to create a win-win experience based on understanding, accepting disagreements, and working toward resolution, not establishing who is right and wrong. The actual process of conflict management can involve tasks such as helping students separate the problem from the person, enhance tolerance for individual differences, create insight into how relationships deteriorate, learn how to sensitively respond to conflict rather than abrasively react, and become aware of choices and options.

One method of conflict resolution that can be used in a classroom is the inside-outside fishbowl approach (Nelson, Thomas, & Pierce, 1995). This is an Adlerian-based approach that attempts to foster encouragement and mutual respect among the students. The process involves a facilitator working with a small group of students in a time-limited focused discussion on a topic of concern while the rest of the class listens and provides feedback at the end of the discussion. The fishbowl approach can create opportunities to gain a broad perspective for understanding and resolving conflicts. As in all group work, issues regarding confidentiality and informed consent must be addressed.

Secondary School Counseling. The origins of secondary school counseling can be traced to the vocational guidance movement that began in the early 1900s. Since that time, secondary school counseling has maintained a close identity with vocational and career guidance and counseling. The role and function of secondary school counselors have centered around assisting students in making the transition from public school to post-secondary education, acquiring vocational training, and entering the world of work.

Secondary school counselors tend to be assigned numerous clerical tasks, including scheduling and administrative functions such as assistance with the disciplinary program. The result has been a loss of clear mission (Aubrey, 1982) and a "role mutation" that has seriously damaged the professional image of school counselors (Peer, 1985). Hutchinson, Barrick, and Groves (1986) provide evidence of the role mutation phenomenon cited by Peer (1985) in a study that compared actual and ideal functions of secondary school counselors. According to the study, counselors believe they should ideally provide the traditional counseling activities of personal, academic, and group counseling. In actual practice, scheduling requires more time than any activity except for personal counseling. The authors conclude that counselors are performing noncounseling activities at the expense of more important functions such as group counseling, career and life planning, and classroom guidance. Tennyson et al. (1989) provide support for this observation by noting that scheduling of students appears to be taking a higher priority over the critical functions of promoting developmental guidance and counseling.

When high school counselors do engage in direct counseling services, they are often unable to invest the necessary time and energy because of the large numbers of students and conflicting role demands. Rowe (1989) surveyed the type and extent of involvement high school counselors have with senior high school students. He found that counselors had sessions with 80 percent of the students who went to college. The primary purpose of their contact was to assist with college plans. Unfortunately, counselors averaged only two sessions with each student for a total of 15 minutes. These students received the largest number of contacts—approximately five—regarding college planning from parents and friends. Results of this study suggest that high school counselors are not providing sufficient information about college planning even though it is the main topic they are addressing with senior high school students (Rowe, 1989).

Rural School Counseling.   The role and function of school counseling varies not only according to educational level but also in terms of rural versus urban settings. Sutton and Southworth (1990) report that rural counselors have fewer referral sources and must therefore rely on their own resources and become jacks-of-all-trades. This situation can contribute to rural counselors experiencing more job-related stress than urban school counselors (Sutton & Southworth, 1990). At the same time, they feel more freedom, strength, optimism, and happiness than urban counselors (Sutton & Southworth, 1990). In addition, rural school counselors tend to have more positive relationships with their principals than urban counselors (Sutton & Southworth, 1990). These relationships may result from rural counselors having more contact and involvement with their principals than urban counselors (McIntire, Marion, & Quaglia, 1990).

McIntire, Marion, and Quaglia (1990) note that 40 percent of rural counselors do not work with other counselors and must therefore develop their own support systems. They also suggest that for counselors to be successful in rural settings, they must be aware of the special needs and circumstances of the community and become actively involved in the community.

Rubisch (1995) notes that students in rural schools face special challenges in terms of promoting postsecondary education. Three interrelated problems are academic runoff, low self-esteem, and low career expectations. Academic runoff involves the brightest students leaving the rural community and not returning, which reduces the amount of role models and mentors available for students. This in turn can have an adverse effect on student's self-esteem and career expectations. Rubisch contends that rural school counselors can play a pivotal role in enhancing student's career aspirations by exposing them to postsecondary educational alternatives in junior and middle school, including field trips to college campuses.

Special Skills and Problems

This section discusses the special skills and problems associated with school counseling. These include consultation, counseling exceptional students, and some of the special problems that students face: drug abuse, teenage pregnancy, divorced or single parents, and dropping out of school.

Consultation

Dougherty (1995) defines consultation as "a process in which a human service professional assists a consultee with a work-related (or caretaking-related) problem with a client system, with the goal of helping both the consultee and the client system in some specified way" (p. 9). The individual who functions as a consultee will vary according to the situation and

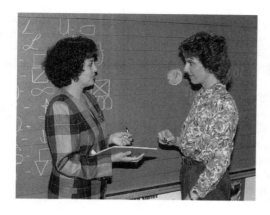

Consultation with teachers is an integral aspect of school counseling.

may be a parent or teacher requesting assistance on how to provide effective discipline for a child so the child can function better at home or school.

Dougherty's (1995) four stages of consultation are summarized as follows.

Stage One: Entry.   Consultation begins with the consultant formulating a relationship with the consultee, determining the nature of the problem, and formulating a contract regarding the nature and scope of the consultation activities.

Stage Two: Diagnosis.   Diagnosis involves making an assessment of the problem and determining possible goals and objectives.

Stage Three: Implementation.   Once a diagnosis is made, an action plan can be formulated, implemented, and evaluated.

Stage Four: Disengagement.   When the goals and objectives have been met, consultation processes can allow for a natural process of disengagement or "winding down" of services.

Dougherty (1995) also identifies the following three models of consultation.

1. *Organizational Consultation* conceptualizes the problem and directs interventions from a systems or organizational perspective.
2. *Mental Health Consultation* conceptualizes the problem and directs interventions with the goal of enhancing mental health of individuals within their organizational structure.
3. *Behavioral Consultation* takes a behavioral perspective (such as social learning theory) in terms of conceptualizing problems and implementing interventions.

Dougherty (1995) notes that these three models are interrelated, and that all consultation to some degree utilizes all three perspectives (that is, focuses on behaviors and the overall system to enhance mental health).

School Consultation.   Hall and Lin (1994) note that consultation is one of the primary functions of the school counselors and involves providing assistance to teachers, parents, and administrators. Hall and Lin developed an integrative model of school consultation based on Dougherty's (1995) four-stage model of consultation (entry, diagnosis, implementation, and disengagement). These authors address some special considerations in school consultation, such as potential confusion in terms of role expectations since the consultant and consultee will typically know each other and work in the same building (for example, counselor-teacher or counselor-administrator). In these instances, they recommend that expectations be made clear during the entry phase of consultation and that the use of empathy, genuineness, respect, and concreteness be used to facilitate this process.

Hall and Lin (1994) suggest that consultation is especially important to the role and function of elementary school counselors. To a large degree, the success of consultation in elementary school can be traced to the pioneering work of Don Dinkmeyer and Jon Carlson. They were able to demonstrate how Adlerian principles could be used effectively in consulting with teachers, administrators, and parents (Dinkmeyer & Carlson, 1973). Dinkmeyer (1971, 1973) developed a collaborative model of consultation called the "C" group model, which can be used with groups of parents and teachers. The "C" group model was designed to create a channel for communication regarding issues pertaining to children, for example, how to deal with children's misbehavior. It was so-called because the forces that operate in the group begin with the letter "C": collaboration, consultation, clarification, confrontation, communication, concern, caring, confidentiality, change, and cohesion.

Opportunities exist for school counselors to provide consultation services at all levels of public schools. Griggs (1988) suggests that school counselors should expand their consultation role to become facilitators of learning. Ferris (1988) also notes that consultation is needed to provide safe, secure, and positive learning environments.

Ritchie and Partin (1994) have conducted a survey of school counselors on the merits of parent education as a consultative service. Results of the survey show wide support for parent education among school counselors. Although 84 percent of the school counselors surveyed recognized the need for parenting consultation, only half have offered training and have an interest in providing this service. There appears to be a gender and grade-level bias in parent education, with more female counselors expressing interest and higher levels of involvement associated with elementary school counseling. Perhaps counselor educators need to focus more on this form of school consultation to enhance involvement in this area.

The following *Personal Note* describes some of the rewards I have experienced in consultation in schools.

A Personal Note

Some of my most rewarding experiences over the years have involved consultation with teachers, parents, and staff. It is really exciting to see these individuals gain skills and confidence that they can use to overcome problems and enhance their life experiences. I see consultation as having the goal of educating for empowerment. In this process I attempt to share information and strategies in a manner that can be easily understood and applied. I begin with sharing tools for understanding problems (such as why children misbehave) because I believe that understanding should always be a prerequisite to change. In addition, I contend that understanding can foster connecting, which in turn can lead to caring between people. And the caring and empathy between people can often be an important first step toward overcoming problems.

Tools for change can then be explored in relation to the clients' concerns. This, as in all phases of consultation, must be a highly individualized process that takes into consideration issues of diversity and the client's phenomenological perspective. In this regard, I believe that for consultation to be successful, it must be something that has meaning in terms of clients' world view and can be integrated into their internal frame of reference. The outcome of consultation is therefore for clients to achieve a heightened state of self-efficacy regarding the development of skills to understand and solve problems.

Counseling Exceptional Students

Issues that relate to counseling exceptional students have had a major impact on school counseling. The term *exceptional* can be defined as applying to "any individual whose physical or behavioral performance deviates so substantially from the norm, either higher or lower, that additional educational and other services may be necessary to meet the individual's needs" (Hardman et al., 1990, p. 14).

Legislative Acts. Several federal laws have been passed which have had a direct impact on exceptional students in terms of identifying and educating exceptional students. Key legislative efforts have included Public Law 94-142, the Americans with Disabilities Act, Section 504 of the Rehabilitation Act, and IDEA legislation. A brief overview of these legislative acts follows.

The passage of the Education for All Handicapped Children Act (Public Law 94-142) in 1975 and the Americans with Disabilities Act (Public Law 101-306) in 1990 had a major impact on education and school counseling. Public Law 94-142 provided for public education within the least restrictive environment for all students with disabilities. Cole (1988) observes that this law has had a dramatic effect on the role of the school counselor. She observes that in many schools, the counselor has become the case manager for exceptional students. This role requires counselors to devote enormous amounts of time to coordination activities such as handling paperwork, attending meetings, and placing students. In addition, counselors have become more involved in providing counseling services to disabled students and their families.

The Americans with Disabilities Act's goal is to ensure civil rights protection to people who have disabilities (Helwig & Holicky, 1994). This landmark legislation prohibits discrimination in employment, public services (including education), transportation, and telecommunication (Parette & Hourcade, 1995). Parette and Hourcade (1995) go on to note that there can be physical, policy, and procedural barriers that can contribute to discrimination against individuals with disabilities. This includes equal access to all public places such as wheelchair ramps providing access to schools and libraries.

Two more recent trends in education relate to Section 504 and IDEA legislation. These two forms of federal legislation are playing key roles in educational reform in terms of individualizing education according to disabilities. These laws are redefining educational policies and procedures, creating enormous opportunities and challenges for educators.

In 1990, PL 94-142 was renamed Individuals with Disabilities Education Act (IDEA). IDEA legislation is updated every three to five years and covers the policies and procedures regarding the assessment, placement, educating, and disciplining of students with a disability. IDEA guidelines are used to qualify students for special education services relating to a number of disabilities such as physical, intellectual, and emotional disabilities. Once students have been placed in special education services, individual education programs (IEP) are developed according to their special needs. IDEA legislation also ensures that disciplinary procedures take into consideration students' disabilities and avoid penalizing students for misbehavior that was the result of a disability. When possible, schools must first attempt to adjust students IEPs to remediate problems associated with misbehavior.

Section 504 of the Rehabilitation Act of 1973 provides additional assistance to disabled students. Students who do not meet the full criteria as disabled according to IDEA may still be considered disabled if they have physical or mental impairments that substantially limit their ability to learn and function at school. These students are not classified as special education students.

Examples of 504 disabilities are medical conditions such as a broken arm or being HIV positive, substance-abuse problems, or students who have attention-deficit hyperactivity disorder but do not qualify for special education. Students who are identified as fulfilling the criteria of 504, are entitled to receive special accommodations regarding their disabilities. For example, if a student has a broken leg, the student can be given extra time to get to class. Other modifications and special considerations can also be required for 504 students such as enhanced physical access to school facilities, individualizing the educational program, and ongoing assessment and reevaluation as a prerequisite to educational placement. As was the case with IDEA, 504 requires disciplinary action to take into consideration students' disabilities. For example, common disciplinary actions such as suspension will probably not be appropriate if the students' misbehavior was due to their disability.

IDEA and 504 legislation offer opportunities and challenges for school counselors. Opportunities are associated with the establishment of policies and procedures that encourage consideration of diversity issues associated with students' disabilities. Individualizing education helps identify special needs and conditions that may undermine the learning process. Individualization of rules and policies can also be a very taxing process for educators. Special challenges that present themselves can include legislative restrictions in discipline, which may impede attempts to keep schools safe from student violence and aggression. School counselors can play an important role in educational reform by ensuring that federal guidelines are applied in a manner that maximizes the learning potential for all disabled students.

School counselors may wish to take a leadership role in terms of emerging legislative acts such as Section 504 and IDEA. Appropriate implementation of these laws is considered a high priority in school districts to ensure dissemination of available federal and state funding, avoid lawsuits and time consuming legal action, and promote safeguards and educational opportunities for students.

Implementation of these federal mandates is an extremely complex process that involves technical skills in legal, mental health, counseling, and administration. School counselors may be particularly well suited to develop expertise in this area since they have a number of these skills and are involved in activities associated with this emerging legislation (for example, developing behavioral management plans relative to disciplinary action).

Additional training and preparation would also be necessary for many school counselors (such as in the area of school law and administration).

Providing coordinating and liaison services for programs such as Section 504 and IDEA could provide an exciting and challenging new dimension to the role and function of the school counselor. It could provide a clear example of school counselors performing a highly specialized and essential service. This could go a long way in disbanding the perception that school counselors lack specialized, essential skills and are therefore in danger of becoming obsolete (see the future trends section at the end of this chapter).

Guidelines for Counseling Exceptional Students. Helwig and Holicky (1994) suggest that school counselors should be familiar with the special needs and services associated with the different types of disabilities. It has therefore become important for school counselors to be aware of the special issues associated with counseling exceptional students.

Perhaps the most basic guideline for counseling exceptional students is to consider that these individuals are more similar to those without disabilities than they are different (McDowell, Coven, & Eash, 1979). Exceptional students should therefore be treated as unique individuals first and people with special needs second. This focus can help counselors become sensitive to individual differences and avoid stereotyping clients in terms of a label.

A second guideline for counselors is being aware of the common problems that exceptional students face. Ciechalski and Schmidt (1995) note that students with exceptionalities often lack social skills and have problems with interpersonal relationships. These authors found that social skill training has a positive effect on the social relationships of exceptional students and that the benefits can be enhanced by involvement with nonspecial education students. Rotatori, Banbury, and Sisterhen (1986) also note that students with exceptionalities also tend to have problems with self-concept, body image, frustration, and dependency.

Bello (1989) suggests that students with disabilities tend to suffer self-concept problems as a result of a history of frustration and failure. These failure-oriented experiences can contribute to irrational beliefs such as "I am not able to do school work"; "People think I'm dumb"; and "In order to be successful, I must be able to do as well as nondisabled people" (Bello, 1989). Bello (1989) therefore recommends that cognitive approaches can play a key role in helping students overcome a failure orientation and improve their self-concept.

Exceptional students, whose bodies have physical abnormalities, may be particularly prone to interpersonal difficulties (Goldberg, 1974). In addition, parents tend to discourage these students from exploring their bodies, contributing to a sense of denial (McDowell, Coven, & Eash, 1979). Rotatori, Banbury, and Sisterhen (1986) therefore recommend that these students be encouraged to explore their bodies and accept their particular disabling condition.

Rotatori, Banbury, and Sisterhen (1986) suggest that exceptional students can become frustrated when they do not feel they can measure up to expectations, a disabling condition limits opportunities for participation, their confidence or competence are threatened, or they do not feel support. Frustration can lead to behavioral problems such as aggression (Talkington & Riley, 1971), sarcasm and cynicism (McDowell, Coven, & Eash, 1979), and stubbornness (Clarizio & McCoy, 1983). Counseling strategies can be directed at resolving the frustration by providing a means for venting the negative emotions and fostering competency skills that prevent frustration (Rotatori, Banbury, & Sisterhen, 1986).

It is not uncommon for parents and teachers to foster dependency in an exceptional student, because they believe the individual is incapable of functioning independently. Overdependent students can lack motivation and experience academic difficulties. They can also be easily influenced by peer pressure, resulting in inappropriate behavior (Rotatori, Banbury, & Sisterhen, 1986). Counseling strategies should be directed at helping these students feel capable, maximizing their self-confidence, and promoting self-reliance.

A third guideline for counseling exceptional students is to be aware of the special needs and counseling strategies associated with the various types of exceptionality. For example, mentally retarded students tend to experience social and emotional problems due to rigid behavior. Behavior therapy has been proven effective with this population to teach self-help skills, enhance social skills, and eliminate inappropriate behavior. Table 14.3 incorporates information from Rotatori et al. (1986) and Parette and Hourcade (1995) to provide a description of the special needs, counseling goals, and associated counseling strategies for nine categories of exceptionality.

A Personal Note

I have found that pet therapy is an excellent tool for working with clients of all ages, especially students with exceptionalities. Pet therapy involves using animals such as dogs, cats, birds, fish, and horses to help individuals overcome various kinds of physical and emotional problems. I first learned of pet therapy from Dr. Herman Salk, the brother of Dr. Jonas Salk, the person who developed the polio vaccine. I met Herman when I worked on the Navajo Indian reservation. He was a veterinarian and had used pet therapy in a wide variety of settings. I was inspired by the passion he had for animals and his method of using pet therapy to overcome communication barriers, foster positive relationships, and enhance social interest.

Over the years, I have used pet therapy in a wide variety of settings such as nursing homes, schools, mental health clinics, and hospitals. My research on pet therapy has shown that it can help promote physical and mental health (Nystul, Emmons, & Cockrell, 1992). For example, hospitalized patients tend to have a higher survival rate and faster recovery if they have a pet to go home to. Pet therapy has also been used to help individuals overcome shyness, aid in self-confidence, and provide a means of working through emotional disorders.

Pet therapy appears to be particularly useful in counseling exceptional students. Pets can provide meaningful stimulation and facilitation of sensory modalities such as seeing eye dogs for the visually impaired. Pets can also be useful with seriously emotionally disturbed students. For example, caring for a pet can help a student overcome problems with anger management. Counselors may also bring a pet to a counseling session to overcome problems with resistance and enhance the counseling relationship. A friend of mine used to bring her parrot to work with her. The parrot was very friendly and would talk to her clients. As you can imagine, she was very popular and always had an abundant supply of students who wanted to see her. Naturally some schools may have policy against bringing pets to school.

I once was treating a suicidal student. With the approval of the parents, I was able to have the student pick a pet out of the local animal shelter and adopt it as her own. I explained to the student that she would be saving a life instead of taking a life. This seemed to bring meaning to her life and the suicidal ideations soon subsided. I have been amazed by the profound effects that pets have on people. I encourage you to explore this exciting dimension to the counseling process.

TABLE 14.3   Counseling Exceptional Children

Disorder	Special Needs or Problems	Counseling Goals	Counseling Strategies
Mentally retarded students (Litton, 1986; Parette & Hourcade, 1995)	High incidence of social-emotional problems due to rigid behavior, restricted life experience, problems perceiving personal and social situations	Improve social adaptation, enhance self-help skills, increase awareness of self and others, assist with development of interpersonal relations skills, promote a positive self-image	Behavior therapy to teach self-help skills, enhance social skills, and eliminate inappropriate behavior Be clear and concise when communicating; limit the number of directions, communicate respect, and provide positive feedback when possible.
Learning-disabled students (Gerber, 1986)	Poor self-concept and self-esteem, tendency to be rejected by peers, a lack of self-appraisal skills, fear of failure, test anxiety; a lack of motivation	Enhance the student's self-esteem and self-concept, promote effective social skills, help overcome fear of failure, promote a positive attitude toward the learning process	Self-concept programs, interpersonal relations training, and cognitive-behavioral approaches to overcome a fear of failure
Mildly behaviorally disordered students (Raiche, Fox, & Rotatori, 1986; Parette & Hourcade, 1995)	Problems with impulse control, aggression, and defiance; emotional problems; hyperactivity; and academic problems	Increase frustration tolerance and self-restraint, help overcome academic difficulties, improve interpersonal relations skills	Cognitive-behavioral techniques to teach anger control, play therapy and group counseling to assist with social-emotional problems, interpersonal relations training to enhance social skills. When a student misbehaves, don't overreact. Also, ask concrete, direct questions.
Speech- or language-disordered students (Kelley & Rotatori, 1986)	Interpersonal problems resulting from exclusion, overprotection, and ridicule; educational difficulties; self-esteem problems; anxiety	Help develop coping mechanisms to deal effectively with negative remarks of peers; help broaden and adapt communication skills to various settings; improve interpersonal relation skills, enhance self-concept and self-esteem; overcome educational difficulties	Cognitive-behavioral approaches to deal effectively with negative remarks, self-concept programs, and communication still development in small groups

continued

TABLE 14.3   Continued

Disorder	Special Needs or Problems	Counseling Goals	Counseling Strategies
Hearing impaired students (Sisterhen & Rotatori, 1986; Parette & Hourcade, 1995)	Language difficulties, including problems with articulation and voice quality, vocabulary, syntax, and grammar; social-emotional problems such as social isolation, emotional immaturity, behavioral problems, difficulty with interpersonal relations, identity problems	Assist with identity formation, encourage independence, help develop appropriate social skills (for example, reduce tendencies to appear physically aggressive)	Behavioral counseling that incorporates social modeling (particularly effective since deaf children tend to follow example set by significant others); guidance programs that focus on self-concept development to promote identity formation. Speak directly to the student and look toward the student (not at an interpreter) to make it clear that your communication is directed at the student. Also, speak slowly and clearly and emphasize nonverbal communication such as facial expressions and gestures.
Visually impaired students (Heinze & Rotatori, 1986)	Low self-confidence, low self-concept, self-criticism, and social isolation	Increase self-confidence, improve self image, and reduce tendencies toward self-criticism and social isolation	Assertiveness training to help increase self-confidence, cognitive behavioral approaches to reduce tendencies toward self-criticism, interpersonal relations training to increase social interest. Introduce yourself before you begin talking and cue the student when a discussion is about to end and you are going to leave. Offer assistance if the student looks confused. If necessary provide assistance that meets the student's needs.

TABLE 14.3   **Continued**

Disorder	Special Needs or Problems	Counseling Goals	Counseling Strategies
Physically disabled students (Griffin, Sexton, Gerber, & Rotatori, 1986; Parette & Hourcade, 1995)	Problems vary according to disability type: some need assistance with basic functioning such as eating, personal hygiene, and locomotion; others need assistance in establishing intimate relationships (including sexuality) or dealing with ridicule	Help identify personal strengths to overcome their physical disability, encourage becoming involved in self-advocacy to foster a sense of self-control over their life	Adlerian counseling to help identify strengths to overcome weaknesses, existential approaches to help discover personal meaning in life, sex education and sex therapy to help deal with sexuality issues. Sit when talking with someone in a wheelchair to maintain appropriate eye contact (that is, not talking down to the student).
Health-impaired students (Griffin, Berger, & Rotatori, 1986)	Health problems such as leukemia, diabetes, asthma, or a seizure disorder, that can interfere with academic functioning or psychosocial development	Alleviate anxiety, depression, and bodily discomfort, maximize bodily functioning, and assist with academic difficulties	Cognitive-behavioral strategies for anxiety and depression; stress management techniques and an exercise program to maximize bodily functioning; family therapy to help with familial factors associated with a seriously ill individual.
Gifted students (Kaufmann, Castellanos, & Rotatori, 1986)	Difficulties with peer relations due to being singled out as the "brain of the class," lack of motivation and underachievement when not challenged	Increase awareness of self and others, enhance problem-solving and decision-making skills, clarify values and personal aspirations, maximize intellectual potential	Appropriate classroom placement to ensure adequate academic challenge; career counseling (including the use of a mentor) to encourage pursuing personal goals and aspirations; personal counseling to increase awareness of self in relation to others.

continued

TABLE 14.3   Continued

Disorder	Special Needs or Problems	Counseling Goals	Counseling Strategies
Abused students (Kennell & Rotatori, 1986)	Multitude of problems such as dependency, anger, depression, anxiety, self-blame, withdrawal, low self-esteem, interpersonal relations; educational problems	Improve self-image, promote positive interpersonal relations skills, assist with anger control, alleviate anxiety and depression, and help overcome educational difficulties	Counseling strategies to focus on helping students realize that they were not responsible for what happened, that the abuse was wrong, and that it will stop; self-concept development programs; cognitive-behavioral approaches to promote anger control and alleviate depression.

Note. From *Counseling Exceptional Students* by A. F. Rotatori, P. J. Gerber, F. W. Litton, & R. A. Fox (Eds.), 1986, New York: Human Sciences Press. Copyright 1986 by Human Sciences Press. Reprinted by permission.

Special Problems

Students do not have to be exceptional to encounter problems in school. They face an increasingly diverse array of problems and challenges as they progress through the school years. McWhirter et al. (1994) have identified the "five Cs of Competency" that are associated with students doing well in life. These qualities are: critical school competencies (including basic academic skills), the concept of self and self-esteem, communication skills, coping skills, and a sense of control. Students who lack these qualities are at a high risk for self-destructive behaviors such as substance abuse, teenage pregnancy, and school drop-out (McWhirter et al., 1994). An overview of these and other problems and challenges follows.

Substance Use and Abuse.   In this discussion, the term substance use refers to alcohol, cigarettes, and illicit drugs such as cocaine, marijuana, or heroin. Substance use among students in the United States continues to rise, with an estimated 5.5 million Americans in need of treatment for substance abuse (Mason, 1996). The cost of substance abuse to society has been estimated in the billions of dollars, and the psychological cost in terms of human suffering is incalculable (Mason, 1996). A survey has shown that 57 percent of high school seniors have used illicit drugs, and more than one-third have used illicit drugs other than marijuana (Newcomb & Bentler, 1989). The use of alcohol and tobacco is even higher, with 66 percent of seniors reporting use within the previous month, and one-fifth reporting daily use of cigarettes (Newcomb & Bentler, 1989). Substance use is increasing among young children. Between 1976 and 1986, drug use tripled for students in grades 1 through 6 (Bennett, 1986). In addition, Hubbard, Brownlee, and Anderson (1988) report that most students initiate substance use during the middle school years. These statistics suggest that elementary and middle schools represent important targets for intervention efforts.

Newcomb and Bentler (1988) have identified factors associated with substance use and abuse. High levels of drug use are related to limited educational pursuits and early marriages. Polydrug use, or the use of many drugs, among teenagers is associated with their later difficulty as young adults in role acquisition, for example, as a spouse or employer. Heavy use of so-called hard drugs is associated with loneliness, drop in social support, psychoticism, and suicidal tendencies.

Newcomb and Bentler (1989) provide information on the etiology, or causes, of substance use and abuse. These authors note that use is prompted most by peer influence, while abuse stems from internal psychological distress. They also identify risk factors associated with substance use and abuse. These include a personal history of drug use, use by peers, a lower socioeconomic level, family dysfunction, a family history of abuse, poor school performance, low self-esteem, lack of abidance with the law, need for excitement, stressful life events, and anxiety and depression.

Children of alcoholics (COA) are a particularly high risk group for developing drug and alcohol problems (Vail-Smith, Knight, & White, 1995). Vail-Smith, Knight, & White (1995) find that a substantial number of elementary school students are COA and require special help. Some of the special problems associated with COA include negative emotions such as anger (Clair & Genest, 1987); low self-esteem (Werner, 1986); and an external locus of control (Werner, 1986). Vail-Smith et al. (1995) note that elementary school counselors are in a particularly good position to provide services to COA. These services could include fostering resiliency skills to help these students cope with family dysfunction (Vail-Smith et al., 1995). In addition, Brake (1988) suggests that group counseling that focuses on the special problems of COA could be beneficial for this population.

Preventive programs for substance abuse have received much attention in the literature. Two studies conducted meta-analyses of the literature. Bangert-Drowns (1988) found none of the existing preventive programs had any appreciable effect on reducing substance use or abuse. Tobler's (1986) review of the research suggested that programs focusing on increased knowledge about drugs and alcohol are not effective in reducing use or abuse. On the positive side, Tobler (1986) found peer programs that included assertiveness, especially refusal skills, and social-skills training prove the most effective in preventing abuse.

Several programs are available to promote assertiveness and social skills. A program called *Children Are People* (Lerner & Naiditch, 1985) can be used at the elementary school level, and the SMART program (Pearson et al., 1985) applies to the middle school level. For teens who have substance abuse problems, the most effective programs are those that promoted alternative activities, such as camping and sports; enhanced confidence and social competence; and provided broadening experiences (Tobler, 1986).

Teenage Pregnancy.   Teenage pregnancies in the United States continue at an alarming rate. Maynard (1996) notes that one million teenagers in the United States become pregnant each year, which is approximately 10 percent of 15- to 19-year-olds. Comparatively, the United States has by far the highest teenage pregnancy rate for an industrialized nation, with it being twice as high as the United Kingdom and 15 times the rate in Japan (Maynard, 1996). The cost of teenage pregnancy to the individual and society can be staggering. Maynard (1996) estimates that the cost to society from such forces as lost wages and social services is between 13 and 19 billion dollars a year. There are other costs to the teenage mothers and

The incidence of teenage pregnancy is increasing

their children, such as a tendency to have low-birth weight and premature babies, having higher rates of school dropouts and lower high-school graduation rates for teenage mothers and their children, having higher rates of abuse and neglect, and having lower lifelong earning for mothers and their children (Maynard, 1996).

Preventive programs can address the special problems associated with teenage pregnancy. Furstenberg, Brooks-Gunn, and Chase-Lansdale (1989) note that the most promising forms of prevention of teenage pregnancy are contraceptive and family-planning services. These authors conclude that other preventive programs that focus on sex education or attempting to change attitudes toward early sexual involvement have had limited success.

Several preventive programs that are implemented after a teenager becomes pregnant have been found to be successful. Prenatal programs have been shown to promote healthy babies for teens (Brooks-Gunn, McCormick, & Heagerty, 1988; Brooks-Gunn et al., 1989). Parent education programs have been used to enhance parenting skills as well as the development of the child (Clewell, Brooks-Gunn, & Benasich, 1989). Emmons and Nystul's (1994) research on the effects of parent education utilizes the PREP for Effective Family Living program (Dinkmeyer et al., 1985) in small groups with pregnant teenagers. They found that the PREP program increases the teenagers' self-concept and fosters democratic parenting attitudes.

MacGregor and Newlon (1987) suggest that the most useful approaches for working with pregnant teenagers include group counseling to provide necessary peer support; parent education after delivery of the baby, but not before; and creative, imaginative prenatal class presentations that encourage active involvement of participants. Berger and Thompson (1995) describe a social inoculation program that involves group work with female adolescents. The groups utilize role-play and discussion and focus on helping these individuals learn how to resist pressures to have sex. Social inoculation is shown to be useful, especially for individuals who are not already sexually active.

Divorced or Single Parents.   Berger and Thompson (1995) contend that high divorce rates are expected to continue into the twenty-first century with only 40 percent of children being reared by both biological parents until they reach 18 years of age. Frieman (1993) suggests that school counselors can play key roles in helping students overcome some of the adverse outcomes associated with divorce and single-parent homes. Active positive involvement in child-rearing by both biological parents can minimize adverse consequences of divorce. Frieman (1993) notes that a special challenge can be to involve the father, since fathers tend to have lower levels of parental involvement (than mothers) before the divorce. Frieman posits that group work with divorced men can be useful to help them become more involved in their children's lives. Topics that may be especially relevant in these groups are common problems of fathers, parenting skills, developmental issues, dealing with negative emotions of anger and jealousy, and information on child care.

Robson (1988) describes variations in the effects of divorce according to the age of the child. Children up to 5 years of age tend to regress by developing feeding and toileting problems. Children from age 6 to 8 initially use denial to cope and later remain hopeful that their parents will get back together. From age 9 to 11, children typically react with shock, surprise, denial, and disbelief. In addition, these children can experience conflicts in loyalty to their parents, often viewing one parent as good and the other as bad. Adolescents from 13 to 18 years of age appear to have increased risk of mental health problems and a negative view of their future, their parents, and their environment. Adolescent females also tend to engage in early heterosexual behavior.

Group counseling has been found effective for dealing with the special issues associated with divorce, for example, alleviating guilt and dealing with anger and feelings of abandonment. Many different kinds of divorce groups have emerged (Bowker, 1982; Hammond, 1981). These groups tend to focus on easing children's level of stress and enhancing their self-esteem. Hammond's (1981) program is typical of these group approaches. It utilizes a structured format that includes a multimedia presentation and exercises providing information on divorce as well as opportunities to process feelings. Burke and DeStreek (1989) have found empirical support for Hammond's approach in terms of enhanced self-concept. Additional research on these groups appears warranted.

Dropping Out of School.

Eggen and Kauchak (1994) estimate that 25 percent or more of the high school class of 2001 will not finish high school. The percentage of school dropouts is even higher for some minority groups (for example, Native American students have the highest rate at 35.5 percent; Garrett, 1995). Students who are at a high risk for dropping out of school are referred to as at-risk students. Eggen and Kauchak (1994) identified common characteristics of at risk students, which include low socioeconomic status (SES), transience, being minority, being male, having English as a second language, and being from divorced families. Students who are at risk not only have a higher tendency to drop out of school, but they also have a tendency to have other problems such as substance abuse, delinquency, low self-esteem, and low motivation and underachievement in school (Eggen & Kauchak, 1994).

An increasing amount of research is focusing on identifying resiliency characteristics that can help students become less vulnerable to academic failure (for example, Alva, 1991; Arellano & Padilla, 1996; & Zimmerman & Arunkumar, 1994). Arellano and Padilla (1996) identify personal and environmental factors that promote academic success in Latino students. These characteristics include parental support and encouragement; role models and mentors; ethnicity as a source of support, pride, and strength; the drive to succeed; and an optimistic outlook. School counselors can attempt to foster resiliency characteristics to maximize academic achievement in students.

Several counseling strategies can address the school dropout phenomenon. Preventive programs can provide special counseling services for students who are at risk for dropping out of school. Bearden, Spencer, and Moracco (1989) have found that males have a higher risk of dropping out of school than females. The authors identify other at-risk characteristics, including low socioeconomic status, a history of previous failures, drug abuse, academic and behavioral problems, poor school attendance, and boredom. Gibson (1989) describes several programs that have been used to work with at-risk students. For example, Florida's Dade County Public Schools uses peer counseling, academic support, and help with educational deficiencies (Dade County Public Schools, 1985). The Los Angeles Unified School District (1985) employs counseling, special tutoring, and vocational assistance. More recently Ruben (1989) has recommended that preventive efforts should be geared to the elementary level by providing classroom guidance programs like Gerler and Anderson's (1986) program called *Success in Schools.*

Future Trends in School Counseling

School counseling appears to be at the crossroads. School counselors are needed more than ever as students experience a complex array of personal and social problems. Yet concerns persist that school counseling cannot deal effectively with these challenges.

Sandhu and Portes (1995) contend that school counseling is in deep trouble as a profession and is in danger of becoming obsolete. These scholars suggest that the fundamental problem facing school counseling is that it tends to be perceived as a nonessential ancillary service that does not require specific expertise to perform. Sandhu and Portes suggest that it is essential for school counselors to become proactive rather than reactive in their roles, priorities, and activities. These individuals describe a proactive model of school counseling that can help move school counseling from the peripheral to the central position in educational reform. Welch and McCarroll (1993) provide additional suggestions on how school counselors can be perceived as more vital to their school and community. They recommend that school counselors must become more involved in the family and community by providing family counseling and becoming a community resource specialist to help link students with appropriate services to meet their needs. They also recommend a shift in emphasis from individual counseling to group work and suggest that counselors utilize a system perspective in conceptualizing the overall functioning of the school.

As noted earlier, school counselors may attempt to receive additional training in areas such as school law and administration to take a leadership role in emerging legislative acts such as Section 504 and IDEA. This would enable school counselors to expand their role in function in an area that is associated with specialized and essential services (for example, interface between discipline and legal mandates and development of behavior management plans).

The College Entrance Examination Board (1987) also concluded that the school counseling profession was in trouble and in need of changes. Based on an examination of school counseling, its report recommended making better use of the school counselor's special skills rather than imposing clerical tasks such as scheduling, increasing support for federal programs that assist disadvantaged students, placing more emphasis on counseling programs at the elementary and middle school level to prevent problems from becoming more serious, and promoting greater involvement of parents in the school counseling program.

Russo and Kassera (1989) note that school counselors have been unsuccessful in clearly communicating the importance of their services. These authors suggest that school counselors should establish a comprehensive ongoing accountability program to overcome these difficulties. They recommend that school counselors could use Wiggins' (1985) accountability program, which includes setting goals, assessing needs, setting priorities, evaluating outcomes, and reporting results.

Green (1988) suggests that image-building activities will play a key role in the future of school counseling. He suggests that school counselors must be accepted as practitioners with specialized knowledge before they can establish professional autonomy. Green (1988) identifies the following activities that could be used to promote a sense of professionalism for school counselors.

- Conduct a survey among colleagues to determine how they perceive the role of the school counselor. This type of peer review is a necessary component of professional behavior.
- Compile a list of professional activities during the previous three years. Determine whether these activities have promoted a professional image, required the special skills of a counselor or simply duplicated services offered by other professionals, and educated others on the complexity of the counselor's role in these activities.
- Provide programs for parents on topics such as parent education, drug abuse, and student achievement.
- Publish a newsletter describing activities of the school counseling program as well as issues that interest students, teachers, and parents.
- Become active in conducting research and writing articles for publication in professional journals.
- Become involved in professional organizations.
- Schedule special consultation days for parents and staff to assist with special needs.
- Provide in-service training to teachers.
- Sponsor a community seminar on a topical issue, for example, teenage pregnancy.

Several authors have commented that school counselors should take a more active role in educational reforms (Kaplan & Geoffroy, 1990; Thomas, 1989). These authors suggest that school counselors can play an important role by promoting a positive school climate. The activities they recommend include encouraging success orientation in the school, fostering self-esteem of teachers and students, and helping integrate cognitive and affective dimensions in the educational process.

Counselor educators can also play an integral role in helping school counseling successfully move forward. Sweeney (1988) notes that school counseling has been deemphasized in most counselor-education programs. The current focus appears to be on providing course work and skills for agency counselors and not school counseling. According to Sweeney (1988), counselor educators have also neglected research on school counseling. For example, the number of articles published in *Counselor Education and Supervision* on the role and function of school counseling has steadily declined. For example, 39 articles appeared on this topic from 1961 to 1968, but none from 1980 to 1988. Besides helping school counselors formulate a professional identity, counselor educators can provide more emphasis on the educational needs of students interested in school counseling.

These studies collectively suggest that school counseling is a profession at risk and in need of dramatic changes. Briefly, school counselors should

- Become proactive in their roles, priorities, and activities
- Use of family-systemic perspective to become more involved in the family and community
- Assume leadership responsibilities for coordinating and acting as a liaison for legislative programs such as Section 504 and IDEA
- Clarify their role and function by encouraging others to focus on their special skills and not on clerical tasks such as scheduling
- Incorporate image-building activities and an ongoing accountability program
- Encourage parents to involve themselves more in their children's counseling programs
- Advocate greater emphasis on elementary and middle school counseling
- Become more actively involved in the school reform movement
- Promote research efforts on special problems such as suicide and depression
- Convince counselor educators to place more emphasis on school counseling

Three trends in the school counseling literature that are receiving an increasing amount of attention are diversity issues, solution-focused counseling, and technology. An overview of these topics follows.

Diversity Issues

School counselors must consider diversity issues in all aspects of counseling. Three examples of diversity issues are culture, religion, and sexual orientation. All facets of society are becoming increasingly multicultural. It is therefore imperative for school counselors to develop the necessary knowledge, skill, and understanding to work with students in a multicultural society. Hobson and Kanitz (1996) note that the recently revised American Counseling Association (1997) Code of Ethics and Standard of Practice advocates that counselors acquire and maintain the necessary multicultural competencies to practice, and that school counselors generally are in need of additional training in this area. Whitledge (1994) goes on to suggest that sensitivity to multicultural issues in schools is necessary to maximize learning in students. School counselors should therefore engage in activities to enhance the school climate by overcoming adverse stereotyping and promoting an acceptance and integration of the student's culture in the overall school curriculum (Whitledge, 1994).

Spiritual and religious issues represent an emerging dimension to school counseling. For example, Miller (1995) identifies special considerations for providing school counseling services to Christian fundamentalist families. He noted that these families tend to respond to a school counselors' referrals with fear and apprehension because they do not believe their religious beliefs will be considered in the counseling process.

School counselors can overcome reluctant tendencies by giving voice to the clients' manner of conceptualizing problems and solutions. For example, it is common for Christian fundamentalists to attribute problems of misbehavior to problems with religion (for example, not spending enough time studying the Bible) (Miller, 1995). When this occurs, school counselors should recognize the role that the church may play in overcoming students' problems. In this process, school counselors must make every effort to listen to their clients' stories in an accepting and nonjudgmental manner. As trust develops, counselors can be in a better position to facilitate the construction of new stories that reflect a movement toward problem resolution and enhanced meaning.

Ribak-Rosenthal and Russell (1994) address another important religious issue in school counseling. Their study found that non-Christian fourth to sixth graders experienced more negative perceptions of themselves and their classroom's social environment than Christian students during the month of December. The study suggested that 20 to 30 percent of the non-Christian students may experience negative emotions during December because it is focused on the celebration of *Christmas* in terms of classroom parties and holiday breaks.

These authors suggested that school counselors could strive to create a positive school climate that recognizes diversity in religion in the schools. In this process, counselors could refer to the school break in December as a holiday vacation and not Christmas vacation. In addition, counselors could create opportunities to recognize other religious holidays and festivities in small- and large-group guidance and counseling activities.

Sexual orientation represents another important diversity issue, with approximately 10 percent of students having gay or lesbian sexual preferences. Unfortunately, sexual orientation has received so little attention in schools that it can be considered "a blind spot in the school mirror" (Marinoble, 1998). In fact, sexual orientation tends to be a subject that is often avoided all together in all aspects of school functioning from the curriculum, to school policies, and even the invitation of guest speakers (Marinoble, 1998). It is not surprising that exclusionary forces such as these contribute to gays and lesbians often feeling like "invisible people" (Ritter & O'Neill, 1995).

Marinoble (1998) identifies some of the special challenges and opportunities that gay and lesbian students pose to school counselors. Challenges include helping these students overcome difficulties associated with being gay or lesbian in a heterosexual-homophobic world. Some of the common problems experienced are identity conflict, feelings of isolation and stigmatization, peer relation problems, and family disruptions. Identity conflicts can in part be due to schools fundamental orientation to recognizing the world in heterosexual terms (Marinoble, 1998). Although the existence of homosexuality is generally ignored, when it is recognized, it tends to have a negative, derogatory connotation. This can contribute to gays and lesbians struggling to define themselves as unique and positive individuals in a tide of negativity.

Gay and lesbian students experience other problems such as isolation and stigmatization, peer relations, and family conflict that can contribute to serious mental health problems. For example, Marinoble (1998) notes that suicide accounts for most of the deaths of gay and lesbian adolescents, occurring at a rate two to three times that of heterosexual teens.

Ritter and O'Neill (1995) also note that gay and lesbian individuals also tend to have problems with spirituality owing to limited access to organized religion. This can compound mental health problems, because people tend to turn to spirituality for strength and support during times of need (Miranti & Burke, 1995).

School counselors are in an ideal position to take a proactive role in assisting gay and lesbian students with their special problems and foster their optimal development. Some of the possible interventions suggested by Cooley (1998), Fontaine (1998), Muller and Hartman (1998), Marinoble (1998), and Ritter and O'Neill (1995) are as follows.

- Promote a school climate (in terms of the curriculum and school policy) that is sensitive and values diversity in sexual orientation.
- Ensure that *all* students have an opportunity to develop a positive self-image, self-acceptance, and personal identity.
- When appropriate, assist students in the process of "coming out" (sharing their sexual orientation with friends and family).
- Utilize individual and group counseling to help gay and lesbian students overcome negative feelings such as isolation and despair.
- Monitor students who are at a high risk for suicide and ensure treatment as necessary.
- Assist students with spiritual needs to promote inner strength and support necessary for problem resolution and movement toward optimal development.

Implementation of these interventions may create serious challenges for school counselors. Schools tend to be a reflection of the culture in which they are created. Successful implementation may therefore require strength and courage to fight against negative forces such as homophobia, racism, stereotyping, discrimination, and prejudice. If schools exist to truly educate *all* students (regardless of race, color, and creed), then school counselors have an opportunity to advocate for school reform necessary to address these important issues.

Brief-Solution-Focused Counseling

Brief-solution-focused models of counseling continue to receive attention from the literature as an innovative alternative to standard approaches to school counseling (Bonnington, 1993; Bruce, 1995; LaFountain, Garner, & Eliason, 1996; and Murphy, 1994). Murphy (1994) summarizes advantages that brief-solution-focused counseling has for school counselors over more traditional counseling methods.

1. It is a strengths approach that focuses on what works and exceptions to problems and therefore promotes collaborative relationships with students, parents, teachers, and staff.
2. It is time-limited, focusing on the present and future rather than lengthy excursions into past history.
3. Its goal of small concrete changes (such as increased class attendance and conflict resolution) is more realistic than more ambitious goals such as personality change.
4. It recognizes the importance of students being aware of the need for change as a prerequisite for change.

Bruce (1995) and Murphy (1994) describe tasks associated with brief-solution-focused counseling in school counseling. Collectively they suggest that school counselors should first establish a positive counseling relationship. This of course is important regardless of the approach that is being used. Second, assess the problem in concrete behavioral terms and identify exceptions to the problem (that is, examples of when the problem does not occur). Third, identify a short-term goal that the student can successfully achieve. Fourth, elaborate on what worked in the past (the exceptions to the problem identified in step 2), and use this information to develop a new approach for the student. Fifth, evaluate the new approach with methods such as the scaling technique (on a 1:10 scale with 1 being the worst and 10 being the best, how would you rate the situation now?), and make changes to the new approach as necessary. And sixth, empowering students to use the brief-solution-focused method to deal with future problems.

There has been a limited amount of research that has evaluated the efficacy of brief-solution-focused counseling. Littrell, Malia, and Vanderwood (1995) found brief-solution-focused counseling (one session with high school students) to be as effective as brief-problem-focused counseling in terms of decreasing the degree of undesired feelings but took less time. Brief-solution-focused and other forms of brief counseling appear to offer much to school counselors who are continually faced with large numbers of students to provide counseling services.

Use of Technology

Technological advances offer numerous opportunities and challenges to school counselors. Challenges relate to the inherent difficulties of trying to keep up with the escalating changes in technology (for example, the computer you just purchased is already out of date). Opportunities include being able to do the job of school counseling better and more efficiently. Technologies such as multimedia authoring (the use of at least two media simultaneously such as image processing, graphics production, sound editing, and three-dimensional modeling) are the wave of the future for state-of-the-art delivery of counseling programs to students (Gerler, 1995). There are limitless other possibilities for the use of technologies in school counseling. Some of these are to enable students to use laser disc and CD-ROMs, electronic links with the Internet, and other technologies to take an active role in their counseling by exploring such topics as career exploration, drug and alcohol abuse, and prejudice (Casey, 1995).

A growing number of school counselors are also finding that the Internet can be an excellent tool to communicate with other school counselors regarding issues from counseling theory to crucial matters that they face daily (Gerler, 1995). Counselor educators are also expanding their use of technologies in the schools. Myrick and Sabella (1995) noted that e-mail could be a useful tool in supervision of student interns in school counseling. It could provide a means to send information immediately and directly to one's supervisor without having to wait for a weekly supervision meeting or playing "telephone tag." E-mail supervision also helps students become more succinct in describing what is going on with a particular case and contributes to an enhanced focus in counselor supervision (Myrick & Sabella, 1995).

Summary

School counseling is a dynamic and challenging field in the counseling profession. It can best be understood within the context of a comprehensive K–12 developmental model. In 1990 the ASCA supported this model in a revised role statement, suggesting also that school counselors engage in individual counseling, small-group counseling, large-group guidance, consultation, and coordination activities.

The role of consultation is receiving increasing emphasis in school counseling. Guidelines for counseling exceptional students and students with the special problems of drug abuse, teenage pregnancy, divorced or single parents, and dropping out of school are also important.

School counseling appears to be at a crossroads. Several studies have suggested that changes are needed for school counseling to successfully move forward as a profession. Some of these are becoming more proactive and enhancing family-community involvement; taking leadership responsibility for legislative programs such as Section 504 and IDEA; increasing direct services and reducing clerical activities; putting more emphasis on elementary and middle school counseling to maximize preventive effort; and engaging in image-building activities. In addition, school counselors need to be cognizant of emerging trends such as incorporating a multicultural perspective, using brief-solution-focused counseling, and making effective use of technology.

15 Mental Health Counseling

CHAPTER OVERVIEW

This chapter provides an overview of mental health counseling. Highlights include

- The art and science of mental health counseling
- Professional issues for mental health counselors, including professional organizations and certification
- The role and function of the mental health counselor, including direct and indirect intervention strategies
- Categories of mental health services: "problems of living" and mental disorders
- Strategies for suicidal clients
- Strategies for clients with substance-abuse problems
- Postmodern trends, diversity issues, and managed care

The Art and Science of Mental Health Counseling

Mental health counseling is both an art and science. It is an art for mental health counselors to attempt to walk the tightrope between adjusting to the demands of health-care reform such as managed care and still maintaining a high-quality mental health service. One of the challenges associated with this process is to maintain the philosophical core of mental health counseling (the developmental/preventative perspective) while continuing to be perceived as a viable provider for managed-care organizations, which tend to focus on symptom relief. In addition, it is an art for mental health counseling to make appropriate changes in its philosophical and theoretical orientation to interface effectively with current trends such as postmodernism and issues relating to diversity.

The art of mental health counseling is reflected in the challenging population that this discipline serves (for example, clients with mental disorders such as serious depression, schizophrenia, and substance abuse). Mental health counselors must strive to develop innovative, creative methods to address these challenges. The art of mental health counseling is expressed in the personal characteristics of patience, humbleness, kindness, and compassion.

Clearly, for mental health counselors to be effective they must be affected by their clients and the counseling process.

The science of mental health counseling can be an effective balance to the emotionally charged art of counseling. Without a balance, the art of counseling will not be as effective. In this regard, counselors can become overly enmeshed in their clients' lives, obscuring the boundaries and undermining essential professional objectivity.

Numerous objective practices can contribute to this balance. Some of these are the use of assessment instruments and procedures such as psychological tests and the clinical interview. Research strategies such as qualitative and quantitative methods can also be useful in establishing the science of counseling in mental health counseling. Assessment and research methodologies can help the mental health counselor stand back and evaluate what is going on in the counseling process, provide new direction for innovations in theory and practice, and determine the efficacy of the mental health services being offered.

Professional Issues

Mental health counseling is both an emerging counseling profession represented by mental health counselors and an amorphous job role performed by various members of the helping professions such as counselors, psychologists, psychiatrists, psychiatric nurses, and social workers. Mental health counselors can be defined as individuals whose "primary affiliation and theoretical basis is counseling and not psychiatry, psychology, or social work" (Palmo, 1986, p. 41). Mental health counselors represent the fastest-growing segment of the mental health field (Dingman, 1988). Burtnett (1986) reported that 57 percent of mental health agencies have a mental health counselor. These counselors handle some of the most difficult cases, including crisis intervention (Ivey, 1989), and have therefore become an integral aspect of the mental health delivery system.

Until relatively recently, mental health counselors did not have a professional organization to identify. In 1976, the American Association for Counseling and Development (AACD)—now called the American Counseling Association (ACA)—addressed this need by creating a special division called the American Mental Health Counselors Association (AMHCA). By 1985, the AMHCA had become the largest division of the AACD. Since its inception, the AMHCA has embarked on numerous activities that have contributed to the professional identity of the mental health counselor. Its most important contributions include creating a code of ethics for mental health counselors; publishing the *Journal of Mental Health Counseling,* which provides information regarding the theory, research, and practice of mental health counseling; spearheading a movement for counselor licensure in all states; and setting up national standards for certification of mental health counselors.

Smith and Robinson (1995) note that in 1988 national preparation standards were established for mental health counselors to ensure adequate professional training and recognition in the health-care delivery system (for example, be eligible for third-party insurance reimbursement and participation in managed care). Smith and Robinson delineated the national clinical standards for mental health counselors as follows. Individuals must graduate from a program that is accredited by the Council for Accreditation of Counseling and Related Educational Programs (CACREP) or has CACREP equivalency; have 3,000 hours of experience in the mental health field; have 100 hours of face-to-face supervision; adhere to the AMHCA standards of clinical practice and code of ethics; pass a national clinical exam; successfully have work samples of counseling reviewed (for example, video tapes); and fulfill state licensure requirements.

More than 1400 individuals have been endorsed as Certified Clinical Mental Health Counselors (CCMHC) by the National Academy of Clinical Mental Health Counselors since 1979 (Brooks & Gerstein, 1990). The academy based its standards on criteria deemed essential for independent practice as a mental health provider and also what would be acceptable standards to third-party insurance programs (Brooks & Gerstein, 1990). CCMHC providers have been recognized by the Civilian Health and Medical Program of the Uniformed Services (CHAMPUS) for third-party insurance reimbursement when clients are referred by a physician (Brooks & Gerstein, 1990).

Mental health counselors work in a variety of settings that include private practice, community mental health centers, hospitals, alcohol and drug centers, social service agencies, and business and industry (Brooks & Gerstein, 1990). Hershenson and Power (1987) note an apparent shift in work settings for mental health counselors during the last decade. For example, Weikel and Taylor (1979) reported that in 1978 the highest percentage (39 percent) of AMHCA members worked in community mental health centers, 18 percent in private practice, and the remainder in a variety of other settings, including college counseling centers and as college teachers. Weikel (1985) noted that in 1985, a large percentage of AMHCA members worked in private practice (22 percent), 13 percent in private counseling centers, 13 percent in colleges and universities, only 11 percent in community mental health centers, and the rest in other settings, such as rehabilitation agencies and state and local government. The trend of private practice becoming the dominant work setting for AMHCA members continued in the 1990s (Brooks & Gerstein, 1990).

Several other studies have shown that a high percentage of mental health counselors work in substance-abuse centers (Hosie, West, & MacKey, 1988; Richardson & Bradley, 1985). Hosie, West, and MacKey (1988) reported that the largest percentage of professionals working in substance-abuse centers held a master's degree in counseling or a Master of Social Work (MSW) degree. In addition, Hosie, West, and MacKey (1988) noted that mental health counselors were more likely to hold a position as program director than individuals from other disciplines.

Smith and Robinson (1995) suggest that mental health counselors must continue to receive training in diagnosing and treatment of mental disorders and that this training should emphasize a developmental/preventative perspective. They also suggest that specialty skills (such as marriage and family counseling) could enhance the standing of mental health counselors within the health-care community.

In an era of rapid change within the health-care system, mental health counseling appears to be posed to have greater inclusion and recognition as a mental health provider. In this regard, mental health counseling appears to represent a cost-effective alternative to mental health delivery, which would be very attractive to managed-care organizations. It is imperative that mental health counseling continues to evolve in a manner that corresponds appropriately to the changing needs and challenges of society.

The Role and Function of Mental Health Counselors

Nicholas, Gerstein, and Keller (1988) have noted that mental health counselors perform most of the same tasks that other mental health practitioners do, such as marriage and family counselors, social workers, and psychologists. These tasks include psychoeducational services, clinical or direct services, supervision, administration, program development, and consultation. Two tasks that mental health counselors do not tend to engage in are program evaluation and research. These tasks are often performed by doctoral-level counselors and psychologists (Nicholas, Gerstein, & Keller, 1988).

Brooks and Gerstein (1990) note that while mental health practitioners serve similar functions, they vary in terms of treatment philosophies. These authors found that typically mental health counselors utilize a psychoeducational, developmental, and psychopathological point of view; marriage and family therapists use a systemic orientation; psychologists rely on a psychopathological frame of reference; and social workers adhere to a sociological perspective (Brooks & Gerstein, 1990). Ivey (1989) also differentiates mental health disciplines according to philosophical orientation, noting that mental health counselors define themselves primarily within a developmental perspective, while psychologists adhere to a medical/therapeutic model and social workers focus on the environment. Ginter (1996) provides additional information on the philosophical orientation of mental health counselors. He identifies three pillars of counseling that provide a framework for mental health counseling. These pillars are that counseling is contextually an interpersonal medium, it recognizes the importance of both prevention and remediation, and it has a developmental perspective.

Kelly (1996) looks to the future in terms of the role and function of mental health counselors. He suggests that mental health counselors are attempting to address three broad, interrelated challenges. First, mental health counselors must continue to assert their right to be mental health service providers in a health-care venue that reflects shrinking resources. This challenge can only be met with continued support for mental health counseling licensure and recognition and utilization by managed-care providers. A second challenge facing mental health counselors is to communicate accountability by documented improvement in clients. Research and evaluation will play a key role in this process. And third, mental health counselors must effectively adjust to the changing landscape of the mental health field in terms of technology, diversity, and health-care reform. The evolution and refinement of mental health counseling will enable this profession to continue to be a viable counseling service in the mental health delivery system.

Central to the role and function of mental health counseling is providing direct and indirect intervention strategies.

Direct Intervention Strategies

Mental health counselors provide direct counseling services to clients with a wide range of mental disorders (West, Hosie, & MacKey, 1988). This section addresses two commonly used direct intervention strategies: counseling and crisis intervention.

Counseling.   Mental health counselors utilize a wide range of direct counseling strategies such as individual counseling, group counseling, marriage and family counseling, and substance abuse counseling (NeJedlo, Arrendondo, & Benjamin, 1985; Spruill & Fong, 1990; West, Hosie, & MacKey, 1988). In addition, Spruill and Fong (1990) suggest that there appears to be a shift in emphasis in mental health counseling from preventive approaches to direct counseling services such as individual, group, and family counseling.

Crisis Intervention.   Mental health counselors also provide crisis intervention services (Ivey, 1989; West, Hosie, & MacKey, 1988). George and Cristiani (1995) suggest that crisis intervention is not the same as counseling, even though it is a helping strategy. Its focus is more narrow and superficial, its goals are more modest, and it has a briefer duration than counseling. The following is a four-step model for crisis intervention.

The first step is to determine whether the client is in crisis. To determine whether crisis intervention is necessary, the counselor must first decide if the client is experiencing a personal crisis. Gilliland and James (1997, p. 3) defined a crisis as "a perception of an event or situation as an intolerable difficulty that exceeds the person's resources and coping mechanisms." Puryear (1979) identifies five factors associated with a crisis.

1. The symptoms of stress result in psychological and physiological discomfort.
2. The client feels intense emotions such as feelings of inadequacy, helplessness, panic, or agitation.
3. The client is more concerned with gaining relief from the symptom than with the problem that precipitated the symptom.
4. The client has a reduced ability to function efficiently.
5. The crisis occurs during a short period of time.

Gilliland and James (1997) recommended that the counselor use listening skills during the initial phase of crisis intervention to gain a phenomenological understanding of the client. This practice can also help the counselor determine whether the client is experiencing a crisis. At the same time, it will enable the counselor to establish rapport and communicate support to the client.

The second step in crisis intervention involves assessment, using two separate procedures. First, the counselor must assess the severity of the crisis in terms of the potential for serious harm to the client or others. Gilliland and James (1997) emphasize that the primary goal of crisis intervention is to avoid a catastrophe in which someone would be seriously injured. The second assessment procedure involves determining whether the client is mentally able to take an active role in resolving the crisis situation. A useful tool in this process is a mental status exam (Othmer & Othmer, 1989), which can help determine whether the client is oriented to person, place, and time; free of hallucinations; and capable of coherent thinking. When a client does not appear to be capable of realistic decision making, the counselor may need to take a more active role in the crisis intervention process.

The third step in the crisis intervention model involves action. During a crisis, some form of action will usually be required to restore equilibrium to the client. Providing the client with rest can be an important part of this process. For example, if the client is acutely suicidal, the counselor may work with family members to arrange for the client to be hospitalized.

Once the client receives rest and equilibrium has been restored, counseling strategies can be implemented. The counselor can attempt to identify the precipitating factors associated with the crisis and help the client overcome these problems in the future.

The fourth and final step entails follow-up. Cavanaugh (1982) notes that clients can have delayed reactions to a crisis, which may occur weeks or even months after the precipitating event. It is therefore important to arrange for appropriate follow-up counseling services.

The following *Personal Note* provides an illustration of crisis intervention.

A Personal Note

Mary arrived at an outpatient mental health clinic where I was a counselor and said that she was having trouble sleeping and wanted sleeping pills. She appeared agitated and tearful, and she spoke in a monotone. It soon became clear that there was much more on her mind than her trouble with sleeping. She began to talk about an affair that her husband was having. She went on to say that "because of my religious beliefs," it was necessary for her to kill her three children and herself. Mary reasoned that since her husband had an affair, he had lost his right to have any more contact with his family.

I asked Mary what religion would want her to kill herself and her children. At this point, she seemed to ramble on incoherently. A brief mental status examination showed her to be oriented to person and place—she knew who and where she was—but not to time—she didn't know the day, month, or year. There was no evidence of hallucinations but some possibility of a delusion since she described herself as the "savior" of the family. She intended to kill herself and her children to "save" them all from the sins of her husband.

I then explored the seriousness of her suicidal and homicidal threat. I discovered that she had a gun and planned to use it. Since Mary had a plan and a method of carrying it through, I saw this as a crisis that required immediate action. I became very concerned about the safety of Mary and her children. I decided that it would be best if Mary were hospitalized so that she could receive mental health treatment and be protected from hurting herself or her children.

I emphasized to Mary that I wanted her to be hospitalized for her safety and the safety of her children. Since there was not a mental health code on the Indian reservation where I was working, I could not insist that she be hospitalized. Fortunately, Mary agreed to be admitted to the hospital for a couple of days. For the first 2 days, Mary slept "around the clock," only getting up occasionally for water. After she rested, she said she felt much better. Although Mary was still very angry with her husband, she realized that killing herself and her children would accomplish nothing. Before Mary was discharged from the hospital, she made an appointment with me for individual and marital counseling.

Indirect Intervention Strategies

Hershenson and Power (1987) have identified six indirect activities associated with the mental health counselor's role and function. They can be considered indirect intervention strategies in that they provide an indirect form of treatment. An overview of these activities follows.

Prevention.   Prevention represents the inverse of coping with a crisis (Barclay, 1984). Prevention of mental disorders and the promotion of mental health have been an integral part of the community mental health movement (Matus & Neuhring, 1979). An example of a preventive focus is the holistic health movement, which promotes healthy lifestyles to prevent the development of illness.

Hershenson and Power (1987) identify three types of prevention: primary, secondary, and tertiary.

1. *Primary prevention* evolved from the public health model. It refers to strengthening the resistance of a particular population and offsetting harmful influences before they can make an impact (Caplan, 1964). Primary prevention takes place before a problem has manifested itself or when its symptoms are barely noticeable (Gilbert, 1982). Shaw and Goodyear (1984) note that primary prevention reduces the number of individuals requiring mental health services and is therefore an important aspect of any comprehensive human services program. Unfortunately, primary prevention has historically taken a back seat to other strategies because resources are instead applied to people with existing problems.

2. *Secondary prevention* involves programs that attempt to identify individuals who are at risk for developing certain problems and then prescribing remedial activities to prevent those problems from occurring (McMurty, 1985). For example, there has been some interest in working with children of alcoholics to prevent them from becoming alcoholic.

3. *Tertiary prevention* attempts to avert further consequences of a problem that has already manifested itself (Hershenson & Power, 1987). The present mental health system puts most of its efforts in tertiary prevention, focusing on alleviating existing mental health problems.

Although prevention is clearly a recognized intervention in mental health counseling, it has not been adequately integrated into the training process or practice of mental health counselors (Kiselica & Look, 1993). The disparity between philosophy and practice may be due in part to a lack of insight into the "what and how" of prevention. Apparently, mental health educators and providers lack a clear understanding of what prevention is and how a clinician can engage in this endeavor. In addition, mental health trainees appear to be more interested in remedial interventions such as psychotherapy than prevention. Kiselica and Look suggest that counselor-educators should make a renewed effort to provide adequate training and emphasis on prevention. In this regard, mental health counselors must work together to make primary prevention the principal mode of intervention for mental health counseling. In addition, these authors recommend that increased efforts need to be directed at pursuing grant money for prevention, and journals such as the *Journal of Mental Health Counseling* should make articles on prevention a higher priority.

Advocacy.   Advocacy is another indirect intervention strategy utilized by mental health counselors. *Advocacy* means to plead the cause of another person and follow through with action in support of that cause (Tesolowski, Rosenberg, & Stein, 1983). Hershenson and Power (1987) further explained that "a mental health counselor-advocate is one who is the client's supporter, the advisor, the champion, and if need be, the client's representative in dealing with the court, the police, the social agency, and other organizations that affect one's well-being" (p. 246).

Advocacy is an action-oriented form of intervention in which the counselor does something for the client. This can have a positive impact on the counseling relationship in that the client may perceive the counselor as someone who can get things done. Mental health counselors can function as advocates in many ways, such as working with a human services department to ensure that clients receive benefits to which they are entitled.

Hershenson and Power (1987) have identified the following advocacy skills of mental health counselors.

- *Timing.* Counselors must decide when to be an advocate and when to let the client take the initiative. As a basic rule, counselors should intervene when it becomes clear that the system is not working for the client or even appears to be working against the client.
- *Support.* Counselors must have the support of the system to be capable of working effectively with that system. In this vein, it is important for counselors not to alienate themselves from co-workers. Counselors are more successful when they work in a cooperative manner and avoid being perceived as blindly fighting for another cause.
- *Compromise.* To maintain support from the system, counselors should be flexible and willing to compromise. A give-and-take approach can also yield creative solutions to complex problems.
- *Communication.* Several communication skills can be useful in the role of advocate. It is important to be able to listen and communicate an understanding of different points of view regarding the client. This can promote a cooperative approach. Another communication skill that may be necessary is assertiveness. Occasionally, mental health counselors need to take an assertive position to obtain the desired results. Naturally, this must be done in a tactful, caring fashion to be effective.

Consulting.   Since the passage of the Community Mental Health Act in 1963, consultation has been an important aspect of the mental health worker's role and function (Kurpius, 1978). The act noted that consultation services were to become an essential part of community mental health programs of the future (Hershenson & Power, 1987). This legislation was viewed as an attempt to broaden mental health services to include more developmental and preventive approaches (Kurpius, 1978).

Caplan (1970) provides the following definition of mental health consultation:

> A process of interaction between two professional persons—the consultant, who is a specialist, and the consultee, who invokes the consultant's help in regard to a current work problem with which he is having some difficulty and which he has decided is within the other's area of specialized competence. (p. 19)

Hansen, Himes, and Meier (1990) note that Caplan's definition of mental health consultation has been broadened to include professional consulting with a lay person, for example, a counselor consulting with a parent. In addition, Brown (1993) notes that consultation can involve working with individuals, couples, groups, families, organizations, and larger systems such as communities.

Brown (1993) posits that although consultation holds an important role in the overall philosophy of counseling, it does not appear to be a high priority for counselor-educators or counselors. Brown makes several recommendations that could increase the role that consultation plays in all aspects of the counseling profession, including mental health counseling. First, more effort needs to be made to integrate consultation into the counselor education curriculum in terms of course work and fieldwork experiences (for example, counseling and consultation should both be considered during treatment planning). Second, licensing and accreditation boards should ensure that individuals and programs show evidence of appropriate consultation skills and activities.

The lack of attention to consultation appears to parallel the underutilization of preventative services by mental health counselors (Albee & Ryan-Finn, 1993). It therefore seems imperative that prevention and consultation be linked together so counselors can gain a better understanding of how to promote prevention through consultation. Clearly the interrelationship between theory, research, and practice regarding these concepts requires further development.

Mediation.   Mediation is one of the newest roles of mental health counselors. Many states now offer mediation services to assist individuals who are going through a divorce (Hershenson & Power, 1987).

Witty (1980) defines mediation as the "facilitation of an agreement between two or more disputing parties by an agreed-upon third party" (p. 4). Kessler (1979) and Koopman (1985) note the following components of mediation: each party agrees to utilize the services of a mediator, the outcome is an agreement made by the disputants themselves, conflict resolution is cooperative instead of competitive, the focus is on "where we go from here" as opposed to fault-finding, self-disclosure and empathy are promoted in place of deception and intimidation, decisions are self-imposed instead of imposed by others, and creative alternatives are promoted rather than win-or-lose positions.

Kessler (1979) describes the actual process of mediation as a structured decision-making process that usually lasts one to three sessions. Hershenson and Power (1987) identify the following three steps that a mental health counselor could use to provide structure to the mediation process.

1. The counselor initially provides the necessary structure by establishing a cooperative tone, setting the rules, obtaining a commitment to the process, and providing an overview of what is to come (Kessler, 1979).
2. In this strategic and planning phase, the mediator obtains an overview of the conflict by reviewing all pertinent information. Toward the end of this step, the mediator can begin to develop a specific plan of action with the disputants.
3. The third step is the problem-solving phase, in which the mediator works with the disputants to help them reach a specific agreement. The mediator may use a variety of tactics during this process, including negotiation, creative problem solving, joining meetings, and private caucuses. The final agreement is usually written out by the disputants so they will have a permanent record of the mediation process.

Mentoring.   Mentoring is another relatively new role and function for mental health counselors. Krupp (1982) defines *mentoring* as a process in which a trusted and experienced individual takes a direct interest in the development and education of a younger, less experienced individual. Numerous studies have shown that mentoring has a positive impact on the mentor, the less-experienced individual, and the organization involved (Lynch, 1980; Vaillant, 1977).

Farren, Gray, and Kaye (1984) have identified several guidelines for establishing a mentoring relationship: participation should be voluntary, there should be minimal rules and maximum freedom, the mentor and the less-experienced individual should share and negotiate expectations, and mentors should be rewarded for their efforts.

Education.   The mental health counselor can also function as an educator; a role that may involve indirect and direct intervention strategies. Education is often an important facet of both types of strategies described in this section, as shown in the following examples.

- Counseling can help a client learn how to become more autonomous.
- Crisis intervention may teach a client how to avoid future crises.
- Prevention often occurs through programs that emphasize an educational component such as parent education.
- Advocacy can teach a client how to be assertive without alienating others.
- Consultation may involve inservice training programs that teach special skills, such as how to avoid burnout.
- Mediation can help a client learn how to resolve conflicts in a cooperative fashion.
- Mentoring provides opportunities for a less-experienced individual to learn from a more experienced person.

Categories of Mental Health Services

The majority of mental health services are directed at helping clients who are dealing with problems of living or who have mental disorders. This section provides an overview of the clinical issues associated with these two categories of problems clients typically face.

Problems of Living

Hershenson and Power (1987) define *problems of living* as "aberrations and/or natural rough spots as one moves through the course of the life-span development" (p. 87). Typical problems of living that clients face are relationship difficulties, such as marital problems; lack of meaning in life, such as not feeling valued at work; and problems associated with stress, such as psychosomatic illness. Although mental disorders may contribute to problems of living, a client can have these problems without a recognized mental disorder.

Counseling is the primary treatment strategy used to help clients deal with problems of living. Counseling can help the client deal with specific problems, prevent future problems, and cope with stress. Since problems of living typically do not involve mental disorders, the use of psychoactive drugs is usually not part of the treatment program.

Mental Disorders

A mental disorder can be broadly defined as a dysfunctional behavioral or psychological pattern associated with distress or disability (American Psychiatric Association, 1994). In 1984 the National Institute of Mental Health conducted a survey of mental health problems in the United States ("Mental Disorders," 1984). It was an in-depth study costing $15 million. The study estimated that 40 million people in the United States experience mental health problems at any given time. More specifically it found that

- One in five adults suffered from a recognized mental disorder.
- The three most common disorders in order of incidence were anxiety, substance abuse, and depression.
- Only one out of five people with a mental disorder sought professional help. Those who did tended to seek help from someone at their church or from a family physician.
- Women tended to suffer from phobias and depression, whereas men tended to have problems with alcohol and drugs and antisocial behavior.
- The rates for mental problems were higher for those under 45.
- College graduates tend to be less prone to mental disorders than those who did not graduate from college.

The results of this survey suggest that a large percentage of Americans suffer from mental disorders. Another important implication is that when people experience mental problems, they tend not to utilize mental health services. Instead, they often turn to other professionals, such as physicians or members of the clergy. A challenge for mental health counselors has been to overcome the stigma often associated with mental health services so that individuals will seek help when they need it.

Treating Mental Disorders.   Treatment approaches for mental disorders include the use of psychoactive drugs and counseling. Psychoactive drugs are used by psychiatrists primarily to treat psychosis, depression, and acute anxiety reactions. It is important to note that these medications do not cure a person of a mental disorder. They are used primarily to treat underlying brain chemistry dysfunctions and provide symptom relief such as alleviating depression or anxiety. There are potential dangers, for example, the possibility of clients becoming dependent on these medications, especially in the case of tranquilizers to treat anxiety. There can also be serious side effects, for instance, tardive dyskinesia, an irreversible neurological disorder that can result from the prolonged use of antipsychotic medications.

Although psychoactive medications can have drawbacks and inherent dangers, their benefits usually outweigh the risks. For example, a schizophrenic client who does not receive medication may be overwhelmed by threatening hallucinations, dangerous delusions, or a disruptive thought disorder. Although medication cannot remove these symptoms entirely, it can usually control them to the degree that the client can function in society. Antidepressant medications can also be an important aspect of a treatment program for severely depressed clients, who may require medication to be able to work and engage in daily activities. Medication can also be very useful in treating a severe anxiety reaction, since it can reduce anxiety to a point where the client can cope.

Counseling can also play a vital role in the overall treatment program for mental disorders (see the section on cognitive-behavioral approaches in Chapter 9). Counseling may not be indicated until a client has been medically stabilized by the psychoactive medication. A client can be considered *medically stable* when the symptoms associated with the mental disorder have been reduced to the extent that the client is capable of actively engaging in the counseling process.

Counseling can also be used, of course, to treat mental disorders that do not require medication. The actual counseling strategies will vary according to the unique needs of the client and the clinical indicators associated with the particular mental disorder. The following *Personal Note* describes some of the things I have learned about the treatment of mental disorders.

A Personal Note

Over the years, I have learned many important lessons from clients who had mental disorders. Several clients have said something in particular that I have never forgotten. As I reflect on these cases, their comments symbolize lessons that I learned from them. I will describe five cases, giving the client's statement, a brief description of the situation, and the lesson I learned from each person.

Client's Statement: "Someone said pull my eyes out and I did."

Description of Client's Situation. The client who made this statement was a 25-year-old male who was in jail for theft. A psychiatrist had been asked to make an evaluation because the client was acting strangely. The psychiatrist made a provisional diagnosis of schizophrenia and arranged to have the client admitted to a psychiatric hospital.

The client was not given any antipsychotic medication and was to be transferred to the hospital the next day. That night, he began to hallucinate that he was hearing voices. A "voice" told him to take his eye out, and he did. Then a "voice" said to take the other eye out, and he took it out as well. He was standing and holding his two eyes when a jailer walked by and saw with horror what had happened. The client was immediately taken to a hospital and provided treatment. At the hospital, the client was diagnosed as schizophrenic. I met this man while I was at the hospital checking on several clients. He told me about the voices he had heard, asking him to take his eyes out when he was in jail.

What I Learned. I learned that clients who are actively hallucinating can do serious harm to themselves. Antipsychotic medications must therefore be considered to help control the hallucinations and other psychotic symptoms.

Client's Statement. "Would you like to see the picture I painted?"

Description of Client's Situation. The client was a 23-year-old woman who had a long history of severe depression. I had been providing counseling for the client for about 1 year. Although she had weekly appointments, she often missed them. I was actually surprised when she did make an appointment, because she always seemed so disoriented.

One day, the client walked into the counseling center and said she wanted to see me. She told me she had painted a self-portrait and asked if I would like to see it. I could not believe my eyes. She painted the most beautiful painting I had ever seen!

What I Learned. This client made me realize never to "write off" a client. Regardless of how incapacitated I may think some clients are, I will always remember that they are still capable of doing fantastic things with their lives!

Client's Statement: "There were spiders crawling all over my face and voices telling me I was going to die. I was terrified!"

Description of Client's Situation: This was a 54-year-old female who had been an alcoholic for 26 years. The client was on a drinking binge for 2 weeks and then experienced alcohol hallucinosis, which involved spiders crawling on her face and hearing terrifying voices. The client came to the counseling center the next day and said she would never drink again. I provided weekly counseling services for her over the next year. During that time, the client did not drink. She later moved to another city.

What I Learned. I discovered that the prognosis for overcoming alcoholism is good when the client decides that the costs outweigh the rewards of use. During the first few sessions, it became clear to me that this client had decided that drinking was just not worth it any more.

Client's Statement: "We just caught on fire."

Description of Client's Situation.   The client who made this statement was one of two brothers who caught on fire when they were sniffing gasoline. Both had a long history of inhalant abuse, spanning a five-year period. I had been seeing them in counseling for two years prior to their accident with gasoline. During the years I worked with them, they were hospitalized on numerous occasions for treatment of acute lead poisoning. On one occasion, one of the brothers became psychotic, jumping out of a moving car and running down the street pounding on cars during the 8:00 A.M. rush-hour traffic.

What I Learned.   I learned several things from this case and similar cases involving inhalant dependency. First, I found these individuals have a very difficult time attempting to overcome inhalant dependency. My success rate has been very low with this population: only 1 out of 5 stopped using inhalants while I worked with them.

I soon discovered that lead poisoning can produce serious side effects. For example, both of the brothers I worked with showed significant intellectual impairment. Their overall IQ scores on the Wechsler Adult Intelligence Scale dropped 15 and 20 points respectively over a 12-month interval while they were using inhalants. I also discovered that gasoline sniffing can make a person psychotic. In addition, I learned that lead poisoning was very difficult to treat. I found out that when an individual inhales lead, the lead is absorbed into the bone structure as well as other parts of the body. Unfortunately, the lead tends to remain in the bone structure, gradually releasing lead into the body.

Client's Statement: "I got my meat, my flour, and my Jesus."

Description of Client's Situation.   This was a 45-year-old woman who had been suffering from chronic schizophrenia for 20 years. A residential program had just opened for people who were chronically mentally ill and had no relatives to assist them. I asked the client if she would like to be admitted into the program, and she said, "Yes."

Getting the client admitted into the program was a very long and drawn-out process. It involved filling out numerous forms and dealing with other seemingly endless aspects of the bureaucracy. I was finally told that my client could get into the program. I couldn't wait to tell her the good news.

When I told her she was accepted into the program, she looked puzzled. She then smiled and told me that she didn't want to go. She said, "I got my meat, my flour, and my Jesus." When I asked her what she meant, she said she had plenty of meat to eat and flour to make bread. Then she turned on her portable radio and played a religious station featuring a preacher giving a high-powered sermon. She pointed to the radio, smiled, and said, "That's my Jesus."

What I Learned.   I learned that freedom is essential to human dignity. Whenever possible, people need to have freedom of choice and be able to act on those choices. My job as a counselor was simply to help create choices. When I did create choices for this client, it seemed to bring more meaning to her existence—an existence that she already had.

Strategies for Suicidal Clients

Mental health services must continually adapt to the changes in society. Two mental health problems requiring increasing efforts from mental health counselors and other members of the helping profession are suicidal clients and clients with substance abuse problems. To illustrate the contemporary issues and skills associated with mental health counseling, this section provides an overview of suicide, and the next will cover substance abuse.

The rate of suicides per 100,000 people has increased steadily and dramatically over the past 30 years. In 1950 there were 4.2 suicides per 100,000; in 1974, 10.9; and 1984, 12.8

(Shneidman, 1984). Suicide rates are high across all levels of society. Among girls, the gifted have the highest rate of suicide nationally and are therefore considered to have an especially high risk (Taylor, 1979).

Capuzzi and Nystul (1986) provided a comprehensive overview of suicide—causes, myths, and treatment strategies. The remainder of this section is adapted from that work.

Causes

Shneidman (1984) identifies four theoretical perspectives for understanding the motivation for attempting suicide.

Sociological.   Durkheim (1897) described sociological reasons for suicide that seem to have withstood the test of time. These reasons can be categorized as: (a) *egoistic,* when a person lacks a sense of belonging and therefore lacks a sense of purpose; (b) *altruistic,* when a person is willing to die for a particular cause (for example, Japanese kamikaze pilots); (c) *anomic,* when people believe their relationship with society has been shattered (for example, after being fired from a job); and (d) *fatalistic,* when individuals feel society does not offer any hope for a better future (for example, people who feel trapped in poverty).

Psychodynamic.   Freud (1933) emphasized the role of unconscious forces in personality dynamics. In this regard, he believed that all people have an unconscious death wish that could contribute to suicidal behavior.

Psychological.   Shneidman (1976) provided a psychological perspective of suicide, suggesting that suicide is associated with the following psychological conditions: *acute perturbation,* when an individual is in a heightened state of unhappiness; *heightened inimicality*, the person has negative thoughts and feelings toward the self, such as self-hate and guilt; *constriction of intellectual focus,* characterized by a tunneling of thought processes resulting in an inability to see viable options; and *cessation,* when a person believes that suicide will make the suffering stop.

Constitutional or Biochemical.   The medical model suggests a link between depression and suicide and views depression as having an organic basis. In this model, therefore, suicide can be prevented by using psychoactive medication to restore an individual's biochemical balance.

Myths About Suicide

Numerous myths are associated with suicide. The following are some of the myths and the facts that counteract them, as provided by Capuzzi and Nystul (1986) and Gilliland and James (1997).

- *Suicide is only committed by people with severe psychological problems.* Studies have shown that most individuals who commit suicide had not been diagnosed as having a psychological disorder (Shneidman, Farberow, & Litman, 1976).

- *Suicide usually occurs without warning.* In fact, most suicides are preceded by warning signs. The nature of the warning signs may be a sudden change of behavior, self-destructive behavior, verbal threats of suicide, talk of hopelessness and despair, and depression.
- *People who are suicidal will always be prone to suicide.* In truth, most people who become suicidal do not remain in that state forever. They may be struggling through a temporary personal crisis. Once they work through the crisis, they may never be suicidal again.
- *Discussing suicide may cause the client to want to carry out the act.* The opposite is actually true. Talking with a caring person can often prevent suicide.
- *When a person has attempted suicide and pulls back from it, the danger is over.* Actually, the greatest period of danger is usually during the upswing period, when the person becomes energized following a severe depression and has the energy to commit suicide.

Treatment Strategies

The best strategy for dealing with the suicidal phenomenon would appear to be prevention. One way to prevent suicide is to be aware of the factors associated with suicide. Gilliland and James (1997) have identified several factors, which include the following: the client has a family history of suicide attempts; the client has attempted suicide before; the client has a plan for suicide and the means to carry out the plan; there is a history of unsuccessful medical treatment for a serious illness; or the client has recently experienced a loss through death, divorce, or separation. When several of these factors are present, especially a past history of suicide and a current plan for suicide, a client can be considered a high risk for suicide.

Capuzzi and Nystul (1986) describe crisis intervention strategies and postcrisis strategies that could be used with suicidal clients. Crisis intervention strategies include the procedures described earlier in this chapter and may also involve consideration of hospitalization and psychiatric intervention. It may also be necessary to inform family members of the risk of suicide so the client can be monitored. Postcrisis counseling strategies can be implemented after the client is no longer suicidal. These procedures can include determining what caused the client to become suicidal, developing a treatment program to overcome the precipitating factors, and teaching coping skills to prevent problems in the future. The following *Personal Note* provides additional insights into the suicidal phenomenon.

A Personal Note

When I was the psychologist for an Indian reservation, I provided mental health counseling to more than 100 clients who attempted suicide. Most of these clients were female adolescents who tried to kill themselves by taking large amounts of pills they found in a medicine cabinet.

The thing that surprised me about these clients was that nearly all of them truly seemed to want to die. They did not appear simply to be making a cry for help. Several nearly died when their hearts stopped. Each time, fortunately, the medical team was able to bring the client back from the

continued

grips of death. When these young women regained consciousness, however, almost all of them immediately said something that expressed their disappointment that they had not died.

As I explored their reasons for wanting to die, the majority seemed to believe life had nothing to offer them. They had reached a dead end, with nowhere to go. They felt if they did try to continue living again, things would probably just get worse. There were feelings of futility and sorrow in their words and tone of voice. Their desire for life seemed to be gone, and in its place grew a sense of apathy.

The focus of counseling with these clients was to help them discover some personal meaning in life. Together we worked to cultivate dreams and develop the means to turn those dreams into reality. This process required intensive individual counseling and psychotherapy. In addition, I often utilized couples counseling and family therapy as an important facet of the overall treatment program.

Strategies for Clients with Substance-Abuse Problems

Substance abuse has become a major health problem in the United States as well as many other countries. Alcoholism is considered to be the third most prevalent public health problem in the United States (Pattison & Kaufman, 1982). For some cultures, such as Native Americans, alcoholism ranks first among all health problems (Herring, 1994). Illicit drug use is also widespread in American society and includes use among children and adolescents, as discussed in Chapter 11. A 1982 survey estimated that 32 million Americans smoke marijuana at least once a year, and 20 million use it once a month; over 12 million use cocaine once a year; and several million use a variety of drugs, such as tranquilizers and stimulants, without medical supervision (Polich et al., 1984).

The result of the high prevalence of alcohol and drug use (not counting tobacco) is that approximately 40 percent of hospital admissions and 25 percent of deaths a year in the United States are related to substance abuse, costing society an excess of $300 billion a year in addition to human suffering and lack of productivity (American Psychiatric Association, 1995). The extensive cost and suffering generated by excessive use of alcohol and other drugs is not surprising when noting that approximately half of all highway fatalities involve alcohol; one-third of all new AIDS cases are related to intravenous drug users; and 7.5 to 15 percent of pregnant women have recently used a drug (not counting alcohol) just prior to their first prenatal exam (American Psychiatric Association, 1995).

Substance abuse permeates all levels of society: approximately one-fifth of all Americans have a problem with alcohol or drug abuse at some time in their lives, and one-third of all psychiatric patients have alcohol- or drug-abuse problems (Frances, 1988). Counselors can therefore expect to come into contact with problems relating to drug abuse regardless of the counseling setting where they work.

This section provides an overview of substance abuse, with information relating to diagnosis, special treatment issues, counseling goals, treatment strategies, and prevention of relapses. Since alcoholism is the most prevalent of these problems, particular attention is devoted to that issue.

Diagnosis

Counselors can diagnose substance-abuse problems using DSM-IV (American Psychiatric Association, 1994), which recognizes two mental disorders associated with substance abuse: substance abuse and substance dependence. A diagnosis of substance abuse applies to a client with an impairment in social or occupational functioning. Substance dependence is considered a more serious disorder and is diagnosed when a client shows evidence of physiological withdrawal or tolerance. It is important to note that use of a particular substance like marijuana does not constitute abuse. Instead, the use of the substance must result in impairment in functioning before it should be considered abuse or dependence, a recognized mental disorder.

Questionnaires can also be used as a part of the diagnostic process to determine whether a person is an alcoholic or has a substance-abuse problem. A commonly used questionnaire is the Michigan Alcohol Screening Test (Selzer, 1971). This test has 24 questions that require yes-or-no answers from the respondent.

Some dangers can result, however, from using the DSM-IV system of diagnosis or a questionnaire to label a person as a substance abuser. These systems have either-or definitions of alcoholism in that they provide a result that a client either is or is not an alcoholic. This either-or definition could result in a counselor not providing needed services to a client with a borderline problem.

Pattison and Kaufman (1982) reject the either-or perspective and instead conceptualize alcoholism as a multivariant syndrome. This position suggests that no two alcoholics are alike. Instead, alcoholics represent multiple patterns of dysfunctional use, varying personalities, numerous possibilities for adverse consequences, and various prognoses, and each individual requires a different type of treatment (Pattison & Kaufman, 1982).

According to Lewis, Dana, and Blevins (1994), the multivariant position suggests that substance abuse should be conceptualized on a continuum from nonuse to dependence (see Figure 15.1). Lewis, Dana, and Blevins (1994) note that the continuum model does not imply that people who develop problems will always move steadily along the continuum from left to right. The relationship to the continuum will vary from individual to individual. Some will stay at the same spot; others will move to the right, signifying more serious problems; and some will develop less severe problems, moving to the left on the continuum.

| Nonuse | Moderate nonproblematic use | Heavy nonproblematic use | Heavy use; moderate problems | Heavy use; serious problems | Dependence life and health problems |

FIGURE 15.1   Substance-Abuse Continuum

Source: From *Substance Abuse Counseling: An Individual Approach* by J. A. Lewis, G. A. Blevins, and, R. Q. Dana. Copyright © 1994, Brooks/Cole Publishing Company, Pacific Grove, CA 93950, a division of International Thomson Publishing, Inc. By permission of the publisher.

Lewis, Dana, and Blevins (1994) suggest that counselors can estimate the place where a person is functioning on the continuum by determining the number of problems the person has experienced in relation to substance abuse. Vaillant's (1983) Problem-Drinking Scale can be used to identify problems relating to drinking, including work-related problems, such as excessive tardiness or sick leave or being fired from work; family problems, such as complaints from family members or marital problems; legal problems, such as alcohol-related arrests; and health problems, such as medical disorders, blackouts, and tremors.

Special Treatment Issues

Most of the counseling theories and strategies described in this text can be applied to the treatment of clients with substance-abuse problems. At the same time, some special issues should be considered when working with this population. In this regard, Lewis, Dana, and Blevins (1994) provide the following guidelines for substance-abuse counseling.

- Conceptualize substance-abuse problems on a continuum from nonproblematic to problematic rather than in dichotomous, either-or terms.
- Provide an individualized treatment program in terms of goals and methods.
- Incorporate a multidimensional treatment program that includes social and environmental aspects associated with long-term recovery.
- Select the least intrusive treatment for each client.
- Consider new methods and goals as research findings become available.
- Be sensitive to the individual differences and various needs of diverse client populations.

These guidelines provide a general theoretical framework for working with substance abuse. In addition, there are some unique counseling goals and treatment strategies associated with substance-abuse counseling.

Counseling Goals

Considerable debate exists in the literature as to whether the primary goal of alcohol-abuse counseling should be abstinence or controlled drinking (Fisher, 1982; Marlatt, 1983; Sobell & Sobell, 1984). Proponents of abstinence align themselves with the disease model of alcoholism, contending that alcoholism is a chronic and progressive disease and that abstinence is therefore the only solution. Alcoholics Anonymous (AA) and Narcotics Anonymous (NA) are among the proponents of this position. In contrast, supporters of controlled drinking conceptualize alcoholism from a behavioral perspective, believing that it results from maladaptive learning.

Miller and Munoz (1982) note that controlled drinking will be appropriate only for approximately 15 percent of all alcohol abusers. In addition, Miller and Munoz (1982) identify conditions that should preclude any consideration of controlled drinking as a treatment goal. These include clients who have a medical problem such as a disease of the gastrointestinal system (for example, liver disease), heart disease, or other condition that may be made worse by drinking; are pregnant or trying to become pregnant; tend to lose control of their behavior when they drink; have been physically addicted to alcohol; take medication that is dangerous when combined with alcohol, such as antidepressants or tranquilizers; or are currently abstaining successfully, particularly if there is a family history of alcoholism or a personal history of serious drinking problems.

Counselors who want to consider controlled drinking as a goal for a client should first receive specialized training. Behavioral self-control training is one approach that has received considerable attention, reporting a success rate between 60 and 80 percent (Miller, 1980). This program is educationally oriented and can be used in an outpatient setting. It involves a variety of behavioral techniques, including training the client to identify environmental cues that increase the frequency of drinking, monitoring drinking consumption, and the use of self-reinforcement to control drinking rates.

Aside from the issue of abstinence versus controlled drinking, there are other, more specific goals that counselors should address in developing a comprehensive treatment program. Lewis, Dana, and Blevins (1994) note that substance abuse tends to be associated with social, physiological, family, and financial problems. Considering these related problems, they identify the following goals that counselors could attempt to accomplish in substance-abuse counseling. The counselor can help clients to

- Resolve legal problems
- Attain stability in marriage and family
- Establish and meet educational and career goals
- Improve interpersonal and social skills
- Enhance physical fitness and health
- Develop effective coping mechanisms to deal with stress
- Learn how to recognize and express feelings
- Develop effective problem-solving and decision-making skills
- Establish a social support system
- Develop positive self-esteem and self-efficacy
- Deal effectively with psychological issues such as anxiety and depression
- Create recreational and social outlets

Treatment Strategies

Treatment approaches in substance-abuse counseling vary according to the counselor's theoretical orientation as well as the goals established by the counselor and client. The following overview presents some commonly used treatment approaches.

The Minnesota Model. The Minnesota model has been one of the most widely used forms of treatment for substance abuse. According to Gilliland and James (1997) there are two phases to the Minnesota model. The first phase involves a comprehensive treatment team to evaluate and provide initial treatment pertaining to the unique needs of the client. The second phase typically involves an intensive 28-day inpatient hospitalization directed at all aspects of the client's substance abuses problem (for example, education, recovery, and relapse prevention). In an era of managed care, the 28-day hospitalization is in most instances not a realistic goal for treatment planning. Most managed-care organizations are shifting to an emphasis on outpatient substance-abuse treatment programs.

The Alcoholics Anonymous (AA) Model.   Since AA was founded in 1935, it has developed into the most popular organization for the treatment of alcoholism and other substance abuse problems (Lê, Ingvarson, & Page, 1995). AA incorporates the disease model of alcoholism and is based on the 12 steps of AA, which have a strong religious context. Some of the strengths of AA is that it is run by individuals who have themselves struggled with substance dependence, and it can be a place where people feel accepted and can feel hope and encouragement. It is also a highly accessible organization with outlets available in almost every major city in the world.

There has been some concern that the efficacy of AA has not been determined through empirical research and the religiously oriented terms such as admitting powerlessness are inconsistent with counseling theory and practice (Bristow-Braitman, 1995; Lê, Ingvarson, & Page, 1995). Bristow-Braitman (1995) suggests that cognitive-behavioral counseling could be used to help reframe some of the AA concepts to make them more compatible with traditional counseling approaches. Professional counselors may benefit from a deeper understanding of AA, so they can become more sensitive to the spiritual aspects of counseling and be more supportive of their clients who are attending AA.

The Medical Model.   This approach also adheres to the disease model of alcoholism. Researchers are currently investigating genetic and organic factors, including brain function and physiology, in terms of etiology and treatment of substance-abuse disorders (Nash, 1997). Several medical approaches are used to treat substance-abuse problems, including antiabuse, which causes a violent physical reaction if alcohol is ingested; methadone maintenance to block the withdrawal symptoms associated with heroin use while not producing the euphoric effects; and programs at detoxification centers and in hospitals to allow patients to overcome the withdrawal effects of alcohol under medical supervision.

One new area of research that supports the medical model of substance abuse is the role that the neurotransmitter dopamine plays in the addiction process. Nash (1997) has reviewed the literature on the dopamine hypothesis for addiction (see Volkow et al., 1997). She concludes that recent research suggests that dopamine may be the master molecule of addiction by transmitting pleasure signals in the brain, resulting in feelings of euphoria. According to this theory, although dopamine may play a central role in addiction, other factors such as neurological, biochemical, and social/behavioral forces also contribute to the complex process of addiction.

Cognitive-Behavioral Therapies.   Cognitive-behavioral therapies are effective treatments in substance-abuse counseling (especially alcohol-related problems). A number of research studies have focused on the role of cognitive-behavior therapies in the acquisition of skills necessary to overcome alcohol abuse and dependence (American Psychiatric Association, 1995). Some of these cognitive-behavioral related skills are self-control, interpersonal functioning, self-efficacy, alternative coping mechanisms, and relapse prevention.

Behavioral Therapies.   Behavioral therapies can be used in substance-abuse counseling. Some of the more common behavioral approaches are operant conditioning to reward and punish behaviors associated with abstaining and engaging in substance abuse and systematic desensitization and aversion training to countercondition clients craving for drugs (American Psychiatric Association, 1995).

Individual Psychodynamic/Interpersonal Therapies. The American Psychiatric Association (APA) (1995) has provided some support for the use of psychodynamic and interpersonal therapies in substance-abuse counseling. The APA notes that psychodynamic psychotherapy appears to help prevent relapse in substance abuse. In addition, newer short-term forms of psychodynamic therapy (such as supportive-expressive therapy and interpersonal psychotherapy) are beginning to demonstrate efficacy in substance-abuse counseling (APA, 1995). These newer approaches focus on formulating supportive counseling relationships in which clients can learn the social skills necessary to overcome negative patterns of interpersonal functioning which in turn decrease problems with substance abuse.

Group Therapies. Lewis, Dana, and Blevens (1994) suggest that group counseling has many advantages over other methods of substance-abuse counseling. For example, it can provide an opportunity for group members to offer support and encouragement, generate problem-solving strategies, learn how to apply new skills such as assertiveness, and when necessary break through denial or other processes that interfere with recovery from substance-abuse problems.

Family Therapy. Gilliland and James (1997) contend that it is critical to involve the family in the treatment of substance abuse. Family therapy recognizes that the behavior of each family member must be understood from the perspective of the family system. Drinking or the use of other drugs is therefore not an isolated event but an action that affects the overall functioning of the family.

Numerous concepts have emerged from the family therapy literature that provide insight into the systemic nature of behavior of family members. For example, the concepts "enabling" and "codependency" imply that two individuals (one with a substance-abuse problem such as drinking) could be dependent on maintaining an adversarial relationship regarding the drinking. In this situation it is common for the drinker and the concerned family member to both get secondary gains from their codependency, thereby enabling the drinker to continue drinking (that is, drinkers feel they have an excuse to drink when they "get griped at" and concerned family members can get sympathy from others regarding having to put up with the drinking).

The use of family dynamics can also be used to overcome one of the most difficult barriers to treatment in substance-abuse counseling—denial. It is very common for individuals to deny problems with alcohol or other drugs and resist treatment even when the problem is having a serious adverse effect on their health, family, social life, and work. When this occurs, Johnson's (1986) family-intervention model can be used to help a family confront a family member with the realities of his or her substance-abuse problem. This approach involves training family members to communicate in a clear, caring, and direct manner their concerns regarding how the substance abuse is affecting the individual and the family as a whole. The family-intervention model can be a powerful approach to overcoming denial and motivating the individual to seek help (Gilliland & James, 1997).

Stages of Change

Helping clients successfully engage in the change process is perhaps the most difficult yet important aspect of counseling. Unfortunately, little has been known about how the change process works. This bleak situation is being addressed by the pioneering work of Prochaska, DiClemente, and associates on how the change process relates to overcoming addictive behaviors (see Prochaska, 1994; Prochaska, DiClemente, & Norcross, 1992).

Prochaska, DiClemente, and associates' transtheoretical model of change "postulates that both the cessation of high-risk behaviors and the acquisition of healthier alternatives involve progression through five stages of change: precontemplation, contemplation, preparation, action, and maintenance" (Prochaska, 1994, p. 47). Prochaska, DiClemente, and Norcross, (1992) provide an overview of these five stages of change and the implications they have for developing intervention strategies.

Precontemplation.   During the first stage, clients have no serious plans to engage in the change process. Resistance and denial are common reactions in the precontemplation stage.

Contemplation.   The second stage is characterized by clients being aware that they have a problem and are thinking about making changes but have not quite reached the point of making a commitment to do something. During the contemplation stage, clients seriously considered resolving their problems. They tend to weigh the pros and cons associated with potential changes to help with decision making.

Preparation.   At the preparation stage, clients have unsuccessfully taken some action during the past year and plan to try to work on their problem during the next 30 days.

Action.   Clients have reached the action stage when they have made the necessary changes in their lives to successfully address a particular problem (for example, stop drinking for one day to six months).

Maintenance.   The maintenance stage is characterized by clients attempting to prevent relapse and stabilize their gains. In substance-abuse counseling, maintenance extends from six months to the rest of the client's life.

Change is like the tide. It moves forward and backward as clients progress and relapse. Prochaska, DiClemente, and Norcross (1992) point out that since clients will tend to relapse, it is common to regress back to earlier stages in the change process. Fortunately, people tend to learn from their mistakes and will use this information to help them be more successful as they work their way back through the stages of change.

One of the most important implications of the change model is to identify where clients are in terms of the change process and match their position with the appropriate form of intervention. For example, there is some evidence that suggests that during the precontemplation and contemplation stages experiential, cognitive, and psychoanalytic approaches are the most effective. And during the action and maintenance stage, existential and behavioral theories have the strongest efficacy (Prochaska, Diclemente, & Norcross, 1992).

Prevention of Relapses

A comprehensive treatment program for substance abuse should also include strategies to prevent or deal with a client's relapse, or uncontrolled return to drug or alcohol use. The potential for relapse is a serious problem in substance-abuse counseling. Some estimates suggest that 90 percent of all clients have a relapse within four years following treatment (Polich, Armor, & Braiker, 1981).

Several factors have been related to substance-abuse relapse. Svanum and McAdoo (1989) note that differences in the outcome of a substance-abuse treatment program are related to the presence or absence of a mental disorder besides the substance-abuse disorder. These researchers found that clients with no additional disorders tended to avoid relapse as long as they complied with after-care treatment, especially an exercise program; had a satisfactory job; and had an adequate living arrangement. Clients with multiple mental disorders were more prone to relapse if their emotional disturbance continued after participation in a substance-abuse program. Other factors such as exercise, work, or living conditions do not appear to be related to relapse for these clients. Since a substantial minority of substance-abuse clients suffer from psychopathology such as anxiety and depression (Mirin et al., 1988), substance-abuse programs should include careful screening and treatment for these disorders as part of relapse prevention.

A second factor related to substance-abuse relapse is the lifestyle imbalance that can result from certain life events. Cummings, Gordon, and Marlatt (1980) attempted to determine what types of events precipitated a relapse. They found that negative emotional states were associated with 35 percent of all relapses; interpersonal conflicts were related to 16 percent; and social pressures accounted for 20 percent.

Lewis, Dana, and Blevins (1994) incorporated Marlatt and Gordon's (1985) model of the relapse process into the flowchart shown in Figure 15.2. The flowchart suggests that the relapse process can begin with a lifestyle imbalance, as shown at the left. This can occur when a client experiences a particular problem, such as a setback at work or a relationship problem. The imbalance may cause the client to feel the need for immediate stress release.

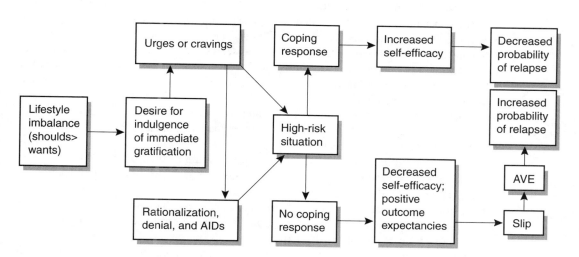

FIGURE 15.2   Relapse Process

Source: Relapse Prevention Maintenance Strategies in the Treatment of Addictive Behaviors, G. A. Marlett and J. R. Gorden, Eds. New York: Guilford Press, 1985.

The client may rationalize taking a drink by thinking, "I deserve a drink, with all that I'm going through." At this point the client may deny having a problem with alcohol and make apparently irrelevant decisions (AIDs). Without the necessary coping skills, the client will experience a decrease in self-efficacy, feeling unable to cope with the situation. This in turn will result in a slip—beginning to drink—creating an abstinence violation effect (AVE). The AVE further undermines the client's self-efficacy, reducing self-confidence. The client may think, "I'm just a hopeless drunk." Such negative thinking can create a self-fulfilling prophesy, leading to an increased probability of a relapse. The flowchart also shows how a substance-abuse counselor can help prevent relapse. The key to preventing a relapse is to teach effective coping skills, such as stress management, which can increase self-efficacy and decrease the probability of relapse.

Current Trends and Perspectives

Several trends impact all aspects of the profession of counseling, including mental health counseling. This section will review three of these emerging trends and perspectives—postmodernism, diversity issues, and issues relating to managed care.

Postmodern Trends

Postmodern trends are beginning to reshape the manner in which mental health counseling is conceptualized and practiced (see special issue in *Journal of Mental Health Counseling, 16*(1), 1994 on constructivist and ecosystemic view and Gutterman, 1996). These emerging trends can be understood by contrasting key concepts of modernism with postmodernism. Modernists view the "self" as autonomous and independent. It therefore follows from a modernist perspective, problems such as depression are caused by internal struggles (for example, intrapsychic conflicts). The modernists' view of the world is objective, with a fixed understanding of knowledge and reality. Research methodology tends to be quantitative, focusing on testing observable, measurable hypotheses. The assessment of clients' problems are understood in terms of cause-and-effect relationships with a focus on content over process (for example, irrational and dysfunctional thinking causes depression and must therefore be analyzed in terms of its content). Goal setting and interventions are generated by mutual agreement between the counselor and client and are reflected in the major counseling theories and approaches.

Postmodern thought broadens the conceptualization of the self to include interpersonal, systemic, and sociocultural forces. Psychological problems, knowledge, and reality are viewed subjectively and are understood in terms of the context in which they are presented (for example, sociocultural milieu). Assessment of clients' problems emphasizes process over content, with a focus on relational/contextual perspectives. Goal setting and intervention strategies often involve exploring clients' narratives and stories and working together to coconstruct new stories that generate personal meaning to life. Research and evaluation methods tend to be qualitative, whereby the counselor and client function as coinvestigators interested in discovering patterns of meaning which can generate insight and understanding. Table 15.1 summarizes the major concepts that differentiate modern from postmodern perspectives.

TABLE 15.1   Comparison of Modern and Postmodern Views

	Modern Views	Postmodern Views
View of the self	Autonomous-independent self	Relational-contextual self
View of knowledge and reality	Fixed-objective concept of knowledge and reality	Subjective-relative concept of knowledge and reality
Assessment of client's problems	Etiology of problems is intrapsychic, with a focus on cause-effect and content (for example, how cognitions effect emotions)	Etiology of problems emphasizes process over content and is focused on relational-contextual perspectives
Goal setting and interventions	Goals are mutually agreed on between counselor and client as reflected in the major counseling theories	Goals and interventions evolve from exploring client's narratives resulting in coconstruction of new stories that generate personal meaning
Research strategies	Quantitative research methodology	Qualitative research methodology

Ecosystemic Mental Health Counseling

Ecosystemic mental health counseling appears to be an attempt to incorporate the major concepts from postmodern trends into a new way of conceptualizing the role and function of the mental health counselor. Sherrard & Amatea (1994, p. 3) define ecosystemic mental health counseling as an approach that "enlarges the field of inquiry and intervention from the individual to the couple, the family, and the larger sociocultural contexts that constitute the individual's environment." Ecosystemic mental health counseling acknowledges the vital role that narrative psychology and counseling as storytelling play in the counseling process (Becvar & Becvar, 1994). In this regard, Daniels and White (1994) suggest that the role of the mental health counselor is directed at exploring the linguistic and language systems of the client resulting in a shift from managing lives to managing conversations.

Mental health counseling recognizes the opportunity that postmodern thought poses for effective integration of theoretical positions. For example, Fong and Lease (1994) suggest that the ecosystemic perspective effectively translates systemic concepts (widely used in marriage and family counseling) into individual and group mental health counseling. Rigazio-DiGilio (1994) addresses the need to integrate theories of development into counseling theories. She provides an in-depth description of how Piaget's theory of cognitive development could be integrated into ecosystemic mental health counseling. Gutterman (1996) provides another example of integration noting that solution-focused counseling was derived from current trends in brief counseling and postmodern/social constructionism. Gutterman contends that solution-focused counseling provides a theoretical framework that can crystallize and bring to focus the unique professional identity of mental health counselors.

Postmodern trends such as ecosystemic mental health counseling are exciting new dimensions of mental health counseling. They appear to offer considerable promise in terms of providing new paradigms for conceptualizing the counseling process. For example, postmodern trends can help create treatment programs that are more comprehensive and holistic in nature and encourage awareness and sensitivity to issues of diversity such as sociocultural forces and gender. Future research activities will need to be directed at the efficacy of postmodern trends as they are integrated into the role and function of mental health counselors.

Diversity Issues

Mental health counseling is attempting to embrace all aspects of diversity so counselors can sensitively and effectively provide mental health services to clients. Culture, gender, individuals with disabilities, and spirituality are examples of diversity in mental health counseling. Locke (1993) suggests that mental health counselors need to increase their efforts to respond to the immense challenges that diversity issues pose in the delivery of mental health services. He suggests that mental health counselors can address these challenges in a number of ways such as increased self-awareness of cultural issues, improved assessment and diagnosis, developing intervention strategies that are more culturally relevant, and increasing awareness and utilization of political forces that impact on psychological functioning.

Cultural issues are critical in all phases of counseling. Substance-abuse counseling provides an illustration of the importance of cultural issues in mental health counseling. Terrell (1993) identifies acculturation, sources of stress, and beliefs and attitudes regarding substance use as important cultural factors which contribute to the development and treatment of substance abuse. Acculturation can play a role in the development of substance abuse in terms of the stress experienced during the acculturation process and as a result of conflicting cultural values regarding substance use. An example of acculturation stress could be Native Americans moving from the reservation to urban areas. Beliefs and attitudes regarding substance abuse can also play a role in treatment. For example, African Americans may resist investing themselves in substance-abuse treatment that adheres to the medical model, contending that substance abuse is not a disease but a condition based on personal choice (Terrell, 1993).

Gender is another important diversity consideration in mental health counseling. In this regard, McDonough and Russell (1994) note that most treatment modalities for substance-abuse counseling have been based on a male model of alcoholism. Research is beginning to suggest that women alcoholics have special needs relating to relationship expectations, development issues, and societal stigma. For example, Terrell (1993) notes that some Hispanic females feel a strong cultural sanction against alcohol use, which could make it difficult to admit to a problem and seek help from mental health services.

Gender and depression is another area of diversity for mental health services. Culberston (1997) provides an international review of the literature on the prevalence of depression in males and females. Culberston's study shows women to have higher ratios of depression compared to men (2:1); women also suffer from the more serious, profound depression at higher rates (between 3:1 and 4:1 for major depression) and the rates of bipolar (manic/depressive) disorders appear to be similar for men and women. Culberston (1997) identifies several factors that could contribute to the different rates of major depression for women and men. Women tend to seek out mental health services more than men, and there is some indication that men tend to "self-medicate" with alcohol and other drugs to deal with problems such as depression. There could also be biological differences in men and women that contribute to higher rates of depression in women. In addition, sociopolitical forces such as child-care demands and lower economic support could contribute to more depression in women than men.

Helwig and Holicky (1994) note that clients with disabilities are an often neglected but important type of diversity that requires careful attention from mental health counselors. Their research suggests that clients with physical disabilities such as spinal cord injuries are also prone to having substance-abuse problems. Although approximately half of these individuals have symptomatology associated with substance abuse, rehabilitation counseling efforts tend to focus on helping the client adjust to the disability with little or no recognition and treatment of the substance abuse. Helwig and Holicky suggest that substance abuse problems should be addressed first to facilitate clients' ability to deal with the challenges of their disability.

Spirituality (which may or not include religion) is an emerging trend in the diversity literature (Bishop, 1995). Spirituality has been conceptualized as a developmental construct endemic to all people that is directed at addressing questions basic to one's existence (Ingersoll, 1995). Recent research has provided a proliferation of support for the positive role that spirituality and religion can play in mental and physical health (Koenig, 1997; Richards & Bergin, 1997; Witmer & Sweeney, 1995). Miranti and Burke (1995) note that people turn to spiritual values as an important source of strength and support in times of great need. And this tendency is especially true as people get older. Richards and Bergin (1997) identify a number of other factors that make spirituality a particularly attractive dimension of the counseling process. Some of the inherent strengths promoted by religion and spirituality include the following.

- It fosters a secure sense of identity that promotes resiliency and helps alleviate stress and anxiety.
- It provides a sense of purpose and meaning to all phases of life including death.
- It encourages positive feelings and thoughts such as hope, healing, optimism, and forgiveness.
- It provides a support system through activities such as church involvement.
- It fosters processes such as prayer and meditation, which promote healing through activities such as communion with the "higher power."
- It encourages healthy lifestyles.

Managed Care

It has become increasingly essential for mental health counselors and other health care professionals to become providers for managed-care organizations in order to access clients' insurance programs, which are evolving in the health-care reform movement. Managed care is essentially an attempt by health organization to control medical costs (Pipal, 1995, p. 323). Its overall aim is to help clients achieve their premorbid levels of functioning and to obtain symptom relief with little interest in developmental or preventive enhancement (Pipal, 1995).

Two facets of managed care that have directly impacted the delivery of mental health services are on the emphasis on diagnosing and the utilization of time-limited solution-focused sessions. In this regard, mental health counselors (and other practitioners) often feel under pressure to conform to managed care's expectations in order to remain a provider. This can involve behaviors that are clearly ethical violations (Bachrach, 1995; Pipal, 1995). Examples of potential ethical problems are making improper diagnoses to gain authorization for services, not ensuring clients' confidentiality through communication with managed-care personnel, providing inadequate services owing to restriction of number of session (usually less than six), and providing services beyond the scope of one's practice.

Wagner and Gartner (1996) suggest that managed care necessitates changes in the counseling process and mental health delivery system. According to Wagner and Gartner, therapists need to function as coaches or teachers and act as catalysts for change. In this mode, clients learn skills from a variety of individuals and practice what they learn in their everyday life experiences. The working-through phase of counseling therefore occurs outside of counseling. In addition, counseling becomes more of an open-ended process involving intermittent or episodic care (Wagner & Gartner, 1996). In this regard, the therapist and client together work within the constraints of managed care to address the client's needs as efficiently as possible (for example, the client may sign up for a certain number of sessions to treat a substance-abuse problem and attempt to seek other assistance at a later date). One facet of counseling that does not appear to be in need of change is the nature of the therapeutic alliance. According to Wagner and Gartner (1996) it is essential for therapists to maintain a positive counseling relationship as advocated by Carl Rogers and others.

Managed care offers many challenges to the mental health counselor and other health practitioners. In an era of increasing pressures for cost containment, it appears to be becoming difficult to provide services that are consistent with the basic standards of practice and that are in the client's best welfare. Former Surgeon General C. Everett Koop voiced this concern when he noted that too much emphasis has been put on the economic/political pressures of health care with little attention to the ethical imperatives for health care reform (Bachrach, 1996).

Summary

Mental health counseling is both an amorphous job role performed by various members of the helping profession and an emerging profession for individuals who identify themselves as mental health counselors.

Professional issues relating to mental health counselors include professional affiliation and certification requirements. The role and function of mental health counselors is to provide direct and indirect counseling services to clients who have either problems of living or mental disorders. Two mental health issues demanding increased attention by mental health counselors and other members of the helping profession are suicidal clients and clients with substance-abuse problems.

Code of Ethics and Standards of Practice

As Approved by Governing Council
April 1997
Effective July 1, 1997

Preamble

The American Counseling Association is an educational, scientific and professional organization whose members are dedicated to the enhancement of human development throughout the life span. Association members recognize diversity in our society and embrace a cross-cultural approach in support of the worth, dignity, potential, and uniqueness of each individual.

The specification of a code of ethics enables the association to clarify to current and future members, and to those served by members, the nature of the ethical responsibilities held in common by its members. As the code of ethics of the association, this document establishes principles that define the ethical behavior of association members. All members of the American Counseling Association are required to adhere to the Code of Ethics and the Standards of Practice. The Code of Ethics will serve as the basis for processing ethical complaints initiated against members of the association.

SECTION A: THE COUNSELING RELATIONSHIP

A.1. CLIENT WELFARE

a. *Primary Responsibility.*

The primary responsibility of counselors is to respect the dignity and to promote the welfare of clients.

b. *Positive Growth and Development.*

Counselors encourage client growth and development in ways that foster the clients' interest and welfare; counselors avoid fostering dependent counseling relationships.

c. *Counseling Plans.*

Counselors and their clients work jointly in devising integrated, individual counseling plans that offer reasonable promise of success and are consistent with abilities and circumstances of clients. Counselors and clients regularly review counseling plans to ensure their continued viability and effectiveness respecting clients' freedom of choice. (See A.3.b.)

d. *Family Involvement.*

Counselors recognize that families are usually important in clients' lives and strive to enlist family understanding and involvement as a positive resource when appropriate.

e. *Career and Employment Needs.*

Counselors work with their clients in considering employment in jobs and circumstances that are consistent with the clients' overall abilities, vocational limitations, physical restrictions, general temperament, interest and aptitude

403

patterns, social skills, education, general qualifications, and other relevant characteristics and needs. Counselors neither place nor participate in placing clients in positions that will result in damaging the interest and the welfare of clients, employers, or the public.

A.2. RESPECTING DIVERSITY

a. *Nondiscrimination.*

Counselors do not condone or engage in discrimination based on age, color, culture, disability, ethnic group, gender, race, religion, sexual orientation, marital status, or socioeconomic status. (See C.5.a., C.5.b., and D.1.i.)

b. *Respecting Differences.*

Counselors will actively attempt to understand the diverse cultural backgrounds of the clients with whom they work. This includes, but is not limited to, learning how the counselor's own cultural/ethnic/racial identity impacts her/his values and beliefs about the counseling process. (See E.8. and F.2.i.)

A.3. CLIENT RIGHTS

a. *Disclosure to Clients.*

When counseling is initiated, and throughout the counseling process as necessary, counselors inform clients of the purposes, goals, techniques, procedures, limitations, potential risks and benefits of services to be performed, and other pertinent information. Counselors take steps to ensure that clients understand the implications of diagnosis, the intended use of tests and reports, fees, and billing arrangements. Clients have the right to expect confidentiality and to be provided with an explanation of its limitations, including supervision and/or treatment team professionals; to obtain clear information about their case records: to participate in the ongoing counseling plans; and to refuse any recommended services and be advised of the consequences of such refusal. (See E.5.a. and G.2.)

b. *Freedom of Choice.*

Counselors offer clients the freedom to choose whether to enter into a counseling relationship and to determine which professional(s) will provide counseling. Restrictions that limit choices of clients are fully explained. (See A.1.c.)

c. *Inability to Give Consent.*

When counseling minors or persons unable to give voluntary informed consent, counselors act in these clients' best interests. (See B.3.)

A.4. CLIENTS SERVED BY OTHERS

If a client is receiving services from another mental health professional, counselors, with client consent, inform the professional persons already involved and develop clear agreements to avoid confusion and conflict for the client. (See C.6.c.)

A.5. PERSONAL NEEDS AND VALUES

a. *Personal Needs.*

In the counseling relationship, counselors are aware of the intimacy and responsibilities inherent in the counseling relationship, maintain respect for clients, and avoid actions that seek to meet their personal needs at the expense of clients.

b. *Personal Values.*

Counselors are aware of their own values, attitudes, beliefs, and behaviors and how these apply in a diverse society and avoid imposing their values on clients. (See C.5.a.)

A.6. DUAL RELATIONSHIPS

a. *Avoid When Possible.*

Counselors are aware of their influential positions with respect to clients, and they avoid exploiting the trust and dependency of clients. Counselors make every effort to avoid dual relationships with clients that could impair professional judgment or increase the risk of harm to clients. (Examples of such relationships include, but are not limited to, familial, social, financial, business, or close personal relationships with clients.) When a dual relationship cannot be avoided, counselors take appropriate professional precautions, such as informed consent, consultation, supervision, and documentation, to ensure that judgment is not impaired and no exploitation occurs. (See F.1.b.)

b. *Superior/Subordinate Relationships.*

Counselors do not accept as clients superiors or subordinates with whom they have administrative, supervisory, or evaluative relationships.

A.7. SEXUAL INTIMACIES WITH CLIENTS

a. *Current Clients.*

Counselors do not have any type of sexual intimacies with clients and do not counsel persons with whom they have had a sexual relationship.

b. *Former Clients.*

Counselors do not engage in sexual intimacies with former clients within a minimum of two years after terminating the counseling relationship. Counselors who engage in such relationship after two years following termination have the responsibility to thoroughly examine and document that such relations did not have an exploitative nature, based on factors, such as duration of counseling, amount of time since counseling, termination circumstances, client's personal history and mental status, adverse impact on the client, and actions by the counselor suggesting a plan to initiate a sexual relationship with the client after termination.

A.8. MULTIPLE CLIENTS

When counselors agree to provide counseling services to two or more persons who have a relationship (such as husband and wife, or parents and children), counselors clarify at the outset which person or persons are clients and the nature of the relationships they will have with each involved person. If it becomes apparent that counselors may be called upon to perform potentially conflicting roles, they clarify, adjust, or withdraw from roles appropriately. (See B.2. and B.4.d.)

A.9. GROUP WORK

a. *Screening.*

Counselors screen prospective group counseling/therapy participants. To the extent possible, counselors select members whose needs and goals are compatible with goals of the group, who will not impede the group process, and whose well-being will not be jeopardized by the group experience.

b. *Protecting Clients.*

In a group setting, counselors take reasonable precautions to protect clients from physical or psychological trauma.

A.10. FEES AND BARTERING

(See D.3.a. and D.3.b.)

a. *Advance Understanding.*

Counselors clearly explain to clients, prior to entering the counseling relationship, all financial arrangements related to professional services including the use of collection agencies or legal measures for nonpayment. (A.11.c.)

b. *Establishing Fees.*

In establishing fees for professional counseling services, counselors consider the financial status of clients and locality. In the event that the established fee structure is inappropriate for a client, assistance is provided in attempting to find comparable services of acceptable cost. (See A.10.d., D.3.a., and D.3.b.)

c. *Bartering Discouraged.*

Counselors ordinarily refrain from accepting goods or services from clients in return for counseling services because such arrangements create inherent potential for conflicts, exploitation, and distortion of the professional relationship. Counselors may participate in bartering only if the relationship is not exploitive, if the client requests

it, if a clear written contract is established, and if such arrangements are an accepted practice among professionals in the community. (See A.6.a.)

d. *Pro Bono Service.*

Counselors contribute to society by devoting a portion of their professional activity to services for which there is little or no financial return (pro bono).

A.11. TERMINATION AND REFERRAL

a. *Abandonment Prohibited.*

Counselors do not abandon or neglect clients in counseling. Counselors assist in making appropriate arrangements for the continuation of treatment, when necessary, during interruptions, such as vacations, and following termination.

b. *Inability to Assist Clients.*

If counselors determine an inability to be of professional assistance to clients, they avoid entering or immediately terminate a counseling relationship. Counselors are knowledgeable about referral resources and suggest appropriate alternatives. If clients decline the suggested referral, counselors should discontinue the relationship.

c. *Appropriate Termination.*

Counselors terminate a counseling relationship, securing client agreement when possible, when it is reasonably clear that the client is no longer benefiting, when services are no longer required, when counseling no longer serves the client's needs or interests, when clients do not pay fees charged, or when agency or institution limits do not allow provision of further counseling services. (See A.10.b. and C.2.g.)

A.12. COMPUTER TECHNOLOGY

a. *Use of Computers.*

When computer applications are used in counseling services, counselors ensure that (1) the client is intellectually, emotionally, and physically capable of using the computer application; (2) the computer application is appropriate for the needs of the client; (3) the client understands the purpose and operation of the computer applications; and (4) a follow-up of client use of a computer application is provided to correct possible misconceptions, discover inappropriate use, and assess subsequent needs.

b. *Explanation of Limitations.*

Counselors ensure that clients are provided information as a part of the counseling relationship that adequately explains the limitations of computer technology.

c. *Access to Computer Applications.*

Counselors provide for equal access to computer applications in counseling services. (See A.2.a.)

SECTION B: CONFIDENTIALITY

B.1. RIGHT TO PRIVACY

a. *Respect for Privacy.*

Counselors respect their clients' right to privacy and avoid illegal and unwarranted disclosures of confidential information. (See A.3.a. and B.6.a.)

b. *Client Waiver.*

The right to privacy may be waived by the client or their legally recognized representative.

c. *Exceptions.*

The general requirement that counselors keep information confidential does not apply when disclosure is required to prevent clear and imminent danger to the client or others or when legal requirements demand that confidential information be revealed. Counselors consult with other professionals when in doubt as to the validity of an exception.

d. *Contagious, Fatal Diseases.*

A counselor who receives information confirming that a client has a disease commonly known to be both communicable and fatal is justified in disclosing information to an identifiable third party, who by his or her relationship with the client is at a high risk of contracting the disease. Prior to making a disclosure the counselor should ascertain that the client has not already informed the third party about his or her disease and that the client is not intending to inform the third party in the immediate future. (See B.1.c. and B.1.f.)

e. *Court Ordered Disclosure.*

When court ordered to release confidential information without a client's permission, counselors request to the court that the disclosure not be required due to potential harm to the client or counseling relationship. (See B.1.c.)

f. *Minimal Disclosure.*

When circumstances require the disclosure of confidential information, only essential information is revealed. To the extent possible, clients are informed before confidential information is disclosed.

g. *Explanation of Limitations.*

When counseling is initiated and throughout the counseling process as necessary, counselors inform clients of the limitations of confidentiality and identify foreseeable situations in which confidentiality must be breached. (See G.2.a.)

h. *Subordinates.*

Counselors make every effort to ensure that privacy and confidentiality of clients are maintained by subordinates including employees, supervisees, clerical assistants, and volunteers. (See B.1.a.)

i. *Treatment Teams.*

If client treatment will involve a continued review by a treatment team, the client will be informed of the team's existence and composition.

B.2. GROUPS AND FAMILIES

a. *Group Work.*

In group work, counselors clearly define confidentiality and the parameters for the specific group being entered, explain its importance, and discuss the difficulties related to confidentiality involved in group work. The fact that confidentiality cannot be guaranteed is clearly communicated to group members.

b. *Family Counseling.*

In family counseling, information about one family member cannot be disclosed to another member without permission. Counselors protect the privacy rights of each family member. (See A.8., B.3., and B.4.d.)

B.3. MINOR OR INCOMPETENT CLIENTS

When counseling clients who are minors or individuals who are unable to give voluntary, informed consent, parents or guardians may be included in the counseling process as appropriate. Counselors act in the best interests of clients and take measures to safeguard confidentiality. (See A.3.c.)

B.4. RECORDS

a. *Requirement of Records.*

Counselors maintain records necessary for rendering professional services to their clients and as required by laws, regulations, or agency or institution procedures.

b. *Confidentiality of Records.*

Counselors are responsible for securing the safety and confidentiality of any counseling records they create, maintain, transfer, or destroy whether the records are written, taped, computerized, or stored in any other medium. (See B.1.a.)

c. *Permission to Record or Observe.*

Counselors obtain permission from clients prior to electronically recording or observing sessions. (See A.3.a.)

d. *Client Access.*

Counselors recognize that counseling records are kept for the benefit of clients and, therefore, provide access to records and copies of records when requested by competent clients unless the records contain information that may be misleading and detrimental to the client. In situations involving multiple clients, access to records is limited to those parts of records that do not include confidential information related to another client. (See A.8., B.1.a., and B.2.b.)

e. *Disclosure or Transfer.*

Counselors obtain written permission from clients to disclose or transfer records to legitimate third parties unless exceptions to confidentiality exist as listed in Section B.1. Steps are taken to ensure that receivers of counseling records are sensitive to their confidential nature.

B.5. RESEARCH AND TRAINING

a. *Data Disguise Required.*

Use of data derived from counseling relationships for purposes of training, research, or publication is confined to content that is disguised to ensure the anonymity of the individuals involved. (See B.1.g. and G.3.d.)

b. *Agreement for Identification.*

Identification of a client in a presentation or publication is permissible only when the client has reviewed the material and has agreed to its presentation or publication. (See G.3.d.)

B.6. CONSULTATION

a. *Respect for Privacy.*

Information obtained in a consulting relationship is discussed for professional purposes only with persons clearly concerned with the case. Written and oral reports present data germane to the purposes of the consultation, and every effort is made to protect client identity and avoid undue invasion of privacy.

b. *Cooperating Agencies.*

Before sharing information, counselors make efforts to ensure that there are defined policies in other agencies serving the counselor's clients that effectively protect the confidentiality of information.

SECTION C: PROFESSIONAL RESPONSIBILITY

C.1. STANDARDS KNOWLEDGE

Counselors have a responsibility to read, understand, and follow the Code of Ethics and the Standards of Practice.

C.2. PROFESSIONAL COMPETENCE

a. *Boundaries of Competence.*

Counselors practice only within the boundaries of their competence, based on their education, training, supervised experience, state and national professional credentials, and appropriate professional experience. Counselors will demonstrate a commitment to gain knowledge, personal awareness, sensitivity, and skills pertinent to working with a diverse client population.

b. *New Specialty Areas of Practice.*

Counselors practice in specialty areas new to them only after appropriate education, training, and supervised experience. While developing skills in new specialty areas, counselors take steps to ensure the competence of their work and to protect others from possible harm.

c. *Qualified for Employment.*

Counselors accept employment only for positions for which they are qualified by education, training, supervised experience, state and national professional credentials, and appropriate professional experience. Counselors hire for professional counseling positions only individuals who are qualified and competent.

d. *Monitor Effectiveness.*

Counselors continually monitor their effectiveness as professionals and take steps to improve when necessary. Counselors in private practice take reasonable steps to seek out peer supervision to evaluate their efficacy as counselors.

e. *Ethical Issues Consultation.*

Counselors take reasonable steps to consult with other counselors or related professionals when they have questions regarding their ethical obligations or professional practice. (See H.1.)

f. *Continuing Education.*

Counselors recognize the need for continuing education to maintain a reasonable level of awareness of current scientific and professional information in their fields of activity. They take steps to maintain competence in the skills they use, are open to new procedures, and keep current with the diverse and/or special populations with whom they work.

g. *Impairment.*

Counselors refrain from offering or accepting professional services when their physical, mental or emotional problems are likely to harm a client or others. They are alert to the signs of impairment, seek assistance for problems, and, if necessary, limit, suspend, or terminate their professional responsibilities. (See A.11.c.)

C.3. ADVERTISING AND SOLICITING CLIENTS

a. *Accurate Advertising.*

There are no restrictions on advertising by counselors except those that can be specifically justified to protect the public from deceptive practices. Counselors advertise or represent their services to the public by identifying their credentials in an accurate manner that is not false, misleading, deceptive, or fraudulent. Counselors may only advertise the highest degree earned which is in counseling or a closely related field from a college or university that was accredited when the degree was awarded by one of the regional accrediting bodies recognized by the Council on Postsecondary Accreditation.

b. *Testimonials.*

Counselors who use testimonials do not solicit them from clients or other persons who, because of their particular circumstances, may be vulnerable to undue influence.

c. *Statements by Others.*

Counselors make reasonable efforts to ensure that statements made by others about them or the profession of counseling are accurate.

d. *Recruiting Through Employment.*

Counselors do not use their places of employment or institutional affiliation to recruit or gain clients, supervisees, or consultees for their private practices. (See C.5.e.)

e. *Products and Training Advertisements.*

Counselors who develop products related to their profession or conduct workshops or training events ensure that the advertisements concerning these products or events are accurate and disclose adequate information for consumers to make informed choices.

f. *Promoting to Those Served.*

Counselors do not use counseling, teaching, training, or supervisory relationships to promote their products or training events in a manner that is deceptive or would exert undue influence on individuals who may be vulnerable. Counselors may adopt textbooks they have authored for instruction purposes.

g. *Professional Association Involvement.*

Counselors actively participate in local, state, and national associations that foster the development and improvement of counseling.

C.4. CREDENTIALS

a. *Credentials Claimed.*

Counselors claim or imply only professional credentials possessed and are responsible for correcting any known misrepresentations of their credentials by others. Professional credentials include graduate degrees in counseling or closely related mental health fields, accreditation of graduate programs, national voluntary certifications, government-issued certifications or licenses, ACA professional membership, or any other credential that might indicate to the public specialized knowledge or expertise in counseling.

b. *ACA Professional Membership.*

ACA professional members may announce to the public their membership status. Regular members may not announce their ACA membership in a manner that might imply they are credentialed counselors.

c. *Credential Guidelines.*

Counselors follow the guidelines for use of credentials that have been established by the entities that issue the credentials.

d. *Misrepresentation of Credentials.*

Counselors do not attribute more to their credentials than the credentials represent and do not imply that other counselors are not qualified because they do not possess certain credentials.

e. *Doctoral Degrees from Other Fields.*

Counselors who hold a master's degree in counseling or a closely related mental health field but hold a doctoral degree from other than counseling or a closely related field do not use the title, "Dr.," in their practices and do not announce to the public in relation to their practice or status as a counselor that they hold a doctorate.

C.5. PUBLIC RESPONSIBILITY

a. *Nondiscrimination.*

Counselors do not discriminate against clients, students, or supervisees in a manner that has a negative impact based on their age, color, culture, disability, ethnic group, gender, race, religion, sexual orientation, or socioeconomic status, or for any other reason. (See A.2.a.)

b. *Sexual Harassment.*

Counselors do not engage in sexual harassment. Sexual harassment is defined as sexual solicitation, physical advances, or verbal or nonverbal conduct that is sexual in nature, that occurs in connection with professional activities or roles, and that either (1) is unwelcome, is offensive, or creates a hostile workplace environment, and counselors know or are told this; or (2) is sufficiently severe or intense to be perceived as harassment to a reasonable person in the context. Sexual harassment can consist of a single intense or severe act or multiple persistent or pervasive acts.

c. *Reports to Third Parties.*

Counselors are accurate, honest, and unbiased in reporting their professional activities and judgments to appropriate third parties including courts, health insurance companies, those who are the recipients of evaluation reports, and others. (See B.1.g.)

d. *Media Presentations.*

When counselors provide advice or comment by means of public lectures, demonstrations, radio or television programs, prerecorded tapes, printed articles, mailed material, or other media, they take reasonable precautions to ensure that (1) the statements are based on appropriate professional counseling literature and practice; (2) the statements are otherwise consistent with the Code of Ethics and the Standards of Practice; and (3) the recipients of the information are not encouraged to infer that a professional counseling relationship has been established. (See C.6.b.)

e. *Unjustified Gains.*

Counselors do not use their professional positions to seek or receive unjustified personal gains, sexual favors, unfair advantage, or unearned goods or services. (See C.3.d.)

C.6. RESPONSIBILITY TO OTHER PROFESSIONALS

a. *Different Approaches.*

Counselors are respectful of approaches to professional counseling that differ from their own. Counselors know and take into account the traditions and practices of other professional groups with which they work.

b. *Personal Public Statements.*

When making personal statements in a public context, counselors clarify that they are speaking from their personal perspectives and that they are not speaking on behalf of all counselors or the profession. (See C.5.d.)

c. *Clients Served by Others.*

When counselors learn that their clients are in a professional relationship with another mental health professional, they request release from clients to inform the other professionals and strive to establish positive and collaborative professional relationships. (See A.4.)

SECTION D: RELATIONSHIPS WITH OTHER PROFESSIONALS

D.1. RELATIONSHIPS WITH EMPLOYERS AND EMPLOYEES

a. *Role Definition.*

Counselors define and describe for their employers and employees the parameters and levels of their professional roles.

b. *Agreements.*

Counselors establish working agreements with supervisors, colleagues, and subordinates regarding counseling or clinical relationships, confidentiality, adherence to professional standards, distinction between public and private material, maintenance and dissemination of recorded information, workload, and accountability. Working agreements in each instance are specified and made known to those concerned.

c. *Negative Conditions.*

Counselors alert their employers to conditions that may be potentially disruptive or damaging to the counselor's professional responsibilities or that may limit their effectiveness.

d. *Evaluation.*

Counselors submit regularly to professional review and evaluation by their supervisor or the appropriate representative of the employer.

e. *In-Service.*

Counselors are responsible for in-service development of self and staff.

f. *Goals.*

Counselors inform their staff of goals and programs.

g. *Practices.*

Counselors provide personnel and agency practices that respect and enhance the rights and welfare of each employee and recipient of agency services. Counselors strive to maintain the highest levels of professional services.

h. *Personnel Selection and Assignment.*

Counselors select competent staff and assign responsibilities compatible with their skills and experiences.

i. *Discrimination.*

Counselors, as either employers or employees, do not engage in or condone practices that are inhumane, illegal, or unjustifiable (such as considerations based on age, color, culture, disability, ethnic group, gender, race, religion, sexual orientation, or socioeconomic status) in hiring, promotion, or training. (See A.2.a. and C.5.b.)

j. *Professional Conduct.*

Counselors have a responsibility both to clients and to the agency or institution within which services are performed to maintain high standards of professional conduct.

k. *Exploitive Relationships.*

Counselors do not engage in exploitive relationships with individuals over whom they have supervisory, evaluative, or instructional control or authority.

l. *Employer Policies.*

The acceptance of employment in an agency or institution implies that counselors are in agreement with its general policies and principles. Counselors strive to reach agreement with employers as to acceptable standards of conduct that allow for changes in institutional policy conducive to the growth and development of clients.

D.2. CONSULTATION

(See B.6.)

a. *Consultation as an Option.*

Counselors may choose to consult with any other professionally competent persons about their clients. In choosing consultants, counselors avoid placing the consultant in a conflict of interest situation that would preclude the consultant being a proper party to the counselor's efforts to help the client. Should counselors be engaged in a work setting that compromises this consultation standard, they consult with other professionals whenever possible to consider justifiable alternatives.

b. *Consultant Competency.*

Counselors are reasonably certain that they have or the organization represented has the necessary competencies and resources for giving the kind of consulting services needed and that appropriate referral resources are available.

c. *Understanding with Clients.*

When providing consultation, counselors attempt to develop with their clients a clear understanding of problem definition, goals for change, and predicted consequences of interventions selected.

d. *Consultant Goals.*

The consulting relationship is one in which client adaptability and growth toward self-direction are consistently encouraged and cultivated. (See A.1.b.)

D.3. FEES FOR REFERRAL

a. *Accepting Fees from Agency Clients.*

Counselors refuse a private fee or other remuneration for rendering services to persons who are entitled to such services through the counselor's employing agency or institution. The policies of a particular agency may make explicit provisions for agency clients to receive counseling services from members of its staff in private practice. In such instances, the clients must be informed of other options open to them should they seek private counseling services. (See A.10.a., A.11.b., and C.3.d.)

b. *Referral Fees.*

Counselors do not accept a referral fee from other professionals.

D.4. SUBCONTRACTOR ARRANGEMENTS

When counselors work as subcontractors for counseling services for a third party, they have a duty to inform clients of the limitations of confidentiality that the organization may place on counselors in providing counseling services to clients. The limits of such confidentiality ordinarily are discussed as part of the intake session. (See B.1.e. and B.1.f.)

SECTION E: EVALUATION, ASSESSMENT, AND INTERPRETATION

E.1. GENERAL

a. *Appraisal Techniques.*

The primary purpose of educational and psychological assessment is to provide measures that are objective and interpretable in either comparative or absolute terms. Counselors recognize the need to interpret the statements in this section as applying to the whole range of appraisal techniques including test and nontest data.

b. *Client Welfare.*

Counselors promote the welfare and best interests of the client in the development, publication, and utilization of educational and psychological assessment techniques. They do not misuse assessment results and interpretations and take reasonable steps to prevent others from misusing the information these techniques provide. They respect the client's right to know the results, the interpretations made, and the basis for their conclusions and recommendations.

E.2. COMPETENCE TO USE AND INTERPRET TESTS

a. *Limits of Competence.*

Counselors recognize the limits of their competence and perform only those testing and assessment services for which they have been trained. They are familiar with reliability, validity, related standardization, error of measurement, and proper application of any technique utilized. Counselors using computer-based test interpretations are trained in the construct being measured and the specific instrument being used prior to using this type of computer application. Counselors take reasonable measures to ensure the proper use of psychological assessment techniques by persons under their supervision.

b. *Appropriate Use.*

Counselors are responsible for the appropriate application, scoring, interpretation, and use of assessment instruments whether they score and interpret such tests themselves or use computerized or other services.

c. *Decisions Based on Results.*

Counselors responsible for decisions involving individuals or policies that are based on assessment results have a thorough understanding of educational and psychological measurement including validation criteria, test research, and guidelines for test development and use.

d. *Accurate Information.*

Counselors provide accurate information and avoid false claims or misconceptions when making statements about assessment instruments or techniques. Special efforts are made to avoid unwarranted connotations of such terms as IQ and grade equivalent scores. (See C.5.c.)

E.3. INFORMED CONSENT

a. *Explanation to Clients.*

Prior to assessment, counselors explain the nature and purposes of assessment and the specific use of results in language the client (or other legally authorized person on behalf of the client) can understand unless an explicit exception to this right has been agreed upon in advance. Regardless of whether scoring and interpretation are completed by counselors, by assistants, or by computer or other outside services, counselors take reasonable steps to ensure that appropriate explanations are given to the client.

b. *Recipients of Results.*

The examinee's welfare, explicit understanding, and prior agreement determine the recipients of test results. Counselors include accurate and appropriate interpretations with any release of individual or group test results. (See B.1.a. and C.5.c.)

E.4. RELEASE OF INFORMATION TO COMPETENT PROFESSIONALS

a. *Misuse of Results.*

Counselors do not misuse assessment results, including test results, and interpretations and take reasonable steps to prevent the misuse of such by others. (See C.5.c.)

b. *Release of Raw Data.*

Counselors ordinarily release data (e.g., protocols, counseling or interview notes, or questionnaires) in which the client is identified only with the consent of the client or the client's legal representative. Such data are usually released only to persons recognized by counselors as competent to interpret the data. (See B.1.a.)

E.5. PROPER DIAGNOSIS OF MENTAL DISORDERS

a. *Proper Diagnosis.*

Counselors take special care to provide proper diagnosis of mental disorders. Assessment techniques (including personal interview) used to determine client care (e.g., locus of treatment, type of treatment, or recommended follow-up) are carefully selected and appropriately used. (See A.3.a. and C.5.c.)

b. *Cultural Sensitivity.*

Counselors recognize that culture affects the manner in which clients' problems are defined. Clients' socioeconomic and cultural experience is considered when diagnosing mental disorders.

E.6. TEST SELECTION

a. *Appropriateness of Instruments.*

Counselors carefully consider the validity, reliability, psychometric limitations, and appropriateness of instruments when selecting tests for use in a given situation or with a particular client.

b. *Culturally Diverse Populations.*

Counselors are cautious when selecting tests for culturally diverse populations to avoid inappropriateness of testing that may be outside of socialized behavioral or cognitive patterns.

E.7. CONDITIONS OF TEST ADMINISTRATION

a. *Administration Conditions.*

Counselors administer tests under the same conditions that were established in their standardization. When tests are not administered under standard conditions or when unusual behavior or irregularities occur during the testing session, those conditions are noted in interpretation, and the results may be designated as invalid or of questionable validity.

b. *Computer Administration.*

Counselors are responsible for ensuring that administration programs function properly to provide clients with accurate results when a computer or other electronic methods are used for test administration. (See A.12.b.)

c. *Unsupervised Test-Taking.*

Counselors do not permit unsupervised or inadequately supervised use of tests or assessments unless the tests or assessments are designed, intended, and validated for self-administration and/or scoring.

d. *Disclosure of Favorable Conditions.*

Prior to test administration, conditions that produce most favorable test results are made known to the examinee.

E.8. DIVERSITY IN TESTING

Counselors are cautious in using assessment techniques, making evaluations, and interpreting the performance of populations not represented in the norm group on which an instrument was standardized. They recognize the effects of age, color, culture, disability, ethnic group, gender, race, religion, sexual orientation, and socioeconomic status on test administration and interpretation and place test results in proper perspective with other relevant factors. (See A.2.a.)

E.9. TEST SCORING AND INTERPRETATION

a. *Reporting Reservations.*

In reporting assessment results, counselors indicate any reservations that exist regarding validity or reliability because of the circumstances of the assessment or the inappropriateness of the norms for the person tested.

b. *Research Instruments.*

Counselors exercise caution when interpreting the results of research instruments possessing insufficient technical data to support respondent results. The specific purposes for the use of such instruments are stated explicitly to the examinee.

c. *Testing Services.*

Counselors who provide test scoring and test interpretation services to support the assessment process confirm the validity of such interpretations. They accurately describe the purpose, norms, validity, reliability, and applications of the procedures and any special qualifications applicable to their use. The public offering of an automated test interpretations service is considered a professional-to-professional consultation. The formal responsibility of the consultant is to the consultee, but the ultimate and overriding responsibility is to the client.

E.10. TEST SECURITY

Counselors maintain the integrity and security of tests and other assessment techniques consistent with legal and contractual obligations. Counselors do not appropriate, reproduce, or modify published tests or parts thereof without acknowledgment and permission from the publisher.

E.11. OBSOLETE TESTS AND OUTDATED TEST RESULTS

Counselors do not use data or test results that are obsolete or outdated for the current purpose. Counselors make every effort to prevent the misuse of obsolete measures and test data by others.

E.12. TEST CONSTRUCTION

Counselors use established scientific procedures, relevant standards, and current professional knowledge for test design in the development, publication, and utilization of educational and psychological techniques.

SECTION F: TEACHING, TRAINING, AND SUPERVISION

F.1. COUNSELOR EDUCATORS AND TRAINERS

a. *Educators as Teachers and Practitioners.*

Counselors who are responsible for developing, implementing, and supervising educational programs are skilled as teachers and practitioners. They are knowledgeable regarding the ethical, legal, and regulatory aspects of the profession, are skilled in applying that knowledge, and make students and supervisees aware of their responsibilities. Counselors conduct counselor education and training programs in an ethical manner and serve as role models for professional behavior. Counselor educators should make an effort to infuse material related to human diversity into all courses and/or workshops that are designed to promote the development of professional counselors.

b. *Relationship Boundaries with Students and Supervisees.*

Counselors clearly define and maintain ethical, professional, and social relationship boundaries with their students, and supervisees. They are aware of the differential in power that exists and the student's or supervisee's possible incomprehension of that power differential. Counselors explain to students and supervisees the potential for the relationship to become exploitive.

c. *Sexual Relationships.*

Counselors do not engage in sexual relationships with students or supervisees and do not subject them to sexual harassment. (See A.6. and C.5.b.)

d. *Contributions to Research.*

Counselors give credit to students or supervisees for their contributions to research and scholarly projects. Credit is given through coauthorship, acknowledgment, footnote statement, or other appropriate means in accordance with such contributions. (See G.4.b. and G.4.c.)

e. *Close Relatives.*

Counselors do not accept close relatives as students or supervisees.

f. *Supervision Preparation.*

Counselors who offer clinical supervision services are adequately prepared in supervision methods and techniques. Counselors who are doctoral students serving as practicum or internship supervisors to master's level students are adequately prepared and supervised by the training program.

g. *Responsibility for Services to Clients.*

Counselors who supervise the counseling services of others take reasonable measures to ensure that counseling services provided to clients are professional.

h. *Endorsement.*

Counselors do not endorse students or supervisees for certification, licensure, employment, or completion of an academic or training program if they believe students or supervisees are not qualified for the endorsement. Counselors take reasonable steps to assist students or supervisees who are not qualified for endorsement to become qualified.

F.2. COUNSELOR EDUCATION AND TRAINING PROGRAMS

a. *Orientation.*

Prior to admission, counselors orient prospective students to the counselor education or training program's expectations including but not limited to the following: (1) the type and level of skill acquisition required for successful completion of the training, (2) subject matter to be covered, (3) basis for evaluation, (4) training components that encourage self-growth or self-disclosure as part of the training process, (5) the type of supervision settings and requirements of the sites for required clinical field experiences, (6) student and supervisee evaluation and dismissal policies and procedures, and (7) up-to-date employment prospects for graduates.

b. *Integration of Study and Practice.*

Counselors establish counselor education and training programs that integrate academic study and supervised practice.

c. *Evaluation.*

Counselors clearly state to students and supervisees, in advance of training, the levels of competency expected, appraisal methods, and timing of evaluations for both didactic and experiential components. Counselors provide students and supervisees with periodic performance appraisal and evaluation feedback throughout the training program.

d. *Teaching Ethics.*

Counselors make students and supervisees aware of the ethical responsibilities and standards of the profession and the students' and supervisees' ethical responsibilities to the profession. (See C.1. and F.3.e.)

e. *Peer Relationships.*

When students or supervisees are assigned to lead counseling groups or provide clinical supervision for their peers, counselors take steps to ensure that students and supervisees placed in these roles do not have personal or adverse relationships with peers and that they understand they have the same ethical obligations as counselor educators, trainers, and supervisors. Counselors make every effort to ensure that the rights of peers are not compromised when students or supervisees are assigned to lead counseling groups or provide clinical supervision.

f. *Varied Theoretical Positions.*

Counselors present varied theoretical positions so that students and supervisees may make comparisons and have opportunities to develop their own positions. Counselors provide information concerning the scientific basis of professional practice. (See C.6.a.)

g. *Field Placements.*

Counselors develop clear policies within their training program regarding field placement and other clinical experiences. Counselors provide clearly stated roles and responsibilities for the student or supervisee, the site supervisor, and the program supervisor. They confirm that site supervisors are qualified to provide supervision and are informed of their professional and ethical responsibilities in this role.

h. *Dual Relationships as Supervisors.*

Counselors avoid dual relationships, such as performing the role of site supervisor and training program supervisor in the student's or supervisee's training program. Counselors do not accept any form of professional services, fees, commissions, reimbursement, or remuneration from a site for student or supervisee placement.

i. *Diversity in Programs.*

Counselors are responsive to their institution's and program's recruitment and retention needs for training program administrators, faculty, and students with diverse backgrounds and special needs. (See A.2.a.)

F.3. STUDENTS AND SUPERVISEES

a. *Limitations.*

Counselors, through ongoing evaluation and appraisal, are aware of the academic and personal limitations of students and supervisees that might impede performance. Counselors assist students and supervisees in securing remedial assistance when needed and dismiss from the training program supervisees who are unable to provide competent service due to academic or personal limitations. Counselors seek professional consultation and document their decision to dismiss or refer students or supervisees for assistance. Counselors assure that students and supervisees have recourse to address decisions made, to require them to seek assistance, or to dismiss them.

b. *Self-Growth Experiences.*

Counselors use professional judgment when designing training experiences conducted by the counselors themselves that require student and supervisee self-growth or self-disclosure. Safeguards are provided so that students and supervisees are aware of the ramifications their self-disclosure may have on counselors whose primary role as teacher, trainer, or supervisor requires acting on ethical obligations to the profession. Evaluative components of experiential training experiences explicitly delineate predetermined academic standards that are separate and not dependent on the student's level of self-disclosure. (See A.6.)

c. *Counseling for Students and Supervisees.*

If students or supervisees request counseling, supervisors or counselor educators provide them with acceptable referrals. Supervisors or counselor educators do not serve as counselor to students or supervisees over whom they hold administrative, teaching, or evaluative roles unless this is a brief role associated with a training experience. (See A.6.b.)

d. *Clients of Students and Supervisees.*

Counselors make every effort to ensure that the clients at field placements are aware of the services rendered and the qualifications of the students and supervisees rendering those services. Clients receive professional disclosure information and are informed of the limits of confidentiality. Client permission is obtained in order for the students and supervisees to use any information concerning the counseling relationship in the training process. (See B.1.e.)

e. *Standards for Students and Supervisees.*

Students and supervisees preparing to become counselors adhere to the Code of Ethics and the Standards of Practice. Students and supervisees have the same obligations to clients as those required of counselors. (See H.1.)

SECTION G: RESEARCH AND PUBLICATION

G.1. RESEARCH RESPONSIBILITIES

a. *Use of Human Subjects.*

Counselors plan, design, conduct, and report research in a manner consistent with pertinent ethical principles, federal and state laws, host institutional regulations, and scientific standards governing research with human subjects. Counselors design and conduct research that reflects cultural sensitivity appropriateness.

b. *Deviation from Standard Practices.*

Counselors seek consultation and observe stringent safeguards to protect the rights of research participants when a research problem suggests a deviation from standard acceptable practices. (See B.6.)

c. *Precautions to Avoid Injury.*

Counselors who conduct research with human subjects are responsible for the subjects' welfare throughout the experiment and take reasonable precautions to avoid causing injurious psychological, physical, or social effects to their subjects.

d. *Principal Researcher Responsibility.*

The ultimate responsibility for ethical research practice lies with the principal researcher. All others involved in the research activities share ethical obligations and full responsibility for their own actions.

e. *Minimal Interference.*

Counselors take reasonable precautions to avoid causing disruptions in subjects' lives due to participation in research.

f. *Diversity.*

Counselors are sensitive to diversity and research issues with special populations. They seek consultation when appropriate. (See A.2.a. and B.6.)

G.2. INFORMED CONSENT

a. *Topics Disclosed.*

In obtaining informed consent for research, counselors use language that is understandable to research participants and that (1) accurately explains the purpose and procedures to be followed; (2) identifies any procedures that are experimental or relatively untried; (3) describes the attendant discomforts and risks; (4) describes the benefits or changes in individuals or organizations that might be reasonably expected; (5) discloses appropriate alternative procedures that would be advantageous for subjects; (6) offers to answer any inquiries concerning the procedures; (7) describes any limitations on confidentiality; and (8) instructs that subjects are free to withdraw their consent and to discontinue participation in the project at any time. (See B.1.f.)

b. *Deception.*

Counselors do not conduct research involving deception unless alternative procedures are not feasible and the prospective value of the research justifies the deception. When the methodological requirements of a study necessitate concealment or deception, the investigator is required to explain clearly the reasons for this action as soon as possible.

c. *Voluntary Participation.*

Participation in research is typically voluntary and without any penalty for refusal to participate. Involuntary participation is appropriate only when it can be demonstrated that participation will have no harmful effects on subjects and is essential to the investigation.

d. *Confidentiality of Information.*

Information obtained about research participants during the course of an investigation is confidential. When the possibility exists that others may obtain access to such information, ethical research practice requires that the possibility, together with the plans for protecting confidentiality, be explained to participants as a part of the procedure for obtaining informed consent. (See B.1.e.)

e. *Persons Incapable of Giving Informed Consent.*

When a person is incapable of giving informed consent, counselors provide an appropriate explanation, obtain agreement for participation and obtain appropriate consent from a legally authorized person.

f. *Commitments to Participants.*

Counselors take reasonable measures to honor all commitments to research participants.

g. *Explanations After Data Collection.*

After data are collected, counselors provide participants with full clarification of the nature of the study to remove any misconceptions. Where scientific or human values justify delaying or withholding information, counselors take reasonable measures to avoid causing harm.

h. *Agreements to Cooperate.*

Counselors who agree to cooperate with another individual in research or publication incur an obligation to cooperate as promised in terms of punctuality of performance and with regard to the completeness and accuracy of the information required.

i. *Informed Consent for Sponsors.*

In the pursuit of research, counselors give sponsors, institutions, and publication channels the same respect and opportunity for giving informed consent that they accord to individual research participants. Counselors are aware of their obligation to future research workers and ensure that host institutions are given feedback information and proper acknowledgment.

G.3. Reporting Results

a. *Information Affecting Outcome.*

When reporting research results, counselors explicitly mention all variables and conditions known to the investigator that may have affected the outcome of a study or the interpretation of data.

b. *Accurate Results.*

Counselors plan, conduct, and report research accurately and in a manner that minimizes the possibility that results will be misleading. They provide thorough discussions of the limitations of their data and alternative hypotheses. Counselors do not engage in fraudulent research, distort data, misrepresent data, or deliberately bias their results.

c. *Obligation to Report Unfavorable Results.*

Counselors communicate to other counselors the results of any research judged to be of professional value. Results that reflect unfavorably on institutions, programs, services, prevailing opinions, or vested interests are not withheld.

d. *Identity of Subjects.*

Counselors who supply data, aid in the research of another person, report research results, or make original data available take due care to disguise the identity of respective subjects in the absence of specific authorization from the subjects to do otherwise. (See B.1.g. and B.5.a.)

e. *Replication Studies.*

Counselors are obligated to make available sufficient original research data to qualified professionals who may wish to replicate the study.

G.4. Publication

a. *Recognition of Others.*

When conducting and reporting research, counselors are familiar with and give recognition to previous work on the topic, observe copyright laws, and give full credit to those to whom credit is due. (See F.1.d. and G.4.c.)

b. *Contributors.*

Counselors give credit through joint authorship, acknowledgment, footnote statements, or other appropriate means to those who have contributed significantly to research or concept development in accordance with such contributions. The principal contributor is listed first and minor technical or professional contributions are acknowledged in notes or introductory statements.

c. *Student Research.*

For an article that is substantially based on a student's dissertation or thesis, the student is listed as the principal author. (See F.1.d. and G.4.a.)

d. *Duplicate Submission.*

Counselors submit manuscripts for consideration to only one journal at a time. Manuscripts that are published in whole or in substantial part in another journal or published work are not submitted for publication without acknowledgment and permission from the previous publication.

e. *Professional Review.*

Counselors who review material submitted for publication, research, or other scholarly purposes respect the confidentiality and proprietary rights of those who submitted it.

Section H: Resolving Ethical Issues

H.1. Knowledge of Standards

Counselors are familiar with the Code of Ethics and the Standards of Practice and other applicable ethics codes from other professional organizations of which they are member or from certification and licensure bodies. Lack of knowledge or misunderstanding of an ethical responsibility is not a defense against a charge of unethical conduct. (See F.3.e.)

H.2. Suspected Violations

a. *Ethical Behavior Expected.*

Counselors expect professional associates to adhere to Code of Ethics. When counselors possess reasonable cause that raises doubts as to whether a counselor is acting in an ethical manner, they take appropriate action. (See H.2.d. and H.2.e.)

b. *Consultation.*

When uncertain as to whether a particular situation or course of action may be in violation of Code of Ethics, counselors consult with other counselors who are knowledgeable about ethics, with colleagues, or with appropriate authorities.

c. *Organization Conflicts.*

If the demands of an organization with which counselors are affiliated pose a conflict with Code of Ethics, counselors specify the nature of such conflicts and express to their supervisors or other responsible officials their commitment to Code of Ethics. When possible, counselors work toward change within the organization to allow full adherence to Code of Ethics.

d. *Informal Resolution.*

When counselors have reasonable cause to believe that another counselor is violating an ethical standard, they attempt to first resolve the issue informally with the other counselor if feasible providing that such action does not violate confidentiality rights that may be involved.

e. *Reporting Suspected Violations.*

When an informal resolution is not appropriate or feasible, counselors, upon reasonable cause, take action, such as reporting the suspected ethical violation to state or national ethics committees, unless this action conflicts with confidentiality rights that cannot be resolved.

f. Unwarranted Complaints.

Counselors do not initiate, participate in, or encourage the filing of ethics complaints that are unwarranted or intend to harm a counselor rather than to protect clients or the public.

H.3. COOPERATION WITH ETHICS COMMITTEES

Counselors assist in the process of enforcing Code of Ethics. Counselors cooperate with investigations, proceedings, and requirements of the ACA Ethics Committee or ethics committees of other duly constituted associations or boards having jurisdiction over those charged with a violation. Counselors are familiar with the ACA Policies and Procedures and use it as a reference in assisting the enforcement of the Code of Ethics.

Standards of Practice

All members of the American Counseling Association (ACA) are required to adhere to the Standards of Practice and the Code of Ethics. The Standards of Practice represent minimal behavioral statements of the Code of Ethics. Members should refer to the applicable section of the Code of Ethics for further interpretation and amplification of the applicable Standard of Practice.

SECTION A: THE COUNSELING RELATIONSHIP

STANDARD OF PRACTICE ONE (SP-1)
NONDISCRIMINATION

Counselors respect diversity and must not discriminate against clients because of age, color, culture, disability, ethnic group, gender, race, religion, sexual orientation, marital status, or socioeconomic status. (See A.2.a.)

STANDARD OF PRACTICE TWO (SP-2)
DISCLOSURE TO CLIENTS

Counselors must adequately inform clients, preferably in writing, regarding the counseling process and counseling relationship at or before the time it begins and throughout the relationship. (See A.3.a.)

STANDARD OF PRACTICE THREE (SP-3)
DUAL RELATIONSHIPS

Counselors must make every effort to avoid dual relationships with clients that could impair their professional judgment or increase the risk of harm to clients. When a dual relationship cannot be avoided, counselors must take appropriate steps to ensure that judgment is not impaired and that no exploitation occurs. (See A.6.a. and A.6.b.)

STANDARD OF PRACTICE FOUR (SP-4)
SEXUAL INTIMACIES WITH CLIENTS

Counselors must not engage in any type of sexual intimacies with current clients and must not engage in sexual intimacies with former clients within a minimum of two years after terminating the counseling relationship. Counselors who engage in such relationship after two years following termination have the responsibility to thoroughly examine and document that such relations did not have an exploitative nature.

STANDARD OF PRACTICE FIVE (SP-5)
PROTECTING CLIENTS DURING GROUP WORK

Counselors must take steps to protect clients from physical or psychological trauma resulting from interactions during group work. (See A.9.b.)

STANDARD OF PRACTICE SIX (SP-6)
ADVANCE UNDERSTANDING OF FEES

Counselors must explain to clients, prior to their entering the counseling relationship, financial arrangements related to professional services. (See A.10.a.-d. and A.11.c.)

STANDARD OF PRACTICE SEVEN (SP-7)
TERMINATION

Counselors must assist in making appropriate arrangements for the continuation of treatment of clients, when necessary, following termination of counseling relationships. (See A.11.a.)

STANDARD OF PRACTICE EIGHT (SP-8)
INABILITY TO ASSIST CLIENTS

Counselors must avoid entering or immediately terminate a counseling relationship if it is determined that they are unable to be of professional assistance to a client. The counselor may assist in making an appropriate referral for the client. (See A.11.b.)

SECTION B: CONFIDENTIALITY

STANDARD OF PRACTICE NINE (SP-9)
CONFIDENTIALITY REQUIREMENT

Counselors must keep information related to counseling services confidential unless disclosure is in the best interest of clients, is required for the welfare of others, or is required by law. When disclosure is required, only information that is essential is revealed and the client is informed of such disclosure. (See B.1.a.-f.)

STANDARD OF PRACTICE TEN (SP-10)
CONFIDENTIALITY REQUIREMENTS FOR SUBORDINATES

Counselors must take measures to ensure that privacy and confidentiality of clients are maintained by subordinates. (See B.1.h.)

STANDARD OF PRACTICE ELEVEN (SP-11)
CONFIDENTIALITY IN GROUP WORK

Counselors must clearly communicate to group members that confidentiality cannot be guaranteed in group work. (See B.2.a.)

STANDARD OF PRACTICE TWELVE (SP-12)
CONFIDENTIALITY IN FAMILY COUNSELING

Counselors must not disclose information about one family member in counseling to another family member without prior consent. (See B.2.b.)

STANDARD OF PRACTICE THIRTEEN (SP-13)
CONFIDENTIALITY OF RECORDS

Counselors must maintain appropriate confidentiality in creating, storing, accessing, transferring, and disposing of counseling records. (See B.4.b.)

STANDARD OF PRACTICE FOURTEEN (SP-14)
PERMISSION TO RECORD OR OBSERVE

Counselors must obtain prior consent from clients in order to electronically record or observe sessions. (See B.4.c.)

STANDARD OF PRACTICE FIFTEEN (SP-15)
DISCLOSURE OR TRANSFER OF RECORDS

Counselors must obtain client consent to disclose or transfer records to third parties unless exceptions listed in SP-9 exist. (See B.4.e.)

STANDARD OF PRACTICE SIXTEEN (SP-16)
DATA DISGUISE REQUIRED

Counselors must disguise the identity of the client when using data for training, research, or publication. (See B.5.a.)

SECTION C: PROFESSIONAL RESPONSIBILITY

STANDARD OF PRACTICE SEVENTEEN (SP-17)
BOUNDARIES OF COMPETENCE

Counselors must practice only within the boundaries of their competence. (See C.2.a.)

STANDARD OF PRACTICE EIGHTEEN (SP-18)
CONTINUING EDUCATION

Counselors must engage in continuing education to maintain their professional competence. (See C.2.f.)

STANDARD OF PRACTICE NINETEEN (SP-19)
IMPAIRMENT OF PROFESSIONALS

Counselors must refrain from offering professional services when their personal problems or conflicts may cause harm to a client or others. (See C.2.g.)

STANDARD OF PRACTICE TWENTY (SP-20)
ACCURATE ADVERTISING

Counselors must accurately represent their credentials and services when advertising. (See C.3.a.)

STANDARD OF PRACTICE TWENTY-ONE (SP-21)
RECRUITING THROUGH EMPLOYMENT

Counselors must not use their place of employment or institutional affiliation to recruit clients for their private practices. (See C.3.d.)

STANDARD OF PRACTICE TWENTY-TWO (SP-22)
CREDENTIALS CLAIMED

Counselors must claim or imply only professional credentials possessed and must correct any known misrepresentations of their credentials by others. (See C.4.a.)

STANDARD OF PRACTICE TWENTY-THREE (SP-23)
SEXUAL HARASSMENT

Counselors must not engage in sexual harassment. (See C.5.b.)

STANDARD OF PRACTICE TWENTY-FOUR (SP-24)
UNJUSTIFIED GAINS

Counselors must not use their professional positions to seek or receive unjustified personal gains, sexual favors, unfair advantage, or unearned goods or services. (See C.5.e.)

STANDARD OF PRACTICE TWENTY-FIVE (SP-25)
CLIENTS SERVED BY OTHERS

With the consent of the client, counselors must inform other mental health professionals serving the same client that a counseling relationship between the counselor and client exists. (See C.6.c.)

STANDARD OF PRACTICE TWENTY-SIX (SP-26)
NEGATIVE EMPLOYMENT CONDITIONS

Counselors must alert their employers to institutional policy or conditions that may be potentially disruptive or damaging to the counselor's professional responsibilities or that may limit their effectiveness or deny clients' rights. (See D.1.c.)

STANDARD OF PRACTICE TWENTY-SEVEN (SP-27)
PERSONNEL SELECTION AND ASSIGNMENT

Counselors must select competent staff and must assign responsibilities compatible with staff skills and experiences. (See D.1.h.)

STANDARD OF PRACTICE TWENTY-EIGHT (SP-28)
EXPLOITIVE RELATIONSHIPS WITH SUBORDINATES

Counselors must not engage in exploitive relationships with individuals over whom they have supervisory, evaluative, or instructional control or authority. (See D.1.k.)

SECTION D: RELATIONSHIP WITH OTHER PROFESSIONALS

STANDARD OF PRACTICE TWENTY-NINE (SP-29)
ACCEPTING FEES FROM AGENCY CLIENTS

Counselors must not accept fees or other remuneration for consultation with persons entitled to such services through the counselor's employing agency or institution. (See D.3.a.)

STANDARD OF PRACTICE THIRTY (SP-30)
REFERRAL FEES

Counselors must not accept referral fees. (See D.3.b.)

SECTION E: EVALUATION, ASSESSMENT, AND INTERPRETATION

STANDARD OF PRACTICE THIRTY-ONE (SP-31)
LIMITS OF COMPETENCE

Counselors must perform only testing and assessment services for which they are competent. Counselors must not allow the use of psychological assessment techniques by unqualified persons under their supervision. (See E.2.a.)

STANDARD OF PRACTICE THIRTY-TWO (SP-32)
APPROPRIATE USE OF ASSESSMENT INSTRUMENTS

Counselors must use assessment instruments in the manner for which they were intended. (See E.2.b.)

STANDARD OF PRACTICE THIRTY-THREE (SP-33)
ASSESSMENT EXPLANATIONS TO CLIENTS

Counselors must provide explanations to clients prior to assessment about the nature and purposes of assessment and the specific uses of results. (See E.3.a.)

STANDARD OF PRACTICE THIRTY-FOUR (SP-34)
RECIPIENTS OF TEST RESULTS

Counselors must ensure that accurate and appropriate interpretations accompany any release of testing and assessment information. (See E.3.b.)

STANDARD OF PRACTICE THIRTY-FIVE (SP-35)
OBSOLETE TESTS AND OUTDATED TEST RESULTS

Counselors must not base their assessment or intervention decisions or recommendations on data or test results that are obsolete or outdated for the current purpose. (See E.11.)

SECTION F: TEACHING, TRAINING, AND SUPERVISION

STANDARD OF PRACTICE THIRTY-SIX (SP-36)
SEXUAL RELATIONSHIPS WITH STUDENTS OR SUPERVISEES

Counselors must not engage in sexual relationships with their students and supervisees. (See F.1.c.)

STANDARD OF PRACTICE THIRTY-SEVEN (SP-37)
CREDIT FOR CONTRIBUTIONS TO RESEARCH

Counselors must give credit to students or supervisees for their contributions to research and scholarly projects. (See F.1.d.)

STANDARD OF PRACTICE THIRTY-EIGHT (SP-38)
SUPERVISION PREPARATION

Counselors who offer clinical supervision services must be trained and prepared in supervision methods and techniques. (See F.1.f.)

STANDARD OF PRACTICE THIRTY-NINE (SP-39)
EVALUATION INFORMATION

Counselors must clearly state to students and supervisees, in advance of training, the levels of competency expected, appraisal methods, and timing of evaluations. Counselors must provide students and supervisees with periodic performance appraisal and evaluation feedback throughout the training program. (See F.2.c.)

STANDARD OF PRACTICE FORTY (SP-40)
PEER RELATIONSHIPS IN TRAINING

Counselors must make every effort to ensure that the rights of peers are not violated when students and supervisees are assigned to lead counseling groups or provide clinical supervision. (See F.2.e.)

STANDARD OF PRACTICE FORTY-ONE (SP-41)
LIMITATIONS OF STUDENTS AND SUPERVISEES

Counselors must assist students and supervisees in securing remedial assistance, when needed, and must dismiss from the training program students and supervisees who are unable to provide competent service due to academic or personal limitations. (See F.3.a.)

STANDARD OF PRACTICE FORTY-TWO (SP-42)
SELF-GROWTH EXPERIENCES

Counselors who conduct experiences for students or supervisees that include self-growth or self-disclosure must inform participants of counselors' ethical obligations to the profession and must not grade participants based on their nonacademic performance. (See F.3.b.)

STANDARD OF PRACTICE FORTY-THREE (SP-43)
STANDARDS FOR STUDENTS AND SUPERVISEES

Students and supervisees preparing to become counselors must adhere to the Code of Ethics and the Standards of Practice of counselors. (See F.3.e.)

SECTION G: RESEARCH AND PUBLICATION

STANDARD OF PRACTICE FORTY-FOUR (SP-44)
PRECAUTIONS TO AVOID INJURY IN RESEARCH

Counselors must avoid causing physical, social, or psychological harm or injury to subjects in research. (See G.1.c.)

STANDARD OF PRACTICE FORTY-FIVE (SP-45)
CONFIDENTIALITY OF RESEARCH INFORMATION

Counselors must keep confidential information obtained about research participants. (See G.2.d.)

STANDARD OF PRACTICE FORTY-SIX (SP-46)
INFORMATION AFFECTING RESEARCH OUTCOME

Counselors must report all variables and conditions known to the investigator that may have affected research data or outcomes. (See G.3.a.)

STANDARD OF PRACTICE FORTY-SEVEN (SP-47)
ACCURATE RESEARCH RESULTS

Counselors must not distort or misrepresent research data nor fabricate or intentionally bias research results. (See G.3.b.)

STANDARD OF PRACTICE FORTY-EIGHT (SP-48)
PUBLICATION CONTRIBUTORS

Counselors must give appropriate credit to those who have contributed to research. (See G.4.a. and G.4.b.)

SECTION H: RESOLVING ETHICAL ISSUES

STANDARD OF PRACTICE FORTY-NINE (SP-49)
ETHICAL BEHAVIOR EXPECTED

Counselors must take appropriate action when they possess reasonable cause that raises doubts as to whether counselors or other mental health professionals are acting in an ethical manner. (See H.2.a.)

STANDARD OF PRACTICE FIFTY (SP-50)
UNWARRANTED COMPLAINTS

Counselors must not initiate, participate in, or encourage the filing of ethics complaints that are unwarranted or intended to harm a mental health professional rather than to protect clients or the public. (See H.2.f.)

STANDARD OF PRACTICE FIFTY-ONE (SP-51)
COOPERATION WITH ETHICS COMMITTEES

Counselors must cooperate with investigations, proceedings, and requirements of the ACA Ethics Committee or ethics committees of other duly constituted associations or boards having jurisdiction over those charged with a violation. (See H.3.)

REFERENCES

The following documents are available to counselors as resources to guide them in their practices. These resources are not a part of the Code of Ethics and the Standards of Practice.

American Association for Counseling and Development/Association for Measurement and Evaluation in Counseling and Development. (1989). The responsibilities of users of standardized tests (revised). Washington, DC: Author.

American Counseling Association. (1988). American Counseling Association Ethical Standards. Alexandria, VA: Author.

American Psychological Association. (1985). Standards for educational and psychological testing (revised). Washington, DC: Author.

American Rehabilitation Counseling Association, Commission on Rehabilitation Counselor Certification, and National Rehabilitation Counseling Association. (1995). Code of professional ethics for rehabilitation counselors. Chicago, IL: Author.

American School Counselor Association. (1992). Ethical standards for school counselors. Alexandria, VA: Author.

Joint Committee on Testing Practices. (1988). Code of fair testing practices in education. Washington, DC: Author.

National Board for Certified Counselors. (1989). National Board for Certified Counselors Code of Ethics. Alexandria, VA: Author.

Prediger, D. J. (Ed.). (1993, March). Multicultural assessment standards. Alexandria, VA: Association for Assessment in Counseling.

SUGGESTED READINGS

Adler, A. (1931). *What life should mean to you.* Boston: Little, Brown.

Adler, A. (1969). *The practice and theory of individual psychology.* Patterson, NJ: Littlefield, Adams.

American Psychological Association. (1975). Carl Rogers on empathy. *The Counseling Psychologist, 5*(2) (entire issue).

Ansbacher, H. L., & Ansbacher, R. R. (Ed.). (1956). *The individual psychology of Alfred Adler.* New York: Basic Books.

Ansbacher, H. L., & Ansbacher, R. R. (Ed.). (1964). *Superiority and social interest.* Evanston, IL: Northwestern University Press.

Arlow, J. A. (1995). Psychoanalysis. In R. J. Corsini & D. Wedding (Eds.), *Current Psychotherapies* (5th ed.) (pp. 15–50). Itasca, IL: Peacock.

Bandura, A. (1986). *Social foundations of thought and action: A social cognitive theory.* Englewood Cliffs, NJ: Prentice-Hall.

Beck, A. T. (1991). Cognitive therapy: A 30-year retrospective. *American Psychologist, 46*(4), 368–375.

Beck, A. T., & Emery, G. (1985). *Anxiety disorders and phobias. A cognitive perspective.* New York: Basic Books.

Beck, A. T., Rush, A. J., Shaw, B. F., & Emery, G. (1979). *Cognitive therapy of depression.* New York: Guilford Press.

Beck, A. T., & Weishaar, M. E. (1995). Cognitive therapy. In R. J. Corsini & D. Wedding (Eds.), *Current psychotherapies* (5th ed.) (pp. 229–261). Itasca, IL: F. E. Peacock.

Berne, E. (1961). *Transactional analysis in psychotherapy.* New York: Grove Press.

Berne, E. (1964). *Games people play.* New York: Grove Press.

Binswanger, L. (1963). *Being-in-the-world. Selected papers of Ludwig Binswanger* (J. Needleman, Trans.). New York: Basic Books.

Buber, M. (1970). *I and Thou* (W. Kaufmann, Trans.). New York: Scribner's.

Bugental, J. F. T. (1965). *The search for authenticity.* New York: Holt, Rinehart, & Winston.

Buirski, P. (Ed.) (1994). *Comparing schools of analytic therapy.* Northvale, NJ: Aronson.

Clarkson, P. (1991). *Transactional analysis psychotherapy: An integrated approach.* London: Routledge.

Dinkmeyer, D., Dinkmeyer, D., Jr., & Sperry, L. (1987). *Adlerian counseling and psychotherapy.* Columbus, OH: Merrill.

Douglas, C. (1995). Analytical psychotherapy. In R. J. Corsini & D. Wedding (Eds.), *Current psychotherapies* (5th ed.) (pp. 95–127). Itasca, IL: F. E. Peacock.

Dryden, W., & DiGiuseppe, R. (1990). *A primer on rational-emotive therapy.* Champaign, IL: Research Press.

Ellis, A. (1994). *Reason and emotion in psychotherapy* (rev. ed.). New York: Birch Lane Press.

Ellis, A. (1995). Rational emotive behavior therapy. In R. J. Corsini & D. Wedding (Eds.), *Current psychotherapies* (5th ed.) (pp. 162–196). Itasca, IL: F. E. Peacock.

Ellis, A. (1996). *Better, deeper, and more enduring brief therapy: The rational emotive behavior therapy approach.* New York: Brunner/Mazel.

Frankl, V. (1963). *Man's search for meaning.* New York: Simon & Schuster (Touchstone).

Frankl, V. (1971). *The doctor and the soul.* New York: Bantam.

Frankl, V. E. (1988). *The will to meaning: Foundations and applications of logotherapy.* New York: Meridian.

Freedman, J., & Combs, G. (1996). *Narrative therapy: The social construction of preferred realities.* New York: Norton.

Freeman, A., Pretzer, J., Fleming, B., & Simon, K. M. (1990). *Clinical applications of cognitive therapy.* New York: Plenum. (Has a great introductory chapter on cognitive therapy.)

Freeman, A., Simon, K. M., Beutler, L. E., & Arkowitz, H. (Eds.) (1989). *Comprehensive handbook of cognitive therapy.* New York: Plenum.

Freud, S. (1953). The interpretation of dreams. In J. Strachey (Ed.), *The standard edition of the complete psychological works of Sigmund Freud, Vols. 4 and 5.* London: Hogarth Press.

Freud, S. (1953). Three essays on sexuality. In J. Strachey (Ed.), *The standard edition of the complete psychological works of Sigmund Freud, Vol. 7.* London: Hogarth Press.

Freud, S. (1960). The psychopathology of everyday life. In J. Strachey, (Ed.), *The standard edition of the complete psychological works of Sigmund Freud, Vol. 6.* London: Hogarth Press.

Freud, S. (1963). Introductory lectures on psycho-analysis. In J. Strachey (Ed.), *The standard edition of the complete psychological works of Sigmund Freud, Vols. 15 and 16.* London: Hogarth Press.

Friedman, S. (Ed.). (1993). *The new language of change: Constructive collaboration in psychotherapy.* New York: Guilford.

Gergen, K. (1985). The social constructionist movement in modern psychology. *American Psychologist, 40,* 266–275.

Gibran, K. (1965). *The prophet.* New York: Alfred A. Knopf.

Glasser, N. (Ed.) (1989). *Control theory in the practice of reality therapy: Case studies.* New York: Harper-Collins.

Glasser, W. (1965). *Reality therapy: A new approach to psychiatry.* New York: Harper & Row.

Glasser, W. (1976). *Positive addictions.* New York: Harper & Row.

Glasser, W. (1981). *Stations of the mind.* New York: Harper & Row.

Glasser, W. (1984). *Take effective control of your life.* New York: Harper & Row.

Glasser, W. (1985). *Control theory.* New York: Harper-Collins. (formerly titled *Take effective control of your life*)

Glasser, W. (1990). *The quality school.* New York: Harper & Row.

Glasser, W. (1994). *The control theory manager.* New York: Harper & Row.

Glasser, W. (1998). *Choice Theory: A new psychology of personal freedom.* New York: HarperCollins.

Glasser, W., & Wubbolding, R. E. (1995). Reality therapy. In R. J. Corsini & D. Wedding (Eds.), *Current psychotherapies* (5th ed.) (pp. 293–321). Itasca, IL: F. E. Peacock.

Guidano, V. F. (1991). *The self in process: Toward a post-rationalist cognitive therapy.* New York: Guilford.

Guidano, V. F., & Liotti, G. (1983). *Cognitive processes and emotional disorders.* New York: Guilford.

Hall, C. (1954). *A primer of Freudian psychology.* Cleveland, OH: World.

Hall, C., & Lindzey, G. (1978). *Theories of Personality* (3rd ed.). New York: John Wiley & Sons.

Hall, C. J., & Norby, J. J. (1973). *A primer of Jungian psychology.* New York: New American Library.

Harris, A. B., & Harris, T. A. (1990). *Staying OK.* New York: Harper & Row.

Harris, T. (1967). *I'm OK, you're OK.* New York: Avon.

Held, B. S. (1995). *Back to reality: A critique of postmodern theory in psychotherapy.* New York: Norton.

Held, B. S. (1996). Solution-focused therapy and the postmodern: A critical analysis. In S. D. Miller, M. A. Hubble, & B. L. Duncan (Eds.), *Handbook of solution-focused brief therapy* (pp. 27–43). San Francisco: Jossey-Bass.

Hoyt, M. F. (Ed.) (1994). *Constructive therapies.* New York: Guilford.

Hoyt, M. F. (Ed.) (1996). *Constructive therapies (Vol. 2),* New York: Guilford.

Jung, C. G. (1961). *Memories, dreams, reflections.* New York: Vintage.

Jung, C. G. (1964). *Man and his symbols.* London: Aldus Books.

Kazdin, A. E. (1994). *Behavior modification in applied settings* (5th ed.). Pacific Grove, CA: Brooks/Cole.

Kierkegaard, S. (1944). *The concept of dread* (W. Lowrie, Trans.). Princeton, NJ: Princeton University Press.

Kischenbaum, H., & Henderson, V. L. (Eds.) (1989). *Carl Rogers: Dialogues.* Boston: Houghton Mifflin.

Korb, M. P., Gorrell, J., & De Riet, V. V. (1989). *Gestalt therapy: Practice and theory* (2nd ed.). New York: Pergamon.

Kuehlwein, K. T., & Rosen, H. (Ed.) (1993). *Cognitive therapies in action: Evolving innovative practice.* San Francisco: Jossey-Bass.

Laing, R. D. (1965). *The divided self.* Baltimore: Pelican.

Lazarus, A. A. (1985). *Casebook of multimodal therapy.* New York: Guilford.

Lazarus, A. A. (1989). *The practice of multimodal therapy.* Baltimore: Johns Hopkins.

Lazarus, A. A. (1995). Multimodal therapy. In R. J. Corsini & D. Wedding (Eds.), *Current psychotherapies* (5th ed.) (pp. 322–355). Itasca, IL: F. E. Peacock.

Lyddon, W. J. (1995). Cognitive therapy and theories of knowing: A social constructionist view. *Journal of Counseling and Development, 73,* 579–585.

Lyddon, W. J. (1995). Forms and facets of constructivist psychology. In R. A. Neimeyer & M. J. Mahoney (Eds.), *Constructivism in psychotherapy* (pp. 69–92). Washington, DC: American Psychological Association.

Mahoney, M. J. (1991). *Human change processes: The scientific foundations of psychotherapy.* New York: Basic Books.

Mahoney, M. J. (Ed.) (1995). *Cognitive and constructive psychotherapies: Theory, research, and practice.* New York: Springer.

Mahoney, M. J., & Freeman, A. (Eds.) (1985). *Cognition and psychotherapy.* New York: Plenum.

Maples, M. F. (1995). Gestalt theory. In D. Capuzzi & D. R. Gross (Eds.), *Counseling and psychotherapy: Theories and interventions.* Columbus, Ohio: Merrill.

May, R. (Ed.). (1961). *Existential Psychology.* New York: Random House.

May, R. (1977). *The meaning of anxiety* (rev. ed.). New York: Norton.

May, R. (1983). *The discovery of being: Writings in existential psychology.* New York: Norton.

May, R. (1991). *The cry for myth.* New York: Norton.

May, R., & Yalom, I. (1995). Existential psychotherapy. In R. J. Corsini & D. Wedding (Eds.), *Current psychotherapies* (5th ed.) (pp. 262–292). Itasca, IL: F. E. Peacock.

McNamee, S., & Gergen, K. J. (Eds.) (1992). *Therapy as social construction.* Newbury Park, CA: Sage.

Meichenbaum, D. (1985). *Stress inoculation training.* New York: Pergamon Press.

Meichenbaum, D. (1986). Cognitive behavior modification. In F. H. Kanfer & A. P. Goldstein (Eds.), *Helping people change: A textbook of methods* (pp. 346–380). New York: Pergamon Press.

Mosak, H. H. (1995). Adlerian psychotherapy. In R. J. Corsini & D. Wedding (Eds.), *Current Psychotherapies* (5th ed.) (pp. 51–94). Itasca, IL: Peacock.

Neimeyer, R. A., & Mahoney, M. J. (Eds.) (1995). *Constructivism in psychotherapy.* Washington, DC: American Psychological Association.

Papadopoulos, R. K., & Saayman, G. S. (1991). *Jung in modern perspective: The master and his legacy.* Dorset, UK: Prism.

Passons, W. R. (1975). *Gestalt approaches in counseling.* New York: Holt, Rinehart, & Winston.

Perls, F. (1969). *Gestalt therapy verbatim.* Moab, UT: Real People Press.

Perls, F. (1969). *In and out of the garbage pail.* Moab, UT: Real People Press.

Pine, F. (1990). *Drive, ego, object, & self: A synthesis for clinical work.* New York: Basic Books.

Poidevant, J. M., & Lewis, H. A. (1995). Transactional analysis theory. In D. Capuzzi & D. R. Gross (Eds.), *Counseling and psychotherapy: Theories and intervention.* Columbus, OH: Merrill.

Prochaska, J. O., & Norcross, J. C. (1994). *Systems of psychotherapy: A transtheoretical approach.* Pacific Grove, CA: Brooks/Cole.

Raskin, N. J., & Rogers, C. R. (1995). Person-centered therapy. In R. J. Corsini & D. Wedding (Eds.), *Current psychotherapies* (5th ed.) (pp. 128–161). Itasca, IL: F. E. Peacock.

Read, H., Fordham, M., & Adler, G. (Eds.). (1953–1978). *Jung's collected works.* Princeton: Princeton University Press.

Robbins, S. B. (1989). Role of contemporary psychoanalysis in counseling psychology. *Journal of Counseling Psychology, 36,* 267–278.

Rogers, C. (1951). *Client-centered therapy.* Boston: Houghton Mifflin.

Rogers, C. (1961). *On becoming a person.* Boston: Houghton Mifflin.

Rogers, C. R. (1989). *The Carl Rogers reader.* H. Kirchenbaum & V. L. Henderson (Eds.). Boston: Houghton Mifflin.

Rosen, H., & Kuehlwein, K. T. (Eds.) (1996). *Constructing realities: Meaning making perspectives for psychotherapists.* San Francisco: Jossey-Bass.

Rycroft, C. (1985). *Psychoanalysis and beyond.* P. Fuller (Ed.). Chicago: University of Chicago Press.

Sartre, J. P. (1956). *Being and nothingness* (H. Barnes, Trans.). New York: Philosophical Library.

Schuyler, D. (1991). *A practical guide to cognitive therapy.* New York: Norton.

Singer, H. A. (1996). *Living with paradox: An introduction to Jungian psychology.* Pacific Grove, CA: Brooks/Cole.

Singer, J. (1991). *Seeing through the visible world: Jung, gnosis, and chaos.* New York: HarperCollins.

Spiegler, M. D., & Guevremont, D. C. (1993). *Contemporary behavior therapy* (2nd ed.). Pacific Grove, CA: Brooks/Cole.

Stewart, I., & Joines, V. (1987). *TA Today: A new introduction to transactional analysis.* Chapel Hill, NC: Lifespace.

Strachey, J. (Ed.). (1953–1974). *The standard edition of the complete psychological works of Sigmund Freud.* London: Hogarth Press.

Teyber, E. (1997). *Interpersonal process in psychotherapy: A relational approach* (3rd. ed.) Pacific Grove, CA: Brooks/Cole.

Van Kaam, A. (1967). Counseling and psychotherapy from the viewpoint of existential psychology. In D. Arbuck (Ed.), *Counseling and psychotherapy: An overview.* New York: McGraw-Hill.

Walen, S. R., DiGiuseppe, R., & Dryden, W. (1992). *A practitioner's guide to rational-emotive therapy* (2nd ed.). New York: Oxford.

Walter, J. L., & Peller, J. E. (1996). Rethinking our assumptions: Assuming anew in a postmodern world. In S. D. Miller, M. A. Hubble, & B. L. Duncan (Eds.), *Handbook of solution-focused brief therapy* (pp. 9–26). San Francisco: Jossey-Bass.

Watson, D. L., & Tharp, R. G. (1993). *Self-directed behavior: Self-modification for personal adjustment* (6th ed.). Pacific Grove, CA: Brooks/Cole.

Wilson, G. T. (1995). Behavior therapy. In R. J. Corsini & D. Wedding (Eds.), *Current Psychotherapies* (5th ed.) (pp. 197–228). Itasca, IL: F. E. Peacock.

Wubbolding, R. E. (1988). *Using reality therapy.* New York: HarperCollins.

Wubbolding, R. E. (1991). *Understanding reality therapy.* New York: Harper & Row (Perennial Library).

Wubbolding, R. E. (1994). *Cycle of managing, supervising, counseling and coaching using reality therapy (chart)* (8th rev.). Cincinnati, OH: Center for Reality Therapy.

Yalom, I. D. (1980). *Existential psychotherapy.* New York: Basic Books.

REFERENCES

Chapter 1

Anastasi, A. (1996). *Psychological testing* (7th ed.). New York: Macmillan.

Ball, F. L. J., & Harassy, B. E. (1984). A survey of the problems and needs of homeless consumers of acute psychiatric services. *Hospital and Community Psychiatry, 35,* 917–921.

Baruth, L. G., & Robinson, E. H. (1987). *An introduction to the counseling profession.* Englewood Cliffs, NJ: Prentice-Hall.

Beck, A. T. (1993). Cognitive therapy: Past, present, and future. *Journal of Consulting and Clinical Psychology, 61*(2), 194–198.

Beers, C. (1908). *A mind that found itself.* New York: Longman Green.

Bergin, A. E. (1991). Values and religious issues in psychotherapy and mental health. *American Psychologist, 46,* 394–403.

Bernstein, B. L., & Kerr, B. (1993). Counseling psychology and the scientist-practitioner model: Implementation and implications. *The Counseling Psychologist, 21*(1), 136–150.

Beutler, L. E., Machado, P. P. P., & Allstetter Neufeldt, S. (1994). Therapist variables. In A. E. Bergin & S. L. Garfield (Eds.), *Handbook of psychotherapy and behavior change* (4th ed.), New York: John Wiley & Sons.

Beutler, L. E., Williams, R. E., Wakefield, P. J., & Entwistle, S. R. (1995). Bridging scientist and practitioner perspective in clinical psychology. *American Psychologist, 50*(12), 984–994.

Brammer, L. M. (1996). *The helping relationship: Process and skills* (6th ed.). Englewood Cliffs, NJ: Prentice-Hall.

Brown, D., & Brooks, L. (1990). Introduction to career development: Origins, evolution and current approaches. In D. Brown & L. Brooks (Eds.), *Career Choice and Development* (2nd ed.). San Francisco: Jossey-Bass.

Claiborn, C. D. (1987). Science and practice: Reconsidering the Pepinskys. *Journal of Counseling and Development, 65*(6), 286–288.

Combs, A., Soper, D., Gooding, C., Benton, J., Dickman, J., & Usher, R. (1969). *Florida studies in the helping professions.* Gainesville: University of Florida Press.

Corey, G., Corey, M. S., & Callanan, P. (1993). *Issues and ethics in the helping professions.* Pacific Grove, CA: Brooks/Cole.

Corsini, R. J., & Wedding, D. (1995). *Current psychotherapies* (5th ed.). Itasca, IL: F. E. Peacock.

Davis, J. L., & Mickelson, D. J. (1994). School counselors: Are you aware of ethical and legal aspects of counseling? *The School Counselor, 42*(1), 5–13.

De Shazer, S. (1994). *Words were originally magic.* New York: Norton.

Dinkmeyer, D. C., & Dinkmeyer, D. C., Jr. (1982). *Developing an understanding of self and others* (DUSO). Circle Pines, MN: American Guidance Service.

Dinkmeyer, D. C., & Losoney, L. E. (1980). *The encouragement book: Becoming a positive person.* Englewood Cliffs, NJ: Prentice-Hall.

Dreikurs, R., & Soltz, V. (1964). *Children: The challenge.* New York: Hawthorn Books.

Dylan, B. (1971). *It's alright ma* [Song]. Los Angeles: Columbia Records.

Edelson, M. (1994). Can psychotherapy research answer this psychotherapist's questions? In P. F. Tally, H. H. Strupp, & S. F. Butler (Eds.), *Psychotherapy research and practice: Bridging the gap.* New York: Basic Books.

Ellis, A. (1994). *Reason and emotion in psychotherapy revised.* New York: Carol Publishing.

Eron, J. B., & Lund, T. W. (1993). How problems evolve and dissolve: Integrating narrative and strategic concepts. *Family Process, 32,* 291–309.

Frazier, S. H. (1985). Responding to the needs of the homeless mentally ill public. *Health Reports, 100,* 462–469.

Freeman, M. A. (1995). Behavioral at-risk contracting in a changing healthcare environment. In G. L. Zieman (Ed.), *The complete capitation handbook: How to design and implement at-risk contracts for behavioral healthcare* (pp. 11–27). Tiburon, CA: CentraLink Publications.

Friedman, S. (1997). *Time-effective psychotherapy: Maximizing outcomes in an era of minimized resources.* Needham Heights, MA: Allyn & Bacon.

Garfield, S. L., & Bergin, A. E. (1994). Introduction and historical overview. In A. E. Bergin & S. L. Garfield (Eds.), *Handbook of psychotherapy and behavior change* (pp. 3–18). New York: John Wiley & Sons.

Gelso, C. J., & Fassinger, R. E. (1990). Counseling psychology: Theory and research on intervention. *American Review of Psychology, 41,* 355–386.

Gergen, K. J. (1982). *Toward transformation is social knowledge*. New York: Springer-Verlag.

Gergen, K. J. (1994). Exploring the postmodern. *American Psychologist, 49*(5), 412–416.

Haase, J. E., Britt, T., Coward, D. D., Kline, N., & Penn, P. E. (1992). Simultaneous analysis of spiritual perspective, hope, acceptance and self-transcendence. *Images, 24*(2), 141–147.

Hannon, K. (1996, May 13). Upset? Try cybertherapy. *U.S. News and World Report, 120,* 81–83.

Havens, L. (1994). Some suggestions for making research more applicable to clinical practice. In P. F. Talley, H. H. Strupp, & S. F. Butler (Eds.), *Psychotherapy research and practice: Bridging the gap* (pp. 88–98). New York: Basic Books.

Herman, K. C. (1993). Reassessing predictors of therapist competence. *Journal of Counseling and Development, 72,* 29–32.

Howard, G. S. (1991). Culture tales: A narrative approach to thinking, cross-cultural psychology, and psychotherapy. *American Psychologist, 46*(3), 187–197.

Ingersoll, R. E. (1995). Spirituality, religion, and counseling: Dimensions and relationships. In M. T. Burke & J. G. Miranti (Eds.) *Counseling: The spiritual dimension* (pp. 5–18). Alexandria, VA: American Counseling Association.

Kirk, M. A. (1997, January). Current perceptions of counseling and counselor education in cyberspace. *Counseling Today, 39,* 17–18.

Kottler, J. A., & Brown, R. W. (1985). *Introduction to therapeutic counseling*. Monterey, CA: Brooks/Cole.

Kroll, J., & Sheehan, W. (1989). Religious beliefs and practices among fifty-two psychiatric inpatients in Minnesota. *American Journal of Psychiatry, 67–72,* 146.

Langs, R. (1985). *Madness and cure*. New York: Newconcept Press.

Lyddon, W. J. (1995). Cognitive therapy and theories of knowing: A social constuctionist view. *Journal of Counseling and Development, 73,* 579–585.

Mahoney, M. J. (1988). Constructive metatheory: 1. Basic Features and historical foundations. *International Journal of Personal Construct Psychology, 1,* 1–35.

Mahoney, M. J. (Ed.) (1995). *Cognitive and constructive psychotherapies: Theory, research, and practice*. New York: Springer.

Maling, M. S., & Howard, K. I. (1994). From research to practice to research to.... In P. F. Talley, H. H. Strupp, & S. F. Butler (Eds.), *Psychotherapy research and practice: Bridging the gap*. New York: Basic Books.

McFadden, J. (1996). A transcultural perspective: Reaction to C. H. Patterson's "Multicultural counseling: From diversity to universality." *Journal of Counseling and Development, 74*(3), 232–235.

Meichenbaum, D., Fitzpatrick, D. (1992). A constructivist narrative perspective on stress and coping: Stress inoculation applications. In L. Golderger & S. Breznitz (Eds.), *Handbook of stress*. New York: Free Press.

Minton, H. L., & Schneider, F. W. (1981). *Differential Psychology*. Monterey, CA: Brooks/Cole.

Miranti, J., & Burkem, M. T. (1995). Spirituality: An integral component of the counseling process. In M. T. Burke & J. G. Miranti (Eds.), *Counseling: The spiritual dimension* (pp. 1–4). Alexandria, VA: American Counseling Association.

Monahan, J. (1993). Limiting therapist exposure to Tarasoff liability: Guidlines for risk containment. *American Psychologist, 43* (3), 242–250.

Nystul, M. S. (1986). Reaching in—reaching out: Counseling an autistic child. *American Mental Health Counselors Association Journal, 8,* 18–26.

Nystul, M. S. (1987). Creative arts therapy and the existential encounter. *The Creative Child and Adult Quarterly, 12*(3), 243–249.

Nystul, M. S. (1995). A problem solving approach to counseling: Integrating Adler's and Glasser's theories. *Elementary School Guidance and Counseling, 29*(4), 297–302.

Pate, R. H., & Miller-Bondi, A. (1995). Religious beliefs and practice: An integral aspect of multicultural awareness. In M. T. Burke & J. G. Miranti (Eds.), *Counseling: The spiritual dimension*. Alexandria, VA: American Counseling Association.

Patterson, C. H. (1996). Multicultural counseling: From diversity to universality. *Journal of Counseling and Development, 74*(3), 227–231.

Pedersen, P. B. (Ed.) (1991). Multiculturalism as a fourth force in counseling (special issue). *Journal of Counseling and Development, 70.*

Pepinsky, H. B., & Pepinsky, P. N. (1954). *Counseling: Theory and practice*. New York: Ronald Press.

Peterson, D. R. (1995). The reflective educator. *American Psychologist, 50*(12), 975–983.

Pincus, H. A., Goodwin, F. K., Barchas, J. D., Cohen, D. J., Judd, L. L., Meltzer, H. Y., & Vaillant, G. E. (1989). The future of the science of psychiatry. In J. A. Talbott (Ed.), *Future directions for psychiatry*. Washington, DC: American Psychiatric Press.

Pope, K. S., & Vetter, V. A. (1992). Ethical dilemmas encountered by members of the American Psychological Association, *American Psychologist. 47*(3), 397–411.

Raimy, V. (1950). *Training in clinical psychology*. Englewood Cliffs, NJ: Prentice-Hall.

Richards, P. S., & Bergin, A. E. (1997). *Strategy for counseling and psychotherapy*. Washington, DC: American Psychological Association.

Rogers, C. (1981). *A way of being*. Boston: Houghton Mifflin.

Rosenhan, D. L., & Seligman, M. E. P. (1995). *Abnormal Psychology* (3rd ed.). New York: W. W. Norton.

Russell, R. L., & Lucariello, J. (1992). Narrative, yes; narrative ad infinitum, no! *American Psychologist, 47*(5), 671–672.

Scott, C. N., Kelly, F. D., & Tolbert, B. L. (1995). Realism, constructivism, and the individual psychology of Alfred Adler. *Individual Psychology: The Journal of Adlerian Theory, Research, and Practice, 51*(1), 5–20.

Sexton, T. L., & Whiston, S. C. (1994). The status of the counseling relationship: An empirical review, theoretical implications and research directions. *The Counseling Psychologist, 22*(1), 6–78.

Shafranske, E. P. (Ed.). (1996). *Religion and clinical practice of psychology*. Washington, DC: American Psychological Association.

Smith, M. B. (1994). Selfhood at risk: Postmodern perils and the perils of postmodernism. *American Psychologist, 49*(5), 405–411.

Solomon, J. (1996). Breaking the silence. *Newsweek,* May 20, 20–24.

Stricker, G., & Trierweiler, S. J. (1995). The local clinical scientist: A bridge between science and practice. *American Psychologist, 50*(12), 995–1002.

Strong, S. R. (1968). Counseling: An interpersonal influence process. *Journal of Counseling Psychology, 15,* 215–224.

Sue, D. W., Ivey, A. E., & Pedersen, P. B. (1996). *A theory of multicultural counseling and therapy*. Pacific Grove, CA: Brooks/Cole.

Wiggins-Frame, M. (1998). The ethics of counseling via the Internet. *The Family Journal: Counseling and Therapy for Couples and Families, 5*(4), 328–330.

Yager, J. (1989). A futuristic view of psychiatry. In J. Yager (Ed.), *The future of psychiatry as a medical specialty*. Washington, DC: American Psychiatric Press.

Chapter 2

Abelson, R., & Nielson, K. (1967). History of ethics. In P. Edwards (Ed.), *The encyclopedia of philosophy, Vol. 3*. New York: Macmillan.

American Association for Counseling and Development (AACD). (1997). *Ethical standards* (rev. ed.). Falls Church, VA: Author.

American Association for Marriage and Family Therapy (AAMFT). (1991). *AAMFT code of ethical principles for marriage and family therapists*.

American Psychological Association (APA). (1992). *Ethical standards of psychologists* (rev. ed.). Washington, DC: Author.

Ansell, C. A. (1987). *Ethical practices workbook*. Santa Monica, CA: Association for Advanced Training in the Behavioral Sciences.

Appelbaum, P. S. (1993). Legal liability and managed care. *American Psychologist, 48*(3), 251–257.

Association for Specialists in Group Work (ASGW). (1990). Ethical guidelines for group counselors. *The Journal for Specialists in Group Work, 15*(2), 119–126.

Baier, K. (1958). *The moral point of view*. Ithaca, NY: Cornell University.

Baruth, L. B., & Huber, C. H. (1985). *Counseling and psychotherapy: Theoretical analyses and skill applications*. Columbus, OH: Merrill/Macmillan.

Bednar, R. L., Bednar, S. C., Lambert, M. J., & Waite, D. R. (1991). *Psychotherapy with high-risk clients: Legal and professional standards*. Pacific Grove, CA: Brooks/Cole.

Bishop, D. R. (1995). Religious values as cross-cultural issues in counseling. In M. T. Burke & J. G. Miranti (Eds.), *Counseling: The spiritual dimension* (pp. 59–72). Alexandria, VA: American Counseling Association.

Brooks, D. K., & Gerstein, L. H. (1990). Counselor credentialing and interprofessional collaboration. *Journal of Counseling and Development, 68,* 477–484.

Cohen, E. D. (1990). Confidentiality, counseling, and clients who have AIDS: Ethical foundations of a model rule. *Journal of Counseling and Development, 68,* 282–287.

Congdon, D. (1987). *Professional issues*. Santa Monica, CA: Association for Advanced Training in Behavioral Sciences.

Corey, G. E. (1996). *Theory and practice of counseling and psychotherapy* (5th ed.). Monterey, CA: Brooks/Cole.

Corey, G. E., Corey, M. S., & Callanan, P. (1998). *Issues and ethics in the helping profession* (5th ed.). Monterey, CA: Brooks/Cole.

Corey, G. E., Corey, M., Callanan, P., & Russell, J. M. (1982). Ethical considerations in using group techniques. *Journal for Specialists in Group Work, 7,* 140–148.

Corey, G., Williams, G. T., & Moline, M. E. (1995). Ethical and legal issues in group counseling. *Ethics and Behavior, 5*(2), 161–183.

Cummings, N. A. (1990). The credentialing of professional psychologists and its implication for other mental health disciplines. *Journal of Counseling and Development, 68,* 485–490.

Denkowski, K. M., & Denkowski, G. C. (1982). Client-counselor confidentiality: An update. *Personnel and Guidance Journal, 60,* 371–375.

DePauw, M. E. (1986). Avoiding ethical relations: A timeline perspective for indivdual counseling. *Journal of Counseling and Development, 64*(5), 303–310.

Everett, C. A. (1990). Where have all the "gypsies" gone? *Journal of Counseling and Development, 68,* 507–510.

Everstine, L., Everstine, D. S., Heymann, G. M., True, R. H., Frey, D. H., Johnson, H. G., & Seiden, R. H. (1980). Privacy and confidentiality in psychotherapy. *American Psychologist, 9,* 828–840.

Forester, J. R. (1977). What shall we do about credentialing? *Personnel and Guidance Journal, 55,* 573–576.

George, R. L., & Cristiani, T. S. (1990). *Counseling: Theory and practice* (3rd ed.). Englewood Cliffs, NJ: Prentice-Hall.

Gillian, C. (1982). *A different voice: Psychological theory and women's development.* Cambridge, MA: Harvard University Press.

Grant, B. (1992). The moral nature of psychotherapy. In M. T. Burke & J. G. Miranti (Eds.), *Ethical and spiritual values in counseling* (pp. 27–36). Alexandria, VA: American Counseling Association.

Gray, L. A., & Harding, A. K. (1988). Confidentiality limits with clients who have the AIDS virus. *Journal of Counseling and Development, 66*(5), 219–223.

Gross, D. R., & Robinson, S. E. (1987). Ethics, violence, and counseling: Hear no evil, see no evil, speak no evil? *Journal of Counseling and Development, 65*(7), 340–344.

Gumper, L. L., & Sprenkle, D. H. (1981). Privileged communication in therapy: Special problems for the family and couples therapist. *Family Process, 20,* 11–23.

Herlihy, B., & Sheeley, V. L. (1987). Privileged communication in selected helping professions: A comparison among statutes. *Journal of Counseling and Development, 65*(9), 479–483.

Herrington, B. S. (1979). Privilege denial in joint therapy. *Psychiatric News, 14*(1), 1–9.

Huber, C. H. (1994). *Ethical, legal, and professional issues in the practice of marriage and family therapy* (2nd ed.). Columbus, OH: Merrill/Macmillan.

Huey, W. (1986). Ethical concerns in school counseling. *Journal of Counseling and Development, 64*(5), 321–322.

Keeton, W. P. (1984). *Prosser and Keeton on the law of torts* (5th ed.). St. Paul, MN: West.

Kitchener, K. S. (1984). Ethics in counseling psychology: Distinctions and directions. *Counseling Psychologist, 12,* 15–18.

Kitchener, K. S. (1985). Ethical principles and ethical decisions in student affairs. In H. J. Canon & R. D. Brown (Eds.), *Applied ethics: Tools for practitioners.* San Francisco: Jossey-Bass.

Knapp, S. (1980). A primer on malpractice for psychologists. *Professional Psychology, 11,* 606–612.

Leslie, R. (1991). Psychotherapist-patient privilege clarified. *The California Therapist,* July/August, 11–19.

Mabe, A. R., & Rollins, S. A. (1986). The role of a code of ethical standards in counseling. *Journal of Counseling and Development, 64*(5), 294–297.

Mardirosian, K., McGuire, J. M., Abbott, D. W., & Blau, B. I. (1990). The effects of enhanced informal consent in a profile pregnancy counseling center. *Journal of Counseling and Development, 69,* 39–41.

Margolin, G. (1982). Ethical and legal considerations in marriage and family therapy. *American Psychologist, 7,* 788–801.

McFadden, J., & Brooks, D. K. (1983). *Counselor licensure action packet.* Alexandria, VA: American Association for Counseling and Development.

Meara, N. M., Schmidt, L. D., & Day, J. D. (1996). Principles and virtues: A foundation for ethical decisions, policies, and character. *The Counseling Psychologist, 24*(1), 4–77.

Melton, G. B. (1988). Ethical and legal issues in AIDS-related practice. *American Psychologist, 43*(11), 941–947.

Monahan, J. (1993). Limiting therapist exposure to Tarasoff liability: Guidelines for risk containment. *American Psychologist, 48*(3), 242–250.

Paradise, L. V., & Kirby, P. C. (1990). Legal issues in group work: Some perspectives on the legal liability of group counseling in private practice. *The Journal for Specialists in Group Work, 15*(2), 114–118.

Patterson, C. H. (1992). Values in counseling and psychotherapy. In M. T. Burke & J. G. Miranti (Eds.), *Ethical and spiritual values in counseling* (pp. 107–120). Alexandria, VA: American Counseling Association.

Pedersen, P. B. (1997). The cultural context of the American Counseling Association Code of Ethics. *Journal of Counseling and Development, 76*(1), 23–28.

Remley, T. P. (1991). *Preparing for court appearances.* Alexandria, VA: American Association for Counseling and Development.

Reynolds, M. (1976). Threats to confidentiality. *Social Work, 21,* 108–113.

Shulte, J. M. (1992). The morality of influencing in counseling. In M. T. Burke & J. G. Miranti (Eds.), *Ethical and spiritual values in counseling* (pp. 107–120). Alexandria, VA: American Counseling Association.

Stanard, R., & Hazler, R. (1995). Legal and ethical implications of HIV and duty to warn for counselors:

Does Tarasoff apply? *Journal of Counseling and Development, 73*(4), 397–400.

Tarasoff v. Board of Regents of the University of California, 13 Cal. 3d 177, 529 P.2d 553 (1974), vacated, 17 Cal. 3d 425, 551 P.2d 334 (1976).

Thompson, C. L., & Rudolph, L. B. (1997). *Counseling children* (3rd ed.). Pacific Grove, CA: Brooks/Cole.

Van Hoose, W. H. (1980). Ethics in counseling. *Counseling and Human Development, 13*(1), 1–12.

Chapter 3

Adler, A. (1964). *Social interest: A challenge to mankind.* New York: Capricorn Books. (original work published 1929)

Adler, A. (1969). *The practice and theory of individual psychology.* Patterson, NJ: Littlefield, Adams.

Al-Darmaki, F., & Kivlighan, D. M., Jr. (1993). Congruence in client-counselor expectations for relationship and the working alliance, *Journal of Counseling Psychology, 40*(4), 379–384.

Andersen, B., & Andersen, W. (1985). Client perceptions of counselors using positive and negative self-involving statements. *Journal of Counseling Psychology, 32,* 462–465.

Anderson, H., & Goolishian, H. (1992). The client is the expert: A not-knowing approach to therapy. In S. McNamee & K. J. Gergen (Eds.), *Therapy as social construction* (pp. 25–39). Newbury Park, CA: Sage.

Angle, S. S., & Goodyear, R. K. (1984). Perception of counselors' qualities: Impact of subjects' self-concepts, counselor gender, and counselor introductions. *Journal of Counseling Psychology, 31,* 576–579.

Argyle, M. (1981). The contribution of social interaction research to social skills training. In J. D. Wine & M. D. Syme (Eds.), *Social Competence.* New York: Guilford.

Barrett-Lennard, G. T. (1981). The empathy cycle: Refinement of a nuclear concept. *Journal of Counseling Psychology, 28,* 91–100.

Beck, A. T., Sokol, L., Clark, D. A., Berchick, R., & Wright, F. (1992). A crossover study of focused cognitive therapy for panic disorder. *American Journal of Psychiatry, 149,* 778–783.

Berenson, B., & Mitchell, K. (1968). Therapeutic conditions for therapist-initiated confrontation. *Journal of Clinical Psychology, 24,* 363–364.

Bernstein, B. L., & Figioli, S. W. (1983). Gender and credibility introduction effects on perceived counselor characteristics. *Journal of Counseling Psychology, 30,* 506–513.

Beutler, L. E., Cargo, M., & Arizmendi, T. G. (1986). Therapist variables in psychotherapy process and outcome. In S. L. Garfield & A. E. Bergin (Eds.), *Handbook of psychotherapy and behavior change.* New York: John Wiley & Sons.

Beutler, L. E., Machado, P. P. P., & Neufeldt, S. A. (1994). Therapist variables. In A. E. Bergin & S. L. Garfield (Eds.), *Handbook of psychotherapy and behavior change* (4th ed.). New York: John Wiley & Sons.

Bitter, J. R., & Corey, G. (1996). Family systems therapy. In G. Corey, *Theory and practice of counseling and psychotherapy* (5th ed.). Pacific Grove, CA: Brooks/Cole.

Blocher, D. H. (1974). *Developmental counseling* (2nd ed.). New York: Ronald Press.

Bordin, E. S. (1979). The generalizability of the psychoanalytic concept of the working alliance. *Psychotherapy: Theory, Research and Practice, 16,* 252–260.

Carkhuff, R. R. (1969). *Helping and human relations* (Vols. 1–2). New York: Holt, Rinehart, & Winston.

Carkhuff, R. R. (1971). *The development of human resources.* New York: Holt, Rinehart, & Winston.

Carlsen, M. B. (1995). Meaning-making and creative aging. In R. A. Neimeyer & M. J. Mahoney (Eds.), *Constructivism in psychotherapy.* Washington, DC: American Psychological Association.

Collins, N. L., & Miller, L. C. (1994). Self-disclosure and liking: A meta-analytic review. *Psychological Bulletin, 116*(3), 457–475.

Chandler, C. K., Holden, J. M., & Kolander, C. A. (1995). Counseling for spiritual wellness: Theory and practice. In M. T. Burke & J. G. Miranti (Eds.), *Counseling: The spiritual dimension* (pp. 41–58). Alexandria, VA: American Counseling Association.

Cormier, L. S., & Hackney, H. (1993). *The professional counselor: A process guide to helping.* Englewood Cliffs, NJ: Prentice-Hall.

Cormier, W. H., & Cormier, L. S. (1991). *Interviewing strategies for helpers* (3rd ed.). Monterey, CA: Brooks/Cole.

Corrigan, J. D., Dell, D. M., Lewis, K. N., & Schmidt, L. D. (1980). Counseling as a social influence process: A review [monograph]. *Journal of Counseling Psychology, 27,* 395–441.

Curran, J., & Loganbell, C. R. (1985). Factors affecting the attractiveness of a group leader. *Journal of College Student Personnel, 24,* 250–255.

Danish, S. J., D'Augelli, A. R., & Brock, G. W. (1976). An evaluation of helping skill training: Effects on helpers' verbal responses. *Journal of Counseling Psychology, 23,* 259–266.

De Shazer, S. *Key solutions in brief therapy.* New York: Norton.

De Shazer, S. (1991). *Putting difference to work.* New York: Norton.

Devine, D. A., & Fernald, P. S. (1973). Outcome effects of receiving a preferred, randomly assigned, or non-referred therapy. *Journal of Consulting and Clinical Psychology, 41,* 104–107.

Dinkmeyer, D., & McKay, G. (1989). *Systematic training for effective parenting (STEP)* (3rd. ed.). Circle Pines, MN: American Guidance Service.

Dixon, D. N., & Glover, J. A. (1984). *Counseling: A problem solving approach.* New York: John Wiley & Sons.

Dobson, K. (1989). A meta analysis of the efficacy of cognitive therapy for depression. *Journal of Consulting and Clinical Psychology, 57,* 414–419.

Dorn, F. J., & Day, B. J. (1985). Assessing change in self-concept: A social psychological approach. *American Mental Health Counselors Association Journal, 7,* 180–186.

Durrant, M. (1995). *Creative strategies for school problems: Solutions for psychologists and teachers.* New York: Norton.

Egan, G. (1994). *The skilled helper: A model for systematic helping and interpersonal relating* (5th ed.). Monterey, CA: Brooks/Cole.

Erikson, E. H. (1968). *Identity, youth, and crises.* New York: W. W. Norton.

Erickson, M. (1954). Special techniques on brief hypnotherapy. *Journal of Clinical and Experimental Hypnosis, 2,* 109–129.

Erickson, M. H. (1954). Pseudo-orientation in time as a hypnotherapeutic procedure. *Journal of Clinical and Experimental Hypnosis, 2,* 261–283.

Fisch, R., Weakland, J. H., & Segal, L. (1982). *The tactics of change: Doing therapy briefly.* San Francisco: Jossey-Bass.

Foa, E. B., Rothbaum, B. O., Riggs, D. S., & Murdock, T. B. (1991). Treatment of posttraumatic stress disorder in rape victims: A comparison between cognitive-behavioral procedures and counseling. *Journal of Consulting and Clinical Psychology, 59,* 715–723.

Freud, S. (1969). *A general introduction to psychoanalysis.* New York: Simon & Schuster.

Friedman, S. (1997). *Time-effective psychotherapy: Maximizing outcomes in an era of minimized resources.* Boston: Allyn & Bacon.

Garfield, S. L., & Bergin, A. E. (1971). Therapeutic conditions and outcome. *Journal of Abnormal Psychology, 77,* 108–114.

Gazda, G. M., Asbury, F., Blazer, F., Childress, W., & Walters, R. (1979). *Human relations development: A manual for educators.* Boston: Allyn & Bacon.

Gelso, C. J., & Carter, J. A. (1985). The relationship in counseling and psychotherapy: Components, consequences, and theoretical antecedents. *The Counseling Psychologist, 13,* 155–243.

Gelso, C. J., & Fretz, B. R. (1992). *Counseling psychology.* Orlando, FL: Holt, Rinehart, & Winston.

George, R. L., & Cristiani, T. S. (1995). *Counseling: Theory and practice* (3rd ed.). Englewood Cliffs, NJ: Prentice-Hall.

Gladstein, G. (1983). Understanding empathy: Integrating counseling, developmental and social psychology perspectives. *Journal of Counseling Psychology, 30,* 467–482.

Glasser, W. (1965). *Reality therapy.* New York: Harper & Row.

Glasser, W. (1989). Control theory in the practice of reality therapy. In N. Glasser (Ed.), *Control theory in the practice of reality therapy: Case studies* (pp. 1–15). New York: Harper & Row.

Greenson, R. R. (1967). *Technique and practice of psychoanalysis.* New York: International University Press.

Gutterman, J. T. (1996). Farewell to families: Language systems in the postmodern era. *The Family Journal: Counseling and Therapy for Couples and Families, 4*(2), 139–142.

Hackman, H. W., & Claiborn, C. D. (1982). An attributional approach to counselor attractiveness. *Journal of Counseling Psychology, 29,* 224–231.

Haley, J. (1984). *Ordeal therapy: Unusual ways to change behavior.* San Francisco: Jossey-Bass.

Heppner, P. P., & Claiborn, C. D. (1989). Social influence research in counseling: A review and critique [monograph]. *Journal of Counseling Psychology, 36,* 365–387.

Heppner, P. P., & Dixon, D. N. (1981). A review of the interpersonal influence process in counseling. *Personnel and Guidance Journal, 59,* 542–550.

Heppner, P. P., & Heesacker, M. (1983). Perceived counselor characteristics, client expectations, and client satisfaction with counseling. *Journal of Counseling Psychology, 30,* 31–39.

Heppner, P. P., & Krauskopf, C. J. (1987). An information-processing approach to personal problem solving. *The Counseling Psychologist, 15,* 371–447.

Homans, G. C. (1962). *Sentiments and activities.* New York: The Free Press of Glencoe.

Humphrey, F. G. (1983). *Marital therapy.* Englewood Cliffs, NJ: Prentice-Hall.

Ivey, A. (1971). *Microcounseling: Innovations in interviewing training.* Springfield, IL: Charles C. Thomas.

Ivey, A. E. (1994). *Intentional interviewing and counseling: Facilitating client development* (3rd ed.). Pacific Grove, CA: Brooks/Cole.

Jourard, S. M. (1958). *Personal adjustment: An approach through the study of healthy personality.* New York: Macmillan.

Kanfer, F. H., & Busemeyer, J. R. (1982). The use of problem solving and decision making in behavior therapy. *Clinical Psychology Review, 2,* 239–266.

Kivlighan, D. M. (1990). Relation between counselors' use of intentions and clients' perception of working alliance. *Journal of Counseling Psychology, 37,* 27–32.

Kokotovic, A. M., & Tracey, T. J. (1990). Working alliance in the early phase of counseling. *Journal of Counseling Psychology, 37,* 16–21.

Koss, M. P., & Shiang, J. (1994). Research on brief psychotherapy. In A. E. Bergin & S. L. Garfield, *Handbook of psychotherapy and behavior change* (4th ed.). New York: John Wiley & Sons.

Kottler, J. A., & Brown, R. W. (1996). *Introduction to therapeutic counseling* (3rd ed.). Monterey, CA: Brooks/Cole.

La Crosse, M. B. (1980). Perceived counselor social influence and counseling outcomes: Validity of the Counselor Rating Form. *Journal of Counseling Psychology, 27,* 320–327.

La Fromboise, T. D., & Dixon, D. N. (1981). American Indian perceptions of trustworthiness in a counseling interview. *Journal of Counseling Psychology, 28,* 135–139.

Lamb, D. H. (1985). A time-frame model of termination in psychotherapy. *Psychotherapy, 22,* 604–609.

Lazarus, A. A. (1993). Tailoring the therapeutic relationship, or being an authentic chameleon. *Psychotherapy, 30*(3), 404–407.

Linder, R. (1954). *The fifty-minute hour.* New York: Bantam Books.

Littrell, J. M., Caffrey, P., & Hopper, G. C. (1987). Counselor's reputation: An important precounseling variable for adolescents. *Journal of Counseling Psychology, 34,* 228–231.

Littrell, J. M., Malila, J. A., & Vanderwood, M. (1995). Single-session brief counseling in a high school. *Journal of Counseling and Development, 73*(4), 451–458.

Mallinckrodt, B., & Helms, J. E. (1986). Effect of disabled counselors' self-disclosure on clients' perceptions of the counselor. *Journal of Counseling Psychology, 33,* 343–348.

Martin, D. G. (1989). *Counseling and therapy skills.* Prospect Heights, IL: Therapy Press.

Maslow, A. H. (1968). *Toward the psychology of being* (2nd ed.). New York: Van Nostrand Reinhold.

McCarthy, P. R. (1982). Differential effects of counselor self-disclosure versus self-involving counselor statements across counselor-client gender pairings. *Journal of Counseling Psychology, 26,* 538–541.

McNeill, B. W., May, R. J., & Lee, V. E. (1987). Perceptions of counselor source characteristics and successful terminators. *Journal of Counseling Psychology, 34,* 86–89.

Merluzzi, T. V., & Brischetto, C. S. (1983). Breach of confidentiality and perceived trustworthiness of counselors. *Journal of Counseling Psychology, 30,* 245–251.

Mintz, J., Luborsky, L., & Auerbach, A. (1971). Dimensions of psychotherapy: A factor-analytic study of ratings of psychotherapy sessions. *Journal of Consulting and Clinical Psychology, 36,* 106–120.

Miranti, J. G., & Burke, M. T. (1995). Spirituality: An integral component of the counseling process. In M. T. Burke & J. G. Miranti (Eds.), *Counseling: The spiritual dimension* (pp. 1–4). Alexandria, VA: American Counseling Association.

Nathan, P. E., & Harris, S. L. (1980). *Psychopathology and society.* New York: McGraw-Hill.

Neimeyer, R. A., & Mahoney, M. J. (1995). *Constructivism in psychotherapy.* Washington, DC: American Psychological Association.

Nystul, M. S. (1979). Three levels of a counseling relationship. *The School Counselor, 26,* 144–148.

Nystul, M. S. (1981). Avoiding roadblocks in counseling. *The Individual Psychologist, 18,* 21–28.

Nystul, M. S. (1994). The use of normalizing and structuring in the counseling process. *Counseling and Human Development, 26*(8), 11–12.

Nystul, M. S. (1995). A problem solving approach to counseling: Integrating Adler's and Glasser's theories. *Elementary School Guidance and Counseling, 29,* 297–302.

O'Hanlon, W. H., & Weiner-Davis, M. (1989). *In search of solutions: A new direction in psychotherapy.* New York: Norton.

Okun, B. F. (1997). *Effective helping interviewing and counseling techniques* (5th ed.). Monterey, CA: Brooks/Cole.

Orlando, D. E., & Howard, K. I. (1986). Process and outcome in psychotherapy. In S. L. Garfield & A. E. Bergin (Eds.), *Handbook of psychotherapy and behavior change.* New York: John Wiley & Sons.

Paradise, L. V., Conway, B. S., & Zweig, J. (1986). Effects of expert and referent influence, physical attractiveness, and gender on perceptions of counselor attributes. *Journal of Counseling Psychology, 33,* 16–22.

Quintana, S. M., & Holahan, W. (1992). Termination in short-term counseling: Comparison of successful and unsuccessful cases. *Journal of Counseling Psychology, 39*(3), 299–305.

Raskin, N. J., & Rogers, C. R. (1995). Person-centered therapy. In R. J. Corsini & D. Wedding (Eds.), *Current psychotherapies* (pp. 128–161). Itasca, IL.: F. E. Peacock.

Richards, P. S., & Bergin, A. E. (1997). *Strategy for counseling and psychotherapy*. Washington, DC: American Psychological Association.

Rogers, C. R. (1957). The necessary and sufficient conditions of therapeutic personality change. *Journal of Counseling Psychology, 21,* 95–103.

Rogers, C. R. (1970). *On encounter groups*. New York: Harper & Row.

Rogers, C. R. (1980). *A way of being*. Boston: Houghton Mifflin.

Rogers, C. R., Gendlin, E. T., Kiesler, D. J., & Truax, C. B. (1967). *The therapeutic relationship and its impact: A study of psychotherapy with schizophrenics*. Madison: University of Wisconsin Press.

Roll, S. A., Crowley, M. A., & Rappl, L. E. (1985). Client perceptions of counselor's nonverbal behavior: A reevaluation. *Counselor Education and Supervision, 24,* 234–243.

Rosenhan, D. L., & Seligman, M. E. P. (1995). *Abnormal Psychology* (3rd ed.). New York: W. W. Norton.

Sager, C. (1976). *Marriage contracts and couple therapy*. New York: Brunner/Mazel.

Sexton, T. L., & Whiston, S. C. (1994). The status of the counseling relationship: An empirical review, theoretical implications, and research directions. *The Counseling Psychologist, 22*(1), 6–78.

Sloane, B., Staples, F., Cristol, A., Yorkston, N., & Whipple, K. (1975). *Psychotherapy versus behavior therapy*. Cambridge, MA: Harvard University Press.

Smith, D. C. (1993). Exploring the religious-spiritual needs of the dying. *Journal of Counseling and Values, 37,* 71–77.

Steenbarger, B. N. (1992). Toward science-practice integration in brief counseling and therapy. *The Counseling Psychologist, 20*(3), 403–450.

Strohmer, D. C., & Biggs, D. A. (1983). Effects of counselor disability status on disabled subjects' perceptions of counselor attractiveness and expertness. *Journal of Counseling Psychology, 30,* 202–208.

Strong, S. R. (1968). Counseling: An interpersonal influence process. *Journal of Counseling Psychology, 15,* 215–224.

Strong, S. R., & Claiborn, C. D. (1982). *Change through interaction*. New York: John Wiley & Sons.

Sue, D. W., Ivey, A. E., & Pedersen, P. B. (1996). *A theory of multicultural counseling and therapy*. Pacific Grove, CA: Brooks/Cole.

Sue, S., Zane, N., & Young, K. (1994). Research on psychotherapy with culturally diverse populations. In A. E. Bergin & S. L. Garfield (Eds.), *Handbook of psychotherapy and behavior change* (4th ed.) (pp. 783–820). New York: John Wiley & Sons.

Suit, J. L., & Paradise, L. V. (1985). Effects of metaphors and cognitive complexity on perceived counselor characteristics. *Journal of Counseling Psychology, 32,* 23–28.

Thompson, R. A. (1996). *Counseling techniques: Improving relationships with others, ourselves, our families, and our environment*. Washington, DC: Accelerated Development.

Truax, C. B., & Carkhuff, R. R. (1967). *Toward effective counseling and psychotherapy*. Chicago: Aldine.

Truax, C. B., & Mitchell, K. M. (1971). Research on certain therapist interpersonal skills in relation to process and outcome. In A. E. Bergin & S. L. Garfield (Eds.), *Handbook of psychotherapy and behavior change*. New York: John Wiley & Sons.

Tyson, J. A., & Wall, S. M. (1983). Effect of inconsistency between counselor verbal and nonverbal behavior on perceptions of counselor attributes. *Journal of Counseling Psychology, 30,* 433–437.

Chapter 4

Allport, G. W., & Ross, J. M. (1967). Personal religious orientation and prejudice. *Journal of Personality and Social Psychology, 5,* 432–443.

American Psychiatric Association. (1994). *Diagnostic and statistical manual of mental disorders* (4th ed.). Washington, DC: American Psychiatric Association.

Anastasi, A. (1997). *Psychological testing* (7th ed.). New York: Macmillan.

Baruth, L. G., & Huber, C. H. (1985). *Counseling and psychotherapy: Theoretical analyses and skill application*. Columbus, OH: Merrill/Macmillan.

Beutler, L. E., Machado, P. P. P., & Neufeldt, S. A. (1994). Therapist variables. In A. E. Bergin & S. L. Garfield (Eds.), *Handbook of psychotherapy and behavior change* (4th ed.) (pp. 229–269). New York: John Wiley & Sons.

Bigler, E. D., & Ehrfurth, J. W. (1981). The continued inappropriate singular use of the Bender Visual Motor Gestalt Test. *Professional Psychology, 12,* 562–569.

Bray, D. W., Campbell, R. J., & Grant, D. L. (1974). *Formative years in business: A long-term AT&T study of managerial lives*. New York: John Wiley & Sons.

Cattell, R. B. (1949). *Culture-fair intelligence tests.* Champaign, IL: Institute for Personality and Ability Testing.

Clark, A. J. (1995). Projective techniques in the counseling process. *Journal of Counseling and Development, 73*(3), 311–316.

Ellis, A. (1996). *Better, deeper and more enduring brief therapy.* New York: Brunner/Mazel.

Freud, S. (1953). Fragment of an analysis of a case of hysteria. In J. Strachey (Ed.), *The standard edition of the complete psychological works of Sigmund Freud, Vol. 7* (pp. 3–122). London: Hogarth.

Garfield, S. L. (1994). Research on client variables in psychotherapy. In A. E. Bergin & S. L. Garfield (Eds.), *Handbook of psychotherapy and behavior change* (4th ed.) (pp. 190–228). New York: John Wiley & Sons.

Gergen, K. J. (1994). Exploring the postmodern. *American Psychologist, 49*(5), 412–416.

Goldman, L. (1990). Qualitative assessment. *The Counseling Psychologist, 18,* 205–213.

Goodyear, R. K. (1990). Research on the effects of test interpretation: A review. *The Counseling Psychologist, 18,* 240–257.

Hamann, E. E. (1994). Clinicians and diagnosis: Ethical concerns and clinician competence. *Journal of Counseling and Development, 72*(3), 259–260.

Hershenson, D. B., Power, P. W., & Waldo, M. (1996). *Community counseling: Contemporary theory and practice.* Needham Heights, MA: Allyn & Bacon.

Hohenshill, T. H. (1996). Editorial: Role of assessment and diagnosis in counseling. *Journal of Counseling and Development, 75*(1), 64–67.

Huebner, L. A. (1980). Interaction of student and campus. In E. Delworth, G. Hanson, & Associates, *Student services: A handbook for the profession* (pp. 117–155). San Francisco: Jossey-Bass.

Ivey, A. E. (1994). *Intentional interviewing and counseling* (3rd ed.). Monterey, CA: Brooks/Cole.

Jewell, D. A. (1989). Cultural and ethnic issues. In S. Wetzler & M. M. Katz (Eds.), *Contemporary approaches to psychological assessment* (pp. 299–309). New York: Brunner/Mazel.

Jones, A. S., & Gelso, C. J. (1988). Differential effects of style of interpretation: Another look. *Journal of Counseling Psychology, 35,* 363–369.

Jones, J. V., Jr. (1995). Constructivism and individual psychology: Common ground for dialogue. *Individual Psychology: The Journal of Adlerian Theory, Research, and Practice, 51*(3), 231–243.

Jongsma, A. E., & Petersen, L. M. (1995). *The complete psychotherapy treatment planner.* New York: John Wiley & Sons.

Kottler, J. A., & Brown, R. W. (1996). *Introduction to therapeutic counseling* (3rd ed.), Monterey, CA: Brooks/Cole.

Lazarus, A. A. (1995). Multimodal therapy. In R. J. Corsini & D. Wedding, *Current Psychotherapies* (5th ed.) (pp. 322–355). Itasca, IL: F. E. Peacock.

Lazarus, A. A. (1997). *Brief but comprehensive psychotherapy.* New York: Springer.

Lazarus, A. L., & Beutler, L. E. (1993). On technical eclecticism. *Journal of Counseling and Development, 71*(4), 381–385.

Lopez, F. M., Jr. (1966). *Evaluating executive decision making.* New York: American Management Association.

Makover, R. B. (1992). Training psychotherapists in hierarchical treatment planning. *Journal of Psychotherapy Practice and Research, 1*(4), 337–350.

May, T. M. (1990). An evolving relationship. *The Counseling Psychologist, 18,* 266–270.

McMillan, J. H. (1984). Culture-fair tests. In R. Corsini (Ed.), *Encyclopedia of Psychology* (pp. 335–336). New York: John Wiley & Sons.

Mercer, J. R. (1977). *SOMPA: System of Multicultural Pluralistic Assessment.* New York: Psychological Corp.

Miller, G. M. (1982). Deriving meaning from standardized tests: Interpreting test results to clients. *Measurement and Evaluation in Guidance, 15,* 87–94.

Miller, M. J., & Cochran, J. R. (1979). Evaluating the use of technology in reporting SCII results to students. *Measurement and Evaluation in Guidance, 12,* 166–173.

Nathan, P. E., & Harris, S. L. (1980). *Psychopathology and society* (2nd ed.). New York: McGraw-Hill.

Newmark, C. S. (1985). *Major psychological assessment instruments.* Boston: Allyn & Bacon.

Office of Strategic Services. (1948). *Assessment of men.* New York: Holt, Rinehart, & Winston.

Oliver, L. W. (1977). Evaluating career counseling outcome for three modes of test interpretation. *Measurement and Evaluation in Guidance, 10,* 153–161.

Othmer, E., & Othmer, S. C. (1989). *The clinical interview: Using DSM-III-R.* Washington, DC: American Psychiatric Press.

Penrose, L. S., & Raven, J. C. (1936). A new series of perceptual tasks: Preliminary communication. *British Journal of Medical Psychology, 16,* 97–104.

Rawlins, M. E., Eberly, C. G., & Rawlins, L. D. (1991). Infusing counseling skills in test interpretation. *Counselor Education and Supervision, 31,* 109–120.

Reynolds, C. R. (1982). The problem of bias in psychological assessment. In C. R. Reynolds & T. B. Gutkin, *The Handbook of School Psychology.* New York: John Wiley & Sons.

Richards, P. S., & Bergin, A. E. (1997). *Strategy or counseling and psychotherapy.* Washington, DC: American Psychological Association.

Rosenhan, D. L., & Seligman, M. E. P. (1995). *Abnormal Psychology* (3rd ed.). New York: W. W. Norton.

Sampson, J. P. (1990). Computer-assisted testing and the goals of counseling psychology. *The Counseling Psychologist, 18,* 227–239.

Seligman, L. (1990). *Selecting effective treatments: A comprehensive, systematic guide to treating adult mental disorders.* San Francisco: Jossey-Bass.

Shea, M. T., Pilkonis, P. A., Beckham, E., Collins, J. F., Elkin, I., Sotsky, S. M., & Docherty, J. P. (1990). Personality disorders and treatment outcome in the NIMH Treatment of Depression Collaborative Research Program. *American Journal of Psychiatry, 147,* 711–718.

Smart, D. W., & Smart, J. F. (1997). DSM-IV and culturally sensitive diagnosis: Some observations for counselors. *Journal of Counseling and Development, 75*(5), 392–398.

Spitzer, R. L., Gibbon, M., Skodol, A. E., Williams, J. B., & First, M. B. (1994). *The DSM-IV Casebook* (4th ed.). Washington, DC: American Psychiatric Press.

Sue, D. W., Ivey, A. E., & Pedersen, P. B. (1996). *A theory of multicultural counseling and therapy.* Pacific Grove, CA: Brooks/Cole.

Sundberg, N. D. (1977). *Assessment of persons.* Englewood Cliffs, NJ: Prentice-Hall.

Taylor, S. E., & Brown, J. D. (1988). Illusion and well-being: A social psychological perspective on mental health. *Psychological Bulletin, 103,* 193–210.

Topper, M. D. (1985). Navajo "alcoholism": Drinking, alcohol abuse, and treatment in a changing cultural environment. In L. A. Bennett & G. M. Ames, (Eds.), *The American experience with alcohol: Contrasting cultural perspectives.* New York: Plenum Press.

Trzepacz, P. T., & Baker, R. (1993). *The psychiatric mental status examination.* New York: Ford University Press.

Vernon, P. E., & Parry, J. B. (1949). *Personnel selection in the British forces.* London: University of London Press.

Walsh, W. B. (1990). Putting assessment in context. *The Counseling Psychologist, 18,* 262–265.

Watkins, C. E., & Campbell, V. L. (1990). Testing and assessment in counseling psychology. *The Counseling Psychologist, 18,* 189–197.

Wilkerson, C. D. (1967). The effects of four methods of test score presentation to eighth-grade students. *Dissertation Abstracts International.* 1318A (order number 67–12661).

Woody, R. H., Hansen, J. C., & Rossberg, R. H. (1989). *Counseling psychology: Strategies and services.* Pacific Grove, CA: Brooks/Cole.

Young, M. E. (1992). *Counseling methods and techniques: An eclectic approach.* Columbus, OH: Merrill.

Chapter 5

Atkinson, D. R. (1993). Who speaks for cross-cultural counseling research? *The Counseling Psychologist, 21*(2), 218–224.

Beutler, L. E., Williams, R. E., Wakefield, P. J., & Entwistle, S. R. (1995). Bridging scientist and practitioner perspective in clinical psychology. *American Psychologist, 50*(12), 984–994.

Borg, W. B., & Gall, M. D. (1989). *Educational research: An introduction* (5th ed.). New York: Longman.

Charles, C. M. (1995). *Introduction to educational research* (2nd ed.). White Plains, NY: Longman.

Consumer Reports. (1995, November). Mental health: Does therapy help? pp. 734–739.

Dreikurs, R., & Soltz, V. (1964). *Children: The challenge.* New York: Hawthorn.

Elkin, I., Shea, T., Watkins, J. T., Imber, S. D., Stotsky, S. M., Collins, J. F., Glass, D. R., Pilkonis, P. A., Leber, W. R., Docherty, J. P., Fiester, S. J., & Parloff, M. B. (1989). National Institute of Mental Health Treatment of Depression Collaborative Research Program. General effectiveness of treatments. *Archives of General Psychiatry, 46,* 971–982.

Eysenck, H. J. (1965). The effects of psychotherapy. *Journal of Consulting Psychology, 16,* 319–324.

Gardill, M. C., & Browder, D. M. (1995). Teaching stimulus classes to encourage independent purchasing by students with severe behavior disorders. *Education and Training in Mental Retardation and Developmental Disabilities, 30,* 254–269.

Garfield, S. L. (1983). *Clinical psychology. The study of personality and behavior* (2nd ed.). New York: Aldine.

Gibson, R. L. (1977). Counseling and annual guidance committee report. Unpublished manuscript, North Central Association of Colleges and Schools.

Goldfried, M. R., & Wolfe, B. E. (1996). Psychotherapy practice and research: Repairing a strained alliance. *American Psychologist, 51*(10), 1007–1016.

Goldman, L. (1989). Moving counseling research into the 21st century. *The Counseling Psychologist, 17,* 81–85.

Gordon, J., & Shontz, F. (1990). Representative case research: A way of knowing. *Journal of Counseling and Development, 69,* 62–66.

Helms, J. E. (1989). At long last: Paradigms for cultural psychology research. *The Counseling Psychologist, 17,* 98–100.

Hershenson, D. B., Power, P. W., & Waldo, M. (1996). *Community counseling.* Needham Heights, MA: Allyn & Bacon.

Hill, C. E. (1992). An overview of four measures developed to test the Hill process model: Therapist intentions, therapist response modes, client reactions, and client behaviors. *Journal of Counseling and Development, 70,* 728–737.

Hill, C. E., & Corbett, M. M. (1993). A perspective on the history of process and outcome research in counseling psychology. *Journal of Counseling Psychology, 40*(1), 3–24.

Hill, C. E., Thompson, B. J., & Williams, E. N. (1997). A guide to conducting consensual qualitative research. *The Counseling Psychologist, 25*(4), 517–572.

Hoshmand, L. L. S. (1989). Alternate research paradigms: A review and teaching proposal. *The Counseling Psychologist, 17,* 3–80.

Hoshmand, L. T. (1985). Phenomenological-based groups for developmentally disabled adults. *Journal of Counseling and Development, 64*(2), 147–148.

Kidder, L. H., Judd, C. M., & Smith, E. R. (1986). *Research methods in social relations.* New York: Holt, Rinehart, & Winston.

Lambert, M. J. (1991). Introduction to psychotherapy research. In L. E. Beutler & M. Crago (Eds.), *Psychotherapy research. An international review of programmatic studies* (pp. 1–11). Washington, DC: American Psychological Association.

Lambert, M. J., & Bergin, A. E. (1994). The effectiveness of psychotherapy. In A. E. Bergin & S. L. Garfield (Eds.), *Handbook of psychotherapy and behavior change* (4th ed.). New York: John Wiley & Sons.

Levitt, E. E. (1957). The results of psychotherapy with children: An evaluation. *Journal of Consulting Psychology, 21,* 189–196.

Lincoln, Y. S., & Guba, E. G. (1985). *Naturalistic inquiry.* Beverly Hills, CA: Sage.

Mahrer, A. R. (1988). Discovery-oriented psychotherapy research: Rationale, aims, and methods. *American Psychologist, 43,* 694–702.

McKenzie, V. M. (1986). Ethnographic findings on West Indian–American clients. *Journal of Counseling and Development, 65,* 40–44.

McNeilly, C. L., & Howard, K. I. (1991). The effects of psychotherapy: A reevaluation based on dosage. *Psychotherapy Research, 1,* 74–78.

Mio, J. S., & Iwamasa, G. (1993). To do, or not to do: That is the question for white cross-cultural researchers. *The Counseling Psychologist, 21*(2), 197–212.

Pedersen, P. (1993). The multicultural dilemma of white cross-cultural researchers. *The Counseling Psychologist, 21*(2), 229–232.

Seligman, L. (1986). The manuscript evaluation process used by AACD journals. *Journal of Counseling and Development, 65*(4), 189–192.

Seligman, M. E. P. (1995). The effectiveness of psychotherapy: The consumer reports study, *American Psychologist, 50*(12), 965–974.

Smith, M. L., & Glass, G. J. (1977). Meta-analysis of psychotherapy outcome studies. *American Psychologist, 32,* 752–760.

Smith, M. L., Glass, G. V., & Miller, T. I. (1980). *The benefits of psychotherapy.* Baltimore: Johns Hopkins University Press.

Stile, S. W. (1993). *N=1 handbook: Designs for inquiry in special education and related services.* Dubuque, IA: Kendall/Hunt.

Sue, D. W., Ivey, A. E., & Pedersen, P. B. (1996). *A theory of multicultural counseling and therapy.* Pacific Grove, CA: Brooks/Cole.

VandenBos, G. R. (1996). Outcome assessment of psychotherapy. *American Psychologist, 51*(10), 1005–1006.

Wilkinson, W. K., & McNeil, K. (1996). *Research for the helping professions.* Pacific Grove, CA: Brooks/Cole.

Chapter 6

Allport, G. W. (1954). *The nature of prejudice.* Cambridge, MA: Addison-Wesley.

Anastasi, A., & Urbina, S. (1997). *Psychological testing* (7th ed.). New York: Prentice-Hall.

Ansbacher, H. L., & Ansbacher, R. R. (Eds.). (1956). *The individual psychology of Alfred Adler.* New York: Basic Books.

Atkinson, D. R., Morten, G., & Sue, D. W. (1998). *Counseling American minorities: A cross-cultural perspective* (5th ed.). Dubuque, IA: William C. Brown.

Atkinson, D. R., & Thompson, C. E. (1992). Racial, ethnic, and cultural variables in counseling. In S. D. Brown & R. W. Lent (Eds.). *Handbook of counseling*

psychology (2nd ed.) (pp. 349–382). New York: John Wiley & Sons.

Ballou, M. (1996). MCT theory and women. In D. W. Sue, A. E. Ivey, & P. B. Pedersen (Eds.). *A theory of multicultural counseling and therapy* (pp. 236–246). Pacific Grove, CA: Brooks/Cole.

Bandler, R., & Grinder, J. (1975). *The structure of magic, Vol. 1.* Palo Alto, CA: Science and Behavior Books.

Barret, R. L. (1995). The spiritual journey: Explorations and implications for counselors. In M. Burke & J. G. Miranti (Eds.), *Counseling: The Spiritual Dimensions.* Alexandria, VA: American Counseling Association.

Baruth, L. G., & Manning, M. L. (1991). *Multicultural counseling and psychotherapy: A lifespan perspective.* New York: Macmillan.

Berrigan, L. P., & Garfield, S. L. (1981). Relationships of missed psychotherapy appointments to premature termination and social class. *The British Journal of Clinical Psychology, 20,* 239–242.

Berry, G. W., & Sipps, G. J. (1991). Interactive effects of counselor-client similarity and client self-esteem on termination type and number of sessions. *Journal of Counseling Psychology, 38*(2), 120–125.

Beutler, L. E., Machado, P. P. P., & Neufeldt, S. A. (1994). Therapist variables. In A. E. Bergin & S. L. Garfield (Eds.), *Handbook of psychotherapy and behavior change* (4th ed.) (pp. 229–269). New York: John Wiley & Sons.

Bishop, D. R. (1995). Religious values as cross-cultural issues in counseling. In M. T. Burke & J. G. Miranti (Eds.), *Counseling: The spiritual dimension* (pp. 59–72). Alexandria, VA: American Counseling Association.

Black, J., & Underwood, J. (1998). Young, female, and gay: Lesbian students and the school environment. *Professional School Counseling, 1*(3), 15–20.

Browning, C., Reynolds, A., & Dworkin, S. H. (1991). Affirmative psychotherapy with lesbian women. *The Counseling Psychologist, 19*(2), 177–196.

Burke, M. T., & Miranti, J. G. (1992). *Ethical and spiritual values in counseling.* Alexandria, VA: American Counseling Association.

Burke, M. T., & Miranti, J. G. (1995). *Counseling: The spiritual dimension.* Alexandria, VA: American Counseling Association.

Casas, J. M., & Pytluk, S. D. (1995). Hispanic identity development: Implications for research and practice. In J. G. Ponterotto, J. M. Casas, L. A. Suzuki, & C. M. Alexander (Eds.), *Handbook of multicultural counseling* (pp. 155–180). Thousand Oaks, CA: Sage.

Cass, V. C. (1979). Homosexual identity formation: a theoretical model. *Journal of Homosexuality, 4,* 219–235.

Choney, S. K., Berryhill-Paapke, E., & Robbins, R. R. (1995). The acculturation of American Indians: Developing frameworks for research and practice. In J. G. Ponterotto, J. M. Casas, L. A. Suzuki, & C. M. Alexander (Eds.), *Handbook of multicultural counseling* (pp. 73–92). Thousand Oaks, CA: Sage.

Cronbach, L. J. (1984). *Essentials of psychological testing.* New York: Harper & Row.

Cross, W. E., Jr. (1995). The psychology of nigrescence: Revising the Cross model. In J. G. Ponterotto, J. M. Casas, L. A. Suzuki, & C. M. Alexander (Eds.), *Handbook of multicultural counseling* (pp. 93–122). Thousand Oaks, CA: Sage.

Dinkmeyer, D., & McKay, G. (1989). *Systematic training for effective parenting (parent's handbook)* (3rd ed.). Circle Pines, MN: American Guidance Service.

Dryden, W. (1987). Theoretically consistent eclecticism: Humanizing a computer "addict." In J. C. Norcross (Ed.), *Casebook of eclectic psychotherapy* (pp. 221–237). New York: Brunner/Mazel.

Dworetzky, J. P. (1996). *Introduction to child development* (6th ed.). New York: ITP.

Ellis, A. (1995). Rational emotive behavior therapy. In R. J. Corsini & D. Wedding (Eds.), *Current psychotherapies* (5th ed.) (pp. 162–196). Itasca, IL: F. E. Peacock.

Enns, C. Z. (1993). Twenty years of counseling and therapy: From naming biases to implementing multifaceted practice. *The Counseling Psychologist, 21*(1), 3–87.

Fassinger, R. E. (1991). The hidden minority: Issues and challenges in working with lesbian women and gay men. *The Counseling Psychologist, 19*(2), 157–176.

Garfield, J. C., Weiss, S. I., & Pollack, E. A. (1973). Effects of the child's social class on school counselors' decision-making. *Journal of Counseling Psychology, 20,* 166–168.

Garfield, S. L. (1994). Research on client variables in psychotherapy. In A. E. Bergin & S. L. Garfield (Eds.), *Handbook of psychotherapy and behavior change* (4th ed.) (pp. 190–228). New York: John Wiley & Sons.

Gelso, C. J., & Fassinger, R. E. (1990). Counseling psychology: Theory and research on intervention. *Annual Review of Psychology, 41,* 387–416.

Genia, V. (1994). Secular psychotherapists and religious clients: Professional considerations and recommendations. *Journal of Counseling and Development, 72*(4), 395–398.

Geoseffi, D. (1993). *On prejudice: A global perspective.* New York: Doubleday.

Gibran, K. (1965). *The prophet.* New York: Alfred A. Knopf.

Gilbert, L. A. (1992). Gender and counseling psychology: Current knowledge and directions for research and social action. In S. D. Brown & R. W. Lent (Eds.), *Handbook of counseling psychology* (2nd ed.) (pp. 383–418). New York: John Wiley & Sons.

Gilligan, C. (1982). *In a Different Voice.* Cambridge, MA: Harvard University Press.

Gilligan, C. (1991). Women's psychological development: Implications for psychotherapy. In C. Gilligan, A. Rogers, & D. Tolman (Eds.), *Women, girls, and psychotherapy: Reframing resistance.* Binghamton, NY: Haworth Press.

Ginter, E. J. (1988). Stagnation in eclecticism: The need to recommit to a journey. *Journal of Mental Health Counseling, 10,* 3–8.

Harrar, L. (Producer). (1984). *Make my people live: The crises in Indian health* [Television broadcast]. Boston, MA: Public Broadcasting System, NOVA.

Helms, J. E. (1986). Expanding racial identity theory to cover the counseling process. *Journal of Counseling Psychology, 33,* 62–64.

Helms, J. E. (1995). An update of Helms's White and people of color racial identity models. In J. G. Ponterotto, J. M. Casas, L. A. Suzuki, & C. M. Alexander (Eds.), *Handbook of multicultural counseling* (pp. 181–198). Thousand Oaks, CA: Sage.

Herring, R. D. (1990). Nonverbal communication: A necessary component of cross-cultural counseling. *Journal of Multicultural Counseling and Development, 18*(4), 172–179.

Ho, D. Y. F. (1995). Internalized culture, culturocentrism, and transcendence. *The Counseling Psychologist, 23*(1), 4–24.

Hoffmann, T., Dana, R., & Bolton, B. (1985). Measured acculturation and MMPI-168 performance of Native American adults. *Journal of Cross-Cultural Psychology, 16*, 243–256.

Ibrahim, F. A. (1991). Contribution of cultural worldview to generic counseling and development. *Journal of Counseling and Development, 70*(1), 13–19.

Ibrahim, F. A. (1993). Existential world view theory: Transcultural Counseling. In J. McFadden (Ed.), *Transactional counseling* (pp. 23–57). Alexandria, VA: ACA Press.

Ibrahim, F. A., & Kahn, H. (1984). *Scale to assess world views.* Unpublished manuscript, University of Connecticut, Storrs, CT.

Ibrahim, F. A., & Kahn, H. (1987). Assessment of world views. *Psychological Reports, 60*, 163–176.

Ingersoll, R. E. (1995). Spirituality, religion, and counseling: Dimensions and relationships. In M. T. Burke & J. G. Miranti (Eds.), *Counseling: The spiritual dimension* (pp. 5–18). Alexandria, VA: American Counseling Association.

Kerwin, C., & Ponterotto, J. G. (1995). Biracial identity development: Theory and research. In J. G. Ponterotto, J. M. Casas, L. A. Suzuki, & C. M. Alexander (Eds.), *Handbook of multicultural counseling* (pp. 181–198). Thousand Oaks, ÇA: Sage.

Kopp, S. B. (1971). *Guru: Metaphors from a psychotherapist.* Palo Alto, CA: Science and Behavior Books.

Lazarus, A. A. (1995). Multimodal therapy. In R. J. Corsini & D. Wedding (Eds.), *Current Psychotherapies* (5th ed.) (pp. 322–355). Itasca, IL: F. E. Peacock.

Lazarus, A. A., & Beutler, L. E. (1993). On technical eclecticism. *Journal of Counseling and Development, 71*(4), 381–385.

Lee, C. C. (1991). Cultural dynamics: Their importance in multicultural counseling. In C. C. Lee & B. L. R. Richardson (Eds.), *Multicultural issues in counseling: New approaches to diversity.* Alexandria, VA: American Association for Counseling and Development.

Lee, C. C., Oh, M. Y., & Mountcastle, A. R. (1992). Indigenous models of helping in nonwestern countries: Implications for multicultural counseling. *Journal of Multicultural Counseling and Development, 20*, 1–10.

Lee, D. (1984). Counseling and culture: Some issues. *Personnel and Guidance Journal, 62*, 592–597.

Lee, S. D. (1968). *Social class bias in the diagnosis of mental illness.* Doctoral dissertation, University of Oklahoma. Ann Arbor, MI: University Microfilms No. 68–6959.

Lonner, W. J. (1985). Issues in testing and assessment in cross-cultural counseling. *The Counseling Psychologist, 13*(4), 599–614.

Lynn, S. J., & Garske, J. P. (1985). *Contemporary psychotherapies: Models and methods.* Columbus, OH: Merrill/Macmillan.

Maslow, A. H. (1968). *Toward a psychology of being.* Princeton, NJ: Van Nostrand.

McBride, M. C., & Martin, G. E. (1990). A framework for eclecticism: The importance of theory to mental health counseling. *Journal of Mental Health Counseling, 12*, 495–505.

McFadden, J. (1996). A transcultural perspective: Reaction to C. H. Patterson's "multicultural counseling: from diversity to universality." *Journal of Counseling and Development, 74*(3), 232–235.

McWhirter, E. H. (1994). *Counseling for empowerment.* Alexandria, VA: American Counseling Association.

Mendoza, R. H. (1989). An empirical scale to measure type and degree of acculturation in Mexican-American adolescents and adults. *Journal of Cross-Cultural Psychology, 20*, 372–385.

Minton, H. L., & McDonald, G. J. (1984). Homosexual identity formation as a developmental process. *Journal of Homosexuality, 9*, 91–104.

Miranti, J. G., & Burke, M. T. (1995). Spirituality: An integral component of the counseling process. In M. T. Burke & J. G. Miranti (Eds.), *Counseling: The spiritual dimension* (pp. 1–4). Alexandria, VA: American Counseling Association.

Morrow, D., Worthington, E. L., & McCullough, M. E. (1993). Observers' perceptions of a counselor's treatment of a religious issue. *Journal of Counseling and Development, 71*(4), 452–456.

Moyerman, D. R., & Forman, B. D. (1992). Acculturation and adjustment: A meta-analytic study. *Hispanic Journal of Behavioral Sciences, 14*, 163–200.

Myers, L. J., Speight, S. L., Highlen, P. S., Cox, C. I., Reynolds, A. L., Adams, E. M., & Hanley, C. P. (1991). Identity development and worldview: Toward an optimal conceptualization. *Journal of Counseling and Development, 70*(1), 54–63.

Nelson, M. L., & Holloway, E. L. (1990). Relation of gender to power and involvement in supervision. *Journal of Counseling Psychology, 37*, 473–481.

Norcross, J. C., & Newman, C. F. (1992). Psychotherapy integration: Setting the context. In J. C. Norcross & M. R. Goldfried (Eds.), *Handbook of psychotherapy integration* (pp. 3–45). New York: Basic Books.

Norcross, J. C., Prochaska, J. O., & Gallagher, K. M. (1989). Clinical psychologists in the 1980's: II. Theory research, and practice. *The Clinical Psychologist, 42,* 45–53.

Nystul, M. S. (1978). Adler as a Sherlockian. *The Individual Psychologist, 15*(1), 41–45.

Nystul, M. S. (1981). Avoiding roadblocks in counseling. *The Individual Psychologist, 18,* 21–28.

Pate, R. H., & Bondi, A. M. (1992). Religious beliefs and practice: An integral aspect of multicultural awareness. *Counselor Education and Supervision, 32*(2), 108–115.

Patterson, C. H. (1989). Eclecticism in psychotherapy: Is integration possible: *Psychotherapy, 26*(2), 157–161.

Patterson, C. H. (1996). Multicultural counseling: From diversity to universality. *Journal of Counseling and Development, 74*(3), 227–231.

Pedersen, P. B. (1987). Ten frequent assumptions of cultural ·bias in counseling. *Journal of Multicultural Counseling and Development, 15*(1), 16–24.

Pedersen, P. (1988). *A handbook for developing multicultural awareness.* Alexandria, VA: American Association for Counseling and Development.

Pedersen, P. B. (1991). Multiculturalism as a generic approach to counseling. *Journal of Counseling and Development, 70*(1), 6–12.

Ponterotto, J. G., & Casas, J. M. (1991). *Handbook of racial/ethnic minority counseling research.* Springfield, IL: Charles C. Thomas.

Richards, P. S., & Bergin, A. E. (1997). *Strategy for counseling and psychotherapy.* Washington, DC: American Psychological Association.

Richardson, T. Q., & Molinaro, K. L. (1996). White counselor self-awareness: A prerequisite for developing multicultural competence. *Journal of Counseling and Development, 74*(3), 238–242.

Ridley, C. R., Mendoza, D. W., & Kanitz, B. E. (1994). Multicultural training: Reexamination, operationalization, and integration. *The Counseling Psychologist, 22*(2), 227–289.

Ritter, K. Y., & O'Neill, C. W. (1995). Moving through loss: The spiritual journey of gay men and lesbian women. In M. T. Burke & J. G. Miranti (Eds.), *Counseling: The spiritual dimension* (pp. 127–141). Alexandria, VA: American Counseling Association.

Rogers, C. (1951). *Client-centered therapy.* Boston: Houghton Mifflin.

Rowe, W., Behrens, J. T., & Leach, M. M. (1995). Racial/ethnic identity and racial consciousness: Looking back and looking forward. In J. G. Ponterotto, J. M. Casas, L. A. Suzuki, & C. M. Alexander (Eds.), *Handbook of multicultural counseling* (pp. 218–235). Thousand Oaks, CA: Sage.

Sandhu, D. S. & Aspy, C. B. (1997). *Counseling for prejudice prevention and reduction.* Alexandria, VA: American Counseling Association.

Shakespeare, W. (1938). *The works of William Shakespeare: Gathered into one volume.* New York: Oxford University Press.

Shannon, J. W., & Woods, W. J. (1991). Affirmative psychotherapy for gay men. *The Counseling Psychologist, 19*(2), 197–215.

Sire, J. W. (1976). *The universe next door.* Downers, IL: Intervarsity.

Smart, J. F., & Smart, D. W. (1995). Acculturative stress: The experience of the Hispanic immigrant. *The Counseling Psychologist, 23*(1), 25–42.

Smith, D. C. (1993). Exploring the religious-spiritual needs of the dying. *Counseling and Values, 37*(2), 71–77.

Snell, W. E., Jr., Hampton, B. R., & McManus, P. (1992). The impact of counselor and participant gender on willingness to discuss relational topics: Development of the relationship disclosure scale. *Journal of Counseling and Development, 70,* 409–416.

Sodowsky, G. R., Kwan, K. L. K., & Pannu, R. (1995). Ethnic identity of Asians in the United States. In J. G. Ponterotto, J. M. Casas, L. A. Suzuki, & C. M. Alexander (Eds.), *Handbook of multicultural counseling* (pp. 123–154). Thousand Oaks, CA: Sage.

Sue, D. W. (1978). World views and counseling. *The Personnel and Guidance Journal, 56,* 458–462.

Sue, D. W. (1981). *Counseling the culturally different: Theory and practice.* New York: John Wiley & Sons.

Sue, D. W., Bermier, T. E., Durran, A., Feinberg, L., Pedersen, P., Smith, E. T., & Vasquez-Nuttall, E. (1982). Position paper: Cross-cultural counseling competencies. *The Counseling Psychologist, 10*(2), 45–52.

Sue, D. W., Ivey, A. E., & Pedersen, P. B. (1996). *A theory of multicultural counseling and therapy.* Pacific Grove, CA: Brooks/Cole.

Sue, D. W., & Sue, D. (1977). Barriers to effective cross-cultural counseling. *Journal of Counseling Psychology, 24,* 420–429.

Sue, D. W., & Sue, D. (1990). *Counseling the culturally different* (2nd ed.). New York: John Wiley & Sons.

Sue, S. (1988). Psychotherapeutic services for ethnic minorities. *American Psychologist, 43*(4), 301–308.

Suinn, R. M., Rickard-Figueroa, K., Lew, S., & Vigil, S. (1987). The Suinn-Lew Asian Self-Identity Acculturation scale: An initial report. *Education and Psychological Measurement, 47,* 401–407.

Topper, M. D. (1985). Navajo "alcoholism": Drinking, alcohol abuse, and treatment in a changing cultural environment. In L. A. Bennett & G. M. Ames (Eds.), *The American experience with alcohol: Contrasting cultural perspectives.* New York: Plenum Press.

Towberman, D. B. (1992). Client-counselor similarity and the client's perception of the treatment environment. *Journal of Offender Rehabilitation, 18*(½), 159–171.

Trevino, J. G. (1996). Worldview and change in cross-cultural counseling. *The Counseling Psychologist, 24*(2), 198–215.

Usher, C. H. (1989). Recognizing cultural bias in counseling theory and practice: The case of Rogers. *Journal of Multicultural Counseling and Development, 17,* 62–71.

Vontress, C. E. (1973). Counseling the racial and ethnic minorities. *Focus on Guidance, 5*(6), 1–10.

Vontress, C. E. (1988). An existential approach to cross-cultural counseling. *Journal of Multicultural Counseling and Development, 16,* 73–83.

Wachtel, P. L. (1991). From eclecticism to synthesis: Towards a more seamless psychotherapeutic integration. *Journal of Psychotherapy Integration, 1*(1), 43–54.

Watts, R. E. (1993). Developing a personal theory of counseling: A brief guide for students. *Texas Counseling Association Journal,* Spring, 103–104.

Weighill, V. E., Hodge, J., & Peck, D. F. (1983). Keeping appointments with clinical psychologists. *British Journal of Clinical Psychology, 22,* 143–144.

Westgate, C. E. (1996). Spiritual wellness and depression. *Journal of Counseling and Development, 75*(1), 26–35.

Westwood, M. J., & Ishiyama, F. I. (1990). The communication process as a critical intervention for client change in cross-cultural counseling. *Journal of Multicultural Counseling and Development, 18*(4), 163–171.

Wogan, M., & Norcross, J. C. (1985). Dimensions of therapeutic skills and techniques: Empirical identification, therapist correlates, and predictive utility. *Psychotherapy, 22,* 63–74.

Worthington, E. L., Jr. (1989). Religious faith across the life span: Implications for counseling and research. *The Counseling Psychologist, 17,* 555–612.

Chapter 7

Adler, A. (1969). *The practice of individual psychology.* Patterson, NJ: Littlefield, Adams.

Adler, K. (1972). Techniques that shorten psychotherapy. *Journal of Individual Psychology, 28,* 155–168.

Allan, J., & Brown, K. (1993). Jungian play therapy in elementary school. *Elementary School Guidance and Counseling, 28*(1), 30–41.

Ansbacher, H. L. (1989). Adlerian psychology: The tradition of brief psychotherapy. *Individual Psychology: The Journal of Adlerian Theory, Research, and Practice, 45*(1&2), 26–33.

Ansbacher, H. L., & Ansbacher, R. R. (Ed.). (1956). *The individual psychology of Alfred Adler.* New York: Basic Books.

Ansbacher, H. L., & Ansbacher, R. R. (Ed.). (1964). *Superiority and social interest.* Evanston, IL: Northwestern University Press.

Arlow, J. A. (1995). Psychoanalysis. In R. J. Corsini (Ed.), *Current psychoanalysis* (5th ed.). Itasca, IL: F. E. Peacock.

Baker, E. L. (1985). *Psychoanalysis and psychoanalytic psychotherapy.* In S. J. Lynn & J. P. Garske (Eds.), *Contemporary psychotherapies: Models and methods.* Columbus, OH: Merrill/Macmillan.

Barth, K., Nielson, G., Haver, B., Havik, O. E., Molstad, E., Rogge, H., & Statun, M. (1988). Comprehensive assessment of change in patients treated with short-term dynamic psychotherapy: An overview. *Psychotherapy Psychosomatic, 50,* 141–150.

Bowlby, J. (1973). *Attachment and loss, Vol. 2. Separation, anxiety and anger.* New York: Basic.

Carmichael, K. D. (1994). Sand play as an elementary school strategy. *Elementary School Guidance and Counseling, 28*(4), 302–307.

Corey, G. (1982). *Theory and practice of counseling and psychotherapy* (2nd ed.). Pacific Grove, CA: Brooks/Cole.

Corey, G. (1996). *Theory and practice of counseling and psychotherapy* (6th ed.). Pacific Grove, CA: Brooks/Cole.

Corsini, R. J. (1977). Individual education. *Journal of Individual Psychology, 33,* 295–349.

Corsini, R. J. (1979). Individual education. In E. Ignas & R. J. Corsini (Eds.), *Alternate educational systems* (pp. 200–256). Itasca, IL: F. E. Peacock.

Davanloo, H. (1978). *Basic principles and techniques in short-term dynamic psychotherapy.* New York: SP Medical and Scientific Books.

Davanloo, H. (1984). Intensive short-term dynamic psychotherapy. In H. Kaplan and B. Sadock (Eds.), *Comprehensive textbooks of psychiatry.* Baltimore, MD: Williams & Wilkins.

Dinkmeyer, D., & Carlson, J. (1984). *Training in marriage enrichment.* Circle Pines, MN: American Guidance Service.

Dinkmeyer, D. C., & Dinkmeyer, D., Jr. (1982). *Developing understanding of self and others.* DUSO-1 Revised, DUSO-2 Revised. Circle Pines, MN: American Guidance Service.

Dinkmeyer, D., & Dinkmeyer, D. C., Jr. (1985). Adlerian psychotherapy and counseling. In S. Lynn & J. P. Garske (Eds.), *Contemporary psychotherapies: Models and methods.* Columbus, OH: Merrill/Macmillan.

Dinkmeyer, D., Dinkmeyer, D., Jr., & Sperry, L. (1987). *Adlerian counseling and psychotherapy.* Columbus, OH: Merrill/Macmillan.

Dinkmeyer, D., & Dreikurs, R. (1963). *Encouraging children to learn: The encouragement process.* Englewood Cliffs, NJ: Prentice-Hall.

Dinkmeyer, D., & Losoncy, L. (1980). *The encouragement book: Becoming a positive person.* Englewood Cliffs, NJ: Prentice-Hall.

Dinkmeyer, D., & McKay, G. (1989). *Systematic training for effective parenting (STEP)* (3rd ed.). Circle Pines, MN: American Guidance Service.

Dinkmeyer, D., McKay, G. D., & Dinkmeyer, D., Jr. (1980). *Systematic training for effective teaching.* Circle Pines, MN: American Guidance Service.

Donne, J. (1952). *The complete poetry and selected prose of John Donne.* New York: Random House.

Douglas, C. (1995). Analytical psychotherapy. In R. J. Corsini & D. Wedding (Eds.), *Current psychotherapies* (5th ed.) (pp. 95–127). Itasca, IL: F. E. Peacock.

Dreikurs, R. (1949). The four goals of children's misbehavior. *Nervous Child, 6,* 3–11.

Dreikurs, R. (1971). *Social equality: The challenge of today.* Chicago: Henry Regnery.

Dreikurs, R., Corsini, R. J., Lowe, R., & Sonstegard, M. (1959). *Adlerian family counseling.* Eugene, OR: University of Oregon Press.

Dreikurs, R., & Soltz, N. (1964). *Children: The challenge.* New York: Hawthorn.

Ellis, A. (1962). *Reason and emotion in psychotherapy.* New York: Lyle Stuart.

Erikson, E. H. (1950). *Childhood and society.* New York: W. W. Norton.

Estes, C. P. (1992). *Women who run with the wolves.* New York: Ballantine Books.

Fadiman, J., & Frager, R. (1976). *Personality and personal growth.* New York: Harper & Row.

Feist, J. (1985). *Theories of personality.* New York: Holt, Rinehart, & Winston.

Freud, S. (1972). *The interpretation of dreams.* New York: Avon Books.

Garske, J. P., & Molteni, A. L. (1985). Brief psychodynamic psychotherapy: An integrative approach. In S. J. Lynn & J. P. Garske (Eds.), *Contemporary psychotherapies.* Columbus, OH: Merrill/Macmillan.

Glasser, W. (1965). *Reality therapy: A new approach to psychiatry.* New York: Harper & Row.

Glover, E. (1950). *Freud or Jung.* New York: W. W. Norton.

Goldfried, M. R., Greenberg, L. S., & Mormar, C. (1990). Individual psychotherapy: Process and outcome. *Annual Review of Psychology, 41,* 659–688.

Hall, C. S. (1954). *A primer of Freudian psychology.* New York: World Publishing.

Hall, C. S., & Lindzey, G. (1978). *Theories of personality* (3rd ed.). New York: John Wiley & Sons.

Harris, A. S. (1996). *Living with paradox: An introduction to Jungian psychology.* Pacific Grove, CA: Brooks/Cole.

Henry, W. P., Strupp, H. H., Schacht, T. E., & Gaston, L. (1994). Psychodynamic approaches. In A. E. Bergin & S. L. Garfield (Eds.), *Handbook of psychotherapy and behavior change* (4th ed.) (pp. 467–508). New York: John Wiley & Sons.

Jones, J. V., Jr. (1995). Constructivism and individual psychology: Common ground for dialogue. *Individual Psychology: The Journal of Adlerian Theory, Research, and Practice, 51*(3), 231–243.

Jung, C. (1928). *Contributions to analytic psychology.* New York: Harcourt.

Kaufmann, Y. (1989). Analytical psychotherapy. In R. J. Corsini (Ed.), *Current psychotherapies* (4th ed.). Itasca, IL: F. E. Peacock.

Kern, R., Gfroerer, K., Summers, Y., Curlette, W., & Matheny, K. (1996). Life-style, personality, and stress coping. *Individual Psychology: The Journal of Adlerian Theory, Research, and Practice, 52*(1), 42–53.

Kernberg, O. F. (1976). *Object-relations theory and clinical psychoanalysis.* New York: Jason Aronson.

Kohut, H. (1971). *The analysis of the self.* New York: International University Press.

Mahoney, M. J. (1991). *Human change processes.* Delran, NJ: Basic.

Mahoney, M. J., & Lyddon, W. J. (1988). Recent developments in cognitive approaches to counseling and psychotherapy. *The Counseling Psychologist, 16*(2), 190–234.

Malan, D. (1976). *The frontier of brief psychotherapy.* New York: Basic Books.

Malan, D. H. (1980). The most important development since the discovery of the unconscious. In H. Davanloo (Ed.), *Short-term dynamic psychotherapy.* New York: Aronson.

Maniacci, M. P. (1996). An introduction to brief therapy of the personality disorders. *Individual Psychology: The Journal of Adlerian Theory, Research, and Practice, 52*(2), 158–168.

Mann, J. (1973). *Time-limited psychotherapy.* Cambridge, MA: Harvard University Press.

Mann, J. (1981). The core of time-limited psychotherapy: Time and central issue. In S. H. Budman (Ed.), *Forms of brief therapy.* New York: Guilford Press.

Marziali, E. (1984). Predictions of outcomes of brief psychotherapy from therapist interpretive interventions, *Archives of General Psychiatry, 41,* 301–304.

McCrae, R. R., & Costa, P. T., Jr. (1989). Reinterpreting the Myers-Briggs Type Indicator from the perspective of the five-factor model of personality. *Journal of Personality, 57*(1), 17–40.

Meyer, A. (1957). *Psychobiology: A science of man.* Springfield, IL: Charles C. Thomas.

Mills, J. A., Bauer, G. P., & Miars, R. D. (1989). Use of transference in short-term dynamic psychotherapy. *Psychotherapy, 26*(3), 112–119.

Mormar, C. R., & Horowitz, M. J. (1988). Diagnosis and phase-oriented treatment of post-traumatic stress disorder. In J. F. Wilson, Z. Harel, & B. Kahana

(Eds.), *Human adaption to extreme stress: From Holocaust to Viet Nam.* New York: Plenum.

Mosak, H. (1991). Where have all the normal people gone? *Individual Psychology: The Journal of Adlerian Theory, Research, and Practice, 47*(4), 437–446.

Mosak, H. (1995). Adlerian psychotherapy. In R. J. Corsini (Ed.), *Current psychotherapies* (5th ed.) (pp. 51–94), Itasca, IL: F. E. Peacock.

Myers, I. B., & McCaulley, M. H. (1985). *Manual: A guide to the development and use of the Myers-Briggs Type Indicator.* Palo Alto: Consulting Psychologist Press.

Nergaard, M. O., & Silberschatz, G. (1989). *The effects of shame, guilt, and the negative reaction in brief dynamic psychotherapy.*

Nystul, M. S. (1985). The use of motivation of modification techniques in Adlerian psychotherapy. *Individual Psychology: The Journal of Adlerian Theory, Research, and Practice, 44*(2), 199–209.

Nystul, M. S. (1988). An interview with Dr. Shulman. *Individual Psychology: The Journal of Adlerian Theory, Research, and Practice, 44*(2), 210–216.

Nystul, M. S. (1991). An interview with Jon Carlson. *Individual Psychology: The Journal of Adlerian Theory, Research, and Practice, 47*(4), 498–503.

Nystul, M. S. (1994). Increasing the positive orientation to Adlerian psychotherapy: Redefining the concept of "basic mistakes." *Individual Psychology: The Journal of Adlerian Theory, Research, and Practice, 50*(3), 271–278.

Patterson, C. H. (1986). *Theories of counseling and psychology.* New York: Harper & Row.

Prochaska, J. O. (1984). *Systems of psychotherapy: A transtheoretical analysis.* Chicago, IL: The Dorsey Press.

Prochaska, J. O., & Norcross, J. C. (1994). *Systems of psychotherapy: A transtheoretical analysis.* Pacific Grove, CA: Brooks/Cole.

Rapaport, D. (1958). The theory of ego autonomy: A generalization. *Bulletin of Menninger Clinic, 22,* 13–35.

Read, H., Fordham, M., & Adler, G. (Eds.). (1953–1978). *Jung's collected works.* Princeton: Princeton University Press.

Saayman, G. S., Faber, P. A., & Saayman, R. V. (1988). Archetypal factors revealed in the study of marital breakdown: A Jungian perspective. *Journal of Analytical Psychology, 33,* 253–276.

Samuels, A. (1985). *Jung and the post-Jungians.* London: Routledge & Kegan Paul.

Samuels, A. (1989). Analysis and pluralism: The politics of psyche. *Journal of Analytical Psychology, 34,* 33–51.

Scott, C. N., Kelly, F. D., & Tolbert, B. L. (1995). Realism, constructivism, and the individual psychology of Al-

fred Adler. *Individual Psychology: The Journal of Adlerian Theory, Research, and Practice, 51*(1), 4–20.

Sherman, R., & Dinkmeyer, D. (1987). *Systems of family therapy: An Adlerian integration.* New York: Brunner/Mazel.

Shulman, B. H. (1973). *Contributions to individual psychology.* Chicago: Alfred Adler Institute.

Shulman, B. H. (1985). Cognitive therapy and the individual psychology of Alfred Adler. In M. J. Mahoney & A. Freeman (Eds.), *Cognition and psychotherapy* (pp. 46–62). New York: Plenum.

Sifneos, P. E. (1979). *Short-term dynamic psychotherapy.* New York: Plenum.

Sifneos, P. (1984). The current status of individual short-term dynamic psychotherapy and its future. *American Journal of Psychotherapy, 38*(4), 472–483.

Sonstegard, M. A., Hagerman, H., & Bitter, J. (1975). Motivation modification: An Adlerian approach. *The Individual Psychologist, 12,* 17–22.

Sperry, L. (1987). ERIC: A cognitive map for guiding brief therapy and health care counseling. *Individual Psychology, 43*(2), 237–241.

Sperry, L. (1989). Varieties of brief therapy: An introduction. *Individual Psychology: The Journal of Adlerian Theory, Research, and Practice, 45*(1&2), 1–2.

Spiegelman, J. M. (1989). The one and the many: Jung and the post-Jungians. *Journal of Analytical Psychology, 34,* 53–71.

Strachey, J. (Ed.). (1953–1974). *The standard edition of the complete psychological works of Sigmund Freud.* London: Hogarth Press.

Strupp, H. H. (1992). The future of psychodynamic psychotherapy. *Psychotherapy, 29*(1), 21–27.

Sue, D. W., Ivey, A. E., & Pedersen, P. B. (1996). *A theory of multicultural counseling and therapy.* Pacific Grove, CA: Brooks/Cole.

Sullivan, B. F., & Schwebel, A. I. (1996). Birth-order position, gender, and irrational relationship beliefs. *Individual Psychology: The Journal of Adlerian Theory, Research, and Practice, 52*(1), 54–64.

Sullivan, H. S. (1953). *The interpersonal theory of psychiatry.* New York: Norton.

Thompson, L. W., Gallagher, D., & Breckenridge, J. S. (1987). Comparative effectiveness of psychotherapies for depressed elders. *Journal of Consulting and Clinical Psychology, 55,* 385–390.

Watkins, E. (1984). The individual psychology of Alfred Adler: Towards an Adlerian vocational theory. *Journal of Vocational Behavior, 24,* 27–48.

Chapter 8

Ascher, L. M. (1979). Paradoxical intention in the treatment of urinary retention. *Behavior Research and Therapy, 17,* 267–270.

Ascher, L. M., & Efran, J. S. (1978). The use of paradoxical intention in a behavioral program for sleep onset insomnia. *Journal of Consulting and Clinical Psychology, 46,* 547–550.

Bertoia, J., & Allan, J. (1988). Counseling seriously ill children: Use of spontaneous drawings. *Elementary School Guidance and Counseling,* 206–221.

Boswell, B. (1983). Adapted dance for mentally retarded children: An experimental study (Doctoral dissertation, Texas Women's University, 1983). *Dissertation Abstracts International, 43*(9–A), 2925.

Brace, K. (1992). I and Thou in interpersonal psychotherapy. *The Humanistic Psychologist, 20*(1), 41–57.

Bruscia, K. E. (1987). *Improvisational models of music therapy.* Springfield, IL: Charles C. Thomas.

Buber, M. (1970). *I and thou* (W. Kaufmann, Trans.). New York: Scribner's.

Bugental, J. (1976). *The search for existential identity.* San Francisco, CA: Jossey-Bass.

Clarke, J., & Evans, E. (1973). Rhythmical intention as a method of treatment for cerebral-palsied patients. *Australia Journal of Physiotherapy, 19–20,* 57–64.

Clarke, K., & Breeberg, L. (1986). Differential effects of the Gestalt two chair intervention and problem solving in resolving decisional conflict. *Journal of Counseling Psychology, 33,* 48–53.

Cole, I. (1982). Movement negotiations with an autistic child. *Arts in Psychotherapy, 9,* 49–53.

Corey, G. (1996). *Theory and practice of counseling and psychotherapy* (5th ed.). Pacific Grove, CA: Brooks/ Cole.

Cramer, D. (1994). Self-esteem and Rogers' core conditions in close friends: A latent variable path analysis of panel data. *Counseling Psychology Quarterly, 7*(3), 321–337.

Cripe, F. F. (1986). Rock music as therapy for children with attention deficit disorder: An exploratory study. *Journal of Music Therapy, 23,* 30–37.

Dowd, E. T., & Sanders, D. (1994). Resistance, reactance, and the difficult client. *Canadian Journal of Counseling, 28*(1), 13–24.

Eidson, C. E., Jr. (1989). The effects of behavioral music therapy on the generalization of interpersonal skills from sessions to the classroom by emotionally handicapped middle school students. *Journal of Music Therapy, 26*(4), 206–221.

Fleshman, B., & Fryrear, J. L. (1981). *The arts in therapy.* Chicago, IL: Nelson-Hall.

Frankl, V. (1963). *Man's search for meaning.* New York: Washington Square Press.

Frankl, V. E. (1967). *Psychotherapy and existentialism: Selected papers on logotherapy.* New York: Simon & Schuster (Touchstone).

Frankl, V. E. (1971). *The doctor and the soul.* New York: Bantam.

Frankl, V. (1978). *The unheard cry for meaning.* New York: Simon & Schuster (Touchstone).

Gelso, C. J., & Carter, J. A. (1985). The relationship in counseling and psychotherapy: Components, consequences, and theoretical antecedents. *The Counseling Psychologist, 13,* 155–243.

Gelso, C. J., & Fritz, B. R. (1992). *Counseling Psychology,* Orlando, FL: Holt, Rinehart, & Winston.

Gergen, K. (1994). *Realities and relationships.* Cambridge: Harvard University Press.

Gibbons, A. C. (1984). A program for noninstitutionalized, mature adults: A description. *Activities, Adaptation, and Aging, 6,* 71–80.

Gibbons, A. C. (1988). A review of literature for music development/education and music therapy with the elderly. *Music Therapy Perspectives, 5,* 33–40.

Goldfried, M. R., Greenberg, L. S., & Mormar, C. (1990). Individual psychotherapy: Process and outcome. In M. R. Rosenzweig & L. W. Porter (Eds.), *Annual review of psychology.* Palo Alto, CA: Annual Reviews.

Greenberg, L., Elliott, R., & Lietaer, G. (1994). Research on experiential psychotherapies. In A. E. Bergin & S. L. Garfield (Eds.), *Handbook of psychotherapy and behavior change* (4th ed.). New York: John Wiley & Sons.

Guinan, J., & Foulds, M. (1970). Marathon groups: Facilitator of personal growth? *Journal of Consulting Psychology, 17,* 145–149.

Gunning, S., & Holmes, T. (1973). Dance therapy with psychotic children. *Archives of General Psychiatry, 28,* 707–713.

Hale, S. (1990). Sitting on memory's lap. *The Arts in Psychotherapy, 17*(3), 269, 274.

Heppner, P. P., Rogers, M. E., & Lee, L. A. (1984). Carl Rogers: Reflections on his life. *Journal of Counseling and Development, 63,* 14–20.

Hollingdale, R. J. (1978). *Twilight of the idols and the anti-christ.* New York: Penguin Books.

Ingersoll, R. E. (1995). Spirituality, religion, and counseling: Dimensions and relationships. In M. T. Burke & J. G. Miranti (Eds.), *Counseling: The spiritual dimension* (pp. 5–18). Alexandria, VA: American Counseling Association.

Irwin, E. C. (1987). Drama: The play's the thing. *Elementary School Guidance and Counseling, 276*–283.

Isenberg-Grzeda, C. (1988). Music therapy assessment: A reflection of professional identity. *Journal of Music Therapy, 25*(3), 156–169.

James, M. R. (1988). Music therapy values clarification: A positive influence on perceived locus of control. *Journal of Music Therapy, 25*(4), 206–215.

Johnson, D. R. (1984a). Establishing the creative arts therapies as an independent profession. *The Arts in Psychotherapy, 11,* 209–212.

Johnson, D. R. (1984b). Perspectives, projects, and training facilities. *Journal of Mental Imagery, 7*(1), 105–109.

Jung, C. G. (1959). *The archetypes and the collective unconscious.* Princeton, NJ: Princeton University Press.

Kenny, A. (1987). An arts activity approach: Counseling the gifted, creative, and talented. *The Gifted Child Today, 10*(3), 22–37.

Kramer, E. (1987). Sublimation and art therapy. In J. A. Rubin (Ed.), *Approaches to art therapy: Theory and technique.* New York: Brunner/Mazel.

Lasseter, J., Privette, G., Brown, C. G., & Duer, J. (1989). Dance as treatment approach with a multi-disabled child: Implications for school counseling. *The School Counselor, 36,* 310–315.

Levitsky, A., & Simkin, J. S. (1972). Gestalt therapy. In L. N. Solomon & B. Berzon (Eds.), *New perspectives on encounter groups* (pp. 245–253). San Francisco: Jossey-Bass.

Martin, D. G. (1989). *Counseling and therapy skills* (2nd ed.). Prospect Heights, IL: Therapy Press.

May, R. (1953). *Man's search for himself.* New York: Norton.

May, R. (1961). *Existential psychology.* New York: Random House.

May, R. (1977). *The meaning of anxiety* (rev. ed.). New York: Norton.

Merrill, C., & Andersen, S. (1993). A content analysis of person-centered expressive therapy outcomes. *The Humanistic Psychologist, 21,* 354–363.

Moreno, J. L. (1946). *Psychodrama, Vol. 1.* Beacon, NY: Beacon House.

Moreno, J. (1988). Multicultural music therapy: The world music connection. *Journal of Music Therapy, 25*(1), 17–27.

Nystul, M. S. (1977). The use of music in counseling and psychotherapy. *The Individual Psychologist, 14,* 45–50.

Nystul, M. S. (1978). The use of creative arts therapy within Adlerian psychotherapy. *The Individual Psychologist, 15,* 11–18.

Nystul, M. S. (1979). Integrating current psychotherapies into Adlerian psychotherapy. *The Individual Psychologist, 16,* 23–29.

Nystul, M. S. (1980). Nystulian play therapy: Applications of Adlerian psychology. *Elementary School Guidance and Counseling, 15,* 22–30.

Nystul, M. S. (1985). Reaching in—reaching out: Treatment of an autistic child. *Mental Health Counselor's Association Journal, 8,* 18–26.

Nystul, M. S. (1987). Creative arts therapy and the existential encounter. *The Creative Child and Adult Quarterly, 12*(3), 243–249.

Nystul, M. S., & Musynska, E. (1976). Adlerian treatment of a classical case of stuttering. *Journal of Individual Psychology, 32,* 194–202.

Passons, W. R. (1975). *Gestalt approaches in counseling.* New York: Holt, Rinehart, & Winston.

Perls, F. (1969a). *Gestalt therapy verbatim.* Moab, UT: Real People Press.

Perls, F. (1969b). *In and out of the garbage pail.* Moab, UT: Real People Press.

Polk, E. (1977). Dance therapy with special children. In K. Mason (Ed.), *Dance therapy: Focus on dance VII* (pp. 56–58). Washington, DC: American Alliance for Health, Physical Education, and Recreation.

Prochaska, J. O., & Norcross, J. C. (1994). *Systems of psychotherapy: A transtheoretical analysis.* Pacific Grove, CA: Brooks/Cole.

Raskin, N. J., & Rogers, L. R. (1995). Person-centered therapy. In R. J. Corsini (Ed.), *Current psychotherapies* (5th ed.) (pp. 154–194). Itasca, IL: F. E. Peacock.

Rhyne, J. (1987). Gestalt art therapy. In J. A. Rubin (Ed.), *Approaches to art therapy: Theory and technique.* New York: Brunner/Mazel.

Riordan, R. J., & Wilson, L. S. (1989). Bibliotherapy: Does it work? *Journal of Counseling and Development, 67,* 506–508.

Robbins, A. (1985). Working towards the establishment of creative arts therapies as an independent profession. *The Arts in Psychotherapy, 12,* 67–70.

Rogers, C. (1939). *The clinical treatment of the problem child.* Boston: Houghton Mifflin.

Rogers, C. (1942). *Counseling and psychotherapy.* Boston: Houghton Mifflin.

Rogers, C. (1951). *Client-centered therapy.* Boston: Houghton Mifflin.

Rogers, C. (1957). The necessary and sufficient condition of therapeutic personality change. *Journal of Consulting Psychology, 21,* 95–103.

Rogers, C. (1961). *On becoming a person.* Boston: Houghton Mifflin.

Rogers, C. R., Gendlin, E. T., Kiesler, D. J., & Truax, C. B. (1967). *The therapeutic relationship and its impact:*

A study of psychotherapy with schizophrenics. Madison: University of Wisconsin Press.

Roth, E. A. (1987). A behavioral approach to art therapy. In J. A. Rubin (Ed.), *Approaches to art therapy: Theory and technique.* New York: Brunner/Mazel.

Rubin, J. A. (1987). Freudian psychoanalytic theory: Emphasis on uncovering and insight. In J. A. Rubin (Ed.), *Approaches to art therapy: Theory and technique.* New York: Brunner/Mazel.

Rubin, J. A. (1988). Art counseling an alternative. *Elementary School Guidance and Counseling,* 180–185.

Sherwood-Hawes, A. (1995). Nontraditional approaches to counseling and psychotherapy. In D. Capuzzi & D. R. Douglas (Eds.), *Counseling and psychotherapy: Theories and interventions.* Columbus, Ohio: Merrill.

Silver, R. A. (1987). A cognitive approach to art therapy. In J. A. Rubin (Ed.), *Approaches to art therapy: Theory and technique.* New York: Brunner/Mazel.

Sparks, R. W., & Deck, J. W. (1994). Melodic intonation therapy. In R. Chapey (Ed.), *Language intervention strategies in adult aphasia* (pp. 368–379). Baltimore, MD: Williams & Wilkins.

Stabler, B. (1984). *Children's drawings.* Chapel Hill, NC: Health Science Consortium.

Starker, S. (1988). Psychologists and self-help books: Attitudes and prescriptive practices of clinicians. *American Journal of Psychotherapy, 42,* 448–455.

Talerico, C. J. (1986). The expressive arts and creativity as a form of therapeutic experience in the field of mental health. *The Journal of Creative Behavior, 20*(4), 229–247.

Turner, R. M., & Ascher, L. M. (1979). Controlled comparison of progressive relaxation, stimulus control, and paradoxical intention therapies for insomnia. *Journal of Consulting and Clinical Psychology, 47,* 500–508.

Usher, C. H. (1989). Recognizing cultural bias in counseling theory and practice: The case of Regus. *Journal of Multicultural Counseling and Development, 17,* 62–71.

Wadeson, H. (1980). *Art psychotherapy.* New York: John Wiley & Sons.

Watkins, C. E. (1993). Person-centered theory and the contemporary practice of psychological testing. *Counseling Psychology Quarterly, 6*(1), 59–67.

Wells, N. F., & Stevens, T. (1984). Music as a stimulus for creative fantasy in group psychotherapy with young adolescents. *The Arts in Psychotherapy, 11,* 71–76.

Wilson, L. (1987). Symbolism and art therapy: Theory and clinical practice. In J. A. Rubin (Ed.), *Approaches to art therapy: Theory and technique.* New York: Brunner/Mazel.

Wislocki, A. (1981). Movement is their medium: Dance movement methods in special education. *Milieu Therapy, 1,* 49–54.

Yontey, G. M., & Simkin, J. S. (1989). Gestalt therapy. In R. J. Corsini (Ed.), *Current psychotherapies* (4th ed.) (pp. 323–361). Itasca, IL: F. E. Peacock.

Zaccaria, J. S., & Moses, J. A. (1968). *Facilitating human development through reading: The use of bibliotherapy through teaching and counseling.* Champaign, IL: Stipes.

Chapter 9

Allen, J., & Allen, B. (1989). Stroking: Biological underpinnings and direct observations. *Transactional Analysis Journal, 19,* 26–31.

Ayllon, T., & Azrin, N. (1968). *The token economy: A motivation system for therapy and rehabilitation.* New York: Appleton-Century-Crofts.

Bandura, A. (1974). Behavior theory and the models of man. *American Psychologist, 29,* 859–869.

Bandura, A. (1977). *Social learning theory.* Englewood Cliffs, NJ: Prentice-Hall.

Bandura, A. (1982). Self-efficacy mechanism in human agency. *American Psychologist, 37*(2), 122–167.

Bandura, A. (1986). *Social foundations of thought and actions: A social cognitive theory.* Englewood Cliffs, NJ: Prentice-Hall.

Bandura, A. (1989). Human agency in social cognitive theory. *American Psychologist, 44*(9), 1175–1184.

Bandura, A., Reese, L., & Adams, N. E. (1982). Microanalysis of actions and fear arousal as a function of differential levels of perceived self-efficacy. *Journal of Personality and Social Psychology, 43*(1), 5–21.

Beck, A. T. (1987). Cognitive therapy. In J. K. Zeig (Ed.), *The evolution of psychotherapy* (pp. 149–178). New York: Brunner/Mazel.

Beck, A. T. (1991). Cognitive therapy: A 30-year retrospective. *American Psychologist, 46*(4), 368–375.

Beck, A. T., & Emery, G. (1985). *Anxiety disorders and phobias: A cognitive perspective.* New York: Basic Books.

Beck, A. T., Rush, A., Shaw, B., & Emery, G. (1979). *Cognitive therapy of depression.* New York: Guilford Press.

Beck, A. T., & Weishaar, M. E. (1989). Cognitive therapy. In R. J. Corsini (Ed.), *Current psychotherapies* (4th ed.) (pp. 285–320). Itasca, IL: F. E. Peacock.

Beck, A. T., & Weishaar, M. E. (1995). Cognitive therapy. In R. J. Corsini & D. Wedding (Eds.), *Current psychotherapies* (5th ed.) (pp. 229–261). Itasca, IL: F. E. Peacock.

Beck, A., Wright, F. D., Newman, C. F., & Liese, B. (1993). *Cognitive therapy of substance abuse.* New York: Guilford Press.

Berne, E. (1961). *Transactional analysis in psychotherapy.* New York: Grove Press.

Berne, E. (1964). *Games people play.* New York: Grove Press.

Blackburn, I. M., Bishop, S., Glen, A. I. M., Whalley, L. J., & Christie, J. E. (1981). The efficacy of cognitive therapy in depression: A treatment trial using cognitive therapy and pharmacotherapy, each alone and in combination. *British Journal of Psychiatry, 139,* 181–189.

Blackburn, I. M., Eunson, K. M., & Bishop, S. (1986). A two-year naturalistic follow-up of depressed patients treated with cognitive therapy, pharmacotherapy, and a combination of both. *Unpublished manuscript.* Royal Edinburgh Hospital, Scotland.

Bowlby, J. (1973). *Attachment and loss: Vol. 2. Separation, anxiety and anger.* New York: Basic Books.

Bowlby, J. (1988). *A secure base.* New York: Basic Books.

Brady, J. P. (1980). Some views on effective principles of psychotherapy. In M. Goldfried (Ed.)., *Cognitive Therapy and Research, 4,* 271–306.

Bredehoft, P. (1990). Self-esteem: A family affair. *Transactional Analysis Journal, 20,* 111-116.

Chambless, D. L., & Gillis, M. M. (1993). Cognitive therapy of anxiety disorders. *Journal of Consulting and Clinical Psychology, 61,* 248–260.

Corey, G. (1996). *Theory and practice of counseling and psychotherapy* (5th ed.). Pacific Grove, CA: Brooks/Cole.

Davis-Berman, J. (1988). Self-efficacy and depressive symptomatology in older adults: An exploratory study. *International Journal of Aging and Human Development, 27*(1), 35–43.

Dobson, K. S. (1989). A meta-analysis of the efficacy of cognitive therapy for depression. *Journal of Consulting and Clinical Psychology, 57*(3), 414–419.

Dusay, J., & Dusay, K. M. (1989). Transactional analysis. In R. Corsini (Ed.), *Current psychotherapies* (4th ed.). Itasca, IL: F. E. Peacock.

Ellis, A. (1962). *Reason and emotion in psychotherapy.* New York: Lyle Stuart.

Ellis, A. (1977). The basic clinical theory of rational-emotive therapy. In A. Ellis & R. Grieger (Eds.), *RET handbook of rational-emotive therapy* (pp. 3–34). New York: Springer.

Ellis, A. (1986). Comments on Gloria. *Psychotherapy, 23,* 647–648.

Ellis, A. (1993, Summer). RET becomes REBT. *IRETletter,* pp. 1, 4.

Ellis, A. (1995). Rational-emotive behavior therapy. In R. Corsini (Ed.)., *Current psychotherapies* (5th ed.) (pp. 162–196). Itasca, IL: F. E. Peacock.

Ellis, A. (1996). *Better, deeper and more enduring brief therapy.* New York: Brunner/Mazel.

Ellis, A., & Harper, R. (1975). *A new guide to rational living* (rev. ed.). Hollywood: Wilshire Books.

Elkin, I., Shea, M. T., Watkins, J. T., Imber, S. D., Sotsky, S. M., Collins, J. F., Glass, D. R., Pilkonis, P. A., Leber, W. R., Docherty, J. P., Fiester, S. J., & Parloff, M. B. (1989). NIMH Treatment of Depression Collaborative Research Program: I. General effectiveness of treatments. *Archives of General Psychiatry, 46,* 971–982.

Emmelkamp, P. M. G. (1994). Behavior therapy with adults. In A. E. Bergin & S. L. Garfield, *Handbook of psychotherapy and behavior change* (4h ed.) (pp. 379–427). New York: John Wiley & Sons.

Gergen, K. J. (1982). *Toward transformation in social knowledge.* New York: Springer-Verlag.

Gilligan, C. (1982). *In a different voice: Psychological theory and women's development.* Cambridge, MA: Harvard University Press.

Gilligan, C. (1990). Joining the resistance: Psychology, politics, girls, and women. *Michigan Quarterly Review, 29*(4), 501–536.

Gintner, G. G., & Poret, M. K. (1987). Factors associated with maintenance and relapse following self-management training. *The Journal of Psychology, 122* (1), 79–87.

Glasser, W. (1961). *Mental health or mental illness?* New York: Harper & Row.

Glasser, W. (1965). *Reality therapy: A new approach to psychiatry.* New York: Harper & Row.

Glasser, W. (1969). *Schools without failure.* New York: Harper & Row.

Glasser, W. (1976). *Positive addiction.* New York: Harper & Row.

Glasser, W. (1980). Reality therapy: An explanation of the steps of reality therapy. In N. Glasser (Ed.), *What are you doing? How people are helped through reality therapy.* New York: Harper & Row.

Glasser, W. (1981). *Stations of the mind.* New York: Harper & Row.

Glasser, W. (1984). *Take effective control of your life.* New York: Harper & Row.

Glasser, W. (1985). *Control theory: A new explanation of how we control our lives.* New York: Harper & Row (Perennial Paperback).

Glasser, W. (1986). *Control theory in the classroom.* New York: Harper & Row.

Glasser, W. (1990). *The quality school.* New York: Harper & Row.

Glasser, W. (1998). *Choice Theory: A new psychology of personal freedom.* New York: HarperCollins.

Glasser, W., & Wubbolding, R. E. (1995). Reality therapy. In R. J. Corsini & D. Wedding (Eds.), *Current psychotherapies* (5th ed.). Itasca, IL: F. E. Peacock.

Gooding, P. R., & Glasgow, R. E. (1985). Self-efficacy and outcome expectations as predictors of controlling smoking status. *Cognitive Therapy and Research, 9,* 583–590.

Hollon, S. D., DeRubeis, R. J., Evans, M. D., Wiemer, M. J., Garvey, M. J., Grove, W. M., & Tuason, V. B. (1992). Cognitive therapy and pharmacotherapy for depression: Singly and in combination. *Archives of General Psychiatry, 49,* 774–781.

Hollon, S. D., & Beck, A. T. (1994). Cognitive and cognitive behavioral therapies. In A. E. Bergin & S. L. Garfield, *Handbook of psychotherapy and behavioral change* (4th ed.) (pp. 428–466). New York: John Wiley & Sons.

Hollon, S. D., Evans, M. D., & DeRubeis, R. (1983). The cognitive-pharmacotherapy project: Study design, outcome, and clinical follow-up. Paper presented at the World Congress of Behavior Therapy. Washington, DC.

Honeyman, A. (1990). Perceptual changes in addicts as a consequence of reality therapy based on group treatment. *Journal of Reality Therapy, 9*(2), 53–59.

Ivey, A. (1996, June). The spirit and the challenge: Postmodernity or reality? *Counseling Today,* p. 33.

Johnson, E., Baker, S. B., Kapola, M., Kiselica, M. S., & Thompson, E. C. III. (1989). Counseling self-efficacy and counseling competency in preparaticum training. *Counselor Education and Supervision, 28,* 205–218.

Kanfer, F. H., & Goldstein, A. P. (1986). Introduction. In F. H. Kanfer & A. P. Goldstein (Eds.), *Helping people change: A textbook of methods* (3rd ed.) (pp. 1–18). New York: Pergamon.

Kazdin, A. E. (1978). *History of behavior modification: Experimental foundations of contemporary research.* Baltimore: University Park Press.

Klerman, G. L., & Weissman, M. M. (Eds.). (1993). *New applications of interpersonal psychotherapy.* Washington, DC: American Psychiatric Press.

Klerman, G. L., Weissman, M. M., Rounsaville, B. J., & Chevron, E. S. (1984). *Interpersonal psychotherapy of depression.* New York: Basic Books.

Kovacs, M., Rush, A. J., Beck, A. T., & Hollon, S. D. (1981). Depressed outpatients treated with cognitive therapy or pharmacotherapy. *Archives of General Psychiatry, 38,* 33–39.

Lee, C. (1982). Self-efficacy as a predictor of performance in competitive gymnastics. *Journal of Sports Psychology, 4,* 405–409.

Livneh, H., & Wright, P. E. (1995). Rational-Emotive Theory. In D. Capuzzi & D. R. Gross (Eds.), *Counseling and psychotherapy: Theories and interventions* (pp. 325–350). Columbus, OH: Merrill.

Lyddon, W. J. (1995). Cognitive therapy and theories of knowing: A social constructionist view. *Journal of Counseling and Development, 73*(6), 579–585.

Lyons, L. C., & Woods, P. J. (1991). The efficacy of rational-emotive therapy: A quantitative review of the outcome research. *Clinical Psychology Review, 11,* 357–369.

Mahoney, M. J. (1995). Continuing evolution of cognitive sciences and psychotherapies. In R. A. Neimeyer & M. J. Mahoney (Eds.), *Constructivism in psychotherapy* (pp. 39–68). Washington, DC: American Psychological Association.

Mahoney, M. J. (1991). *Human change processes: The scientific foundations of psychotherapy.* New York: Basic Books.

Mahoney, M. J., & Lyddon, W. J. (1988). Recent developments in cognitive approaches to counseling and psychotherapy. *The Counseling Psychologist, 16*(2), 190–234.

Maldonado, A. (1982). Terapia de conducta y depresion: Un analisis experimental de los modelos conductal y cognitivo (Cognitive and behavioral therapy for depression. Its efficacy and interaction with pharmacological treatment). *Revista de psicologia general y aplicada, 37*(1), 31–56.

McAuley, E. (1985). Modeling and self-efficacy: A test of Bandura's model. *Journal of Sports Psychology, 7,* 283–295.

Meichenbaum, D. H. (1972). Cognitive modifications of test-anxious college students. *Journal of Consulting and Clinical Psychology, 39,* 370–390.

Meichenbaum, D. (1977). *Cognitive-behavior modification: An integrative approach.* New York: Plenum.

Meichenbaum, D. (1985). *Stress inoculation training.* New York: Pergamon.

Meichenbaum, D. (1986). Cognitive behavior modification. In F. H. Kanfer & A. P. Goldstein (Eds.), *Helping people change: A textbook of methods* (pp. 346–380). New York: Pergamon.

Meyer, A. (1957). *Psychobiology: A science of man.* Springfield, IL: Charles C. Thomas.

Miller, C. A., & Capuzzi, D. (1984). A review of transactional analysis outcome studies. *American Mental Health Counselors Association Journal, 6*(1), 30–41.

Murphy, G. E., Simons, A. D., Wetzel, R. D., & Lustman, P. J. (1983). Cognitive therapy and pharmacotherapy: Singly and together in the treatment of depression. *Archives of General Psychiatry, 41,* 33–41.

Nicki, R. M., Remington, R. M., & MacDonald, G. A. (1984). Self-efficacy, nicotine fading/self-monitoring and cigarette-smoking behavior. *Behavior Research and Therapy, 22,* 477–485.

Nietzel, M. T., Russell, R. L., Hemmings, K. A., & Gretter, M. L. (1987). The clinical significance of psychotherapy for unipolar depression: A meta-analytic approach to social comparison. *Journal of Consulting and Clinical Psychology, 55,* 156–161.

Nykodym, N., Rund, W., & Liverpool, P. (1986). Quality circles: Will transactional analysis improve their effectiveness? *Transactional Analysis Journal, 16,* 182–187.

Nystul, M. S. (1985). An interview with Dr. Albert Ellis. *Individual Psychology: The Journal of Adlerian Theory, Research, and Practice, 41*(2), 243–254.

Palmatier, L. L. (1990). Reality therapy and brief strategic interactional therapy. *Journal of Reality Therapy, 9*(2), 3–17.

Pavlov, I. P. (1906). The scientific investigation of the psychical faculties of processes in the higher animals. *Science, 24,* 613–619.

Poidevant, J. M., & Lewis, H. A. (1995). Transactional analysis theory. In D. Capuzzi and D. R. Gross (Eds.), *Counseling and psychotherapy: Theories and interventions.* Columbus, OH: Merrill.

Prochaska, J. O., & Norcross, J. C. (1994). *Systems of psychotherapy: A transtheoretical analysis.* Pacific Grove, CA: Brooks/Cole.

Raskin, P. A., & Israel, A. C. (1981). Sex role imitation in children: Effects of sex of child, sex of model, and sex role appropriateness of modeled behavior. *Sex Roles, 7*(11), 1067–1077.

Rimm, D. C., & Cunningham, H. M. (1985). Behavior therapies. In S. J. Lynn & J. P. Garske (Eds), *Contemporary psychotherapies.* Columbus, OH: Merrill/Macmillan.

Simons, A. D., Murphy, G. E., Levine, J. L., & Wetzel, R. D. (1986). Cognitive therapy and pharmacotherapy: Sustained improvement over one year. *Archives of General Psychiatry, 43,* 43–48.

Skinner, B. F. (1938). *The behavior of organisms.* New York: Appleton-Century-Crofts.

Skinner, B. F. (1953). *Science and human behavior.* New York: Macmillan.

Skinner, B. F. (1961). *Cumulative record.* New York: Appleton-Century-Crofts.

Skinner, B. F. (1990). Can psychology be a science of mind? *American Psychologist, 45,* 1206–1210.

Smith, M. L., Glass, G. V., & Miller, T. I. (1980). *The benefits of psychotherapy.* Baltimore: Johns Hopkins University Press.

Spencer, G. (1977). Effectiveness of an introductory course in TA. *Transactional Analysis Journal, 7,* 346–349.

Sue, D. W., Ivey, A. E., & Pedersen, P. B. (1996). *A theory of multicultural counseling and therapy.* Pacific Grove, CA: Brooks/Cole.

Sullivan, H. S. (1953). *The interpersonal theory of psychiatry.* New York: Norton.

Sullivan, H. S. (1968). *The interpersonal theory of psychiatry.* New York: Norton.

Swan, G. E., & MacDonald, M. D. (1978). Behavior therapy in practice: A national survey of behavior therapists. *Behavior Therapy, 9,* 799–807.

Tanaka-Matsumi, J., & Higginbotham, H. N. (1994). Clinical application of behavior therapy across ethnic and cultural boundaries. *The Behavior Therapist, 17*(6), 123–126.

Teasdale, J. D., Fennell, M. J. V., Hibbert, G. A., & Amies, P. L. (1984). Cognitive therapy for major depressive disorder in primary care. *British Journal of Psychiatry, 144,* 400–406.

Teyber, E. (1997). *Interpersonal process in psychotherapy: A relational approach* (3rd ed.). Pacific Grove, CA: Brooks/Cole.

Weinberg, R. S., Hughes, H. H., Critelli, J. W., England, R., & Jackson, A. (1984). Effects of pre-existing and manipulated self-efficacy on weight loss in a self-control program. *Journal of Research in Personality, 18,* 352–358.

Weinrach, S. G. (1988). Cognitive therapist: A dialogue with Aaron Beck. *Journal of Counseling and Development, 67*(3), 159–164.

Weinrach, S. G. (1995). Rational emotive behavior therapy: A tough-minded therapy for a tender-minded profession. *Journal of Counseling and Development, 73*(3), 296–300.

Wilson, G. T. (1995). Behavior therapy. In R. J. Corsini (Ed.), *Current psychotherapies* (5th ed.) (pp. 197–228). Itasca, IL: F. E. Peacock.

Wilson, G. T., & Fairburn, C. G. (1993). Cognitive treatments for eating disorders. *Journal of Consulting and Clinical Psychology, 61,* 261–269.

Wolpe, J. (1958). *Psychotherapy by reciprocal inhibition.* Stanford, CA: Stanford University Press.

Wolpe, J. (1973). *The practice of behavior therapy* (2nd ed.). New York: Pergamon Press.

Wubbolding, R. (1986). *Reality therapy training.* Cincinnati: Center for Reality Therapy.

Wubbolding, R. E. (1990). *Expanding reality therapy: Group counseling and multicultural dimensions.* Cincinnati, OH: Real World Publications.

Wubbolding, R. E. (1991). *Understanding reality therapy.* New York: Harper & Row.

Wubbolding, R. E. (1995). Reality therapy theory. In D. Capuzzi & D. R. Douglas (Eds.), *Counseling and psychotherapy: Theories and interventions* (pp. 385–424). Columbus, OH: Merrill.

Zerin, M. (1988). An application of the drama triangle to family therapy. *Transactional Analysis Journal, 18,* 94–101.

Chapter 10

Ackerman, N. W. (1937). The family as a social and emotional unit. *Bulletin of the Kansas Mental Hygiene Society, 12*(2).

Ackerman, N. W. (1956). Interlocking pathology in family relationships. In S. Rado & G. Daniels (Eds.), *Changing conceptions of psychoanalytical medicine.* New York: Grune & Stratton.

Ackerman, N. W. (1966). *Treating the troubled family.* New York: Basic Books.

Ackerman, N. W. (1970). *Family therapy in transition.* Boston: Little, Brown.

Andersen, T. (1991). *The reflecting team: Dialogues and dialogues about the dialogues.* New York: Norton.

Andersen, T. (1992). Reflections on reflecting with families. In S. McNamee & K. J. Gergen (Eds.), *Therapy as social construction* (pp. 54–68). Newbury Park, CA: Sage.

Anderson, H., & Goolishian, H. (1992). The client is the expert: A not-knowing approach to therapy. In S. McNamee & K. J. Gergen (Eds.), *Therapy as social construction* (pp. 25–39). Newbury Park, CA: Sage.

Avis, J. M. (1986). Feminist issues in family therapy. In F. P. Piercy, D. H. Sprenkle, & Associates (Eds.), *Family therapy sourcebook* (pp. 213–242). New York: Guilford Press.

Bednar, R. L., Burlingame, G. M., & Masters, K. S. (1988). Systems of family treatment: Substance or semantics? *Annual Review of Psychology, 39,* 401–434.

Beutler, L. (1983). *Eclectic psychotherapy: A systematic approach.* New York: Pergamon Press.

Bitter, J. R., & Corey, G. (1996). Family systems therapy. In G. Corey, *Theory and practice of counseling and psychotherapy* (5th ed.) (pp. 365–446). Pacific Grove, CA: Brooks/Cole.

Boen, D. L. (1988). A practitioner looks at assessment in marital counseling. *Journal of Counseling and Development, 66*(10), 484–486.

Brown, D. (1997). Implications of cultural values for cross-cultural consultation with families. *Journal of Counseling and Development, 76*(1), 29–35.

Carter, B., & McGoldrick, M. (1988). Overview: The changing family life cycle—A framework for family therapy. In B. Carter & M. McGoldrick (Eds.), *The changing family life cycle: A framework for family therapy* (2nd ed.). New York: Allyn & Bacon.

Coleman, S. (1985). *Failures in family therapy.* New York: Guilford Press.

Cummings, N. A. (1990). The credentialing of professional psychologists and its implication for the other mental health disciplines. *Journals of Counseling and Development, 68,* 485–490.

Dana, R. H. (1993). *Multicultural assessment perspectives for professional psychology.* Boston: Allyn & Bacon.

De Shazer, S. (1991). *Putting difference to work.* New York: Norton.

Dinkmeyer, D., & Carlson, J. (1984). *Time for a better marriage.* Circle Pines, MN: American Guidance Service.

Dinkmeyer, D., & McKay, G. (1989). *Systematic training for effective parenting (STEP): The parent's handbook* (3rd ed.). Circle Pines, MN: American Guidance Service.

Dinkmeyer, D., & McKay, G. (1990). *Systematic training for effective parenting of teens* (2nd ed.). Circle Pines, MN: American Guidance Service.

Dunn, R. L., & Schwebel, A. I. (1995). Meta-analytic review of marital therapy outcome research. *Journal of Family Psychology, 9*(1), 58–68.

Duvall, E. M. (1957). *Family development.* Philadelphia: Lippincott.

Duvall, E. M. (1977). *Marriage and family development* (5th ed.). Philadelphia: Lippincott.

Ebert, B. (1978). The healthy family. *Family Therapy, 5*(3), 227–232.

Elkaim, M. (1982). From the family approach to the socio-political approach. In F. Kaslow (Ed.), *The international book of family therapy* (pp. 331–357). New York: Brunner/Mazel.

Enns, C. Z. (1988). Dilemmas of power and equality in marital and family counseling: Proposals for a feminist perspective. *Journal of Counseling and Development, 67*(4), 242–248.

Enns, C. Z. (1993). Twenty years of feminist counseling and therapy. *The Counseling Psychologist, 21*(1), 3–87.

Epstein, E. S., & Loos, V. E. (1989). Some irreverent thoughts on the limits of family therapy: Towards a language-based explanation of human systems. *Journal of Family Psychology, 2*(4), 405–421.

Everett, C. A. (1990). The field of marital and family therapy. *Journal of Counseling and Development, 68,* 498–502.

Fisher, B. L., & Sprinkle, D. H. (1978). Therapists' perceptions of healthy family functioning. *International Journal of Family Counseling, 19*(4) 9–18.

Foucault, M. (1980). *Power/knowledge: Selected interviews and other writings.* New York: Pantheon Books.

Framo, J. L. (1981). The integration of marital therapy with family of origin sessions. In A. Gurman & D. Kniskern (Eds.), *Handbook of family therapy.* New York: Brunner/Mazel.

Framo, J. (1992). *Family of origin theory: An intergenerational approach.* New York: Brunner/Mazel.

Friedlander, M. L., & Highlen, P. S. (1984). A spatial view of the interpersonal structure of family interviews: Similarities and differences across counselors. *Journal of Counseling Psychology, 31,* 477–487.

Friedlander, M. L., Highlen, P. S., & Lassiter, W. L. (1985). Content analytic comparison of four expert counselors' approach to family treatment: Ackerman, Bowen, Jackson, and Whitaker. *Journal of Counseling Psychology, 32*(2), 171–180.

Giblin, P., & Chan, J. (1995). A feminist perspective. *The Family Journal: Counseling and Therapy for Couples and Families, 3*(3), 234–238.

Gibran, K. (1965). *The prophet.* New York: Harper & Row.

Gilligan, C. (1982). *In a different voice.* Cambridge, MA: Harvard University Press.

Glick, I., Clarkin, J., & Kessler, D. (1987). *Marital and family therapy* (3rd ed.). Orlando, FL: Grune & Stratton.

Golann, S. (1987). On description of family therapy. *Family Process, 26,* 331–340.

Goldenberg, I., & Goldenberg, H. (1995). Family therapy. In R. J. Corsini & D. Wedding (Eds.), *Current psychotherapies* (5th ed.) (pp. 356–385). Itasca, IL: F. E. Peacock.

Goldenberg, I., & Goldenberg, H. (1996). *Family therapy: An overview* (4th ed.). Monterey, CA: Brooks/Cole.

Goldner, V. (1985). Feminism and family therapy. *Family Process, 24,* 31–47.

Gottman, J. M. *Why marriages succeed or fail.* New York: Simon & Schuster.

Gottman, J. M., Coan, J., Carrere, S., & Swanson, C. (1998). Predicting marital happiness and stability from newlywed interactions. *Journal of Marriage and the Family, 60*(1), 5–22.

Gurman, A. S., & Kniskern, D. P. (1981). Family therapy outcome research: Knowns and unknowns. In A. S. Gurman & D. P. Kniskern (Eds.), *Handbook of family therapy.* New York: Brunner/Mazel.

Haley, J. (1963). *Strategies of psychotherapy.* New York: Grune & Stratton.

Haley, J. (1971). Approaches to family therapy. In J. Haley (Ed.), *Changing families: A family therapy reader.* New York: Grune & Stratton.

Haley, J. (1973). *Uncommon psychiatric techniques of Milton H. Erickson.* New York: W. W. Norton.

Haley, J. (1976). *Problem-solving therapy.* San Francisco: Jossey-Bass.

Haley, J. (1980). *Leaving home.* New York: McGraw-Hill.

Hayes, S. G. (1995). Infusing diversity into family and couples counseling. *The Family Journal: Counseling and Therapy for Couples and Families, 3*(3), 231–233.

Hazelrigg, M. D., Cooper, H. M., & Borduin, C. M. (1987). Evaluating the effectiveness of family therapies: An integrative review and analysis. *Psychological Bulletin, 101*(3), 428–442.

Horne, A. M., & Ohlsen, M. M. (1982). Introduction: The family and family counseling. In M. Horne & M. M. Ohlsen (Eds.), *Family counseling and therapy.* Itasca, IL: F. E. Peacock.

Humphrey, F. G. (1983). *Marital therapy.* Englewood Cliffs, NJ: Prentice-Hall.

Johnson, A. C. (1995). Resiliency mechanisms in culturally diverse families. *The Family Journal: Counseling and Therapy for Couples and Families, 3*(4), 316–324.

Kovacs, L. (1988). Couple therapy: An integrated developmental and family system model. *Family Therapy, 15*(2), 133–155.

L'Abate, L. (1986). *Systematic family therapy.* New York: Brunner/Mazel.

Lebow, J. L., & Gurman, A. S. (1995). Research assessing couple and family therapy. *Annual Review of Psychology, 46,* 27–57.

Liddle, H. (1982). On the problems of eclecticism: A call for epistemological clarification and human-scale theories. *Family Process, 21,* 243–250.

Lowe, R. N. (1982). Adlerian/Dreikursian family counseling. In A. M. Horne & M. M. Ohlsen (Eds.), *Family counseling and therapy.* Itasca, IL: F. E. Peacock.

Madanes, C. (1981). *Strategic family therapy.* San Francisco: Jossey-Bass.

Madanes, C. (1984). *Behind the one-way mirror: Advances in the practice of strategic therapy.* San Francisco: Jossey-Bass.

Minuchin, S. (1974). *Families and family therapy.* Cambridge, MA: Harvard University Press.

Minuchin, S. (1984). *Family kaleidoscope.* Cambridge, MA: Harvard University Press.

Moon, S. M., Dillon, D. R., & Sprenkle, D. H. (1990). Family therapy and qualitative research. *Journal of Marital and Family Therapy, 16*(4), 357–373.

Myers, L. J. (1988). *Understanding an Afrocentric worldview: Introduction to optimal psychology.* Dubuque, IA: Kendall/Hunt.

Nichols, M. (1984). *Family therapy: Concepts and methods.* New York: Gardner Press.

Nichols, M. (1987a). The individual in the system. *Family Therapy Networker, 11*(2), 33–38, 85.

Nichols, M. (1987b). *The self in the system: Expanding the limits of family therapy.* New York: Brunner/Mazel.

Nichols, W. (1988). *Marital therapy: An integrative approach.* New York: Brunner/Mazel.

Nichols, W. C., & Everett, C. A. (1986). *Systematic family therapy: An integrative approach.* New York: Guilford Press.

Nystul, M. S. (1988). Marathon family counseling. *Individual Psychology: The Journal of Adlerian Theory, Research, & Practice, 44*(2), 210–216.

O'Hanlon, W. H., & Weiner-Davis, M. (1989). *In search of solutions: A new direction in psychotherapy*. New York: Norton.

Paniagua, F. A. (1996). Cross-cultural guidelines in family therapy practice. *The Family Journal: Counseling and Therapy for Couples and Families, 4*(2), 127–138.

Raffa, H., Sypek, J., & Vogel, W. (1990). Commentary on reviews of "outcome" studies of family and marital psychotherapy. *Contemporary Family Therapy, 12* (1), 65–73.

Rawlings, E. I. (1993). Reflections on "twenty years of feminist counseling and therapy." *The Counseling Psychologist, 21*(1), 88–91.

Rothenberg, P. S. (1995). *Race, class, and gender in the United States: An integrated study*. New York: St. Martin's Press.

Russell, T., & Madsen, D. H. (1985). *Marriage counseling report user's guide*. Champaign, IL: Institute for Personality and Ability Testing.

Satir, V. M. (1982). The therapist and family therapy: Process model. In A. M. Horne & M. M. Ohlsen (Eds.), *Family counseling and therapy*. Itasca, IL: F. E. Peacock.

Satir, V. M. (1983). *Conjoint family therapy* (3rd ed.). Palo Alto, CA: Science and Behavior Books.

Satir, V. M. (1988) *The new peoplemaking*. Palo Alto, CA: Science and Behavior Books.

Schultz, C., & Nystul, M. S. (1980). Mother-child interaction behavior as an outcome of theoretical models of parent group education. *Journal of Individual Psychology, 36,* 16–29.

Schultz, C., Nystul, M. S., & Law, H. (1980). Attitudinal outcomes of theoretical models of parent group education. *Journal of Individual Psychology, 37,* 107–112.

Selvini-Palazzoli, M. (1980). Why a long interval between sessions? The therapeutic control of the family-therapist suprasystem. In M. Andolfi & I. Zwerling (Eds.), *Dimensions of family therapy*. New York: Guilford Press.

Senge, P. M. (1990). *The fifth discipline: The art and practice of the learning organization*. New York: Doubleday/Currency.

Shadish, W. R., Ragsdale, K., Glaser, R. R., & Montgomery, L. M. (1995). The efficacy and effectiveness of marital and family therapy: A perspective from meta-analysis. *Journal of Marital and Family Therapy, 21*(4), 345–360.

Sherrard, P. A. D., & Amatea, E. S. (1995). Ecosystem theory. In D. Capuzzi & D. R. Gross (Eds.), *Counseling and psychotherapy: Theories and Interventions* (pp. 425–470). Columbus, OH: Merrill.

Shields, C. G. (1986). Critiquing the new epistemologies: Towards minimum requirements for scientific theory of family therapy. *Journal of Marital and Family Therapy, 12,* 359–372.

Sholevar, G. (1985). Marital therapy. In H. Kaplan & B. Sadock (Eds.), *Comprehensive textbook of psychiatry IV* (Vol. 2). Baltimore: Williams & Wilkins.

Smith, R. L. (1994). Directions in marriage and family graduate level training. *Counselor Education and Supervision, 34,* 180–183.

Smith, R. L., Carlson, J., Stevens-Smith, & Dennison, M. (1995). Marriage and family counseling. *Journal of Counseling and Development, 2*(74), 154–157.

Snyder, D. K. (1981). *Marital Satisfaction Inventory (MSI)*. Los Angeles: Western Psychological Services.

Solomon, M. A. (1973). A developmental, conceptual premise for family therapy. *Family Process, 12,* 179–188.

Sperry, L. (1989). Assessment in marital therapy: A couples-centered biopsychosocial approach. *Individual Psychology: The Journal of Adlerian Theory, Research, and Practice, 45,* 446–451.

Sperry, L., & Carlson, J. (1991). *Marital therapy: Integrating theory and technique*. Denver, CO: Love.

Stinnet, N., & DeFrain, J. (1985). *Secrets of strong families*. Boston: Little, Brown.

Stuart, R. B. (1983). *Couples' pre-counseling inventory, counselor's guide*. Champaign, IL: Research Press.

Taylor, R. M., & Morrison, L. P. (1984). *Taylor-Johnson temperament analysis manual*. Los Angeles: Psychological Publications.

Von Bertalanffy, L. V. (1968). *General systems theory: Foundations, development, application*. New York: Braziller.

Watts, R. E., Trusty, J., & Mee-Gaik, L. (in press). Characteristics of healthy families as a model of systemic social interest. *The Canadian Journal of Adlerian Psychology*.

Watzlawick, P., Weakland, J. H., & Fisch, R. (1974). *Change: Principles of problem formation and problem resolution*. New York: Norton.

Whitaker, C. A. (1976). The hindrance of theory in clinical work. In P. J. Guerin (Ed.), *Family therapy: Theory and practice*. New York: Gardner Press.

Whitaker, C. A. (1977). Process techniques of family therapy. *Interaction, 1,* 4–19.

Whitaker, C. A., & Bumberry, W. M. (1988). *Dancing with the family: A symbolic-experiential approach*. New York: Brunner/Mazel.

White, M., & Epston, D. (1990). *Narrative means to therapeutic ends*. New York: Norton.

Wilcoxon, S. A. (1985). Healthy family functioning: The other side of family pathology. *Journal of Counseling and Development, 63,* 495–499.

Chapter 11

Achenback, T. M., & Edelbrock, C. S. (1983). *Manual for the child behavior checklist and revised child behavior profile.* Burlington, VT: University of Vermont, Department of Psychiatry

Adams, J. H. (1997). *Perspectives of the oldest-old concerning resilience across the life span.* Unpublished dissertation. NMSU, Las Cruces, NM.

Adler, A. (1930). *The education of children.* South Bend, IN: Gateway Editions.

Ainsworth, M. D. S. (1989). Attachments beyond infancy. *American Psychologist, 44,* 709–716.

Ainsworth, M. D. S. (1991). Attachment and other affectional bonds across the life cycle. In C. M. Parkes, J. Stevenson-Hinde, P. Marris (Eds.), *Attachment across the life cycle* (pp. 33–51). New York: Tavistock/Routledge.

Ainsworth, M. D. S., Blehar, M. C., Waters, E., Wall, S. (1978). *Patterns of attachment: A psychological study of the strange situation.* Hillsdale. NJ: Lawrence Erlbaum.

Allan, J., & Brown, K. (1993). Jungian play therapy in elementary schools. *Elementary School Guidance and Counseling, 28*(1), 30–41.

Allen, S. F., & Stoltenberg, C. D. (1995). Psychological separation of older adolescents and young adults from their parents: An investigation of gender differences. *Journal of Counseling and Development, 73*(5), 542–546.

Alper, J. (1986, May). Depression at an early age. *Science, 86,* 44–50.

Altmann, E. O., & Gotlib, I. H. (1988). The social behavior of depressed children: An observational study. *Journal of Abnormal Child Psychology, 16,* 29–44.

American Psychiatric Association. (1980). *Diagnostic and statistical manual of mental disorders* (3rd ed.). Washington, DC: Author.

American Psychiatric Association. (1987). *Diagnostic and statistical manual of mental disorders* (3rd ed. rev.). Washington, DC: Author.

American Psychiatric Association. (1994). *Diagnostic and statistical manual of mental disorders* (4th ed.). Washington, DC: Author.

Asarnow, J. R., & Calan, J. W. (1985). Boys with peer adjustment problems: Social cognitive processes. *Journal of Counseling and Clinical Psychology, 53,* 80–87.

Axline, V. M. (1964). *Dibs: In search of self.* Boston: Houghton Mifflin.

Axline, V. M. (1974). *Play therapy.* New York: Houghton Mifflin.

Berger, K. S., & Thompson, R. A. (1995). *The developing person through childhood and adolescence* (4th ed.). New York: Worth Publishers.

Bergman, L. R., & Magnusson, D. (1997). A person-oriented approach in research on developmental psychopathology. *Development and Psychopathology, 9,* 291–319.

Blocher, D. H. (1987). *The professional counselor.* New York: Macmillan.

Blustein, D. L., Prezioso, M. S., & Schultheiss, D. P. (1995). *The Counseling Psychologist, 23*(3), 416–432.

Bowlby, J. (1969/1982). *Attachment and loss. Vol I: Attachment.* London: Tavistock.

Bowlby, J. (1988a). *A secure base: Parent-child attachments and healthy human development.* New York: Basic Books.

Bowlby, J. (1988b). Developmental psychiatry comes of age. *The American Journal of Psychiatry, 145,* 1–10.

Bradford, E., & Lyddon, W. J. (1994). Assessing adolescent and adult attachment: An update. *Journal of Counseling and Development, 73*(2), 215–219.

Brennan, K. A., Shaver, P. R., & Tobey, A. N. (1991). Attachment styles, gender, and parental problem drinking. *Journal of Social and Personal Relationships, 8,* 451–466.

Brockman, M. P. (1987). Children and physical abuse. In A. Thomas & J. Grimes (Eds.), *Children's needs: Psychological perspectives* (pp. 418–427). Washington, DC: The National Association of School Psychologists.

Brown, G. W., & Harris, T. (1978). *Social origins of depression.* London: Tavistock.

Bruner, J. S. (1973). *Beyond the information given: Studies in the psychology of knowing.* New York: Norton.

Buck, J. N. (1949). The H-T-P technique: A qualitative and scoring manual, Part 2. *Journal of Clinical Psychology, 5,* 37–76.

Campbell, C. A. (1993). Play, the fabric of elementary school counseling programs. *Elementary School Guidance and Counseling, 28*(1), 10–16.

Carlson, G. A., & Cantwell, D. P. (1979). A survey of depressive symptoms in a child and adolescent psychiatric population. *Journal of the American Academy of Child Psychiatry, 18,* 587–599.

Carmichael, K. D. (1994). Sand play as an elementary school strategy. *Elementary School Guidance and Counseling, 28*(4), 302–307.

Carnelley, K. B., Pietromonaco, P. R., & Jaffe, K. (1994). Depression, working models of others, and relationship functioning. *Journal of Personality and Social Psychology, 66,* 127–140.

Cashwell, C. S., & Vacc, N. A. (1996). Family functioning and risk behaviors: Influences on adolescent delinquency. *The School Counselor, 44*(2), 105–114.

Chambers, W. J., Puig-Antich, J., & Tabrizi, M. A. (1978, Oct.). *The ongoing development of the Kiddie-SADS (schedule for affective disorders and schizophrenia for school-age children)*. Paper presented at the meeting of the American Academy of Child Psychiatry. San Diego, CA.

Chiles, A., Miller, M. L., & Cox, G. B. (1980). Depression in an adolescent delinquent population. *Archives of General Psychiatry, 37*, 1179–1184.

Chu, L., & Powers, P. A. (1995). Synchrony in adolescence. *Adolescence, 30*(118), 453–461.

Cicchetti, D., Ackerman, B. P., & Izard, C. E. (1995). Emotions and emotion regulation in developmental psychopathology. *Development and Psychopathology, 7*, 1–10.

Cochran, J. L. (1996). Using play and art therapy to help culturally diverse students overcome barriers to school success. *The School Counselor, 43*(4), 287–298.

Cole, J. D., & Kupersmidt, J. B. (1983). A behavioral analysis of emerging social status in boys' groups. *Child Development, 54*, 1400–1416.

Cole, O. A., & Rehm, L. P. (1986). Family interaction patterns and childhood depression. *Journal of Abnormal Child Psychology, 14*, 297–314.

Collins, B. G., & Collins, T. M. (1994). Child and adolescent mental health: Building a system of care. *Journal of Counseling and Development, 72*(3), 239–243.

Committee for Economic Development. (1991). *The unfinished agenda: A new vision for child development and education*. New York: Author.

Costello, A. J., Edelbrock, C. S., Dulcan, M. K., & Kalas, R. (1984). *Testing of the NIMH Diagnostic Interview Schedule for Children (DISC) in a Clinical Population* (Contract No. DB-81-0027, final report to the Center for Epidemiological Studies, National Institute for Mental Health). Pittsburgh: University of Pittsburgh.

Costello, A. J., Edelbrock, C., Kalas, R., Kessler, M. D., & Klaric, S. H. (1982). *The NIMH Diagnostic Interview Schedule for Children (DISC)*. Unpublished interview schedule, Department of Psychiatry, University of Pittsburgh.

Craig, C. J. (1996). *Human development* (7th ed.). Englewood Cliffs, NJ: Prentice-Hall.

Daly, M., & Wilson, M. (1983). *Sex, evolution, and behavior* (2nd ed.). Boston, MA: Willard Grant Press.

Damon, L., & Waterman, J. (1986). Parallel group treatment of children and their mothers. In K. MacFarlane & J. Waterman (Eds.), *Sexual abuse of young children*. New York: Guilford Press.

Digdon, N., & Gotlib, I. H. (1985). Developmental considerations in the study of childhood depression. *Developmental Review, 5*, 162–199.

Dinkmeyer, D., & McKay, G. (1989). *Systematic training for effective parenting* (3rd ed.). Circle Pines, MN: American Guidance Service.

Dodge, K. A. (1983). Behavioral antecedents of peer social station. *Child Development, 54*, 1386–1399.

Dreikurs, R., & Soltz, V. (1964). *Children: The challenge.* New York: Hawthorn/Dutton.

Durlak, J. A., Fuhrman, T., & Lampman, C. (1991). Effectiveness of cognitive-behavioral therapy for maladapting children: A meta-analysis. *Psychological Bulletin, 110*, 204–214.

Dworetzky, J. P. (1996). *Introduction to child development* (6th ed.). New York: ITP.

Dysinger, B. J. (1993). Conflict resolution for intermediate children. *The School Counselor, 40*(4), 301–308.

Eccles, J. S., Midgley, C., Wigfield, A., Buchanan, C. M., Reuman, D., Flanagan, C., & Iver, D. M. (1993). Development during adolescence: The impact of stage-environment fit on young adolescents' experiences in schools and families. *American Psychologist, 48*, 90–101.

Edelbrock, C., & Costello, A. J. (1988). Structured psychiatric interviews for children. In M. Rutter, A. H. Tuma, & I. S. Lann (Eds.), *Assessment and diagnosis in child psychopathology* (pp. 82–112). New York: Guilford Press.

Elkind, D. (1984). *All grown up and no place to go.* Reading, MA: Addison-Wesley.

Elliott, D. S., Huizinga, D., & Ageton, S. S. (1985). *Explaining delinquency and drug use.* Beverly Hills, CA: Sage.

Ellis, P. L. (1982). Empathy: A factor in antisocial behavior. *Journal of Abnormal Child Psychology, 10*, 123–133.

England, L. W., & Thompson, C. L. (1988). Counseling child sexual abuse victims: Myths and realities. *Journal of Counseling and Development, 66*, 370–373.

Erikson, E. H. (1963). *Childhood and society* (2nd ed.). New York: Norton.

Erikson, E. H. (1968). *Identity, youth, and crisis.* New York: Norton.

Feinauer, L. L. (1990). Relationship of treatment to adjustment in women sexually abused as children. *The American Journal of Family Therapy, 17*(4), 326–334.

Feldman, R. A., Caplinger, T. E., & Wodarski, S. S. (1981). The St. Louis conundrum: Prosocial and antisocial boys together. Unpublished manuscript.

Field, T., Healy, B., Goldstein, S., Perry, S., Bendell, D., Schanberg, S., Zimmerman, E. A., & Kuhn, C. (1988). Infants of depressed mothers show "depressed" behavior even with nondepressed adults. *Child Development, 59*, 1569–1579.

Freud A. (1928). Introduction to the technique of child analysis. *Nervous and Mental Disease Monograph No. 48.* New York.

Garland, A. F., & Zigler, E. (1993). Adolescent suicide prevention. *American Psychologist, 48*(2), 169–182.

Gibbs, N. (1995). The EQ factor. *Time,* October 2, 1995, 60–68.

Gilligan, C. (1982). *In a different voice: Psychological theory and women's development.* Cambridge, MA: Harvard University Press.

Gilligan, C. (1987). Adolescent development reconsidered. In C. Irwin (Ed.), *Adolescent social behavior and health.* San Francisco: Jossey-Bass.

Gilligan, C. (1990). Joining the resistance: Psychology, politics, girls, and women. *Michigan Quarterly Review, 29*(4), 501–536.

Gilligan, C. (1991). Women's psychological development: Implications for psychotherapy. *Women in Therapy, 11,* 5–31.

Glasser, W. (1969). *Schools without failure.* New York: Harper & Row.

Goldston, S. E., Yager, J., Heinicke, C. M., & Pynoos, R. S. (Eds.). (1990). *Preventing mental health disturbances in childhood.* Washington, DC: American Psychiatric Press.

Goleman, D. (1997). *Emotional intelligence.* New York: Bantam.

Hall, G. S. (1904). *Adolescence.* New York: Appleton.

Hammer, C., & Zupan, B. A. (1984). Self-schemas, depression, and the processing of personal information in children. *Journal of Experimental Child Psychology, 37,* 598–608.

Hammond, W. R., & Yung, B. (1993). Psychology's role in the public health response to assaultive violence among young African-American men. *American Psychologist, 48*(2), 142–154.

Harrar, L. (1984). *Make my people live: The crisis in Indian health.* Public Broadcasting System: NOVA.

Harris, D. E. (1963). *Children's drawings as measures of intellectual maturity.* A revision and extension of Goodenough Draw-A-Man Test. San Diego, CA: Harcourt Brace Jovanovich.

Hart, S. N., & Brassard, M. R. (1987). A major threat to children's mental health: Psychological maltreatment. *American Psychologist, 42,* 160–165.

Hazan, C., & Shaver, P. R. (1990). Love and work: An attachment-theoretical perspective. *Journal of Personality and Social Psychology, 59,* 270–280.

Hazelrigg, M. D., Cooper, H. M., & Borduin, C. M. (1987). Evaluating the effectiveness of family therapies: An integrative review and analysis. *Psychological Bulletin, 101,* 428–442.

Hazzard, A., King, H. E., & Webb, C. (1986). Group therapy with sexually abused adolescent girls. *American Journal of Psychotherapy, 40*(2), 213–223.

Herjanic, B., & Reich, W. (1982). Development of a structured psychiatric interview for children: Agreement between child and parent of individual symp-toms. *Journal of Abnormal Child Psychology, 10,* 307–324.

Herman, J. L. (1986). *Father-daughter incest.* Cambridge, MA: Harvard University Press.

Horst, E. A. (1995). Reexamining gender issues in Erikson's stages of identity and intimacy. *Journal of Counseling and Development, 73*(3), 271–278.

Huba, G. J., & Bentler, P. M. (1983). Causal models of the development of law abidance and its relationship to psychosocial factors and drug use. In W. S. Lauger & J. M. Day (Eds.), *Personality theory, moral development, and criminal behavior* (pp. 164–215). Lexington, MA: Lexington Books.

Johnston, V. S., & Oliver-Rodriguez, J. C. (1997). Facial beauty and the late positive component of event-related potential. *Journal of Sex Research, 34-2,* 188–198.

Kadushin, A., & Martin, J. A. (1981). *Child abuse: An interactional event.* New York: Columbia University Press.

Kandel, D. B. (1973). Adolescent marijuana use: Role of parents and peers. *Science, 181,* 1067–1081.

Kanner, L. (1962). *Child psychiatry* (3rd ed.). Springfield, IL: Charles C. Thomas.

Kazdin, A. E. (1985). *Treatment of antisocial behavior in children and adolescents.* Homewood, IL: Dorsey Press.

Kazdin, A. E. (1987). Treatment of antisocial behavior in children: Current status and future directions. *Psychological Bulletin, 102,* 187–203.

Kazdin, A. E. (1988). Childhood depression. In E. J. Mash & L. Terdal (Eds.), *Behavioral assessment of childhood disorders* (2nd ed.) (pp. 157–196). New York: Guilford Press.

Kazdin, A. E. (1989). Developmental psychopathology: Current research, issues, and directions. *American Psychologist, 44*(2), 180–187.

Kazdin, A. (1993). Adolescent mental health: Prevention and treatment programs. *American Psychologist, 48*(2), 127–141.

Kazdin, A. E. (1994). *Behavior modification in applied settings.* Pacific Grove, CA: Brooks/Cole.

Kazdin, A. E., Bass, D., Ayers, W. A., & Rodgers, A. (1990). Empirical and clinical focus of child and adolescent psychotherapy research. *Journal of Consulting and Clinical Psychology, 58,* 729–740.

Kazdin, A. E., Bass, D., Siegel, T., & Thomas, C. (1989). Cognitive-behavioral therapy and relationship therapy in the treatment of children referred for antisocial behavior. *Journal of Consulting and Clinical Psychology, 57*(4), 522–535.

Kitchur, M., & Bell, R. (1989). Group psychotherapy with preadolescent sexual abuse victims: A literature review and description of an inner-city group. *International Journal of Group Psychotherapy, 39*(3), 285–310.

Klein, M. (1960). *The psychoanalysis of children.* New York: Grove Press.

Knoff, H. M., & Prout, H. T. (1985). *The kinetic drawing system for family and school.* Los Angeles, CA: Western Psychological Services.

Kobak, R. R., & Hazan, C. (1991). Attachment in marriage: Effects of security and accuracy of working models. *Journal of Personality and Social Psychology, 60,* 861–869.

Kohlberg, L (1963). Development of children's orientation towards a moral order. 1. Sequence in the development of moral thought. *Vita Human, 6,* 11–36.

Kohlberg, L. (1973). Continuities in childhood and adult moral development revisited. In P. B. Baltes & K. W. Schair (Eds.), *Life-span developmental psychology: Personality and socialization.* New York: Academic Press.

Kohlberg, L. (1981). *The philosophy of moral development.* New York: Harper & Row.

Kottman, T., & Johnson, V. (1993). Adlerian play therapy: A tool for school counselors. *Elementary School Guidance and Counseling, 28*(1), 42–51.

Kottman, T., Lingg, M., & Tisdell, T. (1995). Gay and lesbian adolescents: Implications for Adlerian therapists. *Individual Psychology: The Journal of Adlerian theory, research, and practice, 51*(2), 114–128.

Kovacs, M. (1981). Rating scales to assess depression in school-aged children. *Acta Parlopsychiatrica, 46,* 305–315.

Kovacs, M. (1982). *The Interview Schedule for Children (ISC):* Unpublished interview schedule, Department of Psychiatry, University of Pittsburgh.

Kovacs, M. (1989). Affective disorders in children and adolescents. *American Psychologist, 44,* 209–215.

Kovacs, M., Gatsonis, C., Marsh, J., & Richards, C. (1988). Intellectual and cognitive development in childhood-onset depressive disorders: A longitudinal study. Manuscripts submitted for publication.

Krause, A. M., & Haverkamp, B. E. (1996). Attachment in adult child-older parent relationships: Research, theory, and practice. *Journal of Counseling and Development, 75*(2), 83–92.

Kupersmidt, J. B., & Patterson, C. J. (1991). Childhood peer rejection, aggression, withdrawal, and perceived competence as predictors of self-reported behavior problems in preadolescence. *Journal of Abnormal Child Psychology, 19,* 437–449.

Landreth, G. L. (1993). Child-centered play therapy. *Elementary School Guidance and Counseling, 28*(1), 17–29.

Lang, M., & Tisher, M. (1978). *Children's depression scale.* Victoria, Australia: Australian Council for Educational Research.

LeVine, E., & Sallee, A. (1992). *Listen to our children: Clinical theory and practice* (2nd ed.). Dubuque, IA: Kendall-Hunt.

Loeber, R., Schmaling, K. B. (1985). Empirical evidence for overt and covert patterns of antisocial conduct problems: A meta-analysis. *Journal of Abnormal Child Psychology, 13,* 337–352.

Lopez, F. G. (1995). Contemporary attachment theory: An introduction with implications for counseling psychology. *The Counseling Psychologist, 23*(3), 395–415.

Lyddon, W. J., Bradford, E., & Nelson, J. P. (1993). Assessing adolescent and adult attachment: A review of current self-report measures. *Journal of Counseling and Development, 71*(4), 390–395.

Maslow, A. (1968). *Towards a psychology of being.* New York: Van Nostrand.

Mayer, J. D., & Geher, G. (in press). Emotional intelligence and the identification of emotion. *Intelligence.*

Mayer, J. D., & Salovey, P. (in press). What is emotional intelligence? In P. Salovey and D. Sluyter (Eds.), *Emotional development, emotional literacy, and emotional intelligence.* New York: Basic Books.

McMahon, R. J., & Forehand, R. (1988). Conduct disorders. In E. J. Mash & L. G. Terdal (Eds.), *Behavioral assessment of childhood disorders* (2nd ed.) (pp. 105–156). New York: Guilford Press.

Milich, R., & Dodge, K. A. (1984). Social information processing in child psychiatric population. *Journal of Abnormal Child Psychology, 12,* 471–490.

Milner, J. S. (1986). *The child abuse potential inventory: Manual* (rev. ed.). Webster, NC: Psytec Corporation.

Mischel, W., Shoda, Y., & Rodriguez, M. L. (1989). Delay of gratification in children. *Science, 244,* 933–938.

Nystul, M. S. (1980). Nystulian play therapy: Applications of Adlerian psychology. *Elementary School Guidance & Counseling, 15*(22), 30.

Nystul, M. S. (1980). Systematic training for effective parenting: STEP in Australia. *Australian Child and Family Welfare, 1–2,* 32–34.

Nystul, M. S. (1982a). The effects of systematic training for effective patenting on parental attitudes. *The Journal of Psychology, 112,* 63–66.

Nystul, M. S. (1982b). Ten Adlerian patenting principles applied to the Navajos. *Individual Psychology: The Journal of Adlerian Theory, Research, & Practice, 38,* 183–198.

Nystul, M. S. (1984). Positive parenting leads to self-actualizing children. *Individual Psychology: The Journal of Adlerian Theory, Research, and Practice, 40,* 177–183.

Nystul, M. S. (1986a). Reaching in-reaching out: Treatment of an autistic child. *Mental Health Counselor's Association Journal, 8,* 18–26.

Nystul, M. S. (1986b). The hidden reason behind children's misbehavior. *Elementary School Guidance and Counseling, 20,* 188–193.

Nystul, M. S. (1987). Strategies of parent-centered counseling of the young. *The Creative Child and Adult Quarterly, 12*(2), 103–111.

Nystul, M. S. (in press). The role of parental emotions in parenting. In R. F. Watts (Ed.), *Innovative techniques in marriage and family therapy.* Alexandria, VA: American Counseling Association.

O'Brien, S. (1983). *Child pornography.* Dubuque, IA: Kendall/Hunt.

O'Connor, M. (1992). Psychotherapy with gay and lesbian adolescents. In S. Dworkin & F. Gutierrez (Eds.), *Counseling gay men and lesbians: Journey to the end of the rainbow.* Alexandria, VA: AACD.

Orenchuk-Tomiuk, N., Matthey, G., & Christensen, C. P. (1990). The resolution model: A comprehensive treatment framework in sexual abuse. *Child Welfare, 69*(5), 417–431.

Orton, G. L. (1997). *Strategies for counseling with children and their parents.* Pacific Grove, CA: Brooks/Cole.

Papalia, D. E., & Olds, S. W. (1995). *Human Development* (6th ed.). New York: McGraw-Hill.

Parr, G. D., & Ostrovsky (1991). The role of moral development in deciding how to counsel children and adolescents. *The School Counselor, 39,* 14–19.

Patterson, G. R. (1982). *Coercive family process.* Eugene, OR: Castalia.

Patterson, G. R., DeBaryshe, R. D., & Ramsey, E. (1989). A developmental perspective on antisocial behavior. *American Psychologist, 44*(2), 329–335.

Petersen, A. C., Compas, B. E., Brooks/Gunn, J., Stemmler, M., Ey, S., & Grant, K. E. (1993). Depression in adolescence. *American Psychologist, 48*(2), 155–168.

Piaget, J. (1952). *The origins of intelligence in children* (M. Cook, Trans.). New York: Norton.

Piaget, J. (1965). *The moral judgment of the child* (M. Gabain, Trans.). New York: Free Press. (Original work published 1936)

Pistole, M. C. (1993). Attachment relationships: Self-disclosure and trust. *Journal of Mental Health Counseling, 15,* 94–106.

Polansky, N., Chalmers, M., Buttenwieser, E., & Williams, D. (1981). *Damaged parents. An anatomy of child neglect.* Chicago: University of Chicago Press.

Puig-Antich, J., Perel, J. M., Lupatkins, W., Chambers, W. J., Tabrizi, M. A., King, J., Goetz, R., Davies, M., & Stiller, R. L. (1987). Imipramine in prepubertal major depressive disorders. *Archives of General Psychiatry, 44,* 81–89.

Quay, H. C., & Petersen, D. R. (1983). *Interim manual for the revised behavior problem checklist.* Unpublished manuscript, University of Miami.

Radbill, S. X. (1980). Children in a world of violence: A history of child abuse. In C. H. Kempe & R. E. Helfer (Eds.), *The battered child.* Chicago: University of Chicago.

Rak, C. F., & Patterson, L. E. (1996). Promoting resilience in at-risk children. *Journal of Counseling and Development, 74*(4), 368–373.

Reams, R., & Friedrich, W. N. (1983). *Play therapy: A review of outcome research.* Seattle: University of Washington, Department of Psychology.

Reynolds, W. M., & Coats, K. I. (1986). A comparison of cognitive-behavioral therapy and relocation training for the treatment of depression in adolescents. *Journal of Counseling and Clinical Psychology, 54,* 653–660.

Rice, K. G. (1990). Attachment in adolescence: A narrative and meta-analytic review. *Journal of Youth and Adolescence, 19,* 511–536.

Rice, K. G., & Meyer, A. L. (1994). Preventing depression among young adolescents: Preliminary process results of a psycho-educational program. *Journal of Counseling and Development, 73*(2), 145–152.

Ricks, M. H. (1985). The social transmission of parental behavior. Attachment across generations. *Monograph of the Society for Research on Child Development, 50,* 211–227.

Robins, L., Helzer, J. E., Croughan, J., & Ratcliff, K. S. (1981). National Institute of Mental Health diagnostic interview schedule: Its history, characteristics, and validity. *Archives of General Psychiatry, 38,* 381–389.

Rogers, C. (1951). *Client-centered therapy.* Boston, MA: Houghton Mifflin.

Rogers, F., & Sharapan, H. (1993). Play. *Elementary School Guidance and Counseling, 28*(1), 10–16.

Rutter, M. (1996). Transitions and turning points in developmental psychopathology: As applied to the age span between childhood and mid-adulthood. *International Journal of Behavioral Development, 19*(3), 603–626.

Rutter, M., Dunn, J., Plomin, R., Simonoff, E., Pickles, A., Maughan, B., Ormel, J., Meyer, J., & Eaves, L. (1997). Integrating nature and nurture: Implications of person-environment correlations and interactions for developmental psychopathology. *Development and Psychopathology, 9,* 335–364.

Sakolske, D. H., & Janzen, H. L. (1987). Dependency. In A. Thomas & J. Grimes (Eds.), *Children's needs: Psychological perspectives* (pp. 157–166). Washington, DC: The National Association of School Psychologists.

Salkind, N. (1994). *Child development* (7th ed.). San Diego, CA: HBJ.

Salovey, P., & Mayer, J. D. (1990). Emotional intelligence. *Imagination, Cognition, and Personality, 9-3,* 185–211.

Schultz, C., & Nystul, M. S. (1980). Mother-child interaction behavior as an outcome of theoretical models of parent group education. *Journal of Individual Psychology, 36,* 16–29.

Seligman, M. (1991). *Learned optimism.* New York: Knopf.

Shaver, P. R., & Brennan, K. A. (1992). Attachment styles and the "big five" personality traits: Their connections with each other and with romantic relationship outcomes. *Personality and Social Psychology Bulletin, 18,* 536–545.

Shoda, Y., Mischel, W., & Peake, P. K. (1990). Predicting adolescent cognitive and self-regulatory competencies from preschool delay of gratification: Identifying diagnostic conditions. *Developmental Psychology, 26,* 978–986.

Simpson, J. A., Rholes, W. S., & Nelligan, J. S. (1992). Support-seeking and support-giving within couples in an anxiety-provoking situation: The role of attachment styles. *Journal of Personality and Social Psychology, 62,* 434-446.

Snyder, J. J. (1977). Reinforcement analysis of interaction in problem and nonproblem families. *Journal of Abnormal Psychology, 86,* 528–535.

Spitz, R. (1946). Anaditic depression. *Psychoanalytic Study of the Child, 2,* 113–117.

Sroufe, L. A. (1997). Psychopathology as an outcome of development. *Development and Psychopathology, 9,* 251–268.

Sroufe, L. A., & Cooper, R. G. (1996). *Child development: Its nature and course.* New York: McGraw-Hill.

Stabler, B. (1984). *Children's drawings.* Chapel Hill, NC: Health Sciences Consortium.

Stern, M., & Newland, L. M. (1994). Working with children: Providing a framework for the roles of counseling psychologist. *The Counseling Psychologist, 22*(3), 402–425.

Sternberg, R. J., Wagner, R. K., Williams, W. M., & Horvath, J. A. (1995). Testing common sense. *American Psychologist, 50*(11), 912–926.

Straus, M. A., Gelles, R. J., & Steinmetz, S. (1980). *Behind closed doors. Violence in the American family.* Garden City, NY: Doubleday/Anchor.

Strober, M., Hanna, G., & McCracken, J. (1989). Bipolar illness. In C. Last & M. Hersens (Eds.), *Handbook of child psychiatric diagnosis.* New York: Wiley.

Takanishi, R. (1993). The opportunities of adolescence— research, interventions, and policy. *American Psychologist, 48,* 85–87.

Talbutt, L. C. (1986). The abused child. In L. B. Golden & D. Capuzzi (Eds.), *Helping families help children.* Springfield, IL: Charles C. Thomas.

Thompson, C. L., & Rudolph, L. B. (1997). *Counseling children* (3rd ed.). Pacific Grove, CA: Brooks/Cole.

Thompson, R. A., & Wilcox, B. L. (1995). Child maltreatment research. *American Psychologist, 50*(9), 789–793.

Thorndike, E. L. (1920). Intelligence and its uses. *Harper's Magazine, 140,* 227–235.

Tremblay, R. E., LeBlanc, M., & Schwartzman, A. E. (1988). The predictive power of first-grade peer and teacher ratings of behavior: Sex differences in antisocial behavior and personality at adolescence. *Journal of Abnormal Child Psychology, 16,* 571–583.

Tuma, J. M. (1989). Mental health services in children: The state of the art. *American Psychologist, 44*(2), 188–199.

Van Slyck, M., Stern, M., & Zak-Place, J. (1996). Promoting optimal adolescent development through conflict resolution education, training, and practice: An innovative approach for counseling psychologist. *The Counseling Psychologist, 24*(3), 433–461.

Vernon, A. (1995). Working with children, adolescents, and their parents: Practical application of developmental theory. *Counseling and Human Development, 27*(7), 1–12.

Wagner, W. G. (1994). Counseling with children: An opportunity for tomorrow. *The Counseling Psychologist, 22*(3), 381–401.

Wagner, W. G. (1996). Optimal development in adolescence: What it is and how it can be encouraged? *The Counseling Psychologist, 24*(3), 360–399.

Wahler, R. G., & Dumas, J. E. (1987). Family factors in childhood psychopathology: Toward a coercion neglect model. In T. Jacob (Ed.), *Family interaction and psychopathology.* New York: Plenum Press.

Wakefield, J. C. (1997). When is development disordered? Developmental psychopathology and the harmful dysfunction analysis of mental disorder. *Development and Psychopathology, 9,* 193–229.

Wastell, C. A. (1996). Feminist developmental theory: Implications for counseling. *Journal of Counseling and Development, 74*(6), 575–581.

Weiner, I. B. (1992). *Psychological disturbance in adolescence.* New York: Wiley.

Weissberg, R. P., Caplan, M., & Harwood, R. L. (1991). Promoting competent young people in competence-enhancing environments: A systems-based perspective on primary prevention. *Journal of Consulting and Clinical Psychology, 59,* 830–841.

Weisz, J. R., Weiss, B., & Donenberg, G. R. (1992). The lab versus the clinic: Effects of child and adolescent psychotherapy. *American Psychologist, 47*(12), 1578–1585.

Werner, E. E. (1992). The children of Kauai: Resiliency and recovery in adolescence and adulthood. *Journal of Adolescent Health, 13,* 262–268.

Werner, E. E., & Smith, R. S. (1982). *Vulnerable but not invincible: A longitudinal study of resilient children and youth.* New York: McGraw-Hill.

Werner, E. E. & Smith, R. S. (1992). *Overcoming the odds: High risk children from birth to adulthood.* Ithaca, NY: Cornell University Press.

White, J. A., & Allers, C. T. (1994). Play therapy with abused children: A review of the literature. *Journal of Counseling and Development, 72*(4), 390–394.

Wilson, J. Q., & Hernstein, R. J. (1985). *Crime and human nature.* New York: Simon & Schuster.

Wolfe, D. A. (1988). Child abuse and neglect. In E. J. Mash & L. G. Terdal (Eds.), *Behavioral assessment of childhood disorders* (2nd ed.) (pp. 627–679). New York: Guilford Press.

Wright, R. (1994). *The moral animal: The new science of evolutionary psychology.* New York: Pantheon Books.

Chapter 12

Addington, J. (1992). Separation groups. *Journal for Specialists in Group Work, 17,* 20–28.

Aiello, T. J. (1979). Short-term group therapy of the hospitalized psychotic, In P. Olsen & H. Grayson (Eds.), *Short-term approaches to psychotherapy.* New York: Human Sciences Press.

Baruth, L. G., & Robinson, E. H. III. (1987). *An introduction to the counseling profession.* Englewood Cliffs, NJ: Prentice-Hall.

Bonner, H. (1959). *Group Dynamics.* New York: Ronald Press.

Brabender, V. (1985). Time-limited impatient group therapy: A developmental model. *International Journal of Group Psychotherapy, 35,* 373–390.

Brown, B. M. (1995). THe bill of rights for people with disabilities in group work. *Journal for Specialists in Group Work, 20*(2), 71–75.

Burlingame, G. M., & Fuhriman, A. (1990). Time-limited group therapy. *The Counseling Psychologist, 18*(1), 93–118.

Coe, D. M., & Zimpfer, D. G. (1996). Infusing solution-oriented theory and techniques into group work. *Journal for Specialists in Group Work, 21*(1), 49–57.

Corey, G. (1995). *Theory and practice of group counseling* (4th ed.). Pacific Grove, CA: Brooks/Cole.

Corey, M. S., & Corey, G. (1997). *Groups: Process and practice* (5th ed.). Pacific Grove, CA: Brooks/Cole.

Couch, R. D. (1994, February). Changes in the theory and practice of individual psychotherapy by the year 2003. *The Advocate,* p. 6.

Couch, R. D. (1995). Four steps for conducting a pregroup screening interview. *Journal for Specialists in Group Work, 20*(1), 18–25.

Couch, R. D., & Childers, J. H., Jr. (1989). A discussion of differences between group therapy and family therapy: Implications for counselor training and practice. *Journal for Specialists in Group Work, 14*(4), 226–231.

de Shazer, S. (1985). *Keys to solution in brief therapy.* New York: Norton.

de Shazer, S. (1988). *Clues: Investigating solutions in brief therapy.* New York: Norton.

Elliot, G. (1989). An interview with George M. Gazda. *Journal for Specialists in Group Work, 14*(3), 131–140.

Forester-Miller, H. (1989). Dr. Irvin Yalom discusses group psychotherapy. *Journal for Specialists in Group Work, 14*(4), 196–201.

Fuhriman, A., & Burlingame, G. M. (1990). Consistency of matter: A comparative analysis of individual and group process variables. *The Counseling Psychologist, 18*(1), 6–63.

Gazda, G. M. (1989). *Group counseling: A developmental approach* (4th ed.). Boston: Allyn & Bacon.

Gilligan, C. (1982). *In a different voice: Psychological theory and women's development.* Cambridge, MA: Harvard University Press.

Gregg, C. (1994). Group work with single fathers. *Journal for Specialists in Group Work, 19,* 95–101.

Hines, M. (1988). Similarities and differences in group and family therapy. *Journal for Specialists in Group Work, 13*(4), 173–179.

Horne, A. M. (1993). Telling stories: The ecosystem model (Editorial). *Journal for Specialists in Group Work, 18,* 98.

Horne, A. M. (1995). Changes and challenges in group work. *Journal for Specialists in Group Work, 20*(2), 67–68.

Horne, A. M. (1996). The changing world of group work. *Journal for Specialists in Group Work, 21*(1), 2–3.

Jacobs, E. E., Harvill, R. L., & Masson, R. L. (1997). *Group counseling: Strategies and skills* (3rd ed.). Pacific Grove, CA: Brooks/Cole.

Johnson, I. H., Torres, J. S., Coleman, V. D., & Smith, M. C. (1995). Issues and strategies in leading cultural diverse counseling groups. *Journal for Specialists in Group Work, 20*(3), 143–150.

Juhnke, G. A., & Osborne, W. L. (1997). The solution-focused debriefing group: An integrated postviolence group intervention for adults. *Journal for Specialists in Group Work, 22*(1), 66–76.

Kottler, J. A. (1994). Working with difficult group members. *Journal for Specialists in Group Work, 19*(1), 3–10.

Lynn, S. J., & Frauman, D. (1985). Group psychotherapy. In S. J. Lynn & F. P. Garske (Eds.), *Contemporary psychotherapies: Model and methods* (pp. 419–458). Columbus, OH: Merrill.

McRae, M. B. (1994). Interracial group dynamics: A new perspective. *Journal for Specialists in Group Work, 19*(3), 168–174.

Mitchell, J. T., & Everly, G. S. (1993). *Critical Incident Stress Debriefing: An operations manual for the prevention of traumatic stress among emergency services and disaster workers.* Ellicott City, MD: Chevron.

Nelson-Jones, R. (1992). *Group leadership: A training approach.* Pacific Grove, CA: Brooks/Cole.

Ohlsen, M. M. (1970). *Group counseling.* New York: Holt, Rinehart, & Winston.

Patterson, J. B., McKenzie, B., & Jenkins, J. (1995). Creating accessible groups for individuals with disabilities. *Journal for Specialists in Group Work, 20*(2), 76–82.

Rittenhouse, J. A. (1997). Feminist principles in survivor's groups: Out-of-group contact. *Journal for Specialists in Group Work, 22*(2), 111–119.

Schultz, W. C. (1977). *FIRO-B* (2nd ed.). Palo Alto, CA: Consulting Psychologists Press.

Sklare, G., Keener, R., & Mas, C. (1990). Preparing members for "here and now" group counseling. *Journal for Specialists in Group Work, 15*(3), 141–148.

Thompson, R. A. (1993). Posttraumatic stress and posttraumatic loss debriefing: Brief strategic intervention for survivors of sudden loss. *The School Counselor, 41,* 16–22.

Unger, R. (1989). Selection and composition criteria in group psychotherapy. *Journal for Specialists in Group Work, 14*(3), 151–157.

Vacc, N. A. (1989). Group counseling: C. H. Patterson—A personalized view. *Journal for Specialists in Group Work, 14*(1), 4–15.

Vinson, M. L. (1995). Employing family therapy in group counseling with college students: Similarities and a technique employed in both. *Journal for Specialists in Group Work, 20*(4), 240–252.

Waldo, M., & Bauman, S. (1998). Regrouping the categorization of group work: A goals and process (GAP) matrix for groups. *Journal for Specialists in Group Work, 23-2,* 215–224.

Walter, J., & Peller, J. (1992). *Becoming solution-focused in brief therapy.* New York: Brunner/Mazel.

Whitaker, C. A., & Keith, D. V. (1981). Symbolic-experiential family therapy. In A. S. Gurman & D. P. Kniskern (Eds.), *Handbook of family therapy* (pp. 187–225). New York: Brunner/Mazel.

Yalom, I. D. (1995). *The theory and practice of group psychotherapy* (4th ed.). New York: Basic Books.

Yalom, I. D., & Lieberman, M. (1971). A study of encounter group casualties. *Archives of General Psychiatry, 25,* 16–30.

Chapter 13

Arbona, C. (1996). Career theory and practice in a multicultural context. In M. L. Savickas & W. B. Walsh (Eds.), *Handbook of care theory and practice.* Palo Alto, CA: Davies-Black.

Axelson, J. A. (1997). *Counseling and development in a multicultural society* (3rd ed.). Belmont, CA: Wadsworth.

Bandura, A. (1986). *Several foundations of thought and action: A social cognition theory.* Englewood Cliffs, NJ: Prentice-Hall.

Bandura, A. (1989). Human agency in social cognitive theory. *American Psychologist, 44*(9), 1175–1184.

Bansberg, B., & Sklare, J. (1986). *The career decision diagnostic assessment.* Monterey, CA: CTB/McGraw-Hill.

Betz, N. E. (1994). Self-concept theory in career development and counseling. *The Career Development Quarterly, 43*(1), 32–42.

Betz, N. E., & Hackett, G. (1986). Applications of self-efficacy theory to understanding career choice behavior. *Journal of Social and Clinical Psychology, 4,* 279–289.

Birk, J. M., & Brooks, L. (1986). Required skills and training needs of recent counseling psychology graduates. *Journal of Counseling Psychology, 33,* 320–325.

Blustein, D. L. (1987). Integrating career counseling and psychotherapy: A comprehensive treatment strategy. *Psychotherapy, 24,* 794–799.

Blustein, D. L., & Spengler, P. M. (1995). Personal adjustment: Career counseling and psychotherapy. In

W. B. Walsh & S. H. Osipow (Eds.), *Handbook of Vocational Psychology* (2nd ed.) (pp. 295–329). Hillsdale, NJ: Erlbaum.

Bonett, R. M. (1994). Marital status and sex: Impact on self-efficacy. *Journal of Counseling and Development, 73*(2), 187–190.

Brooks, L. (1990). Recent developments in theory building. In D. Brown, L. Brooks, & Associates (Eds.), *Career choice and development* (2nd ed.). San Francisco, CA: Jossey-Bass.

Brown, D. (1987). The status of Holland's theory of vocational choice. *Career Development Quarterly, 36,* 13–23.

Carson, A., & Mowsesian, R. (1990). Some remarks on Gati's theory of career decision-making models. *Journal of Counseling Psychology, 37*(4), 502–507.

Carter, R. T., & Swanson, J. L. (1990). The validity of the Strong Interest Inventory with Black Americans: A review of the literature. *Journal of Vocational Behavior, 36,* 195–209.

Chartrand, J. M. (1996). Linking theory and practice: A sociocognitive interactional model for career counseling. In M. L. Savickas & W. B. Walsh (Eds.), *Handbook of career counseling theory and practice* (pp. 121–134). Palo Alto, CA: Davies-Black.

Chung, Y. B. (1995). Career decision making of lesbian, gay, and bisexual individuals. *The Career Development Quarterly, 44*(2), 178–190.

Drummond, R. J. (1992). *Appraisal procedures for counselors and helping professionals* (2nd ed.). Columbus, Ohio: Merrill.

Dungy, G. (1984). Computer-assisted guidance: Determining who is ready. *Journal of College Student Personnel, 25,* 539–546.

Engels, D. W., Minor, C. W., Sampson, J. P., & Splete, H. H. (1995). Career counseling specialty: History, development, and prospect. *Journal of Counseling and Development, 74*(2), 134–138.

Fassinger, R. E. (1995). From invisibility to integration: Lesbian identity in the workplace. *The Career Development Quarterly, 44*(2), 148–167.

Feller, R. W. (1995). Action planning for personal competitiveness in the "broken workplace." *Journal of Employment Counseling, 32,* 154–163.

Festinger, L. (1957). *A theory of cognitive dissonance.* Stanford, CA: Stanford University Press.

Fitzgerald, L. F., & Rounds, J. B. (1989). Vocational behavior, 1988: A critical analysis. *Journal of Vocational Behavior, 35,* 105–163.

Fosterling, F. (1980). Attributional aspects of cognitive behavior modification: A theoretical approach and suggestions for techniques. *Cognitive Therapy and Research, 24,* 27–37.

Gati, I. (1986). Making career decisions: A sequential elimination approach. *Journal of Counseling Psychology, 33,* 408–417.

Gati, I. (1990a). Interpreting and applying career decision-making models: Comments on Carson and Mowsesian. *Journal of Counseling Psychology, 32*(4), 508–514.

Gati, I. (1990b). Why, when, and how to take into account the uncertainty involved in career decisions. *Journal of Counseling Psychology 37*(3), 277–280.

Gati, I. (1994). Computer-assisted career counseling: Dilemmas, problems, and possible solutions. *Journal of Counseling and Development, 73*(1), 51–56.

Gati, I., Fassa, N., & Houminer, D. (1995). Applying decision theory to career counseling practice: The sequential elimination approach. *Career Development Quarterly, 43,* 211–220.

Gati, I., & Tikotzki, Y. (1989). Strategies for collection and processing of occupational information in making career decisions. *Journal of Counseling Psychology, 35*(3), 430–439.

Goodman, J. (1994). Career adaptability in adults: A construct whose time has come. *The Career Development Quarterly, 43*(1), 74–84.

Gottfredson, L. S. (1981). Circumscription and compromise: A developmental theory of occupational aspirations. *Journal of Counseling Psychology Monograph, 28,* 545–579.

Gysbers, N. C., & Moore, E. J. (1987). *Career counseling: Skills and techniques for practitioners.* Englewood Cliffs, NJ: Prentice-Hall.

Hackett, G., & Betz, N. E. (1981). A self-efficacy approach to the career development of women. *Journal of Vocational Behavior, 18,* 326–339.

Hackett, G., & Byars, A. M. (1996). Social cognitive theory and the career development of African American women. *The Career Development Quarterly, 4*(4), 322–340.

Hanson, J. C., & Campbell, D. P. (1985). *Manual for the SVIB-SCII* (4th ed.). Palo Alto, CA: Consulting Psychologists Press.

Harmon, L. W. (1996). A moving target: The widening gap between theory and practice. In M. L. Savickas & W. B. Walsh (Eds.), *Handbook of career counseling theory and practice* (pp. 37–44). Palo Alto, CA: Davies-Black.

Harmon, L. W., Hansen, J. C., Borgen, F. H., & Hammer, A. L. (1994). *Strong Interest Inventory: Application and technical guide.* Palo Alto, CA: Consulting Psychologists Press.

Haviland, M. G., & Hanson, J. C. (1987). Criterion validity of the Strong-Campbell Interest Inventory for American Indian college students. *Measurement and*

Evaluation in Counseling and Development, 19, 196–201.

Henderson, S., Hesketh, B., & Tuffin, K. (1988). A test of Gottfredson's theory of circumscription. *Journal of Vocational Behavior, 32,* 37–48.

Heppner, M. J., & Johnston, J. A. (1985). Computerized career guidance and information systems: Guidelines for selection. *Journal of College Students Personnel, 26,* 156–163.

Herr, E. L. (1996). Toward the convergence of career theory and practice: Mythology, issues, and possibilities. In M. L. Savickas & W. B. Walsh (Eds.), *Handbook of career counseling theory and practice* (pp. 13–36). Palo Alto, CA: Davies-Black.

Hesketh, B., Elmslie, S., & Kaldor, W. (1990). Career compromises: An alternative account to Gottfredson's theory. *Journal of Counseling Psychology, 37* (1), 49–56.

Hill, C. E., Tanney, M. F., & Leonard, M. M. (1977). Counselor reactions to female clients: Type of problem, age of client, and sex of counselor. *Journal of Counseling Psychology, 24,* 60–65.

Hilton, T. L. (1962). Career decision making. *Journal of Counseling Psychology, 9,* 291–298.

Holland, J. L. (1973). *Making vocational choices: A theory of careers.* Englewood Cliffs, NJ: Prentice-Hall.

Holland, J. L. (1985a). *Making vocational choices: A theory of vocational personalities and work environments* (2nd ed.). Englewood Cliffs, NJ: Prentice-Hall.

Holland, J. L. (1985b). *Manual for the vocational preference inventory.* Odessa, FL: Psychological Assessment Resources.

Holland, J. L. (1992). *Making vocational choices: A theory of vocational personalities and work environments* (2nd ed.). Odessa, FL: Psychological Assessment Resources.

Holland, J. L. (1994). *Self-directed search.* Odessa, FL: Psychological Assessment Resources.

Holland, J. L. (1996). Exploring careers with a typology: What we have learned and some new directions. *American Psychologist, 51*(4), 397–406.

Holland, J. L., Daieger, D. C., & Power, P. G. (1980). Some diagnostic scales for research in decision making and personality: Identity information and barriers. *Journal of Personality and Social Psychology, 39,* 1191–1200.

Holland, J. L., Johnston, J. A., & Asama, N. F. (1994). More evidence for the relationship between Holland's personality types and personality variables. *Journal of Career Assessment, 2,* 331–340.

Holt, P. A. (1989). Differential effects of status and interest in the process of compromise. *Journal of Counseling Psychology, 36,* 42–47.

Jepsen, D. A. (1996). Relationships between developmental career counseling theory and practice. In M. L. Savickas & W. B. Walsh (Eds.), *Handbook of career counseling theory and practice,* Palo Alto, CA: Davies-Black.

Johnston, J. A., Buescher, K. L., & Heppner, M. J. (1988). Computerized career information and guidance systems: Caveat emptor. *Journal of Counseling and Development, 57*(1), 39–41.

Kivlighan, D. M., Johnston, J. A., Hogan, R. S., & Mauer, E. (1994). Who benefits from computerized career counseling? *Journal of Counseling and Development, 27*(3), 289–292.

Kivlighan, D. M., Jr., & Shapiro, R. M. (1987). Holland type as a predictor of benefit from self-help career counseling. *Journal of Counseling Psychology, 34* (3), 326–329.

Kjos, D. (1995). Linking career counseling to personality disorders. *Journal of Counseling and Development, 73*(6), 592–597.

Krumboltz, J. D. (1979). A social learning theory of career decision making. In A. M. Mitchell, F. B. Jones, & J. D. Krumboltz (Eds.), *Social learning theory and career decision making.* Cranston, RI: Carroll.

Krumboltz, J. D. (1994). The career beliefs inventory. *Journal of Counseling and Development, 72*(4), 424–428.

Krumboltz, J. D. (1996). A learning theory of career counseling. In M. L. Savickas & W. B. Walsh (Eds.), *Handbook of career counseling theory and practice* (pp. 55–80). Palo Alto, CA: Davies-Black.

Kuder, G. F. (1964). *Kuder general interest survey: Manual.* Chicago: Science Research Associates.

Lapan, R. T., Boggs, K. R., & Morrill, W. H. (1989). Self-efficacy as a mediator of investigative and realistic general occupational themes on the Strong-Campbell Interest Inventory. *Journal of Counseling Psychology, 36,* 176–182.

Larson, J. H., Busby, D. M., Wilson, S., Medora, N., & Allgood, S. (1994). The multidimensional assessment of career decision problems: The career decision diagnostic assessment. *Journal of Counseling and Development, 72*(3), 323–328.

Lent, R. W., Brown, S. D., & Hackett, G. (1994). Toward a unifying social cognitive theory of career and academic interest, choice, and performance. *Journal of Vocational Behavior, 45,* 79–122.

Lent, R. W., & Hackett, G. (1987). Career self-efficacy: Empirical status and future divisions. *Journal of Vocational Behavior, 30,* 347–382.

Leong, F. T. L., & Chou, E. L. (1994). The role of ethnic identity and acculturation in the vocational behavior of Asian Americans: An integrative review. *Journal of Vocational Behavior, 44,* 155–172.

Leung, S. A., & Plake, B. S. (1990). A choice dilemma approach for examining the relative importance of sex type and prestige preferences in the process of career choice compromise. *Journal of Counseling Psychology, 37*(4), 399–406.

Levinson, E. M. (1994). Current vocational assessment models for students with disabilities. *Journal of Counseling and Development, 73*(1), 94–101.

Luzzo, D. A. (1996). A psychometric evaluation of the career decision-making self-efficacy scale. *Journal of Counseling and Development, 74*(3), 276–279.

Matsui, T., Ikeda, H., & Ohnishi, R. (1989). Relations of sex-typed socializations to career self-efficacy expectations of college students. *Journal of Vocational Behavior, 35,* 1–16.

Matsui, T., & Onglatco, M-L. (1992). Career self-efficacy as a moderator of the relation between occupational stress and strain. *Journal of Vocational Behavior, 41,* 79–88.

Maze, M. (1984). How to select a computerized guidance system. *Journal of Counseling and Development, 63*(3), 158–162.

Melnick, R. R. (1975). Counseling responses as a function of method of problem presentation and type of problem. *Journal of Counseling Psychology, 22,* 108–112.

Mitchell, L. K., & Krumboltz, J. D. (1987). The effects of cognitive restructuring and decision-making training on career indecision. *Journal of Counseling and Development, 66,* 171–174.

Mitchell, L. K., & Krumboltz, J. D. (1990). Social learning approach to career decision making: Krumboltz's theory. In D. Brown, L. Brooks, & Associates (Eds.), *Career choice and development* (2nd ed.). San Francisco, CA: Jossey-Bass.

Morrow, P. C., Mullen, E. J., & McElvoy, J. C. (1990). Vocational behavior, 1989: The year in review. *Journal of Vocational Behavior, 37,* 121–195.

Oliver, L. W., & Spokane, A. R. (1983). Research integration: Approaches, problems and recommendations for research reporting. *Journal of Counseling Psychology, 30,* 252–257.

Oliver, L. W., & Spokane, A. R. (1988). Career-intervention outcome: What contributes to clients' gain? *Journal of Counseling Psychology, 35*(4), 447–462.

Osipow, S. H. (1987). Counseling psychology: Theory, research, and practice in career counseling. *Annual Review of Psychology, 38,* 257–278.

Osipow, S. H. (1990). Convergence in theories of career choice and development: Review and prospects. *Journal of Vocational Behavior, 36,* 122–131.

Osipow, S. H. (1996). *Theories of career development* (4th ed.). Englewood Cliffs, NJ: Prentice-Hall.

Parson, F. (1909). *Choosing a vocation.* Boston: Houghton Mifflin.

Phillips, S. D., & Blustein, D. L. (1994). Readiness for career choices: Planning, exploring, and deciding. *The Career Development Quarterly,* 63–73.

Phillips, S. D., Cairo, P. C., Blustein, D. L., & Myers, R. A. (1988). Career development and behavior, 1987: A review. *Journal of Vocational Behavior, 33,* 119–184.

Prince, J. P. (1995). Influences on the career development of gay men. *The Career Development Quarterly, 44*(2), 148–167.

Raskin, P. M. (1987). *Vocational counseling: A guide for the practitioner.* New York: Teacher's College Press.

Richardson, M. S. (1996). From career counseling to counseling/psychotherapy and work, job, and career. In M. L. Savickas & W. B. Walsh (Eds.), *Handbook of career counseling theory and practice* (pp. 347–360). Palo Alto, CA; Davies-Black.

Roe, A. (1956). *The psychology of occupations.* New York: Wiley.

Roe, A., & Lunneborg, P. W. (1990). Personality development and career choice. In D. Brown, L. Brooks, & Associates (Eds.), *Career choice and development.* San Francisco, CA: Jossey-Bass.

Salomone, P. R. (1988). Career counseling. Steps and stages beyond Parsons. *Career Development Quarterly, 36,* 218–221.

Sampson, J. P. (1994). Factors influencing the effective use of computer-assisted career guidance: The North American experience. *British Journal of Guidance and Counselling, 22*(1), 91–106.

Sampson, J. P., Jr., Shahnasarian, M., & Reardon, R. C. (1987). Computer-assisted career guidance: A national perspective on the use of DISCOVER and SIGI. *Journal of Counseling and Development, 65*(8), 416–419.

Savickas, M. L. (1989). Annual review: Practice and research in career counseling and development. *The Career Development Quarterly, 38,* 100–134.

Savickas, M. L. (1994). A festschrift for Donald E. Super. *The Career Development Quarterly, 43*(1), 3.

Savickas, M. L. (1996). A framework for linking career theory and practice. In M. L. Savickas & W. B. Walsh (Eds.), *Handbook of career counseling theory and practice* (pp. 191–208). Palo Alto, CA: Davies-Black.

Savickas, M. L., & Walsh, W. B. (1996). Toward convergence between career theory and practice. In M. L. Savickas & W. B. Walsh (Eds.), *Handbook of career counseling theory and practice* (pp. xi–xvi). Palo Alto, CA: Davies-Black.

Seligman, L. (1994). *Developmental career counseling and assessment* (2nd. ed.). Thousand Oaks, CA: Sage.

Sharf, R. S. (1997). *Applying career development theory to counseling* (2nd ed.). Pacific Grove, CA: Brooks/Cole.

Slaney, R. B., & Russell, J. E. A. (1987). Perspectives on vocational behavior, 1986: A review. *Journal of Vocational Behavior, 31,* 111–173.

Spengler, P. M., Blustein, D. L., & Strohmer, D. C. (1990). Diagnostic and treatment overshadowing of vocational problems by personal problems. *Journal of Counseling Psychology, 37*(4), 372–381.

Stoltz-Loike, M. (1996). Annual review: Practice and research in career development and counseling—1995. *The Career Development Quarterly,* 99–140.

Super, D. E. (1957). *The psychology of careers.* New York: Harper & Row.

Super, D. E. (1970). *Work values inventory.* Boston: Houghton Mifflin.

Super, D. E. (1980). A life-span, life space approach to career development. *Journal of Vocational Behavior, 16,* 282–298.

Super, D. E. (1990). A life-span, life space approach. In D. Brown, L. Brooks, & Associates (Eds.). *Career choice and development* (2nd ed.). San Francisco, CA: Jossey-Bass.

Swanson, J. L. (1992). Vocational behavior, 1989–1991; life-span career development and reciprocal interaction of work and nonwork. *Journal of Vocational Behavior, 41,* 101–161.

Taylor, N. B., & Pryor, R. G. L. (1985). Exploring the process of compromise in career decision making. *Journal of Vocational Behavior, 27,* 171–190.

Thompson, J. M., Flynn, R. J., & Griffith, S. A. (1994). Congruence and coherence as predictors of congruent employment outcomes. *The Career Development Quarterly, 42,* 271–281.

Wagner, E. (1971). Structural analysis: A theory of personality based on projective techniques. *Journal of Personality Assessment, 35,* 422–435.

Walsh, W. B., & Srsic, C. (1995). Annual Review: Vocational behavior and career development—1994. *Career Development Quarterly, 44*(2), 98–145.

Watkins, C. E., Jr., Lopez, F. G., Campbell, V. L., & Himmell, C. D. (1986). Contemporary counseling psychology: Results of a national survey. *Journal of Counseling Psychology, 33,* 301–309.

Watkins, C. E., Jr., Schneider, L. J., Cox, J. R. H., & Reinberg, J. A. (1987). Clinical psychology and counseling psychology: On similarities and differences revisited. *Professional Psychology: Research and Practice, 18,* 530–535.

Watkins, C. E. Jr., & Subich, L. M. (1995). Annual Review, 1992–1994: Career development, reciprocal work/non-work interaction, and women's workforce participation. *Journal of Vocational Behavior, 47,* 109–163.

Watts, A. G. (1996). Toward a policy for lifelong career development: A transatlantic perspective. *The Career Development Quarterly, 45*(1), 41–53.

Weinrach, S. G., & Srebalus, D. J. (1990). Holland's theory of careers. In D. Brown, L. Brooks, & Associates (Eds.), *Career Choice and Development* (2nd ed.). San Francisco, CA: Jossey-Bass.

Yost, E., & Corbishley, M. (1987). *Career counseling: A psychological approach.* San Francisco, CA: Jossey-Bass.

Zunker, V. G. (1997). *Career counseling: Applied concepts of life planning* (5th ed.). Monterey, CA: Brooks/Cole.

Zytowski, D. G. (1985). *Kuder Occupational Interest Survey Form DD Manual Supplement.* Chicago: Science Research Associates.

Zytowski, D. G. (1994). A super contribution to vocational theory: Work values. *The Career Development Quarterly, 43*(1), 25–31.

Zytowski, D. G., & Warman, R. E. (1982). The changing use of tests in counseling. *Measurement and Evaluation in Guidance, 15,* 147–152.

Chapter 14

Alva, S. A. (1991). Academic invulnerability among Mexican-American students: The importance of protective resources and appraisals. *Hispanic Journal of Behavioral Sciences, 13*(1), 18–34.

American Counseling Association. (1997). *Code of ethics and standards of practice.* Alexandria, VA: Author.

Arellano, A. R., & Padilla, A. M. (1996). Academic invulnerability among a select group of Latino university students. *Hispanic Journal of Behavioral Sciences, 18*(4), 485–507.

ASCA Role Statement (1990). *American School Counselor Association role statement.* Alexandria, VA: ASCA.

Aubrey, R. F. (1982). A house divided: Guidance and counseling in 20th century America. *The Personnel and Guidance Journal, 761,* 198–204.

Baker, S. (1995). Qualitative research has a place in the school counseling literature. *The School Counselor, 42*(5), 339–340.

Bangert-Drowns, R. L. (1988). The effects of school-based substance abuse education: A meta-analysis. *Journal of Drug Education, 18,* 243–264.

Bearden, L. J., Spencer, W. A., & Moracco, J. C. (1989). A study of high school dropouts. *The School Counselor, 37,* 113–120.

Bello, G. A. (1989). Counseling handicapped students: A cognitive approach. *The School Counselor, 36,* 298–304.

Bennett, W. J. (1986). *What works: Schools without drugs.* Washington, DC: U.S. Department of Education.

Berger, K. S., & Thompson, R. A. (1995). *The developing person through the childhood and adolescence* (4th ed.). New York: Worth.

Bergin, J. J., Miller, S. E., Bergin, J. W., & Koch, R. E. (1990). The effects of a comprehensive guidance model on a rural school's counseling program. *Elementary School Guidance & Counseling, 25*(1), 37–45.

Blocher, D. H. (1974). *Developmental counseling* (2nd ed.). New York: Roland Press.

Blocher, D. H. (1987). *The professional counselor.* New York: Macmillan.

Bonebrake, C. R., & Borgers, S. B. (1984, February). Counselor role as perceived by counselors and principals. *Elementary School Guidance & Counseling,* 194–199.

Bonnington, S. B. (1993). Solution-focused brief therapy: Helpful interventions for school counselors. *The School Counselor, 41*(2), 126–128.

Borders, D. L., & Drury, R. D. (1992). Comprehensive school counseling programs: A review for policy makers and practitioners. *Journal of Counseling and Development, 70*(4), 487–498.

Bowker, M. (1982). Children of divorce: Being in between. *Elementary School Guidance & Counseling, 17,* 126–130.

Brake, K. J. (1988). Counseling young children of alcoholics. *Elementary School Guidance & Counseling, 23,* 106–111.

Brooks-Gunn, J., McCormick, M. C., Gunn, R. W., Shorter, T., Wallace, C. Y., & Heagerty, M. C. (1989). Outreach as casefindings: The process of locating low-income pregnant women. *Medical Care, 27*(2), 95–102.

Brooks-Gunn, J., McCormick, M. C., & Heagerty, M. C. (1988). Preventing infant mortality and morbidity: Developmental perspectives. *American Journal of Orthopsychiatry, 58,* 288–296.

Bruce, M. A. (1995). Brief counseling: An effective model for change. *The School Counselor, 42*(5), 353–363.

Burke, D. M., & DeStreek, L. V. (1989). Children of divorce: An application of Hammond's group counseling for children. *Elementary School Guidance & Counseling, 24,* 112–118.

Campbell, C. A. (1993). Play, the fabric of elementary school counseling programs. *Elementary School Guidance and Counseling, 28*(1), 10–16.

Campbell, C. A., & Dahir, C. A. (1997). *The National Standards for School Counseling Programs.* Alexandria, VA: ASCA.

Capuzzi, D. (1988). Personal and social competency: Developing skills for the future. In G. R. Walz & J. C. Bleuer (Eds.), *Building strong school counseling programs.* Alexandria, VA: American Association for Counseling and Development.

Carmichael, K. D. (1994). Sand play as an elementary school strategy. *Elementary School Guidance and Counseling, 28*(4), 302–307.

Casey, J. A. (1995). Developmental issues for school counselors using technology. *Elementary School Guidance and Counseling, 30*(1), 26–34.

Ciechalski, J. C., & Schmidt, M. W. (1995). The effects of social skills training on students with exceptionalities. *Elementary School Guidance and Counseling, 29*(3), 217–222.

Clair, D., & Genest, M. (1987). Variables associated with the adjustment of offspring of alcoholic fathers. *Journal of Studies on Alcohol, 48,* 345–356.

Clarizio, H. F., & McCoy, G. F. (1983). *Behavior disorders in children.* New York: Harper & Row.

Clewell, B. C., Brooks-Gunn, J., & Benasich, A. A. (1989). Evaluating child-related outcomes of teenage parenting programs. *Family Relations, 38*(2), 201–209.

Cole, C. G. (1988). The school counselor: Image and impact, counselor role and function, 1960s to 1980 and beyond. In G. R. Walz & J. C. Bleuer (Eds.), *Building strong school counseling programs.* Alexandria, VA: American Association for Counseling and Development.

College Entrance Examination Board. (1987). *Keeping options open: Recommendations, final reports of the commission on precollege guidance and counseling.* New York: Author.

Cooley, J. J. (1998). Gay and lesbian adolescents: Presenting problems and the counselor's role. *Professional School Counseling, 1*(3), 30–34.

Conger, J. J., & Peterson, A. C. (1984). *Adolescence and youth: Psychological development in a changing world.* New York: Harper & Row.

Dade County Public Schools. (1985). *Dropout prevention/ reduction programs and activities* (p. 22). Miami, FL: Author.

Dahir, C. (1997). National standards for school counseling programs: A pathway to excellence. *The ASCA Counselor, 35*(2), 11.

Dinkmeyer, D. C. (1971). The "C" group: Integrating knowledge and experience to change behavior. *The Counseling Psychologist, 3,* 63–72.

Dinkmeyer, D. C. (1973). The parent "C" group. *Personnel and Guidance Journal, 52,* 4.

Dinkmeyer, D., & Carlson, J. (1973). *Consultation: Facilitating human potential and processes.* Columbus, OH: Merrill/Macmillan.

Dinkmeyer, D., McKay, G., Dinkmeyer, D., Jr., Dinkmeyer, J. S., & Carlson, J. (1985). *PREP for effective family living. Student handbook.* Circle Pines, MN: American Guidance Service.

Dougherty, A. M. (1995). *Consultation: Practice and perspectives in school and community settings* (2nd ed.). Pacific Grove, CA: Brooks/Cole.

Dysinger, B. J. (1993). Conflict resolution for intermediate children. *The School Counselor, 40*(4), 301–308.

Eggen, P., & Kauchak, D. (1994). *Educational psychology: Classroom connections* (2nd ed.). Columbus OH: Merrill.

Emmons, R., & Nystul, M. S. (1994). The effects of a prenatal course including PREP for effective family living on self-esteem and parenting attitudes of adolescents: A brief report. *Adolescence, 29,* 935–938.

Erikson, E. H. (1963). *Childhood and society* (2nd ed.). New York: W. W. Norton.

Ferris, P. A. (1988). Future directions for elementary/middle school counseling. In G. R. Walz & J. C. Bleuer (Eds.), *Building strong school counseling programs.* Alexandria, VA: American Association for Counseling and Development.

Fontaine, J. H. (1998). Evidencing a need: School counselor's experiences with gay and lesbian students. *Professional School Counseling, 1*(3), 8–14.

Frieman, B. B. (1993). Children of divorced parents: Action steps for the counselor to involve fathers. *Elementary School Guidance and Counseling, 28*(3), 197–205.

Furstenberg, F. F., Jr., Brooks-Gunn, J., & Chase-Lansdale, L. (1989). *Unplanned parenthood: The social consequences of teenage childbearing.* New York: Free Press.

Garrett, M. W. (1995). Between two worlds: Cultural discontinuity in the dropout of Native American youth. *The School Counselor, 42*(3), 186–195.

George, P. S. (1986). The counselor and modern middle-level schools: New roles in new schools. *The School Counselor, 33*(3), 178–188.

Gerber, P. J. (1986). Counseling the learning disabled. In A. F. Rotatori, P. J. Gerber, F. W. Litton, & R. A. Fox (Eds.), *Counseling exceptional students.* New York: Human Sciences Press.

Gerler, E. R., Jr. (1995). Advancing elementary and middle school counseling through computer technology. *Elementary School Guidance and Counseling, 30* (1), 8–15.

Gerler, E. R., & Anderson, R. F. (1986). The effects of classroom guidance on children's success in school. *Journal of Counseling and Development, 65,* 78–81.

Gibson, R. L. (1989). Prevention and the elementary school counselor. *Elementary School Guidance & Counseling, 24,* 30–36.

Gilligan, C. (1982). *In a different voice: Psychological theories and women's development.* Cambridge, MA: Harvard University Press.

Ginter, E. J., Scalise, J. J., & Presse, N. (1990). The elementary school counselor's role: Perceptions of teachers. *The School Counselor, 38,* 19–23.

Goldberg, R. T. (1974). Adjustment of children with invisible and visible handicaps. *Journal of Counseling Psychology, 21,* 428–432.

Good, G. E., Fischer, A. R., Johnston, J. A., Jr., & Heppner, P. P. (1994). Norman C. Gysbers: A proponent of comprehensive school guidance programs. *Journal of Counseling and Development, 73*(2), 115–120.

Green, R. L. (1988). Image-building activities for the elementary school counselor. *Elementary School Guidance & Counseling, 22*(3), 186–191.

Griffin, H. C., Berger, C., & Rotatori (1986). Counseling the health impaired student. In A. F. Rotatori, P. J. Gerber, F. W. Litton, & R. A. Fox (Eds.), *Counseling exceptional students.* New York: Human Sciences Press.

Griffin, H. C., Sexton, D., Gerber, P. J., & Rotatori, A. F. (1986). Counseling the physically handicapped child. In A. F. Rotatori, P. J. Gerber, F. W. Litton, & R. A. Fox (Eds.), *Counseling exceptional students.* New York: Human Sciences Press.

Griggs, S. A. (1988). The counselor as facilitator of learning. In G. R. Walz & J. C. Bleuer (Eds.), *Building strong school counseling programs.* Alexandria, VA: American Association for Counseling and Development.

Gysbers, N. (1988). Career guidance: A professional heritage and future challenge. In G. R. Walz & J. C. Bleuer (Eds.), *Building strong school counseling programs.* Alexandria, VA: American Association for Counseling and Development.

Gysbers, N., & Henderson, P. (1988). *Developing and managing your school guidance program.* Alexandria, VA: American Association for Counseling and Development.

Hall, A. S., & Lin, M. J. (1994). An integrative consultation framework: A practical tool for elementary school counselors. *Elementary School Guidance and Counseling, 29*(1), 16–27.

Hamachek, D. (1995). Self-concept and school achievement: Interaction dynamics and a tool for assessing the self-concept component. *Journal of Counseling and Development, 73*(4), 419–425.

Hammond, J. (1981). *Group counseling for children of divorce: A guide for the elementary school.* Ann Arbor, MI: Cranbrook.

Hardesty, P. H., & Dillard, J. M. (1994). The role of elementary school counselors compared with their middle and secondary school counterparts. *Elementary School Guidance and Counseling, 29*(2), 83–91.

Hardman, M. L., Drew, C. J., Egan, M. W., & Wolf, B. (1990). *Human exceptionality* (3rd ed.). Boston: Allyn & Bacon.

Havighurst, R. J. (1972). *Developmental tasks and education* (3rd ed.). New York: David McKay.

Heinze, A., & Rotatori, A. F. (1986). Counseling the visually handicapped child. In A. F. Rotatori, P. J. Gerber, F. W. Litton, & R. A. Fox (Eds.), *Counseling exceptional students*. New York: Human Sciences Press.

Helwig, A. A., & Holicky, R. (1994). Substance abuse in persons with disabilities: Treatment considerations. *Journal of Counseling and Development, 72*(3), 227–233.

Hobson, S. M., & Kanitz, H. M. (1996). Multicultural counseling: An ethical issue for school counselors. *The School Counselor, 43*(4), 245–255.

Hubbard, R. L., Brownlee, R. F., & Anderson, R. (1988). Initiation of alcohol and drug abuse in the middle school years. *Elementary School Guidance & Counseling, 23,* 118.

Hughey, K. F., Gysbers, N. C., & Starr, M. (1993). Evaluating comprehensive school guidance programs. *The School Counselor, 41*(1), 31–35.

Hutchinson, R. L., Barrick, A. L., & Groves, M. (1986). Functions of secondary school counselors in the public schools: Ideal and actual. *The School Counselor, 34*(2), 87–91.

Ivey, A. (1986). *Developmental therapy: Theory and practice*. San Francisco: Jossey-Bass.

Kaplan, L. S., & Geoffroy, K. E. (1990). Enhancing the school climate: New opportunities for the counselor. *The School Counselor, 38,* 7–12.

Kaufmann, F. A., Castellanos, Z. F., & Rotatori, A. F. (1986). Counseling the gifted child. In A. F. Rotatori, P. J. Gerber, F. W. Litton, & R. A. Fox (Eds.), *Counseling exceptional students*. New York: Human Sciences Press.

Kelley, R. H., & Rotatori, A. F. (1986). Counseling the language-disordered child. In A. F. Rotatori, P. J. Gerber, F. W. Litton, & R. A. Fox (Eds.), *Counseling exceptional students*. New York: Human Sciences Press.

Kennel, S. E., & Rotatori, A. F. (1986). Counseling the abused child. In A. F. Rotatori, P. J. Gerber, F. W. Litton, & R. A. Fox (Eds.), *Counseling exceptional students*. New York: Human Sciences Press.

LaFountain, R. M., Garner, N. E., & Eliason, G. T. (1996). Solution-focused counseling groups: A key for school counselors. *The School Counselor, 43*(4), 256–267.

Lerner, R., & Naiditch, B. (1985). *Children are people*. St. Paul, MN: Children are People.

Litton, F. W. (1986). Counseling the mentally retarded clinic. In A. F. Rotatori, P. J. Gerber, F. W. Litton, & R. A. Fox (Eds.), *Counseling exceptional students*. New York: Human Sciences Press.

Littrell, J. M., Malia, J. A., & Vanderwood, M. (1995). Single-session brief counseling in a high school. *Journal of Counseling and Development, 73,* 451–458.

Los Angeles Unified School District. (1985). Dropout prevention and recovery. Los Angeles, CA: Author.

MacGregor, J., & Newlon, B. J. (1987). Description of a teenage pregnancy program. *Journal of Counseling and Development, 65,* 447.

Marinoble, R. M. (1998). Homosexuality: A blind spot in the school mirror. *Professional School Counseling, 1*(3), 4–7

Mason, M. J. (1996). Evaluation of an alcohol and other drug use prevention training program for school counselors in a predominantly Mexican American school district. *The School Counselor, 43*(4), 308–316.

Maynard, R. A. (1996). *Kids having kids: A Robin Hood foundation special report on the costs of adolescent childbearing*. New York: The Robin Hood Foundation.

McDowell, W., Coven, A., & Eash, V. (1979). The handicapped: Special needs and strategies for counseling. *Personnel and Guidance Journal, 58,* 228–232.

McIntire, Marion, & Quaglia, R. (1990). Rural school counselors: Their communities and schools. *The School Counselor, 37,* 166–172.

McWhirter, J. J., McWhirter, B. T., McWhirter, A. M., & McWhirter, E. H. (1994). High- and low-risk characteristics of youth: The five Cs of competencies. *Elementary School Guidance and Counseling, 28*(3), 188–196.

Miller, D. R. (1995). The school counselor and Christian fundamentalist families. *The School Counselor, 42* (4), 317–320.

Miller, G. D. (1989). What roles and functions do elementary school counselors have? *Elementary School Guidance & Counseling, 24,* 77–88.

Morse, C. L., & Russell, T. (1988). How elementary counselors see their role: An empirical study. *Elementary School Guidance & Counseling, 23*(1), 44–62.

Muller, L. E., & Hartman, J. (1998). Group counseling for sexual minority youth. *Professional School Counseling, 1*(3), 38–41.

Muro, J. J. (1981). On target—on top. *Elementary School Guidance & Counseling, 15,* 307–314.

Murphy, J. J. (1994). Working with what works: A solution-focused approach to school behavior problems. *The School Counselor, 42*(1), 59–65.

Myrick, R. D. (1987). *Developmental guidance and counseling. A practical approach.* Minneapolis, MN: Educational Media.

Myrick, R. D., & Sabella, R. A. (1995). Cyberspace: New place for counselor supervision. *Elementary School Guidance and Counseling, 30*(1), 35–44.

Nelson, M. D., Thomas, J. V., & Pierce, K. A. (1995). Inside-outside: A classroom discussion model for conflict resolution. *The School Counselor, 42*(5), 399–404.

Neukrug, E. S., Barr, C. G., Hoffman, L. R., & Kaplan, L. S. (1993). Developmental counseling and guidance: A model for use in your school. *The School Counselor, 40*(5), 356–362.

Newcomb, M. D., & Bentler, P. M. (1988). *Consequences of adolescent drug use: Impact on the lives of young adults.* Newbury Park, CA: Sage.

Newcomb, M. D., & Bentler, P. M. (1989). Substance use and abuse among children and teenagers. *American Psychologist, 44*(2), 242–248.

Newcomb, N. S. (1994). Music: A powerful resource for the elementary school counselor. *Elementary School Guidance and Counseling, 29*(2), 150–155.

Nystul, M. S., Emmons, R., & Cockrell, K. (1992). The use of pet therapy in counseling. *New Zealand Journal of Counseling, 14*(1), 32–35.

Oklahoma State Department of Education. (1988). *Building skills for tomorrow: A developmental guidance model.* Oklahoma City: State Board of Affairs.

Paisley, P. O., & Benshoff, J. M. (1996). Applying developmental principles to practice: Training issues for the professional development of school counselors. *Elementary School Guidance and Counseling, 30*(3), 163–169.

Paisley, P. O., & Borders, (1995). School counseling: An emerging specialty. *Journal of Counseling and Development, 74*(2), 150–153.

Paisley, P. O., & DeAngelis-Peace, S. (1995). Developmental principles: A framework for school counseling programs. *Elementary School Guidance and Counseling, 30*(2), 85–93.

Parette, H. P., & Hourcade, J. J. (1995). Disability etiquette and school counselors: A common sense approach toward compliance with the Americans with Disabilities Act. *The School Counselor, 52*(3), 224–233.

Parsons, F. (1909). *Choosing a vocation.* Boston: Houghton Mifflin.

Pearson, J., Lunday, B., Rohrbach, L., & Whitney, D. (1985). *Project SMART: A social approach to drug abuse prevention.* Unpublished curriculum guide, University of Southern California, Health Behavior Research Institute, Los Angeles, CA.

Peer, G. G. (1985). The status of secondary school guidance: A national survey. *The School Counselor, 32*(3), 181–189.

Piaget, J. (1955). *The language and thought of the child.* New York: New American Library. (Original work published 1923)

Public Law 94-142, *The Education for All Handicapped Children Act of 1975* is coded at 20 U.S.C. Sec. 613 et. seq. and its implementing regulations at 45 C.F.R. Part 121a. (1975).

Raiche, B. M., Fox, R., & Rotatori, A. F. (1986). Counseling the mildly behaviorally disordered child. In A. F. Rotatori, P. J. Gerber, F. W. Litton, & R. A. Fox (Eds.), *Counseling exceptional students.* New York: Human Sciences Press.

Ribak-Rosenthal, N., & Russell, T. T. (1994). Dealing with religious differences in December: A school counselor's role. *Elementary School Counseling and Guidance, 28*(4), 295–301.

Ritchie, M. H., & Partin, R. L. (1994). Parent education and consultation activities of school counselors. *The School Counselor, 41*(3), 165–170.

Ritter, K. Y., & O'Neill, C. W. (1995). Moving through loss: The spiritual journey of gay men and lesbian women. In M. T. Burke & J. G. Miranti (Eds.), *Counseling: The spiritual dimension* (pp. 127–141). Alexandria, VA: American Counseling Association.

Robson, B. E. (1988). Changing family patterns: Developmental impacts on children. In J. Carlson & J. Lewis (Eds.), *Counseling the adolescent: Individual, family and school interventions.* Denver, CO: Love.

Rogers, C. R. (1942). *Counseling and psychotherapy.* Boston: Houghton Mifflin.

Rotatori, A. F., Banbury, M., & Sisterhen, D. (1986). Overview of counseling exceptional students. In A. F. Rotatori, P. J. Gerber, F. W. Litton, & R. A. Fox (Eds.), *Counseling exceptional students.* New York: Human Sciences Press.

Rotatori, A. F., Gerber, P. J., Litton, F. W., & Fox, R. A. (Eds.). (1986). *Counseling exceptional students.* New York: Human Sciences Press.

Rowe, F. A. (1989). College students' perceptions of high school counselors. *The School Counselor, 36,* 260–264.

Ruben, A. M. (1989). Preventing school dropouts through classroom guidance. *Elementary School Guidance & Counseling, 24,* 21–29.

Rubisch, J. C. (1995). Promoting postsecondary education in rural schools. *The School Counselor, 42*(5), 404–409.

Russo, T. J., & Kassera, W. (1989). A comprehensive needs-assessment package for secondary school guidance programs. *The School Counselor, 36,* 265–269.

Sandu, D. S., & Portes, P. R. (1995). The proactive model of school counseling. *International Journal for the Advancement of Counselling, 18,* 11–20.

Sisterhen, D., & Rotatori, A. F. (1986). Counseling the hearing-impaired child. In A. F. Rotatori, P. J. Gerber, F. W. Litton, & R. A. Fox (Eds.), *Counseling exceptional students.* New York: Human Sciences Press.

Sutton, J. M., Jr., & Southworth, R. S. (1990). The effect of the rural setting on school counselors. *The School Counselor, 37,* 173–178.

Sweeney, T. J. (1988). Building strong school counseling programs: Implications for counselor preparation. In G. R. Walz & J. C. Bleuer (Eds.), *Building strong school counseling programs.* Alexandria, VA: American Association for Counseling and Development.

Talkington, L. W., & Riley, J. B. (1971). Reduction diets and aggression in institutionalized mentally retarded patients. *American Journal of Mental Deficiency, 76,* 370–372.

Tennyson, W. W., Miller, G. D., Skovholt, T. G., & Williams, R. C. (1989). Secondary school counselors: What do they do? What is important? *The School Counselor, 36,* 253–259.

Thomas, M. D. (1989). The role of the secondary school counselor: The counselor in effective schools. *The School Counselor, 36,* 249–252.

Tobler, N. S. (1986). Meta-analysis of 143 adolescent drug prevention programs: Quantitative outcome results of program participants compared to a control or comparison group. *Journal of Drug Issues, 16,* 537–568.

Vail-Smith, K., Knight, S. M., & White, D. M. (1995). Children of substance abusers in the elementary school: A survey of counselor perceptions. *Elementary School Guidance & Counseling, 29*(3), 163–176.

Wallis, C. (1985, December 9). Children having children. *Time,* 78–90.

Welch, I. D., & McCarroll, L. (1993). The future role of school counselors. *The School Counselor, 41*(1), 48–53.

Werner, E. E. (1986). Resident offspring of alcoholics: A longitudinal study from birth to age 18. *Journal of Studies on Alcoholism, 47,* 34–41.

Whitledge, J. (1994). Cross-cultural counseling: Implications for school counselors in enhancing student learning. *The School Counselor, 41*(5), 314–318.

Wiggins, J. D. (1985). Six steps towards counseling program accountability. *NASSP Bulletin, 69*(485), 28–31.

Zimmerman, M. A., & Arunkumar, R. (1994). Resiliency research: Implications for schools and policy. *Social Policy Report: Society for research in child development, 8*(4), 1–17.

Chapter 15

Albee, G. W., & Ryan-Finn, K. D. (1993). An overview of primary prevention. *Journal of Counseling and Development, 72*(2), 115–123.

Amatea, E. S., & Sherrard, P. A. D. (1994). The ecosystemic view: A choice of lenses. *Journal of Mental Health Counseling, 16*(1), 6–21.

American Psychiatric Association. (1994). *Diagnostic and statistical manual of mental disorders* (4th ed. revised). Washington, DC: Author.

American Psychiatric Association. (1995). Practice guidelines for the treatment of patients with substance use disorders: alcohol, cocaine, opioids. *American Journal of Psychiatry (Supplement), 152*(11), 3–59.

Bachrach, L. L. Managed care: I. Delimiting the concept. *Psychiatric Service, 46*(12), 1229–1230.

Barclay, J. R. (1984, April). Primary prevention and assessment. *The Personnel and Guidance Journal,* 475–478.

Becvar, R. J., & Becvar, D. S. (1994). The ecosystemic story: A story about stories. *Journal of Mental Health Counseling, 16*(1), 22–32.

Bishop, D. R. (1995). Religious values as cross-cultural issues in counseling. In M. T. Burke & J. G. Miranti (Eds.), *Counseling: The spiritual dimension* (pp. 59–72.) Alexandria, VA: American Counseling Association.

Bristow-Braitman, A. (1995). Addiction recovery: 12-step programs and cognitive-behavioral psychology. *Journal of Counseling and Development, 73*(4), 414–418.

Brooks, D. K., & Gerstein, L. H. (1990). Counselor credentialing and interpersonal collaboration. *Journal of Counseling and Development, 68,* 477–484.

Brown, D. (1993). Training consultants: A call to action. *Journal of Counseling and Development, 72*(2), 139–143.

Burtnett, F. E. (1986). *Staffing patterns in mental health agencies and organizations.* Unpublished report, American Association for Counseling and Development, Alexandria, VA.

Caplan, G. (1964). *Principles of preventive psychiatry.* New York: Basic Books.

Caplan, G. (1970). *The theory and practice of mental health consultation.* New York: Basic Books.

Capuzzi, D., & Nystul, M. S. (1986). The suicidal adolescent. In L. B. Golden & D. Capuzzi (Eds.), *Helping families help children: Family interventions with school-related problems* (pp. 23–32). Springfield, IL: Charles C. Thomas.

Cavanaugh, M. E. (1982). *The counseling experience.* Monterey, CA: Brooks/Cole.

Culbertson, F. M. (1997). Depression and gender: An international review. *American Psychologist, 52*(1), 25–31.

Cummings, C., Gordon, J. R., & Marlatt, G. A. (1980). Relapse: Prevention and prediction. In W. R. Miller (Ed.), *The addictive behaviors.* New York: Pergamon Press.

Daniels, M. H., & White, L. J. (1994). Revisiting Auerswald's conundrum—A response to Fong and Lease, and Lanning. *Journal of Mental Health Counseling, 16*(2), 217–225.

Dingman, R. L. (Ed.). (1988). *Licensure for mental health counselors.* Huntington, WV: Marshall University Press.

Durkheim, E. (1897). *Suicide: A study in sociology.* Glencoe, IL: Free Press.

Farren, C., Gray, J. D., & Kaye, B. C. (1984). Mentoring: A boom to career development. *The Personnel and Guidance Journal, 61,* 20–24.

Fisher, K. (1982, November). Debate rages on 1973 Sonell study. *APA Monitor,* pp. 8–9.

Fong, M. L., & Lease, S. H. (1994). Constructivist alternatives: The case for diversity and integration in mental health counseling. *Journal of Mental Health Counseling, 16*(1), 120–124.

Frances, R. J. (1988). Update on alcohol and drug disorder treatment. *Journal of Clinical Psychiatry, 49*(9), 13–17.

Freud, S. (1933). New introductory lectures on psychoanalyses. In J. Strachey (Ed. and Trans.), *The complete psychological works, Vol. 22.* New York: Norton.

George, R. L., & Cristiani, T. S. (1995). *Counseling: Theory and practice* (4th ed.). Englewood Cliffs, NJ: Prentice-Hall.

Gilbert, N. (1982, July). Policy issues in primary prevention. *Social Work,* 293–296.

Gilliland, B. E., & James, R. K. (1997). *Crisis intervention strategies.* (3rd ed.). Pacific Grove, CA: Brooks/Cole.

Ginter, E. J. (1996). Three pillars of mental health counseling: Watch in what you step. *Journal of Mental Health Counseling, 18*(2), 99–107.

Gutterman, J. T. (1996). Doing mental health counseling: A social constructionist re-vision. *Journal of Mental Health Counseling, 18*(3), 228–252.

Hansen, J. C., Himes, B. S., & Meier, S. (1990). *Consultation: Concepts and practices.* Englewood Cliffs, NJ: Prentice-Hall.

Helwig, A. A., & Holicky, R. (1994). Substance abuse in persons with disabilities: Treatment considerations. *Journal of Counseling and Development, 72*(3), 227–233.

Herring, R. D. (1994). Substance use among Native American Indian Youth: A selected review of causality. *Journal of Counseling and Development, 72*(6), 578–584.

Hershenson, D. B., & Power, P. W. (1987). *Mental health counseling.* New York: Pergamon Press.

Hosie, T. W., West, J. D., & MacKey, J. A. (1988). Employment and roles of mental health counselors in substance-abuse centers. *Journal of Mental Health Counseling, 10*(3), 188–198.

Ingersoll, R. E. (1995). Spirituality, religion, and counseling: Dimensions and relationships. In M. T. Burke & J. G. Miranti (Eds.), *Counseling: The spiritual dimension* (pp. 5–18). Alexandria, VA: American Counseling Association.

Ivey, A. E. (1989). Mental health counseling: A developmental process and profession. *Journal of Mental Health Counseling, 11*(1), 26–35.

Johnson, V. E. (1986). *Intervention: A professional guide.* Minneapolis, MN: Johnson Institute.

Kelly, K. R. (1996). Looking to the future: Professional identity, accountability, and change. *Journal of Mental Health Counseling, 18*(3), 195–199.

Kessler, S. (1979, November). Counselor as mediator. *The Personnel and Guidance Journal,* 194–197.

Kiselica, M. S., & Look, C. (1993). Mental health counseling and prevention: Disparity between philosophy and practice? *Journal of Mental Health Counseling, 15*(1), 3–14.

Koenig, H. G. (1997). *Is religion good for your health? The effects of religion on physical and mental health.* New York: Haworth Press.

Koopman, E. J. (1985). The education and training of mediators. In S. Grebs (Ed.), *Divorce and family mediation.* Rockville, MD: Aspen Systems.

Krupp, J. (1982). *Mentoring as a means to personnel growth and improved school climate: A research report.* Colchester, CT: Project Rise.

Kurpius, D. (1978). Consultation theory and process: An integrated model. *The Personnel and Guidance Journal, 56,* 335–378.

Lê, C., Ingvarson, E. P., & Page, R. C. (1995). Alcoholics anonymous and the counseling profession: Philosophies in conflict. *Journal of Counseling and Development, 73*(6), 603–609.

Lewis, J. A., Dana, R. Q., & Blevins, G. A. (1994). *Substance abuse counseling: An individualized approach* (2nd ed.). Pacific Grove, CA: Brooks/Cole.

Locke, D. C. (1993). Diversity in the practice of mental health counseling: *Journal of Mental Health Counseling, 15*(3), 228–231.

Lynch, S. (1980). The mentor link: Bridging education and employment. *Journal of College Placement, 40,* 44–47.

Marlatt, G. A. (1983). The controlled drinking controversy: A commentary. *American Psychologist, 38,* 1097–1110.

Marlatt, G. A., & Gordon, J. R. (Eds.). (1985). *Relapse prevention.* New York: Guilford Press.

Matus, R., & Neuhring, E. M. (1979). Social workers in primary prevention: Action and ideology in mental health. *Community Mental Health Journal, 15,* 33–38.

McDonough, R. L., & Russell, L. (1994). Alcoholism in women: A holistic, comprehensive care model. *Journal of Mental Health Counseling, 16*(4), 459–474.

McMurty, S. C. (1985, January–February). Secondary prevention of child maltreatment: A review. *Social Work,* 42–46.

Mental disorders may affect 1 in 5. (1984, October 3). *Washington Post,* p. A1.

Miller, W. R. (1980). Treating the problem drinker. In W. R. Miller (Ed.), *The addictive behaviors: Treatment of alcoholism, drug abuse, smoking, and obesity.* New York: Pergamon Press.

Miller, W. R., & Munoz, R. F. (1982). *How to control your drinking.* Albuquerque, NM: University of New Mexico Press.

Miranti, J. G., & Burke, M. T. (1995). Spirituality: An integral component of the counseling process. In M. T. Burke & J. G. Miranti (Eds.), *Counseling: The spiritual dimension* (pp. 1–4). Alexandria, VA: American Counseling Association.

Mirin, S. M., Weiss, R. D., Michael, J., & Griffin, M. L. (1988). Psychopathology in substance abusers: Diagnosis and treatment. *American Journal of Drug and Alcohol Abuse, 14*(2), 139–157.

NeJedlo, R. J., Arredondo, P., & Benjamin, L. (1985). *Imagine: A visionary model for the counselors of tomorrow.* Alexandria, VA: Association for Counselor Education and Supervision.

Nicholas, D., Gerstein, L., & Keller, K. (1988). Behavioral medicine and the mental health counselor. Roles and interdisciplinary collaboration. *Journal of Mental Health Counseling, 10,* 79–94.

Othmer, E., & Othmer, S. C. (1989). *The clinical interview: Using DSM-III-R.* Washington, DC: American Psychiatric Press.

Palmo, A. J. (1986). Professional identity of the mental health counselor. In A. J. Palmo & W. J. Weikel (Eds.), *Foundations of mental health counseling.* Springfield, IL: Charles C. Thomas.

Pattison, E. M., & Kaufman, E. (1982). The alcoholism syndrome: Definitions and models. In E. M. Pattison & E. Kaufman (Eds.), *Encyclopedic handbook of alcoholism* (pp. 3–30). New York: Gardner Press.

Pipal, J. E. (1995). Managed care: Is it the corpse in the living room? An Expose. *Psychotherapy, 32*(2), 323–332.

Polich, J. M., Armor, D. M., & Braiker, H. B. (1981). *The course of alcoholism: Four years after treatment.* New York: Wiley.

Polich, J. M., Ellickson, P. L., Reuter, P., & Kahan, J. P. (1984). *Strategies for controlling adolescent drug use.* Santa Monica, CA: Rand.

Prochaska, J. O., DiClemente, C. C., & Norcross, J. C. (1992). In search of how people change: Applications to addictive behaviors. *American Psychologist, 47*(9), 1102–1114.

Puryear, D. A. (1979). *Helping people in crisis.* San Francisco: Jossey-Bass.

Richards, P. S., & Bergin, A. E. (1997). *Strategy for counseling and psychotherapy.* Washington, DC: American Psychological Association.

Richardson, B. K., & Bradley, L. J. (1985). *Community agency counseling: An emerging specialty in counselor education programs.* Alexandria, VA: American Association for Counseling and Development Foundation.

Rigazio-DiGilio, S. A. (1994). A co-constructive-developmental approach. *Journal of Mental Health Counseling, 16*(1), 43–74.

Selzer, M. L. (1971). Michigan alcoholism screening test: The quest for a new diagnostic instrument. *American Journal of Psychiatry, 127,* 1653–1658.

Shaw, M. D., & Goodyear, R. K. (1984, April). Introduction to special issues on primary prevention. *The Personnel and Guidance Journal,* 444–445.

Sherrard, P. A. D., & Amatea, E. S. (1994). Looking through the looking glass: A preview. *Journal of Mental Health Counseling, 16*(1), 3–5.

Shneidman, E. S. (1976). A psychological theory of suicide. *Psychiatric Annals, 6,* 51–66.

Shneidman, E. S. (1984). Suicide. In R. Corsini (Ed.), *Encyclopedia of Psychology, Vol. 3.* New York: Wiley.

Shneidman, E. S., Farberow, N. L., & Litman, R. E. (1976). *The psychology of suicide.* New York: Aronson.

Smith, H. B., & Robinson, G. P. (1995). Mental health counseling: Past, present, and future. *Journal of Counseling and Development, 74*(2), 158–162.

Sobell, M. B., & Sobell, L. C. (1984). The aftermath of heresy: A response to Pendery et al.'s (1982) critique of "Individualized Behavior Therapy for Alcoholics." *Behavior Research and Therapy, 22,* 413–447.

Spruill, D. A., & Fong, M. L. (1990). Defining the domain of mental health counseling: From identity confusion to consensus. *Journal of Mental Health Counseling, 12*(1), 12–23.

Taylor, R. (1979). *The gifted and the talented.* CO: Educational Consultant Agency.

Terrell, M. D. (1993). Ethnocultural factors and substance abuse: Toward culturally sensitive treatment models. *Psychology of Addictive Behaviors, 7*(3), 162–167.

Tesolowski, D. G., Rosenberg, H., & Stein, R. J. (1983, July, August, September). Advocacy intervention: A responsibility of human service professionals. *Journal of Rehabilitation,* 12–17.

Vaillant, G. E. (1977). *Adaptation to life.* Boston: Little, Brown.

Valliant, G. E. (1983). *The natural history of alcoholism.* Cambridge, MA: Harvard University Press.

Volkow, N. D., Wong, G. J., Fischman, M. W., Foltin, R. W., Fowler, J. S., Abumrad, N. N., Vitkuns, S., Logan, J., Gatley, S. J., Poppas, N., Hitzemann, R., & Shea, C. E. (1997). Relationship between subjective effects of cocaine and dopamine transporter occupancy. *Nature, 6627,* 827–833.

Wagner, J., & Gartner, C. G. (1996). *Psychiatric Services, 47*(1), 15–20.

Weikel, W. J. (1985). The American Mental Health Counselors Association. *Journal of Counseling and Development, 63,* 457–460.

Weikel, W. J., & Taylor, S. S. (1979). AMHCA: Membership profile and five journal preferences. *AMHCA Journal, 1,* 89–94.

West, J. D., Hosie, T. W., & Mackey, J. A. (1988). The counselor's role in mental health: An evaluation. *Counselor Education and Supervision, 27,* 233–239.

Witmer, J. M., & Sweeney, J. T. (1995). A holistic model for wellness and prevention over the life span. In M. T. Burke & J. G. Miranti (Eds.), *Counseling: The spiritual dimension* (pp. 19–40). Alexanderia, VA: American Counseling Association.

Witty, C. (1980). *Mediation and society. Conflict management in Lebanon.* New York: Academic.

CREDITS

pages 98–100: Spitzer, R. L., Gibbon, M., Skodol, A. E., Williams, T. B., & First, M. B. (Eds.). (1900). In *Casebook: A learning companion to the D.S.M.IV.* Washington, DC: American Psychiatric Press.

pages 143–144: Reprinted from Pedersen, P. B. (1987). Ten frequent assumptions of cultural bias in counseling. *Journal of Multicultural Counseling and Development, 15*(1): 16–24. © ACA. Reprinted with permission. No further reproduction authorized without written permission of the American Counseling Association.

page 149: Sue, D. W., Bernier, T. E., Durran, A., Feinberg, L., Pedersen, P., Smith, E. T., & Vasquez-Nuhall, E. (1982). Position paper: Cross-cultural counseling competencies. *The Counseling Psychologist, 10,* 45–52. Copyright © 1982 by Sage Publications. Reprinted by permission of Sage Publications, Inc.

page 308: Fuhriman, A., & Burlingame, G. M. (1990). Consistency of matter: A comparative analysis of individual and group process variables. *The Counseling Psychologist, 18,* 6–63. Copyright © 1982 by Sage Publications. Reprinted by permission of Sage Publications, Inc.

pages 312–313: Burlingame, G. M. & Fuhriman, A. (1990). Time-limited group therapy. *The Counseling Psychologist, 18,* 93–118. Copyright © 1982 by Sage Publications. Reprinted by permission of Sage Publications, Inc.

page 328: From Samuel H. Osipow & Louise F. Fitzgerald. *Theories of career development,* 4th ed. © 1996, Allyn & Bacon.

Appendix A: Reprinted from *Codes of Ethics and Standards of Practice* (1997). © ACA. Reprinted with permission. No further reproduction authorized without written permission of the American Counseling Association.

NAME INDEX

SUBJECT INDEX